BASIC CONSTRUCTION
TECHNIQUES
for Houses and Small Buildings
Simply Explained

Prepared by the U. S. Navy

(Bureau of Naval Personnel)

Dover Publications, Inc., New York

PREFACE

This book is intended to serve as an aid for men who are seeking to acquire the theoretical knowledge and operational skills required of candidates for advancement to Builder Third Class and Builder Second Class. As one of the Rate Training Manuals, this book was prepared by the Training Publications Division of the Naval Personnel Program Support Activity, Washington, D.C. Information and material provided by numerous manufacturers is gratefully acknowledged. Technical assistance was provided by the Naval Facilities Engineering Command; the Naval Schools Construction, Davisville, Rhode Island; the Naval Schools Construction, Port Hueneme, California; Construction Training Unit, Gulfport, Mississippi; and Naval Examining Center, Great Lakes, Illinois.

Published in Canada by General Publishing Company, Ltd., 30 Lesmill Road, Don Mills, Toronto, Ontario.

Published in the United Kingdom by Constable and Company, Ltd., 10 Orange Street, London WC 2.

This Dover edition, first published in 1972, is an unabridged republication of the sixth revised edition as published by the Training Publications Division of the Naval Personnel Program Support Activity in 1970 under the title *Builder 3 & 2*. This work was prepared by the Bureau of Naval Personnel, Department of the Navy, as Rate Training Manual NAVPERS 10648-F.

International Standard Book Number: 0-486-20242-9
Library of Congress Catalog Card Number: 70-189351

Manufactured in the United States of America
Dover Publications, Inc.
180 Varick Street
New York, N.Y. 10014

CONTENTS

CREDITS

The illustrations listed below are included in this edition of Builder 3 & 2 through the courtesy of the designated sources. Permission to use these illustrations is gratefully acknowledged. Permission to reproduce illustrations and other materials in this publication must be obtained from the source.

Source	Figures
Butler Manufacturing Company	15-7 through 15-26
D. Van Nostrand Company, Inc.	5-20
Delta Manufacturing Company	8-83
Douglas Fir Plywood Association	9-6, 9-7
Eugene Dietzgen Company	3-2
Great Lakes Steel Corporation	15-1 through 15-6
Hilti Fastening Systems, Inc.	8-95, 8-99, 8-100, 8-101
John T. Wiley and Sons, Inc.	4-9 through 4-11, 4-14
Keuffel and Esser Company	3-4
National Tank and Pipe Company	16-73, 16-75 through 16-78
Oliver Machinery Company	8-84
Theo. Audel and Company	8-9, 8-10, 8-16
Thor Power Tool Company	6-39, 6-40

CHAPTER 1
PREPARATION FOR ADVANCEMENT

This training manual has been prepared for men of the Navy and of the Naval Reserve who are studying for advancement to the rates of Builder 3 and Builder 2. The occupational, professional, or technical quals for the Builder rating that were used as a guide in the preparation of this training manual were current through change 6 (1971) to the Manual of Qualifications for Advancement, NavPers 18068-B. Therefore, changes in the qualifications occurring after change 6 to NavPers 18068-B are not necessarily reflected in the information given here.

This chapter gives information on the enlisted rating structure, the Builder rating, requirements and procedures for advancement, and references that will help you in working for advancement. Information on how to make the best use of this training manual also is included. It is strongly recommended that you study this chapter carefully before beginning intensive study of the remainder of this training manual.

Chapter 2 of this manual presents a general overview of the construction field. Chapters 3 and 4 explain the use of the engineer's level for grading and excavating. Chapter 5 concerns material handling and scaffolding. Chapter 6 will introduce you to concrete as a building material together with the forms that are required to cast concrete for form walls, columns, girders, beams, and floors. Chapter 7 covers masonry units and the tools and equipment needed to erect them. Chapter 8 describes the tools and equipment used in woodworking. Chapter 9 will explain the types of woods and their usage. Chapters 10 through 14 will introduce you to framing and finish carpentry, various techniques, and the various materials used. Chapter 15 describes prefabricated and other advanced base structures. Chapter 16 describes heavy construction tools and timbers and how they are used. Chapter 17 will provide general information concerning logging operations. Chapter 18 will introduce you to paints and preservatives and how they are applied. Chapter 19 of this training manual concerns construction safety supervision in general

and some specific safety points not covered elsewhere in the manual.

THE ENLISTED RATING STRUCTURE

The two main types of ratings in the present enlisted rating structure are general ratings and service ratings.

GENERAL RATINGS identify broad occupational fields of related duties and functions. Some general ratings include service ratings; others do not. Both Regular Navy and Naval Reserve personnel may hold general ratings.

SERVICE RATINGS identify subdivisions or specialties within a general rating. Although service ratings can exist at any petty officer level, they are most common at the PO3 and PO2 levels. Both Regular Navy and Naval Reserve personnel may hold service ratings.

THE BUILDER RATING

The Builder rating is now a general rating as are all others in the Group VIII ratings. Builders construct, maintain, and repair wooden and concrete structures. They select and position piles for waterfront structures. Builders also mix, place, finish, and cure concrete.

NAVY ENLISTED CLASSIFICATION CODES

The Builder rating is a source of a number of NECs (Navy Enlisted Classification Codes). NECs reflect special knowledge and skills in certain ratings. The NEC Coding System is designed to facilitate management control over enlisted skills by accurately identifying billets and personnel. It also helps ensure maximum skill utilization in distribution and detailing. The following NECs may be earned by Builders at certain grade levels by satisfactorily completing an applicable course of instruction at a Navy Class "C" school.

1. CONCRETE TECHNICIAN, BU-5901—He performs duties related to concrete construction, including: Formwork, reinforcement, placement methods, related tools, equipment,

1

accessories, transportation, storage and handling of related materials. Lays out and sets up concrete batch plants, block plants and precast yard operation; directs concrete paving machine operations; prepares simple designs, sketches, and specifications, estimates materials, equipment, and manpower requirements; supervises and trains crews in concrete construction.

The NEC BU-5901 is assigned only to E-5 and above who are graduates of the applicable course of instruction which, at this writing, is under development. The course of instruction, when officially established, will be offered by a Class "C" school at the Naval Schools Construction, Gulfport, Mississippi.

2. MASONRY TECHNICIAN, BU-5902—He performs duties related to masonry construction, including bricklaying, blocklaying, stone setting, tile setting, and plastering (portland cement and gypsum). Prepares simple designs, sketches and specifications, and estimates materials, equipment and manpower requirements; supervises and trains masonry construction crews.

The NEC BU-5902 is assigned only to E-5 and above who are graduates of the applicable course of instruction which, at this writing, is under development. The course of instruction, when officially established, will be offered by a Class "C" school at the Naval School Construction, Gulfport, Mississippi.

3. MILLWORKER, BU-5904—He operates required woodworking machines and handtools for fabrication of cabinets and millwork products from rough lumber. He uses jigs, gages and templates for assembly type production; prepares simple designs and sketches; and estimates and schedules shop workload to meet construction requirements; supervises and trains carpenter shop crews. This NEC is assigned only to E-5 and above who are graduates of the applicable course of instruction. The course is offered at the Naval Schools Construction, Davisville, Rhode Island.

4. HEAVY CONSTRUCTION TECHNICIAN, BU-5906—He performs duties related to construction of timber structures, cofferdams, seawalls, jetties and breakwaters. He directs pile driving operations utilizing all types of piles and pile driving rigs, prepares simple designs, sketches and specifications; estimates materials, equipment, and manpower requirements; supervises and trains heavy construction crews.

The NEC BU-5906 is assigned only to E-5 and above who are graduates of the applicable course of instruction which, at this writing, is under development. The course of instruction, when officially established, will be offered by a Class "C" school at the Naval School Construction, Davisville, Rhode Island.

5. TOOL AND EQUIPMENT TECHNICIAN, BU-5908—He installs, maintains and repairs sawmill and building trades shop equipment. He maintains and repairs portable, powered handtools associated with construction skills; gums, sharpens cutting tools; maintains files of manufacturer's maintenance and spare parts lists; coordinates stocking and procurement of parts; establishes preventive maintenance schedules; and records data on major parts. This NEC is assigned only to E-5 and above who are graduates of the applicable course of instruction. This course is offered at the Naval Schools Construction, Davisville, Rhode Island.

6. CONSTRUCTION PLANNER AND ESTIMATOR SPECIALIST, EA-5515—He plans and estimates material, manpower, and equipment requirements for various construction jobs; and performs scheduling, procurement, production control and management reporting of construction projects.

The NEC EA-5515 is assigned not only to BUs, but also to EAs, SWs, CEs, and UTs at E-5 level and above, who are graduates of the applicable course of instruction. The applicable course is ENGINEERING AIDS (PLANNING AND ESTIMATING), Class C, A-412-012, 014, or 016. It is offered at the Naval Schools Construction, Port Hueneme, California.

TYPES OF BILLETS

The great majority of Builders are serving in mobile construction battalions, most of which are engaged in overseas base construction. Outside the battalions, a number of Builders are frequently assigned to a variety of billets in the Public Works Departments of naval shore activities. In addition, especially well qualified Builders are assigned instructor duty at the Builder school in Port Hueneme, California, and at the Builder school in Davisville, Rhode Island.

Geographical Location

The Navy, as you know, maintains a large number of activities within the United States, mostly along the coastlines. As a Builder, you may work at almost any one of them, either as a member of a unit of the Fleet operating at the station, or as a member of the station force itself.

In the Atlantic area you may be assigned to duty in Turkey, Spain, Italy, Ireland, Newfoundland, or even Iceland or Greenland. You may also work in Bermuda or at a number of other islands: Cuba, Trinidad, Antigua, Turks Island, and so on. You may have the opportunity to winter over in Antarctica.

In the Pacific area you may be assigned duties in Okinawa, Japan, Alaska, Guam, Saipan, or the Philippines. You may even work in Thailand, Cambodia, Viet Nam, or Indonesia.

Units of the Fleet

As a Builder, you may not expect to be assigned to duty as a member of a ship's company. There is a possibility that you may be assigned to an amphibious construction battalion, but you will most likely be assigned to a mobile construction battalion, or a detachment thereof, or to other activities related to the Fleet Construction Force such as a CBBU, CBC, regimental headquarters, or Construction Force headquarters. In a mobile construction battalion, you may be assigned to B, C, or D company, depending upon the needs of the battalion. These companies are rifle companies for military purposes. From a construction standpoint, B company is a special construction (or shops) company and C and D companies are general construction companies.

Duty at Overseas Bases

In general, you may expect to work in your rate if assigned to a shore activity outside the United States. As a rule, you will work with foreign nationals, or civil service workers. As you advance in rate, you may be afforded the opportunity to serve as a member of a Seabee Team. Only men of the highest caliber are chosen for duty as Seabee Team members.

A Seabee Team normally consists of 12 men with an officer in charge of the team. Members of a Seabee Team undergo about 16 weeks of rigorous training. During this period, members learn to speak the foreign language of the country to which they are going to deploy. Also, a team member learns about another rating; for example, a BU in a team may spend two weeks at the UT school learning the fundamentals of plumbing or boilers.

After their training is complete, Seabee Teams are deployed to a foreign country to assist the people of that country. Some of the ways the Seabee Teams assist a country is to show personnel of an area or village how to dig a water well, how to construct wooden bridges, and in general how to improve their living conditions. Seabee Teams endeavor to win the friendship and admiration of the countries they serve in. There could be many more meritorious things said about the Seabee Teams, but in this book, space does not permit. For further information on the duties of a Seabee Team member, see your first class or chief.

The Public Works Department

When you are assigned to duty at a shore activity, either within the United States or overseas, you will most likely be assigned to the Public Works Department of the station. Most stations which have more than about 100 men and 15 or 20 buildings have a Public Works Department (which administers and maintains public works and utilities), except that in some localities Public Works Centers have been established. These Centers perform the public works duties for a number of Navy activities in the vicinity of the Center. The Public Works Department is headed by the Public Works Officer, who is an officer of the Civil Engineer Corps. The organization and staffing of the Department varies considerably, depending on the size, location, and mission of the activity.

The larger Public Works Departments are generally divided into Administrative and Technical Divisions (Administrative, Engineering, Maintenance Control, and sometimes Housing) and Operating Divisions (Maintenance, Utilities, and Transportation). The Operating Divisions are usually headed by a CEC officer who has the title Shops Engineer. A smaller station might have only three divisions: Administrative, Engineering, and Shops. The Shops Division usually has a Maintenance Branch.

Some Public Works Departments, particularly at small, isolated stations, may be staffed entirely by military personnel, but most Public Works Departments, both in the United States and overseas, are staffed largely by civilians. The Administrative and Technical Divisions (except for Maintenance Control) are mainly staffed with civil service workers classed as "GS," or "per annum," or "white collar" employees. The Operating Divisions are mainly staffed with civil service workers classed as "wage board," or "per diem," or "blue collar" employees. Supervisory blue collar employees have titles such as (in ascending order of responsibility) Snapper, Head, Leadingman, Quarterman, and Chief Quarterman. Very large stations may also have Master Mechanics and Foreman Mechanics. At bases overseas, foreign nationals may be hired to work in the Public Works Department. They may be employed directly as a special category of civil service worker, or they may be utilized as contract labor through the negotiation of a labor contract with the host government of the country involved.

Duty Within the U. S.

As stated before, if you are assigned to shore activity within the U. S. you will most likely be assigned to Public Works; but this is not always the case. In areas where there is a large stable supply of manpower, most of the maintenance work is done by blue collar employees. Therefore, you may be assigned to the master-at-arms force, special services, the salvage yard, the commissary, or to any of a great variety of jobs.

Your chances of working at your trade are much better in areas where there is a relative shortage of manpower. In these areas, you may expect to be assigned to the Maintenance Division or the Maintenance Branch of the Shops Division. Some Public Works Officers prefer to organize two separate lines of authority: one for civilians and one for the military personnel. In this case you may expect to be assigned to a division frequently called the Military Division. Other Public Works Officers prefer to integrate the civilians and military completely; in the latter case you may work beside a civilian and report to a BU1 who reports to a Quarterman who, in turn, answers to the Shops Engineer who is an officer. There are some activities which are staffed completely by military personnel because the mission is highly classified; if you are assigned to a station of this type you may expect to work within your rating.

PRACTICAL LEADERSHIP ASPECTS

Your status as a Constructionman might be roughly described as that of a relatively unskilled construction worker with little or no responsibility for the training and supervision of subordinates. Your status as a Builder Third will be that of a more highly skilled construction worker with a larger responsibility for the training and supervision of subordinates.

In short, when you become a petty officer you become a link in the chain of command which extends from the battalion CO down through the various officer grades and petty officer rates to the nonrated men in the battalion. Your responsibilities are more than just giving orders and seeing that work is done. You also have a responsibility for sharing your knowledge with others. When you become a petty officer, the Navy expects you to do your part in the training of the men under you.

The general principles of military leadership and supervision, many of which are also applicable in the Builder's technical field, are described at length in Military Requirements for Petty Officers 3 & 2, NavPers 10056-B, especially in Chapter 11, Military Leadership. After you have read this chapter closely, try to think of ways in which you can apply the information it contains to your technical duties as a Builder Third or Second.

On the purely technical side, the Builder petty officer must possess the leadership qualities required to train and supervise a crew of subordinates who are capable of producing, under his supervision, construction work of the first quality, performed in accordance with drawings and specifications, and completed on or ahead of schedule. As a Builder Third your crews will be small; they will increase in size as you rise through the rates, until finally, as a Chief Builder, you may have the final enlisted responsibility for a large construction project.

As is the case with practically any type of technical leadership, an essential requirement is the possession of a vast amount of technical knowledge and technical skill. Along with this must go the capacity for extending this knowledge and skill to subordinates, plus the ability to organize both the job and the men in the manner which will best expedite the work and develop each man's particular knowledge and skill.

An indispensable part of leadership is the confidence and respect of your subordinates. To gain the confidence and respect of your men, it is important, among other things, that you show an interest in others; know your job; be friendly and courteous; and give praise and compliments where deserved.

ADVANCEMENT

Some of the rewards of advancement are easy to see. You get more pay. Your job assignments become more interesting and more challenging. You are regarded with greater respect by officers and enlisted personnel. You enjoy the satisfaction of getting ahead in your chosen Navy career.

But the advantages of advancement are not yours alone. The Navy also profits. Highly trained personnel are essential to the functioning of the Navy. By each advancement, you increase your value to the Navy in two ways. First, you become more valuable as a specialist in your own rating. And second, you become more valuable as a person who can train others and thus make far-reaching contributions to the entire Navy.

HOW TO QUALIFY FOR ADVANCEMENT

What must you do to qualify for advancement? The requirements may change from time to time, but usually you must:

1. Have a certain amount of time in your present grade.

2. Complete the required military and occupational training manuals.

3. Demonstrate your ability to perform all the PRACTICAL requirements for advancement by completing the Record of Practical Factors, NavPers 1414/1. In some cases the Record of Practical Factors may contain the old form number, NavPers 760.

4. Be recommended by your commanding officer, after the petty officers and officers supervising your work have indicated that they consider you capable of performing the duties of the next higher rate.

5. Demonstrate your KNOWLEDGE by passing written examinations on the occupational and military qualification standards for advancement.

Some of these general requirements may be modified in certain ways. Figure 1-1 gives a more detailed view of the requirements for advancement of active duty personnel; figure 1-2 gives this information for inactive duty personnel.

Remember that the qualifications for advancement can change. Check with your division officer or training officer to be sure that you know the most recent qualifications.

Advancement is not automatic. Even though you have met all the requirements, including passing the written examinations, you may not be able to "sew on the crow" or "add a stripe." The number of men in each rate and rating is controlled on a Navy-wide basis. Therefore,

the number of men who may be advanced is limited by the number of vacancies that exist. When the number of men passing the examination exceeds the number of vacancies, some system must be used to determine which men may be advanced and which may not. The system used is the "final multiple" and is a combination of three types of advancement systems.

Merit rating system
Personnel testing system
Longevity, or seniority, system

The Navy's system provides credit for performance, knowledge, and seniority, and, while it cannot guarantee that any one person will be advanced, it does guarantee that all men within a particular rating will have equal advancement opportunity.

The following factors are considered in computing the final multiple:

Factor	Maximum Credit
Examination score	80
Performance factor (Performance evaluation)	50
Length of service (years × 1)	20
Service in pay grade (years × 2)	20
Medals and awards	15
	185

All of the above information (except the examination score) is submitted to the Naval Examining Center with your examination answer sheet. After grading, the examination scores, for those passing, are added to the other factors to arrive at the final multiple. A precedence list, which is based on final multiples, is then prepared for each pay grade within each rating. Advancement authorizations are then issued, beginning at the top of the list, for the number of men needed to fill the existing vacancies.

HOW TO PREPARE FOR ADVANCEMENT

What must you do to prepare for advancement? You must study the qualifications for advancement, work on the practical factors, study the required Rate Training Manuals, and study other material that is required for advancement in your rating. To prepare for advancement, you will need to be familiar with (1) the Quals Manual, (2) the Record of Practical Factors, (3)

REQUIREMENTS*	E1 to E2	E2 to E3	#† E3 to E4	#E4 to E5	† E5 to E6	† E6 to E7	† E7 to E8	† E8 to E9
SERVICE	4 mos. service— or completion of	6 mos. as E-2.	6 mos. as E-3.	12 mos. as E-4	24 mos. as E-5.	36 mos. as E-6. 8 years total enlisted service.	36 mos as E-7. 8 of 11 years total service must be enlisted.	24 mos. as E-8. 10 of 13 years total service must be enlisted.
SCHOOL	Recruit Training.		Class A for PR3, DT3, PT3, AME 3, HM 3, PN 3, FTB 3, MT 3,			Class B for AGC MUC, MNC. ††		
PRACTICAL FACTORS	Locally prepared check-offs.	Record of Practical Factors, NavPers 1414/1, must be completed for E-3 and all PO advancements.						
PERFORMANCE TEST			Specified ratings must complete applicable performance tests before taking examinations.					
ENLISTED PERFORMANCE EVALUATION	As used by CO when approving advancement.		Counts toward performance factor credit in advancement multiple.					
EXAMINATIONS**	Locally prepared tests.	See below.	Navy-wide examinations required for all PO advancements.				Navy-wide, selection board.	
RATE TRAINING MANUAL (INCLUDING MILITARY REQUIREMENTS)			Required for E-3 and all PO advancements unless waived because of school completion, but need not be repeated if identical course has already been completed. See NavPers 10052 (current edition).				Correspondence courses and recommended reading. See NavPers 10052 (current edition).	
AUTHORIZATION	Commanding Officer	Naval Examining Center						

* All advancements require commanding officer's recommendation.

† 1 year obligated service required for E-5 and E-6; 2 years for E-7, E-8 and E-9.

Military leadership exam required for E-4 and E-5.

** For E-2 to E-3, NAVEXAMCEN exams or locally prepared tests may be used.

†† Waived for qualified EOD personnel.

Figure 1-1.—Active duty advancement requirements.

REQUIREMENTS *	E1 to E2	E2 to E3	E3 to E4	E4 to E5	E5 to E6	E6 to E7	E8	E9
TOTAL TIME IN GRADE	4 mos.	6 mos.	6 mos.	12 mos.	24 mos.	36 mos. with total 8 yrs service	36 mos. with total 11 yrs service	24 mos. with total 13 yrs service
TOTAL TRAINING DUTY IN GRADE †	14 days	14 days	14 days	14 days	28 days	42 days	42 days	28 days
PERFORMANCE TESTS			Specified ratings must complete applicable performance tests before taking examination.					
DRILL PARTICIPATION	Satisfactory participation as a member of a drill unit in accordance with BUPERSINST 5400.42 series.							
PRACTICAL FACTORS (INCLUDING MILITARY REQUIREMENTS)	Record of Practical Factors, NavPers 1414/1, must be completed for all advancements.							
RATE TRAINING MANUAL (INCLUDING MILITARY REQUIRE MENTS)	Completion of applicable course or courses must be entered in service record.							
EXAMINATION	Standard Exam	Standard Exam required for all PO Advancements. Also pass Military Leadership Exam for E-4 and E-5.					Standard Exam, Selection Board.	
AUTHORIZATION	Commanding Officer	Naval Examining Center						

* Recommendation by commanding officer required for all advancements.
† Active duty periods may be substituted for training duty.

Figure 1-2.—Inactive duty advancement requirements.

a NavPers publication called Training Publications for Advancement, NavPers 10052, and (4) applicable Rate Training Manuals. The following sections describe them and give you some practical suggestions on how to use them in preparing for advancement.

Quals Manual

The Manual of Qualifications for Advancement, NavPers 18068B (with changes), gives the minimum occupational and military qualification standards for advancement to each pay grade within each rating. This manual is usually called the "Quals Manual," and the qualifications themselves are often called "quals." The qualification standards are of two general types: (1) military qualification standards and (2) occupational qualification standards.

MILITARY STANDARDS are requirements that apply to all ratings rather than to any one particular rating. Military requirements for advancement to third class and second class petty officer rates deal with military conduct, naval organization, military justice, security, watch standing, and other subjects which are required of petty officers in all ratings.

OCCUPATIONAL STANDARDS are requirements that are directly related to the work of each rating.

Both the military requirements and the occupational qualification standards are divided into subject matter groups; then, within each subject matter group, they are divided into PRACTICAL FACTORS and KNOWLEDGE FACTORS. Practical factors are things you must be able to DO. Knowledge factors are things you must KNOW in order to perform the duties of your rating.

In most subject matter areas, you will find both practical factor and knowledge factor qualifications. In some subject matter areas, you may find only one or the other. It is important to remember that there are some knowledge aspects to all practical factors, and some practical aspects to most knowledge factors. Therefore, even if the Quals Manual indicates that there are no knowledge factors for a given subject matter area, you may still expect to find examination questions dealing with the knowledge aspects of the practical factors listed in that subject matter area.

You are required to pass a Navywide military/leadership examination for E-4 or E-5, as appropriate, before you take the occupational examinations. The military/leadership examinations are administered on a schedule determined by your commanding officer. Candidates are required to pass the applicable military/leadership examination only once. Each of these examinations consists of 100 questions based on information contained in Military Requirements for Petty Officer 3 and 2, NavPers 10056 (current edition) and in other publications listed in Training Publications for Advancement, NavPers 10052 (current edition).

The Navywide occupational examinations for pay grades E-4 and E-5 will contain 150 questions related to occupational areas of your rating.

If you are working for advancement to second class, remember that you may be examined on third class qualifications as well as on second class qualifications.

The Quals Manual is kept current by means of changes. The occupational qualifications for your rating which are covered in this training manual were current at the time the manual was printed. By the time you are studying this manual, however, the quals for your rating may have been changed. Never trust any set of quals until you have checked it against an UP-TO-DATE copy in the Quals Manual.

Record of Practical Factors

Before you take the servicewide examination for advancement, there must be an entry in your service record to show that you have qualified in the practical factors of both the military qualifications and the occupational qualifications. The RECORD OF PRACTICAL FACTORS, mentioned earlier, is used to keep a record of your practical factor qualifications. This form is available for each rating. The form lists all practical factors, both military and occupational. As you demonstrate your ability to perform each practical factor, appropriate entries are made in the DATE and INITIALS columns.

Changes are made periodically to the Manual of Qualifications for Advancement, and revised forms of NavPers 1414/1 are provided when necessary. Extra space is allowed on the Record of Practical Factors for entering additional practical factors as they are published in changes to the Quals Manual. The Record of Practical Factors also provides space for recording demonstrated proficiency in skills which are within the general scope of the rating but which are not identified as minimum qualifications for advancement.

Until completed, the NavPers 1414/1 is usually held by your division officer; after completion, it is forwarded to the personnel office for insertion in your service record. If you are transferred before qualifying in all practical factors, the incomplete form should be forwarded with your service record to your next duty station. You can save yourself a lot of trouble by making sure that this form is actually inserted in your service record before you are transferred. If the form is not in your service record, you may be required to start all over again and requalify in the practical factors which have already been checked off.

NavPers 10052

Training Publications for Advancement, NavPers 10052 (revised), is a very important publication for any enlisted person preparing for advancement. This bibliography lists required and recommended Rate Training Manuals and other reference material to be used by personnel working for advancement.

NavPers 10052 is revised and issued once each year by the Bureau of Naval Personnel. Each revised edition is identified by a letter following the NavPers number. When using this publication, be SURE that you have the most recent edition.

If extensive changes in qualifications occur in any rating between the annual revisions of NavPers 10052, a supplementary list of study material may be issued in the form of a BuPers Notice. When you are preparing for advancement, check to see whether changes have been made in the qualifications for your rating. If changes have been made, see if a BuPers Notice has been issued to supplement NavPers 10052 for your rating.

The required and recommended references are listed by pay grade in NavPers 10052. If you are working for advancement to third class, study the material that is listed for third class. If you are working for advancement to second class, study the material that is listed for second class; but remember that you are also responsible for the references listed at the third class level.

In using NavPers 10052, you will notice that some Rate Training Manuals are marked with an asterisk (*). Any manual marked in this way is MANDATORY—that is, it must be completed at the indicated rate level before you can be eligible to take the servicewide examination for advancement. Each mandatory manual may be completed by (1) passing the appropriate enlisted correspondence course that is based on the mandatory training manual; (2) passing locally prepared tests based on the information given in the training manual; or (3) in some cases, successfully completing an appropriate Class A school.

Do not overlook the section of NavPers 10052 which lists the required and recommended references relating to the military qualification standards for advancement. Personnel of ALL ratings must complete the mandatory military requirements training manual for the appropriate rate level before they can be eligible to advance.

The references in NavPers 10052 which are recommended but not mandatory should also be studied carefully. ALL references listed in NavPers 10052 may be used as source material for the written examinations, at the appropriate rate levels.

Rate Training Manuals

There are two general types of Rate Training Manuals. RATING manuals (such as this one) are prepared for most enlisted ratings. A rating manual gives information that is directly related to the occupational qualifications of ONE rating. SUBJECT MATTER manuals or BASIC manuals give information that applies to more than one rating.

Rate Training Manuals are revised from time to time to keep them up to date technically. The revision of a Rate Training Manual is identified by a letter following the NavPers number. You can tell whether any particular copy of a training manual is the latest edition by checking the NavPers number and the letter following this number in the most recent edition of List of Training Manuals and Correspondence Courses, NavPers 10061. (NavPers 10061 is actually a catalog that lists all current training manuals and correspondence courses; you will find this catalog useful in planning your study program.)

Each time a Rate Training Manual is revised, it is brought into conformance with the official publications and directives on which it is based; but during the life of any edition, discrepancies between the manual and the official sources are almost certain to arise because of changes to the latter which are issued in the interim. In the performance of your duties, you should always refer to the appropriate official publication or directive. If the official source is listed in NAVPERS 10052, the Naval Examining Center uses it as a source of questions in preparing the fleetwide examinations for advancement. In case of discrepancy between any publications listed in NAVPERS 10052 for a given rate, the Examining Center will use the most recent material.

Rate Training Manuals are designed to help you prepare for advancement. The following suggestions may help you to make the best use of this manual and other Navy training publications when you are preparing for advancement.

1. Study the military qualifications and the occupational qualifications for your rating before you study the training manual, and refer to the quals frequently as you study. Remember, you are studying the manual primarily in order to meet these quals.

2. Set up a regular study plan. It will probably be easier for you to stick to a schedule if you can plan to study at the same time each day. If possible, schedule your studying for a time of day when you will not have too many interruptions or distractions.

3. Before you begin to study any part of the manual intensively, become familiar with the entire book. Read the preface and the table of contents. Check through the index. Look at the appendixes. Thumb through the book without any particular plan, looking at the illustrations and reading bits here and there as you see things that interest you.

4. Look at the training manual in more detail, to see how it is organized. Look at the table of contents again. Then, chapter by chapter, read the introduction, the headings, and the subheadings. This will give you a pretty clear picture of the scope and content of the book. As you look through the book in this way, ask yourself some questions:

• What do I need to learn about this?
• What do I already know about this?
• How is this information related to information given in other chapters?
• How is this information related to the qualifications for advancement?

5. When you have a general idea of what is in the training manual and how it is organized, fill in the details by intensive study. In each study period, try to cover a complete unit—it may be a chapter, a section of a chapter, or a subsection. The amount of material that you can cover at one time will vary. If you know the subject well, or if the material is easy, you can cover quite a lot at one time. Difficult or unfamiliar material will require more study time.

6. In studying any one unit—chapter, section, or subsection—write down the questions that occur to you. Many people find it helpful to make a written outline of the unit as they study, or at least to write down the most important ideas.

7. As you study, relate the information in the training manual to the knowledge you already have. When you read about a process, a skill, or a situation, try to see how this information ties in with your own past experience.

8. When you have finished studying a unit, take time out to see what you have learned. Look back over your notes and questions. Maybe some of your questions have been answered, but perhaps you still have some that are not answered. Without looking at the training manual, write down the main ideas that you have gotten from studying this unit. Don't just quote the book. If you can't give these ideas in your own words, the chances are that you have not really mastered the information.

9. Use enlisted correspondence courses whenever you can. The correspondence courses are based on Rate Training Manuals or on other appropriate texts. As mentioned before, completion of a mandatory Rate Training Manual can be accomplished by passing an enlisted correspondence course based on the Rate Training Manual. You will probably find it helpful to take other correspondence courses, as well as those based on mandatory manuals. Taking a correspondence course helps you to master the information given in the training manual, and also helps you see how much you have learned.

10. Think of your future as you study Rate Training Manuals. You are working for advancement to third class or second class right now, but some day you will be working toward higher rates. Anything extra that you can learn now will help you both now and later.

SOURCE OF INFORMATION

Besides training manuals, NavPers 10052 lists official publications on which you may be examined. You should not only study the sections required, but should become as familiar as possible with all publications you use.

One of the most useful things you can learn about a subject is how to find out more about it. No single publication can give you all the information you need to perform the duties of your rating. You should learn where to look for accurate, authoritative, up-to-date information on all subjects related to the military requirements for advancement and the occupational qualifications of your rating.

Some publications are subject to change or revision from time to time—some at regular intervals, others as the need arises. When using any publication that is subject to change or revision, be sure that you have the latest edition. When using any publication that is kept current by means of changes, be sure you have a copy in which all official changes have been made. Studying canceled or obsolete information will not help you to do your work or to advance; it is likely to be a waste of time, and may even be seriously misleading.

GOVERNMENT PUBLICATIONS

There are various government publications which you may find useful as sources of reference. A number of publications issued by the Naval Facilities Engineering Command (NAVFAC) which will be of interest to personnel in the Group VIII ratings are listed in the Index of Naval Facilities Engineering Command Publications, NAVFAC P-349 (updated semiannually). A publications program is one of the principal communications media used by NAVFAC to provide a ready reference of current technical and administrative data for use by its subordinate units. NAVFAC publications are listed in alphabetical and numerical order in NAVFAC P-349; copies of NAVFAC P-349 may be obtained through proper channels from the Naval Supply Depot, 5801 Tabor Avenue, Philadelphia, Pennsylvania 19120.

Some of the BuPers publications that you need to study or refer to as you prepare for advancement have been discussed earlier in this chapter. Three additional BuPers publications needed to help you succeed in your occupation as a Builder are discussed in the following paragraphs.

Basic Handtools, NavPers 10085-A, is especially helpful because it contains a great deal of information on the use and care of various types of handtools not covered in Builder 3 & 2, NavPers 10648-F.

Blueprint Reading and Sketching, NavPers 10077-C, contains information and drawings that will be extremely helpful to you in learning to read and work from shop and/or construction drawings and specifications.

Mathematics, Vol. 1; NavPers 10069-C, is also helpful to you because it contains basic information that is needed in using formulas and in making simple computations.

In addition, you may find it useful to consult the Rate Training Manuals prepared for other Group VIII (Construction) ratings. Reference to these manuals will add to your knowledge of the duties of other men in the Construction ratings.

Some of the U. S. Army technical manuals (TMs) may contain information that will help you in your work. TMs are easily ordered through the normal naval supply procurement system.

COMMERCIAL PUBLICATIONS

There is a wealth of information for the construction field contained in reports, pamphlets, handbooks, and texts published by manufacturers, trade associations, technical and professional societies, and commercial publishing houses. Much of this literature will be available to you at the station library, the Public Works Department, or the battalion office or library.

TRAINING FILMS

Training films available to naval personnel are a valuable source of supplementary information on many technical subjects. Films that may be of interest are listed in the United States Navy Film Catalog, NAVAIR 10-1-777.

When selecting a film, note its date of issue listed in the Film Catalog. As you know procedures sometimes change rapidly. Thus some films become obsolete rapidly. If a film is obsolete only in part, it may still have sections that are useful, but it is important to note procedures that have changed. If there is any doubt, verify current procedures by looking them up in the appropriate source.

CHAPTER 2
DRAWINGS AND SPECIFICATIONS

A building project may be broadly divided into two major phases: (1) the DESIGN phase, and (2) the CONSTRUCTION phase. In accordance with a number of considerations, of which the function and desired appearance of the building are perhaps the most important, the architect first conceives the building in his mind's eye, as it were, and then sets his concept down on paper in the form of PRESENTATION drawings. Presentation drawings are usually done in PERSPECTIVE, by employing the PICTORIAL drawing techniques described in NavPers 10077-C, Blueprint Reading and Sketching.

Next the architect and the engineer, working together, decide upon the materials to be used in the structure and the construction methods which are to be followed. The engineer determines the loads which supporting members will carry and the strength qualities the members must have to bear the loads. He also designs the mechanical systems of the structure, such as the lighting, heating, and plumbing systems. The end-result of all this is the preparation of architectural and engineering DESIGN SKETCHES. The purpose of these sketches is to guide draftsmen in the preparation of CONSTRUCTION DRAWINGS.

The construction drawings, plus the SPECIFICATIONS to be described later, are the chief sources of information for the supervisors and craftsman responsible for the actual work of construction. Construction drawings consist mostly of ORTHOGRAPHIC views, prepared by draftsmen who employ the standard technical drawing techniques, and who use the sumbols and other designations, explained in MIL-STD-14A, MIL-STD-17B (part 1), and MIL-STD-100A. You should make a thorough study of symbols before proceeding further with this chapter. Figure 2-1 illustrates the conventional symbols for the more common types of material used on structures. Figure 2-2 shows the more common symbols used for doors and windows.

Before you can interpret construction drawings correctly, you must also have some knowledge of the structure and of the terminology for common structural members.

STRUCTURES

The main parts of a structure are the LOAD-BEARING STRUCTURAL MEMBERS, which support and transfer the loads on the structure while remaining in equilibrium with each other. The places where members are connected to other members are called JOINTS. The sum total of the load supported by the structural members at a particular instant is equal to the total DEAD LOAD plus the total LIVE LOAD.

The total dead load is the total weight of the structure, which gradually increases, of course, as the structure rises, and remains constant once it is completed. The total live load is the total weight of movable objects (such as people, furniture, bridge traffic or the like) which the structure happens to be supporting at a particular instant.

The live loads in a structure are transmitted through the various load-bearing structural members to the ultimate support of the earth as follows. Immediate or direct support for the live loads is provided by HORIZTONAL members; these are in turn supported by VERTICAL members; which in turn are supported by FOUNDATIONS and/or FOOTINGS; and these are, finally, supported by the earth.

The ability of the earth to support a load is called the SOIL BEARING CAPACITY; it is determined by test and measured in pounds per square foot. Soil bearing capacity varies considerably with different types of soil, and a soil of given bearing capacity will bear a heavier load on a wide foundation or footing than it will on a narrow one.

VERTICAL STRUCTURAL MEMBERS

Vertical structural members are high-strength columns; they are sometimes called PILLARS in buildings. Outside wall columns and inside bottom-floor columns, usually rest directly on footings. Outside-wall columns usually extend from the footing or foundation to the roof line. Inside bottom-floor columns extend upward from footings or foundations to horizontal members which in turn support the

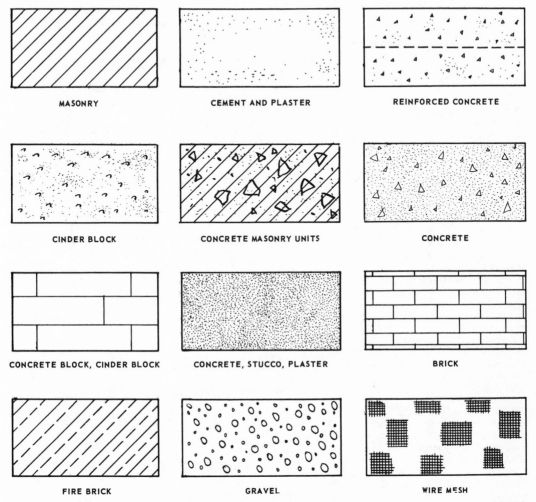

MASONRY

CEMENT AND PLASTER

REINFORCED CONCRETE

CINDER BLOCK

CONCRETE MASONRY UNITS

CONCRETE

CONCRETE BLOCK, CINDER BLOCK

CONCRETE, STUCCO, PLASTER

BRICK

FIRE BRICK

GRAVEL

WIRE MESH

45.271

Figure 2-1.—Material symbols.

first floor. Upper floor columns usually are located directly over lower floor columns.

A PIER in building construction might be called a short column. It may rest directly on a footing, or it may be simply set or driven in the ground. Building piers usually support the lowermost horizontal structural members.

In bridge construction a pier is a vertical member which provides intermediate support for the bridge superstructure.

The chief vertical structural members in light frame construction are called STUDS. They are supported on horizontal members called SILLS or SOLE PLATES, and are topped by horizontal members called TOP PLATES or RAFTER PLATES. CORNER POSTS are enlarged studs, as it were, located at the building corners. In early FULL-FRAME construction a corner post was usually a solid piece of larger timber. In most modern construction BUILT-UP

13

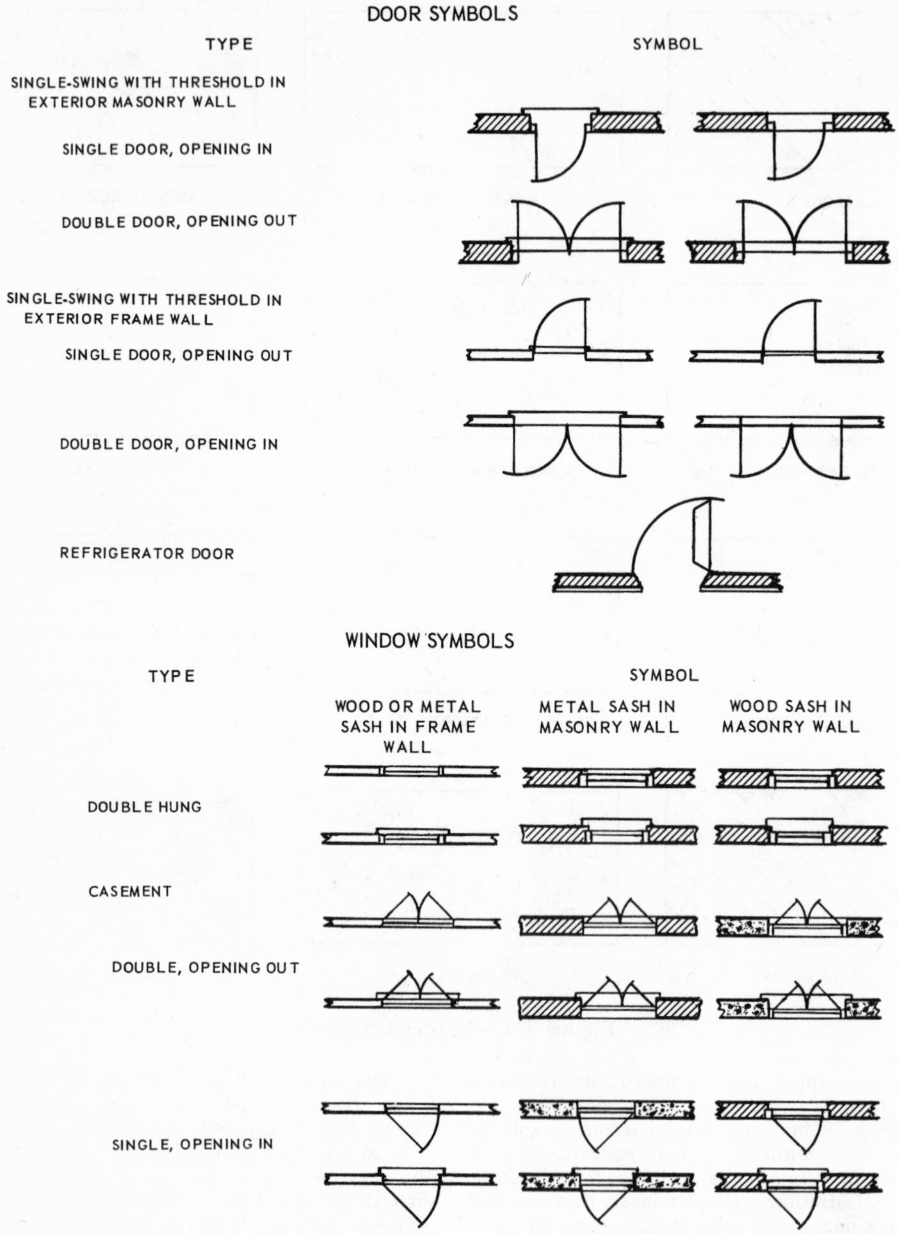

DOOR SYMBOLS

TYPE	SYMBOL

SINGLE-SWING WITH THRESHOLD IN
EXTERIOR MASONRY WALL

SINGLE DOOR, OPENING IN

DOUBLE DOOR, OPENING OUT

SINGLE-SWING WITH THRESHOLD IN
EXTERIOR FRAME WALL

SINGLE DOOR, OPENING OUT

DOUBLE DOOR, OPENING IN

REFRIGERATOR DOOR

WINDOW SYMBOLS

TYPE	SYMBOL		
	WOOD OR METAL SASH IN FRAME WALL	METAL SASH IN MASONRY WALL	WOOD SASH IN MASONRY WALL
DOUBLE HUNG			
CASEMENT			
DOUBLE, OPENING OUT			
SINGLE, OPENING IN			

65.112

Figure 2-2.—Architectural symbols (door and windows).

14

corner posts are used, consisting of various numbers of ordinary studs, nailed together in various ways.

HORIZONTAL STRUCTURAL MEMBERS

In technical terminology, a horizontal load-bearing structural member which spans a space, and which is supported at both ends, is called a BEAM. A member which is FIXED at one end only is called a CANTILEVER. Steel members which consist of solid pieces of the regular structural steel shapes are called beams, but a type of steel member which is actually a light truss is called an OPEN-WEB STEEL JOIST or a BAR STEEL JOIST.

Horizontal structural members which support the ends of floor beams or joists in wood frame construction are called SILLS, GIRTS, or GIRDERS, depending on the type of framing being done and the location of the member in the structure. Horizontal members which support studs are called SILL or SOLE PLATES. Horizontal members which support the wall-ends of rafters are called RAFTER PLATES. Horizontal members which assume the weight of concrete or masonry walls above door and window openings are called LINTELS.

TRUSSES

A beam of given strength, without intermediate supports below, can support a given load over only a certain maximum span. If the span is wider than this maximum, intermediate supports, such as a column must be provided for the beam. Sometimes it is not feasible or possible to install intermediate supports. When such is the case, a TRUSS may be used instead of a beam.

A beam consists of a single horizontal member. A truss, however, is a framework, consisting of two horizontal (or nearly horizontal) members, joined together by a number of vertical and/or inclined members. The horizontal members are called the UPPER and LOWER CHORDS; the vertical and/or inclined members are called the WEB MEMBERS.

ROOF MEMBERS

The horizontal or inclined members which provide support to a roof are called RAFTERS. The lengthwise (right angle to the rafters) member which support the peak ends of the rafters in a roof is called the RIDGE. (The ridge may be called the Ridge board, the Ridge PIECE, or the Ridge pole.) Lengthwise members other than ridges are called PURLINS. In wood frame construction the wall ends of rafters are supported on horizontal members called RAFTER PLATES, which are in turn supported by the outside wall studs. In concrete or masonry wall construction, the wall ends of rafters may be anchored directly on the walls, or on plates bolted to the walls.

CONSTRUCTION DRAWINGS

Construction drawings are drawings in which as much construction information as possible is presented GRAPHICALLY, or by means of pictures. Most construction drawings consist of ORTHOGRAPHIC views. GENERAL drawings consist of PLANS AND ELEVATIONS, drawn on a relatively small scale. DETAIL drawings consist of SECTIONS and DETAILS, drawn on a relatively large scale.

PLANS

A PLAN view is, as you know, a view of an object or area as it would appear if projected onto a horizontal plane passed through or held above the object or area. The most common construction plans are PLOT PLANS (also called SITE PLANS), FOUNDATION PLANS, FLOOR PLANS, and FRAMING PLANS.

A PLOT PLAN shows the contours, boundaries, roads, utilities, trees, structures, and any other significant physical features pertaining to or located on the site. The locations of proposed structures are indicated by appropriate outlines or floor plans. By locating the corners of a proposed structure at given distances from a REFERENCE or BASE line (which is shown on the plan and which can be located on the site), the plot plan provides essential data for those who will lay out the building lines. By indicating the elevations of existing and proposed earth surfaces (by means of CONTOUR lines), the plot plan provides essential data for the graders and excavators.

A FOUNDATION PLAN (fig. 2-3) is a plan view of a structure projected on a horizontal plane passed through (in imagination, of course) at the level of the tops of the foundations. The plan shown in figure 2-3 tells you that the main foundation of this structure will consist of a rectangular 12-in. concrete block wall, 22 ft

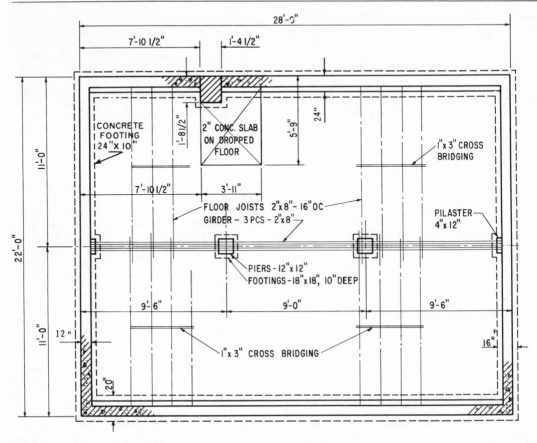

Figure 2-3.—Foundation plan.

45.513

wide by 28 ft long, centered on a concrete foot-ing 24 in. wide. Besides the outside wall and footing, there will be two 12-in. square piers, centered on 18-in. square footings, and located on center 9 ft 6 in. from the end wall building lines. These piers will support a ground floor center-line girder.

A FLOOR PLAN (also called a BUILDING PLAN) is developed as shown in figure 2-4. Information on a floor plan includes the lengths, thicknesses, and character of the building walls at that particular floor, the widths and locations of door and window openings, the lengths and character of partitions, the number and arrange-ment of rooms, and the types and locations of utility installations. A typical floor plan is shown in figure 2-5.

FRAMING PLANS show the dimensions, numbers, and arrangement of structural mem-bers in wood frame construction. A simple FLOOR FRAMING PLAN is superimposed on the foundation plan shown in figure 2-3. From this foundation plan you learn that the ground-floor joists in this structure will consist of 2 x 8's, lapped at the girder, and spaced 16 in. O. C. The plan also shows that each row of joists is to be braced by a row of 1 x 3 cross bridging. For a more complicated floor fram-ing problem, a framing plan like the one shown in figure 2-6 would be required. This plan

PERSPECTIVE VIEW OF A
BUILDING SHOWING   CUTTING
PLANE WXY

PREVIOUS PERSPECTIVE VIEW AT
CUTTING PLANE WXYZ,
TOP REMOVED

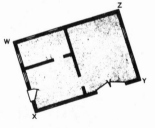

DEVELOPED FLOOR PLAN
WXYZ

45.514

Figure 2-4.—Floor plan development.

shows, among other things, the arrangement of joists and other members around stair wells and other floor openings.

A WALL FRAMING PLAN gives similar information with regard to the studs, corner posts, bracing, sills, plates, and other structural members in the walls. Since it is a view on a vertical plane, a wall framing plan is not a plan in the strict technical sense. However, the practice of calling it a plan has become a general custom.   A ROOF FRAMING PLAN gives similar information with regard to the rafters, ridge, purlins, and other structural members in the roof.

A UTILITY PLAN is a floor plan which shows the layout of a heating, electrical, plumbing, or other utility system. Utility plans are used primarily by the ratings responsible for the utilities, but they are important to the Builder as well. Most utility installations require the leaving of openings in walls, floors, and roofs for the admission or installation of utility features. The Builder who is placing a concrete foundation wall must study the utility plans to determine the number, sizes, and locations of the openings he must leave for utilities.

Figure 2-7 shows a heating plan. Figure 2-8 shows an electrical plan.

ELEVATIONS

ELEVATIONS show the front, rear, and sides of a structure projected on vertical planes parallel to the planes of the sides. Front, rear, right side, and left side elevations of a small building are shown in figure 2-9.

As you can see, the elevations give you a number of important vertical dimensions, such as the perpendicular distance from the finish floor to the top of the rafter plate and from the finish floor to the tops of door and window finished openings. They also show the locations and characters of doors and windows. Dimensions of window sash and dimensions and character of lintels, however, are usually set forth in a WINDOW SCHEDULE.

A SECTION view is a view of a cross-section, developed as indicated in figure 2-10. By general custom, the term is confined to views of cross-sections cut by vertical planes. A floor plan or foundation plan, cut by a horizontal plane, is, technically speaking, a section view as well as a plan view, but it is seldom called a section.

The most important sections are the WALL sections. Figure 2-11 shows three wall sections for three alternate types of construction for the building shown in figures 2-3, 2-5, 2-7 and 2-8.   The angled arrows marked "A" in figure 2-5 indicate the location of the cutting plane for the sections.

The wall sections are of primary importance to the supervisors of construction and to the craftsmen who will do the actual building. Take the first wall section, marked "masonry construction," for example. Starting at the bottom, you learn that the footing will be concrete, 2 ft wide and 10 in. high.   The vertical distance of the bottom of the footing below FINISHED GRADE (level of the finished earth surface around the house) "varies"—meaning that it will depend on the soil-bearing capacity at the particular site. The foundation wall will consist of

17

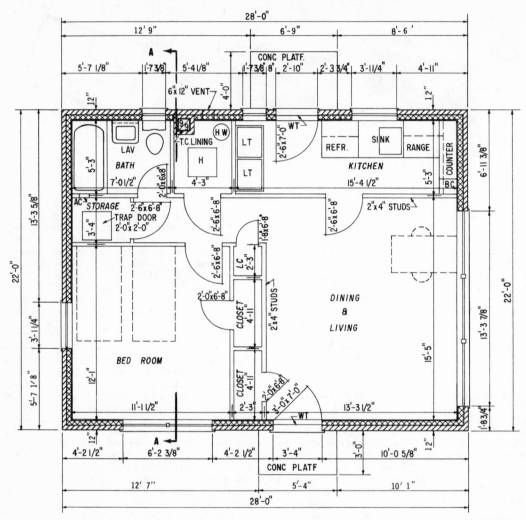

Figure 2-5.—Floor plan.

45.515(54)A

12-in. CMU, centered on the footing. Twelve-inch blocks will extend up to an unspecified distance below grade, where a 4-in. brick FACING (dimension indicated in the middle wall section) begins. Above the line of the bottom of the facing, it is obvious that 8-in. instead of 12-in. blocks will be used in the foundation wall.

The building wall above grade will consist of a 4-in. brick FACING TIER, backed by a BACKING TIER of 4-in. cinder blocks. The floor joists, consisting of 2 x 8's placed 16 in. O.C., will be anchored on 2 x 4 sills bolted to the top of the foundation wall. Every third joist will be additionally secured by a 2 x 1/4 STRAP ANCHOR embedded in the cinder block backing tier of the building wall.

The window (window B in the plan front elevation, fig. 2-9) will have a finished opening

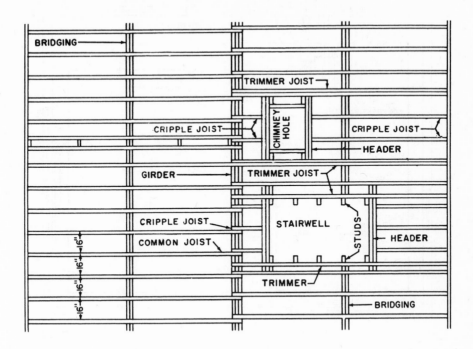

65.114

Figure 2-6.—Floor framing plan.

4 ft 2-5/8 in. high. The bottom of the opening will come 2 ft 11-3/4 in. above the line of the finished floor. As indicated in the wall section, (fig. 2-11) 13 masonry COURSES (layers of masonry units) above the finished floor line will amount to a vertical distance of 2 ft 11-3/4 in. As also indicated, another 19 courses will amount to the prescribed vertical dimension of the finished window opening.

Window framing details, including the placement and cross-sectional character of the lintel, are shown. The building wall will be carried 10-1/4 in., less the thickness of a 2 x 8 RAFTER PLATE, above the top of the window finished opening. The total vertical distance from the top of the finished floor to the top of the rafter plate will be 8 ft 2-1/4 in. Ceiling joists and rafters will consist of 2 x 6's, and the roof covering will consist of composition shingles laid on wood sheathing.

Flooring will consist of a wood finisher floor laid on a wood subfloor. Inside walls will be finished with plaster on lath (except on masonry wall which would be with or without lath as directed). A minimum of 2 vertical feet of crawl space will extend below the bottoms of the floor joists.

The middle wall section in figure 2-11 gives you similar information for a similar building constructed with wood frame walls and a DOUBLE-HUNG window. The third wall section shown in the figure gives you similar information for a similar building constructed with a steel frame, a casement window, and a concrete floor finished with asphalt tile.

DETAILS

DETAIL drawings are drawings which are done on a larger scale than that of the general drawings, and which show features not appearing at all, or appearing on too small a scale, on the general drawings. The wall sections just described are details as well as sections, since

19

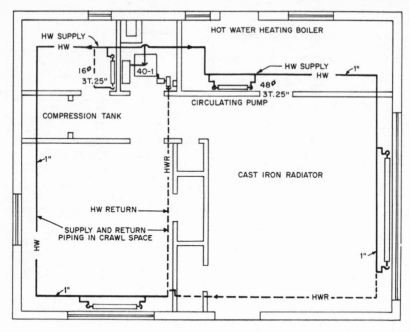

45.515(54)B

Figure 2-7.—Heating plan.

they are drawn on a considerable larger scale than the plans and elevations. Framing details at doors, windows, and cornices, which are the most common types of details, are practically always sections.

Details are included whenever the information given in the plans, elevations, and wall sections is not sufficiently "detailed" to guide the craftsmen on the job. Figure 2-12 shows some typical door and window wood framing details, and an eave detail for a very simple type of CORNICE. You should study these details closely to learn the terminology of framing members.

SPECIFICATIONS

The construction drawings contain much of the information about a structure which can be presented GRAPHICALLY (that is, in drawings). A very considerable amount of information can be presented this way, but there is more information which the construction supervisors and artisans must have and which is not adaptable to the graphic form of presentation. Information

of this kind includes quality criteria for materials (maximum amounts of aggregate per sack of cement, for example), specified standards of workmanship, prescribed construction methods, and the like.

Information of this kind is presented in a list of written SPECIFICATIONS, familiarly known as the "SPECS." A list of specifications usually begins with a section on GENERAL CONDITIONS. This section starts with a GENERAL DESCRIPTION of the building, including the type of foundation, type or types of windows, character of framing, utilities to be installed, and the like. Next comes a list of DEFINITIONS of terms used in the specs, and next certain routine declarations of responsibility and certain conditions to be maintained on the job.

SPECIFIC CONDITIONS are grouped in sections under headings which describe each of the major construction phases of the job. Separate specifications are written for each phase, and the phases are then combined to more or less follow the usual order of construction sequences on the job. A typical list of sections under "Specific Conditions" follows:

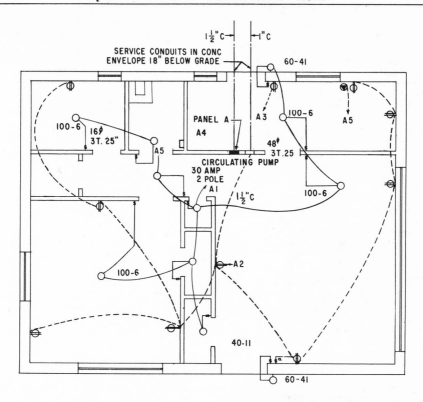

26.6(133E)

Figure 2-8.—Electrical plan.

2.—EARTHWORK 3.—CONCRETE 4.—MASONRY 5.—MISCELLANEOUS STEEL AND IRON 6.—CARPENTRY AND JOINERY 7.—LATHING AND PLASTERING 8.—TILE WORK 9.—FINISH FLOORING 10.—GLAZING 11.—FINISHING HARDWARE 12.—PLUMBING 13.—HEATING 14.—ELECTRICAL WORK 15.—FIELD PAINTING.

A section under "Specific Conditions" usually begins with a subsection of GENERAL REQUIREMENTS which apply to the phase of construction being considered. Under Section 6, CARPENTRY AND JOINERY, for example, the first section might go as follows:

6-01. GENERAL REQUIREMENTS. All framing, rough carpentry, and finishing woodwork required for the proper completion of the building shall be provided. All woodwork shall be protected from the weather, and the building shall be thoroughly dry before the finish is placed. All finish shall be dressed, smoothed, and sandpapered at the mill, and in addition shall be hand smoothed and sandpapered at the building where necessary to produce proper finish. Nailing shall be done, as far as practicable, in concealed places, and all nails in finishing work shall be set. All lumber shall be S4S (meaning, "surfaced on 4 sides"); all materials for millwork and finish shall be kiln-dried; all rough and framing lumber shall be air- or kiln-dried. Any cutting, fitting, framing, and blocking necessary for the accommodation of other work shall be provided. All nails, spikes, screws, bolts, plates, clips, and other fastenings and rough hardware necessary for the proper completion of the building shall be provided.

21

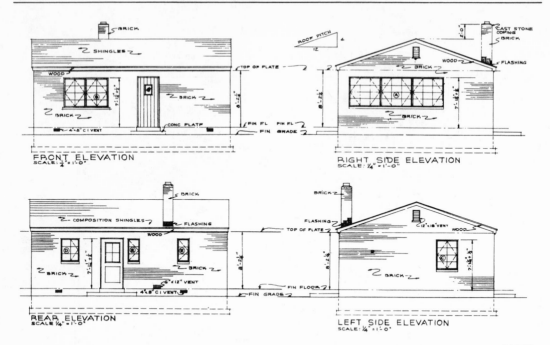

45.518

Figure 2-9.—Elevations.

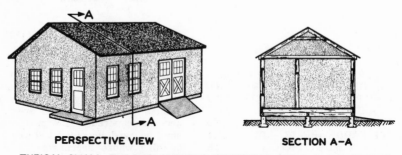

PERSPECTIVE VIEW   SECTION A-A

TYPICAL SMALL BUILDING SHOWING CUTTING PLANE A-A AND SECTION
DEVELOPED FROM THE CUTTING PLANE

45.520

Figure 2-10.—Development of a section view.

All finishing hardware shall be installed in accordance with the manufacturers' directions.
Calking and flashing shall be provided where
indicated, or where necessary to provide weathertight construction.

Next after the General Requirements for
Carpentry and Joinery, there is generally a
subsection on "Grading," in which the kinds and
grades of the various woods to be used in the
structure are specified. Subsequent subsections

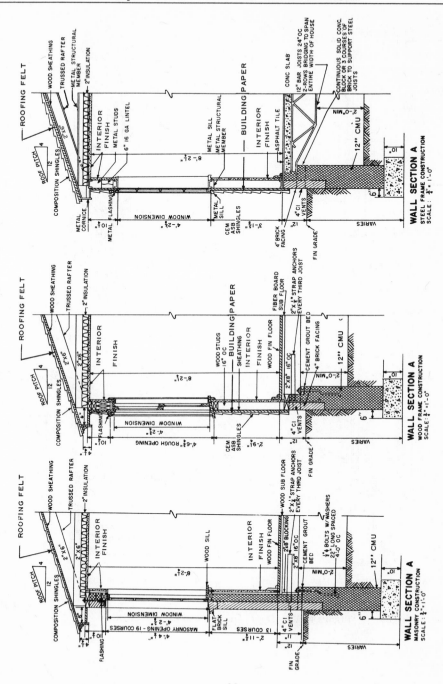

Figure 2-11.—Wall sections

45.521

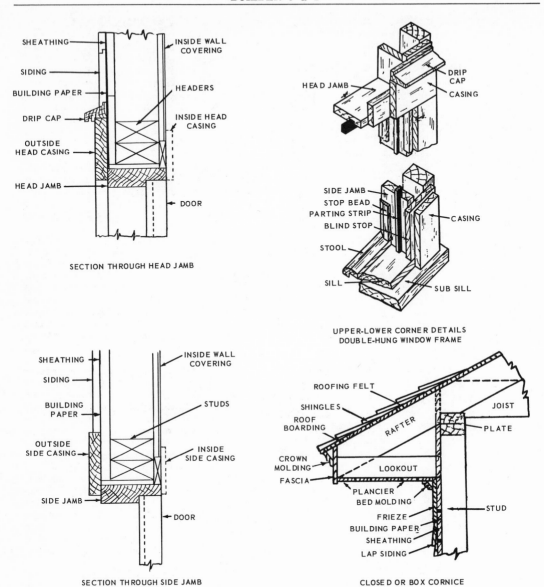

SHEATHING

SIDING

BUILDING PAPER

DRIP CAP

OUTSIDE
HEAD CASING

HEAD JAMB

INSIDE WALL
COVERING

HEADERS

INSIDE HEAD
CASING

DOOR

SECTION THROUGH HEAD JAMB

HEAD JAMB

DRIP
CAP

CASING

SIDE JAMB
STOP BEAD
PARTING STRIP
BLIND STOP

CASING

STOOL

SILL

SUB SILL

UPPER-LOWER CORNER DETAILS
DOUBLE-HUNG WINDOW FRAME

SHEATHING

SIDING

BUILDING
PAPER

OUTSIDE
SIDE CASING

SIDE JAMB

INSIDE WALL
COVERING

STUDS

INSIDE
SIDE CASING

DOOR

SECTION THROUGH SIDE JAMB

ROOFING FELT

SHINGLES

ROOF
BOARDING

CROWN
MOLDING

FASCIA

JOIST

RAFTER

PLATE

LOOKOUT

PLANCIER
BED MOLDING

FRIEZE

BUILDING PAPER

SHEATHING

LAP SIDING

STUD

CLOSED OR BOX CORNICE

45.501:.502

Figure 2-12.—Door, window and eave details.

specify various quality criteria and standards of workmanship for the various aspects of the rough and finish carpentry work, under such headings as FRAMING; SILLS, PLATES, AND GIRDERS; FLOOR JOISTS AND ROOF RAFTERS; STUDDING; and so on. An example of one of these subsections follows:

6-07. STUDDING for walls and partitions shall have doubled plates and doubled stud caps. Studs shall be set plumb and not to exceed 16-in. centers and in true alignment; they shall be bridged with one row of 2 x 4 pieces, set flatwise, fitted tightly, and nailed securely to each stud. Studding shall be doubled around openings and the heads of openings shall rest on the inner studs. Openings in partitions having widths of 4 ft and over shall be trussed. In wood frame construction, studs shall be trebled at corners to form posts.

From the above samples, you can see that a knowledge of the relevant specifications is as essential to the construction supervisor and the construction artisan as a knowledge of the construction drawings.

With very few exceptions, the material used by the SEABEES is covered by a Government spec, a NavFac spec, a Federal spec, or a Military spec. Commercial specs may be used in conjunction with Government specs for specialized types.

It is very important that the proper spec be used to cover the material requested. In cases in which the material is not covered by a Government spec, the ASTM (American Society for Testing Materials) spec or some other approved commercial spec may be used. It is EXTREMELY IMPORTANT in using specifications to cite all amendments, including the latest changes.

As a rule, the specs are provided for each project by the A/E (ARCHITECT-ENGINEERS). These are the OFFICIAL guidelines approved by the Chief of NavFac or his representative for use during construction. These requirements should NOT be deviated from without prior approval from proper authority. This approval is usually obtained by means of a change order. When there is disagreement between the specifications and drawings, the specifications should normally be followed; however, check with higher authority in each case.

BUILDER'S MATHEMATICS

The Builder has many occasions for the employment of the processes of ordinary arithmetic, and he must be thoroughly familiar with the methods of determining the areas and volumes of the various plane and solid geometrical figures. Only a few practical applications and a few practical suggestions, will be given here.

RATIO AND PROPORTION

Ratio and proportion and the manner of solving proportional equations are explained in Mathematics, vol. 1. There are a great many practical applications of ratio and proportion in the construction field. A few examples are as follows:

Some dimensions on construction drawings (such as, for example, distances from base lines and elevations of surfaces) are given in ENGINEER'S instead of CARPENTER's measure. Engineer's measure is measure in feet and decimal parts of a foot, or in inches and decimal parts of an inch, such as 100.15 ft or 11.14 in. Carpenter's measure is measure in yards, feet, inches, and even-denominator fractions of an inch, such as 1/2 in., 1/4 in., 1/16 in., 1/32 in., and 1/64 in.

You must know how to convert an engineer's measure given on a construction drawing to a carpenter's measure. Besides this, it will often happen that calculations you make yourself may produce a result in feet and decimal parts of a foot, which result you will have to convert to carpenter's measure. To convert engineer's to carpenter's measure you can use ratio and proportion as follows:

Let's say that you want to convert 100.14 ft to feet and inches to the nearest 1/16 in. The 100 you don't need to convert, since it is already in feet. What you need to do, first, is to find out how many twelfths of a foot (that is, how many inches) there are in 14/100 ft. Set this up as a proportional equation as follows: $x:12::14:100$.

You know that in a proportional equation the product of the means equals the product of the extremes. Consequently, $100x = (12 \times 14)$, or 168. Then $x = 168/100$, or 1.68 in. Next question is, how many 16ths of an in. are there in 68/100 in.? Set this up, too, as a proportional equation, thus: $x:16::68:100$. Then $100x = 1088$, and $x = 10\ 88/100$ sixteenths. Since 88/100 of a sixteenth is more than one-half of a sixteenth, you ROUND OFF by calling it 11/16. In 100.14 ft, then, there are 100 ft 1 11/16 in. For example:

A.   means
              x:12::14:100
              ⎵⎵⎵⎵⎵⎵⎵
              Extremes

Product of extremes = product of means:

$$100 \; x = 168$$
$$x = 1.68 \text{ IN.}$$

B. x:16::68:100

$$100 \, x = 1088$$

$$x = 10.88$$

$$x = 10 \frac{88}{100} \text{ sixteenths}$$

Rounded off to 11/16

Another way to convert engineer's measurements to carpenter's measurements is to multiply the decimal portion of a foot by 12 to get inches; multiply the decimal by 16 to get the fraction of an inch.

There are many other practical applications of ratio and proportion in the construction field. Suppose, for example, that a table tells you that, for the size and type of brick wall you happen to be laying, 12,321 bricks and 195 cu ft of mortar are required per every 1000 sq ft of wall. How many bricks and how much mortar will be needed for 750 sq ft of the same wall? You simply set up equations as follows; for example:

Brick: x:750::12,321:1000
Mortar: x:750::195:1000

Brick: $\dfrac{X}{750} = \dfrac{12,321}{1000}$ Cross multiply

$$1000 \, X = 9,240,750 \quad \text{Divide}$$
$$X = 9,240.75 = 9241 \text{ Brick.}$$

Mortar: $\dfrac{X}{750} = \dfrac{195}{1000}$ Cross multiply

$$1000 \, X = 146,250 \quad \text{Divide}$$
$$X = 146.25 = 146 \, 1/4 \text{ cu ft}$$

Suppose, for another example, that the ingredient proportions by volume for the type of concrete you are making are 1 cu ft cement to 1.7 cu ft sand to 2.8 cu ft coarse aggregate. Suppose you know as well, by reference to a table, that ingredients combined in the amounts indicated will produce 4.07 cu ft of concrete. How much of each ingredient will be required to make a cu yd of concrete?

Remember here, first, that there are not 9, but 27 (3 ft x 3 ft x 3 ft) cu ft in a cu yd. Your proportional equations will be as follows:

Cement: x:27::1:4.07

Sand: x:27::1.7:4.07

Coarse aggregate: x:27::2.8:4.07

Cement: x:27::1:4.07

$$\frac{x}{27} = \frac{1}{4.07}$$

$$4.07 \, x = 27$$

$$x = 6.63 \text{ cu ft Cement}$$

Sand: x:27::1.7:4.07

$$\frac{x}{27} = \frac{1.7}{4.07}$$

$$4.07 \, x = 45.9$$

$$x = 11.28 \text{ cu ft Sand}$$

Coarse aggregate: x:27::2.8:407

$$\frac{x}{27} = \frac{2.8}{4.07}$$

$$4.07 \, x = 75.6$$

$$x = 18.57 \text{ cu ft Coarse aggregate}$$

ARITHMETICAL OPERATIONS

The formulas for finding the area and volume of geometric figures are expressed in algebraic equations which are called formulas. A few of the more important formulas and their mathematical solutions will be discussed in this section.

To get an area, you multiply 2 linear measures together, and to get a volume you multiply 3 linear measures together. The linear measures you multiply together must all be expressed in the SAME UNITS; you cannot, for example, multiply a length in feet by a width in inches to get a result in square feet or in square inches.

Dimensions of a feature on a construction drawing are not always given in the same units. For a concrete wall, for example, the length and height are usually given in feet and the thickness in inches. Furthermore, you may want to get a result in units which are different from any shown on the drawing. Concrete volume, for example, is usually expressed in cubic yards, while the dimensions of concrete work are given on the drawings in feet and inches.

You can save yourself a good many steps in calculating by using fractions to convert the original dimension units into the desired end-result units. Take 1 in., for example. To express 1 in. in feet, you simply put it over 12, thus: 1/12 ft. To express 1 in. in yards, you simply put it over 36, thus: 1/36 yd. In the same manner, to express 1 ft in yards you simply put it over 3, thus 1/3 yd.

Suppose now that you want to calculate the number of cu yd of concrete in a wall 32 ft long by 14 ft high by 8 in. thick. You can express all these in yards and set up your problem thus:

$$\frac{32}{3} \times \frac{14}{3} \times \frac{8}{36}$$

Next you can cancel out, thus:

$$\frac{\overset{16}{\cancel{32}}}{3} \times \frac{\cancel{14}}{3} \times \frac{8}{\underset{9}{\cancel{36}}} = \frac{896}{81}$$

Dividing 896 by 81, you get 11.06 cu yds of concrete in the wall.

The right triangle is a triangle which contains one right (90°) angle. The following letters will denote the parts of the triangle indicated in figure 2-13—a = altitude, b = base, c = hypotenuse.

In solving a right triangle, the length of any side may be found if the lengths of the other two sides are given. The combinations of 3-4-5 (lengths of sides) or any multiple of these combinations will come out to a whole number. The following examples show the formula for finding

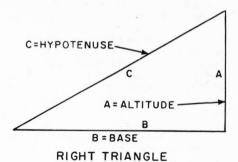

RIGHT TRIANGLE

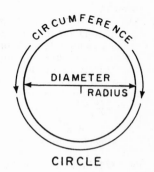

CIRCLE

133.1

Figure 2-13.—Right triangle and circle.

each side. Each of these formulas is derived from the master formula $c^2 = a^2 + b^2$.

(1) Find c when a = 3, and b = 4.

$$c = \sqrt{a^2 + b^2} = \sqrt{3^2 + 4^2} = \sqrt{9 + 16} = \sqrt{25} = 5$$

(2) Find a when b = 8, and c = 10.

$$a = \sqrt{c^2 - b^2} = \sqrt{10^2 - 8^2} = \sqrt{100 - 64} = \sqrt{36} = 6$$

(3) Find b when a = 9, and c = 15.

$$b = \sqrt{c^2 - a^2} = \sqrt{15^2 - 9^2} = \sqrt{225 - 81} = \sqrt{144} = 12.$$

There are tables from which the square roots of numbers may be found; otherwise, they may be found arithmetically as explained later in this chapter.

Areas And Volumes Of
Geometric Figures

This section on areas and volumes of geo-metric figures will be limited to the most com-monly used geometric figures. Reference books, such as Mathematics, Vol. 1, are available for additional information if needed. Areas are expressed in square units and volumes in cubic units.

1. A circle is a plane figure bounded by a curved line every point of which is the same distance from the center.
    a. The curved line is called the circum-ference.
    b. A straight line drawn from the center to any point on the circumference is called a radius. (r = 1/2 the diameter.)
    c. A straight line drawn from one point of the circumference through the center and terminating on the opposite point of the circumference is called a diam-eter. (d = 2 times the radius.) See figure 2-13.
    d. The area of a circle is found by the following formulas: $A = \pi r^2$ or $A = .7854 d^2$. (π is pronounced pie = 3.1416 or 3 1/7, .7854 is 1/4 of π.) Example: Find the area of a circle whose radius is 7". $A = \pi r^2 = 3\ 1/7 \times 7^2 = 22/7 \times 49 = 154$ sq in. If you use the second formula you obtain the same results.
    e. The circumference of a circle is found by multiplying π times the diameter or 2 times π times the radius. Example: Find the circumference of a circle whose diameter is 56 inches. $C = \pi d = 3.1415 \times 56 = 175.9296$ inches.
2. The area of a right triangle is equal to one-half the product of the base by the altitude. (Area = 1/2 base x altitude.) Example: Find the area of a triangle whose base is 16" and altitude 6". Solution:

$$A = 1/2\ bh = 1/2 \times 16 \times 6 = 48 \text{ sq in.}$$

3. The volume of a cylinder is found by mul-tiplying the area of the base times the height. ($V = 3.1416 \times r^2 \times h$). Example: Find the vol-ume of a cylinder which has a radius of 8 in. and a height of 4 ft. Solution:

$$8 \text{ in} = \frac{2}{3} \text{ ft and } \left(\frac{2}{3}\right) 2 = \frac{4}{9} \text{ sq ft.}$$

$$V = 3.1416 \times \frac{4}{9} \times 4 = \frac{50.2656}{9} = 5.59 \text{ cu ft.}$$

4. The volume of a rectangular solid equals the length x width x height. (V = lwh.) Exam-ple: Find the volume of a rectangular solid which has a length of 6 ft, a width of 3 ft, and a height of 2 ft. Solution:

$$V = lwh = 6 \times 3 \times 2 = 36 \text{ cu ft.}$$

5. The volume of a cone may be found by multiplying one-third times the area of the base times the height.

$$\left(V = \frac{1}{3} \pi r^2 h\right)$$

Example: Find the volume of a cone when the radius of its base is 2 ft and its height is 9 ft. Solution:

$$\pi = 3.1416,\ r = 2,\ 2^2 = 4$$

$$V = \frac{1}{3} r^2 h = \frac{1}{3} \times 3.1416 \times 4 \times 9 = 37.70 \text{ cu ft.}$$

Powers And Roots

1. Powers—When we multiply several num-bers together, as 2 x 3 x 4 = 24, the numbers 2, 3, and 4 are factors and 24 the product. The operation of raising a number to a power is a special case of multiplication in which the fac-tors are all equal. The power of a number is the number of times the number itself is to be taken as a factor. Example: 2^4 is 16. The second power is called the square of the number, as 3^2. The third power of a number is called the cube of the number, as 5^3. The exponent of a number is a number placed to the right and above a base to show how many times the base is used as a factor. Example:

$$4^3 \leftarrow \text{ exponent} = \\ \leftarrow \text{ base}$$

$$4 \times 4 \times 4 = 64.$$

2. Roots—To indicate a root, use the sign $\sqrt{\ }$, which is called the radical sign. A small figure, called the index of the root, is placed in the opening of the sign to show which root is to be taken. The square root of a number is one of the two equal factors into which a number is

divided. Example: $\sqrt{81} = \sqrt{9 \times 9} = 9$. The cube root is one of the three equal factors into which a number is divided. Example: $\sqrt[3]{125} = \sqrt[3]{5 \times 5 \times 5} = 5$.

Square Root

1. The square root of any number is that number which, when multiplied by itself, will produce the first number. For example; the square root of 121 is 11 because 11 times 11 equals 121.

2. How to extract the square root arithmetically:

$$\begin{array}{r} 95. \\ \sqrt{9025} \quad \sqrt{90'25.} \end{array}$$

$$: -81$$

$$\begin{array}{r} 180 : \quad 925 \\ +5 : \quad -925 \\ \hline 185 : \quad 000 \end{array}$$

a. Begin at the decimal point and divide the given number into groups of 2 digits each (as far as possible), going from right to left and/or left to right.

b. Find the greatest number (9) whose square is contained in the first or left hand group (90). Square this number (9) and place it under the first pair of digits (90), then subtract.

c. Bring down the next pair of digits (25) and add it to the remainder (9).

d. Multiply the first digit in the root by 20 and use it as a trial divisor (180). This trial divisor (180) will go into the new dividend (925) five times. This number, 5 (second digit in the root), is added back to the trial divisor, obtaining the true divisor (185).

e. The true divisor (185) is multiplied by the second digit (5) and placed under the remainder (925). Subtract and the problem is solved.

f. If there is still a remainder and you want to carry the problem further, add zeros (in pairs) and continue the above process.

Coverage Calculations

You will frequently have occasion to estimate the number of linear feet of boards of a given size, or the number of tiles, asbestos shingles, and the like, required to cover a given area. Let's take the matter of linear feet of boards first.

What you do here is calculate, first, the number of linear feet of board required to cover 1 sq ft. For boards laid edge-to-edge, you base your calculations on the total width of a board. For boards which will lap each other, you base your calculations on the width laid TO THE WEATHER, meaning the total width minus the width of the lap.

Since there are 144 sq in. in a sq ft, linear footage to cover a given area can be calculated as follows. Suppose your boards are to be laid 8 in. to the weather. If you divide 8 in. into 144 sq in., the result (which is 18 in., or 1.5 ft) will be the linear footage required to cover a sq ft. If you have, say, 100 sq ft to cover, the linear footage required will be 100 x 1.5, or 150 ft.

To estimate the number of tiles, asbestos shingles, and the like required to cover a given area, you first calculate the number of units required to cover a sq ft. Suppose, for example, you are dealing with 9 in. x 9 in. asphalt tiles. The area of one of these is 9 in. x 9 in. or 81 sq in. In a sq ft there are 144 sq in. If it takes 1 to cover 81 sq in., how many will it take to cover 144 sq in.? Just set up a proportional equation, as follows.

$$1:81::x:144$$

When you work this out, you will find that it takes 1.77 tiles to cover a sq ft. To find the number of tiles required to cover 100 sq ft, simply multiply by 100. How do you multiply anything by 100? Just move the decimal point 2 places to the right. Consequently, it takes 177 9 x 9 asphalt tiles to cover 100 sq ft of area.

Board Measure

BOARD MEASURE is a method of measuring lumber in which the basic unit is an abstract volume 1 ft long by 1 ft wide by 1 in. thick. This abstract volume or unit is called a BOARD FOOT.

There are several formulas for calculating the number of board feet in a piece of given dimensions. Since lumber dimensions are most frequently indicated by width and thickness in inches and length in feet, the following formula is probably the most practical.

$$\frac{\text{Thickness in in. x width in in. x length in ft}}{12}$$

= board feet

Suppose you are calculating the number of board feet in a 14-ft length of 2 x 4. Applying the formula, you get:

$$\frac{\overset{1}{\cancel{2}} \text{ x } \overset{2}{\cancel{4}} \text{ x } 14}{\underset{3}{\cancel{12}}} = \frac{28}{3} = 9 \text{ 1/3 bd ft}$$

The chief practical use of board measure is in cost calculations, since lumber is bought and sold by the board foot. Any lumber less than 1 in. thick is presumed to be 1 in. thick for board measure purposes. Board measure is calculated on the basis of the NOMINAL, not the ACTUAL, dimensions of lumber. As explained in chapter 9, the actual size of a piece of dimension lumber (such as a 2 x 4, for example) is usually less than the nominal size.

CHAPTER 3

THE ENGINEER'S LEVEL

You should be familiar with the various types of drawings which the Builder may use as an aid when laying out structures to conform to the location, size, shape, and quality specified by the designer. If you are not familiar with such drawings, review the applicable portions of Blueprint Reading and Sketching, NavPers 10077-C, before studying this chapter. In this chapter, you will learn how to use the information available on drawings, along with the related layout methods, in locating and laying out building lines and/or establishing elevations.

ELEVATION AND REFERENCE

The ELEVATION of any object is its vertical distance above or below an established height on the earth's surface. This established height is referred to as a REFERENCE PLANE, or simple REFERENCE. The most commonly used reference plane for elevations is MEAN (or average) SEA LEVEL, which has been assigned an assumed elevation of 000.0 ft. However, the reference plane for a construction project is usually the height of some permanent or semi-permanent object in the immediate vicinity, such as the rim of a manhole cover, a road, or the finish floor of an existing structure. This object may be given its relative sea-level elevation, if that happens to be known; or it may be given a convenient, arbitrarily assumed elevation, usually a whole number such as 100.0 ft. An object of this type, with a given, known, or assumed elevation which is to be used in determining the elevations of other points, is called a BENCH MARK.

DIFFERENTIAL LEVELING

The most common procedure for determining elevations in the field, or for locating points at specified elevations, is known as DIFFEREN-TIAL LEVELING. This procedure, as its name implies, is nothing more than finding the vertical DIFFERENCE between the known or assumed elevation of a bench mark and the elevation of the point in question. Once the difference is measured, it can be added to, or subtracted from (depending on the circumstances), the bench mark elevation to determine the elevation of the new point.

Figure 3-1, illustrates the principle of differential leveling. The instrument shown in the center represents an ENGINEER'S LEVEL. This optical instrument (described in more detail below) provides a perfectly level line of sight through a telescope which can be trained in any direction. Point A in the figure is a bench mark (it could be a concrete monument, a wooden stake, a sidewalk curb, or any other of a variety of objects) having a known elevation of 365.01 ft. Point B is a ground surface point whose elevation is desired.

The first step in finding the elevation point of Point B is to determine the elevation of the line-of-sight of the instrument. This is known as the height of instrument, and is often written and referred to as simply H.I. To determine the H.I. you would take a BACKSIGHT on a LEVEL ROD held vertically on the bench mark (B.M. or BM), as shown, by a RODMAN. A backsight (B.S. or BS) is always taken after a new instrument set-up by sighting back to a known elevation in order to get the new H.I. A leveling rod is a rod which is graduated upward from 0 at its base in feet with appropriate subdivisions of feet.

In figure 3-1, the backsight reading is 11.56 ft. It follows then, that the elevation of the line-of-sight (that is, the H.I.) must be 11.56 feet greater than the bench mark elevation, Point A. Therefore, the H.I. is 365.01 ft + 11.56 ft, or 376.57 ft as indicated.

Next, you would train the instrument ahead on another rod (or more usually, on the same rod carried ahead) held vertically on B. This is known as taking a FORESIGHT. After reading a foresight (F.S. or FS) of 1.42 ft on the rod, it follows that the elevation at point B must be 1.42 ft lower than the H.I. Therefore, the elevation of Point B is 376.57 ft - 1.42 ft, or 375.15 ft.

31

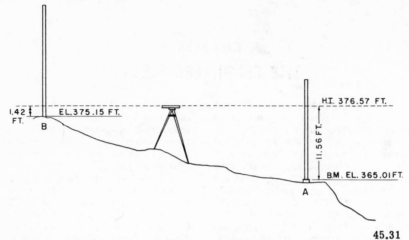

EL.375.15 FT.

1.42 FT.

B

HI. 376.57 FT.

11.56 FT.

BM. EL. 365.01 FT.

A

45.31

Figure 3-1.—Procedure for differential leveling.

THE ENGINEER'S LEVEL

The ENGINEER'S LEVEL is the instrument most commonly used to attain the level line of sight required for differential leveling. There are three types: the DUMPY LEVEL, SELF-LEVELING LEVEL, and the WYE LEVEL. Each type is mounted for use on a TRIPOD, usually with adjustable legs. See figure 3-2. Mounting is done by engaging threads at the base of the instrument (called the FOOTPLATE) with the threaded HEAD on the tripod. The dumpy level and the self-leveling level are the ones most frequently used in ordinary leveling, however, the wye level is also carried in the battalion equipment allowance.

DUMPY LEVEL

Figure 3-3 shows a DUMPY LEVEL and its nomenclature. Notice that the telescope is rigidly fixed to the supporting frame, whereas the telescope of the wye level (discussed later in this chapter) is held by rings which can be opened for removal. This is the major difference in these two levels.

Inside the telescope is a ring of diaphragm known as the RETICLE (not shown), which supports the CROSSHAIRS. The crosshairs are brought into exact focus by manipulating the knurled EYEPIECE FOCUSING RING near the EYEPIECE, or, on some models, the eyepiece itself. If the crosshairs get out of horizontal

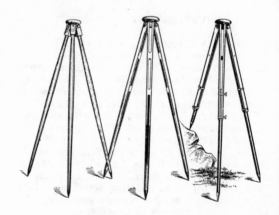

29.243AX

Figure 3-2.—Tripods.

adjustment, it can be made horizontal again by slackening the RETICLE ADJUSTING SCREWS and turning the screws in the appropriate direction.

The object to which you are sighting is called a TARGET, regardless of its shape. The target is brought into clear focus by manipulating the FOCUSING KNOB shown on top of the telescope. The telescope can only be rotated horizontally, but before it can be rotated, the AZIMUTH CLAMP must be released. When you have trained the telescope as nearly on the target as

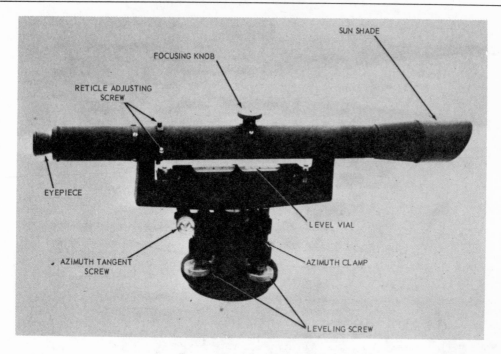

29.245A

Figure 3-3.—Dumpy Level.

you can get it, you tighten the azimuth clamp. Then you bring the vertical crosshair into exact alignment on the target by rotating the AZIMUTH TANGENT SCREW.

The LEVEL VIAL, LEVELING HEAD, LEVELING SCREWS, and FOOTPLATE are all used to adjust the instrument to a perfectly level line of sight, once it is mounted on the tripod.

SELF-LEVELING LEVEL

The self-leveling level (also called automatic level) is a timesaving invention used in leveling operations. The self-leveling level has completely eliminated the use of the tubular spirit level. (An excess amount of time was needed to center the bubble in the tubular spirit level, and the bubble had to be reset quite often during operation.)

The self-leveling level is equipped with a small bull's eye level and three leveling screws. The leveling screws, which set on a triangular foot plate, are used to (approximately) center the bubble of the bull's eye level. The line of

sight automatically becomes horizontal and remains horizontal as long as the bubble remains approximately centered.

There is a prismatic device located within the self-leveling level (called a "compensator") that makes all this possible. This compensator is suspended on fine, non-magnetic wires. The action of gravity on the compensator causes the optical system to swing into position which defines a horizontal sight. This horizontal line of sight is maintained despite a slight out-of-level of the telescope, or even when a slight disturbance occurs on the instrument.

A self-leveling level is shown in figure 3-4.

WYE LEVEL

The telescope of the WYE LEVEL, unlike that of the dumpy level, is supported in two rings which can be opened, allowing the telescope to be turned end-for-end or to be rotated. These rings (see Fig. 3-5) are called WYE RINGS, as the lower portion of each ring resembles the letter Y and it is from these rings

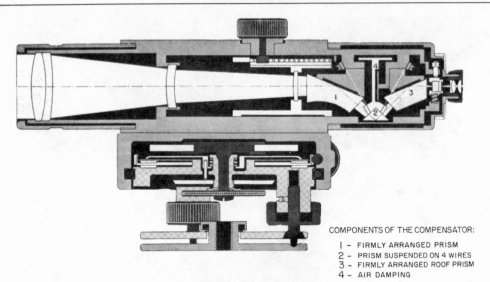

COMPONENTS OF THE COMPENSATOR:

1 - FIRMLY ARRANGED PRISM
2 - PRISM SUSPENDED ON 4 WIRES
3 - FIRMLY ARRANGED ROOF PRISM
4 - AIR DAMPING

45.750X

Figure 3-4.—Self-Leveling Level.

34

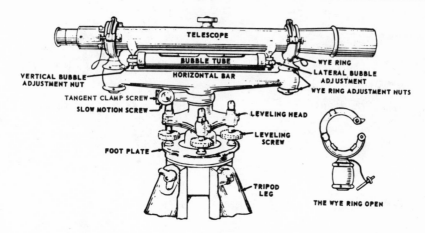

29.244

Figure 3-5.—Wye Level.

that the level gets its name. The level vial on the wye level can be adjusted vertically or horizontally by means of the VERTICAL (or LATERAL) ADJUSTMENT NUTS. There are also WYE RING ADJUSTMENT NUTS for raising and lowering the wye rings. All of these features exist to provide the possibility of fine adjustments for high-precision leveling. For most ordinary leveling that you will do, the wye level has no particular advantage over the dumpy or self-leveling level.. Because it has many more features capable of getting out of adjustment, or of being damaged by wear or hard use, it is seldom used when the dumpy and self-leveling levels are available.

CARE OF LEVELS

An engineer's level is a precision instrument containing many delicate and some fragile parts. It must be handled gently and with the greatest care at all times, and it must never be subjected to shock or jar. Movable parts (if not locked or clamped in place) should work easily and smoothly. If a movable part resists normal pressure, there is something wrong somewhere, and if you FORCE the part to move you will probably damage the instrument. You will also cause wear and/or damage if you tighten clamps, screws, and the like excessively.

The ONLY proper place to stow the instrument when it is detached from the tripod, is in its own carrying box or case. The carrying case is designed to reduce the effect of jarring to a minimum, and it is strongly made and well padded to protect the instrument from damage. Before stowing, the azimuth clamp and leveling screws should be slightly tightened to prevent movement of parts inside the box. When being transported in a vehicle, the case containing the instrument should be placed as nearly as possible midway between the front and rear wheels. This is the point where jarring of the wheels has the least effect on the chassis.

NEVER lift the instrument out of the case by grasping the telescope. Wrenching the telescope in this manner will damage a number of delicate parts. Instead, lift it out by reaching down and grasping the foot plate or the level bar.

When the instrument, attached to the tripod, is to be carried from one point to another, the azimuth clamp and level screws should be set up tight enough to prevent part motion during the transport, but loose enough to allow a "give" in case of an accidental bump against some object or other. When you are carrying the instrument over terrain which is free of possible contacts (across an open field, for example), you may carry it over your shoulder, like a rifle. When there are obstacles, however, you should carry it as shown in figure 3-6. Carried in this manner, the instrument is always visible to you, and this makes it possible for you to avoid striking it against obstacles.

45.93

Figure 3-6.—Safest carrying procedure
where obstacles exist.

SETTING UP A LEVEL

The first step in setting up, after selecting
the proper location, is to set up the tripod.
This is done by spreading two legs a convenient
distance apart, and then bringing the third leg
to a position which will bring the PROTECTOR
CAP (covering the TRIPOD HEAD THREADS)
about level when the tripod stands on all legs.
Then unscrew the protector cap, exposing the
threaded head, and place it in the carrying case
where it will not get lost or dirty.

Lift the instrument out of the carrying case
by the footplate—NOT by the telescope. Set it
squarely and gently on the tripod head threads
and engage the HEAD NUT THREADS under the
footplate by rotating the footplate clockwise. If
the threads will not engage smoothly, they may
be cross-threaded or dirty. DO NOT FORCE
them if you encounter resistance, but instead,
back off and, after checking to see that they are
clean, square up the instrument and try again
gently. Screw the head nut up firmly but not
too tightly. Setting up too tightly causes eventual wearing of the threads, and makes unthread-
ing difficult. After you have attached the instrument, thrust the leg tips into the ground far
enough to ensure that each leg has stable support, taking care to maintain the footplate as
near level as possible. With the instrument
mounted and the legs securely positioned in the
soil, the thumbscrews at the top of each leg
should be firmly tightened to prevent any possible movement.

Quite frequently the Builder must set up on
a hard, smooth surface such as a concrete
pavement. Therefore, steps must be taken to

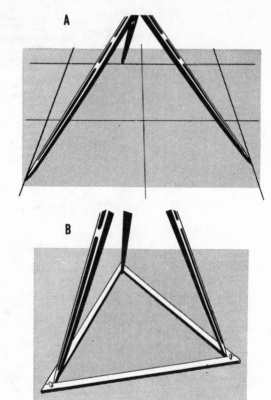

45.94

Figure 3-7.—Methods of preventing
tripod legs from spreading.

prevent the legs from spreading. Figure 3-7
shows two good ways of doing this. In view A,
the tips of the legs are inserted in joints in the
pavement. In view B, the tips are held by a
wooden triangle called a floor triangle.

LEVELING A LEVEL

To function accurately, the level must provide a line of sight which is PERFECTLY HOR-
IZONTAL (that is, LEVEL) in any direction the
telescope is trained. To ensure this, the instrument must be leveled as follows.

As already explained, when the tripod and
instrument are first set up, the footplate should
be made as nearly level as possible. Next,

train the telescope over a pair of diagonally opposite leveling screws and clamp it in that position. Then manipulate the leveling thumbscrews, as shown in figure 3-8, so as to bring the bubble in the level vial exactly into the marked center position.

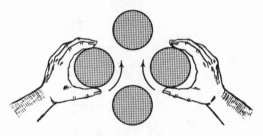

45.95

Figure 3-8.—Manipulating level screws.

The thumbscrews are manipulated by simultaneously turning them in opposite directions, a procedure which shortens one SPIDER LEG (threaded member running through the thumbscrew) while it lengthens the other. It is helpful to remember that the level vial bubble will move in the same direction that your left thumb moves while you rotate the thumbscrews. To put this another way: when your left thumb pushes the thumbscrew CLOCKWISE, the bubble will move towards your left hand; when you turn the left thumbscrew COUNTERCLOCKWISE, the bubble moves toward your right hand.

After leveling the telescope over one pair of screws, train it over the other pair and repeat the process. As a check, set the telescope over pairs in all four possible positions and ascertain that the bubble centers exactly in each.

LEVELING RODS

LEVELING RODS are used to measure the precise vertical distance between the object or point in question and the exactly level line-of-sight of the instrument. For example, in Fig. 3-1, the leveling, rod was held at points A and B and vertical heights of 11.56 ft and 1.42 ft were read respectively. There are two general types of leveling rods. These are the DIRECT READING type (also called SELF-READING type) and the TARGET-READING type. Since most target-reading rods can also be read direct, it is really more accurate to say that most leveling rods are direct-reading and some are also equipped for target-reading.

Philadelphia Rod

Perhaps the most frequently used leveling rod is the PHILADELPHIA rod shown in figure 3-9. The face of the rod is shown to the left; the back to the right. The rod consists of two sliding sections which can be fully extended to a total length of 13.10 ft. When the sections are entirely closed, the total length is 7.10 ft. For direct readings (that is, for readings on the face of the rod) of up to 7.10 ft and 13.10 ft, it is used extended and read on the back, by the rodman.

In direct readings it is the man at the instrument who reads, through the telescope, the graduation on the rod intercepted by the crosshair. In TARGET readings on the face of the rod it is the RODMAN who reads the graduation on the rod intercepted by a TARGET. In figure 3-9 the target does not appear; it is shown however, in figure 3-10. As you can see, it is a sliding, circular, red-and-white device which can be moved up or down the rod and clamped in position. It is placed by the rodman on signals given by the instrumentman.

The rod shown in the figures is graduated in feet and hundredths of a foot. Each even foot is marked with a large red numeral, and between each pair of adjacent red numerals the intermediate tenths of a foot are marked with smaller black numerals. Each intermediate hundredth of a foot between each pair of adjacent tenths is indicated by the top or bottom of one of the short, black dash graduations.

DIRECT READING.—In direct reading, readings are taken directly from the face of the rod only. In almost all instances, this would be the type of reading made by a Builder. As markings on the rod represent 0.01 ft, accuracy can only be maintained to 0.01 ft; however, with a little practice, an intermediate reading of 0.005 (a little under 1/16 in.) can be easily estimated. Suppose, for example, that for a direct reading on the rod shown in figure 3-10 the crosshair intercepted the rod at the point where the 0 on the target is shown in the figure. This point lies somewhere between 5.00 ft and 6.00 ft, since the large, red 6 appears above. The black 8 and 9 indicate that the reading also lies between 5.80 ft and 5.90 ft. Counting the bottoms and tops of the dashes up from the top of the

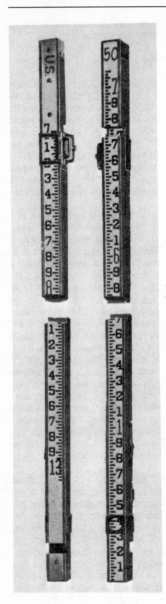

29.265A
Figure 3-9:—Face and back of
Philadelphia leveling rod.

5.80 dash, you will count 4 hundredths of a foot
before you get to the target zero. Therefore,

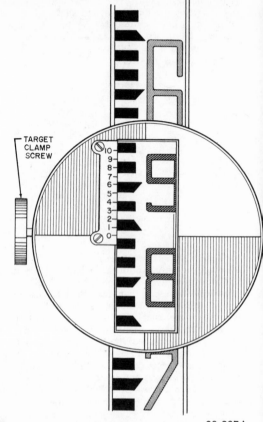

TARGET
CLAMP
SCREW

29.267A
Figure 3-10.—Philadelphia rod set for target
reading of less than 7.000 ft.

the reading to the nearest 0.01 ft is 5.84 ft. If
a little closer reading is necessary you could
estimate this to be about 5.845 ft as the 0 line
looks to be about half-way between the 5.84
dash and 5.85 dash. Actually, you will find in
the next few paragraphs that this reading is
exactly 5.843 ft which is just about 1/64 of an
inch difference and normally acceptable.

TARGET READING.—There are three situations in which target reading rather than direct
reading is done on the face of the rod: when
the rod is too far from the level to be read directly through the telescope; when a reading to
the nearest 0.001 ft, rather than to the nearest

0.01 ft, is desired (a VERNIER on the target, or on the back of the rod, makes this possible as explained shortly); and when the instrumentman desires to ensure against the possibility of reading the wrong foot (large red letter) designation on the rod.

For target readings up to 7.000 ft, the rod is used fully closed, and the rodman, on signals from the instrumentman, sets the target at the point where its horizontal axis is intercepted by the crosshair as seen through the telescope. He then clamps it in place with the TARGET SCREW CLAMP shown in figure 3-10. If reading to only the nearest 0.01 ft is desired, he reads the graduation indicated by the target horizontal axis; in figure 3-10, this reading is 5.84 ft.

If reading to the nearest 0.001 ft is desired, the rodman reads the VERNIER (small scale running from 0 to 10) on the target. The 0 on the vernier indicates that the reading lies between 5.840 ft and 5.850 ft. To determine how many thousandths of a foot over 5.840 there are, you examine the graduations on the vernier to determine which one is most exactly in line with a graduation (top or bottom of a black dash) on the rod. In figure 3-10 this graduation on the vernier is the 3; therefore, the reading to the 0.001 ft. is 5.843 ft.

For target readings of more than 7.000 ft the procedure is a little different. If you look at the right-hand view of figure 3-4 (showing the BACK of the rod), you will see that only the back of the UPPER section is graduated, and that it is graduated DOWNWARD from 7.000 ft at the top to 13.09 ft at the bottom. You can also see that there is a ROD VERNIER fixed to the top of the LOWER section of the rod. This vernier is read against the graduations on the back of the upper section.

For a target reading of more than 7.000 ft, the rodman first clamps the target at the upper section of the rod. Then, on signals from the instrumentman, he extends the rod upward to the point where the horizontal axis of the target is intercepted by the crosshair. He then clamps the rod, using the ROD CLAMP SCREW shown in figure 3-11, and reads the vernier on the BACK of the rod, also shown in that figure. In this case the 0 on the vernier indicates a certain number of thousandths more than 7.100 ft. REMEMBER THAT IN THIS CASE YOU READ THE ROD AND THE VERNIER DOWN FROM THE TOP, NOT UP FROM THE BOTTOM. To determine the thousandths, determine which

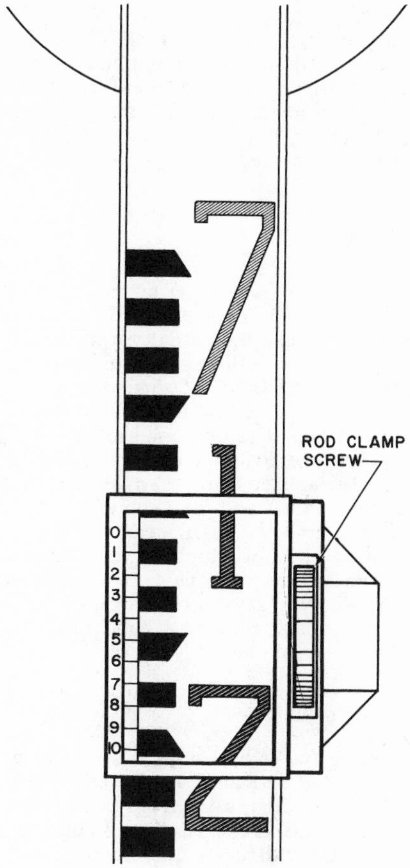

ROD CLAMP
SCREW

29.267B
Figure 3-11.—Philadelphia rod target reading of more than 7.000 ft.

vernier graduation lines up most exactly with a graduation on the rod. In this case it is the 7; therefore, the rod reading is 7.107 ft.

Other Types of Rods

There are several other types of leveling rods, which differ from the Philadelphia only in details. The FRISCO rod, for direct reading only, is available with 2 sections or with 3 sections. The DETROIT rod is available with 3 or 4 sections which, instead of sliding, are joined

end-to-end, fishing-rod style. The ARCHI-
TECT'S rod (also called ARCHITECT'S AND
BUILDER'S rod) is a 2-section rod similar to
the Philadelphia, but graduated in feet and
inches to the nearest 1/8 in., rather than deci-
mally. Readings to the nearest 1/64 in. can be
made with the vernier.

Rod Levels

A rod reading is accurate only if the rod is
perfectly PLUMB (vertical) at the time of the
reading. If the rod is out of plumb, the reading
will be greater than the actual vertical distance
between the H.I. and the base of the rod.

The use of a ROD LEVEL ensures a vertical
rod. A BULL'S-EYE rod level is shown in figure 3-12. When it is held as shown (on a part
of the rod where readings are not being taken,
to avoid interference with the instrumentman's
view of the scale), and the bubble is centered,
the rod is plumb. A VIAL rod level has two
spirit vials, each of which is mounted on the
upper edge of one of a pair of hinged metal
LEAVES. The vial level is used like the bull's-
eye level, except that two bubbles must be
watched instead of one.

Care of Leveling Rods

A leveling rod is a precision instrument and
must be treated as such. Most rods are made
of carefully selected, kiln-dried, well-seasoned
hardwood. Scale graduations and numerals on
some are painted directly on the wood; on most
rods, however, they are painted on a metal
strip attached to the wood. Unless a rod is
handled at all times with great care, the painted
scale will soon become scratched, dented, worn,
or otherwise marked and obscured. Accurate
readings on a scale in this condition are difficult.

Allowing an extended sliding-section rod to
close "on the run," by permitting the upper
section to drop, may jar the vernier scale out
of position or otherwise injure the rod. Always
close an extended rod by easing the upper section down gradually.

A rod will read accurately only if it is perfectly straight. It follows from this that anything which might bend or warp the rod must be
avoided. Do not lay a rod down flat unless it is
supported throughout, and never, of course, use
a rod for a seat, a lever, or a pole vault. In

45.40
Figure 3-12.—Bull's-eye
rod level.

short, never use a rod for any purpose except
the one for which it is designed.

Store a rod not in use in a DRY place, to
avoid warping and swelling caused by dampness.
Always wipe off a wet rod before putting it away.
If there is dirt on the rod, RINSE it off but do
not SCRUB it off. If a soap solution must be
used (to remove grease, for example), make it
a very mild one. The use of strong soap solution will soon cause the paint on the rod to degenerate.

Protect a rod as much as possible against
prolonged exposure to strong sunlight. Such
exposure causes paint to CHALK—meaning to
degenerate into a chalk-like substance which
detaches from the surface.

CARPENTER'S RULE AND "STORY POLE"

For much of the work done at advance bases,
extreme accuracy is relatively unimportant. It
is therefore often useful and expedient to take
direct readings from an extended carpenter's
rule. To help keep the rule from bending, it
should be held against a stiff board, such as a
1 x 2.

When several readings must be made at the
same height (such as setting screeds for a
slab, or certain heights that must be checked at

regular intervals, a "story pole" can be used. This is nothing more than a 1 x 2 with the proper elevations already marked on it.

Suppose, for example, you were placing 2 x 4 screeds for a concrete slab. Let's assume that the slab elevation is to be 2 ft higher than a nearby manhole cover, which we will give an assumed elevation of 100.00 ft. Naturally, the proposed slab elevation will be 102.00 ft. After setting up the instrument, have a rodman hold the pole on the bench mark (manhole cover) and then direct him to make a mark on the pole where the crosshair crosses it. As a rodman, you might find it convenient to use a combination square as a target. This mark of course is the present H.I. Next, a mark is made two feet up from the bottom. This is the proposed deck elevation. The story pole now has all the information required to set the screeds. Whenever the pole is held vertically, with the H.I. mark in alignment with the level's crosshair, the 2 ft mark will indicate the height at which the screeds should be set. Very few decks, however, are over two feet thick and you will probably find that the two feet protruding below the deck will get in the way while using the pole. Rather than cutting it off, it would be better to make another pole with the bottom representing the floor height. In this manner, wherever it is placed on the screed the crosshair should intersect the H.I. mark. Don't throw away the original. It will be needed throughout the project to establish wall heights, window and door heights, courses of siding, etc. Each day after a new instrument set up, a new H.I. must be found.

LEVELING TECHNIQUES

Various techniques for using the level will develop with experience; however, in this section we will only discuss the techniques that we believe are essential to the Builder rating. If you as a Builder find that you need more information concerning leveling techniques, refer to the latest edition of Engineering Aid 3 & 2.

BALANCING SHOTS

No matter how carefully an instrument is leveled, the line of sight through the telescope is likely to be not quite exactly horizontal. The error which this introduces is directly proportional to the distance between the level and the object sighted—meaning that the error increases as the distance increases. To help overcome the INSTRUMENTAL ERROR we should take BALANCING SHOTS.

Balancing shots are nothing more than equalizing, as much as possible, the backsight and foresight distances by selecting setup points which are as nearly as possible equidistant from the points backsighted and foresighted.

Assume, for example, that you took a backsight on a rod held on a BM, which is 350 horizontal feet away from the level, and read 7.50 ft. There you take a foresight on a rod held on a point, which is also 350 horizontal feet away from the level, and read 11.5 ft. Now suppose that, because of instrument error, both of these readings are slightly less than they should be. Because of the equal BS and FS distances, however, they are less by exactly the same amount.

However, if the BS and FS distances were radically different, the effect of instrumental error on BS and FS would also be radically different. For this reason, shots must always be balanced as nearly as possible when accurate elevations are required.

TURNING POINTS

In the case shown in figure 3-1, you were able to determine the desired elevation from a single instrument setup, because the difference in elevation between the bench mark and the point was small enough to make this possible. However, figure 3-13 shows a situation in which the difference in elevation is too large for a single setup.

What you do in such a case is determine the elevations of as many intermediate TURNING POINTS as you need to bring the instrument to a setup point from which you can read a rod set on the summit. You started here by setting up at a point on the slope where you could get a pretty high backsight reading on a rod set on the bench mark. The backsight reading was 12.02 ft; therefore, the H.I. at the first setup was 100.00 + 12.02, or 112.02 ft. You then trained the telescope ahead, in the direction of the summit, and had the rod set up on a point where you could get a low reading of 2.06 ft. The elevation of this point is 112.02 - 2.06, or 109.96 ft. This point is the first turning point (T.P.). You can see in the figure how it was used to backsight on from the next forward setup, and how the elevation of a second T.P. was obtained. From a third setup, between this T.P. and the summit, it was possible to determine the elevation of the summit.

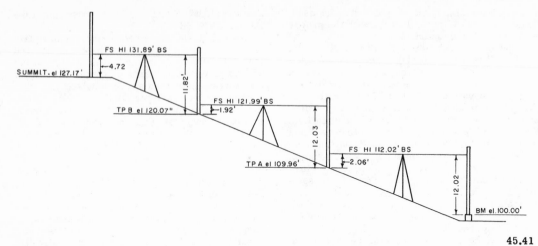

45.41

Figure 3-13.—A series of turning points.

SELECTION OF TURNING POINTS

Suppose you want to determine the elevation of a certain point A. The nearest point of known elevation is a certain BM. Because of distance, steepness of slope, or both, you have to make the run by way of a series of intermediate TP's. Somebody else has determined the elevation of the BM, but each of the TP's is a point whose elevation you must determine yourself. The accuracy of the elevation you determine for point A will depend on the accuracy with which you determine the elevation of each intermediate TP.

For most ordinary leveling it is customary to limit BS and FS distances to a maximum of 300 horizontal ft. Consequently, the first setup point should be not more than 300 ft from the BM, and the first TP should be about the same distance from the setup point (if the required accuracy calls for balancing shots).

In general, TP's and setup points should be selected so as to make rod readings as small as possible—meaning that the best setup point is one at which the difference in elevation between the BM and the H.I. is as small as possible, and the best TP is one with an elevation as near that of the H.I. as possible.

The reason why small rod readings are desirable is this. If a rod is held slightly out of plumb, each reading on the rod will be larger by a certain amount than it should be, and this amount increases as the size of the rod reading

increases. Suppose, for example, that a rodman holds a rod so far out of plumb as to cause it to read 12.01 ft when it would have read 12.00 ft if it were plumb. The error for a 12.00-ft distance, then, is 0.01 ft. For a 2.00-ft distance on the same rod held in the same manner, however, the error would equal the value of x in the equation $12.00:0.01::2.00:x$, or only about 0.002 ft.

A selected TP must be STABLE—meaning that it must furnish a firm, unyielding support for the base of the rod. This prevents the rod from settling into the ground between instrument setups. When you cannot avoid working in soft, yielding ground, the base of the rod should be placed on a stake driven flush with the ground, or, on a specially made TURNING POINT PIN or TURNING POINT PLATE as those illustrated in fig. 3-14.

FIELD NOTES

It is not often that you will be required to keep FIELD NOTES; however, if you had to make the level run illustrated in figure 3-13 you should keep a record in a FIELD NOTE-BOOK similar to that shown in figure 3-15. The lefthand page shown is called the DATA page, the right-hand page the REMARKS page. On the data page there are, from left to right, columns headed Sta. (for station), B.S. (for backsight), H.I. (for height of instrument), F.S. (for foresight), and Elev. (for elevation). The first entry

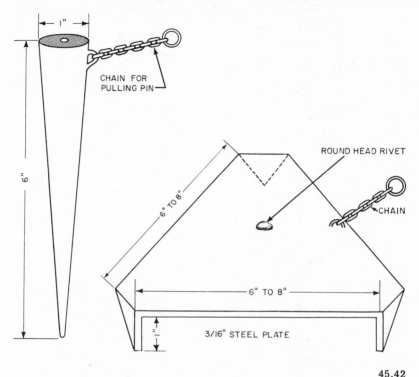

CHAIN FOR PULLING PIN

1"

6"

ROUND HEAD RIVET

6" TO 8"

CHAIN

6" TO 8"

3/16" STEEL PLATE

45.42

Figure 3-14.—Turning point pin and turning point plate.

under Sta. is the starting point, the bench mark, entered as B.M. 1. Beside this entry, under Elev., is the bench mark elevation of 100.00 ft. The first B.S. reading, on the rod held on the B.M., is 12.02, as entered beside B.M. 1 in the column headed B.S. The H.I. of 100.00 + 12.02, or 112.02, is entered under H.I.

The first turning point, T.P. 1, is entered in the Sta. column below B.M. 1. The foresight on that T.P., which read 2.06 ft, is entered in the F.S. column, and the elevation of the T.P., computed by subtracting the F.S. of 2.06 ft from the H.I. of 112.02 ft, is entered (109.96 ft) in the column headed "Elev." You can see how the notes follow through to the summit elevation of 127.17 ft.

Note the check on the mathematics. This check is based on the fact that the difference between the sum of the foresight readings and the sum of the backsight readings should equal the difference between the starting B.M. elevation and the summit elevation. The sum of the

B.S. readings is 35.87 ft; the sum of the F.S. readings is 8.70 ft; and the difference is 35.87 - 8.70, or 27.17 ft. The difference between the starting B.M. elevation and the summit elevation is 127.17 - 100.00, or 27.17 ft. Therefore, the check on the mathematics is satisfactory.

As a check on the precision with which the work was done, the line of levels was run back again from the summit to the B.M. As you can see, this resulted in an elevation for the B.M. which is 0.02 ft higher than its actual elevation. Whether or not this discrepancy would be considered too large would depend on the order of precision required in the level run. For most preliminary Builder leveling purposes, it would probably be considered satisfactory.

SIGNALS

During fieldwork, it is essential that you communicate with the other members of the survey party over considerable distances.

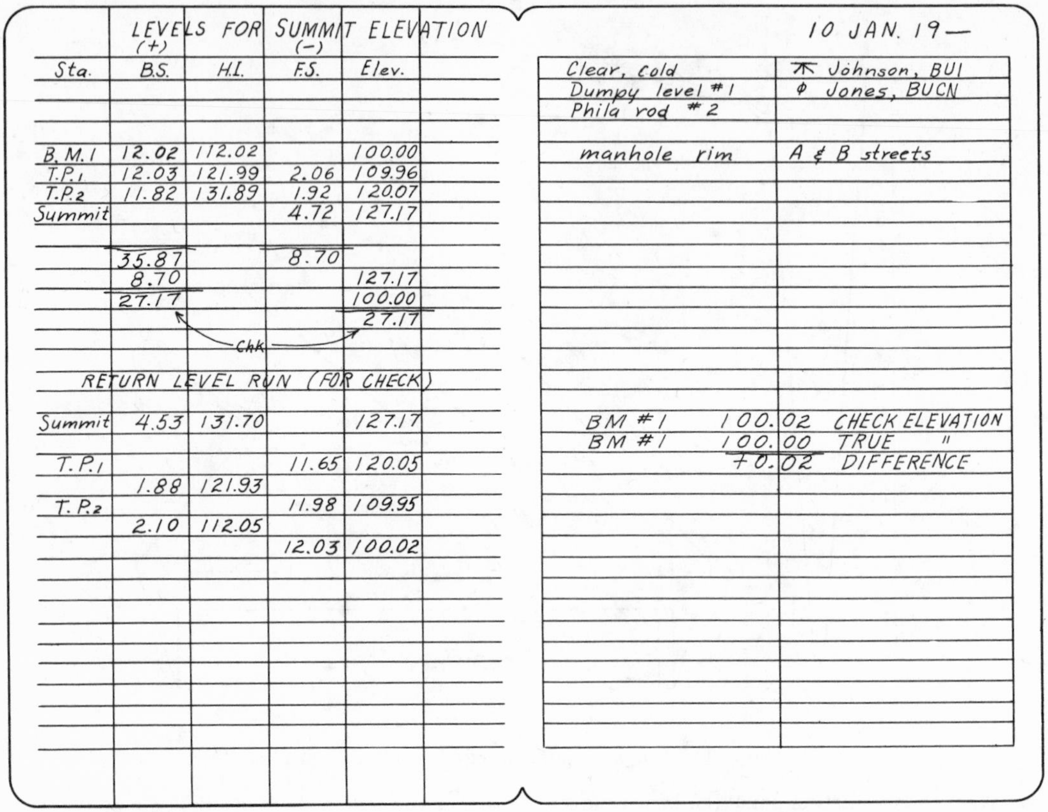

Sta.	B.S. (+)	H.I.	F.S. (−)	Elev.			
LEVELS FOR SUMMIT ELEVATION							10 JAN. 19—
						Clear, cold	🏹 Johnson, BU1
						Dumpy level #1	ϕ Jones, BUCN
						Phila rod #2	
B.M.1	12.02	112.02		100.00		manhole rim	A & B streets
T.P.1	12.03	121.99	2.06	109.96			
T.P.2	11.82	131.89	1.92	120.07			
Summit			4.72	127.17			
	35.87		8.70				
	8.70			127.17			
	27.17			100.00			
				27.17			
	—Chk—						
RETURN LEVEL RUN (FOR CHECK)							
Summit	4.53	131.70		127.17		BM #1	100.02 CHECK ELEVATION
						BM #1	100.00 TRUE "
T.P.1			11.65	120.05			+0.02 DIFFERENCE
	1.88	121.93					
T.P.2			11.98	109.95			
	2.10	112.05					
			12.03	100.02			

45.7.37

Figure 3-15.—Field notes for differential leveling.

Sometimes you may be close enough to use voice communication; more often you will use hand signals. Avoid shouting; it is the sign of a beginner. Standard voice signals between instrumentman and rodman (or vice versa) must be used at all times to avoid misunderstanding. Recommended hand signals are illustrated in figures 3-16 and 3-17. Those illustrated are recommended but any set of signals mutually agreed upon and understood by all members of the party can also be used. It is important to face the person being signaled. Sometimes, if it is difficult for you to see the instrumentman, he will hold white flagging in his hand when giving signals. When signals are given over snow-covered areas, red or orange flagging is more appropriate. Explanations of the hand signals shown in figure 3-16 are as follows:

ALL RIGHT. When the alignment is OK for a plumb line, range pole, a stake, hub or any other device used as a target, or when the instrumentman has finished all activities at your location, he will motion "all right" by waving his arms up and down while extending them out from his sides. If the instrumentman, in aligning a target, extends his arms sidewards without waving them, it means that the target should be held steady while a quick check of its position is being made.

MOVE RIGHT OR LEFT. This signal is given by moving the appropriate hand outward from the shoulder. This is given by the instrumentman when lining-in a target on a predetermined line. A slow motion of the hand means that you must move a long distance; a quick short motion means that you must move a short distance.

44

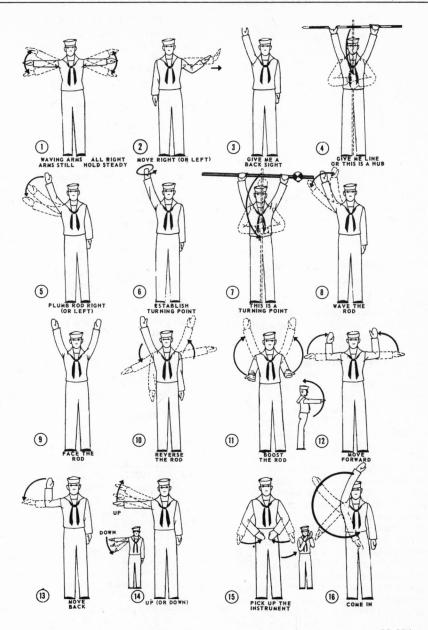

29.271

Figure 3-16.—Surveyor's hand signals.

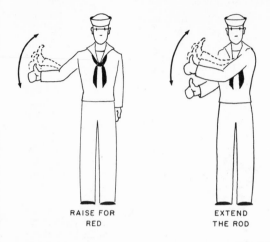

RAISE FOR
RED

EXTEND
THE ROD

117.29

Figure 3-17.—Additional hand signals.

GIVE ME A BACKSIGHT. This signal is done by extending one arm upward, palm of the hand forward when the instrumentman wants a target held at a previously located point.

GIVE ME A LINE OR THIS IS A HUB. This signal is accomplished by holding a range pole horizontally overhead, then moving it to a vertical position in front of the body. When the signal is intended to indicate a hub, place the range pole on the point indicating the exact station. This signal is given by the rodman or the instrumentman when he wants the range pole lined-in on a previously determined line, or to indicate that a hub has been established and the instrumentman is to measure an angle to the station. Sometimes the range pole tip is set on the ground to act as a pivot and the pole is swayed slowly to the left and right until the instrumentman picks up the signal.

PLUMB THE ROD. To plumb the rod to the desired direction (right or left), the signal is given by extending the appropriate arm upward and moving the hand in the direction the top of the rod must be moved to make it vertical.

ESTABLISH A TURNING POINT. This signal is given by extending an arm upward and making a circular motion. The instrumentman usually gives this signal when he wants a turning point established during level operations, or when he wants a hub established during traversing operations.

THIS IS A TURNING POINT. This signal is given by the rodman to indicate a turning point, using a leveling rod as described for the range pole above.

WAVE THE ROD. This signal is accomplished by extending one arm upward, palm of the hand forward, and waving the arm slowly from side to side. The instrumentman gives this signal to indicate that he wants the rodman to move the top of the leveling rod forward and backward slowly, about one foot each way from the vertical. This is done so that the instrumentman can get the lowest reading.

FACE THE ROD. To give this signal, the instrumentman extends both his arms upward to indicate to the rodman that the leveling rod is faced in the wrong direction.

REVERSE THE ROD. Its meaning is obvious. This signal is given by the instrumentman holding one arm upward and the other downward, and reversing their positions with full side-arm swings. "Reversed rod generally happens when the rodman is not paying full attention to his work."

BOOST THE ROD. This signal is given by swinging both arms forward and upward, palms of the hands upward. The instrumentman uses this signal when he wants the leveling rod raised and held with its bottom end at a specified distance, usually about 3 feet above the ground.

MOVE FORWARD. The instrumentman gives this signal by extending the arms sideward, palms up, then swinging the forearms upward.

MOVE BACK. This signal is given by the instrumentman holding one upper arm extended sideward, hand and forearm extended vertically, and moving the hand and forearm outward until the whole arm is extended horizontally.

UP, OR DOWN. This signal is given by extending one arm horizontally and moving it upward or downward. This directs the rodman to slide the target up or down on the rod.

PICK UP THE INSTRUMENT. This signal is accomplished by imitating the motions of picking up an instrument and putting it on the shoulder. This signal is given by the party chief or other responsible member of the party, directing the instrumentman to move forward to the point that has just been established.

COME IN. This signal is given by the chief of the party at the end of the day's work, and at other times as necessary.

The meaning of the signals shown in figure 3-17 are as follows:

RAISE FOR RED/READING. This signal is given by the instrumentman in level operations when he cannot ascertain the immediate whole-foot mark after he reads the tenths and hundredths of a foot. This usually happens when the rodman is very near the instrument or if something is in the way to obscure the whole-foot mark. When the rodman is very near, the instrumentman can naturally just tell him to raise the rod slowly; however, this is difficult to do when you are working around equipment or machines that are in operation.

EXTEND THE ROD. This signal is given by the instrumentman when there is a need to extend an adjustable rod. This happens when the height of the instrument becomes greater than the standard length of the unextended adjustable level rod.

There are other optional signals sometimes used when the necessity arises. If you know the standard signals, you will have no trouble picking up the new ones as you need them.

Signals for numerals are not standardized. Here is a simple system of numerals that is frequently used:

ONE—Right arm extended diagonally down to right from body.
TWO—Right arm extended straight out from body.
THREE—Right arm extended diagonally up and out from right shoulder.
FOUR—Left arm extended diagonally up and out from left shoulder.
FIVE—Left arm extended straight out from body.
SIX—Left arm extended diagonally down to left from body.
SEVEN—Both arms extended diagonally down and out from body.
EIGHT—Both arms extended straight out from body.
NINE—Both arms extended diagonally up and out from body.
ZERO—Hit top of head with up-and-down motion of palm.

Make sure to orient yourself properly when receiving signals for the numerals 1 through 6; your left is to the right of the signalman. The other numerals can be read without thinking of right or left.

ERRORS AND MISTAKES IN LEVELING

You might think that an error and a mistake are much the same thing; however, in surveyor's technical terminology there is a distinction. An error, in the technical sense, is an inaccuracy cause by built-in circumstances, while a mistake is, simply, a "boner," such as subtracting a BS reading from, instead of adding it to, a BM elevation to determine the H.I.

An INSTRUMENTAL error is one caused by an imperfection, maladjustment, or malfunction in the instrument used. A rod, for example, which indicated 5.00 ft when it was actually measuring only 4.99 ft would contain an instrumental error. Similarly, a level on which the bubble in the vial centered when the telescope was not actually level would contain an instrumental error. The error in the rod could not be eliminated; it would have to be compensated for, by applying a correction to every reading taken on the rod. Fortunately, rods seldom contain significant instrumental errors, and for the purposes for which a Builder is usually using a rod, you may assume the rod to be free of error. Similarly, the level you use is checked periodically by an EA or Instrumentman for proper level adjustment.

PERSONAL errors exist as a result of natural limitations on the powers of the human senses. When, for example, you align, by eye, the horizontal crosshair in a level telescope with a point on a distant rod, your alignment is never absolutely exact. You must reduce personal errors to a minimum by care and practice.

The commonest personal error in leveling occurs as a result of holding the level rod out of plumb. Other common personal errors are as follows:

Failure to center the bubble in the level tube vial exactly when the instrument is being leveled.

Failure to bring the image of the crosshair and/or image of the rod into clear focus. If these images are out of focus, the reading cannot be made with exactness.

Failure, in target reading, to clamp the target or the upper section of rod securely before making the reading, so that the target or upper section of rod changes position slightly before the reading is made.

Most personal errors can be reduced, but few can be eliminated entirely. Mistakes, however, can and must be avoided. Common mistakes made in leveling are:

Setting the rod on the wrong BM or TP, or on a point mistaken for a BM or TP.

Misreading the rod, as previously described.

Recording readings incorrectly, such as recording the right figures in the wrong column or the wrong figures in the right one.

Incorrect computing. This includes, besides all the common types of arithmetical mistakes, the common mistakes of subtracting instead of adding a BS or adding instead of subtracting an FS. To avoid this one, it is a good idea to develop the habit of calling a BS a "plus-sight" and a FS a "minus-sight."

CHAPTER 4

GRADING AND EXCAVATING

The term GRADE is used in several different senses in construction. In one sense it refers to the steepness of a slope; a slope, for example, which rises 3 vertical feet for every 100 horizontal feet has a grade of 3 percent. Although the term "grade" is commonly used in this sense, the more accurate term for indicating steepness of slope is GRADIENT.

In another sense the term "grade" simply means surface. On a wall section, for example, the line which indicates the ground surface level outside the building is marked GRADE or GRADE LINE.

The elevation of a surface at a particular point is a GRADE ELEVATION. A grade elevation may refer to an existing, natural earth surface or a hub or stake used as a reference point, in which case the elevation is that of EXISTING GRADE or EXISTING GROUND; or it may refer to a proposed surface to be created artificially, in which case the elevation is that of PRESCRIBED GRADE, PLAN GRADE, or FINISHED GRADE.

Operations concerning grading and excavating are discussed in this chapter. As a Builder, you will find the information especially useful in performing various duties, such as setting grade stakes, laying out building lines, setting batter boards, and determining dimensions of excavations according to specifications. Special attention is given on measures for preventing slides and cave-ins and safety precautions relating to excavations.

GRADING

Grade elevations of the surface area around a structure are indicated on the plot plan. Because a natural earth surface is usually irregular in contour, existing grade elevations on such a surface are indicated by CONTOUR LINES on the plot plan—that is, by lines which indicate points of equal elevation on the ground. Contour lines which indicate existing grade are usually made dotted; however, existing contour lines on maps are sometimes represented by SOLID LINES. If the prescribed surface to be created artificially will be other than a horizontal-plane surface, prescribed grade elevations will be indicated on the plot plan by solid contour lines.

On a level, horizontal-plane surface the elevation is, of course, the same at all points. Grade elevation of a surface of this kind cannot be indicated by contour lines, because each contour line indicates an elevation different from that of each other contour line. Therefore, a prescribed level surface area, to be artificially created, is indicated on the plot plan by outlining the area and inscribing inside the outline the prescribed elevation, such as "First Floor Elevation 127.50".

GRADE STAKES

The first earth-moving operations for a structure usually involve the artificial creation of a level area of prescribed elevation at and adjacent to the place where the structure will be built. This GRADING operation involves removing earth from areas which are higher than the prescribed elevation (CUT) and filling earth into areas which are below the prescribed elevation (FILL).

To guide the earth-moving crew, a sufficient number of GRADE STAKES must be driven in the area, the number depending mainly on the extent of irregularity of the existing surface. Grade stakes usually consist of about 18-inch lengths (depending on the amount to be cut) of 1 x 2, marked on the side with lumber crayon (called KEEL by the surveyors) as follows:

A stake driven at a point where the elevation of existing grade coincides with that of prescribed grade is simply marked GRD (for "grade"), indicating to the earth-moving crew that the surface here is already at prescribed grade elevation, and no cut or fill is required. A stake driven at a point where the elevation of existing grade is greater than that of prescribed grade is marked with a C (for cut), followed by a figure indicating the difference between the two elevations. In writing this figure it is customary to indicate decimal subdivisions of feet, not by a decimal point, but by raising and underlining the figures which indicate the decimal subdivisions. For example: for a cut of 6.25 ft you should write C 6$\underline{25}$ not C 6.25. A stake driven at a point where the elevation of prescribed grade is greater than that of existing grade is marked with an F (for fill), followed by the figures which indicate the difference between the two elevations.

GRADE ROD AND GROUND ROD

The elevation of prescribed grade at each point where a grade stake will be driven is obtained from the plot plan. Once this is known, all you need to know to mark the stake correctly is the elevation of existing ground at the point. You should have learned in the preceding chapter how to determine this by differential leveling, using the engineer's level. However, in setting grade stakes you often set a number of stakes from a single instrument setup, and in such a case you speed up the computational procedure by applying values called GRADE ROD and GROUND ROD.

GRADE ROD is simply the difference between the prescribed elevation of the point and the H. I. If you are setting stakes for a level surface area, grade rod will be the same for all points sighted from the same instrument setup point. This will not be the case, of course, if the prescribed elevation differs at different points. Once you have determined the H. I., grade rod can be calculated in advance for all points to be sighted from a particular instrument setup point.

GROUND ROD is simply the rod reading you get on a particular point. When you know the grade rod (difference between plan elevation and H.I.) and the ground rod (read on a rod set on the point) for a particular point, you can rapidly determine the mark for the stake by applying rules as follows:

The H.I. is always greater than the elevation of existing ground at the point (if it were less, you couldn't read a rod on the point from that particular setup), but it may be greater or less than the elevation of prescribed grade. If the H.I. is LESS than the elevation of prescribed grade (see fig. 4-1), the difference in elevation between existing ground and prescribed grade (which is what you need to know to mark the stake) amounts to the SUM of grade rod and ground rod. and the stake should be marked with an F.

For example, in figure 4-1, the elevation of the prescribed grade is 131.12 ft; the H.I. is 127.62 ft. The grade rod is therefore 131.12 - 127.62, or 3.50 ft, and the H.I. is less than prescribed grade elevation. You can see that fill must be put in at this point, and that the vertical depth of fill equals the sum of ground rod plus grade rod, or 5.60 ft + 3.50 ft, or 9.10 ft. Therefore you would mark the stake F 9$\underline{10}$.

If the H.I. is GREATER than the prescribed grade elevation (see figs. 4-2 and 4-3), the difference in elevation between existing and prescribed grade (that is, the vertical depth of cut or fill) equals the DIFFERENCE between ground rod and grade rod. Whether the stake should be marked with a C or an F depends upon which of the two, ground rod or grade rod, is the larger.

If ground rod is larger than grade rod (fig. 4-2), the stake takes an F. Here the difference between existing ground elevation and prescribed grade elevation equals the difference between

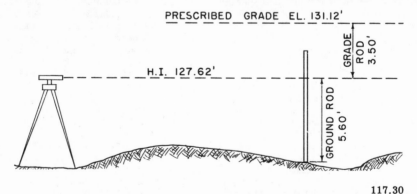

PRESCRIBED GRADE EL. 131.12'

H.I. 127.62'

GRADE ROD 3.50'

GROUND ROD 5.60'

117.30

Figure 4-1.—H.I. less than prescribed grade elevation.

50

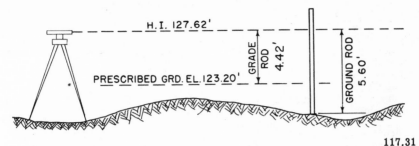

Figure 4-2.—H.I. greater than prescribed grade elevation
with larger ground rod.

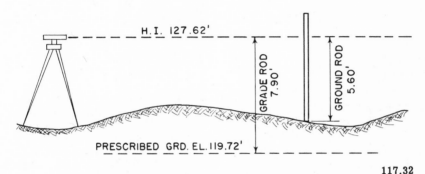

Figure 4-3.—H.I. greater than prescribed grade elevation
with larger grade rod.

ground rod and grade rod, or 5.60 - 4.42, or
1.18. Ground rod is larger than grade rod, and
you can see that fill is required to bring the
ground line up to grade. Therefore, you would
mark this stake F 1$\underline{18}$.

If grade rod is larger than ground rod (fig.
4-3), the stake takes a C. Here again the difference between existing ground elevation and
prescribed grade elevation equals the difference
between grade rod and ground rod, or 7.90 -
5.60, or 2.30 ft. Grade rod is larger than
ground rod, and you can see that cut is required
to bring the ground line down to grade. Therefore you would mark this stake C 2$\underline{30}$.

EXCAVATING

Grading means, generally speaking, the earth-
moving required to create a surface of desired
grade elevation at and adjacent to the place
where a structure will be erected. After this
has been accomplished, further earthmoving is
usually required. If the structure is to have a
below-grade basement, for example, earth
lying within the building lines must be removed
down to the prescribed finished basement floor
elevation, less the thickness of the basement
floor paving and subfill. After this earth is
removed, further earth may have to be removed
for footings under the foundation walls. This
type of earth-removal is generally known as
EXCAVATING.

LAYING OUT BUILDING LINES

Before foundation and footing excavation for
a building can begin, the building lines must be
laid out to determine the boundaries of the
excavations. Points shown on the plot plan (such
as building corners) are located at the site from
a system of HORIZONTAL CONTROL points
established by the battalion EAs. This system
consists of a framework of stakes, driven pipes,
or other markers, located at points of known

horizontal location. A point in the structure (such as a building corner) is located on the ground by reference to one or more nearby horizontal control points.

We can't describe here all the methods of locating a point with reference to a horizontal control point of known horizontal location. We'll just take as an illustrative example the situation shown in figure 4-4. This figure shows two horizontal control points, consisting of MONUMENTS A and B. The term "monument," incidentally, doesn't necessarily mean an elaborate stone or concrete structure. In structural horizontal control it simply means any relatively permanently located object, either artificial (such as a driven length of pipe) or natural (such as a tree), of known horizontal location.

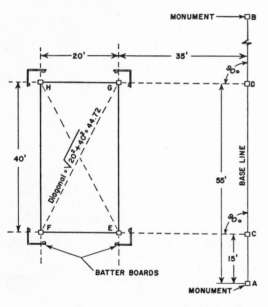

117.40

Figure 4-4.—Locating building corners.

In figure 4-4 the straight line from A to B is a control BASE LINE, from which the building corners of the structure can be located. Corner E, for example, can be located by first measuring 15 ft along the base line from A to locate point C; then measuring off 35 ft on CE, laid off at 90° to (that is, perpendicular to) AB. By extending CE another 20 ft, you can locate building corner F. Corners G and H can be similarly

located along a perpendicular run from point D, which is itself located by measuring 55 ft along the base line from A.

Perpendicular by Pythagorean Theorem

The easiest and most accurate way to locate points on a line or to turn a given angle (such as 90°) from one line to another is by the use of a surveying instrument called a TRANSIT. However, if you don't have a transit, you can locate the corner points by tape measurements by applying the Pythagorean theorem. First stretch a cord from monument A to monument B, and locate points C and D by tape measurements from A. Now, if you examine figure 4-4 you will observe that straight lines connecting points C, D, and E would form a right triangle with one side 40 ft long and the adjacent side 35 ft long. By the Pythagorean theorem, the length of the hypotenuse of this triangle (the line ED) would equal the square root of $35^2 + 40^2$, which is about 53.1 ft. Because the figure EGCD is a rectangle, the diagonals both ways (ED and CG) are equal; therefore, the line from C to G should also measure 53.1 ft. If you have one man hold the 53.1-ft mark of a tape on D, have another hold the 35-ft mark of another tape on C, and have a third man walk away with the joined 0-ft ends, when the tapes come taut the joined 0-ft ends will lie on the correct location for point E. The same procedure, but this time with the 53.1-ft length of tape running from C and the 35-ft length running from D, will locate corner point G. Corner points F and H can be located by the same process, or by extending CE and DG 20 ft.

Perpendicular by 3:4:5 Triangle

If you would rather avoid the square root calculations required for the Pythagorean theorem method, you can apply the basic fact that any triangle with sides in the proportions of 3:4:5 is a right triangle. In locating point E (for example), you know that this point lies 35 feet from C on a line perpendicular to the base line. You also know that a triangle with sides 30 and 40 ft long and a hypotenuse 50 ft long is a right triangle.

To get the 40-ft side, you would measure off 40 ft from C along the base line; in figure 4-4, the segment from C to D happens to measure 40 ft. Now if you run a 50-ft tape from D and a 30-ft tape from C, the joined ends will lie on a line perpendicular from the base line, 30 ft from C. Drive a hub at this point, and extend the line to E (5 more feet) by stretching a cord from C across the mark on the hub.

Checking Rectangular Layout

You always check a rectangular layout for its accuracy by "checking the diagonals." The diagonals of any rectangle are equal. You check the layout by tape-measuring the diagonals—if the layout is correct, the two diagonals will measure the same (or very nearly the same) distance. If you wish to know the value of the correct diagonal length, you may compute it by using the Pythagorean theorem; as you can see, the diagonals for the structure shown in figure 4-4 should measure 44.72 ft.

BATTER BOARDS

Hubs driven at the exact locations of building corners will, of course, be disturbed as soon as excavation for foundations begins. To preserve the corner locations, and also to provide a reference for measurement down to prescribed elevations, BATTER BOARDS are erected as shown in figure 4-5.

Each pair of boards is nailed to three 2 x 4 corner stakes, as shown. The stakes are driven far enough outside the building lines so that they will not be disturbed during excavating. The top edges of the boards are located at a specific elevation, usually some convenient number of whole feet above a significant prescribed elevation (such as that of the top of the foundation). Cords located directly over the lines through corner hubs (placed by holding plumb bobs on the hubs) are nailed to the batter boards. Figure 4-5 shows how a corner point can be located in the excavation by dropping a plumb bob from the point of intersection between two cords.

In addition to their function in horizontal control, batter boards are also used for vertical control. The top edge of a batter board is placed at a specific elevation. Elevations of features in the structure (such as foundations, floors, and the like) may be located by measuring downward or upward from the cords stretched between the batter boards.

You should always make sure that you have complete information as to exactly what lines and elevations are indicated by the batter boards.

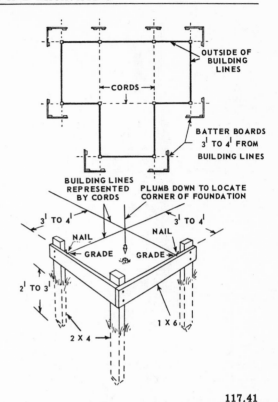

117.41
Figure 4-5.—Batter boards.

DIMENSIONS OF EXCAVATIONS

With regard to the dimensions of cellar or basement excavations, the specifications usually say something like the following:

Excavations shall extend 2' 0" outside of all basement wall planes and to 9" below finished planes of basement floor levels.

The 2-ft space is the customary allowance made for working space outside the foundation walls, it is a space which must be backfilled after the foundations have set. The 9 in. below finished planes of basement floor levels is the usual allowance for basement floor thickness (usually about 3 in.) plus thickness of cinder or other fill placed under the basement floor (usually about 6 in.).

The actual depth below grade to which a basement excavation must be carried is determined by study of a wall section like the one shown in figure 4-6. This section shows that the depth

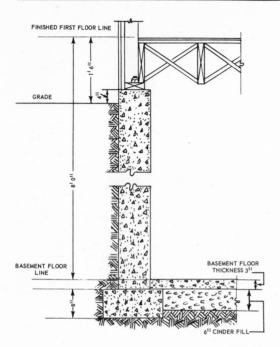

FINISHED FIRST FLOOR LINE

1'6"

GRADE

8'0"

BASEMENT FLOOR LINE

BASEMENT FLOOR THICKNESS 3"

1'8"

6" CINDER FILL

117.42

Figure 4-6.—Wall section, showing excavation depth data.

of the basement excavation below grade would in this case equal 8 ft 0 in. (vertical distance between basement and first floor finished planes), minus 1 ft 6 in. (vertical distance between surface grade and first floor finished plane), plus 9 in. (3 in. pavement floor plus 6 in. cinder fill), or 7 ft 3 in.

The top of the footing comes level with the top of the 6-in. cinder fill. However, the footing is 2 in. deeper than the fill. Therefore, the footing excavation would be carried 2 in. lower than the basement floor elevation, or to 7 ft 5 in. below grade.

If a specific elevation were prescribed for the finished first floor line, then the basement floor and footing excavation would be carried down to the corresponding elevation, without reference to surface grade. Suppose, for example, that the specified elevation for the finished first floor line were 163.50 ft. Obviously, the elevation to which the basement floor elevation would be carried would be 163.50 -(8 ft +3 in. +6 in.), or 163.50 -(8 ft +0.25 ft +0.50 ft),

or 154.75 ft. The elevation to which the footing excavation would be carried would be 163.50 ft -(8 ft + 0.25 ft + 0.67 ft), or 154.58 ft. Suppose the batter board cords were at elevation 165.00 ft. Then the vertical distance from the cords to the bottom of the basement floor excavation would be 165.00 ft - 154.75 ft, or 10.25 ft, or 10 ft 3 in. The vertical distance from the cords to the bottom of the footing excavation would be 165.00 - 154.58, or 10.42 ft, or 10 ft 5 in.

Excavations should never, of course, be carried below the proper depths. If a basement floor or footing excavation is by mischance so carried, however, the error should not ordinarily be corrected by refilling. It is almost impossible to attain the necessary load-bearing density by compacting the refill unless special, carefully controlled procedures are used. For a basement floor excavation a relatively small error should be corrected by increasing the vertical dimension of the subfloor fill by the amount of the error. For a footing excavation the error should be corrected by increasing the vertical dimension of the footing by the amount of the error. Both of these mean, of course, additional and unnecessary expense for the extra material.

PREVENTION OF SLIDES AND CAVE-INS

When your work involves excavation, there are definite precautions that should be observed to prevent accidents.

To avoid slides or cave-ins, the sides of excavations 4 feet or more in depth should be supported by substantial and adequate sheathing, sheet piling, bracing, shoring, etc., or the sides sloped to the angle of repose. The angle of repose is the angle, measured from the horizontal, of the natural slope of the side of a pile of granular material formed by pouring grains or particles through a funnel, practically without impact. The angle of repose varies with the moisture content and the type of earth or other material. For ordinary earth, the angle of repose varies from about 20 to 45 degrees, corresponding to slopes of from about 2.8:1 to 1:1. The sides of an excavation do not consist of poured particles, however; many types of earth, because of their cohesive qualities, will stand vertically without failure. But, because of the nonuniformity of most soils, the times and places of local and intermittent cave-ins and slides cannot ordinarily be predicted.

Therefore, it is conservative and safe to require laying the bank back to the angle of repose, or natural slope, of the material being excavated.

It is seldom practical to slope the sides of foundation and footing excavations to the angle of repose. Therefore, any such excavation 4 ft deep or more must be supported as specified. Many people wonder about this, in view of the fact that most adult males are a good deal more than 4 ft tall. The reason lies in the fact that a man needs to be buried ONLY TO CHEST LEVEL to suffocate in a cave-in. The pressure against his chest makes breathing impossible, and if his chest isn't freed within a minute or two, he will suffocate, even though head and shoulders are out in the air. This is a terrible way to die, and a man dies this way, somewhere in the world, in an excavation which should have been supported but wasn't, nearly every day.

Sheathing

SHEATHING consists of wooden planks, placed edge-to-edge either horizontally or vertically. Horizontal planking is used for excavations with plane faces, vertical planking when it is necessary to follow curved faces. Sheathing is supported by longitudinal WALES or RANGERS which are nailed to the sheathing and which bear against transverse SHORES or BRACES.

Sheathing must be progressively installed and braced as every 4-ft stage of depth is reached. Vertical and horizontal wood sheathing are illustrated in figure 4-7.

Sheet Piling

SHEET PILING is driven before the work of excavation begins. Steel sheet piling will be described in a later chapter. Wooden sheet piling consists of 2-in., 3-in., or 4-in. planks, beveled at the lower end to facilitate penetration of the soil. Also, the lower ends are cut at an angle, as shown in figure 4-8, so as to cause the edge of a pile being driven to bear against the edge of one previously driven. Obviously, care must be taken to place a pile with this angle inclined in the proper direction. The bevel on the lower end-edge, too, must face toward the excavation. As a pile is driven, it tends to slant off in the direction away from

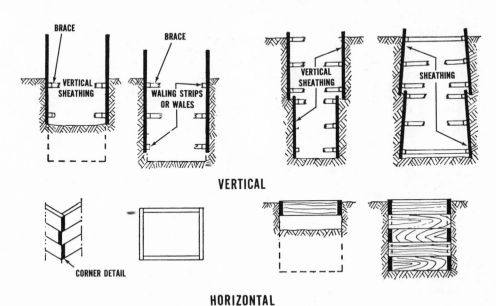

VERTICAL

HORIZONTAL

117.43

Figure 4-7.—Vertical and horizontal sheathing.

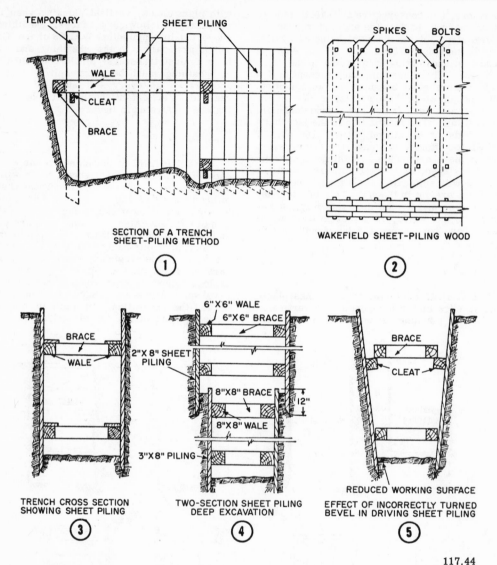

TEMPORARY

SHEET PILING

WALE

CLEAT

BRACE

SECTION OF A TRENCH
SHEET-PILING METHOD

①

SPIKES   BOLTS

WAKEFIELD SHEET-PILING WOOD

②

BRACE

WALE

TRENCH CROSS SECTION
SHOWING SHEET PILING

③

6"X6" WALE

6"X6" BRACE

2"X8" SHEET
PILING

8"X8" BRACE

12"

8"X8" WALE

3"X8" PILING

TWO-SECTION SHEET PILING
DEEP EXCAVATION

④

BRACE

CLEAT

REDUCED WORKING SURFACE

EFFECT OF INCORRECTLY TURNED
BEVEL IN DRIVING SHEET PILING

⑤

117.44

Figure 4-8.—Wooden sheet piling.

the bevel. If the bevel is incorrectly turned away from the excavation, the excavation will progressively narrow as shown in figure 4-8 (5).

In WAKEFIELD sheet piling, each pile consists of three planks, bolted together with the center plank offset for tongue-and-groove joining as shown in figure 4-8 (2).

To set wooden piles for driving, you first dig a shallow notch along the excavation line, wide enough to admit the bottoms of the piles and deep enough to hold them upright. For additional upright support, lay pairs of wales along the notch and stake them in position. If the piles are too long to stand this way, the wales must be braced in elevated position.

In favorable soil a 2-in. sheet pile can be driven to a depth of about 16 ft, a 3-in. sheet pile to about 24 ft, and a 4-in. sheet pile to about 32 ft. When piles are too short to cover full excavation depth, they are driven in stages called SECTIONS, as shown in figure 4-8 (4).

SUPPORT FOR ADJACENT STRUCTURES

The removal of material near the foundations of a structure may threaten the stability of the foundations. When this is a possibility, temporary supports must be provided before excavation reaches the dangerous stage.

Shoring

A common method of providing support is by the use of up to 12 x 12 timbers called SHORES, inclined against the wall to be supported and extending across the excavation to a temporary FOOTING consisting of a framework or mat of timbers laid on the ground. The upper ends of the shores may be fitted into openings cut in the wall, or they may butt against a timber bolted to the wall. Steel SADDLES may be placed in openings cut in concrete or masonry walls to support lifting or steadying shores.

It is good practice to set shores as nearly vertical as possible, to reduce lateral thrust against the wall. Heads of shores should, whenever possible, be located at floor levels, to minimize the danger of pushing the wall in.

Provision for inducing a lift or thrust in the shores is usually made by inserting jacks between the bases of the shores and the footing. Figure 4-9 shows a standard steel SCREW JACK. One of these may apply a lift of as much as 100 tons. When a single screw jack is used with a shore, a hole is bored in the base of the shore to admit the threaded portion of the jack, and the arrangement is called a PUMP. For a larger lifting effect, a pair of jacks are attached to a short timber called a CROSSHEAD. Pump and crosshead arrangements are illustrated in figure 4-10.

An advantage of the crosshead arrangement is that after a lift has been applied, the crosshead can be blocked and the jacks removed for use elsewhere.

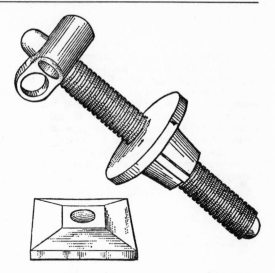

117.45X

Figure 4-9.—Standard steel screw jack.

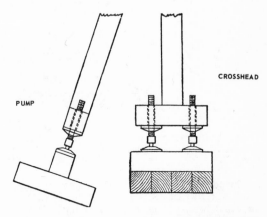

CROSSHEAD

PUMP

117.46X

Figure 4-10.—Pump and crosshead.

HYDRAULIC jacks provide a much stronger lift than screw jacks, but cannot be used to support a load over a length of time. However, with a pair of hydraulic jacks in crosshead arrangement, as many shores as desired can be set up and blocked in a short time and with a minimum of labor.

Needling

Figure 4-11 shows a project which involves a construction procedure known as UNDER-PINNING. The feature marked W is a wall, resting on a footing BB. Excavation is to be carried down to the level indicated by the horizontal dotted line, which means that the earth supporting the footing BB is to be completely removed. The existing wall is to be supported during this procedure, and subsequently a new foundation wall extended upward from the footing shown below. This is the process known as underpinning.

and proper interpretation generally proves very costly. Soil samples should be properly taken, and the results interpreted by trained engineers. The depth and character of the soil should be determined, and it should be ascertained that a suitable stratum is not underlain by softer material.

After the preliminary investigations have been made, a pit DDDD is excavated down to the level of the top of the proposed new footing. At the bottom of this pit a layer of heavy timbers FF is laid on a layer of thick planks. At grade level on the other side of the wall a similar platform is laid. Holes are cut in the wall and

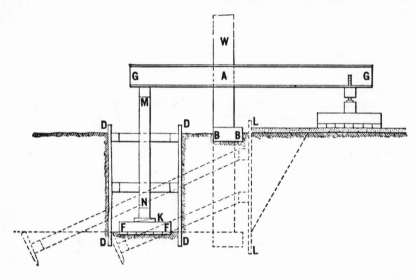

117.47X

Figure 4-11.—Needling and underpinning.

Support for the wall will be provided by a series of NEEDLES, that is, of heavy timbers or steel beams, inserted horizontally through holes cut in the wall, and wedged or jacked upward so as to assume the weight of the wall. In figure 4-11 the member marked GG is a needle. The needling and underpinning procedure shown in that figure would be carried out about as follows.

Before actual underpinning operations are begun, complete preliminary investigations are made, especially with regard to soil bearing capacity. Too much emphasis cannot be placed upon this point. The neglect of adequate study

the needles are inserted, each supported at the pit end by vertical timber and blocks MN and at the other end by a screw jack. The lift at the pit end is obtained by driving wedges at K, at the other end by the jack.

Before the material under the wall is excavated, sheet piles are driven at LL. As excavation proceeds downward, these are shored up as shown, to prevent a slide caused by the weight of the nearby grade-level platform.

Obviously, only that portion of the wall which is directly above a needle will receive direct support from the needle. Other portions of the wall above the needles will receive indirect support by oblique transfer of the needles' upward thrust through the material; however, some parts of the wall above the needles will receive no support at all. Consider, for example, the section of needled brick wall shown in figure 4-12. The oblique corbel outward of the upward thrust of the needles through the material is indicated by the line AAAAA. Only the portion of the wall above this line is receiving support from the needles. All of the wall below this line will be hanging when the support under the footing is removed. The hanging part will be held up to some extent by cohesion to the supported part, but it is important for you to know that this is all the support it will have. In a brick wall, of course, cohesion of this type would be slight; in a reinforced concrete wall it would be much greater. Sometimes the hanging part of a needled wall is preserved by chaining or wiring it firmly up to the supported part.

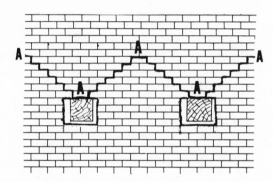

117.48

Figure 4-12.—Line of demarcation between supporting and hanging brick wall in underpinning.

When the new footing has been constructed and the new wall carried up to the old wall, joining the wall sections in a manner which will allow a transfer of the weight of the supported wall from the needles to the new wall without settlement presents a problem. In the case of a brick wall, WEDGING STONES may be inserted in the new wall, at needle level, as shown in figure 4-13. As the last course of brick between the old wall and the new is laid, the joint is compacted as tightly as possible by driving pieces of slate into the mortar, and steel wedges are driven home between the wedging stones, to transfer most of the weight of the wall to the new underpinning. The jack is then backed

off to release the needle, and the needle is removed.

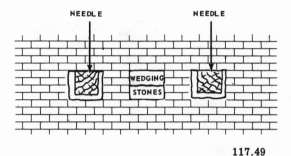

117.49

Figure 4-13.—Wedging stones.

FIGURE-4 Needling

In the method of needling just described the needle is used as a beam—meaning that it is supported at both ends and sustains a downward load in the middle. Figure 4-14 shows a situation in which this method of needling is not feasible, probably because the erection of a supporting platform for the inner end of the needle inside the building is not feasible. In this case the FIGURE-4 method of needling is being used, with the needle serving as a CANTILEVER rather than as a beam.

EXCAVATION SAFETY

Burial alive in an excavation slide or cave-in is a terrible accident which occurs in the construction industry with scandalous frequency. Application of the basic excavation safety rule—that any excavation 4 ft or more in depth must be protected by one of the prescribed methods—would reduce this frequency almost to nil. There are additional safety rules, most of which have the same basic purpose; that is, to prevent slides or cave-ins. Some of these rules are as follows:

Any trees, boulders, or other surface encumbrances located close enough to create a hazard must be removed before excavation begins.

If it is necessary to bring power shovels, derricks, trucks, large quantities of supplies, or other heavy objects or materials near an excavation, the face of the excavation which is toward the object or material must be ADDITIONALLY shored and braced to resist the additional pressure. NO object or material

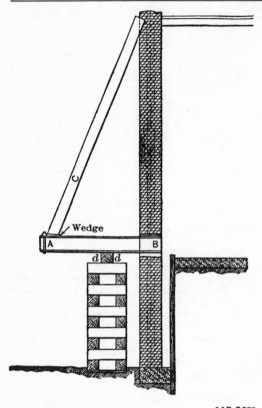

117.50X
Figure 4-14.—Figure-4 method of needling.

should be placed within 2 ft of the edge of an excavation.

When soil against the face of a masonry wall is excavated, it must not be presumed that the wall will, of itself, provide sufficient support against lateral pressure from unexcavated material on the other face. The wall must be adequately shored and braced.

Temporary sheet piling installed to permit construction of a retaining wall must not be removed until the wall has developed full strength—meaning, for a concrete wall, usually 28 days.

Undercutting of earth banks should be done only when it is unavoidable, and then only as the overhang is kept progressively and adequately shored and braced.

Excavations must be inspected after every rainstorm or similar hazard-increasing occurrence, and the protection against slide or cave-in increased if necessary.

No sidewalk may be undermined without being progressively shored to carry a live load of 125 psf. Excavated material must not be piled on sidewalks or walkways.

All timber used for shoring, bracing, sheathing, and sheet piling must be sound, straight-grained timber, of strength and quality equal to that of long-leaf yellow pine or Douglas fir, and free from splits, shakes, large or loose knots, or other strength-impairing defects.

Wooden sheet piling must not be less than 2 in. thick for a depth of up to 16 ft, not less than 3 in. for a depth of up to 24 ft, and not less than 4 in. for a depth of up to 40 ft.

If pedestrian and/or vehicular traffic must be maintained over or near excavations, all proper safeguards, such as bridges, walkways, guardrails, barricades, warning flags, and lights, must be installed.

Entrance to and exit from any excavation over 5 ft deep must be by properly constructed ramp, ladder, stairway, or hoist. Jumping into trenches and the use of bracing and shoring members for climbing must be prohibited.

Tools, materials, and debris must not be left on bridges or walkways over excavations, on shoring and bracing members, near the edges of excavations, or in any other position from which they might fall on men in the excavation below.

Pick and shovel men working in excavations must keep far enough apart to avoid striking each other accidentally with tools.

CHAPTER 5
MATERIALS HANDLING AND SCAFFOLDING

During your stay in the Navy you may be required quite often to help on jobs such as erecting a campsite. No matter how well jobs of this nature have been planned, there is always the need for transportation, stowage, and handling of materials. Sure there has been a great improvement in this area because now you can use power-driven equipment, such as trucks, earthmovers, cranes, forklifts and the like; however, this type of machinery may be late arriving or broken down; therefore, you may have to use the old standbys such as picks, shovels, hods, wheelbarrows and the good old "back."

With this in mind, information is presented in this chapter on the various materials and equipment that should be readily available such as fiber lines, wire rope, scaffolding, and ladders. Information is included on the proper care, inspection, and use of such equipment and materials. A knowledge of this information will help conserve the good old back and minimize injuries on the job.

There is also a section in this chapter on rigging and erecting shear legs and tripods. Remember that no matter what job you are doing there is always a safety factor involved. Be sure to study the safety precautions discussed in this chapter.

FIBER LINES

Fiber line, sometimes called cordage, is made up by twisting vegetable fibers together. A line consists of three elements, fibers, yarns, and strands. (See fig. 5-1.) A number of fibers are twisted together to form yarns. Yarns are twisted together to form a strand. Finally a number of strands are twisted to form a line. The direction of twist for each successive element is reversed. Reverse twisting puts the line in balance and prevents the elements from unlaying when load is suspended on it.

There are three types of fiber line with which you should be familiar. They are the hawser-laid, shroud-laid, and cable-laid lines; each type is illustrated in figure 5-2.

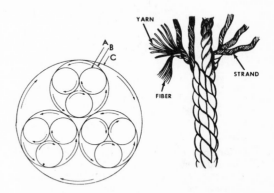

29.172(133F)
Figure 5-1.—Fabrication of fiber line.

HAWSER-LAID LINE generally consists of three strands twisted together, usually in a right-hand direction. A SHROUD-LAID line ordinarily is composed of four strands twisted together in a right-hand direction around a center strand or core, which usually is of the same material but smaller in diameter than the four strands. You will find that shroud-laid line is more pliable and stronger than hawser-laid line. However, shroud-laid line has a strong tendency toward kinking. Therefore, in most instances, it is used on the larger sheaves and drums. This not only prevents kinking, but also makes use of its pliability and strength.

CABLE-LAID line usually consists of three right-hand hawser-laid lines twisted together in a left-hand direction. This type is especially useful in heavy construction work because, if it tends to untwist, it will tend to tighten any regular right-hand screw connection to which it may be attached. Hence, its use provides an added safety feature.

SIZE DESIGNATIONS

Line larger than 1 3/4 inches in circumference is generally designated as to size by its CIRCUMFERENCE in inches. A 6-inch manila

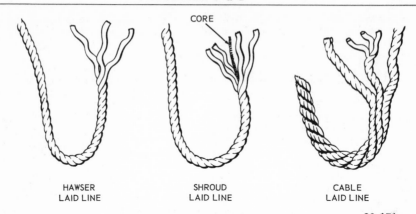

CORE

HAWSER
LAID LINE

SHROUD
LAID LINE

CABLE
LAID LINE

29.171

Figure 5-2.—Three types of fiber line.

line, for instance, would be constructed of manila fibers and measure 6 inches in circumference. Line is available in sizes ranging up to 16 inches in circumference, but 12 inches is about the largest carried in stock. Anything larger is used only on special jobs. (See figure 5-3 for commonly used sizes of line.)

Line 1 3/4 inches or less in circumference is called SMALL STUFF, and is usually designated as to size by the number of THREADS (or yarns) that make up each strand. You may use 6-to-24 threads, but the most commonly used are 9-to-21 threads. You may also hear some small stuff designated by name, without reference to size. One such type is MARLINE, a tarred, 2-strand, left-laid hemp. Marline is the small stuff you will use most for seizings. When you need something stronger than marline, you will use a tarred, 3-strand, left-laid hemp called HOUSELINE.

If you have occasion to order line, you may find that it is designated and ordered by diameter. The catalog may also use the term rope rather than line.

ROPE YARNS for temporary seizings, whippings, and lashings, are pulled from large strands of old line which has outlived its usefulness. Pull yarn from the middle, away from the ends, or it will get fouled.

SAFE WORKING LOAD

To hoist a load of a given size, you should set up a hoisting device with a SAFE WORKING LOAD which is equal to or in excess of the load

MANILA LINE SOME COMMONLY USED SIZES	CIRCUMFERENCE	THREAD
	3/4 "	6
	1 "	9
	1 1/8 "	12
	1 1/4 "	15
	1 1/2 "	21
	1 3/4 "	24
	2 "	
	3 "	
	4 "	
	5 "	
	6 "	

SIZE IS DESIGNATED BY THE CIRCUMFERENCE

127.40

Figure 5-3.—Some commonly used sizes of manila line.

to be hoisted. In order to do this, you must be able to calculate the safe working load of a single line or wire rope of given size, the safe working load of a given purchase which contains line or wire rope of given size, and the minimum size of line or wire rope and the minimum size of hooks or shackles required in a given type of purchase to hoist a given load.

The best sources of information on the safe working load of a single line or wire are the manufacturer's tables, and these should always be used when available. Remember, however, that the values given in manufacturer's tables apply only to NEW line or wire, and that they must be reduced as the line or wire deteriorates with use.

In the absence of tables there are certain "thumb" rules which are well within the margin of safety for standard manila line or the equivalent, and for plow steel wire or the equivalent. In applying the thumb rules, you ADD 30 percent to the value obtained from the formula if the line or wire is brand-new and in A-1 condition. If the line or wire has had a considerable amount of careful use but doesn't show any signs of deterioration, you use the value obtained from the formula. If the line or wire is nearing the stage where it requires replacement, you SUBTRACT 30 percent from the value obtained from the formula.

Where C means the circumference of (distance around) the line in inches, a formula for finding the safe working load (SWL) in pounds is:

$$\text{SWL in pounds} = C^2 \times 150$$

HANDLING AND CARE

If the fiber line you work with is to give safe and dependable service, you must make a special effort to ensure that it is handled and cared for properly. Study the precautions and procedures given here, and make sure you carry them out properly in duties involving fiber line.

Loose ends of fiber line should be whipped or spliced to prevent unlaying of the line. When fiber line is to be cut, put two whippings on the line 1 or 2 inches apart and make the cut between the whippings.

When fiber line is being stored away for either short or long periods, care should be taken to prevent deterioration of the line.

Do not store fiber line in wet or damp places. Dry carefully before storing.

If possible, always store fiber line on gratings or in some other manner that will allow circulation of air through the coil.

Fiber line deteriorates rapidly from continued dampness. Line tends to contract when wet and, unless allowed to do so, may be overstrained and weakened.

Slacken dry, taut lines before they are exposed to rain or damp weather.

Do not cover fiber line unless it is absolutely necessary, as covering holds in any moisture present and prevents discovery of deterioration.

The strength of fiber line decreases rapidly with use because of breakage and slipping of the fibers. The fibers will slip a small amount under each strain in spite of the twisting, and no attempt should be made to load a line to its maximum after it has been used for some time. Breakage of fibers should be avoided as much as possible.

Clean muddy line by washing in water only. Do not use soap because it will take oil out of the line.

Avoid pulling line over sharp edges. Place chafing gear such as a board, folded cardboard, canvas, or part of a firehose between the line and the sharp edge to reduce breakage of the strands.

Sand has an abrasive action on the inner fibers of line. Avoid dragging line through sand or dirt. If sand gets on the line, carefully wash the line in water only.

Wherever possible, use knots that can be untied easily to eliminate the necessity for cutting the line.

Repair broken strands in line as soon as possible.

WIRE ROPE

Wire rope is made of steel or iron wires laid together to form strands. Strands are laid together to form a rope, either wound about each other or wound together about a central core. (See figure 5-4.) The number of strands, number of wires per strand, type of material, and nature of the core will depend on the purpose for which the rope is intended.

The types of wire rope used by the Navy consist of 6, 7, 12, 19, 24, or 37 wires in each strand. Usually, the rope has 6 strands laid around a fiber or steel center.

Two common types of wire rope, 6 x 19 and 6 x 37 rope, are illustrated in figure 5-5. The 6 x 19 type has 6 strands with 19 wires in each strand. This rope is commonly used for rough hoisting and skidding work where abrasion is likely to occur.

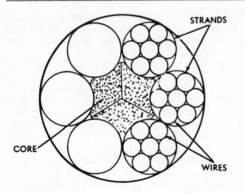

29.172(29C)

Figure 5-4.—Parts of a wire rope.

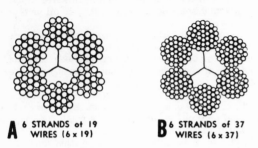

A 6 STRANDS of 19 WIRES (6 x 19)

B 6 STRANDS of 37 WIRES (6 x 37)

29.173(29C)

A. 6 x 19 wire rope.   B. 6 x 37 wire rope.

Figure 5-5.—Two common types of wire rope.

The 6-37 wire rope is a 6-strand rope with 37 wires on each strand. This is the most flexible of the standard 6-strand ropes. For that reason it is particularly suitable when small sheaves and drums are to be used, such as on cranes and similar machinery.

MEASURING WIRE ROPE

Wire rope is designated as to size by its diameter in inches. The true diameter of a wire rope is considered as being the diameter of the circle which will just enclose all of its strands. The correct, as well as incorrect, method of measuring wire rope is illustrated in figure 5-6. Note, in particular, that the RIGHT WAY is to measure from the top on one strand to the top of the strand directly opposite it. The WRONG WAY, as you will note, is to

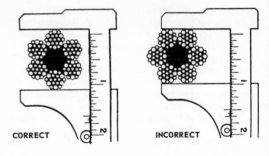

CORRECT   INCORRECT

29.173(133E)

Figure 5-6.—Correct and incorrect methods of measuring wire rope.

measure across two strands side by side. Use calipers to take the measurement; if they are not available, an open end adjustable wrench will do.

To ensure an accurate measurement of the diameter of a wire rope, always measure the rope at three places, at least 5 feet apart. Use the average of the three measurements as the diameter of the rope.

SAFE WORKING LOAD

The term SAFE WORKING LOAD (SWL), as used in reference to wire rope, means the load that can be applied and still obtain most efficient service and also prolong the life of the rope. There are a number of rule of thumb formulas which may be used to compute the strength of a wire rope. The one recommended by NAVFAC is as follows:

$$SWL \text{ (in tons)} = D^2 \times 4$$

In this formula, D represents the diameter of the rope in inches. Suppose you want to find the SWL of a 2-in. rope. Using the formula above, your figures would be:

$$SWL = (2)^2 \times 4$$
$$SWL = 4 \times 4 = 16$$

The answer is 16, meaning that the rope has an SWL of 16 tons.

It is very important to remember that any formula for determining SWL is ONLY A RULE OF THUMB. In computing the SWL of old rope, worn rope, or rope which is otherwise in poor condition, you should reduce the SWL as much as 50 percent, depending on the condition of the rope.

WIRE ROPE FAILURE

Some of the common causes of wire rope failure are listed below.

1. Using incorrect size, construction, or grade.
2. Dragging over obstacles.
3. Improper lubrication.
4. Operating over sheaves and drums of inadequate size.
5. Overriding or cross-winding on drums.
6. Operating over sheaves and drums with improperly fitted grooves or broken flanges.
7. Jumping off sheaves.
8. Subjecting to acid fumes.
9. Improperly attached fitting.
10. Promoting internal wear by allowing grit to penetrate between the strands.
11. Subjecting to severe or continuing overload.
12. Kinking.

BLOCK AND TACKLE

A BLOCK consists of one or more sheaves fitted in a wood or metal frame supported by a hook or shackle inserted in the strap of the block. A TACKLE is an assembly of blocks and lines used to gain a mechanical advantage in lifting or pulling.

In a tackle assembly, the line is reeved over the sheaves of blocks. There are two types of tackle systems: simple and compound. A SIMPLE tackle system is an assembly of blocks in which a single line is used. (See view A, fig. 5-7.) A COMPOUND tackle system is an assembly of blocks in which more than one line is used. (See view B, fig. 5-7.)

TACKLE TERMS

To help avoid confusion in working with tackle, it is important that you be familiar with various technical terms. Here are some commonly used tackle terms which you should know and understand.

A FALL is a line, either fiber line or wire rope, reeved through a pair of blocks to form a tackle. (See fig. 5-8.)

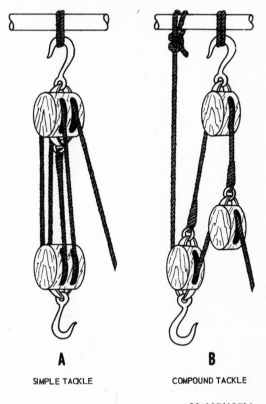

A

SIMPLE TACKLE

B

COMPOUND TACKLE

29.187(127)A
Figure 5-7.—Tackles.

The HAULING PART is the part of the fall leading from one of the blocks upon which the power is exerted. The STANDING PART is the end of the fall which is attached to one of the beckets.

The MOVABLE (or RUNNING) BLOCK of a tackle is the block attached to the object to be moved. The FIXED (or STANDING) BLOCK is the block attached to a fixed object or support. When a tackle is being used, the movable block moves and the fixed block remains stationary.

The term TWO-BLOCKED means that both blocks of a tackle are as close together as they will go. You may also hear this same condition referred to as BLOCK-AND-BLOCK.

To OVERHAUL is to lengthen a tackle by pulling the two blocks apart.

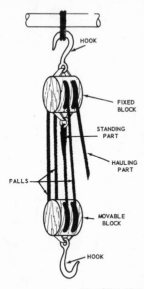

29.187(127)B

Figure 5-8.— Parts of a tackle.

To ROUND IN means to bring the blocks of a tackle toward each other, usually without a load on the tackle (opposite of overhaul).

Don't be surprised if your co-workers use a number of different terms in referring to a tackle. Such terms as LINE-AND-BLOCKS, PURCHASE, and BLOCK-AND-FALLS are typical of other names frequently used for tackle.

BLOCK NOMENCLATURE

The function of the block or blocks in a tackle assembly is to change the direction of pull or provide mechanical advantage or both. The name and location of the principal parts of a fiber line block are shown in figure 5-9.

The FRAME (or SHELL), made of wood or metal, houses the sheaves.

The SHEAVE is a round, grooved wheel over which the line runs. Ordinarily, blocks used in your work will have one, two, three, or four sheaves. Blocks can be obtained, of course, with more than this number of sheaves; blocks have been made with as many as 11 sheaves.

The CHEEKS are the portions of the shell enclosing the sheaves.

The PIN is a metal axle that the sheave turns on. It runs from cheek to cheek through the middle of the sheave.

The BECKET is a metal loop formed at one or both ends of a block; the standing part of the line is fastened to this part.

The STRAPS (one inner and one outer type) are used to enclose the shell, hold the block together, and support the pin on which the sheaves rotate.

The SWALLOW is the opening in the block through which the line passes.

The BREECH is the part of the block opposite the swallow.

CONSTRUCTION OF BLOCKS

Blocks are constructed for use with fiber line or with wire rope. Wire rope blocks are heavily constructed, and have a large sheave containing a deep groove. Fiber line blocks are generally not as heavily constructed as wire rope blocks and have smaller sheaves with shallower wide grooves. A large sheave is necessary with wire rope to prevent sharp bending. Since fiber line has greater flexibility and pliability, it does not require a sheave as large as does the same size of wire rope.

Blocks fitted with one, two, three, or four sheaves are often referred to as single, double, triple, and quadruple blocks, respectively. Blocks are fitted with a varying number of attachments, depending upon their particular use. Some of the most commonly used fittings are hooks, shackles, eyes and rings.

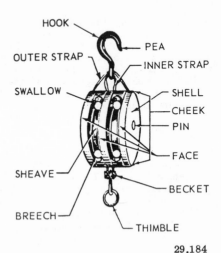

29.184

Figure 5-9.— Nomenclature of a block.

RATIO OF SIZE OF BLOCK TO SIZE OF LINE OR WIRE USED

The size of fiber line blocks is designated by the length in inches of the shell or cheek. The size of standard wire rope blocks is controlled by the diameter of the rope. With nonstandard and special-purpose wire rope blocks, the size is determined by measuring the diameter of one of its sheaves in inches.

Make sure you exercise care in selecting the proper size line or wire for the block to be used. If a fiber line is reeved on to a tackle whose sheaves are below a certain minimum diameter, the line will be distorted and will wear badly in a very short time. A wire rope too large for a sheave will have a tendency to be pinched and damage the sheave. The wire also will be damaged because of too short a radius of bend. A wire rope too small for a sheave lacks the necessary bearing surface, thus placing the strain on only a few strands and shortening the life of the wire.

With fiber line the length of the block used should be about three times the circumference of the line. However, an inch or so either way doesn't matter too much; for example, a 3-inch line may be reeved on to an 8-inch block with no ill effects. As a rule you are more likely to know the block size than you are the sheave diameter. However, it may be said that the sheave diameter should be about twice the size of the circumference of the line used.

Manufacturers of wire issue tables which give the proper sheave diameters to be used with the various types and sizes of wire they manufacture. In the absence of these, a rough thumb rule is that the sheave diameter should be about 20 times the diameter of the wire. Remember that with wire it is DIAMETER rather than circumference, and that this rule refers to the diameter of the SHEAVE rather than the size of the block as with line.

TYPES OF CARGO BLOCKS

Blocks take their names from the purpose for which they are used, from the places they occupy in the rig, or from some other peculiarity in their shape or construction.

Regardless of type, a cargo block is usually named for its location in the cargo rig. The block at the head of the boom through which the whip runs is called the HEAD BLOCK. That at the foot, which fair-leads the wire to the winch, is the HEEL BLOCK. A small single-sheave block in the middle of most booms is referred to as the SLACK WIRE BLOCK, because it keeps the slack in a whip from hanging down in a bight. Blocks in the topping lift are upper and lower TOPPING LIFT BLOCKS.

A fair-lead on cargo gear or elsewhere may be through a CHEEK BLOCK, welded or bolted to the boom, davit, etc., by one side of the frame, called a CHEEK. Incidentally, FAIR-LEADERS serve the purpose of leading lines in the direction desired and changes its direction so that the line or wire rope is delivered fair to a sheave or drum. The fair-lead angle should not exceed about 2 degrees to prevent the line from jumping the sheave and also to prevent undue wear on the line.

Another fair-lead block is the SNATCH BLOCK, which is cut at the swallow, hinged on one side, and fitted with a hasp on the other. A snatch block is shown in figure 5-10. You will find the snatch block about the most useful block in rigging. You can easily place a bight in this block without hauling the whole length of line through the block. TAIL BLOCKS (not illustrated) are single blocks, which generally are used alone with a whip or as a runner.

MECHANICAL ADVANTAGE

The mechanical advantage of a tackle is the term applied to the relationship between the load being lifted and the power required to lift that load. In other words, if a load of 10 pounds requires 10 pounds of power to lift it, the mechanical advantage is one. However, if a load of 50 pounds requires only 10 pounds to lift it, then you have a mechanical advantage of 5 to 1, or 5 units of weight are lifted for each unit of power applied.

The easiest way to determine the mechanical advantage of a tackle is by counting the number of parts of falls at the running block. If there are two parts, the mechanical advantage is two times the power applied (disregarding friction). A gun tackle, for instance, has a mechanical advantage of 2. Therefore, to lift a 200-pound load with a gun tackle would require 100 pounds of power, disregarding friction.

By inverting any tackle, a mechanical advantage of 1 is always gained because the number of parts at the movable block is increased. By inverting a gun tackle (See fig. 5-11) a mechanical advantage of 3 is attained. When a tackle is inverted, the direction of pull is difficult. This

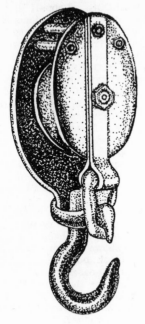

127.54
Figure 5-10.—Snatch block.

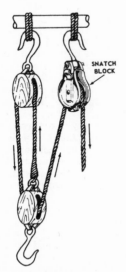

29.187(127)C
Figure 5-11.—Inverted gun tackle.

can easily be overcome by adding a snatch block which changes the direction of the pull, but does not increase the mechanical advantage.

To ascertain the amount of power required to lift a given load by means of a tackle, determine the weight of the load to be lifted and divide that by the mechanical advantage. Example: If it is necessary to lift a 600-pound load by means of a single luff tackle, first determine the mechanical advantage gained by using this type of tackle. Upon examination, it is found that by counting the parts of the falls at the movable block, we have a mechanical advantage of 3. Therefore, by dividing the weight to be lifted, 600 pounds, by the mechanical advantage in this tackle, 3, we find that 200 pounds of power is required to lift a weight of 600 pounds using a single luff tackle.

ALLOWANCE FOR FRICTION

A certain amount of the force applied to a tackle is lost through friction. Friction will develop in a tackle by the lines rubbing against each other, or against the shell of a block. Friction also is caused by the passing of the line over the sheaves, or by the rubbing of the pin against the sheaves. An adequate allowance for the loss due to friction must be added to the weight being lifted in determining the power required to lift a given load. Roughly, 10 percent of the load must be allowed for each sheave in the tackle.

For example, suppose you want to lift a load of 500 lbs with a twofold purchase. Simply take 10 percent of the 500 lbs, which is 50 lbs; and that multiplied by 4 (the number of sheaves) gives you 200 lbs, which is the amount to be added to the load. The total load of 700 lbs is divided by 4, which is the mechanical advantage of a twofold purchase. The answer 175 lbs is the power required to lift the load.

TYPES OF TACKLE

Tackles are designated according to (1) the number of sheaves in the blocks that are used to make the tackle, such as single whip or twofold purchase; or (2) the purpose for which the tackle is used, such as yard tackles or stay tackles. In this section, we will discuss some of the different types of tackle in common use; namely, single whip, runner, gun tackle, single luff, twofold purchase, double luff, and threefold purchase. Before proceeding, we should explain that the purpose of the numbers and arrows in figures 12 through 17 (which follow) is to indicate the sequence and direction in which the standing part of the fall is led in reeving. You may want to refer back to these illustrations when we take up the reeving of blocks in the following section.

A SINGLE WHIP tackle consists of one single sheave block (tail block) fixed to a support with a line passing over the sheave. (See fig. 5-12.) It has no mechanical advantage and if a 100-pound load were to be lifted, it would require a pull of 100 pounds plus an allowance for friction.

A RUNNER (not illustrated) is a single-sheave movable block that is free to move along the line on which it is rove. It has a mechanical advantage of 2.

A GUN TACKLE is made up of two single sheave blocks (fig. 5-13). This tackle got its

29.187.1
Figure 5-13.—Gun tackle.

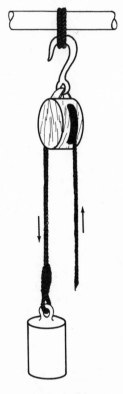

29.187(127)D
Figure 5-12.—Single whip tackle.

name by being used in the old days to haul muzzle-loading guns back into battery after the guns had been fired and reloaded.

As pointed out earlier in this chapter, a gun tackle has a mechanical advantage of 2.

A SINGLE LUFF TACKLE consists of a double and a single block, as indicated in figure 5-14. This type has a mechanical advantage of 3.

A TWOFOLD PURCHASE consists of two double blocks, as illustrated in figure 5-15. It has a mechanical advantage of 4.

A DOUBLE LUFF TACKLE has one triple and one double block. (See fig. 5-16.) A mechanical advantage of 5 is gained by using this tackle.

A THREEFOLD PURCHASE consists of two triple blocks with a mechanical advantage of 6. (See fig. 5-17.)

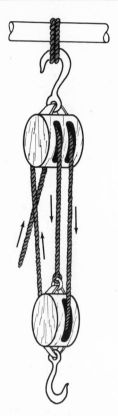

29.187.2
Figure 5-14.—Single luff tackle.

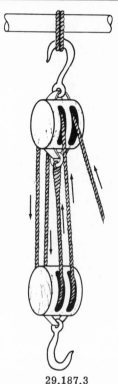

29.187.3
Figure 5-15.—Twofold purchase.

REEVING BLOCKS

In reeving a simple tackle, lay the blocks a few feet apart. The blocks should be placed down with the sheaves at right angles to each other and the becket ends pointing toward each other.

To begin reeving, lead the standing part of the falls through one sheave of the block which has the greatest number of sheaves. If both blocks have the same number of sheaves, begin at the block fitted with the becket. Then pass the standing part around the sheaves from one block to the other, making sure no lines are crossed, until all sheaves have a line passing over them. Now secure the standing part of the falls at the becket of the block containing the least number of sheaves, using a becket hitch

for a temporary securing, or an eye splice for a permanent securing.

With blocks of more than two sheaves, the standing part of the falls should be led through the sheave nearest the center of the block. This method places the strain on the center of the block and prevents the block from toppling and the lines from being cut by rubbing against the edges of the block.

Falls are generally reeved, through 8-inch or 10-inch wood or metal blocks, in such a manner as to have the lower block at right angles to the upper. Two 3-sheave blocks is the usual arrangement, and the method of reeving these is shown in figure 5-18. The hauling part must go through the middle sheave of the upper block, or the block will tilt to the side and the falls jam when a strain is taken. If a 3- and 2-sheave block rig is used, the method of reeving is about the same (fig. 5-19), but here the becket for the dead end must be on the lower rather than the upper block.

29.187(127)E
Figure 5-16.—Double luff tackle.

29.187(127)F
Figure 5-17.—Threefold purchase.

Naturally you must reeve the blocks before you splice in the becket thimble, or you will have to reeve the entire fall through from the opposite end. If the becket block has a grommet (fig. 5-9), it is better to take it out and substitute a heart-shaped thimble for the sake of appearance. Splice it in with a tapered eye splice, and worm, parcel and serve the splice if you want a neat-looking job.

In order to visualize the sequence in reeving blocks, refer again to figures 6 through 11, paying particular attention to the numbers and arrows which indicate where the standing part is led.

SAFE WORKING LOAD OF A TACKLE

You know that the force applied at the hauling part of a tackle is multiplied as many times as there are parts of the fall on the movable block; also that an allowance for friction must be made which adds roughly 10 percent to the weight to be lifted for every sheave in the system. For example, if you are lifting a weight of 100 pounds with a tackle containing five sheaves, you must add 10 percent times 5, or 50 percent, of 100 pounds to the weight in your calculations. In other words, you figure that this tackle is going to lift 150 instead of 100 pounds.

Disregarding friction, the safe working load of a tackle would be equal to the safe working load of the line or wire used, multiplied by the number of parts of the fall on the movable block. To make the necessary allowance for friction, you multiply this result by 10, and then divide what you get by 10 plus the number of sheaves in the system.

For example, let's say you have a three-fold purchase, mechanical advantage six, reeved with a line whose safe working load is, say, 2 tons. Disregarding friction, 6 times 2, or 12 tons, would be the safe working load of this setup.

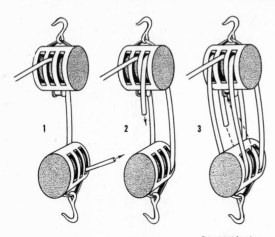

29.187(58)B
Figure 5-18.—Reeving falls—two
3-sheave blocks.

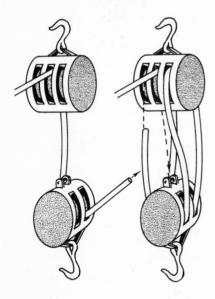

29.187(58)A
Figure 5-19.—Reeving falls—a 3 and 2.

To make the necessary allowance for friction, however, you first multiply 12 by 10, which gives you 120. This you divide by 10 plus 6 (number of sheaves in a three-fold purchase), or 16. The answer is 7-1/2 tons, safe working load.

LIFTING A GIVEN WEIGHT

To find the size of fiber line required to lift a given load use this formula:

$$C \text{ (in inches)} = \sqrt{15} \times P \text{ (tons)}$$

C in the formula is the circumference, in inches, of the line that is safe to use. The number 15 is the conversion factor. P is the weight of the given load, expressed in tons. The radical sign, or symbol, over 15 x P, indicates that you are to find the SQUARE ROOT OF that product.

To square a number means to multiply that number by itself. Finding the square root of a number simply means finding the number which, multiplied by itself, will give you the number whose square root you are seeking. If you do not understand how to work square root, refer to Mathematics, Volume 1, NavPers 10069-B. Now let us figure what size fiber line you would need to hoist a 5-ton load.

$$C = \sqrt{15} \times 5, \text{ or } \sqrt{75}$$

The number which, multiplied by itself, comes nearest to 75 is 8.6. Therefore, a fiber line 8-1/2 inches in circumference will do the job.

The formula for finding the size of wire rope required to lift a given load is:

$$C \text{ (in inches)} = \sqrt{2.5} \times P \text{ (tons)}$$

Work this formula in the way as explained above for fiber line. One point you should be careful not to overlook is that these formulas call for the CIRCUMFERENCE of the wire. You are used to talking about wire rope in terms of its diameter, so remember that circumference is about 3 times the diameter, roughly speaking. You can also determine circumference by the following formula, which is more accurate than rule of thumb: Circumference = diameter times Pi (π). In using this formula, remember that π equals 3.14.

SIZE OF LINE TO USE IN A TACKLE

To find the size of line to use in a tackle for a given load add to the weight to be hoisted one-tenth (or 10 percent) of its value for every sheave in the sytsem. Divide the result you get by the number of parts of the fall at the movable block, and use this result as P in the formula

$$C = \sqrt{15} \times P.$$

For example, let's say you are trying to find the size of fiber line to reeve in a three-fold purchase to lift 10 tons. There are six sheaves in a three-fold purchase, so you add 1/10 x 6, or 6/10 of 10, to the 10 tons. This gives you a theoretical weight to be lifted of 16 tons.

Divide 16 tons by 6 (number of parts on the movable block in a three-fold purchase), and you get about 2 2/3. Using this as P in the

formula $C = \sqrt{15} \times P$, you get:

$$C = \sqrt{15} \times 2\text{-}2/3, \quad \text{or} \quad \sqrt{40}$$

The square root of 40 is about 6.3, so it will take about a 6 1/2 inch line in this purchase to hoist 10 tons safely. As you seldom find three-sheave blocks which will take a line as large as 6 1/2 inch, you will probably have to rig two three-fold purchases with a continuous fall, as shown in figure 5-20. As each of these will have half the load, to find the size of line to use, calculate what size fiber line in a three-fold purchase will lift 5 tons. It works out to about 4 1/2 inches.

TACKLE SAFETY PRECAUTIONS

In hoisting and moving heavy objects, using blocks and tackle, keep SAFETY uppermost in mind. This should include safety for men and materials.

Always check the condition of blocks and sheaves before using them on a job to make sure they are in safe working order. See that the blocks are properly greased. Also, make sure that the line and sheave are the right size for the job.

Remember that sheaves or drums which have become worn or chipped or have corrugated grooves must not be used because they will injure the line. It is very important that you always ascertain whether you have enough mechanical advantage, in the amount of blocks, to make the load as easy to handle as possible.

Sheaves and blocks designed for use with fiber line must NOT be used for wire rope, since they are not strong enough for that service and the wire rope does not fit the sheave grooves. Moreover, sheaves and blocks

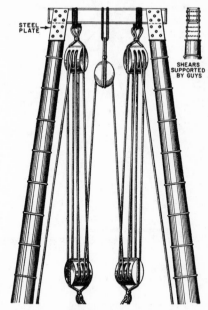

STEEL PLATE

SHEARS SUPPORTED BY GUYS

Courtesy of Knight's Modern Seamanship, 1945, D. Van Nostrant Co., Inc., 250 Fourth Avenue,

29.187(58)HX
Figure 5-20.—Rigging two tackles with a continuous fall.

built for wire rope should NEVER be used for fiber line.

SHEAR LEGS

The SHEAR LEGS are formed by crossing two timbers, poles, planks, pipes, or steel bars and lashing or bolting them together near the top. A sling is suspended from the lashed intersection and is used as a means of supporting the load tackle system. (See fig. 5-21.) In addition to the name SHEAR LEGS, this rig often is referred to simply as a SHEARS. (It has also been called an A-frame.)

The shear legs frequently is used to lift heavy machinery and other bulky objects. It may also be used as end supports of a cableway and highline. The fact that a shears can be quickly assembled and erected is a major reason why it is widely used in field work.

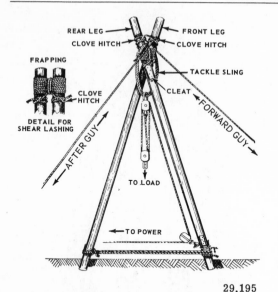

29.195

Figure 5-21.—Shear Legs.

A shears requires only two guys and can be used for working at a forward angle. The forward guy does not have much strain imposed on it during hoisting. This guy is used primarily as an aid in adjusting the drift of the shears and in keeping the top of the rig steady when hoisting or placing a load. The after guy has considerable strain imposed on it during hoisting, and thus should be selected with care. The thrust increases drastically as the shear legs go off the perpendicular. To determine the safe thrust use the formula $T = 4R^4/L^2$.

RIGGING

In rigging the shears, place your two spars or poles on the ground parallel to each other and with their butt ends even. Next, put a large block under the tops of the legs just below the point of lashing, and place a small block between the tops at the same point. To facilitate handling of the lashing, now separate the poles a distance equal to about one-third the diameter of one pole.

As lashing material, use 18 or 21 thread stuff. In applying the lashing, first make a clove hitch around one of the legs. Then take about 8 or 9 turns around both legs above the hitch,

working towards the top of the legs. Remember to wrap the turns tightly so that the finished lashing will be smooth and free of kinks. To apply the frapping (tight lashings), make 2 or 3 turns around the lashing between the legs; then, with a clove hitch, secure the end of the line to the other leg just below the lashing (fig. 5-21).

Now cross the legs of the shears at the top and separate the butt ends of the two legs so that the spread between them is equal to one-half the height of the shears. Dig shallow holes, about 1 foot deep, at the butt end of each leg. The butts of the legs should be placed in these holes in erecting the shears. Placing the legs in the holes will keep them from kicking out in operations where the shears is at an angle other than vertical.

The next step is to form the sling for the hoisting falls. To do this, take a short length of line or wire rope, pass it a sufficient number of times over the cross at the top of the shears, and tie the ends together.

Now reeve a set of blocks and place the hook of the upper block through the sling; then secure the hook by mousing. Fasten a snatch block to the lower part of one of the legs, as indicated in figure 5-21.

If you need to move the load horizontally by moving the head of the shears, you must rig a tackle in the after guy near its anchorage.

The guys—one for forward guy and one after guy—are secured next to the top of the shears. Secure the forward guy to the rear leg and the after guy to the front leg, using a clove hitch in both instances. (See fig. 5-21.)

ERECTING

Several men are needed for safe, efficient erection of the shears, the number being determined largely by the size of the rig. To help ensure good results, the erection crew should lift the top of the frame and walk it up by hand until the after guy tackle system takes over the load. When this point is reached, complete the raising of the shears into final position by hauling in on the tackle.

Remember to secure the forward guy to its anchorage before raising the legs and maintain a slight tension on the line to control the movement. Also, after the shears has been raised, lash the butt ends with chain, line, or boards to keep them from spreading when a load is applied.

TRIPOD

A tripod consists of three legs of equal length, which are lashed together at the top. (See fig. 5-22.) The fact that the tripod can only be used where hoisting is vertical, places it at a distinct disadvantage in comparison with other hoisting devices. Its use will be limited primarily to jobs that involve hoisting over wells, mine shafts, or other excavations.

A major advantage of the tripod is its great stability. In addition, it requires no guys or anchorages, and its load capacity is approximately 1 1/2 times greater than for shears made of the same size timbers.

The legs of a tripod generally are made of timber poles or pipes. Materials used for lashing include fiber line, wire rope, and chain. Metal

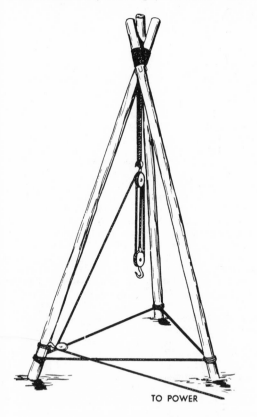

TO POWER

29.196

Figure 5-22.—Tripod.

rings joined with short chain sections are also available for insertion over the top of the tripod legs.

RIGGING

The strength of a tripod depends largely on the strength of the material used for lashing, as well as the amount of lashing used. The following procedure for lashing applies to line 3 inches in circumference or smaller. For extra heavy loads, use more turns than specified in the procedure given here; for light loads, use fewer turns than specified here.

As the first step of the procedure, take three spars of equal length and place a mark near the top of each to indicate the center of the lashing. Now lay two of the spars parallel with their TOPS resting on a skid (or block). Place the third spar between the two, with the BUTT end resting on a skid. Position the spars so that the lashing marks on all three are in line. Leave an interval between the spars equal to about one-half the diameter of the spars. This will keep the lashing from being drawn too tight when the tripod is erected.

With the 3-inch line, make a clove hitch around one of the outside spars; put it about 4 inches above the lashing mark. Then make 8 or 9 turns with the line around all three spars. (See part A, fig. 5-23.) In making the turns, remember to maintain the proper amount of space between the spars.

Now make 1 or 2 close frapping turns around the lashing between each pair of spars. Do not draw the turns too tight. Finally, secure the end of the line with a clove hitch on the center spar just above the lashing, as shown at A, figure 5-23.

There is another method of lashing a tripod which you may find preferable to the method just given. It may be used in lashing slender poles up to 20 feet in length, or when some means other than hand power is available for erection.

First place the three spars parallel to each other, leaving an interval between them slightly greater than twice the diameter of the line to be used. Rest the top of each pole on a skid so that the end projects about 2 feet over the skid. Then line up the butts of the three spars, as indicated at B, figure 5-23.

Next, make a clove hitch on one outside leg at the bottom of the position the lashing will occupy, which is about 2 feet from the end. Now proceed to weave the line over the middle leg,

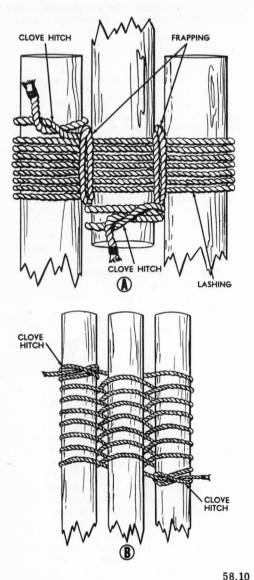

CLOVE HITCH   FRAPPING

CLOVE HITCH

Ⓐ

LASHING

CLOVE
HITCH

CLOVE
HITCH

Ⓑ

58.10

Figure 5-23.—Lashings for a tripod.

under and around the other outside leg, under the middle leg, over and around the first leg, and so forth, until completing about 8 or 9 turns.

Finish the lashing by forming a clove hitch on the other outside leg. (See B, fig. 5-23.)

ERECTING

In the final position of an erected tripod, it is important that the legs be spread an equal distance apart. The spread between legs must be not more than two-thirds, nor less than one-half the length of a leg. Small tripods, or those lashed according to the first procedure given in the preceding section, may be raised by hand. Here are the main steps which make up the hand-erection procedure.

Start by raising the top ends of the three legs about 4 feet, keeping the butt ends of the legs on the ground. Now cross the tops of the two outer legs and position the top of the third or center leg so that it rests on top of the cross.

A sling for the hoisting tackle can be attached readily by first passing the sling over the center leg, and then around the two outer legs at the cross. Place the hook of the upper block of a tackle on the sling, and secure the hook by mousing.

The raising operation can now be completed. To raise an ordinary tripod, a crew of about eight men may be required. To help ensure best results in raising the tripod, see that the legs are lifted from the center. Also, remember to push in on the legs as they are being lifted. After getting the tripod in its final position, lash the legs near the bottom with line or chain to keep them from shifting. (See fig. 5-22.) Sometimes boards, rather than line or chain, may be used to hold the legs in place.

Where desirable, a leading block for the hauling part of the tackle may be lashed to one of the tripod legs, as indicated in figure 5-22.

In erecting a large tripod, you may need a small gin pole to aid in raising the tripod into position. When called on to assist in the erection of a tripod lashed according to the alternate lashing procedure described in the preceding section, the first thing to do is to raise the tops of the legs far enough from the ground to permit spreading them apart. Use guys or tag lines to help hold the legs steady while they are being raised. Now, with the legs clear of the ground, cross the two outer legs and place the center leg so that it rests on top of the cross. Then attach the sling for the hoisting tackle. Here, as with a small tripod, simply pass the sling over the center leg and then around the two outer legs at the cross.

SCAFFOLDING

As the working level on a structure rises above the reach of men standing on the ground, temporary elevated platforms called SCAF-FOLDS are erected to support the craftmen, their tools and materials.

There are several types of wood scaffolds in use today, but they are rapidly being replaced by the ready-made steel bracket type. Of the wood type scaffolds in use, there is the one which is suspended from above and called a swinging scaffold, whereas the one supported below is called a pole scaffold. Now, let us take a brief look at the construction of the various scaffolds that you may use from time to time.

SPECIFICATIONS FOR SCAFFOLD MEMBERS

The poles on a job-built pole scaffold should not exceed 40 ft in height. If higher poles than this are required, the scaffolding must be designed by an engineer.

For a light-duty (not over 25 lbs per sq ft) scaffold, either single-pole or double-pole, the minimum lumber dimensions are as follows:

Poles: 24-ft or less, 2 x 4; 24-ft to 40 ft, 2 x 6
Putlogs: 2 x 6 on edge
Ledgers: 2 x 6
Braces: 1 x 4
Planking: 2 x 10
Guardrails: 2 x 4

For a heavy-duty (25 to 75 lbs per sq ft) single-pole scaffold the minimum dimensions are as follows:

Poles: 24-ft or less, 2 x 6; 24-ft to 40-ft, doubled 2 x 4
Putlogs: doubled 2 x 4, or 2 x 8 on edge
Ledgers: 2 x 8
Braces: 1 x 6
Planking: 2 x 10
Guardrails: 2 x 4

For a heavy-duty double-pole scaffold the minimum lumber dimensions are as follows:

Poles: 24-ft or less, 2 x 6; 24-ft to 40-ft: for load from 25 to 50 lb per sq ft, double 2 x 4; for load from 50 to 75 lb per sq ft, double 2 x 6
Putlogs: 2 x 8 on edge
Ledgers: 2 x 8
Braces: 1 x 6
Planking: 2 x 10
Guardrails: 2 x 6

The longitudinal maximum pole spacing for a light-duty scaffold is 7 ft 6 in. For a heavy-duty scaffold it is 7 ft.

The transverse maximum pole spacing for a light- or heavy-duty independent-pole scaffold with poles up to 24 ft is 6 ft 6 in. For a light-duty independent-pole scaffold with poles 24 to 40 ft the transverse maximum pole spacing is 7 ft. For a heavy-duty independent-pole scaffold with poles 24 to 40 ft the transverse maximum spacing is 10 ft.

For a single-pole light- or heavy-duty scaffold the pole spacing from the wall should be from 3 to 5 feet.

For a light-duty scaffold the maximum ledger vertical spacing is 7 ft. For a heavy-duty scaffold the maximum ledger vertical spacing is 4 ft 6 in.

SCAFFOLD CONSTRUCTION REQUIREMENTS

Construction requirements for pole scaffolds are as follows:

All poles must be set up perfectly plumb.

The lower ends of poles must not bear directly on a natural earth surface. If the surface is earth, a board footing 2 in. thick by from 6 to 12 in. wide (depending on the softness of the earth) must be placed under the poles.

If poles must be spliced, splice plates must not be less than 4 ft long, not less than the width of the pole wide, and each pair of plates must have a combined thickness not less than the thickness of the pole. Adjacent poles must not be spliced at the same level.

A ledger must be long enough to extend over two pole spaces, and it must overlap the poles at the ends by at least 4 in. Ledgers must be spliced by overlapping and nailing AT POLES-never between poles. If platform planks are raised as work progresses upward, the ledgers and putlogs on which the planks previously rested must be left in place to brace and stiffen the poles.

For a heavy-duty scaffold, ledgers must be supported by cleats nailed or bolted to the poles, as well as by being themselves nailed to the poles.

A single putlog must be set with the longer section dimension vertical, and putlogs must be long enough to overlap the poles by at least 3 in. They should be both face nailed to the poles and toenailed to the ledgers. When the inner end of the putlog butts against the wall (as it does in a single-pole scaffold), it must be supported by a 2 x 6 bearing block not less than 12 in. long, notched out the width of the putlog and securely nailed to the wall. The inner end of the putlog should be nailed to both the bearing block and the wall. If the inner end of a putlog is located in a window opening, it must be supported on a stout plank nailed across the opening. If the inner end of a putlog is nailed to a building stud, it must be supported on a cleat of the same thickness as the putlog, nailed to the stud.

A platform plank must never be less than 2 in. thick. Edges of planks should be close enough together to prevent tools or materials from falling through the opening. A plank must be long enough to extend over 3 putlogs, with an overlap of at least 6 in. But not more than 12 in.

SWINGING SCAFFOLDS

The simplest type of swinging scaffold is one which consists simply of a stout plank (minimum thickness 2 in.) with a couple of transverse HORNS nailed or bolted to the under side, near the ends. The stage hangs from a couple of lines, (minimum size, 2 in.) which lead up and over or through some supporting device (such as a pair of shackles secured to outriggers at the roof line) and back to the stage.

Figure 5-24 shows the method of bending a bowline to a stage by means of a SCAFFOLD HITCH. A stage provides a convenient means for working down from upward (painting down a wall from roof line to ground level, for instance), but since you can't hoist yourself aloft on a stage, it's no good for working from down upward.

When the rig shown in figure 5-25 is hooked to the tackles, you can move up or down at will, simply by heaving in or slacking out on the tackles. The two projecting timbers to which the tackles will be attached are called OUTRIGGERS.

Figure 5-26 shows you a single-pole wood scaffold. Study the figure closely until you have learned the names of the various parts. Figure 5-27 shows you a double-pole wood scaffold, and figure 5-28 shows you a double-pole steel

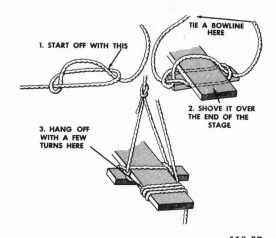

1. START OFF WITH THIS

TIE A BOWLINE HERE

2. SHOVE IT OVER THE END OF THE STAGE

3. HANG OFF WITH A FEW TURNS HERE

118.37

Figure 5-24.—Making a scaffold hitch.

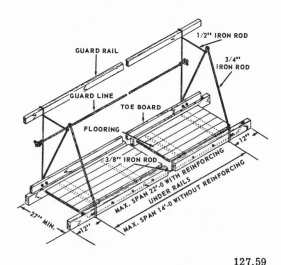

GUARD RAIL

1/2" IRON ROD

3/4" IRON ROD

GUARD LINE

TOE BOARD

FLOORING

3/8" IRON ROD

MAX. SPAN 22'-0 WITH REINFORCING UNDER RAILS

MAX. SPAN 14'-0 WITHOUT REINFORCING

27" MIN.

12"

12"

127.59

Figure 5-25.—Swinging scaffold.

scaffold being constructed. The double-pole scaffold (steel or wood) which is completely independent of the main structure, is used for the erection of sheathing, siding and the like. (A light-duty scaffold, designed for loads not more than 25 lbs per sq ft, is used by builders, painters, and others using relatively light materials. A heavy-duty scaffold, designed for loads from 25 to 75 lbs per sq ft, is used by masons and other

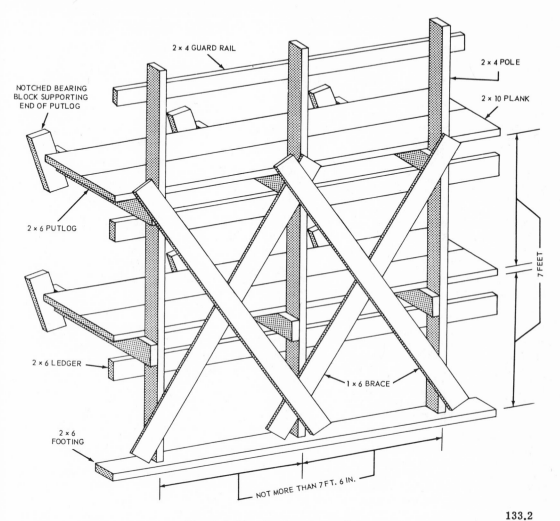

2 x 4 GUARD RAIL

NOTCHED BEARING
BLOCK SUPPORTING
END OF PUTLOG

2 x 4 POLE

2 x 10 PLANK

2 x 6 PUTLOG

7 FEET

2 x 6 LEDGER

1 x 6 BRACE

2 x 6
FOOTING

NOT MORE THAN 7 FT. 6 IN.

133.2

Figure 5-26.—Single-pole scaffold.

workers in heavy materials.) Several types of patent independent scaffolding are available for simple and rapid erection as shown in figure 5-28. The scaffold uprights are braced with diagonal members as shown in figure 5-29, and the working level is covered with a platform of planks. All bracing must form triangles and the base of each column requires adequate footing plates for bearing area on the ground. The patented steel scaffolding is usually erected by placing the two uprights on the ground and inserting the diagonal members. The diagonal members have end fittings which permit rapid locking in position. The first tier is set on steel bases on the ground, and a second tier is placed in the same manner on the first tier with the bottom of each upright locked to the top to the lower tier. A third and fourth upright can be

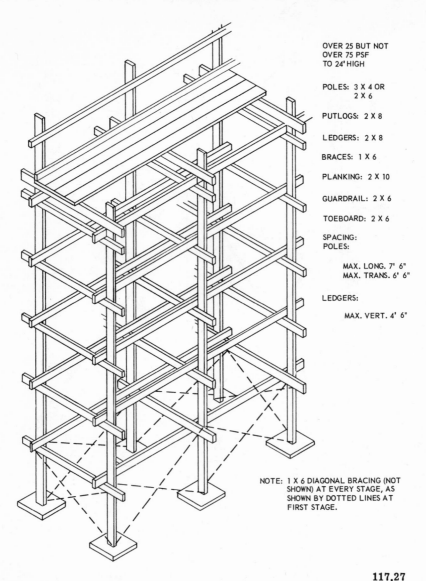

OVER 25 BUT NOT
OVER 75 PSF
TO 24' HIGH

POLES: 3 X 4 OR
2 X 6

PUTLOGS: 2 X 8

LEDGERS: 2 X 8

BRACES: 1 X 6

PLANKING: 2 X 10

GUARDRAIL: 2 X 6

TOEBOARD: 2 X 6

SPACING:
POLES:

MAX. LONG. 7' 6"
MAX. TRANS. 6' 6"

LEDGERS:

MAX. VERT. 4' 6"

NOTE: 1 X 6 DIAGONAL BRACING (NOT
SHOWN) AT EVERY STAGE, AS
SHOWN BY DOTTED LINES AT
FIRST STAGE.

117.27
Figure 5-27.—Heavy-duty independent-pole scaffold, diagonal bracing not shown.

placed on the ground level and locked to the first set with diagonal bracing. The scaffolding can be built as high as desired, but high scaffolding should be tied in to the main structure.

NAILING POLE SCAFFOLDS

The safety of a wood scaffold (or of any wood structure, for that matter) depends upon the

133.247

Figure 5-28.—Assembling prefabricated independent scaffolding.

nails as well as upon the timbers selected. Nails smaller than 8d common should not be used in scaffolds. All nails should be driven full length, and in directions which will ensure that the pull is across, not along, the length of the nail. Nails should be placed not less than half their lengths from the ends of boards, and not less than one-quarter their lengths from the edges of boards.

81

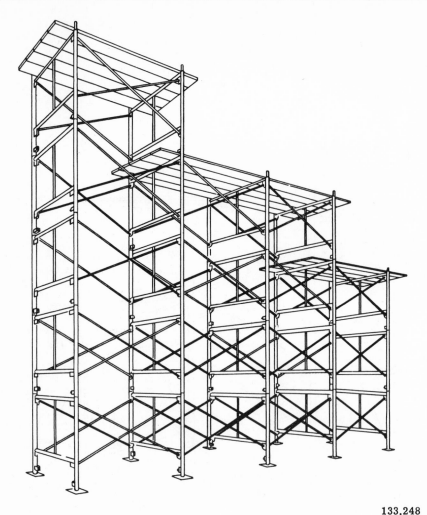

133.248

Figure 5-29.—Prefabricated independent scaffolding.

FRAMED PORTABLE-SUPPORTED SCAFFOLD

Scaffolding which is used in the renovation and installation of high ceilings is shown in figure 5-30. This type of scaffold is self-supporting and can be easily moved as the occasion demands. The construction of this form of scaffolding consists of four uprights, and cross and diagonal braces. (See figure 5-30.) An excellent scaffold can be constructed to provide three elevated platforms in order to expedite the erection of 40' x 100' Quonset huts or similar buildings. Figure 5-31 illustrates this type of scaffolding. You'll notice that this scaffolding is made by adding two platform structures to the framed portable scaffold shown in figure 5-30.

In order to make the framed portable-supported scaffold, a rectangular frame is

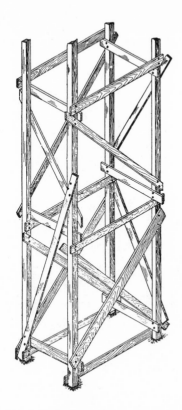

133.3

Figure 5-30.—Detail of a framed
portable scaffold.

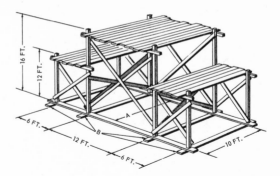

133.4

Figure 5-31.—Typical scaffold for the rib construction of a 40' x 100' Quonset hut.

of 1" x 4" or 1" x 6" material. Four outriggers
or supports are secured to the uprights to which
planking of 2" x 12" material is made fast to
form the horizontal elevated deck.

Four 4" x 4" uprights (two on each side) with
diagonal braces are then nailed to the foundation
pieces at their intersection with the end skids.
These uprights should be cut 12 feet in length and
may be secured by fastening them to the foundation pieces with 90-degree angle irons and lag
screws. The diagonal braces should be of 1" x
4" or 1" x 6" material. The two end platforms
are constructed in the same manner as the center
platform. All planking must be securely nailed
to the horizontal outriggers or supports.

STEEL AND ALUMINUM SCAFFOLDING

Steel and aluminum scaffolding is used to
speed up construction and maintenance operations. For interior work and erection, there
are many types. Figure 5-32 shows the type of
scaffolding used around most construction sites
because this type can be disassembled and
transported whenever necessary. They are
mounted on steel casters, with brakes and adjustable supports, which permit quick movement and positioning of each tower. This
scaffolding is equipped with special, trussed
planks, 12 feet long, which are so placed as to
enable workmen to be within comfortable and
safe working distance of all building connections.

BRACKET SCAFFOLDING

The type of scaffolding discussed in this section is considered as the bracket type scaffolding.

constructed with four skids, 12 feet long. Make
the skids of 2" x 8" material and fasten them
to two foundation pieces of 2" x 6" material, 24
feet in length. The four skids, indicated in
figure 5-31 as B, are fastened to the foundation
pieces A in such a manner as to have their ends
extend 1 foot on each side of the foundation
pieces. This increases the stability of the scaffolding. The two center skids are spaced 12 feet
apart, and the two end skids, 6 feet from the
center skids.

Four 4" x 4" uprights, with diagonal cross
braces, are then nailed to the foundation pieces
at their intersection with the center skids.
These uprights should be 16 feet long. To make
these uprights even more secure, use 90-degree
angle irons and lag screws to fasten them to
the foundation. The diagonal braces should be

133.5

Figure 5-32.—The scaffolding used for interior work and erection of a construction project.

This type of scaffolding has certain advantages over the ones previously discussed; it is easier to erect, involves less labor, and requires less material. This type scaffold can be easily constructed of wood and, in some areas, is readily available in prefabricated steel.

Caution is a must when fastening steel bracket scaffolding in place with nails, because the nails must be driven as not to break the heads. Nails with broken heads are definitely unsafe for scaffolds. Some brackets are even fastened to the wall with spikes while others may be hooked around a stud. The latter type of bracket is safe, but requires the making of a hole in the sheathing for withdrawal of the bracket. To fasten another type steel bracket you need to bore a hole in a 2 x 4 crosspiece nailed to the inside of a stud.

The most simple bracket and yet sturdy is the wooden bracket and the Builder can construct it on the job. Some wooden brackets are fastened to the wall and some are not. The ones not fastened to the wall are supported by 2 x 4's

set at an angle of 45 degrees. The brackets are held in place and kept from tipping or sliding on the wall by using cross braces of 1 x 6 material.

SCAFFOLDING SAFETY

The following scaffolding safety precautions must be observed by all men working on scaffolds, or tending other men who are working on scaffolds. Builder petty officers must not only observe the safety precautions themselves, but also promulgate them to their men and ensure that the men observe them.

Standard scaffolds suitable to the work at hand must be provided and used. The use of makeshift substitutes is prohibited.

All scaffolds must be maintained in a safe condition, and a scaffold must not be altered or disturbed while in use. Personnel must not be allowed to use damaged or weakened scaffolds.

Structural members, supporting lines and tackles, and other scaffold equipment must be inspected daily before work on scaffolding is started.

When men working on a scaffold are directly below other men working above, the men below must be sheltered against possible falling objects by a protective covering. The men below MUST wear protective headgear.

If the frequent presence of personnel directly under a scaffold is unavoidable, a protective covering must be set up under the scaffold. A passageway or thoroughfare under a scaffold must have both overhead and side protection.

Access to scaffolds must be by standard stairs or fixed ladders only.

The erection, alteration, and dismantling of scaffolds must be done under the supervision of men who are experienced in scaffold work.

When scaffolding is being dismantled it should be cleaned, and ready for storage or use. Scaffolding that is not ready for use should never be stored.

Work on scaffolds should be secured during storms or high winds, or when scaffolds are covered with ice or snow.

Unstable objects, such as barrels, boxes, loose brick, building blocks, must not be used to support scaffold planking.

No scaffold may be used for the storage of materials in excess of those currently required for the job.

Tools not in immediate use on scaffolds must be stowed in containers, to prevent tools left adrift from being knocked off. Tool containers must be lashed or otherwise secured to the scaffolds.

Scaffolds must be kept clear of accumulations of tools, equipment, materials, and rubbish.

If part of a scaffold must be used as a loading or landing stage for materials, the scaffold must be additionally braced and reinforced at and around the landing stage area.

Throwing objects to or dropping them from scaffolds is absolutely prohibited. Hand lines must be used for raising or lowering objects which cannot be passed hand-to-hand.

A standard guardrail and toeboard should be provided on the open side of the platform on all single-pole and independent-pole scaffolds.

If the space between the scaffold and building is more than 18 inches, a standard guardrail should be erected on the building side.

No person should remain on the rolling scaffold while it is being moved.

When a light-duty portable scaffold is formed of planks supported or hitched on trestle ladders, the base of the ladder should be secured against opening up to the full spread before laying on the planks.

A scaffold must NEVER be overloaded. Scaffolds are built in the following strength categories: (1) extra heavy duty, (2) heavy duty, (3) light duty, and (4) an intermediate category between light and heavy, for scaffolds used by stucco workers and by lathers and plasterers. The maximum uniform safe working load per sq ft of platform for each of these categories is as follows:

Extra-heavy-duty (stone
   mason's scaffold)......... 75 lbs.
Heavy-duty (stone setters and
   bricklayers............. 50 lbs.
Light-duty (carpenter's and
   miscellaneous).......... 25 lbs.
Intermediate (stucco workers
   and plasterers) .... 30 lbs.

To get the load per sq ft of platform of a pile of materials on a platform, divide the total weight of the pile by the number of sq ft of platform it covers.

LADDERS

A sufficient supply of ladders, as indicated by the nature of the work, must be provided at the site before construction can begin. However, the use of ladders, where scaffolds, platforms, or other substantial working levels could have been provided, has caused many serious accidents. Work actually performed on ladders should be confined to an unavoidable minimum.

TYPES OF LADDERS

A number of different types of ladders are available for construction today. Among the various types which you may use frequently in construction work are single portable ladders and extension ladders.

A SINGLE PORTABLE ladder is a ladder of one section which may be used at various locations. This type should not exceed 30 feet in length. In the placement of a ladder, careful consideration must be given the need for placing it at a safe angle against the wall or other fixed object to be scaled. In case of a single portable ladder, remember that: UNLESS the ladder is securely fastened or a man is holding it, the base should be one-fourth the ladder length from the vertical plane of the top support. Where the rails extend above the top landing the ladder length to the top support only is considered. (See fig. 5-33.)

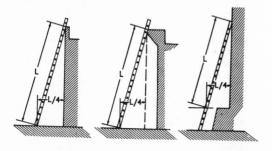

127.61

Figure 5-33.—Correct angles for ladder placement.

The clearance space IN BACK of a single portable ladder should always be sufficient to obtain a secure foothold on the rungs. A back clearance of at least 6 inches is recommended. The clearance space IN FRONT of the ladder should be such that it will not be necessary to assume a cramped or unnatural position when climbing. A front clearance of at least 30 inches is recommended.

If a portable ladder is to be used on smooth floors, concrete walks, or sloping surfaces, make sure it is equipped with nonslipping bases or that other suitable means is provided to prevent displacement while in use. Single portable ladders not constructed for use as sectional ladders must not be spliced together to form a longer ladder.

An EXTENSION ladder is one consisting of two sliding sections which can be adjusted to different heights. No extension ladder may contain more than two sections, and no such ladder may be extended to more than 60 ft. An extension ladder must be so constructed as to bring the RUNGS (horizontal members) of overlapping parts of sections opposite each other when the ladder is locked in extended position. Again, when an extended ladder is placed in position for use, the horizontal distance from the vertical plane of the upper support to the base should be one-fourth of the ladder length.

For extension lengths up to 38 ft the minimum section overlap should be 3 ft; for lengths from 38 to 44 ft it should be 4 ft; and for lengths from 44 to 60 ft it should be 5 ft.

Most requirements for a ladder are satisfied with the single portable and extension types. However, the fixed ladder and the stepladder may be required under certain conditions.

A FIXED ladder is one which is fastened to a structure in a more or less permanent manner. Top, bottom, and intermediate fastenings must be used as required. The RAILS (vertical members) of a fixed ladder must extend at least 36 in. above the top landing. If landing at the top requires passing between the rails, rungs above the landing must be removed.

A STEPLADDER is a portable ladder which opens out, saw horse-fashion, for self-support. The maximum permissible height for a stepladder is 16 ft. Stepladders must always be used fully opened, and they should not be used as regular working platforms.

LADDER SAFETY

Here are a few important safety precautions which apply to ladders in general.

Ladders should be inspected at regular and frequent intervals. Ladders with weakened, broken, or missing treads, rungs, or cleats, or broken or "splintered" side rails should not be used.

Ladders should be kept coated with a clear shellac or other transparent material, or treated with linseed oil. Painting with opaque (nontransparent) paint is forbidden.

Separate ladders for ascending and descending should be provided in a building construction of more than 2 stories in height, or where traffic is heavy.

Where a ladder is installed wide enough to permit traffic in both directions at the same time, a center rail should be provided. One side of the ladder should be plainly marked "up" and the other side "down".

Ladders used in passageways, driveways, or thoroughfares should be guarded by barricades (guardrails). Doors which open adjacent to portable ladders should be locked or otherwise blocked or guarded while the ladder remains in use.

Ladders should be placed so that the rails have a secure footing and a substantial support at or near the top.

Ladders should not be placed against sash, window panes, or unstable supports such as loose boxes or barrels. The use of ladders during a storm or in a high wind should be avoided unless absolutely necessary, in which case the ladder should be securely lashed in position.

If a ladder is to be placed against a window frame, a board should first be spiked across the side rails at the top.

Ladders should not be placed or used in elevator shafts or hoistways. Should such a procedure be necessary, the ladders should be protected from objects from operation at higher elevations in or adjoining the shaft.

Ladders should not be left standing, especially on the outside, for long periods of time unless securely anchored at both top and bottom.

Ladders should be handled carefully when being lowered. They should not be allowed to drop on their sides or to fall heavily endwise on one rail.

Ladders consrtucted of metal should not be used near electricity.

Until such time as satisfactory specification for portable metal ladders approved by the Navy Department is issued, the use of such ladders is not recommended. These ladders should not be used within four feet of any electrical wiring or equipment. All portable metal ladders should be marked with signs or decals reading CAUTION—DO NOT USE NEAR ELECTRICAL EQUIPMENT. Such signs should be placed on the inside rails between the third and fourth rungs.

When ascending or descending a ladder, the user should always face the ladder.

No one should go or down a ladder without the free use of both hands. If handling material, a rope should be used.

No one should run up or down a ladder, or slide down a ladder, at any time.

Before attempting to climb a ladder, workmen should remove oil or grease from the soles of their shoes.

When doing maintenance work above the ground, workmen should always use a safety belt, with a lifeline tied of long enough for necessary movement, but short enough to prevent falls.

Single portable ladders over 30 ft in length should not be used.

Fixed ladder should be securely held in place by top, bottom, and intermediate fastenings as required.

Sloping ladders which require climbing on the under side of the ladder should not be used.

Rails of ladders fixed to top landings should extend a distance of at least 36 inches above the landing. Rungs above the landing should be omitted when it is necessary to pass through the ladder. Landing platforms should be provided where a person must step a greater distance than 14 inches from ladder to roof, tank, etc.

MATERIALS HANDLING SAFETY

An attempt to describe in detail the large variety of methods by which the large variety of materials used in construction are transported, hoisted, stored, and otherwise handled, would require a book in itself. Earth, for example, is moved by devices which range in power and complexity from the ancient and honorable hand shovel to the power shovel capable of scooping out many yards at a bite.

Only a very general treatment of the subject of materials handling can be presented here. Since the chief emphasis will be placed on materials handling safety, we'll give the discussion that general title. However, in discussing materials handling safety, a good deal about materials handling methods will be said as well.

ACCIDENT CAUSES

Surveys seem to indicate that the major portion of the accidents which occur during construction operations are accidents which happen in the course of materials handling. Handling by hand seems to produce more accidents than handling by mechanical equipment, but mechanical equipment accidents usually produce greater damage and more severe personal injury. Nevertheless, the human element is the basic cause of the great majority of accidents. Very few accidents have been caused by equipment defects which a reasonably careful inspection would not have revealed.

PERSONAL PROTECTION

All personnel engaged in materials handling operations should wear approved safety shoes, the wearing of sandals, open-toe shoes, or thin-soled shoes should be absolutely prohibited. Foot guards and leg guards should be worn when the nature of the material being handled indicates a necessity for such protection.

Gloves should be worn by men engaged in carrying, lifting, or moving objects which are sharp, splintery, or otherwise hazardous to the bare hands. Men handling acids, caustics, or strong solvents should wear suitable approved gloves, rubber aprons, acid-resistant boots, and goggles or face shields.

All personal protective equipment should be issued clean, and it should be kept clean while in use. A life line and safety belt should be worn when working on high elevations, to prevent falling.

Finger rings should not be worn by men engaged in materials handling.

HAND-HANDLING PRECAUTIONS

Personnel with existing hernias, or with a history of repeated back-strain, should report the fact to their superiors. Such personnel should not be assigned to hand-handling of heavy materials.

All personnel engaged in hand-handling should be instructed in the proper method of lifting a heavy object. This method may be roughly defined as "lifting with the legs and not with the back." The lifter should stand close to the load, with feet solidly placed and slightly apart. He should then lower himself to grasping position by SQUATTING, NOT by STOOPING. After grasping the load firmly, he should raise both it and himself by STRAIGHTENING HIS LEGS. During the whole procedure, the back should be kept as nearly vertical as possible.

A man rolling a drum should always PUSH it AWAY from him. Drums should always be hand-handled up an incline by PARBUCKLING. (See fig. 5-34.)

Before any material is hand-handled, it should be inspected for sharp edges, protruding points, or any other factors likely to cause personal injury. If the factors cannot be eliminated, adequate personal protection must be provided. Face shields or goggles should be worn when removing steel strapping.

WHEELBARROW/BUGGY/HAND-TRUCK PRECAUTIONS

A hand truck, wheelbarrow, or buggy must never be so heavily loaded as to create a danger that it may take charge on a ramp or incline.

A wheelbarrow or buggy with a loose, cracked, or broken handle, or one with a twisted or out-of-round wheel, should be taken out of service at once and not used again until repaired.

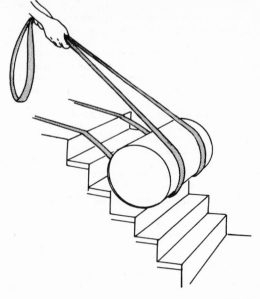

133.7

Figure 5-34.—Parbuckling.

Gloves or knuckle guards should be worn by men who are steering wheelbarrows through narrow passageways.

A wheelbarrow should be so loaded as to place the center of gravity of the load as far forward as possible. The purpose of this is to remove as much of the weight as possible from the handles. Handles should be lifted like any other load should be lifted—with the leg muscles, not with the back muscles.

A wheelbarrow or buggy should always be PUSHED, not pulled. The practice of running with an empty wheelbarrow has caused many injuries by stumbling over or falling against the wheelbarrow, and should never be done.

Wheelbarrows should not be overloaded, especially when used on ramps.

Wheelbarrows should never be left in such a position that they can readily tip over or fall, or should never be left where persons or traffic can run into them.

RIGGING/HOISTING SAFETY

The material in this section relates principally to weight-handling equipment. Equipment of this kind ranges in power and complexity all the way from a simple hand-operated single whip to a 400-ton floating crane. The care, maintenance, and operation of power equipment is, of course, a responsibility of a different rating than yours, but you and your men must work in the close vicinity of such equipment, and you should therefore know how to do so in safety.

PRINCIPAL CAUSES OF ACCIDENTS

About 80 percent of all accidents involving equipment used in construction work and weight-handling are caused by unsafe practices of operating, maintenance, and other personnel involved in the operation of the equipment. It is possible for these personnel to perform their tasks on or about the equipment in an unsafe manner many times over a long period without accident. Eventually they become convinced that their unsafe practices actually are safe. Inevitably, their continued violation of the safety rules results in accidents.

The predominant unsafe practices and hazardous conditions in the operation of heavy construction equipment are listed below. Operators of all such equipment should study this list carefully, noting particularly the hazards connected with their own work. They should also heed seriously the instructions and warnings of their supervisors regarding safe practices to be followed during operation, making every effort to avoid accidents from any of these major causes:

backing and turning machines, swinging booms, lowering buckets, and performing similar operations without looking, warning, or signaling;

getting on and off equipment carelessly while it is in operation, or riding equipment when not authorized to do so;

operating equipment with defective brakes, clutches, cables, or other improperly functioning parts;

working or walking under skips, buckets, or loads;

failing to adjust controls properly before attempting to crank an engine;

oiling, adjusting, or repairing equipment while it is in operation;

using equipment with unguarded or inadequately guarded engine fans and other dangerous moving parts;

failing to use personal protective devices or clothing such as goggles, safety shoes, gloves, and hard hats;

failing to properly block equipment or heavy parts while repairing equipment;

operating equipment in a thoughtless or unsafe manner, such as moving too fast over rough ground or working too near the edge of a soft fill;

operating cranes too close to power lines without adequate watches and supervision;

failing to secure equipment, brakes, booms, and movable parts before repairing, leaving, or moving the machine;

poor housekeeping either on the equipment itself or in the operating area;

overloading the equipment.

SIGNALS AND SIGNAL SAFETY

ONE MAN, and ONE MAN ONLY, should be designated as official signalman for the operator of a piece of hoisting equipment, and both the signalman and the operator must be thoroughly familiar with the standard hand signals. Whenever possible, the signalman should wear some distinctive article of dress, such as a bright-colored helmet. He must maintain himself at all times in the position from which he can best observe the load and the men working on it, while remaining himself clearly visible to the operator. Figure 5-35 shows the standard hand signals for hoisting equipment. Some of the signals shown apply only to mobile equipment; others only to a piece of equipment with a boom which can be raised, lowered, and swung in a circle.

The signals shown are self-explanatory, with a few possible exceptions. The two-arm hoist and lower signals are used when the signalman desires to control the speed of hoisting or lowering. The one-arm hoist or lower signal allows the operator to take the load right on up, or to lower it right on down.

To DOG OFF the load and boom means to set the brakes so as to lock both the hoisting mechanism and the boom hoist mechanism. The signal is given when circumstances require that the load be left hanging motionless in the air for some time.

With exception of the EMERGENCY STOP signal, which may be given by anyone who perceives a necessity for it, and which must be obeyed instantly by the operator, only the official signalman should be permitted to make signals.

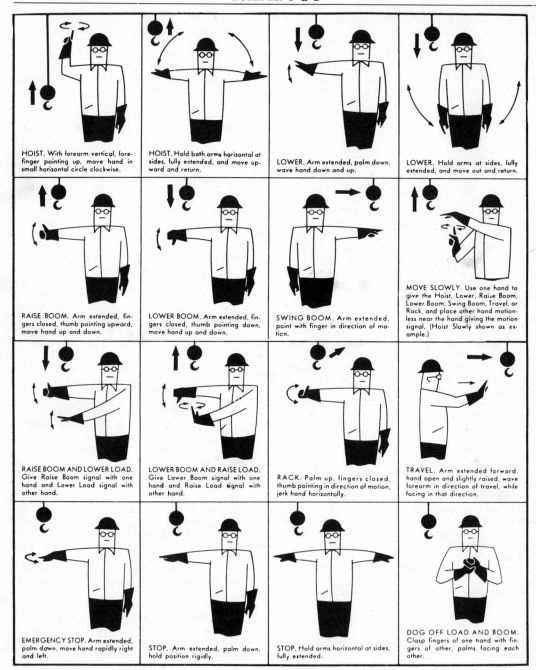

Figure 5-35.—Standard signals to crane operators.

29.86

The signalman is responsible for making sure that members of the crew remove their hands from slings, hooks, and loads before giving a signal. He should also make sure that all persons are clear of bights and snatch clock lines.

HOOKING-ON SAFETY

The most common way of attaching a load to a lifting hook is to put a SLING around the load and hang the sling off on the hook. (See fig. 5-36.) A sling may be made of line, wire, or wire rope with an eye in each end, (also called a STRAP) or an ENDLESS SLING. (See fig. 5-37.) Both of these types are described and illustrated in Constructionman, NavPers 10630-D. When a sling is passed through its own bight or eye, or shackled or hooked to its own standing part, so that it tightens around the load like a lasso when the load is lifted, the sling is said to be CHOKED, or it may be called a CHOKER as shown in figures 5-36 and 5-37. A two-legged sling which supports the load at two points is called a BRIDLE as shown in figure 5-38.

The following safety rules must be promulgated to and observed by all hands engaged in hooking on.

The man in charge of hooking on must know the safe working load of the rig and the weight of every load to be hoisted. The hoisting of any load heavier than the safe working load of the rig must be absolutely prohibited.

When a cylindrical metal object such as a length of pipe, a gas cylinder, or the like, is hoisted in a choker bridle, each leg of the bridle should be given a round turn around the load before it is hooked or shackled to its own part. The purpose of this is to ensure that the legs of the bridle will not slide together along the load, thereby upsetting the balance and possibly dumping the load.

The point of strain on a hook must never be at or near the point of the hook.

When using a choker which includes a shackle, the BOW, never the PIN, of the shackle must ride on the standing part of the choker. If the pin rode on the standing part of the choker, it might unthread as the choker drew tight.

HOISTING SAFETY

Before the HOIST signal is given, the man in charge must be sure that the load will balance evenly in the sling.

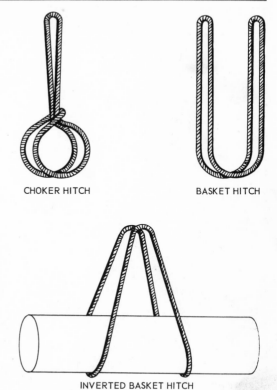

CHOKER HITCH   BASKET HITCH

INVERTED BASKET HITCH

29.190

Figure 5-36.—Ways of hitching on a sling.

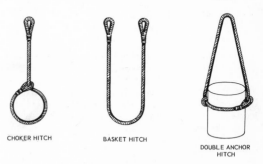

CHOKER HITCH BASKET HITCH DOUBLE ANCHOR HITCH

29.191

Figure 5-37.—Ways of hitching on straps.

Before the HOIST signal is given, the man in charge should be sure that the lead of the whip or

CHAIN SAFETY

All hoisting chains shall be inspected at frequent intervals for such defects as stretch, wear, gouge marks, open welds or fractures as indicated by very fine surface cracks, and shall be removed from hoisting service when such defects are found. Chains are less reliable than manila or wire rope as they break without any warning. Chains which have stretched more than 5 percent in any five link section shall be discarded. Chains, which in any individual link show wear greater than 25 percent of the thickness of the metal, shall be removed from service. Chains shall not be stored where they will be run over by tractors, trucks, or other equipment. Makeshift repairs such as splicing with bolts shall not be used on hoisting chain or chain slings. Chains should not be subject to sudden shock while in use. Loads shall not be lifted with a kinked or knotted chain. Attachments or fittings for chains should be of the type, grade, and size suitable for service with size of chain used.

Wrought iron chain shall be annealed by qualified personnel at least annually and a record of such treatment maintained. Alloy chain shall never be annealed.

Hooks and rings used with chain should have at least as great strength as the chain. Hooks should be given a visual inspection at the beginning of each workday and prior to lifting the full rated load. Hooks bent to the extent that the throat opening is increased more than 15 percent or the point is more than 10° out of plane shall be discarded. They shall not be put back in service.

Safety latch hooks in good condition should be used in operations where there is danger of catching the load on an obstruction and where heavy, stiff slings are used; also where ammunition and explosives are being handled. This applies particularly to hoisting buckets, cages or skips and particularly in shaft work.

LOAD PLACING SAFETY

Loads must not be placed and left at any point closer than 4 ft to 8 in. from the nearer rail of a railroad track or crane track, or in any position where they would impede or prevent access to firefighting equipment.

Whenever materials are being loaded or unloaded from any vehicle by crane, the vehicle operators and all other persons except the rigging crew should stand clear.

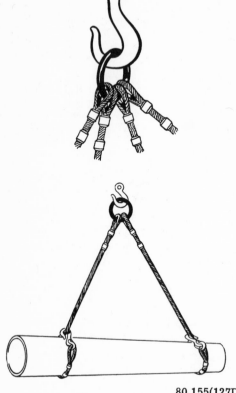

80.155(127D)
Figure 5-38.—Bridles.

falls is vertical. If it is not, the load will take a swing as it leaves the deck.

As the load leaves the deck, the man in charge must watch carefully for kinked or fouled falls or slings. If any such are observed, the load must be lowered at once for clearing.

Tag lines must be used to guide and steady a load whenever there is a possibility that the load might get out of control.

Before any load is hoisted, it must be inspected carefully for loose parts or objects which might drop as the load goes up.

All personnel must be cleared from and kept out of any area which is under a suspended load, or over which a suspended load may pass.

NEVER walk or run under a suspended load.

Whenever materials are placed in work or storage areas, dunnage or shoring must be provided as necessary to prevent tipping of the load or shifting of the materials.

Men must stand well clear of loads which tend to spread out when landed.

When slings are being heaved out from under a load, men must stand well clear to avoid a backlash, and also to avoid a toppling or a tip of the load which might be caused by fouling of a sling.

STORING AND HANDLING SAFETY

All material in bags, containers, or bundles, and any other material which is stored in tiers, should be stacked, blocked, interlocked, and limited in height, so as to produce a stable pile which will not topple, slide, or collapse. Material stored inside buildings under construction should not be placed within 6 feet of any hoistway or other floor opening. When walls are not yet constructed, material piled on any above-ground open floor should not be piled within 10 feet of the outside wall lines. Material should not be piled against columns, and floors should be shored up under piles whose weight exceeds the maximum designed live load of the floors.

If material must be piled in thoroughfares, piles must be located where they will present the least possible hazard to and interference with traffic. Vehicle traffic must be warned by barricades and red flags by day and by red lights at night.

CHAPTER 6
CONCRETE

Concrete, as you probably know is an artificial stone made by mixing cement and sand with gravel, broken stone, or other aggregate. However, concrete is not fully obtained that way, because these materials must be mixed with sufficient water to cause the cement to set and bind the entire mass.

There are various types of concrete used during construction operations such as precast, prestressed and many others. No matter how the concrete is expected to be used, the makeup is basically the same the world over. So in this chapter we will explain the physical characteristics and properties of concrete materials, the selection of proportions for concrete mixtures, the ways of mixing and transporting concrete, the use of forms and joints, and the reinforcing, placing, finishing, and curing of concrete.

There may be other jobs considered more dangerous than working with concrete, but we believe concrete still deserves its share of safety measures, so we have provided some information on concrete safety along with a few hints on supervision.

CHARACTERISTICS

CONCRETE is a synthetic construction material made by mixing CEMENT, FINE AGGREGATE (usually sand), COARSE AGGREGATE (usually gravel or crushed stone) and water together in proper proportions. The product is not concrete unless all four of these ingredients are present. A mixture of cement, sand, and water, without coarse aggregate, is not concrete but MORTAR or GROUT. Never fall into the common error of calling a CONCRETE wall or floor a CEMENT wall or floor. There is no such thing as a cement wall or floor.

The fine and coarse aggregate in a concrete mix are called the INERT ingredients; the cement and water are the ACTIVE ingredients. The inert ingredients and the cement are thoroughly mixed together first. As soon as the water is added, a chemical reaction between the water and the cement begins, and it is this reaction (which is called HYDRATION) that causes the concrete to harden.

Always remember that the hardening process is caused by hydration of the cement by the water, not by a DRYING OUT of the mix. Instead of being dried out, the concrete must be kept as moist as possible during the initial hydration process. Drying out would cause a drop in water content below the amount required for satisfactory hydration of the cement.

The fact that the hardening process has nothing whatever to do with a drying out of the concrete is clearly shown by the fact that concrete will harden just as well under water as it will in the air.

CONCRETE AS BUILDING MATERIAL

Concrete may be cast into bricks, blocks, and other relatively small building units which are used in concrete MASONRY construction which is covered in the next chapter. This chapter is concerned with the concrete itself and the casting of larger structural components.

The proportion of concrete to other materials used in building construction has greatly increased in recent years, to the point where large, multistory modern buildings are constructed entirely of concrete, with concrete footings, foundations, columns, walls, girders, beams, joists, floors, and roofs.

STRENGTH OF CONCRETE

The COMPRESSIVE strength of concrete is very high, but its TENSILE strength (meaning its ability to resist stretching, bending, or twisting) is relatively low. Consequently, concrete which must resist a good deal of stretching, bending, or twisting (such as concrete in beams, girders, walls, columns, and the like) must be REINFORCED with steel. Concrete which must resist compression only may not require reinforcement.

As will be seen later, the most important factor controlling the strength of concrete is the WATER-CEMENT RATIO, or the proportion of water to cement in the mix.

94

DURABILITY OF CONCRETE

The DURABILITY of concrete means the extent to which the material is capable of resisting the deterioration caused by exposure to service conditions. Ordinary structural concrete which is to be exposed to the element must be watertight and weather-resistant. Concrete which is subject to wear (such as floor slabs and pavements) must be capable of resisting abrasion.

It has been found that the major factor controlling durability is strength—in other words, the stronger the concrete is, the more durable it will be. As mentioned previously, the chief factor controlling strength is the water-cement ratio, but the character, size, and grading (distribution of particle sizes between the largest permissible coarse and the smallest permissible fine) of the aggregate also have important effects on both strength and durability. Given a water-cement ratio which will produce maximum strength consistent with workability requirements, maximum strength and durability will still not be attained unless the sand and coarse aggregate consist of well-graded, clean, hard, and durable particles, free from undesirable substances (see fig. 6-1).

WATERTIGHTNESS OF CONCRETE

The ideal concrete mix would be one made with just the amount of water required for complete hydration of the cement. This would be a DRY mix, however, too stiff to pour in forms. A mix which is fluid enough to be poured in forms always contains a certain amount of water over and above that which will combine with the cement, and this water will eventually evaporate, leaving voids or pores in the concrete.

Even so, penetration of the concrete by water would still be impossible if these voids were not interconnected. They are interconnected, however, as a result of a slight sinking of solid particles in the mix during the hardening period. As these particles sink, they leave water-filled channels which become voids when the water evaporates.

The larger and more numerous these voids are, the more the watertightness of the concrete will be impaired. Since the size and number of the voids vary directly with the amount of water used in excess of the amount required to hydrate the cement, it follows that to keep the concrete as watertight as possible, you must not use more water than the minimum amount required to attain the necessary degree of workability.

GENERAL REQUIREMENTS FOR GOOD CONCRETE

The first requirement for good concrete is, of course, a supply of good cement of a type suitable for the work at hand. Next is a supply of satisfactory sand, coarse aggregate, and water. Everything else being equal, the mix with the best-graded, strongest, best-shaped, and cleanest aggregate will make the strongest and most durable concrete.

The amount of cement, sand, coarse aggregate, and water required for each batch must be carefully weighed or measured in accordance with Naval Facilities Engineering Command (NavFac) Specification 13Y series.

The best-designed, best-graded, and highest-quality mix in the world will not make good concrete if it is not WORKABLE enough to fill the form spaces thoroughly. On the other hand, too much fluidity will result in certain defects. Improper handling during the whole concrete-making process (from the initial aggregate handling to the final placement of the mix) will cause segregation of aggregate particles by sizes, resulting in nonuniform, poor concrete.

Finally, the best-designed, best-graded, highest-quality, and best-placed mix in the world will not produce good concrete if it is not properly CURED—meaning, properly protected against loss of moisture during the earlier stages of setting.

CONCRETE INGREDIENTS

The essential ingredients of concrete are cement, aggregate, and water which react chemically in a process called hydration to form another material having useful strength. Hardening of concrete is not the result of the drying of the mix as seen from the fact that fresh concrete placed under water will harden despite its completely submerged state. The mixture of cement and water is called cement paste, but such a mixture, in large quantities, is prohibitively expensive for practical construction purposes.

CEMENT

Most cement used today is PORTLAND cement, which is usually manufactured from

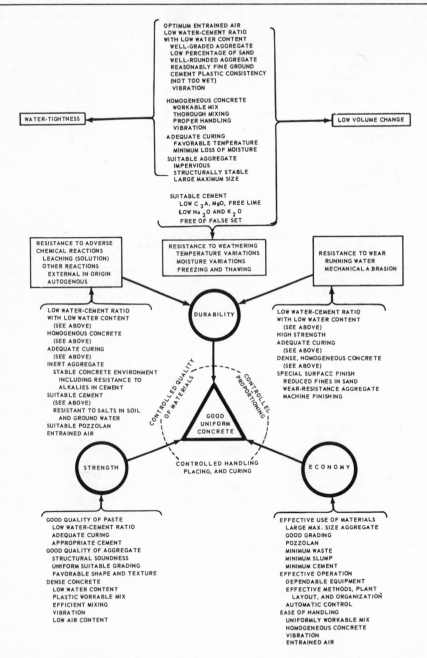

Figure 6-1.—The principal properties of good concrete.   117.83

limestone mixed with shale, clay, or marl. The properly proportioned raw materials are pulverized and fed into kilns, where they are heated to a temperature of 2700°F and maintained at that temperature for a certain time. As a result of certain chemical changes produced by the heat, the material is transformed into a clinker. The clinker is then ground down so fine that it will pass through a sieve containing 40,000 openings per square inch.

There are a number of types of portland cement, of which the most common are types I through V and air-entrained.

Types

References to cement can be assumed to mean "portland cement," which is the primary type used in concrete. There are five common types of portland cement in use today. The type of construction, chemical type of the soil, economy, and the requirements for use of the finished concrete are factors which influence the selection of the type of cement to be used. The different types of cement are discussed below:

Type I (normal portland cement) is used for all general types of construction. It is used in pavement and sidewalk construction, reinforced concrete buildings and bridges, railways, tanks, reservoirs, sewers, culverts, water pipes, masonry units, and soil-cement mixtures. In general, it is used when concrete is not subject to special sulfate hazard or where the heat generated by the hydration of the cement will not cause an objectionable rise in temperature.

Type II (modified portland cement) has a lower heat of hydration than type I, and lower heat generated by the hydration of the cement improved resistance to sulfate attack. It is intended for use in structures of considerable size where cement of moderate heat of hydration will tend to minimize temperature rise, as in large piers, heavy abutments, and heavy retaining walls and when the concrete is placed in warm weather. In cold weather when the heat generated is helpful, type I cement may be preferable for these uses. Type II cement is also intended for places where an added precaution against sulfate attack is important, as in drainage structures where the sulfate concentrations are higher than normal, but not usually severe.

Type III (high-early-strength portland cement) is used where high strengths are desired at very early periods. It is used where it is desired to remove forms as soon as possible, to put the concrete in service as quickly as possible, and in cold weather construction to reduce the period of protection against low temperatures. High strengths at early periods can be obtained more satisfactorily and more economically using high-early-strength cement than using richer mixes of type I cement. Type III develops strength at a faster rate than other types of cement, such as:

28-day strength for types I and II, which is reached by Type III in about 7 days.

7-day strength for types I and II, while Type III takes about 3 days.

Type IV (low-heat portland cement) is a special cement for use where the amount and rate of heat generated must be kept to a minimum. This type of cement was first developed for use on the Hoover Dam. It develops strength at a slow rate and should be cured and protected from freezing for at least 21 days. For this reason it is unsuitable for structures of ordinary dimensions, and is available only on special order from a manufacturer.

Type V (sulfate-resistant portland cement) is a cement intended for use only in structures exposed to high alkali content. It has a slower rate of hardening than normal portland cement. The sulfates react chemically with the hydrated lime and the hydrated calcium aluminate in the cement paste. This reaction results in considerable expansion and disruption of the paste. Cements which have a low content of calcium aluminate have a great resistance to sulfate attack. Thus, type V portland cement is used exclusively for situations involving severe sulfate concentrations.

Air-entrained portland cement is a special cement that can be used with good results for a variety of conditions. It has been developed to produce concrete that has a resistance to freeze-thaw action and scaling caused by chemicals applied for severe frost and ice removal. In this cement, very small quantities of air-entraining materials are added as the clinker is being ground during manufacturing. Concrete made with this cement contains minute, well-distributed and completely separated air bubbles. The bubbles are so minute that it is estimated there are many millions of them in a cubic foot of concrete. Air bubbles provide space for water to expand due to freezing, without damage to the concrete. Air-entrained concrete has been used in pavements in the northern states for about

25 years with excellent results. Air-entrained concrete also reduces the amount of water loss and the capillary and water-channel structure. The agent may be added to types I, II, III portland cement. The manufacturer will specify the percentage of air-entrainment which can be expected in the concrete. An advantage of using air-entrained cement is that it can be used and batched like normal cement.

Storage of Cement

Portland cement is packed in cloth or paper sacks, each of which contains 94 lbs of cement. A 94-lb sack of cement amounts to about 1 cu ft by loose volume.

Cement will retain its quality indefinitely if it does not come in contact with moisture. If it is allowed to absorb appreciable moisture in storage, it will set more slowly and its strength will be reduced. Sacked cement should be stored in warehouses or sheds made as watertight and airtight as possible. All cracks in roof and walls should be closed, and there should be no opening between walls and roof. The floor should be above ground to protect the cement against dampness. All doors and windows should be kept closed.

Sacks should be stacked against each other to prevent circulation of air between them, but they should not be stacked against outside walls. If stacks are to stand undisturbed for long intervals, they should be covered with tarpaulins.

When shed or warehouse storage cannot be provided, sacks which must be stored in the open should be stacked on raised platforms and covered with waterproof tarps. The tarps should extend beyond the edges of the platform so as to deflect water away from the platform and the cement.

Cement sacks which have been stacked in storage for long periods sometimes acquire a hardness called WAREHOUSE PACK. This can usually be loosened up by rolling the sack around. No cement should be used which has lumps or is not free flowing.

AGGREGATE

The material which is combined with cement and water to make concrete is called AGGREGATE. Aggregate helps to increase the strength of concrete while reducing the shrinking tendencies of the cement. Not only does aggregate aid in the strength of concrete, but it is also used as a filler for economical purposes. The aggregate is divided into FINE (usually consisting of sand) and COARSE. For most ordinary building concrete, the coarse aggregate usually consists of gravel or crushed stone, running not more than about 1 1/2 in. in size. In massive structures like dams, however, the coarse aggregate may include natural stones or rocks ranging up to 6 in. or more in size.

What might be called the fundamental structural mechanics of a concrete mix are about as follows. The large, solid coarse aggregate particles form the basic structural members of the concrete. The voids between the larger coarse aggregate particles are filled by smaller particles, and the voids between the smaller particles are filled by still smaller particles, until finally the voids between the smallest coarse aggregate particles are filled by the largest fine aggregate particles. In turn, the voids between the largest fine aggregate particles are filled by smaller fine aggregate particles, the voids between the smaller fine aggregate particles by still smaller particles, and so on. You can see from this that the better the aggregate is GRADED (that is, the better the distribution of particle sizes), the more solidly all voids will be filled, and the denser and stronger will be the concrete.

The cement and water form a paste which binds the aggregate particles solidly together when it hardens. In a well graded, well designed, and well mixed batch each aggregate particle is thoroughly coated with cement water paste, so that each particle is solidly bound to adjacent particles when the cement-water paste hardens.

Gradation

The existing GRADATION, or distribution of particle sizes from coarse to fine, in a supply of fine or coarse aggregate is determined by extracting a representative sample of the material, screening the sample through a series of sieves ranging in size from coarse to fine, and determining the percentage of the total sample which is retained on (fine aggregate), or which passes (coarse aggregate), each sieve. This procedure is called making a SIEVE ANALYSIS.

The size of a fine aggregate sieve is designated by a number which corresponds to the number of meshes to the linear inch that the sieve contains. Obviously, then, the higher the number, the finer the sieve. The most commonly used fine-aggregate sieves are the Nos. 4, 8, 16, 30, 50, 100, and 200. Any material retained on the No. 4 sieve is considered coarse aggregate, and any material which will pass the No. 200 sieve is too fine to be used in concrete. When an analysis reveals the presence of a substantial percentage of material which will pass the No. 200, the aggregate must be washed before being used.

The finest coarse-aggregate sieve is the same No. 4 used as the coarsest fine-aggregate sieve. With this exception, a coarse-aggregate sieve is designated by the size of one of its openings. The sieves commonly used are 1 1/2-in., 3/4-in., 1/2-in., 3/8-in., and No. 4.

Experience and experiments have shown that for ordinary building concrete certain particle distributions seem consistently to produce the best results. For fine aggregate the recommended distribution of particle sizes from No. 4 to No. 100 is shown in table 6-1.

Table 6-1.—Recommended Distribution of Particle Sizes

Sieve Number	Percent retained on square mesh laboratory sieves
3/8"	0
No. 4	18
No. 8	27
No. 16	20
No. 30	20
No. 50	10
No. 100	4

117.178

The percentages given are CUMULATIVE, meaning that each is a percentage of the TOTAL SAMPLE, not of the amount remaining on a particular sieve. For example: suppose the total sample weighs 1 lb. Place this on the No. 4 sieve, and shake the sieve until nothing more will go through. If what is left on the sieve weighs 0.05 lb, then 5 percent of the total sample was retained on the No. 4 sieve. Place what passed through on the No. 8 sieve and shake that one. Suppose you find that what stays on the sieve weighs 0.1 lb. Since 0.1 lb is 10 percent of 1 lb, it follows that 10 percent of the total sample was retained on the No. 8 sieve.

The nominal size of coarse aggregate to be used is usually specified as a range between a minimum and a maximum size, as: "2 in. to No. 4," "1 in. to No. 4," "2 in. to 1 in.," and so on. The recommended particle size distributions vary with maximum and minimum nominal size limits, as shown in table 6-2.

A blank space in table 6-2 indicates a sieve which is not required in the indicated analysis. For example: for the 2-in. to No. 4 nominal size there are no values listed under the 4-in., the 3 1/2-in., and the 3-in. sieves. The reason for this is simply the fact that, since 100 percent of this material should pass a 2 1/2-in. sieve, the use of sieves coarser than the 2 1/2-in. is superfluous. For the same size designation, there are no values listed under the 1 1/2-in., the 3/4-in., and the 3/8-in. sieves. This is because experience has shown that it is not necessary to use these sieves when making this particular analysis.

Note that when you are analyzing coarse aggregate you determine the percentage of material which PASSES a sieve, not the percentage which is retained on a sieve.

Quality Criteria

Since from 66 to 78 percent of the volume of the finished concrete consists of aggregate, it is imperative that the aggregate measure up to certain minimum quality standards. It should consist of clean, hard, strong, durable particles which are free of any chemicals which might interfere with hydration, and of any superfine material which might prevent bond between the aggregate and the cement-water paste. The undesirable substances most frequently found in aggregate are dirt, silt, clay, coal, mica, salts, and organic matter. Most of these can be removed by washing.

Aggregate may be field-tested for an excess of silt, clay, and the like, as follows: fill a quart jar with the aggregate to a depth of 2 in.; add water until the jar is about three-fourths full; shake the jar for 1 minute; and allow it to stand for 1 hour. If at the end of that time more than 1/8 in. of sediment has settled on the top of the aggregate, as shown in figure 6-2, the material should be washed. An easily constructed rig for washing a small amount of aggregate is shown in figure 6-3.

Weak, friable (easily pulverized), or laminated (containing layers) aggregate particles are undesirable. Shale, stones laminated with

Table 6-2.—Recommended Maximum and Minimum Particle Sizes

Size of coarse aggregate, inches	Percentages by weight passing laboratory sieves having square openings										
	4-in.	3 1/2 in.	3-in.	2 1/2 in.	2-in.	1 1/2 in.	1-in.	3/4 in.	1/2 in.	3/8 in.	No. 4
1.5	--	--	--	--	100	95-100	--	35-70	--	10-30	0-5
2	--	--	--	100	95-100	--	35-70	--	10-30	11	0-5
2.5	--	--	100	90-100	--	35-70	--	10-40	--	0-15	0-5
3.5	100	90-100	--	45-80	--	25-50	--	10-30	--	0-15	0-5

133.245

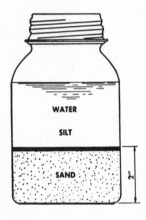

133.249
Figure 6-2.—Quart-jar method of determining silt content of sand.

shale, and most varieties of chert (impure) flintlike rock) are especially to be avoided. For most ordinary concrete work, visual inspection is enough to reveal any weaknesses in the coarse aggregate. For work in which aggregate strength and durability is of vital importance (such as paving concrete), aggregate must be laboratory-tested.

Handling and Storing

A mass of aggregate containing particles of different sizes has a natural tendency toward SEGREGATION, meaning that particles of the same size tend to gather together whenever the material is being loaded, transported, or otherwise disturbed. Aggregate should always be handled and stored by a method which will minimize segregation.

Stockpiles should not be built up in cone shapes, made by dropping successive loads at the same spot. This procedure causes larger aggregate particles to segregate and roll down the sides, leaving the pile with a preponderance of fine at the top and a preponderance of coarse at the bottom. A pile should be built up in layers, each made by dumping successive loads alongside each other.

If aggregate is dropped in a free fall from a clamshell, bucket, or conveyor, some of the fine material may be blown aside, causing a segregation of fines on the lee side of the pile. Conveyors, clamshells, and buckets should be discharged in contact with the pile.

The bottom of a storage bin should always slope at least 50 degrees toward the central outlet. If the slope is less than 50 degrees, segregation will occur as the material is discharged. When a bin is being charged, the material should be dropped from a point directly over the outlet. Material chuted in at an angle, or material discharged against the side of a bin, will segregate. Since a long drop causes both segregation and the breakage of aggregate particles, the length of the drop into a bin should be minimized by keeping the bin as full as possible at all times.

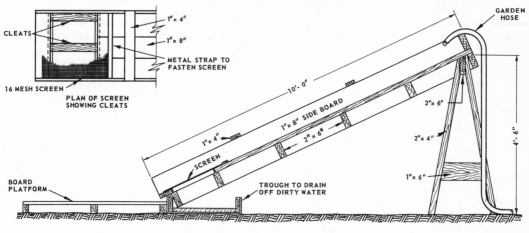

CLEATS

1" x 4"

1" x 8"

METAL STRAP TO
FASTEN SCREEN

16 MESH SCREEN

PLAN OF SCREEN
SHOWING CLEATS

GARDEN
HOSE

10'- 0"

1" x 8" SIDE BOARD

1" x 4"

2" x 6"

SCREEN

2" x 6"

2" x 4"

1" x 6"

4'- 6"

BOARD
PLATFORM

TROUGH TO DRAIN
OFF DIRTY WATER

133.250

Figure 6-3.—Field-constructed rig for washing aggregate.

WATER

The principal function of the water in a concrete mix is to bring about the hardening of the concrete through hydration of the cement. Another essential function, however, is to make the mix workable enough to satisfy the requirements of the job at hand. To attain this result, a mix which is to be poured in forms must contain additional water over and above the amount required for complete hydration of the cement. Too much water, however, will cause a loss of strength by upsetting the water-cement ratio. It will also cause "water gain" on the surface, a condition which leaves a surface layer of weak material called LAITANCE. Also, as previously mentioned, an excess of water will impair the watertightness of the concrete.

Mixing water should be free of any acids, alkalis, or oils which would interfere with the hydration process. Water containing decayed vegetable matter is especially to be avoided. Most specifications require that the mixing water be fit for drinking, since any water fit for drinking is usually satisfactory for concrete.

CONCRETE MIX DESIGN

The ingredient proportions to be used for the concrete on a particular job are usually set forth in the specifications under "CONCRETE-General requirements." A typical specification of this type reads as follows:

"All concrete shall conform to 13Y (series)." For example see table 6-3.

In this specification, one of the FORMULAS for 3000 psi is 5.80 (bag of cement per cu yd), 233 lbs of sand (per bag of cement), 297 lb of coarse aggregate (per bag of cement), and the WATER-CEMENT RATIO is 6.75 gals water to each bag of cement. These proportions are based upon the assumption that the inert ingredients are in a SATURATED SURFACE-DRY condition, meaning that they contain all the water they are capable of absorbing, but no additional FREE water over and above this amount.

This is a condition which almost never exists in the field. The amount of free water in the coarse aggregate is usually small enough to be ignored, but the ingredient proportions set forth in the specs must almost always be adjusted to allow for the existence of free water in the fine aggregate. Furthermore, since free water in the fine aggregate increases its measured volume or weight over that of the sand itself, the specified volume or weight of sand must be increased to offset the volume or weight of the water in the sand. Finally, the number of gallons of water used per sack of cement must be

Table 6-3.—Normal Concrete

Class concrete (figures denote size of coarse aggregate in inches)	Estimated 28-day compressive strength, (pounds per square inch)	Cement factor, bags (94 pounds) of cement per cubic yard of concrete, freshly mixed	Maximum water per bag (94 pounds) of cement (gallons)	Fine aggregate range in percent of total aggregate by weight	Approximate weights of saturated surface-dry aggregates per bag (94 pounds) of cement	
					Fine aggregate (pounds)	Coarse aggregate (pounds)
(1)	(2)	(3)	(4)	(5)	(6)	(7)
B-1	1500	4.10	9.50	42-52	368	415
B-1.5	1500	3.80	9.50	38-48	376	498
B-2	1500	3.60	9.50	35-45	378	567
B-2.5	1500	3.50	9.50	33-43	373	609
B-3.5	1500	3.25	9.50	30-40	378	702
C-1	2000	4.45	8.75	41-51	329	387
C-1.5	2000	4.10	8.75	37-47	338	467
C-2	2000	3.90	8.75	34-44	338	529
C-2.5	2000	3.80	8.75	32-42	332	565
C-3.5	2000	3.55	8.75	29-39	334	648
D-0.5	2500	5.70	7.75	50-60	282	231
D-0.75	2500	5.30	7.75	45-55	288	288
D-1	2500	5.05	7.75	40-50	279	341
D-1.5	2500	4.65	7.75	36-46	287	413
D-2	2500	4.40	7.75	34-42	288	471
D-2.5	2500	4.25	7.75	32-40	287	509
D-3.5	2500	4.00	7.75	29-37	285	578
E-0.5	3000	6.50	6.75	50-58	238	203
E-0.75	3000	6.10	6.75	45-53	240	249
E-1	3000	5.80	6.75	40-48	233	297
E-1.5	3000	5.35	6.75	36-44	239	359
E-2	3000	5.05	6.75	33-41	241	410
E-2.5	3000	4.90	6.75	31-39	238	441
E-3.5	3000	4.60	6.75	28-36	237	503

133.246

reduced to allow for the free water in the sand—that is to say, the amount of water actually added at the mixer must be the specified amount per sack, LESS the amount of free water which is already in the ingredients in the mixer.

Except as otherwise specified in the project specifications, concrete shall be proportioned by weighing and shall conform to NavFac Specification 13Y (series). See table 6-3 for normal concrete.

Material Estimate

A handling loss factor is added when ordering materials for jobs. An additional 5 percent of material is added for jobs requiring 200 or more cubic yards of concrete, and 10 percent is added for smaller jobs. (This loss factor is based on materials estimate after requirements have been calculated.) Additional loss factors may be added where conditions indicate the necessity for excessive handling of materials before batching.

When tables, such as table 6-4, are not available for determining quantities of material required for 1 cubic yard of concrete, the following rule, known as the 3/2's rule may be used for rough approximation. (The rule states that to produce a given volume of concrete, the combined amounts of cement, sand, and gravel are 1-1/2 times the volume of the concrete pour.) Since the void spaces between the coarse aggregate are filled with sand particles, and the voids between the sand particles are similar filled with cement, the total volume occupied by the three components will be less than the sum of their individual volumes. Normally, a mix ratio of 1:2:3 is assumed when using the 3/2's rule. This means that of a total volume, one part will be cement, two parts will be sand, and three parts will be gravel. The amount of water is roughly established by assuming a ratio that assures water tightness—6 gallons per sack; additional water will be needed for wetting down forms and subgrade, washing tools, and curing the concrete. When computing quantities of concrete, the space occupied by embedded objects or steel reinforcement is ignored.

By using the 3/2's rule, we will determine the amount of cement, sand, and gravel required to construct a 45' x 10' x 2' retaining wall. Assume a mix ratio of 1:2:3.

Volume of concrete required:
45 x 10 x 2 = 900 cu ft = 33.3 cu yd. Applying the 3/2's rule and allowing 10 percent handling loss, total volume required is 33.3 x 1.10 x 3/2, or 55 cu yds.
The required volumes needed are:
cement: 1/6 x 55 = 9.17 cu yds
sand: 2/6 x 55 = 18.33 cu yds
gravel: 3/6 x 55 = 27.50 cu yds

Since cement is usually obtained in sacks, you should multiply the volume by 27 and round it to the next larger number.

9.17 x 27 = 247.59 cu ft, or 248 sacks.
The 3/2 rule is not used to estimate materials if the size of the pour is greater than 200 cu yds.

WATER-CEMENT RATIO

The specified ingredient proportions are those which, it has been calculated, will produce an economical concrete of the strength and durability required for the project. Durability is to a large extent controlled by strength—meaning that the stronger the concrete is, the more durable it will be as well. However, the quality of the aggregate, the aggregate grading, and the proportion of fine to coarse also have an important effect on durability.

It has been discovered that the major factor controlling strength, everything else being equal, is the amount of water used per bag of cement. Maximum strength would be obtained by using just the amount of water, and no more, than would be required for the complete hydration of the cement.

As previously mentioned, however, a mix of this type would be too dry to be workable, and therefore a plastic concrete mix always contains more water than the amount required to attain maximum strength. The point for you to remember is that the strength of the concrete decreases as the amount of this extra water increases.

The specified water-cement ratio is the happy medium between the maximum possible strength of the concrete and the necessary minimum requirements as to workability. The strength of building concrete is expressed in terms of the compressive strength in psi (lbs per sq in.) reached after a 7-day set and/or after a 28-day set, usually referred to as PROBABLE AVERAGE 7-DAY STRENGTH and PROBABLE AVERAGE 28-DAY STRENGTH.

SLUMP TEST

The slump test is used to measure the consistency of the concrete. The test is made by using a SLUMP CONE; the cone is made of No. 16 gage galvanized metal with the base 8 inches in diameter, the top 4 inches in diameter, and the height 12 inches. The base and the top are open and parallel to each other and at right angles to the axis of the cone. A tamping rod 5/8 inch in diameter and 24 inches long is also needed. The tamping rod should be smooth and bullet pointed (not a piece of rebar).

133.264

Table 6-4.—Suggested Trial Mixers for Concrete of Medium Consistency with a 3-Inch Slump (SSD Condition)

Maximum size of aggregate, inches	Water, gallon per sack of cement	Water, gallon per cu yd of concrete	Cement, sacks per cu yd of concrete	With Fine Sand—Fineness Modulus 2.20-2.60						With Medium Sand—Fineness Modulus 2.60-2.90						With Coarse Sand—Fineness Modulus 2.90-3.20					
				Fine agg.—per cent of total agg.	Fine agg.—lb per sack of cement	Coarse agg.—lb per sack of cement	Fine agg.—lb per cu yd of concrete	Coarse agg.—lb per cu yd of concrete	Yield, cu ft per sack	Fine agg.—per cent of total agg.	Fine agg.—lb per sack of cement	Coarse agg.—lb per sack of cement	Fine agg.—lb per cu yd of concrete	Coarse agg.—lb per cu yd of concrete	Yield, cu ft per sack	Fine agg.—per cent of total agg.	Fine agg.—lb per sack of cement	Coarse agg.—lb per sack of cement	Fine agg.—lb per cu yd of concrete	Coarse agg.—lb per cu yd of concrete	Yield, cu ft per sack
¾	5	38	7.6	43	170	230	1290	1750	3.56	45	180	220	1370	1670	3.56	47	185	210	1405	1595	3.56
1	5	37	7.4	38	160	255	1185	1890	3.65	40	165	250	1220	1850	3.65	42	175	240	1295	1775	3.65
1½	5	35	7.0	34	150	285	1050	2010	3.86	36	160	290	1120	2030	3.86	38	170	280	1190	1960	3.86
2	5	33	6.6	31	150	320	990	2110	4.09	33	160	325	1055	2140	4.09	35	170	315	1120	2080	4.09
¾	5½	38	6.9	44	195	250	1345	1725	3.91	46	205	240	1415	1655	3.91	48	215	230	1480	1585	3.91
1	5½	37	6.7	41	180	285	1205	1910	4.03	43	190	275	1270	1840	4.03	45	200	265	1340	1775	4.03
1½	5½	35	6.4	37	175	320	1120	2050	4.22	39	185	315	1185	2015	4.22	41	195	305	1250	1950	4.22
2	5½	33	6.0	35	175	370	1050	2220	4.50	37	185	360	1110	2160	4.50	39	195	350	1170	2100	4.50
¾	6	38	6.3	45	215	265	1355	1670	4.29	47	225	255	1420	1605	4.29	49	235	245	1480	1545	4.29
1	6	37	6.2	42	210	290	1300	1800	4.36	44	220	280	1365	1735	4.36	46	230	270	1425	1675	4.36
1½	6	35	5.8	38	200	330	1160	1915	4.66	40	210	320	1220	1855	4.66	42	225	305	1305	1770	4.66
2	6	33	5.5	34	195	385	1075	2120	4.91	36	210	370	1155	2035	4.91	38	220	360	1210	1980	4.91
¾	6½	38	5.8	45	230	280	1335	1625	4.66	47	240	270	1390	1565	4.66	49	250	260	1450	1510	4.66
1	6½	37	5.7	42	225	310	1285	1765	4.74	44	235	300	1340	1710	4.74	46	245	290	1395	1655	4.74
1½	6½	35	5.4	38	215	350	1160	1890	5.00	40	225	340	1215	1835	5.00	42	235	330	1270	1780	5.00
2	6½	33	5.1	34	210	410	1070	2090	5.30	36	225	395	1150	2015	5.30	38	235	385	1200	1965	5.30
¾	7	38	5.4	46	250	295	1350	1595	5.00	48	260	285	1405	1540	5.00	50	275	270	1485	1460	5.00
1	7	37	5.3	43	245	320	1300	1695	5.10	45	255	310	1350	1645	5.10	47	265	300	1405	1590	5.10
1½	7	35	5.0	39	235	365	1175	1825	5.40	41	245	355	1225	1775	5.40	43	260	340	1300	1700	5.40
2	7	33	4.7	35	230	430	1080	2020	5.75	37	245	415	1150	1950	5.75	39	255	405	1200	1905	5.75
¾	7½	38	5.1	47	270	305	1375	1555	5.30	49	280	295	1428	1505	5.30	51	295	280	1505	1428	5.30
1	7½	37	4.9	43	260	340	1275	1665	5.51	45	270	330	1325	1615	5.51	47	280	320	1370	1570	5.51
1½	7½	35	4.7	39	250	385	1175	1810	5.75	41	260	375	1220	1760	5.75	43	275	360	1295	1690	5.75
2	7½	33	4.4	36	250	450	1100	1980	6.14	38	265	435	1165	1915	6.14	40	280	420	1230	1850	6.14
¾	8	38	4.8	48	295	315	1415	1510	5.63	50	305	305	1465	1465	5.63	52	315	295	1510	1415	5.63
1	8	37	4.6	44	280	360	1290	1655	5.87	46	295	345	1355	1585	5.87	48	305	335	1405	1540	5.87
1½	8	35	4.4	40	270	410	1190	1805	6.14	42	285	395	1255	1740	6.14	44	300	380	1320	1670	6.14
2	8	33	4.1	37	275	475	1130	1950	6.59	39	290	460	1189	1885	6.59	41	305	445	1250	1825	6.59

*Increase or decrease water per cu. yd. of concrete by 3% for each increase or decrease of 1 in. in slump; recalculate quantities of cement and aggregate to maintain the quality of concrete. For stone sand, increase percentage of sand by 3 and water by 15 lb. per cu. yd. of concrete. For less workable concrete, as in pavements, decrease percentage of sand by 3 and water by 8 lb. per cu. yd. of concrete.

Samples of concrete for test specimens should be taken at the mixer or, in the case of ready-mixed concrete, from the transportation vehicle during discharge. The sample of concrete from which test specimens are made will be representative of the entire batch. Such samples should be obtained by repeatedly passing a scoop or pail through the discharging stream of concrete, starting the sampling operation at the beginning of discharge and repeating the operation until the entire batch is discharged. The sample being obtained should be transported to the testing site. To counteract segregation the concrete should be mixed with a shovel until the concrete is uniform in appearance. The location in the work of the batch of concrete being sampled should be noted for future reference. In the case of paving concrete, samples may be taken from the batch immediately after depositing on the subgrade. At least five samples should be taken from different portions of the pile and these samples should be thoroughly mixed to form the test specimen.

The cone should be dampened and placed on a flat, moist nonabsorbent surface. From the sample of concrete obtained, the cone should immediately be filled in three layers, each approximately one-third the volume of the cone. In placing each scoopful of concrete the scoop should be moved around the top edge of the cone as the concrete slides from it, in order to ensure symmetrical distribution of concrete within the cone. Each layer should be RODDED IN, as shown in figure 6-4, with 25 strokes. The strokes should be distributed uniformly over the cross section of the cone and should penetrate into the underlying layer. The bottom layer should be rodded throughout its depth.

When the cone has been filled to a little more than full, strike off the excess concrete, flush with the top, with a straightedge. The cone should be immediately removed from the concrete by raising it carefully in a vertical direction. The slump should then be measured to the center of the slump immediately by determining the difference between the height of the cone and the height at the vertical axis of the specimen as shown in figure 6-5.

The consistency should be recorded in terms of inches of subsidence of the specimen during the test, which is called slump. Slump equals 12 inches of height after subsidence.

After the slump measurement is completed, the side of the mix should be tapped gently with the tamping rod. The behavior of the concrete

MOIST, FLAT
NONABSORBENT
SURFACE

45.573
Figure 6-4.—Charging slump cone for slump test.

under this treatment is a valuable indication of the cohesiveness, workability, and placeability of the mix. If the mix is well-proportioned, tapping will only cause it to slump lower, without crumbling apart or segregating by the dropping of larger aggregate particles to a lower level in the mix. If the concrete crumbles apart, it is over-sanded; if it segregates, it is undersanded.

WORKABILITY

A mix must be WORKABLE enough to fill the form spaces completely of its own accord, or with the assistance of a reasonable amount of shoveling, spading, and vibrating. Since a fluid or "runny" mix will do this more readily than a dry or "stiff" mix, it follows that workability varies directly with fluidity. The workability of a mix is determined by the slump test. The amount of the slump, in inches, is the measure of the concrete's workability—the more the slump, the higher the workability.

45.574(45B)

Figure 6-5.—Slump test.

The slump can be controlled by a change in any one or all of the following: gradation of aggregates, proportions of aggregates, or moisture content. (If the moisture content should change, you should add more cement to maintain the proper W/C ratio.

The desired degree of workability is attained by running a series of trial batches, using various amounts of fines to coarse aggregate, until a batch is produced in which the slump is as desired, provided you stay within the percentages as listed in column 5 of table 6-3. Once the amount of increase or decrease required to produce the desired slump is determined, the aggregate proportions, not the water proportion, in the field mix should be altered to conform. If the water proportion were changed, the water-cement ratio would be upset.

Never yield to the temptation to throw in more water without making the corresponding adjustment in the cement content, and make sure that men who are spreading a stiff mix by hand do not ease their labors this way without telling you about it.

As you gain experience you will discover that adjustments in workability can be made by making minor changes in the amount of fines in the fine aggregate or of coarses in the coarse aggregate; also by making minor changes in the proportion of fine to coarse. In general, everything else remaining the same, an increase in the proportion of fines stiffens a mix, and an increase in the proportion of coarse loosens a mix.

Before you alter the proportions set forth in the specification, you must, of course, find out from higher authority whether or not you are allowed to make any such alterations, and if you are, what the permissible limits are beyond which you must not go.

GROUT

As previously mentioned, concrete consists of four essential ingredients: water, cement, sand, and coarse aggregate. A mixture of water, cement, sand, and lime is not concrete but MORTAR. Mortar, which is used chiefly for bonding masonry units together, will be discussed in the next chapter.

The term GROUT refers to a water-cement mixture (called NEAT CEMENT GROUT) or a water-sand-cement mixture (called SAND-CEMENT GROUT) used to plug holes or cracks in concrete, to seal joints, to fill spaces between machinery bed plates and concrete foundations, and for similar plugging or sealing purposes. The consistency of grout may range from stiff (about 4 gals water per sack of cement) to fluid (as many as 10 gals water per sack of cement), depending upon the nature of the grouting job at hand.

BATCHING

When bagged cement is being used, the field mix proportions are usually given in terms of designated amounts of fine and coarse aggregate per bag (or per 94 lbs) of cement. The amount of material which is mixed at a time is called a BATCH, and the size of a batch is usually designated by the number of bags of cement it contains, as: a 4-bag batch, a 6-bag batch, and so on.

The process of weighing out or measuring out the ingredients for a batch of concrete is called BATCHING. When mixing is to be done by hand, the size of the batch will depend upon the number of men who are available to turn it with hand shovels. When mixing is to be done by machine, the size of the batch will depend upon the rated capacity of the mixer. The rated capacity of the mixer is given in terms of cubic feet of MIXED CONCRETE, not of batched ingredients.

MEASURING CEMENT

Since it is known that a bag of cement contains 94 lbs by weight and about 1 cu ft by loose volume, a batch formula for bagged cement is usually based upon the highest even number of bags that will produce a batch within the capacity of the men (hand mixing) or the machine (machine mixing). You can use rules 38, 41, and 42, for calculating the amount of material needed for the mix without a great deal of paperwork. These rules will be explained herein. Rule 38 is used in the mixing of mortar. Rule 41 is used in calculating the quantities of materials for concrete when the size of the coarse aggregate is not over one inch. Rule 42 is used when the size of the coarse aggregate is not over 2 1/2 inches. (Coarse aggregates over one inch in size are termed rock in concrete work.) These three calculating rules will not give the accurate amount of required materials for large construction jobs; you will have to use the absolute volume or weight formulae. (The tables mentioned in 13Yh (series) show the yield per bag of cement for each of the many ingredient formulas they contain.) However, in most cases you can use these rules of thumb to quickly calculate the quantities of required materials.

It has been found that it takes about 38 cubic feet of raw materials to make 1 cubic yard of mortar. In using the 38 calculating rule for mortar take the rule number and divide it by the sum of the quantity figures specified in the mix. For example, let's assume that the building specifications call for a 1:3 mix for mortar $1 + 3 = 4$ - $38 \div 4 = 9 \ 1/2$. You will then need 9 1/2 bags or 9 1/2 cubic feet of cement. In order to calculate the amount of fine aggregates (sand), you simply multiply 9 1/2 by 3. The product 28 1/2 cubic feet is the amount of sand you need to mix one cubic yard of mortar using a 1:3 mix. The sum of the two required quantities should equal the calculating rule 38. Therefore, you can always check in order to see if you are using the correct amounts. In the above example, 9 1/2 bags of cement plus 28 1/2 cubic feet of sand, equal 38.

Rules 41 and 42, for calculating the amount of raw materials needed to mix 1 cubic yard of concrete, are worked in the same manner. For example, let's assume that the specifications called for a 1:2:4 mix with 2-inch coarse aggregates:

$1 + 2 + 4 = 7$ - $42 \div 7 = 6$ - bags or cubic feet of cement.
$6 \times 2 = 12$ - cubic feet of sand.
$6 \times 4 = 24$ - cubic feet of coarse aggregates.
$6 + 12 + 24 = 42$ - your calculations have been proven correct.

Frequently, it will be necessary to convert these volumes in cubic feet to weights in pounds. These conversions are easy. Multiply the required cubic feet of cement by 94 pounds, remembering that 1 cubic foot or one standard bag of cement weighs 94 pounds. The average weight of dry-compacted, fine aggregate or gravel is 105 pounds per cubic foot, while the average weight of dry-compacted, coarse aggregate over 1 inch in size—termed rock—is 100 pounds. Therefore, you multiply the quantity of coarse gravel in cubic feet by 105 when using the rule 41 for coarse gravels or aggregates. When the calculating rule 42 is used, multiply the cubic feet of required rock by 100 in order to figure the amount of needed rock in pounds.

MEASURING WATER

The water-measuring controls on a machine concrete mixer will be described later in this chapter. Water measurement for hand-mixing may be done with a 14-qt bucket, marked off on the inside in gallons, half-gallons, and quarter-gallons.

NEVER add water to the mix without measuring it carefully, and always remember that the amount of water actually placed in the mix varies according to the amount of free water that is already in the aggregate. This means that if the aggregate is wet by a rainstorm, the proportion of water in the mix may have to be changed.

MEASURING AGGREGATE

The accuracy of aggregate measurement by volume depends upon the accuracy with which the amount of the "bulking" caused by moisture in the aggregate can be determined. The amount of bulking varies, not only with different moisture contents, but also with different gradations. Fine sand, for example, is bulked more than coarse sand by the same moisture content. Furthermore, moisture content itself varies from time to time, and a rather small variation causes a rather large change in the amount of bulking. For these and other reasons, aggregate should be measured by weight rather than by volume whenever possible.

To make grading easier, to keep segregation low, and to ensure that each batch is uniform, coarse aggregate should be stored in and measured from separate piles or hoppers, in each of which the ratio of maximum to minimum particle size should not exceed 2:1 for a maximum nominal size larger than 1 in. and 3:1 for a maximum nominal size smaller than 1 in. A mass of aggregate with a nominal size of 1 1/2 in. to 1/4 in., for example, should be separated into one pile or hopper containing 1 1/2 in. to 3/4 in., and another pile or hopper containing 3/4 in. to 1/4 in. A mass with a nominal size of 3 in. to 1/4 in. should be separated into one pile or hopper containing 3 in. to 1 1/2 in., another containing 1 1/2 in. to 3/4 in., and a third containing 3/4 in. to 1/4 in.

BATCHING PLANT

On large jobs the aggregate is stored and weighed out in an aggregate BATCHING PLANT (usually shortened to "batch plant") like the one shown in figure 6-6. A batch plant is, whenever possible, located near and used in conjunction with a CRUSHING AND/OR SCREENING plant. In a crushing and screening plant, stone is crushed into various particle sizes, which are then screened into separate piles. In a screening plant, the aggregate in its natural state is screened by sizes into separate piles.

The batch plant, which is usually a portable affair that can be knocked down and moved from site to site, is generally set up adjacent to the pile of screened aggregate. The plant may include separate hoppers for several sizes of fine and coarse aggregate; it may include one hopper for fine aggregate and another for coarse aggregate; or it may include one or more DIVIDED hoppers, each containing two or more separate compartments for different sizes of aggregate.

Each storage hopper or storage hopper compartment can be discharged into a WEIGH BOX, which can in turn be discharged into a mixer or a batch truck. When a specific weight of aggregate is called for, the operator sets the weight on a beam scale. He then opens the discharge chute on the storage hopper. When the desired weight has been reached in the weigh box, the scale beam rises and the operator closes the storage hopper discharge chute. He then

29.153
Figure 6-6.—Aggregate batching plant.

opens the weigh box discharge chute, and the aggregate discharges into the mixer or batch truck. Batch plant aggregate storage hoppers are usually loaded with clamshell-equipped cranes.

MIXING CONCRETE

Mixing concrete is done by one of the two methods, by hand or by machine. No matter which method is used, a well established procedure must be followed if you expect the finished concrete to be of good quality. An oversight in this phase of concrete construction, whether through lack of competence or inattention to detail, cannot be overcome later.

MIXING BY HAND

A batch which is to be hand-mixed by a couple of men should not be much larger than about a cubic yard. The equipment required consists of a watertight metal or wooden platform, two shovels, a metal-lined measuring box, and a graduated bucket for measuring the water.

The mixing platform should measure about 10 ft by 12 ft. For a wood platform the boards should be at least 1-in. tongue-and-groove, the tongue-and-groove joints being required for watertightness. The boards should be nailed to 2 x 4 joists spaced not less than 2 and not more than 3 ft O.C. A strip of 2 x 2 should be nailed along the outer edges, to prevent water or fluid material from flowing off the platform. For the same reason, the platform must be level.

Mix the sand and cement together first, using the following procedure. Let's say that the batch is to consist of 2 bags of cement, 5.5 cu ft of sand, and 6.4 cu ft of coarse aggregate. Dump 3 cu ft of sand on the platform first, spread it out in a layer, and dump a bag of cement over it. Spread the cement out in a layer, and dump the rest of the sand (2.5 cu ft) over it. Then dump the other sack of cement on top of the lot. This use of alternate layers of sand and cement reduces the amount of shoveling required for complete mixing.

Men doing the mixing should face each other from opposite sides of the pile, and they should work from the outside to the center, turning the material as many times as is necessary to produce a uniform color throughout. When the cement and sand have been completely mixed, the pile should be leveled off and the coarse material should be added and mixed in by the necessary number of turnings.

The pile should next be troughed in the center, and the mixing water, carefully measured, should be poured into the trough. The dry materials should then be turned into the water, with great care taken to ensure that none of the water escapes. When all the water has been taken up, the batch should be mixed to a uniform consistency. At least four complete turnings are usually required.

MIXING BY MACHINE

A concrete mixer is designated as to size by its RATED CAPACITY, expressed in terms of the volume of mixed concrete—not of batched ingredients—it can mix in a single batch. Rated capacities run from as small as 2 cu ft to as large as 7 cu yd (189 cu ft). For most ordinary building construction the most commonly used mixer is the 16-S (fig. 6-7) with a capacity of 16 cu ft.

The 16-S concrete mixer is a self-contained unit capable of producing 16 cubic feet of concrete plus a 10 percent overload per batch. The hourly production capacity will vary between

29.151
Figure 6-7.—Model 16-S concrete mixer.

10- and 15-cubic yards depending on the efficiency of the personnel. Aggregate larger than 3 inches will damage the mixer. The mixer consists of a frame which is equipped with wheels and towing tongue for easy movement, an engine, a power loader skip, mixing drum, water tank, and auxiliary water pump. The mixer may be used as a central mixing plant.

Charging the Mixer

There are two ways of charging concrete mixers, by hand and with the mechanical skip. The 16-S mixer is equipped with a mechanical skip. The cement, sand, and gravel are placed in the skip and then dumped into the mixer together while the water runs into the mixing drum on the side opposite the skip. The mixing water is measured from a storage tank on top of the mixer a few seconds before the skip is dumped to wash the mixer between batches. The coarse aggregate is placed in the skip first, the cement next and the sand is placed on top to prevent excessive loss of cement as the batch enters the mixer.

A cement bag should be emptied onto the skip by cutting the under side of the bag lengthwise with a linoleum knife and then pulling the sack clear of the cement.

Mixing Time

The mixing time for a 1-cu yd batch is 1 1/2 minutes. Another 15 seconds should be allowed for each additional 1/2 cu yd or fraction thereof. The water should be started into the drum a few seconds before the skip begins to dump, so that the inside of the drum will get a wash-out before the batched ingredients go in. The mixing period should be measured from the time all the batched ingredients are in, provided that all the water is in before one-fourth of the mixing time has elapsed.

Discharging the Mixer

When the material is ready for discharge from the mixer, the discharge chute is moved into place to receive the concrete from the drum of the mixer. In some cases, dry concrete has a tendency to carry up to the top of the drum and not drop down in time to be deposited on the chute. Very wet concrete may not carry up high enough to be caught by the chute. This condition can be corrected by adjusting the speed of the mixer. For very wet concrete, the speed of the drum should be increased and for dry concrete, it should be slowed down.

Cleaning and Maintaining the Mixer

The mixer should be cleaned daily when it is in continuous operation or following each period of use if it is in operation less than a day. If the outside of the mixer is kept coated with form oil, the cleaning process can be speeded up. The outside of the mixer should be washed with a hose and all accumulated concrete should be knocked off. If the blades of the mixer become worn, or coated with hardened concrete, mixing action will be less efficient. Badly worn blades should be replaced. Hardened concrete should not be allowed to accumulate in the mixer drum. The mixer drum must be cleaned out whenever it is necessary to shut down for more than 1 1/2 hours. Place a volume of coarse aggregate in the drum equal to one-half of the capacity of the mixer and allow it to revolve for about 5 minutes. Discharge the aggregate and flush out the drum with water. Do not pound the discharge chute, drum shell, or skip to remove aggregate or hardened concrete, for concrete will more readily adhere to the dents and bumps created.

For complete instructions on the operation, adjustment, and maintenance of the mixer, study the manufacturer's manual.

HANDLING AND TRANSPORTING CONCRETE

If mixed plastic concrete is carried by the ordinary type of vehicle (dump truck, for example), there is a strong tendency for the larger aggregate particles to segregate by settling to the bottom. To avoid this, ready-mixed concrete is usually delivered to a job by a transit-mix truck.

When ready-mixed concrete is carried by the ordinary type of carrier (such as a dump truck, wheelbarrow, or buggy), any jolting of the carrier increases the natural tendency of the concrete to segregate. Carriers should therefore be equipped with pneumatic tires whenever possible, and the surface over which they travel should be as smooth as possible.

A long free fall will cause concrete to segregate. If the concrete must be discharged at a level more than 4 ft above the level of placement, it should be dumped into an ELEPHANT TRUNK like the one shown in figure 6-8.

Segregation also occurs whenever discharged concrete is allowed to glance off a surface, such as the side of a form or of a chute. Wheelbarrows, buggies, and conveyors should therefore be discharged so as to cause the concrete to fall clear.

Concrete should be transported by chute for short distances only, since it tends to segregate and also to dry out, when handled in this manner. For a mix of average workability, the best slope for a chute is about 1 ft of rise to 2 or 3 ft of run. For a mix of this type, a steeper slope will cause segregation, while a flatter slope will cause the concrete to run slowly or not at all. For a stiffer mix, a steeper slope will be required.

READY MIX

On some jobs, such as large highway jobs, it is possible to use a batch plant which contains its own mixer. A plant of this type discharges ready-mixed concrete into dump trucks or agitator trucks, which haul it to the construction site. An agitator truck carries the mix in a revolving chamber much like the one on a mixer. Keeping the mix agitated en route prevents segregation of aggregate particles. Seabees have

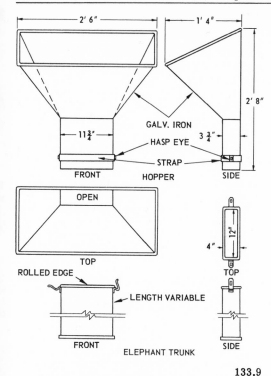

133.9

Figure 6-8.—Chute or down-pipe used to
check free fall of concrete.

used concrete pavers as central mixing plants, stationing the paver adjacent to a cut so that trucks may be driven under the bucket boom.

A ready-mix plant is usually portable, so that it can follow the job along. It must be certain, of course, that a truck will be able to deliver the mix at the site before it starts to set. The interval between the time when the water is introduced at the mixer and the time when the truck discharges the mix into the forms must not be longer than 1 1/2 hours.

TRANSIT MIX

A TRANSIT MIX truck is a traveling concrete mixer. The truck carries a mixer and a water tank, from which the driver can, at the proper time, introduce the required amount of water into the mix. The truck picks up the dry ingredients at the batch plant, together with a slip which tells him how much water is to be introduced into the mix. As a rule it is his best policy to wait until he arrives at the site and is sure they are ready there to receive the mix before he introduces the water and starts mixing the concrete. Usually, however, he keeps the mixer revolving slowly en route, to prevent segregation of particles in the dry aggregate. All Seabee battalions are equipped with transit mix trucks. Of the various mixing procedures, the transit mix method is the most widely used on all but the smallest jobs assigned to a battalion.

FORMWORK

Most structural concrete is made by placing (called CASTING) plastic concrete into spaces enclosed by previously constructed FORMS. The plastic concrete hardens into the shape outlined by the forms, after which the forms are usually removed.

Forms for concrete structures must be tight, rigid, and strong. If the forms are not tight, there will be a loss of paste which may cause weakness or a loss of water which may cause SAND STREAKING. The forms must be strong enough and well-braced enough to resist the high pressure exerted by the concrete.

Forms, or parts of forms, are often omitted when a firm earth surface exists which is capable of supporting and/or molding the concrete. In most footings, for example, the bottom of the footing is cast directly against the earth and only the sides are molded in forms. Many footings are cast with both bottom and sides against the natural earth. In this case however, the specifications usually call for larger footings. A foundation wall is often cast between a form on the inner side and the natural earth surface on the outer side.

FORM MATERIALS

Form material should be of wood, plywood, steel, or other approved material, except that forms for concrete pavement other than on curves should be metal, and on curves, flexible or curved forms of metal or wood may be used. Wood forms, for surfaces exposed to view in the finished structure and requiring a standard finish, should be tongue-and-groove boards or plywood. For exposed surfaces, undressed square-edge lumber may be used. Forms for surfaces requiring special finishes should be plywood or tongue-and-groove boards, or should be lined with plywood, a non-absorptive hard-pressed fiberboard, or other approved material.

Tongue-and-groove boards should be dressed to a uniform thickness, evenly matched, and free from loose knots, holes, and other defects which would affect the concrete finish. Plywood, other than for lining, should be concrete-form plywood not less than 5/8 inch thick. Surfaces of steel forms should be free from irregularities, dents, and sags.

FORMWORK NOMENCLATURE

Strictly speaking, it is only those parts of the formwork which directly mold the concrete that are correctly referred to as the "forms." The rest of the formwork consists of various bracing and tying members used to strengthen the forms and to hold them rigidly in place.

Wall, column, and floor slab forms were formerly built by joining boards edge-to-edge, but built-up forms have been largely replaced by plywood forms. Plywood forms are tighter, more warp-resistant, and easier to construct than board forms, and they can be re-used oftener and more conveniently.

In the following discussion of the various common types of forms, you should study the illustrations until you have learned the names of all the formwork members.

FOOTING FORMS

When possible, the earth should be excavated so as to form a mold for concrete wall footings. Otherwise, forms must be constructed. In most cases, footings for columns are square or rectangular. The four sides should be built and erected in panels. The earth must be thoroughly moistened before the concrete is placed. The panels for the opposite sides of the footing are made to exact footing width. The 1-inch thick sheathing is nailed to vertical cleats spaced on 2-foot centers. See (a) in figure 6-9 which shows a typical form for a large footing. Two-inch dressed lumber should be used for the cleats and cleats spaced 2 1/2 inches from each end of the panel as shown. The other pair of panels (b), figure 6-9 have two end cleats on the inside spaced the length of the footing plus twice the sheathing thickness. The panels are held together by No. 8 or 9 soft black annealed iron wire wrapped around the center cleats. All reinforcing bars must be in place before the wire is installed. The holes on each side of the cleat permitting the wire to be wrapped around the cleat should be less than one-half inch in diameter to prevent leakage of mortar through the hole. The panels may be held in place with form nails until the tie wire is installed. All

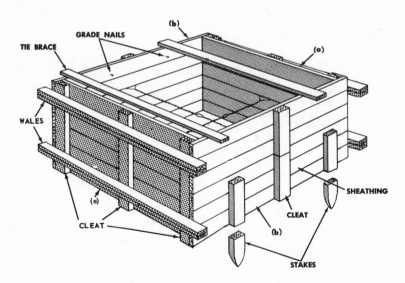

133.251

Figure 6-9.—Typical large footing form.

form (duplex) nails should be driven from the outside if possible to make stripping easier. For forms 4 feet square or larger, stakes should be driven as shown. These stakes and 1 x 6 boards nailed across the top prevent spreading. The side panels may be higher than the required depth of footing since they can be marked on the inside to indicate the top of the footing. If the footings are less than 1 foot deep and 2 feet square, the forms can be constructed of 1-inch sheathing without cleats. Boards for the sides of the form are cut and nailed as shown in figure 6-10. The form can be braced and no wire ties are needed.

Sometimes it may be necessary to place a footing and a small pier at the same time. The form for this type of concrete construction is shown in figure 6-11. The units are similar to the one shown in figure 6-9. Support for the upper form must be provided in such a way that it does not interfere with the placement of concrete in the lower form. This is accomplished by nailing a 2 by 2 or 4 by 4 to the lower form as shown. The top form is then nailed to these support pieces.

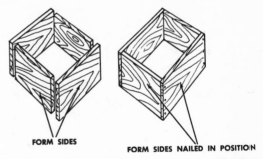

FORM SIDES   FORM SIDES NAILED IN POSITION

133.252

Figure 6-10.—Typical small footing form.

Form work for a wall footing is shown in figure 6-12 and methods of bracing the form are given in figure 6-13. The sides of the forms are made of 2-inch lumber having a width equal to the depth of the footing. These pieces are held in place with stakes and are maintained the correct distance apart by spreaders. The short brace shown at each stake holds the form in line.

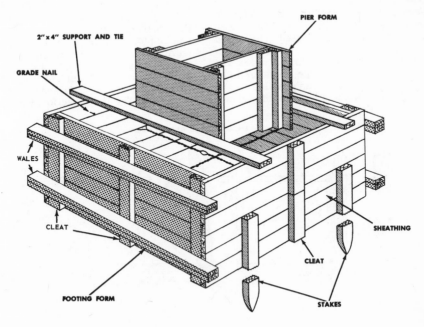

133.253

Figure 6-11.—Typical footing and pier form.

113

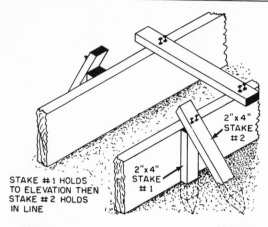

STAKE #1 HOLDS
TO ELEVATION THEN
STAKE #2 HOLDS
IN LINE

2"x4"
STAKE
#2

2"x4"
STAKE
#1

133.254

Figure 6-12.—Typical wall footing forms.

WALL FORMS

Figure 6-14 shows a wall form without wales. The studs are usually backed by wales as shown in figure 6-15.

Wall forms are usually additionally reinforced against displacement by the use of TIES. Two types of simple wire ties, used with wood SPREADERS, are shown in figure 6-16. The wire is passed around the studs, the wales and through small holes bored in the sheathing. The spreader is placed as close as possible to the studs, and the tie is set taut by the wedge shown

in the upper view, or by twisting with a small toggle as shown in the lower view. When the concrete reaches the level of the spreader, the spreader is knocked out and removed. The parts of the wire which are inside the forms remain in the concrete; the outside surplus is cut off after the forms are removed.

Wire ties and wooden spreaders have been largely replaced by various manufactured devices in which the function of the tie and the spreader are combined. Figure 6-17 shows one of these, called a SNAP TIE. These ties are made in various sizes to fit various wall thicknesses. The tie holders can be removed from the tie rod. The rod goes through small holes bored in the sheathing, and also through the wales, which are usually doubled for that purpose. Tapping the tie holders down on the ends of the rod brings the sheathing to bear solidly against the spreader washers. (To prevent the tie holder from coming loose, drive a duplex nail in the provided hole.) After the concrete has hardened, the tie holders can be detached to strip the forms. After the forms are stripped, a special wrench is used to break off the outer sections of rod, which break off at the breaking points, located about 1 in. inside the surface of the concrete. Small surface holes remain, which can be plugged with grout if necessary.

Another type of wall form tie is the TIE ROD shown in figure 6-18. The rod in this type consists of three sections: an inner section which is threaded on both ends, and two threaded outer sections. The inner section, with the cones set

SPREADER NAILED TO FORM SIDES

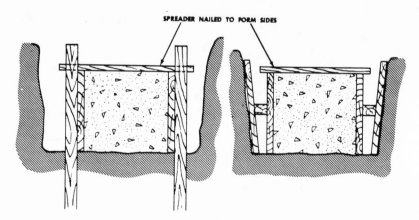

133.255

Figure 6-13.—Methods of bracing footing forms.

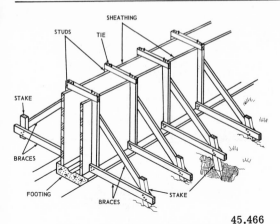

45.466

Figure 6-14.—Wall form without wales.

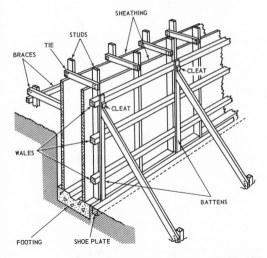

29.128

Figure 6-15.—Wall form with wales.

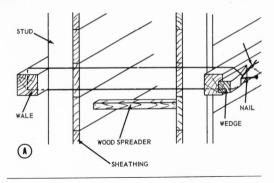

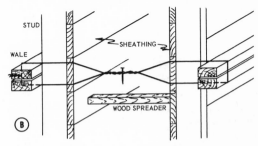

133.10

Figure 6-16.—Wire ties for wall forms.

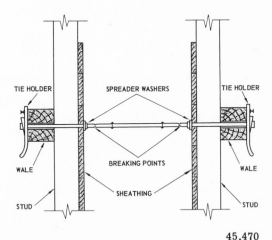

45.470

Figure 6-17.—Snap tie.

to the thickness of the wall, is placed between the forms, and the outer sections are passed through the wales and sheathing and threaded into the cone nuts. The clamps are then threaded up on the outer sections to bring the forms to bear against the cone nuts. After the concrete hardens, the clamps are loosened and the outer sections of rod are removed by threading them out of the cone nuts. After the forms are stripped, the cone nuts are removed from the concrete by threading them off the inner sections

of rod with a special wrench. The cone-shaped surface holes which remain may be plugged with

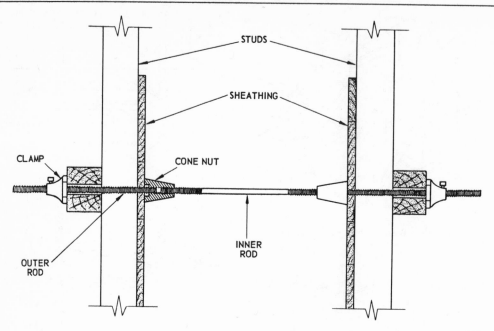

Figure 6-18.—Tie rod.

45.471

grout. The inner sections of rod remain in the concrete. The outer sections and the cone nuts may be re-used indefinitely.

Wall forms are usually constructed as separate panels, each made by nailing sheathing to a number of studs. Panels are joined to each other in line as shown in figure 6-19. A method of joining panels at a corner is shown in figure 6-20.

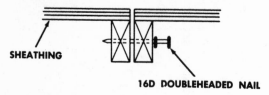

Figure 6-19.—Joining wall form panels together in line.

133.11

COLUMN FORM

Figure 6-21 shows a column form. Since the rate of placing in a column form is very high,

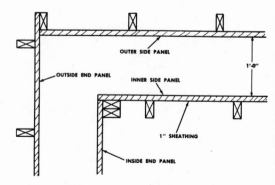

Figure 6-20.—Method of joining wall form panels at a corner.

133.12

and since the bursting pressure exerted on the form by the concrete increases directly with the rate of placing, a column form must be securely braced by the yokes shown in the figure. Since the bursting pressure is greater at the bottom of the form than it is at the top, the yokes are

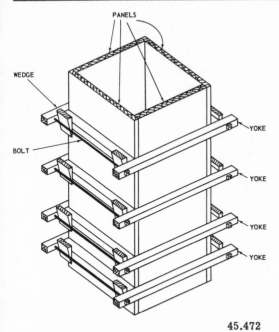

45.472

Figure 6-21.—Column form.

placed closer together at the bottom than they are at the top.

The panels for the form are made up first, by nailing the yoke members to the sheathing. On two panels the yoke members come flush with the edges of the sheathing; on the other two they project beyond the edges as shown. Bolt holes are bored in these projections as shown, and bolts are inserted as shown to back up the wedges which are driven to tighten the yokes.

BEAM AND GIRDER FORMS

The type of construction to be used for beam forms depends upon whether the form is to be removed in one piece or whether the sides are to be stripped and the bottom left in place until such time as the concrete has developed enough strength to permit removal of the shoring. The latter type beam form is preferred and details for this type are shown in figure 6-22. Beam forms are subjected to very little bursting pressure but must be shored up at frequent intervals to prevent sagging under the weight of the fresh concrete.

The bottom of the form has the same width as the beam and is in one piece for the full width. The sides of the form should be 1-inch thick tongue and groove sheathing and should lap over the bottom as shown. The sheathing is nailed to 2- by 4-inch struts placed on 3-foot centers. A 1- by 4-inch piece is nailed along the struts. These pieces support the joist for the floor panel, as shown in figure 6-23. The beam sides of the form are not nailed to the bottom but are held in position by continuous strips as shown in detail E. The cross pieces nailed on top serve as spreaders. After erection, the slab panel joists hold the beam sides in position. Girder forms are the same as beam forms except that the sides are notched to receive the beam forms. Temporary cleats should be nailed across the beam opening when the girder form is being handled.

The entire method of assembling beam and girder forms is illustrated in figure 6-23. The connection of the beam and girder is illustrated in detail D. The beam bottom butts up tightly against the side of the girder form and rests on a 2- by 4-inch cleat nailed to the girder side. Detail C shows the joint between beam and slab panel and details A and B show the joint between girder and column. The clearances given in these details are needed for stripping and also to allow for movement that will occur due to the weight of the fresh concrete. The 4 by 4 posts used for shoring the beams and girders should be spaced so as to provide support for the concrete and forms and wedged as shown in detail E.

OILING AND WETTING FORMS

Before concrete is placed in forms which are to be stripped, the forms must be coated with a suitable form oil or other material which will prevent bond between the forms and the concrete. Almost any light-bodied petroleum oil makes a satisfactory bond-preventer for wood forms. The use of oil however, should be avoided where finished concrete surfaces are to be painted. However, for forms which are to be re-used a compound is preferable which will not only prevent bond but also protect the form material.

On plywood forms, lacquer is preferred to ordinary oil. Commercial lacquers and similar preparations are also good. If the forms are to be re-used a good many times, painting is a good way to preserve them.

117

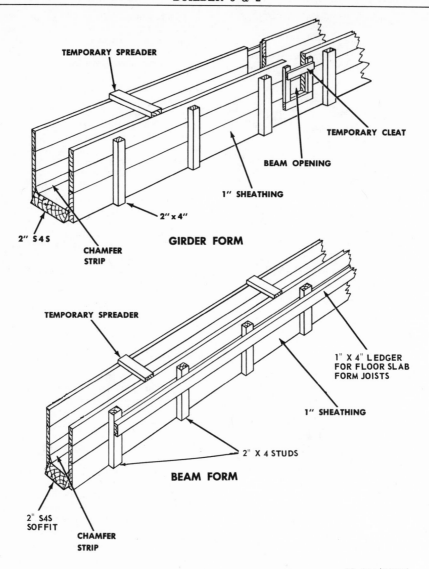

Figure 6-22.—Typical beam and girder forms.

Ordinary petroleum oils which are satisfactory for wood forms may not prevent bond between concrete and steel forms. For steel forms certain specially compounded petroleum oils, such as synthetic castor-oil, and some types of marine engine oils, should be used.

Since any form oil dropped on the reinforcing steel (see next section) will prevent bond between the steel and the concrete, forms should be oiled before the steel is set in place. Column panels and wall form panels must be oiled before they are erected. Surfaces which are to be

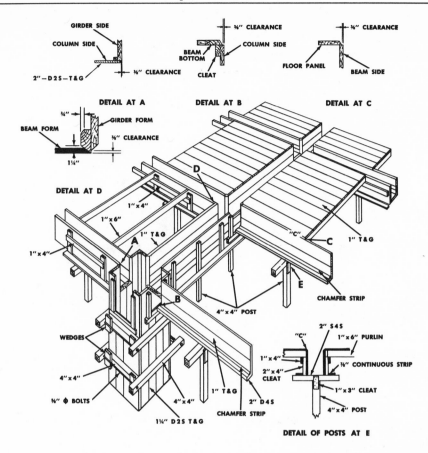

133.256

Figure 6-23.—Assembly of beam and floor forms.

oiled must be smooth, and the oil (which may be applied by brush, sprayer, or swab) must cover evenly and without holidays.

If form oil or its equivalent is not available, the forms may be thoroughly wetted to help prevent sticking. This method of bond-prevention should be used only when a suitable bond-preventing compound is unobtainable.

REINFORCED CONCRETE

Concrete is strong in compression, but relatively weak in tension. The reverse is true for slender steel bars and when the two materials are used together one makes up for the deficiency of the other. When steel is embedded in concrete in a manner which assists it in carrying imposed loads, the combination is known as reinforced concrete. The steel may consist of welded wire mesh or expanded metal mesh, but commonly consists of steel bars called REINFORCING BARS.

Before placing reinforcing steel in forms, all form oiling should be completed. Oil on reinforcing bars is objectionable because it reduces the bond between the bars and the concrete. Use a piece of burlap to clean the bars of rust, scale, grease, mud, or other foreign matter. A tight film of rust or mill scale is not objectionable.

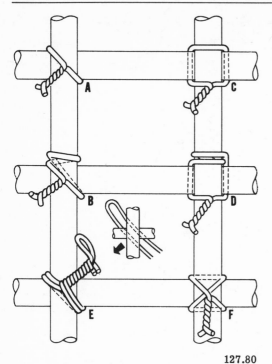

127.80

Figure 6-24.—Types of ties.

When you are tying reinforcing bars you must have a supply of tie wire available. There are several ways you can carry your tie wire. One way is to coil it to a diameter of 18 inches, then slip it around your neck and under one arm as shown in figure 6-25. This leaves a free end for tying. Coil enough wire so it weighs about 9 pounds.

127.81

Figure 6-25.—Carrying tie wire.

There are several types of ties that can be used with deformed bars; some are more effective than others. Figure 6-24 illustrates the six types used by the Seabees: A. Snap tie or simple tie; B. Wall tie; C. Saddle tie; D. Saddle tie with twist; E. Double strang single tie; and F. Cross tie or figure eight tie. As a Builder, you will only be concerned with the snap tie and saddle tie.

When making the SNAP TIE or SIMPLE TIE, the wire is simply wrapped once around the two crossing bars in a diagonal manner with the two ends on top, and these are twisted together with a pair of sidecutters until they are very tight against the bars. Then the loose ends of the wire are cut off. This tie is used mostly on floor slabs. When making the SADDLE TIE, the wires pass halfway around one of the bars on either side of the crossing bar and are brought squarely or diagonally around the crossing bar, with the ends twisted together and cut off. This tie is used on special location (walls).

Another way to carry tie wire is to take pieces of wire about 9 inches long, fold them and hook one end in your belt; then you can pull the wires out as needed. The tools you will use in tying reinforcing bars include a 6-foot folding rule; sidecutters; leather gloves; 50-foot tape measure; and keel crayon, either yellow, red, or blue.

The proper location for the reinforcing bars is usually given on drawings. In order for the structure to withstand the loads it must carry, place the steel in the position shown. Secure the bars in position in such a way that when placing the concrete, they will not move. This can be accomplished by the use of the reinforcing bar supports shown in figures 6-26, 6-27, and 6-28.

Footings and other principal structural members which are against the ground should have at least 3 inches of concrete between steel and

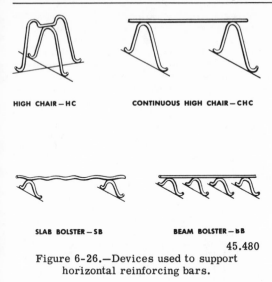

HIGH CHAIR—HC   CONTINUOUS HIGH CHAIR—CHC

SLAB BOLSTER—SB   BEAM BOLSTER—BB

45.480

Figure 6-26.—Devices used to support
horizontal reinforcing bars.

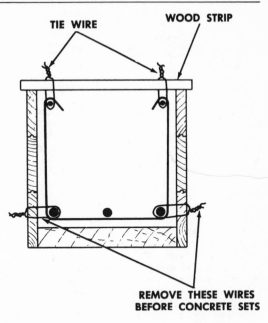

TIE WIRE   WOOD STRIP

REMOVE THESE WIRES
BEFORE CONCRETE SETS

127.83.2

Figure 6-28.—Beam reinforcing steel
hung in place.

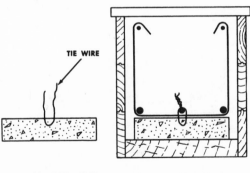

TIE WIRE

PRECAST CONCRETE BLOCK   METHOD OF USING CONCRETE
BLOCK

127.83.1

Figure 6-27.—Precast concrete block used
for reinforcing steel support.

ground. If the concrete surface is to be in contact with the ground or exposed to the weather after removal of the forms, the protective covering of concrete over the steel should be 2 inches. It may be reduced to 1 1/2 inches for beams and columns, and 3/4-inch for slabs and interior wall surfaces, but it should be 2 inches for all exterior wall surfaces.

Specifications and designs are usually used when lapping wire mesh. However, as a rule of thumb, 1 complete lap is usually sufficient with a minimum of 2 inches between laps. Whenever the rule of thumb is not allowed, use the end and side lap method.

In the end lap method, the wire mesh is lapped by overlapping one full mesh measured from the end of longitudinal wires in one piece to the end of longitudinal wires in the adjacent piece, and then tying the two pieces at 1' 6" centers with a snap tie.

In the side method, the two longitudinal side wires are placed one alongside and overlapping the other, and then are tied with a snap tie every 3 feet.

Where splices in reinforcing steel are not dimensioned on the drawings, the bars should be lapped not less than 30 times the bar diameter, nor less than 12 inches.

The stress in a tension bar can be transmitted through the concrete and into another adjoining bar by a lap splice of proper length. The lap is expressed as the number of bar diameters. If the bar is #2 make the lap at least 12 inches. Tie the bars together with a snap tie as shown in figure 6-29.

LAP AT LEAST 30 X BAR DIAMETER

127.85

Figure 6-29.—Bars spliced by lapping.

The minimum clear distance between parallel bars in beams, footings, walls, and floor slabs should be not less than 1 inch, nor less than one and one-third times the largest size aggregate particle in the concrete. In columns, the clear distance between parallel bars should be not less than one and one-half times the bar diameter, 1 1/2 times the maximum size of the coarse aggregate, nor 1 1/2 inches.

The support for reinforcing steel in floor slabs is shown in figure 6-30. The height of the slab bolster is determined by the concrete protective cover required. Concrete blocks made of sand-cement mortar can be used in place of the slab bolster. Wood blocks should never be used for this purpose if there is any possibility that the concrete can become wet and if the construction is of a permanent type. Bar chairs of a type shown in figure 6-30 can be obtained in heights up to 6 inches. If a height greater than this is required, make the chair of No. 0 soft annealed iron wire. Tie the bars together at frequent intervals with a snap tie where they cross to hold the bars firmly in position.

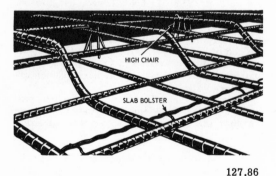

HIGH CHAIR

SLAB BOLSTER

127.86

Figure 6-30.—Reinforcing steel for a floor slab.

Steel for column ties may be assembled with the verticals into cages, by laying the vertical bars for one side of the column horizontally across a couple of sawhorses. The proper

number of ties are slipped over the bars, the remaining vertical bars are added, and then the ties are spaced out as required by the placing plans. A sufficient number of intersections are wired together to make the assembly rigid, so that it may be hoisted and set as a unit.

After the column is raised it is tied to the dowels or reinforcing steel carried up from below. This holds it firmly in position at the base. The column form is erected and the reinforcing steel is tied to the column form at 5-foot intervals, as shown in figure 6-31.

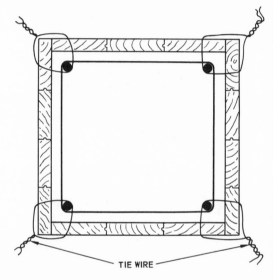

TIE WIRE

127.83.4

Figure 6-31.—Securing column reinforcing steel against displacement.

The use of metal supports to hold beam reinforcing steel in position is shown in figure 6-32. Note the position of the beam bolster. The stirrups are tied to the main reinforcing steel with a snap tie. Wherever possible you should assemble the stirrups and main reinforcing steel outside the form and then place the assembled unit in position. Wood blocks should be substituted for the metal supports only if there is no possibility of the concrete becoming wet or if the construction is known to be temporary. Precast concrete blocks, as shown in figure 6-27, may be substituted for metal

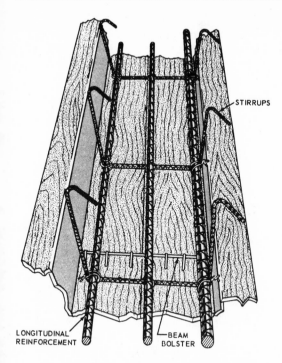

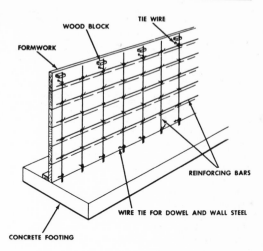

127.88

Figure 6-33.—Steel in place in a wall.

LONGITUDINAL REINFORCEMENT

BEAM BOLSTER

STIRRUPS

45.481

Figure 6-32.—Beam reinforcing steel supported on beam bolsters.

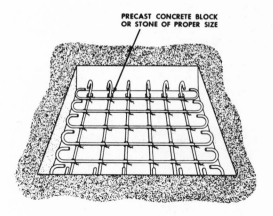

127.89

Figure 6-34.—Steel in place in a footing.

supports or, if none of the types of bar supports described above seems suitable, the method shown in figure 6-28 may be used.

Placement of steel in walls is the same as for columns except that the steel is erected in place and not preassembled. Horizontal steel is tied to vertical steel at least three times in any bar length. Steel in place in a wall is shown in figure 6-33. The wood block is removed when the form has been filled up to the level of the block. For high walls, ties in between the top and bottom should be used.

Steel is placed in footings very much as it is placed in floor slabs. Stones, rather than steel supports, may be used to support the steel at the proper distance above the subgrade. Steel mats in small footings are generally preassembled and placed after the forms have been set. A typical arrangement is shown in figure 6-34. Steel mats in large footings are constructed in place.

PLACING CONCRETE

Concrete will not attain its maximum possible strength, density, and uniformity unless proper methods are used to place it in the forms. Proper methods are methods which will ensure the thorough filling of all form spaces, while at the same time confining segregation to a minimum.

The general rule with regard to placement is that each separate load of concrete should be placed as nearly as possible in the position it is to occupy permanently. In a slab form, for example, loads should NOT be dumped in the center of the form and then shoveled or otherwise spread out to the sides. Instead, placement should begin along an edge, and successive loads should be dumped adjacent to each other, so as to reduce to a minimum the necessity for further handling. The more concrete is handled, the more it segregates (fig. 6-35).

Concrete should be deposited in layers whenever possible, and each layer should be consolidated (described later) before the next layer is placed on top of it. For reinforced concrete walls layers should be from 6 to 12 in. deep. A high wall form should be filled to within 1 ft of the top, after which 1 hour should be allowed for settling. The form should then be overfilled about 2 or 3 in. above the top. The excess concrete above the top of the form will be high in water content, and therefore low in strength. This excess is struck off after the concrete has stiffened slightly.

A wall, beam, or girder form should be filled from the ends toward the center; meaning, that in a beam form (for example) the first load should be placed at one end, the second load at the other end, the third load next to the first, the fourth load next to the second, and so on.

Before any concrete is placed, the forms must be cleaned of all rubbish and carefully checked for strength tightness, and proper alignment.

CONSOLIDATING CONCRETE

If concrete were simply placed in a form and left to harden without further treatment, the end-product would contain a number of defects. Large numbers of air bubbles (called honeycomb) entrapped in the material would make for inadequate density. Surfaces would show inadequate coverage of coarse aggregate, with rock pockets (clusters of exposed coarse aggregate particles) showing here and there. Small or intricate form spaces would not be completely filled, and the reinforcing steel would not be solidly bonded to the concrete at all points.

To eliminate these and other defects, concrete must be CONSOLIDATED. Consolidation may be accomplished by using a hand SPADING TOOL or a mechanical VIBRATOR. In spading, the spading tool is shoved down along the inside surface of the form (fig. 6-36), through the layer

133.13

Figure 6-35.—Placing concrete with a bucket.

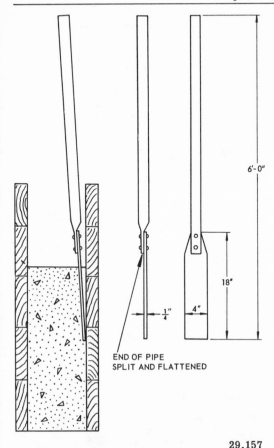

6'-0"

18"

$\frac{1}{4}$"   4"

END OF PIPE
SPLIT AND FLATTENED

29.157

Figure 6-36.—Consolidation by spading
and the spading tool.

BEFORE VIBRATION

AFTER VIBRATION

Figure 6-37.—The use of a vibrator
to consolidate concrete.   29.158

to be spaded and several inches into the layer previously placed. The handle is then worked back and forth several times until there is reason to believe that all the air has been expelled from the concrete, and that all the form spaces have been well filled.

Consolidation is effectively accomplished by use of mechanical vibrators, as shown in figure 6-37. With vibrators it is possible to place mixtures too stiff to be placed in any other way. In most structures, concrete with a 1- or 2-inch slump can be deposited. Stiff mixtures require less cement and are therefore more economical. Moreover, there is less danger of segregation and excessive bleeding. The mix must not be so stiff that an excessive amount of labor is required to place it. External vibrators and internal vibrators are available. The internal vibrator involves insertion of a vibrating element into the concrete. The external type is applied to the forms. It is powered by an electric motor, gasoline engine, or compressed air. The internal vibrator should be inserted in the concrete at intervals of approximately 18 inches for 5 to 15 seconds to allow some overlap of the area vibrated at each insertion. The vibrator should pass through the layer being placed and penetrate the layer below for several inches to ensure a good bond between the layers. Under normal conditions there is little likelihood of damage from the vibration of lower layers provided the disturbed concrete in these lower layers again becomes plastic under the vibratory action. Sufficient vibration has taken place when a thin line of mortar appears along the form near the vibrator, and when the coarse aggregate has sunk into the concrete. Overvibration should be guarded against. Internal vibrators will gouge the forms if they come in contact with them. Mixes that can be easily consolidated by spading should not be vibrated for the vibration may cause segregation. If the concrete has a slump of 5 or 6 inches, it should not be vibrated. Vibrators must not be used to move concrete over long distances within the form. Some hand spading or puddling should be used along with the vibration. In addition to one man operating the vibrator, there should also be a man spading.

FINISHING CONCRETE

The concrete finishing process may be performed in many ways, depending on the effect desired. Occasionally only correction of surface defects, filling of bolt holes or cleaning is necessary. Unformed surfaces may require only screeding to proper contour and elevation, or a broomed, floated, or troweled finish may be specified. Each step of the finishing operation is discussed below.

SCREEDING

The first step in finishing a slab is called SCREEDING. A hand-operated strike-off board and the method of using it are shown in figure 6-38. The chief purpose of screeding is to level the surface of the slab by striking off the excess concrete. The strike-off board rides on the edges of the side forms or on wood or metal strips (screeds) set up for this purpose. The two men give the strike-off board a sawing motion while moving it along the slab.

Screeding by means of mechanical equipment is shown in figure 6-39.

The vibrating screed is being used more and more in construction for striking off concrete

133.14

Figure 6-38.—Screeding by hand.

133.15X
Figure 6-39.—Mechanical screeding.

pass if required. The vibration is normally transmitted through the length of the beam directly to the concrete.

Screeds are pulled by either ropes or pipe handles by a man at each end. The speed at which it is pulled is directly related to the slump of the concrete—the less the slump, the slower the speed—the more the slump, the faster the speed. The finishing screed, having no transverse (crosswise) movement of the beam, is merely drawn directly forward riding on the forms or rails. See figure 6-39. Whether the screed is electric motor or gas engine operated, in either case a method is provided to quickly start or stop the screed's vibration. This is important to prevent overvibration when the screed might be standing still.

The concrete is usually placed from 15' to 20' ahead of the strikeboard and shoveled as close as possible to its final resting place. The screed is then put into operation and pulled along by two men (one at each end of the screed). See figure 6-40. It is very important, that sufficient concrete is kept in front of the screed. Should the concrete be below the level of the screed beam, voids or bare spots will appear on the concrete surface as the screed passes over the slab. Should this occur, a shoveful or so of concrete is thrown on the bare spot, and the screed is lifted up and carried back for a second pass. In some cases, the screed crew will endeavor to work out the void or bare spot with a hand-operated bull float, rather than make the second pass with the screed. It may be found that intermediate vibration speeds are more desirable for particular mixes and different length beams. Generally, the stiffer the mix and the longer the beam, the greater the vibration speed required. Then, too, the speed at which the screed is moved will affect the resulting finish of the slab. After a few minutes of operation, a satisfactory vibration speed and pulling speed can be established. After the vibratory finishing screed has passed over the slab, the surface is then ready for broom or burlap finishing.

Where possible, it is advisable to lay out or engineer the concrete slab specifically for use of a vibratory finishing screed. Forms should be laid out in lanes of equal widths, so that the same length screed can be used on all lanes or slabs. It should also be planned, if possible, that any vertical columns will be next to the forms, so that the screed can easily be lifted or maneuvered around the column.

slabs on highways, bridge decks, and deck slabs. The screed, incorporating the use of vibration, permits the use of stronger and more economical, low slump concrete as it strikes off this relatively dry material smoothly and quickly. The advantages of vibration are two-fold—greater density and stronger concrete. Not only do vibratory finishing screeds give a better finish, and reduce maintenance, but they also save considerable time due to the speed at which they operate. Then, too, as far as the men are concerned, screeds are much less fatiguing to operate than hand strike-offs.

A vibratory finishing screed usually consists of a beam or beams with a gasoline engine or an electric motor and vibrating mechanism which is generally mounted in the center of the beam. Most screeds, are exceedingly heavy and equipped with wheels, and a raising device to facilitate rolling it back for a second pass. However, there are lightweight screeds which are not equipped with wheels, and are easily lifted by two men and set back for the second

133.16X

Figure 6-40.—Pulling a mechanical screed.

The following are the important advantages of using a vibratory finishing screed:

Allow the use of low slump concrete resulting in stronger slabs.

Reduce and sometimes eliminate the necessity of bull-floating.

Increase the density of the concrete resulting in a superior wearing surface.

In the case of floor slabs, they make it possible to start troweling sooner since drier mixes can be used which set up more quickly.

FLOATING

If a smoother surface is required than the one obtained by screeding, the surface should be worked sparingly with a wood or metal float or finishing machine. A wood float and the method of using it is shown in figure 6-41. This process should take place shortly after screeding and while the concrete is still plastic and workable. High spots are eliminated, low spots filled in, and enough mortar is brought (floated) to the surface to produce the desired finish. The concrete must not be overworked while it is still plastic, to avoid bringing an excess of

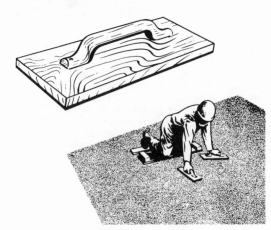

29.162

Figure 6-41.—Wood float and floating operation.

water and mortar to the surface. This fine material will form a thin weak layer that will scale or wear off under usage. Where a coarse texture is desired as the final finish, it is usually necessary to float the surface a second time after it has partially hardened so that the required surface will be obtained. In slab construction long-handled wood floats are used as shown in figure 6-42. The steel float is used the same way as the wood float but it gives the finished concrete a much smoother surface. Steel floating should begin when the water sheen disappears from the concrete surface, to avoid cracking and dusting of the finished concrete. Cement or water should not be used to aid in finishing the surface.

29.163

Figure 6-42.—Long-handling wood float and floating operation.

TROWELING

If a dense, smooth finish is desired, floating must be followed by steel troweling at some time after the moisture film or sheen disappears from the floated surface and when the concrete has hardened enough to prevent fine material and water from being worked to the surface. This step should be delayed as long as possible. Excessive troweling too early tends to produce crazing and lack of durability; too long a delay in troweling results in a surface too hard to finish properly. The usual tendency is to start to trowel too soon. Troweling should leave the surface smooth, even, and free of marks and ripples. Spreading dry cement on a wet surface to take up excess water is not good practice where a wear-resistant and durable surface is required. Wet spots must be avoided if possible; when they do occur, finishing operations should not be resumed until the water has been absorbed, has evaporated, or has been

mopped up. A surface that is fine-textured but not slippery may be obtained by troweling lightly over the surface with a circular motion immediately after the first regular troweling. In this process, the trowel is kept flat on the surface of the concrete. Where a HARD STEEL-TROWELED FINISH is required, the first regular troweling is followed by a second troweling after the concrete has become hard enough so that no mortar adheres to the trowel and a ringing sound is produced as the trowel passes over the surface. During this final troweling, the trowel should be tilted slightly and heavy pressure exerted to thoroughly compact the surface. Hair cracks are usually due to a concentration of water and fines at the surface resulting from overworking the concrete during finishing operations. Such cracking is aggravated by too rapid drying or cooling. Checks that develop before troweling usually can be closed by pounding the concrete with a hand float. A steel trowel and an edger are shown in A, figure 6-43 and the troweling operation in B, figure 6-43.

29.164

Figure 6-43.—Steel finishing tools and troweling operations.

The mechanical (troweler) finishing machine is used to good advantage on flat slabs with stiff consistency. The concrete must be set enough

129

133.17

Figure 6-44.—Mechanical trowelers.

to support the weight of the machine and the operator. (See fig. 6-44.) Machine finishing is faster than by hand, where the machine will fit in with the type of construction.

BROOMING

A nonskid surface can be produced by brooming the concrete before it has thoroughly hardened. Brooming is carried out after the floating operation. For some floors and sidewalks where severe scoring is not desirable, the broomed finish can be produced with a hair brush after the surface has been troweled to a smooth finish once. Where rough scoring is required, a stiff broom made of steel wire or coarse fiber should be used. Brooming should be done in such a way that the direction of the scoring is at right angles to the direction of the traffic. (See Page 145 for additional finishing information.)

CURING CONCRETE

As previously mentioned, concrete hardens as a result of the HYDRATION of the cement by the water. Freshly placed concrete contains more than enough water to hydrate the cement completely, but if the concrete is not protected against drying out the water content, especially at and near the surface, will drop below that required for complete hydration.

The procedure called CURING is designed to prevent surface evaporation of water during the period between beginning and final set. Concrete takes a beginning set in about 1 hour; a final set takes about 7 days.

Curing is brought about by keeping the concrete surfaces continuously moist. Depending upon the type of structure, this may be done by spraying or ponding; by covering with continually moistened earth, sand, burlap, straw, or by covering with a water-retaining membrane.

Concrete made with ordinary cement should be kept moist for a minimum of 7 days. It should be protected from direct sunlight for at least the first 3 days of the curing period. Wet burlap is excellent for this purpose. Wood forms left in place also furnish good protection against sunlight, but they should be loosened at the time when they might safely be removed, and the space between the forms and the concrete should be flooded with water at frequent intervals.

Curing by ponding is usually confined to large slabs. An earth dike is built around the area to be cured, and the space inside the dike is filled with water.

A highway pavement, laid in the open air and perhaps under a hot sun, is especially likely to dry out rapidly. It is vital that the pavement receive full and continuous protection for the full time set in the specifications, but it is

133.257

Figure 6-45.—Burlap mats used for curing.

during the first few days that pavement is most affected by drying. The first 24 hours are the most important of all.

In hot weather the pavement should be protected as soon as the last finishing operation is completed. This is best accomplished by placing a wet burlap or cotton-mat cover over the concrete and keeping the cover moist by sprinkling with a fine spray as shown in figure 6-45. This procedure will prevent HAIR CHECKS, or fine surface cracks which occur when the surface dries out much faster than the under-lying mass.

The coverings may be either burlap or cotton mats. Burlap covers consist of two or more layers of burlap having a combined weight of 14 ounces or more per square yard in a dry condition. Burlap should either be new or have been used only for curing concrete. Cotton mats and burlap strips should have a length, after shrinkage, at least 1 foot greater than necessary to cover the entire width and edges of the pavement lane. The mats should overlap each other at least 6 inches. The mats should be thoroughly wetted before placing and kept continuously wet and in intimate contact with the pavement edges and surface for the duration of the required curing period.

When using the waterproof-paper blankets or impermeable sheets, the surface of the concrete should be wetted with a fine spray of water and then covered with waterproof-paper blankets (fig. 6-46). Polyethylene coated burlap blankets or polyethylene sheets if available. The burlap of the polyethylene coated burlap should be thoroughly saturated with water before placing. The waterproof-paper blankets, polyethylene coated burlap blankets, or polyethylene sheeting should be in pieces large enough to cover the entire width and edges of the slab. (Polyethylene sheets carefully lapped will eliminate the necessity for two curing treatments. This material is also lighter, cheaper, and more easily handled than polyethylene coated burlap.) The sheets should be placed with the light-colored side up. Adjacent sheets should overlap not less than 12 inches with the lapped edges securely weighted down and cemented or taped to form a continuous cover and a completely closed joint. These coverings must be adequately weighted down to

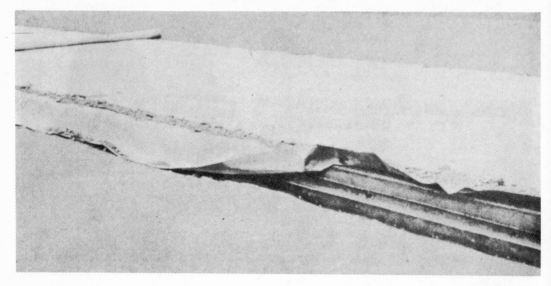

133.258

Figure 6-46.—Waterproof curing paper used after burlap curing.

prevent displacement or billowing from winds. Covering should be folded down over the side of the pavement edges and secured by a continuous bank of earth or other approved means, as shown in figure 6-46. Tears and holes must be patched immediately. The coverings should remain in place during the entire specified curing period.

Hay and straw absorb moisture readily and retain it well. The minimum depth of layer should be at least 6 inches. Whatever wet method of curing is used, the entire pavement from edge to edge must be KEPT wet during the entire curing period.

Much pavement curing is done by the mechanical application of membranes to the surface. The entire exposed surface of the concrete should be uniformly coated with a pigmented membrane curing compound. The curing compounds are either wax or resin-base. The concrete should not be allowed to dry out before the application of membrane. If any drying has occurred, the surface of the concrete should be moistened with a spray of water.

The curing compound is applied to the finished surfaces by an approved automatic spraying machine (fig. 6-47) as soon as the free water has disappeared. The spraying machine should be self-propelled and ride on the side forms or previously constructed pavement, straddling the newly paved lane. The machine should be equipped with spraying nozzle or nozzles that can be so controlled and operated as to completely and uniformly cover the pavement surface with the required amount of curing compound. The curing compound in the storage drum used for the spraying operation should be thoroughly and continuously agitated mechanically throughout the full depth of the drum during the application. Air agitation may be used only to supplement mechanical agitation. Spraying pressure should be sufficient to produce a fine spray and cover the surface thoroughly and completely with a uniform film. Spray equipment must be maintained in first-class mechanical condition and the spray nozzle should be provided with an adequate wind guard. The curing compound should be applied with an overlapping coverage that will give a two-coat application at a coverage of not more than 200 square feet per gallon for both coats.

The application of curing compound by hand-operated pressure sprayers is satisfactory only on odd widths or shapes of slabs and on concrete surfaces exposed by the removal of forms, as authorized. When application is made by

133.259

Figure 6-47.—Application of curing compound.

hand-operated sprayers, the second coat is applied in a direction approximately at right angles to the direction of the first coat. The compound should form a uniform, continuous, cohesive film that will not check, crack, or peel, and be free from pinholes and other imperfections. If discontinuities, pinholes, or abrasions exist, an additional coat should be applied to the affected areas within 30 minutes. Concrete surfaces that are subjected to heavy rainfall within 3 hours after the curing compound has been applied should be resprayed.

Necessary precautions should be taken to assure that the concrete is properly cured at the joints, but that no curing compound enters the joints that are to be sealed with joint-sealing compound. The top of the joint opening and the joint groove at exposed edges should be tightly sealed as soon as the joint-sawing operations have been completed. After application of the seal, the concrete in the region of the joint should be sprayed with curing compound. The method used for sealing the joint groove is also effective in preventing loss of moisture from the joint during the entire specified curing period.

Approved standby facilities for curing concrete pavement should be provided at a location readily accessible to the site of the work. These would be for use in the event of mechanical failure of the spraying equipment or any other conditions that might prevent correct application of the membrane-curing compound at the proper time.

Concrete surfaces to which membrane curing compounds have been applied should be adequately protected for the duration of the entire curing period from pedestrian and vehicular traffic, except as required for joint-sawing operations and surface tests, and from any other possible damage to the continuity of the membrane. Any area covered with curing compound that is damaged by subsequent construction operations within the curing period must be resprayed.

REMOVAL OF FORMS

Forms should, whenever possible, be left in place for the entire curing period (about 7 days). Forms which are to be re-used, however, must be stripped for re-use as soon as possible. In any event, forms must not be stripped until the concrete has hardened enough to hold its own weight and any other weight it may be carrying. The surface must be hard enough to remain uninjured and unmarked when reasonable care is used in stripping the forms.

Under ordinary circumstances, forms for various types of construction may be removed after intervals as follows:

Haunch boards (side forms) on
    girders beams . . . . 1 day
Soffits on girders and beams . . . 7 days
Floor slab forms . . . . 10 days
Wall forms . . . . 1 day
Column forms . . . . 3 days

After removing the forms the concrete should be inspected for surface defects. These defects may be rock pockets, inferior quality, ridges at form joints, bulges, bolt holes and form-stripping damage. Experience has proven that no steps can be omitted or carelessly performed without harming the serviceability of the work. If not properly performed, the repaired area will later become loose, will crack at the edges, and will not be watertight. Sometime repairs may not be necessary, but if they are necessary, they should be done immediately after stripping the forms (within 24 hours).

Various defects can be repaired in various ways; therefore, we will discuss repairing several defects that you may encounter when inspecting new concrete.

RIDGES and BULGES may be repaired by careful chipping followed by rubbing with a grinding stone.

Defective areas such as HONEYCOMB must be chipped out to solid concrete, the edges cut as straight as possible at right angles to the surface or slightly undercut to provide a key at the edge of the patch. If a shallow layer of mortar is placed on top of the honeycomb concrete, moisture will form in the voids and subsequent weathering will cause the mortar to spall off. Shallow patches may be filled with mortar placed in layers not more than 1/2 inch thick. Each layer is given a scratch finish to match the surrounding concrete by floating, rubbing or tooling or on formed surfaces by pressing the form material against the patch while the mortar is still in place.

Large or deep patches may be filled with concrete held in place by forms. These patches should be reinforced and doweled to the hardened concrete (fig. 6-48). Patches usually appear darker than the surrounding concrete. Some white cement should be used in the mortar or concrete used for patching if appearance is

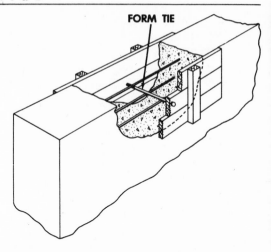

FORM TIE

133.260

Figure 6-48.—Repair of large volumes of concrete.

important. A trial mix should be tried to determine the proportion of white and gray cements to use. Before mortar or concrete is placed in patches, the surrounding concrete should be kept wet for several hours. A grout of cement and water mixed to the consistency of paint should then be brushed into the surfaces to which the new material is to be bonded. Curing should be started as soon as possible to avoid early drying. Damp burlap, tarpaulins and membrane curing compounds are useful for this purpose.

BOLT HOLES should be filled with grout carefully packed into place in small amounts. The grout should be mixed as dry as possible, with just enough water so that it will be tightly compacted when forced into place. Tie rod holes extending through the concrete can be filled with grout with a pressure gun similar to an automatic grease gun.

ROCK POCKETS or honeycomb and other defective concrete should be completely chipped out. The chipped-out hole should have sharp edges and should be so shaped that the grout patch will be keyed in place. This is shown in figure 6-49. The surface of all holes that are to be patched should be kept moist for several hours before applying the grout. Grout should be placed in these holes in layers not over 1/4 inch thick and should be well compacted. The grout should be allowed to set as long as possible before being used, to reduce the amount

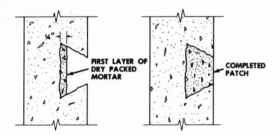

133.261

Figure 6-49.—Repairing concrete with
dry-packed mortar.

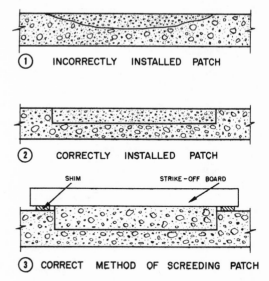

133.262
Figure 6-50.—Patching concrete.

of shrinkage and make a better patch. Each layer should be scratched rough to improve the bond with the succeeding layer, and the last layer smoothed to match the adjacent surface. Where absorptive form lining has been used, the patch can be made to match the rest of the surface by pressing a piece of the form lining against the fresh patch.

Feathered edges around a patch (1, fig. 6-50) will break down. The chipped area should be at least 1 inch deep with the edges at right angles to the surface (2, fig. 6-50). The correct method of screeding a patch is shown in 3, figure 6-50. The new concrete should project slightly beyond the surface of the old concrete. It should be allowed to stiffen and then troweled and finished to match the adjoining surfaces.

CONCRETE SAW

The concrete saw is used to cut longitudinal and transverse joints in finished concrete pavements. Several types of blades are available, the most common of which have either diamond or carborundum cutting surfaces. The diamond blade is used for hard cutting and the carborundum blade for cuts after aggregate has been displaced by vibration. The unit is small and can be operated by one man. (See fig. 6-51.) Once the cut has been started, the machine will provide its own tractive power. A water spray is used to flush the saw cuttings from the cutting area and to cool the cutting blade.

Considering that concrete saws cost almost as much as a new car, it is surprising how little attention is often given to proper breaking-in, maintenance and storage.

You would not take a new car and run it at 90 mph, but many operators will run a new engine at top speed and maximum load from the very beginning.

The following suggestions apply to all makes of concrete saws, and if followed carefully, will prolong their useful life many times.

A new engine should be operated at low speeds (1000-1200 rpm) for an hour without any load. The speed should then be increased gradually over a period of 2 hours until it is up to governed speed. Only after this break-in period should the engine be subjected to any load. If the saw has a water pump (for cooling the saw blade) it should be disconnected during this period.

Always operate the engine at proper governed top speed. Blade life can be seriously reduced if the engine is running too slowly. For the same reason, don't use 12-in. diameter blades on 18-in. blade capacity saws, which have a slower blade shaft speed.

Concrete sawing creates a sludge which is deposited on the engine cooling fan and in the air passages. This can cause serious overheating unless removed regularly. Air cleaners must be inspected daily. Crank case oil should be checked daily and changed every 50 hours. Use only regular gasoline.

Many saws have hydraulic pumps for raising and lowering of the blade and variable speed

133.18

Figure 6-51.—Concrete saw.

transmissions for self-propulsion. It is most important to use the correct oils as specified in these systems. Under no circumstances should brake fluid be added. The transmissions can be damaged seriously if the proper fluid level is not maintained. Always refer to the manufacturers' manual for information on maintenance and repairs of the machine.

Most concrete saws have a slight tendency to lead off from a straight line when sawing, since the blade is located to the right and outside of the four wheels. Therefore, they require a minimum amount of "steering" to keep them cutting in a straight line. However, most saws have an adjustment built in to compensate for lead-off. When steering becomes too hard,

consult the manufacturer's handbook for corrective action.

Two types of blades are used for the cutting of concrete: diamond blades, and abrasive blades.

Diamond blades have segments, made from a sintered mixture of industrial diamonds and metal powders, which are brazed to a steel disc. They are generally used for old concrete, asphalt and green concrete containing the harder aggregates, and must always be used wet. Many grades of diamond blades are available to suit the conditions of the job.

Twelve inch diameter is the most popular size of diamond blades. It allows a depth of cut of about 3 1/4 in. Larger size blades are used for deeper cuts.

Low cost, abrasive blades are now widely used to cut green concrete with some of the softer aggregates such as limestone, dolomite, coral or slag. These blades are made from a mixture of silicon carbide grains and a resin bond, which is pressed and baked. In many cases, even some of the medium hard aggregates can be cut if the step cutting method is employed: two or more saws cut the same joint, but each one cuts only a part of the total depth. This principle is also used on the longitudinal saw which has two individually adjustable cutting heads. When cutting a total depth of 2 1/2 in., the leading blade cuts about an inch deep and the trailing blade, which is slightly narrower, cuts to the remaining depth.

Abrasive blades are made in 14 in. and 18 in. diameters and in various thicknesses to cut joints from 1/4 in. to 1/2 in. wide.

When is the best time to saw green concrete? In the case of abrasive blades, there is only one answer: as soon as the concrete will support the equipment and the joint can be cut with a minimum of raveling. In the case of diamond blades, two factors must be considered. In the interest of long blade life, sawing should be delayed, but control of random cracking makes it necessary to saw at the transverse joints as early as possible. Where transverse joints are spaced closely, every second or third joint can be cut initially and the rest later. Sawing of longitudinal joints can be delayed as much as 7 days or longer.

PLACING CONCRETE IN WATER

If placement of concrete underwater is necessary, it should be done by the best methods available.

Concrete can be placed under water by several methods. For best results, concrete should not be placed in water having a temperature below 45°F and should not be placed in water flowing with a velocity greater than 10 feet per minute, although sacked concrete may be used for water velocities greater than this. If the water temperature is below 45°F, the temperature of the concrete when it is deposited should be above 60°F but in no case above 80°F. If the water temperature is above 45°F, no temperature precautions need be taken. Cofferdams or forms must be tight enough to reduce the current to less than 10 feet per minute through the space to be concreted. Pumping of water should not

be permitted while concrete is being placed or for 24 hours thereafter.

The tremie method involves a device shown in figure 6-52. A tremie is a pipe having a funnel-shaped upper end into which the concrete is fed. The pipe must be long enough to reach from a working platform above water level to the lowest point at which the concrete is to be deposited. Frequently the lower end of the pipe is equipped with a gate, permitting filling before insertion in water. This gate can be opened from above at the proper time. The bottom or discharge end is kept continuously buried in newly placed concrete, and air and water are excluded from the pipe by keeping it constantly filled with concrete. The tremie should be lifted slowly to permit the concrete to flow out. Care must be taken not to lose the seal at the bottom. If lost, it is necessary to raise the tremie, plug the lower end, and lower the tremie into position again. The tremie should not be moved laterally through the deposited concrete. When it is necessary to move the tremie, it should be lifted out of the concrete and moved to the new position, keeping the top surface of the concrete as level as possible. A number of tremies should be used if the concrete is to be deposited over a large area. They should be spaced on 20- to 25-foot centers. Concrete should be supplied at a uniform rate to all tremies with no interruptions at any of them. Pumping from the mixer is the best method of supplying the concrete. Large tremies can be suspended from a crane boom and can be easily raised and lowered with the boom. Concrete that is placed with a tremie should have a slump of about 6 inches and a cement content of seven sacks per cubic yard of concrete. About 50 percent of the total aggregate should be sand and the maximum coarse aggregate size should be from 1 1/2 to 2 inches.

Concrete can be placed at considerable depth below the water surface by means of the open-top BUCKET method. This bucket has a drop bottom and is shown in fig. 6-53 and fig. 6-35. Concrete placed by this method can be slightly stiffer than that placed by the tremie method but it should still contain seven sacks of cement per cubic yard. The bucket is completely filled and the top covered with a canvas flap. The flap is attached to one side of the bucket only. The bucket is lowered slowly into the water so that the canvas will not be displaced. Concrete must not be discharged from the bucket before the surface upon which the concrete is to be placed

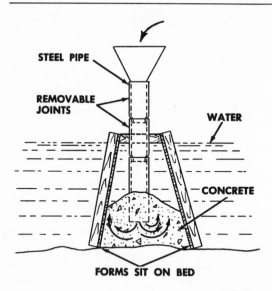

STEEL PIPE

REMOVABLE
JOINTS

WATER

CONCRETE

FORMS SIT ON BED

133.20

Figure 6-52.—Placing concrete under
water with a tremie.

has been reached. Soundings should be made
frequently so that the top surface is kept
level.

In an emergency, concrete can be placed
under water by the SACK method. Jute sacks
of about 1-cubic foot capacity, filled about two-
thirds full, are lowered into the water, preferably
shallow water. These sacks are placed in header
and stretcher course, interlocking the entire
mass. A header course is placed so that the
length of the sack is at right angles to the direction in which the stretcher-course sacks are
laid. Cement from one sack seeps into adjacent
sacks and they are thus bonded together. No
attempt should be made to compact concrete
under water, for experience has shown that the
less the concrete is disturbed after placement,
the better it will be.

PRECAST CONCRETE

Precasting is the fabrication of a structural
member at a place other than its final position
of use. It can be done anywhere although this
procedure is best adapted to a factory or yard.
Job-site precasting is not uncommon for large
projects. Precast concrete can be produced in
several different shapes and sizes, including
piles, girders and roof members. Prestressed
concrete is especially well adapted to precasting
techniques.

Generally, structural members including
standard highway girders, poles, electric poles,

133.19

Figure 6-53.—Placing concrete in water by using the
bucket and the tremie pipe.

masts and building members are precast by factory methods unless the difficulty or impracticability of transportation makes job-site casting more desirable.

PRECAST CONCRETE FLOOR AND ROOF SLABS, WALLS, AND PARTITIONS

The most commonly used precast slabs or panels for FLOOR and ROOF DECKS are the channel and double-T types. See figure 6-54.

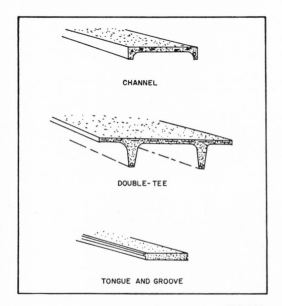

CHANNEL

DOUBLE-TEE

TONGUE AND GROOVE

133.263
Figure 6-54.—Typical precast planks.

The channel slab vary in size with a depth ranging from 9 to 12 inches, width 2 to 5 ft, thickness 1 to 2 inches and have been used in spans up to 50 ft. If desired or needed, the legs of the channels may extend across the ends; and if used in combination with the top-slab it may be stiffened with occasional cross-ribs. Wire mesh may be used in the top slab for reinforcement. The longitudinal grooves located along the top of the channel legs may be grouted to form keys between adjacent slabs.

The double-T slab vary in size from 4 to 6 ft in width, 9 to 16 in depth, and have been used in spans as long as 50 feet also. When the top slab

size range from 1 1/2 to 2 inches in thickness, it should be reinforced with wire mesh.

Welding matching plates are ordinarily used to connect the supporting members to the floor and roof slabs.

Panels precast in a horizontal position, in a casting yard or on the floor of the building, are ordinarily used in the make-up of bearing and nonbearing WALLS and PARTITIONS. These panels are placed in their vertical position by cranes or by the tilt-up procedure.

Usually, these panels are solid reinforced slabs 5 to 8 inches in thickness, and the length vary according to the distances between columns or other supporting members. When windows and door openings are cast in the slabs, extra reinforcements should be installed around the openings.

A concrete floor slab with a smooth regular surface can be used as a casting surface. When casting on the smooth surface, the casting surface should be covered with some form of liquid or sheet material to prevent bonding between the surface and the wall panel. The upper surface of the panel may be finished as regular concrete is finished by troweling, floating, or brooming.

SANDWICH PANELS are panels that consist of two thin dense reinforced concrete face slabs separated by a core of insulating material such as lightweight concrete, cellular glass, plastic foam, or some other rigid insulating material; and these panels are sometimes used for exterior walls to provide additional heat insulation. The thickness of the sandwich panel vary from 5 to 8 inches in thickness and the face slabs are tied together with wire, small rods, or in some other manner. Welded or bolted matching plates are also used to connect the wall panels to the building frame, top and bottom. Calking on the outside and grouting on the inside should be used to make the points between the wall panels watertight.

PRECAST CONCRETE JOISTS, BEAMS, GIRDERS, AND COLUMNS

Small closely spaced beams used in floor construction are usually called JOISTS; however, these same beams whenever used in roof construction are called PURLINS. The cross sections of these beams are shaped like a T or an I. The ones with the inverted T-sections are usually used in composite construction where they support cast-in-place floor or roof slabs.

BEAMS and GIRDERS are terms usually applied to the same members, but the one with the longer span should be referred to as the girder. Beams and girders may be conventional precast design or prestressed. Most of the beams will be I-shaped unless the ends are rectangular. The T-shaped ones can also be used.

Precast concrete COLUMNS may be solid or hollow. If the hollow type is desired, heavy cardboard tubing should be used to form the core. A looped rod is cast in the column footing and projects upward into the hollow core to help hold the column upright. An opening should be left in the side of the column so that the column core can be filled with grout, this way the looped rod becomes embedded to form an anchor. (The opening is dry-packed.)

ADVANTAGES

Precast concrete has the greatest advantage when there are identical members to be cast, because the same forms can be used several times. In addition to using the same forms precast concrete has other advantages such as:

Control on the quality of concrete.
Smoother surfaces, and plastering is not necessary.
Less storage space is needed.
Concrete member can be cast under all weather conditions.
Better protection for curing.
Weather conditions does not affect erection.
Faster erection time.

HANDLING

Precast concrete should not be lifted or otherwise subjected to strain until the concrete has attained the specified strength or until after the specified curing period. Except as otherwise specified, casting forms should not be removed earlier than 24 hours after placing the concrete. Precast concrete moved prior to completion of the curing period or before the concrete has attained specified strength, should be handled according to an approved procedure, with equipment of an approved type. Care should be taken to ensure that the precast member is not overstressed or otherwise damaged during the specified curing period. Precast members, including piles, should not be skidded, rolled, driven, or subjected to full design load until they have attained their 28-day strengths as indicated by cylinders made from the same concrete, at the same time as the precast concrete, and cured in the same manner. Handling of cured precast members should be either as specified or indicated, or as approved.

STEAM CURING

Use of steam curing is particularly advantageous under certain conditions, chiefly because of the higher curing temperature and the fact that moisture conditions are favorable. This type of curing is permitted by NavFac in the manufacture of precast units. Its benefits are also realized in connection with the use of live steam for cold-weather protection of concrete. Steam-cured precast units attain strength so rapidly that the forms can be removed and re-used very soon after concrete placing.

Data on early strength development of concrete cured with steam at various temperatures between 100° and 200°F are presented in figure 6-55. Greatest acceleration in strength gain and minimum loss in ultimate strength are obtained at temperatures between 130° and 165°F. Higher temperatures produce greater strengths at very early ages, but there are severe losses in strength at ages greater than 2 days. Precast concrete pipe is usually cured at temperatures ranging from 100° to 150°F. Under such conditions the loss in ultimate strength is relatively small. Use of steam curing in winter to maintain the required initial concrete temperature of 50°F rarely involves an ambient temperature around the concrete in excess of 100°F.

A delay of 2 to 6 hours prior to steam curing will result in higher strength at 24 hours than would be obtained if steam curing were commenced immediately after filling of the forms. If the temperature is between 100° and 165°F a delay of 2 to 4 hours will give good results; for higher temperatures, the delay should be greater.

It is desirable that the insides and outsides of pipe sections (and both sides of other concrete sections) be simultaneously exposed to the steam curing, especially in cold weather, in order to avoid stress-producing temperature differences in the concrete.

The necessary duration of steam curing depends on the concrete mix, the temperature, and the desired results.

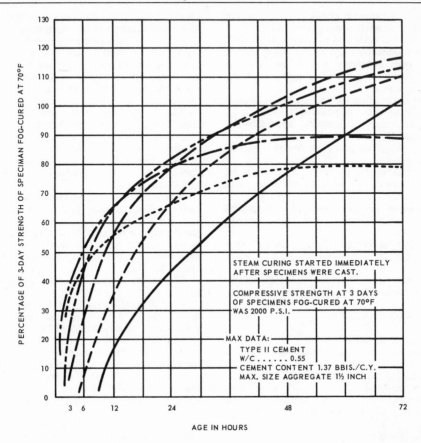

STEAM CURING STARTED IMMEDIATELY
AFTER SPECIMENS WERE CAST.

COMPRESSIVE STRENGTH AT 3 DAYS
OF SPECIMENS FOG-CURED AT 70°F
WAS 2000 P.S.I.

MAX DATA:
TYPE II CEMENT
W/C 0.55
CEMENT CONTENT 1.37 BBIS./C.Y.
MAX. SIZE AGGREGATE 1½ INCH

PERCENTAGE OF 3-DAY STRENGTH OF SPECIMAN FOG-CURED AT 70°F

AGE IN HOURS

133.24

Figure 6-55.—Effect of steam curing at temperatures below 200°F
on the compressive strength of concrete at early ages.

CONCRETE SAFETY

In dealing with any type of work there should be a certain degree of safety involved; so to help you do your concrete work on the safe side we will discuss the various safety precautions concerning concrete.

CONCRETE PLACEMENT AND FORM CONSTRUCTION

Form construction and concrete placement have pecularities in each job, however, certain natural conditions will prevail in all situations. Wet concrete will always develop hydrostatic pressure and strain on forms. Therefore, all stakes, braces, walers, ties, and shebolts should be properly secured before placing any concrete.

The use of safety belts by personnel tying reinforcing bars in high places will expedite the job and provide safety at all time.

Careless nailing and exposed nails in form work cause accidents, all nailing should be correctly placed and secured.

All personnel placing concrete in elevated or high wall forms should wear hard hats, shirt sleeves should be rolled down and gloves should be worn. These precautions are for safety first and also to assist in decreasing the exposure of skin to "cement poisoning."

A supervisor should check all forms for tightness prior to each pour.

If concrete buckets and cranes are used in pouring, each bucket should be provided with a tag line or two, depending on the location. A man should never ride a free swinging concrete bucket during a pour.

Adequate scaffolding should be built to permit men to stand clear of pouring areas.

Tools, particularly hammers, should be inspected frequently.

Mud sills should be placed under shoring that rests in the ground.

Raising of large form panels should not be attempted in heavy gusts of wind either by hand or by crane.

Only workmen actually engaged in stripping the forms should be permitted in the immediate work area.

Stripped forms should be piled immediately to avoid congestion, exposed nails, and other hazards.

Wires under tension should be cut with caution to avoid backlash.

SPOUTING AND CHUTES

All chutes and spouting used in concrete pours should be clean and well supported by proper bracing and guys.

When spouting and chutes run overhead the area beneath must be cleared and barricaded during placing to eliminate the danger of falling concrete or possible collapse causing injuries.

CONCRETE BUCKETS

Concrete buckets must be checked thoroughly before using for proper functioning of discharge gate, sound handles and lift bucket.

All hooks that lift and carry concrete buckets should be moused properly to prevent loss of load. Careful inspection of rigging cables should be routine prior to each pour. Closure hooks will not require mousing.

All concrete handling equipment must be thoroughly cleaned at the end of each work period. It must be remembered that all splattered and set concrete on gear adds to the weight of the dead load cutting the carrying capacity and function of the equipment.

MIXERS AND PAVERS

All gears, chains, and rollers of mixers should be properly guarded. All moving parts cleaned and properly serviced so as to give safe performance of the equipment.

Pavers should be equipped with a loud warning bell to be used in advance of any movement or change of direction. During night operations, all equipment should be equipped with sufficient flood and spot lights to make the perimeter of the operations clearly visible. The pouring bucket and the boom of the paver operating controls should have a synchronized warning device to function automatically with the motion of either the boom or the traveling bucket.

Skip loader cables and brakes must be inspected frequently to prevent injuries caused by falling skips.

Whenever working under an elevated skip is unavoidable, the skip must be shored up to prevent it from falling in the event that the brake should fail or be accidentally released.

The mixer operator must never lower the skip without first making sure that there is no one under it.

The area around the mixer must be kept clear.

Dust protection equipment must be issued to men engaged in handling cement, and the men must wear the equipment when so engaged. Men should stand with backs to the wind whenever possible, to prevent cement and sand from being blown into eyes and faces.

Whenever the mixer drum is being cleaned, the switches must be open, the throttles closed, and the control mechanism locked in the OFF position.

Whenever possible, a flagman or watchman should be stationed near the mixer to warn all hands when a batch truck is backing up to the skip. The watchman should use a whistle to warn any personnel in the danger zone. DANGER—KEEP AWAY signs should be placed where they can readily be seen.

CONCRETE BATCH PLANT OPERATIONS

All personnel working in Batch Plant Area should wear hard hats at all times.

While men are working on or in conveyor line areas, the switches and controls are to be secured and tagged so that no one can engage them until all personnel are clear.

When hoppers are being loaded with clamshell or other loaders, men should stay away from the area of falling aggregate.

The scale operator should be the only man on the scale platform during batching operations.

Housekeeping of charging area is important and men will do all possible to keep the area clean and free of spoiled material or overflow.

Debris in aggregate causes much of the damage to conveyors, so keep the material clean at all times.

When batch operations are conducted at night, good maximum lighting is a must.

Respirators are to be worn by all personnel handling bag or bulk cement.

Any cut or injury should get immediate attention so as to avoid infection.

Particular attention should be given to any rash or other irregularities of the skin as it might indicate "cement poisoning."

Personnel working in Batch Plants should use good eye hygiene as continual neglect of eye care can have serious consequences.

VAPOR TYPES GOGGLES SHOULD BE WORN BY PERSONNEL IN BATCH PLANT OPERATIONS.

HOIST, CRANES, AND DERRICKS

When HOIST, CRANES, and DERRICKS are to be used on a project, the responsibility of operation should be with the Equipment Operator but the responsibility for safe movement, hooking up to the load, and giving of signals should be with the Builder in charge. The supervisory Builder will check all rigging before the signalman will give any signals. The signalman and the Equipment Operator should agree on any special conditions other than standard signals before all operations begin.

The condition of the crane, hoist and derricks and the components parts of each should be inspected by the Equipment Operator daily.

A tagline, or guide rope should be used on loads that are liable to swing while being hoisted. They should be handled by capable men under the direction of the petty officer in charge of the movement.

Care should be exercised to prevent any damage to scaffolds or buildings or existing structures.

Personnel should not ride loads or walk under them while being lifted.

Loads should not be swung or lifted over men working.

Care should be used to keep crane on good footing at all times.

When using a crane, survey the area and be sure that the boom will be clear of electrical wire at all times. The minimum allowable distance from an energized electrical wire is ten (10) feet.

SUPERVISION

Supervision may be defined in a number of ways. The terms "management" and "administration" are related to an overlap with supervision; in fact, supervision is often considered to be a part of management, which is a broader term. We are not concerned with the definitions of these terms here except to indicate in a general way what is included in supervision. Very simply supervision, as the term is used here, means overseeing and directing the work of others.

Supervision, then, means working with people. A good supervisor knows how to get a job done efficiently by getting the most out of his men. This is perhaps the basic difference between a supervisor who is merely technically competent and one who knows how to get maximum production. It is absolutely essential, of course, for a supervisor to be competent in his specialty. Competence alone, however, will rarely get the job done when he has to direct the work of others. As well as doing, knowing and understanding the job to be done, a good supervisor must understand the capabilities of his men, and must know the techniques of good supervision. In short, a good supervisor is a good leader—another term which may be defined in many ways and which has many meanings to different people.

However, there are at least three things that should help you to become a successful supervisor; and they are know your job, know your men, and job analyzation. With these thoughts in mind we will continue our discussion on supervision; beginning with knowing your job.

KNOW YOUR JOB

The Builder Rating cuts across a good many occupational fields—preparing and transporting mix, placing mix, finishing surfaces, removing forms, and batching and paving, to name some of the main specialties involving concrete operations. As you go up in rate, you will learn to become an expert in various fields—probably more of an expert in some than in others, depending upon your experience, talent, and interests. In a construction battalion you may be assigned anyone of a number of supervisory duties with which you must become thoroughly familiar. For example, you might serve as squad leader in a heavy construction platoon of Company C; in this capacity you might direct various concrete operations, form construction and operate the concrete batching plant. Or you might be assigned to supervise other jobs of building construction operations. A construction squad leader may also be assigned to direct framing, painting, masonry and sawmill operations.

Any of the duties listed requires a great deal of technical knowledge of the tools or equipment used in building construction operations. In addition, such duties require a knowledge of flow of work, relationship between projects, and responsibilities of the various persons involved. Certain duties require supervising as many as 25 men. Unless you thoroughly understand lines of authority, the job to be accomplished, the equipment required, limitations of the equipment, and the capabilities of your crew, you are likely to have trouble in meeting schedules and handling your responsibilities properly.

KNOW YOUR CREW

Knowing the job to be done is the first step in achieving maximum production. Knowing your crew is the second step, and thirdly it is as important as knowing the job.

When you learn that a new man is being assigned to your crew, learn what you can about him; ask to see his record. Talk to him when he reports; find out what he has done and likes to do. Finally, observe him closely in various work situations; you will soon learn what type of person he is.

If a new BU3 is assigned to your crew, you can be certain that he has checked out in the practical factors for his rate, and that he has passed the servicewide exam. Without investigation, however, you cannot tell whether he is an expert concrete finished or whether he barely knows how to mix concrete, or whether he is ready for promotion to BU2, or whether he has just made his present rate. His experience and capabilities will have a very important effect upon the assignment that he can handle.

You will not know whether the new man is one whom you can give very brief instructions and expect the job to be done, or whether he requires close supervision in getting the job done.

From the foregoing, it is obvious that a good supervisor needs to know the strong points and weak points of each crew member. You need to know your crew in order to make intelligent decisions about assignments, needed training, and recommendations for advancement in rating among other things.

JOB ANALYZATION

The job to be accomplished should be carefully analyzed to determine the best procedures to get it done most effectively. Assume that you are working on a concrete paving project, the following are factors that you should consider in analyzing the job.

Type of construction. The type of construction is determined by the purpose for which the project is intended. This, of course, will have been determined by higher authority (Battalion Operations). Anyone supervising a concrete crew must know the type of construction required in order to be able to make plans for the amount and type of cement, aggregated requirements, and the like.

Priorities established by work directive. You must know the deadlines for completing your phase of the project. Deadlines, too, will be set forth by higher authority (Battalion Operations). Among other things, these deadlines will determine whether it is necessary to work your crew in shifts.

Equipment and personnel available. A knowledge of equipment and personnel available to do the job is basic to job analysis and planning. You must determine the condition of the equipment to be used and must ascertain the capabilities of the crew assigned to do the job.

The type of materials to be used on the job and their location in relation to the construction site are an important factor to be considered. For example, the aggregate, water, and cement being used in the mix, and the amount of form building necessary.

Amount of concrete mix necessary and the method of finishing required.

Weather and climatic forecasts. Many types of construction operations must come to a halt during heavy rains or other unfavorable weather conditions. In some parts of the world, operations may not be possible during the rainy season. Expected weather conditions, then, have an obvious and important effect upon how the job will proceed.

Method of curing and stripping.

Jobs which can be performed concurrently. In considering the entire project, you can see that certain operations must wait until others are completed. Sometimes it may be possible for other operations to go on at the same time. For example, the preparation of forms might be going on at the same time as concrete paving operations in another location. Considering the personnel and equipment available, you should have as many jobs as possible being performed concurrently if this will speed up completion of the project.

Security requirements. The problems of security will determine whether or not you must post guards around the job site at night. Security requirements can vary tremendously, depending upon the location of the job being performed and whether or not there is a peacetime or wartime situation.

As stated previously supervision is hard to define and even more so in the BU 3 & 2 case. But, we definitely believe that with the proper attitude and workmanship, you can be a very good crew leader.

DUE TO LATE QUAL CHANGES THE FOLLOWING
COPY IS ADDED TO THIS CHAPTER

GRINDING

When properly constructed of materials of good quality, ground floors are dustless, dense, easily cleaned, and attractive in appearance. When grinding is specified, it should be started after the surface has hardened sufficiently to prevent dislodgment of aggregate particles and should be continued until the coarse aggregate is exposed. The machines used should be of approved type with stones that cut freely and rapidly. The floor is kept wet during the grinding process, and the cuttings are removed by squeegeeing and flushing with water. After the surface is ground, airholes, pits, and other blemishes are filled with a thin grout composed of 1 part No. 80-grain carborundum grit and 1 part portland cement. This grout is spread over the floor and worked into the pits with a straightedge, after which it is rubbed into the floor with the grinding machine. When the fillings have hardened for 7 days the floor receives a final grinding to remove the film and to give the finish a polish. All surplus material is then removed by washing thoroughly.

SACK-RUBBED FINISH

A sack-rubbed finish is sometimes necessary when the appearance of formed concrete falls considerably below expectations. This treatment is performed after all required patching and correction of major imperfections have been completed.

The surfaces are thoroughly wetted and sack rubbing is commenced while they are still damp. The mortar used consists of 1 part cement; 2 parts, by volume, of sand passing a No. 16 screen; and enough water so that the consistency of the mortar will be that of a thick cream. It may be necessary to blend the cement with white cement to obtain a color that will match that of the surrounding concrete surface. The mortar is rubbed thoroughly over the area with clean burlap or a sponge rubber float, so as to fill all pits. While the mortar in the pits is still plastic, the surface should be rubbed over with a dry mix of the above proportions and material. This serves to remove all of the excess plastic material and place enough dry material in the pits to stiffen and solidify the mortar so that the fillings will be flush with the surface. No material should remain on the surface except that within the pits. Curing of the surface is then continued.

RUBBED FINISH

A rubbed finish is required when a uniform and attractive surface must be obtained although it is possible to produce a surface of satisfactory appearance without rubbing if plywood or lined forms are used. The first rubbing should be done with coarse carborundum stones as soon as the concrete has hardened so that the aggregate is not pulled out. The concrete should then be cured until final rubbing. Finer carborundum stones are used for the final rubbing. The concrete should be kept damp while being rubbed. Any mortar used to aid in this process and left on the surface should be kept damp for 1 to 2 days after it sets in order to cure properly. The mortar layer should be kept to the minimum as it is likely to scale off and mar the appearance of the surface.

CHAPTER 7
MASONRY

The American Standard Building Code Requirements for Masonry defines masonry as "a built-up construction or combination of building units of such materials as clay, shale, glass, gypsum or stone, set in mortar or plain concrete." However, for our purpose, the commonly accepted definition of masonry, or unit masonry as it is sometimes called, is a construction made up of prefabricated masonry units (such as concrete blocks, structural clay tile, brick) laid in various ways and joined together with mortar.

In the following sections, an explanation is given of various operational techniques, tool usage, and equipment needed by the Builder.

The sections are so written as to explain the various operations needed, to thoroughly complete a wall whether the Builder is to work with concrete block, structural clay tile, stone, or brick.

MASONRY TOOLS AND EQUIPMENT

The mason's tools include trowel, bolster, hammer and jointer; these tools are illustrated in figure 7-1.

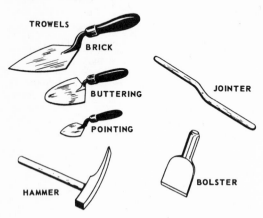

TROWELS
BRICK
BUTTERING
POINTING
HAMMER
JOINTER
BOLSTER

29.164

Figure 7-1.—Mason's trowels, bolster, hammer, and jointer.

The mason's TROWEL may be a BRICK, a BUTTERING, or a POINTING trowel, as shown in figure 7-1. The trowel is used for mixing, placing, and spreading mortar; the hammer is used for tapping masonry units into the beds where necessary, and for chipping and rough-cutting. For smoother cutting the BOLSTER (also called a BRICKCUTTING CHISEL or BRICK SET) shown in the figure is used. Breaking into bats and closures is done with the chisel peen on the MASON's HAMMER shown in the figure. Splitting and rough breaking is done with the head or flat of the hammer.

The JOINTER, of which there are several types besides the one shown in figure 7-1, is used for making various joint finishes which will be described later.

The mason must maintain a constant check on his courses to ensure that they are level and plumb; otherwise the courses will appear wavy and the plane surfaces warped. The equipment for this vital purpose consists of a length of line, a steel square and level, and a straightedge like the one shown in figure 7-2. The square is used to lay out corners and for other right-angle work. The mason's level is used exactly as the carpenter's level is in wood construction. The straightedge is used in conjunction with the level for leveling or plumbing long stretches.

A MORTAR BOARD for holding a supply of ready-to-use mortar should be constructed as shown in figure 7-3. If mortar is to be mixed by hand, it should be mixed in a MORTAR BOX like the one shown in figure 7-4. However, if the box is expected to be used over a period of time, it should be lined with some type of metal. The metal will make mixing easier and also prolong the life of the box. Other required equipment includes shovels, mortar hoes, wheelbarrows, and buckets.

MORTAR

There are two common types of masonry mortar: LIME MORTAR and PORTLAND CEMENT-LIME MORTAR. Lime mortar is normally used only in temporary work, from

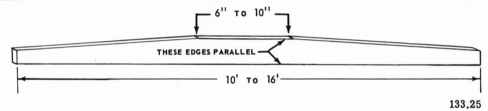

Figure 7-2.—Mason's straightedge.

133.25

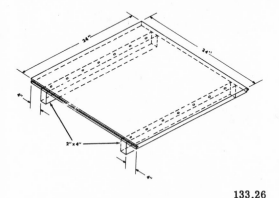

133.26

Figure 7-3.—Mortar board.

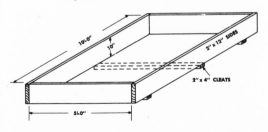

133.27

Figure 7-4.—Mortar box.

which the masonry units are to be salvaged for re-use. It is a mixture of sand, hydrated lime, and water proportioned so as to produce a plastic, workable paste. If the mortar sticks to the tools, add more sand; if it lacks cohesion and fails to adhere to the units, add more lime. If it is too stiff for easy mixing and troweling, add water.

Portland-cement-lime mortar is used for permanent masonry structures. Mortar can be made with portland cement, sand, and water only (leaving out the lime), but mortar of this type is hard to work. The addition of lime

greatly increases the workability and "fatness" of the mortar.

TYPE A portland cement-lime mortar is a strong mortar, intended primarily for use in reinforced masonry structures. The ingredient proportions for this type are approximately as follows:

1 sack cement
3 cu ft damp sand
13 lbs hydrated lime

TYPE B portland cement-lime mortar should not be used for reinforced masonry, but is strong enough for almost all other purposes. The ingredient proportions for this type are approximately as follows:

1 sack cement
6 cu ft damp sand
50 lbs hydrated lime

Sufficient mixing water should be added to obtain the desired consistency. If a large quantity of mortar is required, it should be mixed in a drum-type mixer similar to those used for mixing concrete. The mixing time should not be less than 3 minutes. All dry ingredients should be placed in the mixer first and mixed for 1 minute before adding the water.

Unless large amounts of mortar are required, the mortar is mixed by hand using a mortar box like the one shown in figure 7-4. Care must be taken to mix all the ingredients thoroughly to obtain a uniform texture. As in machine mixing, all dry material should be mixed first. A steel drum filled with water should be kept close to the mortar box for the water supply. A second drum of water should be available for shovels and hoes when not in use.

ESTIMATING THE REQUIRED MATERIALS

You will be able to use rule 38 for calculating the amount of raw material needed to mix one yard of mortar without a great deal of paper

147

work. This calculating rule will not give the accurate amount of required raw materials for large masonry construction jobs; you will have to use the absolute volume or weight formulae. However, in most cases, particularly in advanced base construction, you can use the rule of thumb to quickly estimate the quantities of required raw materials.

Builders have found that it takes about 38 cubic feet of raw materials to make 1 cubic yard of mortar. In using the 38 calculating rule for mortar, take the rule number and divide it by the sum of the quantity figures specified in the mix. For example, let us assume that the building specifications call for a 1 : 3 mix for mortar $1 + 3 = 4—38 \div 4 = 9 \ 1/2$. You will then need 9 1/2 sacks or 9 1/2 cubic feet of cement. In order to calculate the amount of fine aggregates (sand), you simply multiply 9 1/2 by 3. The product 28 1/2 cubic feet is the amount of sand you need to mix one cubic yard of mortar using a 1 : 3 mix. The sum of the two required quantities should always equal the calculating rule 38. Therefore, you can always check in order to see if you are using the correct amounts. In the above example, 9 1/2 sacks of cement, plus 28 1/2 cubic feet of sand, equal 38.

CONCRETE MASONRY

Concrete masonry has become increasingly important as a construction material. Important technological developments in the manufacture and utilization of the units have accompanied the rapid increase in the use of concrete masonry. Concrete masonry walls properly designed and constructed will satisfy varied building requirements including fire, safety, durability, economy, appearance, utility, comfort, and good acoustics.

Concrete masonry units were at one time made only with cinder or slag, small-diameter aggregate, but they are now made for the most part like any other lightweight concrete, except that the maximum diameter of the coarse aggregate is about five-eighths of an inch. Concrete for units which will be exposed to the weather should contain at least 6 sacks of cement per cu yd.

Concrete units may be manufactured either by machine or by hand. A concrete block machine (shown in fig. 7-5) feeds a "dry" mix from a hopper into a mold and tamps it hard enough to allow the mold to be removed at once (as shown in fig. 7-6) and the block to be put aside for setting without losing its shape.

133.29
Figure 7-5.—Block machine.

In the hand method, a plastic mix is poured into sets of iron molds which are stripped after the concrete has set.

Blocks can be steam-cured to 70 percent of 28-day strength in about 15 hours. They can be ordinary damp-cured in about 7 days.

BLOCK SIZES AND SHAPES

Concrete building units are made in sizes and shaped to fit different construction needs. Units are made in full and half-length sizes as shown in figure 7-7. Concrete unit sizes are usually referred to by their nominal dimensions. A unit measuring 7 5/8 inches wide, 7 5/8 inches high and 15 5/8 inches long is referred to as an 8 X 8 X 16 inch unit. When it is laid in a wall with 3/8-inch mortar joints, the unit will occupy a space exactly 16 inches long and 8 inches high. Besides the basic 8 X 8 X 16 units, the illustration shows a smaller partition unit and other units which are used much as cut brick are in brick masonry.

The corner unit is, of course, laid at a corner or at some similar point where a smooth rather than a recessed end is required. The header unit is used in a backing course placed behind a brick face tier header course. Part of the block is cut away to admit the brick headers. The uses of the other specials shown are

133.30

Figure 7-6.—Removing block from
block machine.

self-evident. Besides the shapes shown in figure 7-7, a number of smaller shapes for various special purposes are available. Units may be cut to desired shapes with a bolster or, more conveniently and accurately, with a power-driven masonry saw such as that shown in figure 7-8.

BLOCK MORTAR JOINTS

The sides and the recessed ends of a concrete block are called the SHELL; and the material which forms, as it were, the partitions between the cores is called the WEB. Each of the long sides of a block is called a FACE SHELL, and each of the recessed ends is called an END SHELL. Bed joints on first courses and bed joints in column construction are mortared by spreading a 1-in. layer of mortar. This is called FULL MORTAR BEDDING. For most other bed joints, only the upper edges of the face shells need to be mortared. This is called FACE SHELL MORTAR BEDDING.

The vertical ends of the face shells, on either side of the end shells, are called the EDGES. Head joints may be mortared by buttering both edges of the block being laid, or by buttering one edge on the block being laid and the opposite edge on the block already in place.

MODULAR PLANNING

Concrete masonry walls should be laid out to make maximum use of full- and half-length units, thus minimizing cutting and fitting of units on the job. Length and height of wall, width and height of openings and wall areas between doors, windows, and corners should be planned to use full-size and half-size units which are usually available (fig. 7-9). This procedure assumes that window and door frames are of modular dimensions which fit modular full- and half-size units. Then, all horizontal dimensions should be in multiples of nominal full-length masonry units and both horizontal and vertical dimensions should be designed to be in multiples of 8 inches. Table 7-1 lists nominal length of concrete masonry walls by stretchers and table 7-2 lists nominal height of concrete masonry walls by courses. When units 8 X 4 X 16 are used, the horizontal dimensions should be planned in multiples of 8 inches (half-length units) and the vertical dimensions in multiples of 4 inches. If the thickness of the wall is greater or less than the length of a half unit, a special length unit is required at each corner in each course.

CONCRETE MASONRY WALL

After locating the corners of the wall, the Builder usually checks the layout by stringing out the blocks for the first course without mortar (fig. 7-10). A chalked snapline is useful to mark the footing and align the block accurately. A full bed of mortar is then spread and furrowed with the trowel to ensure plenty of mortar along the bottom edges of the face shells of the block for the first course (fig. 7-11). The corner block should be laid first and carefully positioned (fig. 7-12). All block should be laid with the thicker end of the face shell up to provide a larger mortar-bedding area (fig. 7-13). Mortar is applied only to the ends of the face shells for vertical joints. Several blocks can be placed on end and the mortar applied to the vertical face shells in one operation. Each block is then brought over

Table 7-1.—Nominal Length of Concrete Masonry Walls by Stretchers

(Actual length of wall is measured from outside edge to outside edge of units and is equal to the nominal length minus ⅜″ (one mortar joint).)

No. of stretchers	Nominal length of concrete masonry walls	
	Units 15⅝″ long and half units 7⅝″ long with ⅜″ thick head joints.	Units 11⅝″ long and half units 5⅝″ long with ⅜″ thick head joints.
1	1′ 4″	1′ 0″.
1½	2′ 0″	1′ 6″.
2	2′ 8″	2′ 0″.
2½	3′ 4″	2′ 6″.
3	4′ 0″	3′ 0″.
3½	4′ 8″	3′ 6″.
4	5′ 4″	4′ 0″.
4½	6′ 0″	4′ 6″.
5	6′ 8″	5′ 0″.
5½	7′ 4″	5′ 6″.
6	8′ 0″	6′ 0″.
6½	8′ 8″	6′ 6″.
7	9′ 4″	7′ 0″.
7½	10′ 0″	7′ 6″.
8	10′ 8″	8′ 0″.
8½	11′ 4″	8′ 6″.
9	12′ 0″	9′ 0″.
9½	12′ 8″	9′ 6″.
10	13′ 4″	10′ 0″.
10½	14′ 0″	10′ 6″.
11	14′ 8″	11′ 0″.
11½	15′ 4″	11′ 6″.
12	16′ 0″	12′ 0″.
12½	16′ 8″	12′ 6″.
13	17′ 4″	13′ 0″.
13½	18′ 0″	13′ 6″.
14	18′ 8″	14′ 0″.
14½	19′ 4″	14′ 6″.
15	20′ 0″	15′ 0″.
20	26′ 8″	20′ 0″.

45.730

Table 7-2.—Nominal Height of Concrete Masonry Walls by Courses

(For concrete masonry units 7⅝″ and 3⅝″ in height laid with ⅜″ mortar joints. Height is measured from center to center of mortar joints.)

No. of courses	Nominal height of concrete masonry walls	
	Units 7⅝″ high and ⅜″ thick bed joint	Units 3⅝″ high and ⅜″ thick bed joint
1	8″	4″.
2	1′ 4″	8″.
3	2′ 0″	1′ 0″.
4	2′ 8″	1′ 4″.
5	3′ 4″	1′ 8″.
6	4′ 0″	2′ 0″.
7	4′ 8″	2′ 4″.
8	5′ 4″	2′ 8″.
9	6′ 0″	3′ 0″.
10	6′ 8″	3′ 4″.
15	10′ 0″	5′ 0″.
20	13′ 4″	6′ 8″.
25	16′ 8″	8′ 4″.
30	20′ 0″	10′ 0″.
35	23′ 4″	11′ 8″.
40	26′ 8″	13′ 4″.
45	30′ 0″	15′ 0″.
50	33′ 4″	16′ 8″.

45.731

(fig. 7-14). After three or four blocks have been laid, the mason's level is used as a straightedge to assure correct alignment of the blocks. Then the blocks are carefully checked with the level and brought to proper grade and made plumb by tapping with the trowel handle (fig. 7-15). The first course of concrete masonry should be laid with great care, to make sure it is properly aligned, leveled, and plumbed, and to assure that succeeding courses, and finally the wall, are straight and true.

After the first course is laid, mortar is applied only to the horizontal face shells of the block (face-shell mortar bedding). Mortar for the vertical joints may be applied to the vertical faceshells of the block to be placed or to the block previously laid or both, to ensure well-filled joints (fig. 7-16). The corners of the wall

its final position and pushed downward into the mortar bed and against the previously laid block to obtain a well-filled vertical mortar joint

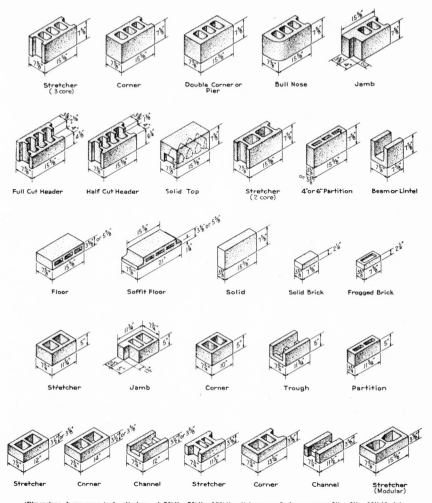

Stretcher (3 core) Corner Double Corner or Pier Bull Nose Jamb

Full Cut Header Half Cut Header Solid Top Stretcher (2 core) 4"or 6"Partition Beam or Lintel

Floor Soffit Floor Solid Solid Brick Frogged Brick

Stretcher Jamb Corner Trough Partition

Stretcher Corner Channel Stretcher Corner Channel Stretcher (Modular)

(Dimensions shown are actual unit sizes. A 7⅝" x 7⅝" x 15⅝" unit is commonly known as an 8" x 8" x 16" block.)

29.142(133F)

Figure 7-7.—Typical sizes and shapes of concrete masonry units.

are built first, usually four or five courses higher than the center of the wall. As each course is laid at the corner, it is checked with a level for alignment, for levelness, and plumbness as shown in figure 7-17. Each block is carefully checked with a level or straightedge to make certain that the faces of the block are all in the same plane to ensure true, straight walls. The use of a story or course-pole, a board with markings 8 inches apart, provides an accurate method of determining the top of the masonry for each course (fig. 7-18). Joints are 3/8-inch thick. Each course, in building the corners, is stepped back a half block and the Builder checks the horizontal spacing of the block by placing his

151

133.31

Figure 7-8.—Masonry saw.

133.265

Figure 7-10.—Stringing out blocks.

WRONG

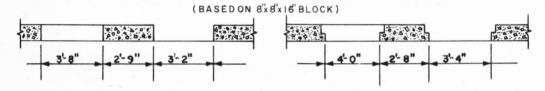

5'-0" 7'-0"

ELEVATION

SHADED PORTION INDICATES CUT MASONRY

RIGHT

4-8 7'-4"

ELEVATION

ALL MASONRY FULL OR HALF SIZE UNITS

(BASED ON 8"x8"x16" BLOCK)

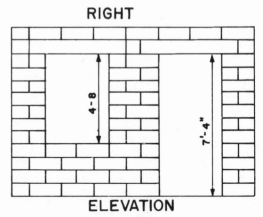

3'-8"   2'-9"   3'-2"

4'-0"   2'-8"   3'-4"

45.728

Figure 7-9.—Planning concrete masonry wall openings.

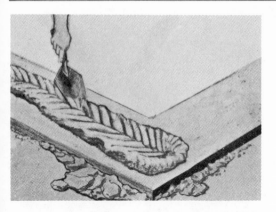

133.266
Figure 7-11.—Spread and furrow mortar bed.

133.268
Figure 7-13.—Blocks buttered for vertical joints.

133.267
Figure 7-12.—Position corner block.

133.269
Figure 7-14.—Positioning block.

level diagonally across the corners of the block (fig. 7-19).

When filling in the wall between the corners, a mason's line is stretched from corner to corner for each course and the top outside edge of each block is laid to this line. The manner of gripping the block is important. It should be tipped slightly towards the Builder so he can see the edge of the course below, enabling him to place the lower edge of the block directly over the course below (fig. 7-20). All adjustments to final position must be made while the mortar is soft and plastic. Any adjustments made after the mortar has stiffened will break the mortar bond and allow the penetration of

water. Each block is leveled and aligned to the mason's line by tapping lightly with the trowel handle. The use of the mason's level between corners is limited to checking the face of each block to keep it lined up with the face of the wall.

To assure good bond, mortar should not be spread too far ahead of actual laying of the block or it will stiffen and lose its plasticity. As each block is laid, excess mortar extruding from the joints is cut off with the trowel (fig. 7-21) and is thrown back on the mortar board to be reworked into the fresh mortar. Dead mortar that has been picked up from the scaffold or from the floor should not be used.

When installing the closure block, all edges of the opening and all four vertical edges of the closure block are buttered with mortar and the closure block is carefully lowered into place

LEVELING BLOCK

PLUMBING BLOCK

133.270

Figure 7-15.—Checking first course of blocks.

133.271

Figure 7-16.—Vertical joints.

either concave or V-shaped. Horizontal joints should be tooled first, followed by striking the vertical joints with a small S-shaped jointer. Mortar burrs remaining after tooling is completed should be trimmed off flush with the face of the wall with a trowel or removed by rubbing with a burlap bag or soft bristle brush.

Wood plates are fastened to tops of concrete masonry walls by anchor bolts 1/2 inch in diameter, 18 inches long and spaced not more than 4 feet apart. The bolts are placed in cores of the top two courses of block with the cores filled with concrete or mortar. Pieces of metal lath placed in the second horizontal mortar joint from the top of the wall and under the cores to be filled (fig. 7-24) will hold the concrete or mortar filling in place. The threaded end of the bolt should extend above the top of the wall.

CONTROL JOINTS

Control joints are continuous vertical joints built into concrete masonry walls to control cracking resulting from unusual stresses. The joints are intended to permit slight wall movement without cracking. Control joints should be laid up in mortar just as any other joint. Full- and half-length block are used to form a continuous vertical joint (fig. 7-25). If they are exposed to the weather or to view, they should

(fig. 7-22). If any of the mortar falls out leaving an open joint, the block should be removed and the procedure repeated.

Weathertight joints and neat appearance of concrete block walls are dependent on proper tooling. The mortar joints should be tooled after a section of the wall has been laid and the mortar has become "thumb-print" hard. Tooling (fig. 7-23) compacts the mortar and forces it tightly against the masonry on each side of the joint. All joints should be tooled

154

ALIGNING

LEVELING

PLUMBING

133.272

Figure 7-17.—Checking each course.

be calked. After the mortar is quite stiff, it should be raked out to a depth of about 3/4 inch to provide a recess for the calking material. A thin, flat calking trowel is used to force the calking compound into the joint. Another type of control joint can be constructed with building paper or roofing felt inserted in the end core of the block and extending the full height of the control joint (fig. 7-26). The paper or felt, cut to convenient lengths and wide enough to

133.273

Figure 7-18.—Use of story or course pole.

133.274

Figure 7-19.—Checking horizontal spacing
of block.

133.275

Figure 7-20.—Adjusting block between corners.

133.276

Figure 7-21.—Cutting off excess mortar.

133.277

Figure 7-22.—Installing closure block.

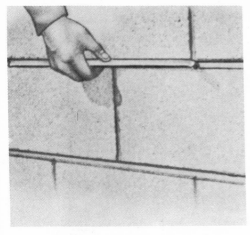

TOOLING HORIZONTAL JOINTS

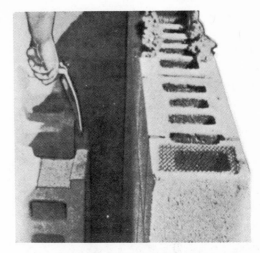

PLACING METAL LATH

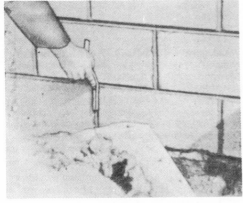

STRIKING VETERICAL JOINTS

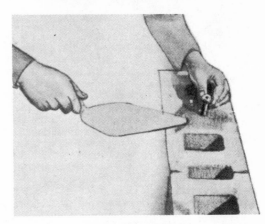

SETTING ANCHOR BOLT

133.278

Figure 7-23.—Tooling mortar joints.

133.279

Figure 7-24.—Installing anchor bolts on top of wall.

extend across the joint, prevents the mortar from bonding on one side of the joint. Sometimes control joint blocks are used if available.

To provide lateral support, metal ties can be laid across the joint in every other horizontal course.

Intersecting Walls

Intersecting concrete block bearing walls should not be tied together in a masonry bond,

except at the corners. Instead, one wall should terminate at the face of the other wall with a control joint at the point. Bearing walls are tied together with a metal tiebar 1/4 x 1 1/4 x 28 inches, with 2-inch right angle bends on each end (fig. 7-27). Tiebars are spaced not over 4 feet apart vertically. Bends at the ends of the tiebars are embedded in cores filled with mortar or concrete. Pieces of metal lath placed under

157

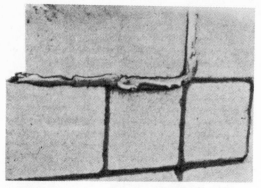

1 FULL AND HALF LENGTH BLOCK FOR JOINT

2 RAKING MORTAR FROM JOINT

133.280

Figure 7-25.—Control joint.

133.281

Figure 7-26.—Paper or felt used for
control joints.

the cores support the concrete or mortar filling as previously shown in figure 7-24.

To tie nonbearing block walls to other walls, strips of metal lath or 1/4-inch mesh galvanized hardware cloth are placed across the joint between the two walls (fig. 7-28), in alternate courses in the wall. When one wall is constructed first, the metal strips are built into the wall and later tied into the mortar joint of the second wall. Control joints are constructed where the two walls meet.

LINTELS

The top of openings for door and windows in masonry construction may be made in two different ways. One is to use a precast concrete lintel; in this way the opening can be formed before the door or window frame is set. The other method is to use the lintel block like that shown in figure 7-29. Here the frame is set in place and the block wall is built around it. Lintel blocks are used across the top. Reinforcing bars and concrete are placed in the lintel blocks. Window and door openings in masonry should be planned to bring the top or bottom of a course in line with the openings.

PATCHING AND CLEANING BLOCK WALLS

Any patching of the mortar joints or filling of holes left by nails or line pins should be done with fresh mortar.

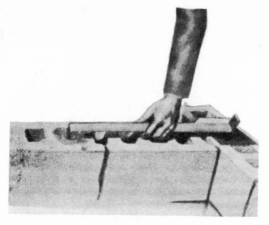

TIEBAR

FILLING CORE WITH MORTAR

133.282
Figure 7-27.—Tieing intersecting bearing walls.

USE OF METAL LATH

MORTAR JOINT BETWEEN WALLS

133.283
Figure 7-28.—Tieing intersecting nonbearing walls.

Hardened, embedded mortar smears cannot be removed and paint cannot be depended on to hide smears, so particular care should be taken to prevent smearing mortar into the surface of the block. Concrete block walls should not be cleaned with an acid wash to remove smears or mortar droppings. Mortar droppings that stick to the block wall should be allowed to dry before removal with a trowel (A, fig. 7-30). Most of the mortar can be removed by rubbing with a small piece of concrete (broken) block after the mortar is dry and hard (B, fig. 7-30). Brushing the rubbed spots will remove practically all of the mortar (C, fig. 7-30).

CUTTING CONCRETE BLOCKS

Concrete blocks are usually made in half sizes, as well as full-length units. However, it

159

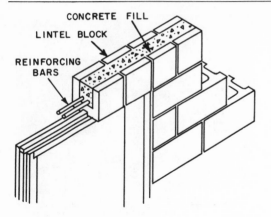

CONCRETE FILL

LINTEL BLOCK

REINFORCING BARS

133.37

Figure 7-29.—Lintel made from blocks.

is sometimes necessary to cut a block to fit a particular location. This can be done in two ways. The block may be scored with a bolster and broken along the score lines. Blocks may also be cut with a masonry saw as shown in figure 7-8. This saw is particularly useful when only a portion of the block is to be cut. For instruction on the operation and maintenance of the concrete saw, study the manufacturer's manual.

REINFORCED BLOCK WALLS

Block walls may be reinforced vertically or horizontally. To reinforce vertically, place reinforcing rods into the cores at the specified spacing and fill the cores with a relatively high slump concrete. Rebars (studs) should be placed at each corner and at both sides of each opening. The vertical rebars should generally be spaced a maximum of 32 inches O.C. in walls. Where splices are required, the bars should be lapped 40 diameters. The concrete should be placed in one continuous pour from foundation to plate line. A cleanout block may be placed in the first course at every rebar (stud) for cleanout of excess mortar and to ensure proper alignment and laps of rebars.

Horizontal rebars should be placed in bond beam units which are laid with the channel up and then filled with concrete. Bond beams may be installed both below windows and at the top of the wall at the plate line. Typically, the reinforcing rebars used may be two 3/8 inch diameter deformed bars (lapped 40 diameters at splices). Lintels formed by placing bond

beam blocks are usually extended 8 inches past each opening. You should always check the specifications carefully for the size and number of rebars to be used. A pilaster block may be used for lateral strength and to provide greater bearing area for beam ends carried on the wall. One type of pilaster is shown in figure 7-31.

Practical experience indicates that control of cracking and wall flexibility can be achieved with the use of horizontal joint reinforcing. The amount of joint reinforcement depends largely upon the type of construction. Horizontal joint reinforcing, where required, should consist of not less than two deformed longitudinal No. 9 (or heavier) cold drawn steel wires. Truss type cross wires should be 1/8 inch diameter (or heavier) of the same quality. Figure 7-32 shows joint reinforcement at a vertical spacing of 16 inches.

The location and details of bond beams, control joints, and joint reinforcing should all be shown on the drawings.

WATERTIGHT BLOCK WALLS

To ensure that block walls below grade will be watertight, they should be covered with plaster and sealed. Plastering consists of applying two 1/4-inch coats of plaster, using 1 : 2 1/2 mortar mix. The wall should be dampened before applying the plaster in order to get a good bond. The first coat should extend from 6 inches above the grade line down to the footing. When it is partially set up, roughen the surface with a wire brush and then allow at least 24 hours. Dampen the wall again before the second coat is applied. After the second coat is applied the wall should be kept damp for 48 hours.

In poorly drained or heavy wet soils the plaster should be covered with two coats of an asphalt waterproofing, brushed on. The wall may be further protected by laying a line of drainage tile around the outside of the footing. Cover the tile joints with pieces of building paper, and cover the tile with about 12 inches of washed gravel before the back filling is done.

STRUCTURAL CLAY TILE MASONRY

Hollow masonry units made of burned clay or shale are called, variously, structural tiles, building tiles, hollow tiles, structural clay tiles, structural clay hollow tiles, and structural clay hollow building tiles. Let's call them BUILDING TILES in this manual. In building

A. REMOVING MORTAR WITH TROWEL

B. USING PIECE OF BROKEN BLOCK

C. BRUSHING

133.284

Figure 7-30.—Patching and cleaning concrete block.

tile manufacture, plastic clay is pugged through a die and the shape which emerges is cut off into units. The units are then burned much as bricks are burned.

The apertures in a building tile, which correspond to the cores in a brick or a concrete block, are called CELLS. The solid sides of a tile are called the SHELL and the perforated

161

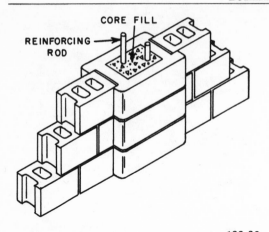

133.38

Figure 7-31.—One type of pilaster.

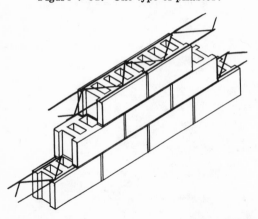

133.39

Figure 7-32.—Masonry wall horizontal
joint reinforcement.

material enclosed by the shell is called the
WEB. A tile which is laid on one of its shell
faces is called a SIDE-CONSTRUCTION tile;
one which is laid on one of its web faces is
called an END-CONSTRUCTION tile. Figures
7-33 and 7-34 show the sizes and shapes of
basic side- and end-construction building units.
Special shapes for use at corners and openings,
or for use as closures, are also available.

PHYSICAL CHARACTERISTICS

The compressive strength of the individual
tile depends upon the materials used and upon
the method of manufacture in addition to the
thickness of the shells and webs. A minimum
compressive strength of tile masonry of 300
pounds per square inch based on the gross section may be expected. The tensile strength of
structural clay tile masonry is small. In most
cases it is less than 10 percent of the compressive strength.

The abrasion resistance of clay tile depends
primarily upon its compressive strength. The
stronger the tile, the greater its resistance to
wearing. The abrasion resistance decreases
as the amount of water absorbed increases.

Structural clay facing tile has excellent
resistance to weathering. Freezing and thawing
action produces almost no deterioration. Tile
that will absorb no more than 16 percent of their
weight of water have never given unsatisfactory
performance in resisting the effect of freezing
and thawing action. Only portland cement-lime
mortar or mortar prepared from masonry
cement should be used if the masonry is exposed
to the weather.

Walls containing structural clay tile have
better heat-insulating qualities than do walls
composed of solid units, due to dead air space
that exists in tile walls. The resistance to
sound penetration of this type of masonry

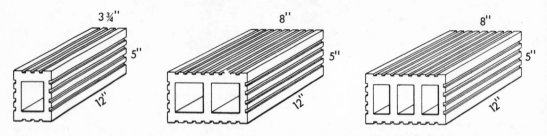

29.143

Figure 7-33.—Standard shapes of side-construction building tiles.

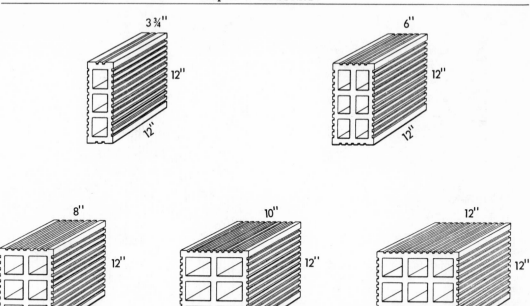

29.144

Figure 7-34.—Standard shapes of end-construction building tiles.

compares favorably with the resistance of solid masonry walls but it is somewhat less.

The fire resistance of tile walls is considerably less than the fire resistance of solid masonry walls. It can be improved by applying a coat of plaster to the surface of the wall. Partition walls of structural clay tile 6 inches thick will resist a fire for 1 hour provided the fire produces a temperature of not more than 1,700°F.

The solid material in structural clay tile weighs about 125 pounds per cubic foot. Since the tile contains hollow cells of various sizes, the weight of tile varies, depending upon the manufacture and type. A 6-inch tile wall weighs approximately 30 pounds per square foot, while a 12-inch weighs approximately 45 pounds per square foot.

USES FOR STRUCTURAL CLAY TILE

Structural clay tile may be used for exterior walls of either the load-bearing or non-load-bearing type. It is suitable for both below-grade and above-grade construction.

Non-load-bearing partition walls of from 4- to 12-inch thickness are frequently made of structural clay tile. These walls are easily built, light in weight, and have good heat- and sound-insulating properties.

Figure 7-35 illustrates the use of structural clay tile as a backing unit for a brick wall. Figure 7-35 also shows the use of header brick to tie the brick tier to the tile used for backing.

MORTAR JOINTS FOR
STRUCTURAL CLAY TILE

In general, the procedure for making mortar joints for structural clay tile is the same as for concrete block.

The bed joint for the end-construction is made by spreading a 1-inch thickness of mortar on the shell of the bed tile but not on the webs. The mortar should be spread for a distance of about 3 feet ahead of the laying of the tile. The position of the tile above does not coincide with the position of the tile below since the head joints are to be staggered as shown in figure 7-36. The web of the tile above will not contact the

163

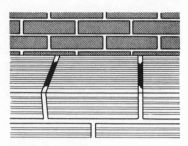

29.148
Figure 7-35.—Structural clay tile used as
a backing unit.

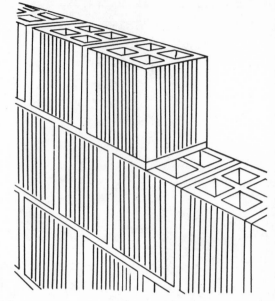

BED JOINT

web of the tile below and any mortar placed on these webs is useless.

The head joint for the end-construction is formed by spreading plenty of mortar along each edge of the tile, as shown in figure 7-36, and then pushing the tile into the mortar bed until in its proper position. Enough mortar should be used to cause excess mortar to squeeze out of the joints. This excess mortar is cut off with a trowel. The head joint need not be a solid joint as recommended for head joints in brick masonry unless the joint is to be exposed to the weather. Clay tile units are heavy, making it necessary to use both hands when placing the tile in position in the wall. The mortar joint should be about 1/2-inch thick, depending upon the type of construction.

The bed joint for the side-construction is made by spreading the mortar to a thickness of about 1 inch for a distance of about 3 feet ahead of the laying of the tile. A furrow need not be made.

There are two methods of laying the head joint. In the first method, as much mortar as will adhere is spread on both edges of tile as shown in figure 7-37. The tile is then pushed into the mortar bed against the tile already in place until in its proper position. Excess mortar is cut off. In the second method, as much mortar as will adhere is placed on the interior edge of the tile already in place and on the opposite edge of the unit being placed. This is also shown in figure 7-37. The tile is then shoved in place and the excess mortar cut off.

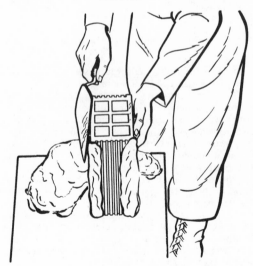

HEAD JOINT

133.286
Figure 7-36.—Laying end-
construction tile.

1 METHOD A FOR MAKING HEAD JOINT

2 METHOD B FOR MAKING HEAD JOINT

133.40(133F)
Figure 7-37.—Laying side-construction tile.

The mortar joints should be about 1/2 inch thick, depending upon the type of construction.

EIGHT-INCH WALL WITH FOUR-INCH STRUCTURAL CLAY TILE BACKING

For this wall there will be six stretcher courses between the header courses. The backing tile is side-constructed 4- by 5- by 12-inch tile. They are 4 inches wide, 5 inches high and 12 inches long. The 5-inch height is equal to the height of two brick courses and a 1/2-inch mortar joint. These tiles are laid with a bed joint such that the top of the tile will be level with every second course of brick. The thickness of the bed joint therefore depends upon the thickness of the bed joint used for the brick.

The first course of the wall is temporarily laid out without mortar as recommended for solid brick walls. This will establish the number of brick required for one course.

As shown in figure 7-38, the first course of the corner lead is identical to the first course of the corner lead for a solid 8-inch brick wall except that one more brick is laid.

All the brick required for the corner lead are laid before any tile is placed. The first course of tile and the completed corner lead are also shown in figure 7-38.

EIGHT-INCH STRUCTURAL CLAY TILE WALL

This wall is constructed of 8- by 5- by 12-inch tile. The length of the tile is 12 inches, the width is 8 inches, and the height is 5 inches. A 2- by 5- by 8-inch soap is used at the corners as shown in figure 7-39. Half-lap bond is used as indicated.

Figure 7-39 also illustrates laying the corner leads by showing that tiles a and b are laid first, then c and d. The level is checked as they are laid. Tiles e and f are laid and their level checked. Tile b must be laid so that it projects 6 inches from the inside corner as shown to provide for the half-lap bond. Corner tiles such as b, g, and h, should be end-construction tile in order to avoid exposure of the open cells at the face of the wall, or a thin end-construction tile, known as a "soap", may be used at the corner as shown. The remainder of the tile in the corner is then laid, and the level of each is checked. After the corner leads are erected, the wall between is laid using the line.

JOINT FINISHING

The exterior surfaces of joints are finished to make the masonry more watertight and to improve its appearance. Concave and V-shaped mortar joints (fig. 7-40) are recommended for walls of exterior concrete masonry in preference to struck or raked joints that form small lodges which may hold water. Some joints can be made

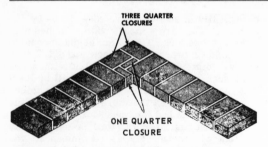

THREE QUARTER
CLOSURES

ONE QUARTER
CLOSURE

FIRST COURSE OF CORNER LEAD, HOLLOW TILE BACKING

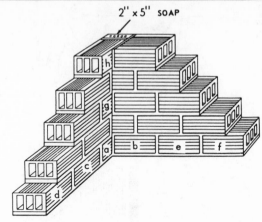

2" x 5" SOAP

133.41
Figure 7-39.—Eight-inch structural clay
tile wall.

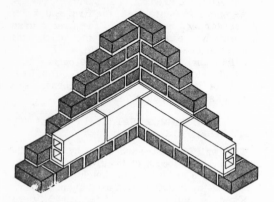

FIRST COURSE OF TILE, HOLLOW TILE BACKING

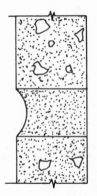

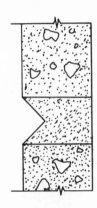

CONCAVE JOINT   V-JOINT

133.43
Figure 7-40.—Tooled mortar joints for
watertight concrete.

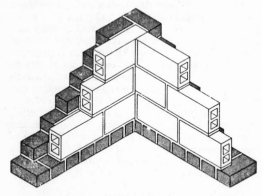

COMPLETE CORNER LEAD, HOLLOW TILE BACKING

133.40(133F)
Figure 7-38.—Corner lead hollow tile backing.

with the trowel, while others have to be made with the jointer. With modular-size masonry units mortar joints will be approximately

3/8-inch thick. Experience has shown that this thickness of joint where properly made helps to produce a weathertight, neat and durable concrete masonry wall.

There is a process called POINTING that may have to be done after jointing has occurred. Pointing is the process of inserting mortar into horizontal and vertical joints after the unit has been laid. Basically, pointing is done to restore or replace deteriorated surface mortar in old work. Pointing of this nature is called TUCK pointing. However, pointing may be necessary for filling holes or correcting defective joints in freshly laid masonry.

STONE MASONRY

Stone masonry is masonry in which the units consist of natural stone. In RUBBLE stone masonry the stones are left in their natural state, without any kind of shaping. In ASHLAR masonry the faces of stones which are to be placed in surface positions are squared, so that the surfaces of the finished structure will be more or less continuous plane surfaces. Both rubble and ashlar work may be either COURSED or RANDOM.

Random rubble is the crudest of all types of stonework. Little attention is paid to laying the stones in courses as shown in figure 7-41. Each layer must contain bonding stones that extend through the wall as shown in figure 7-42. This produces a wall that is well tied together. The bed joints should be horizontal for stability but the "builds" or head joints may run in any direction.

Coursed rubble is assembled of roughly squared stones in such a manner as to produce approximately continuous horizontal bed joints as shown in figure 7-43.

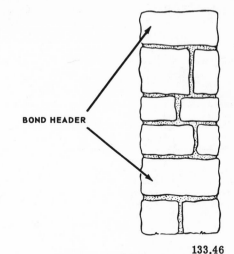

BOND HEADER

133.46

Figure 7-42.—Bond stones.

133.45

Figure 7-43.—Coursed rubble masonry.

133.44

Figure 7-41.—Random rubble masonry.

MATERIALS FOR USE IN STONE MASONRY

The stone for use in stone masonry should be strong, durable, and cheap. Durability and strength depend upon the chemical composition and physical structure of the stone. Some of the more commonly found stones that are suitable are limestone, sandstone, granite, and slate. Unsquared stones obtained from nearby ledges or quarries or even field stones may be used. The size of the stone should be such that two men can easily handle it. A variety of sizes is necessary in order to avoid using large quantities of mortar.

The mortar for use in stone masonry may be composed of portland cement and sand in the proportions of one part cement to three parts sand by volume. Such mortar shrinks excessively and does not work well with the trowel. A better mortar to use is portland cement-lime mortar (table 7-3). Mortar made with ordinary portland cement will stain most types

Table 7-3.—Recommended Mortar Mixes

Proportions by Volume

Type of service	Cement	Hydrated lime	Mortar sand, in damp, loose condition
For ordinary service.	1—masonry cement*	----------	2¼ to 3.
	or		
	1—portland cement.	½ to 1¼--	4½ to 6.
Subject to extremely heavy loads, violent winds, earthquakes, or severe frost action. Isolated piers.	1—masonry cement* plus 1— portland cement	----------	4½ to 6.
	or		
	1—portland cement.	0 to ¼---	2¼ to 3.

*ASTM Specification C 91 Type II.

133.329

of stone. If staining must be prevented, non-staining white portland cement should be used in making the mortar. Lime does not usually stain the stone.

LAYING STONE MASONRY

The wall proper should be laid on a footing of large stones, each of which should be as long as the footing is wide. Some general rules for laying stones are as follows:

Each stone should be laid on its broadest face.

If appearance is a factor, the larger stones should be laid in the lower courses and the size of stones should gradually diminish toward the top of the wall. An exception to this, of course, is work in which the stones are deliberately arranged to form an ornamental pattern, as is the case in much ashlar work.

Masonry stone is classified as absorbent or nonabsorbent. The absorbent type stone must be wetted before placing, to prevent absorption of water and consequent weakening of the mortar; whereas the nonabsorbent type does not need wetting at all.

Stones should be selected and placed so as to make the spaces between stones as small as possible. If large spaces are unavoidable, they must be filled with small stones embedded in mortar.

If a stone must be moved after it has been set in bed mortar, it must be lifted out entirely and reset.

The thickness of bed joints depends upon the size and type of the stone to be set. The only general rule is that the mortar must be thick enough to fill all the spaces between stones.

Head joints are not made by buttering, as with brick, but by slushing with mortar and, if necessary, filling with small stones after 3 or 4 stones have been laid on bed joints.

There should be a bond stone like those shown in figure 7-42 in every 6 to 10 sq ft of wall.

JOINTS AND POINTING

There are two classifications for horizontal joints between stones and they are BED JOINTS or simply BEDS; whereas vertical joints are classified as HEAD JOINTS or BUILDS.

The joints in rubble masonry are neither constant in direction nor uniform in thickness because they are used to fill the spaces between stones of irregular shape.

The joints in ashlar or cut-stone masonry do not exceed 1/2-inch in thickness because the stones are accurately dressed to shape. A joint thickness of 1/4-inch is commonly used whenever ashlar facing is used and a joint thickness of 1/8-inch for interior stonework.

POINTING is whenever the mortar in the horizontal and vertical joints of ashlar masonry is raked out to a depth of about 3/4-inch. Sometimes a special mortar may be used to make a tighter and more attractive joint. The pointing process should not be performed while the wall is being constructed. This process must be done after the mortar has fully set and the wall has received its full load.

Rubble masonry does not require the pointing process; therefore, the joints are usually considered finished whenever the stones are set. However; sometime the joints of rubble masonry are made flush with the surface of the stones thus enabling the Builder to run a narrow bead of colored mortar on the wide joints to give the effect of narrow joints. The wide joint is usually the same color as the stone and the narrow joint a contrasting color. (This operation is also carried on after the mortar has set.)

BRICK MASONRY

Brick masonry is that type of construction in which units of baked clay or shale of uniform size, small enough to be placed with one hand, are laid in courses with mortar joints to form walls of virtually unlimited length and height. Bricks are kiln-baked from various clay and shale mixtures. The chemical and physical characteristics of the ingredients vary considerably; these and the kiln temperatures combine to produce brick in a variety of colors and hardnesses. In some regions, pits are opened and found to yield clay or shale which, when ground and moistened, can be formed and baked into durable brick; in other regions, clays or shales from several pits must be mixed.

The dimensions of a U.S. standard building brick are 2 1/2 X 3 3/4 X 8. The actual dimensions of brick may vary a little because of shrinkage during burning.

BRICK TERMINOLOGY

Frequently the Builder must cut the brick into various shapes. The more common of these are shown in figure 7-44. They are called half or bat, three-quarter closure, quarter closure, king closure, queen closure, and split. They are used to fill in the spaces at corners and such other places where a full brick will not fit.

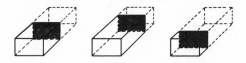

HALF OR BAT   THREE-QUARTER CLOSURE   QUARTER CLOSURE

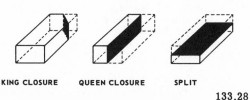

KING CLOSURE   QUEEN CLOSURE   SPLIT

133.28

Figure 7-44.—Nomenclature of common shapes of cut brick.

The six surfaces of a brick are called the face, the side, the cull, the end, and the beds, as shown in figure 7-45.

BRICK CLASSIFICATION

A finished brick structure contains FACE brick (brick placed on the exposed face of the

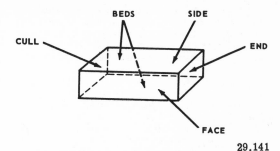

29.141

Figure 7-45.—Names of brick surfaces.

structure) and BACK-UP brick (brick placed behind the face brick). The face brick is often of higher quality than the back-up brick; however, the entire wall may be built of COMMON brick. Common brick is brick which is made from pit-run clay, with no attempt at color control and no special surface treatment like glazing or enameling. Most common brick is red.

Although any surface brick is a face brick as distinguished from a back-up brick, the term face brick is also used to distinguish high-quality brick from brick which is of common brick quality or less. Applying this criterion, face brick is more uniform in color than common brick, and it may be obtained in a variety of colors as well. It may be specifically finished on the surface, and in any case it has a better surface appearance than common brick. It may also be more durable, as a result of the use of select clay and other materials, or as a result of special manufacturing methods.

Back-up brick may consist of brick which is inferior in quality even to common brick. Brick which has been underburned or overburned, or brick made with inferior clay or by inferior methods, is often used for back-up brick.

Still another type of classification divides brick into grades in accordance with the probable climatic conditions to which it is to be exposed, as follows:

GRADE SW is brick designed to withstand exposure to below-freezing temperatures in a moist climate like that of the northern regions of the United States.

GRADE MW is brick designed to withstand exposure to below freezing temperatures in a drier climate than that mentioned in the previous paragraph.

GRADE NW is brick primarily intended for interior or back-up brick. It may be used exposed, however, in regions where no frost action occurs, or in regions where frost action occurs but the annual rainfall is less than 15 inches.

TYPES OF BRICKS

There are many types of brick. Some are different in formation and composition while others vary according to their use. Some commonly used types of brick are:

BUILDING brick, formerly called common brick, is made of ordinary clays or shales and burned in the usual manner in the kilns. These bricks do not have special scorings or markings and are not produced in any special color or surface texture. Building brick is also known as hard and kiln run brick. It is used generally for the backing courses in solid or cavity brick walls. The harder and more durable kinds are preferred for this purpose.

FACE brick are used in the exposed face of a wall and are higher quality units then backup brick. They have better durability and appearance. The most common colors of face brick are various shades of brown, red, gray, yellow, and white.

When bricks are overburned in the kilns, they are called CLINKER brick. This type of brick is usually hard and durable and may be irregular in shape. Rough hard corresponds to the clinker classification.

The dry press process is used to make this class of brick which has regular smooth faces, sharp edges, and perfectly square corners. Ordinarily all PRESS brick are used as face brick.

GLAZED brick has one surface of each brick glazed in white or other color. The ceramic glazing consists of mineral ingredients which fuse together in a glass-like coating during burning. This type of brick is particularly suited for walls or partitions in hospitals, dairies, laboratories or other buildings where cleanliness and ease of cleaning is necessary.

FIRE brick is made of a special type of fire clay which will withstand the high temperatures of fireplaces, boilers and similar usages without cracking or decomposing. Fire brick is generally larger than regular structural brick and often it is hand molded.

CORED bricks are bricks made with two rows of five holes extending through their beds to reduce weight. There is no significant difference between the strength of walls constructed with cored brick and those constructed with solid brick. Resistance to moisture penetration is about the same for both types of walls. The most easily available brick that will meet requirements should be used whether the brick is cored or solid.

SAND-LIME bricks are made from a lean mixture of slaked lime and fine silicious sand molded under mechanical pressure and hardened under steam pressure.

MORTAR FOR BRICK MASONRY

Mortar is used to bond the brick together and unless properly mixed and applied will be the weakest part of brick masonry. Both the strength and resistance to rain penetration of brick masonry walls are dependent to a great degree on the strength of the bond. Water in the mortar is essential to the development of bond and if the mortar contains insufficient water the bond will be weak and spotty. When brick walls leak it is usually through the mortar joints. Irregularities in dimensions and shape of bricks are corrected by the mortar joint.

Mortar should be plastic enough to work with a trowel. The properties of mortar depend largely upon the type of sand used in it. Clean, sharp sand produces excellent mortar. Too much sand in mortar will cause it to segregate, drop off the trowel, and weather poorly.

The selection of mortar for brick construction depends on the use requirements of the structure. For example, the recommended mortar for use in laying up interior non-load-bearing partitions would not be satisfactory for foundation walls. In many cases, the builder relies upon a fixed proportion of cement, lime and sand to provide a satisfactory mortar. The following types of mortar are proportioned on a volume basis:

TYPE M is 1 part portland cement, 1/4 part hydrated lime or lime putty, and 3 parts sand, or 1 part portland cement, 1 part type II masonry cement, and 6 parts sand. This mortar is suitable for general use and is recommended specifically for masonry below grade and in contact with earth, such as foundations, retaining walls, and walks.

TYPE S is 1 part portland cement, 1/2 part hydrated lime or lime putty, and 4 1/2 parts sand, or 1/2 part portland cement, 1 part type II masonry cement and 4 1/2 parts sand. This mortar is also suitable for general use and is recommended where high resistance to lateral forces is required.

TYPE N is 1 part portland cement, 1 part hydrated lime or lime putty, and 6 parts sand, or 1 part type II masonry cement and 3 parts sand. This mortar is suitable for general use in exposed masonry above grade and is recommended specifically for exterior walls subjected to severe exposures.

TYPE O is 1 part portland cement, 2 parts hydrated lime or lime putty, and 9 parts sand, or 1 part type I or type II masonry cement and 3 parts sand. This mortar is recommended for load-bearing walls of solid units where the compressive stresses do not exceed 100 pounds per square inch and the masonry will not be subjected to freezing and thawing in the presence of excessive moisture.

RESISTANCE TO WEATHERING

The resistance of masonry walls to weathering depends almost entirely upon their resistance to water penetration because freezing and thawing action is virtually the only type of weathering that affects brick masonry. With the best workmanship, it is possible to build brick walls that will resist the penetration of rain water during a storm lasting as long as 24 hours accompanied by a 50- to 60-mile-per-hour wind. In most construction, it is unreasonable to expect the type of workmanship required to build a wall that will allow no water penetration. It is advisable to provide some means of taking care of moisture after it has penetrated the brick masonry. Properly designed flashing and cavity walls are two ways of handling moisture that has entered the wall.

Important factors in preventing the entrance of water are tooled mortar joints and caulking around windows and door frames.

The joints between the brick must be solidly filled, especially in the face tier. Slushing or grouting the joints after the brick has been laid does not completely fill the joint. The mortar joint should be tooled to a concave surface before the mortar has had a chance to set up. In tooling, sufficient force should be used to press the mortar tight against the brick on both sides of the mortar joint.

Mortar joints that are tightly bonded to the brick have been shown to have greater resistance to moisture penetration than joints not tightly bonded to the brick.

FIRE RESISTANCE

Fire-resistance tests conducted upon brick walls laid up with portland-cement-lime mortar have made it possible to give fire-resistance periods for various thicknesses of brick walls. A summary is given in table 7-4. The tests

Table 7-4.—Fire Resistance of Brick Load-Bearing Walls Laid with Portland Cement Mortar

Normal wall thickness (inches)	Type of wall	Material	Ultimate fire-resistance period. Incombustible members framed into wall or not framed in members		
			No plaster (hours)	Plaster on one side* (hours)	Plaster on two sides* (hours)
4	Solid	Clay or shale	1¼	1¾	2½
8	Solid	Clay or shale	5	6	7
12	Solid	Clay or shale	10	10	12
8	Hollow rowlock	Clay or shale	2½	3	4
12	Hollow rowlock	Clay or shale	5	6	7
9 to 10	Cavity	Clay or shale	5	6	7
4	Solid	Sand-lime	1¾	2½	3
8	Solid	Sand-lime	7	8	9
12	Solid	Sand-lime	10	10	12

*Not less than ½ inch of 1:3 sanded gypsum plaster is required to develop these ratings.

133.330

were made using the American Society for Testing Materials standard method for conducting fire tests.

GENERAL CHARACTERISTICS
OF BRICK MASONRY

Solid brick masonry walls provide very little insulation against heat and cold. A cavity wall or a brick wall backed with hollow clay tile has much better insulating value.

Because brick walls are exceptionally massive, they have good sound-insulating properties. In general, the heavier the wall, the better will be its sound-insulating value; however, there is no appreciable increase in sound insulation by a wall more than 12 inches thick as compared to a wall between 10 and 12 inches thick. The expense involved in constructing a thicker wall merely to take advantage of the slight increase is too excessive to be worthwhile. Dividing the wall into two or more layers, as in the case of a cavity wall, will increase its resistance to the transmission of sound from one side of the wall to the other. Brick walls are poor absorbers of sound originating within the walls and reflect much of it back into the structure. Sounds caused by impact, as when the wall is struck with a hammer, will travel a great distance along the wall.

Brick masonry expands and contracts with temperature change. Walls up to a length of 200 feet do not need expansion joints. Longer walls need an expansion joint for every 200 feet of wall. The joint can be made as shown in figure 7-46. A considerable amount of the expansion and contraction is taken up in the wall itself.

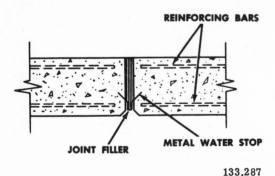

REINFORCING BARS

JOINT FILLER

METAL WATER STOP

133.287

Figure 7-46.—Expansion joint for wall.

For this reason, the amount of movement that theoretically takes place does not actually occur.

The resistance of brick to abrasion depends largely upon its compressive strength, related to the degree of burning. Well-burned brick have excellent wearing qualities.

The weight of brick varies from 100 to 150 pounds per cubic foot depending upon the nature of the materials used in making the brick and the degree of burning. Well-burned brick are heavier than under-burned brick.

BRICKLAYING METHODS

Good bricklaying procedure depends on good workmanship and efficiency. Means of obtaining good workmanship are treated below. Efficiency involves doing the work with the fewest possible motions. The Builder studies his own operations to determine those motions that are unnecessary. Each motion should have a purpose and should accomplish a definite result. After learning the fundamentals, every Builder develops his own methods for achieving maximum efficiency. The work must be arranged in such a way that the Builder is continually supplied with brick and mortar. The scaffolding required must be planned before the work begins. It must be built in such a way as to cause the least interference with other workmen.

Types of Bonds

The word bond, when used in reference to masonry, may have three different meanings:

STRUCTURAL BOND is the method by which individual masonry units are interlocked or tied together to cause the entire assembly to act as a single structural unit. Structural bonding of brick and tile walls may be accomplished in three ways. First, by overlapping (interlocking) the masonry units, second by the use of metal ties imbedded in connecting joints, and third by the adhesion of grout to adjacent wythes of masonry.

MORTAR BOND is the adhesion of the joint mortar to the masonry units or to the reinforcing steel.

PATTERN BOND is the pattern formed by the masonry units and the mortar joints on the face of a wall. The pattern may result from the type of structural bond used or may be purely a decorative one in no way related to the structural bond. There are five basic pattern bonds in common use today as shown in figure 7-47:

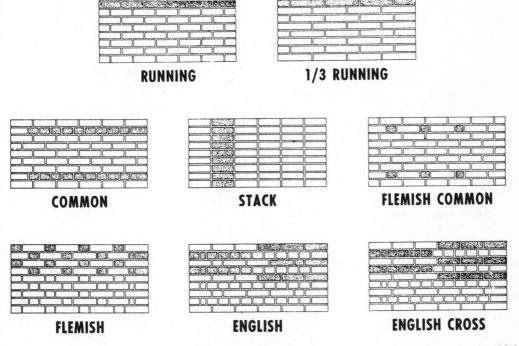

RUNNING   **1/3 RUNNING**

COMMON   **STACK**   **FLEMISH COMMON**

FLEMISH   **ENGLISH**   **ENGLISH CROSS**

133.288

Figure 7-47.—Some types of brick masonry bond.

Running bond, common or American bond, Flemish bond, English bond, and block or stack bond.

RUNNING BOND is the simplest of the basic pattern bonds; the running bond consists of all stretchers. Since there are no headers used in this bond, metal ties are usually used. Running bond is used largely in cavity wall construction and veneered walls of brick, and often in facing tile walls where the bonding may be accomplished by extra width stretcher tile.

COMMON OR AMERICAN BOND is a variation of running bond with a course of full length headers at regular intervals. These headers provide structural bonding as well as pattern. Header courses usually appear at every fifth, sixth, or seventh course depending on the structural bonding requirements. In laying out any bond pattern it is very important that the corners be started correctly. For common bond, a "three-quarter" brick must start each header course at the corner. Common

bond may be varied by using a Flemish header course.

FLEMISH BOND is made up of alternate stretchers and headers, with the headers in alternate courses centered over the stretchers in the intervening courses. Where the headers are not used for the structural bonding, they may be obtained by using half brick, called "blind-headers." There are two methods used in starting the corners. Figure 7-47 shows the so called "Dutch" corner in which a three-quarter brick is used to start each course and the "English" corner in which 2 inch or quarter-brick closures must be used.

ENGLISH BOND is composed of alternate courses of headers and stretchers. The headers are centered on the stretchers and joints between stretchers. The vertical (head) joints between stretchers in all courses line up vertically. Blind headers are used in courses which are not structural bonding courses.

BLOCK OR STACK BOND is purely a pattern bond. There is no overlapping of the units, all vertical joints being aligned. Usually this pattern is bonded to the backing with rigid steel ties, but when 8 inch thick stretcher units are available, they may be used. In large wall areas and in load-bearing construction it is advisable to reinforce the wall with steel pencil rods placed in the horizontal mortar joints. The vertical alignment requires dimensionally accurate units, or carefully prematched units, for each vertical joint alignment. Variety in pattern may be achieved by numerous combinations and modifications of the basic patterns shown.

ENGLISH CROSS OR DUTCH BOND is a variation of English bond and differs only in that vertical joints between the stretchers in alternate courses do not line up vertically. These joints center on the stretchers themselves in the courses above and below.

Masonry Terms

Specific terms are used to describe the various positions of masonry units and mortar joints in a wall (fig. 7-48):

Course. One of the continuous horizontal layers (or rows) of masonry which, bonded together, form the masonry structure.

Wythe. A continuous vertical 4-inch or greater section or thickness of masonry as the thickness of masonry separating flues in a chimney.

Stretcher. A masonry unit laid flat with its longest dimension parallel to the face of the wall.

Header. A masonry unit laid flat with its longest dimension perpendicular to the face of the wall. It is generally used to tie two wythes of masonry together.

Rowlock. A brick laid on its edge (face).

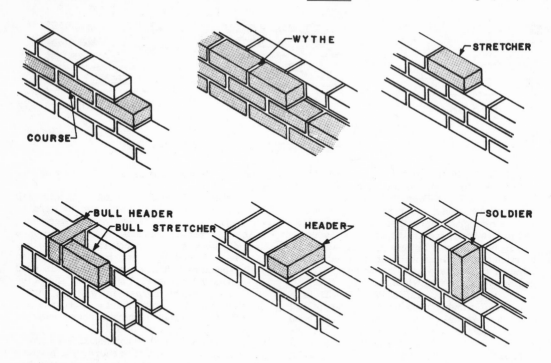

133.289

Figure 7-48.—Masonry units and mortar joints.

Bull-Stretcher. A rowlock brick laid with its longest dimension parallel to the face of the wall.

Bull-Header. A rowlock brick laid with its longest dimension perpendicular to the face of the wall.

Soldier. A brick laid on its end so that its longest dimension is parallel to the vertical axis of the face of the wall.

Metal Ties

Metal ties can be used to tie the brick on the outside face of the wall to the backing courses. These are used when no header courses are installed. They are not as satisfactory as header courses. Typical metal ties are shown in figure 7-49.

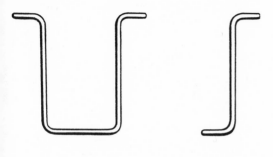

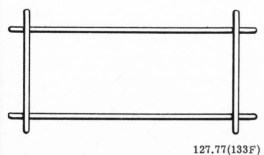

127.77(133F)

Figure 7-49.—Metal ties.

Flashing

Flashing is installed in masonry construction to divert moisture, which may enter the masonry at vulnerable spots, to the outside.

Flashing should be provided under horizontal masonry surfaces such as sills and copings, at intersections of masonry walls with horizontal surfaces such as roof and parapet or roof and chimney, over heads of openings such as doors and windows, and frequently at floor lines, depending upon the type of construction. To be most effective, the flashing should extend through the outer face of the wall and be turned down to form a drop. Weep holes should be provided at intervals of 18 inches to 2 feet to permit the water which accumulates on the flashing to drain to the outside. If, because of appearance, it is necessary to stop the flashing back of the face of the wall, weep holes are even more important than when the flashing extends through the wall. Concealed flashings with tooled mortar joints frequently will retain water in the wall for long periods and, by concentrating moisture at one spot, may do more harm than good.

Mortar Joints and Pointing

The trowel should be held in a firm position. (See fig. 7-50.) The thumb should rest on top of the handle and should not encircle it. A right-handed Builder picks up mortar with the left edge of the trowel from the outside of the pile (fig. 7-51). He picks up the correct amount to spread for one to five bricks, according to the wall space and his skill. A pickup for one brick forms a small windrow along the left edge of the trowel. A pickup for five bricks is a full load for a large trowel. See figure 7-52.

133.290

Figure 7-50.—One way to hold a trowel.

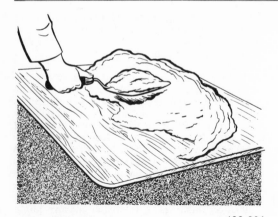

133.291

Figure 7-51.—Proper way to pick up mortar.

133.293

Figure 7-53.—Mortar thrown on brick.

133.292

Figure 7-52.—Trowel full of mortar.

133.294

Figure 7-54.—Mortar spread for a distance of 3 to 5 brick.

Holding the trowel with its left edge directly over the centerline of the previous course, the Builder tilts the trowel slightly and moves it to the right, dropping a windrow of mortar along the wall until the trowel is empty as shown in figures 7-53 and 7-54. In some instances mortar will be left on the trowel when the spreading of mortar on the course below has been completed. When this occurs the remaining mortar is returned to the board. A right-handed Builder works from left to right along the wall.

Mortar projecting beyond the wall line is cut off with the trowel edge (step 1, fig. 7-55) and thrown back on the mortar board, but enough is retained to "butter" the left end of the first brick to be laid in the fresh mortar.

With the mortar spread about 1 inch thick for the bed joint as shown in step 1, figure 7-55, a shallow furrow is made (step 2, fig. 7-55) and the brick pushed into the mortar (step 3, fig. 7-55). If the furrow is too deep, there will be a gap left between the mortar and the brick bedded in the mortar. This gap will reduce the resistance of the wall to water penetration. The mortar for a bed joint should not be spread out too far in advance of the laying. A distance of 4 or 5 bricks is advisable. Mortar that has been spread out too far will dry out before the brick is bedded in it. This results in a poor bond as can be seen in figure 7-56. The mortar must be soft and plastic so that the brick can be easily bedded in it.

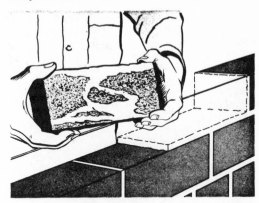

133.296

Figure 7-56.—A poorly bonded brick.

The next step after the bed joint mortar has been spread is the laying of the brick. The brick to be laid is picked up as shown in figure 7-57 with the thumb on one side of the brick and the fingers on the other. As much mortar as will stick is placed on the end of the brick. The

STEP 1

STEP 2

STEP 3

133.295

Figure 7-55.—Bed joint and furrow.

133.297

Figure 7-57.—Proper way to hold a brick.

brick should then be pushed into place so that excess mortar squeezes out at the head joint and at the sides of the wall as indicated in figure 7-58. The head joint must be completely filled with mortar. This can only be done by placing plenty of mortar on the end of the brick. After the brick is bedded, the excess mortar is cut off and used for the next end joint. Surplus mortar should be thrown to the back of the mortar board for retempering if necessary. The proper position of the brick is determined by the use of a cord which can be seen in step 1, figure 7-58.

133.298
Figure 7-58.—Head joint in a stretcher course.

The method of inserting a brick in a space left in a wall is shown in figure 7-59. A thick bed of mortar is spread (step 1, fig. 7-59) and the brick shoved into this deep bed of mortar (step 2, fig. 7-59) until it squeezes out at the top of the joint at the face tier, and at the header joint (step 3, fig. 7-59) so that the joints are full of mortar at every point.

The position of a cross joint is illustrated in figure 7-60. These joints must be completely filled with mortar. The mortar for the bed joint should be spread several brick widths in advance. The mortar is spread over the entire side of the header brick before it is placed in the wall (step 1, fig. 7-60). The brick is then shoved into place so that the mortar is forced out at the top of the joint and the excess mortar cut off, as shown in step 2, figure 7-60.

Figure 7-61 shows the method of laying a closure brick in a header course. Before laying the closure brick, plenty of mortar should be placed on the sides of the brick already in

place (step 1, fig. 7-61). Mortar should also be spread on both sides of the closure brick to a thickness of about 1 inch (step 2, fig. 7-61). The closure brick should then be laid in position without disturbing the brick already in place (step 3, fig. 7-61).

Before laying a closure brick for a stretcher course, the ends of the brick on each side of the opening to be filled with the closure brick should be well covered with mortar (step 1, fig. 7-62). Plenty of mortar should then be thrown on both ends of the closure brick (step 2, fig. 7-62) and the brick laid without disturbing those already in place (step 3, fig. 7-62). If any of the adjacent brick are disturbed they must be removed and relaid. Otherwise, cracks will form between the brick and mortar, allowing moisture into the wall.

There is no hard and fast rule regarding the thickness of the mortar joint. Brick that are irregular in shape may require mortar joints up to 1/2-inch thick. All brick irregularities are taken up in the mortar joint. Mortar joints 1/4 inch thick are the strongest and should be used when the bricks are regular enough to permit it.

Slushed joints are made by depositing the mortar on the head joints in order that the mortar will run down between the brick to form a solid joint. THIS SHOULD NOT BE DONE. Even when the space between the brick is completely filled, there is no way to compact the mortar against the faces of the brick and A POOR BOND WILL RESULT.

Filling exposed joints with mortar immediately after the wall has been laid is called POINTING. Pointing is frequently necessary to fill holes and correct defective mortar joints. The pointing trowel is used for this purpose. (See fig. 7-1.)

Cutting Brick

If a brick is to be cut to exact line the bolster or brick set should be used. When using these tools, the straight side of the cutting edge should face the part of the brick to be saved and also face the Builder. One blow of the hammer on the brick set should be enough to break the brick. Extremely hard brick will need to be cut roughly with the head of the hammer in such a way that there is enough brick left to be cut accurately with the brick set. See figure 7-63.

For normal cutting work, such as is required for making the closures and bats required around openings in walls and for the completion of corners, the brick hammer should be used.

STEP 1

STEP 2   STEP 3

133.299

Figure 7-59.—Laying inside brick.

The first step is to cut a line all the way around the brick with light blows of the hammer head (fig. 7-64). When the line is complete, a sharp blow to one side of the cutting line will split the brick at the cutting line. Rough places are trimmed using the blade of the hammer, as shown in figure 7-64. The brick can be held in the hand while being cut.

Joint Finishes

Exterior surfaces of mortar joints are finished to make the brickwork more waterproof and to improve the appearance. There are several types of joint finishes, as shown in figure 7-65. The more important of these are discussed below. When joints are cut flush with the brick and not finished, cracks are immediately apparent between the brick and the mortar. Although these cracks are not deep, they are undesirable and can be eliminated by finishing or tooling the joint. In every case, the mortar joint should be finished before the mortar has hardened to any appreciable extent. The jointing tool is shown in figure 7-1.

The best joint from the standpoint of weather-tightness is the CONCAVE joint. This joint is made with a special tool after the excess mortar has been removed with the trowel. The tool

179

STEP 1

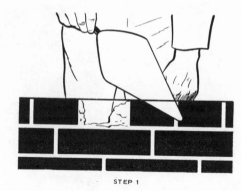

STEP 1

STEP 2

133.300

Figure 7-60.—Making cross joints in
header courses.

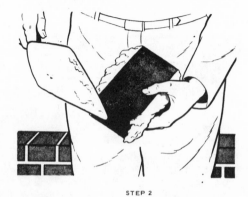

STEP 2

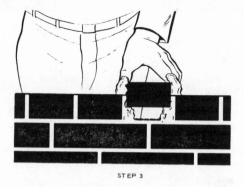

STEP 3

should be slightly larger than the joint. Force is used to press the mortar tight against the brick on both sides of the mortar joint.

The FLUSH joint (fig. 7-65) is made by keeping the trowel almost parallel to the face of the wall while drawing the point of the trowel along the joint.

A WEATHER joint sheds water more easily from the surface of the wall and is formed by pushing downward on the mortar with the top edge of the trowel.

133.301

Figure 7-61.—Making closure joints in
header courses.

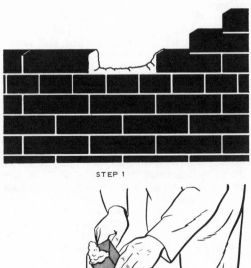

STEP 1

STEP 2

STEP 3

Figure 7-62.—Making closure joints in
stretcher courses.   133.302

133.303

Figure 7-63.—Cutting brick with
a bolster.

BRICK CONSTRUCTION

An attractive brick construction depends upon the interpretation of the plans and the abilities of the Strikers and Builders. Whether building an eight- or twelve-inch wall they must be able to work together and carry out their duties properly.

Striker's Duties

The Striker mixes mortar, carries brick and mortar to the Builder laying brick, and keeps him supplied with these materials at all times. He fills the mortar board and places it in a position convenient for the Builder laying brick. He assists in the laying out and, at times, such as during rapid backup bricklaying, he may lay out brick in a line on an adjacent course so that the Builder needs to move each brick only a few inches in laying backup work.

Wetting brick is also the duty of the Striker. This is done when bricks are laid in warm weather. There are four reasons for wetting brick just before they are laid:

There will be a better bond between the brick and the mortar.

The water will wash dust and dirt from the surface of the brick. Mortar adheres better to a clean brick.

If the surface of the brick is wet, the mortar spreads more evenly under it.

A dry brick may absorb water from the mortar rapidly. This is particularly bad when mortar containing portland cement is used. In order for cement to harden

STRIKING BRICK TO ONE SIDE
OF CUTTING LINE

TRIMMING ROUGH SPOTS

133.304

Figure 7-64.—Cutting brick with a hammer.

properly, sufficient moisture must be present to complete the hydration of the cement. If the brick robs the mortar of too much water, there will not be enough left to hydrate the cement properly.

Builder's Duties

The Builder does the actual laying of the brick. It is his responsibility to lay out the job so that the finished masonry will be properly done. In construction involving walls, he must see that the walls are plumb and the courses level.

Footings

A footing is required under a wall when the bearing capacity of the supporting soil is not sufficient to withstand the wall load without a further means of redistribution. The footing must be wider than the thickness of the wall, as illustrated in figure 7-66. The required footing width and thickness for walls of considerable height or for walls that are to carry a heavy load should be determined by a qualified Builder. Every footing should be below the frost line in order to prevent heaving and settlement of the foundation. For the usual one-story building with an 8-inch-thick wall, a footing 16 inches wide and approximately 8 inches thick is usually enough. Although brickwork footings are satisfactory, footings are normally concrete, leveled on top to receive the brick or stone foundation wall. As soon as the subgrade is prepared, the Builder should place a bed of mortar about 1 inch thick on the subgrade to take up all irregularities. The first course of the foundation is laid on this bed of mortar. The other courses are then laid on this first course.

A column footing for a 12- by 16-inch brick column is shown in figure 7-67. The construction method for this footing is the same as for the wall footing.

Eight-Inch Common Bond Brick Wall

For a wall of given length, the Builder makes a slight adjustment in the width of head joints so that some number of brick, or some number including one half-brick, will just make up the length. The Builder first lays the brick on the foundation without mortar as shown in figure 7-68. The distance between the bricks is equal to the thickness of the head mortar joints. Tables 5, 6, and 7 give the number of courses and horizontal joints required for a given wall height.

The corners are erected first. This is called "laying of leads." The Builder will use these leads as a guide in laying the remainder of the wall.

The first step in laying a corner lead is shown in first step, figure 7-69. Two three-quarter closures are cut and a 1-inch-thick mortar bed is laid on the foundation. The three-quarter closure marked by a in second step, figure 7-69 is pressed down into the mortar bed until the bed joint becomes 1/2 inch thick. Next, mortar is placed on the end

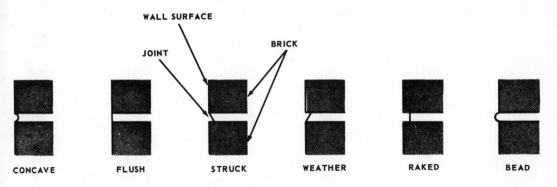

WALL SURFACE

JOINT

BRICK

CONCAVE   FLUSH   STRUCK   WEATHER   RAKED   BEAD

133.305

Figure 7-65.—Joint finishes.

Table 7-5.—Height of Courses: 2 1/4-Inch Brick, 3/8-Inch Joint

Courses	Height	Courses	Height	Courses	Height	Courses	Height	Courses	Height
1	0′ 2⅝″	21	4′ 7⅛″	41	8′ 11⅝″	61	13′ 4⅛″	81	17′ 8⅝″
2	0′ 5¼″	22	4′ 9¾″	42	9′ 2¼″	62	13′ 6¾″	82	17′ 11¼″
3	0′ 7⅞″	23	5′ 0⅜″	43	9′ 4⅞″	63	13′ 9⅜″	83	18′ 1⅞″
4	0′ 10½″	24	5′ 3″	44	9′ 7½″	64	14′ 0″	84	18′ 4½″
5	1′ 1⅛″	25	5′ 5⅝″	45	9′ 10⅛″	65	14′ 2⅝″	85	18′ 7⅛″
6	1′ 3¾″	26	5′ 8¼″	46	10′ 0¾″	66	14′ 5¼″	86	18′ 9¾″
7	1′ 6⅜″	27	5′ 10⅞″	47	10′ 3⅜″	67	14′ 7⅞″	87	19′ 0⅜″
8	1′ 9″	28	6′ 1½″	48	10′ 6″	68	14′ 10½″	88	19′ 3″
9	1′ 11⅝″	29	6′ 4⅛″	49	10′ 8⅝″	69	15′ 1⅛″	89	19′ 5⅝″
10	2′ 2¼″	30	6′ 6¾″	50	10′ 11¼″	70	15′ 3¾″	90	19′ 8¼″
11	2′ 4⅞″	31	6′ 9⅜″	51	11′ 1⅞″	71	15′ 6⅜″	91	19′ 10⅞′
12	2′ 7½″	32	7′ 0″	52	11′ 4½″	72	15′ 9″	92	20′ 1½″
13	2′ 10⅛″	33	7′ 2⅝″	53	11′ 7⅛″	73	15′ 11⅝″	93	20′ 4⅛″
14	3′ 0¾″	34	7′ 5¼″	54	11′ 9¾″	74	16′ 2¼″	94	20′ 6¾″
15	3′ 3⅜″	35	7′ 7⅞″	55	12′ 0⅜″	75	16′ 4⅞″	95	20′ 9⅜″
16	3′ 6″	36	7′ 10½″	56	12′ 3″	76	16′ 7½″	96	21′ 0″
17	3′ 8⅝″	37	8′ 1⅛″	57	12′ 5⅝″	77	16′ 10⅛″	97	21′ 2⅝″
18	3′ 11¼″	38	8′ 3¾″	58	12′ 8¼″	78	17′ 0¾″	98	21′ 5¼″
19	4′ 1⅞″	39	8′ 6⅜″	59	12′ 10⅞″	79	17′ 3⅜″	99	21′ 7⅞″
20	4′ 4½″	40	8′ 9″	60	13′ 1½″	80	17′ 6″	100	21′ 10½″

133.331

of three-quarter closure b and a head joint is formed as described previously. The head joint between the two three-quarter closures should be 1/2 inch thick also. Excess mortar that has been squeezed out of the joints is cut off. The level of the two three-quarter closures should now be checked by means of the plumb rule placed in the positions indicated by the heavy dashed lines in second step, figure 7-69. The edges of both these closure brick must be even with the outside face of the foundation. Next mortar is spread on the side of brick c and it is laid as shown in third step, figure 7-69. Its level is checked using

Table 7-6.—Height of Courses: 2 1/4-Inch Brick, 1/2-Inch Joint

Courses	Height	Courses	Height	Courses	Height	Courses	Height	Courses	Height
1	0' 2¾''	21	4' 9¾''	41	9' 4¾''	61	13' 11¾''	81	18' 6¾''
2	0' 5½''	22	5' 0½''	42	9' 7½''	62	14' 2½''	82	18' 9½''
3	0' 8¼''	23	5' 3¼''	43	9' 10¼''	63	14' 5¼''	83	19' 0¼''
4	0' 11''	24	5' 6''	44	10' 1''	64	14' 8''	84	19' 3''
5	1' 1¾''	25	5' 8¾''	45	10' 3¾''	65	14' 10¾''	85	19' 5¾''
6	1' 4½''	26	5' 11½''	46	10' 6½''	66	15' 1½''	86	19' 8½''
7	1' 7¼''	27	6' 2¼''	47	10' 9¼''	67	15' 4¼''	87	19' 11¼''
8	1' 10''	28	6' 5''	48	11' 0''	68	15' 7''	88	20' 2''
9	2' 0¾''	29	6' 7¾''	49	11' 2¾''	69	15' 9¾''	89	20' 4¾''
10	2' 3½''	30	6' 10½''	50	11' 5½''	70	16' 0½''	90	20' 7½''
11	2' 6¼''	31	7' 1¼''	51	11' 8¼''	71	16' 3¼''	91	20' 10¼''
12	2' 9''	32	7' 4''	52	11' 11''	72	16' 6''	92	21' 1''
13	2' 11¾''	33	7' 6¾''	53	12' 1¾''	73	16' 8¾''	93	21' 3¾''
14	3' 2½''	34	7' 9½''	54	12' 4½''	74	16' 11½''	94	21' 6½''
15	3' 5¼''	35	8' 0¼''	55	12' 7¼''	75	17' 2¼''	95	21' 9¼''
16	3' 8''	36	8' 3''	56	12' 10''	76	17' 5''	96	22' 0''
17	3' 10¾''	37	8' 5¾''	57	13' 0¾''	77	17' 7¾''	97	22' 2¾''
18	4' 1½''	38	8' 8½''	58	13' 3½''	78	17' 10½''	98	22' 5½''
19	4' 4¼''	39	8' 11¼''	59	13' 6¼''	79	18' 1¼''	99	22' 8¼''
20	4' 7''	40	9' 2''	60	13' 9''	80	18' 4''	100	22' 11''

133.332

Table 7-7.—Height of Courses: 2 1/4-Inch Brick, 5/8-Inch Joint

Courses	Height	Courses	Height	Courses	Height	Courses	Height	Courses	Height
1	0' 2⅞''	21	5' 0⅜''	41	9' 9⅞''	61	14' 7⅜''	81	19' 4⅞''
2	0' 5¾''	22	5' 3¼''	42	10' 0¾''	62	14' 10¼''	82	19' 7¾''
3	0' 8⅝''	23	5' 6⅛''	43	10' 3⅝''	63	15' 1⅛''	83	19' 10⅝''
4	0' 11½''	24	5' 9''	44	10' 6½''	64	15' 4''	84	20' 1½''
5	1' 2⅜''	25	5' 11⅞''	45	10' 9⅜''	65	15' 6⅞''	85	20' 4⅜''
6	1' 5¼''	26	6' 2¾''	46	11' 0¼''	66	15' 9¾''	86	20' 7¼''
7	1' 8⅛''	27	6' 5⅝''	47	11' 3⅛''	67	16' 0⅝''	87	20' 10⅛''
8	1' 11''	28	6' 8½''	48	11' 6''	68	16' 3½''	88	21' 1''
9	2' 1⅞''	29	6' 11⅜''	49	11' 8⅞''	69	16' 6⅜''	89	21' 3⅞''
10	2' 4¾''	30	7' 2¼''	50	11' 11¾''	70	16' 9¼''	90	21' 6¾''
11	2' 7⅝''	31	7' 5⅛''	51	12' 2⅝''	71	17' 0⅛''	91	21' 9⅝''
12	2' 10½''	32	7' 8''	52	12' 5½''	72	17' 3''	92	22' 0½''
13	3' 1⅜''	33	7' 10⅞''	53	12' 8⅜''	73	17' 5⅞''	93	22' 3⅜''
14	3' 4¼''	34	8' 1¾''	54	12' 11¼''	74	17' 8¾''	94	22' 6¼''
15	3' 7⅛''	35	8' 4⅝''	55	13' 2⅛''	75	17' 11⅝''	95	22' 9⅛''
16	3' 10''	36	8' 7½''	56	13' 5''	76	18' 2½''	96	23' 0''
17	4' 0⅞''	37	8' 10⅜''	57	13' 7⅞''	77	18' 5⅜''	97	23' 2⅞''
18	4' 3¾''	38	9' 1¼''	58	13' 10¾''	78	18' 8¼''	98	23' 5¾''
19	4' 6⅝''	39	9' 4⅛''	59	14' 1⅝''	79	18' 11⅛''	99	23' 8⅝''
20	4' 9½''	40	9' 7''	60	14' 4½''	80	19' 2''	100	23' 11½''

133.333

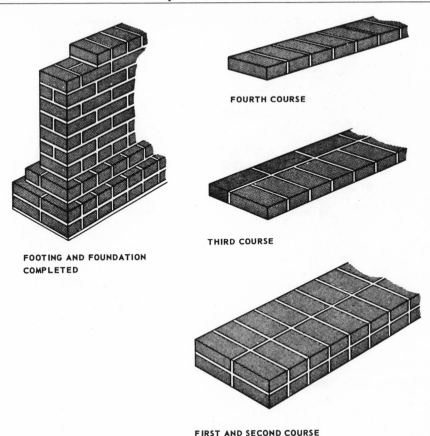

FOURTH COURSE

THIRD COURSE

FOOTING AND FOUNDATION
COMPLETED

FIRST AND SECOND COURSE

133.306

Figure 7-66.—Wall footing.

the plumb rule in the position given in third step, figure 7-69. Its end must also be even with the outside face of the foundation. Brick d is laid and its level and position checked. When brick d is in the proper position, the quarter closures e and f should be cut and placed according to the recommended procedures for laying closure brick. All excess mortar should be removed and the tops of these quarter closures checked to see that they are at the same level as the tops of surrounding brick.

Brick g (fourth step, fig. 7-69) is now shoved into position after mortar has been spread on its face. Excess mortar should be removed. Bricks h, i, j, and k are laid

in the same manner. The level of the brick is checked by placing the plumb rule in the several positions indicated in fourth step, figure 7-69. All brick ends must be flush with the surface of the foundation. Bricks l, m, n, o, and p are then laid in the same manner. The number of leader bricks that must be laid in the first course of the corner lead can be determined from fifth step, figure 7-69. It will be noted that six header bricks are required on each slide of the three-quarter closures a and b.

The second course, a stretcher course, is now laid. Procedure is shown in step 1, figure 7-70. A 1-inch thick layer of mortar should be spread over the first course and a

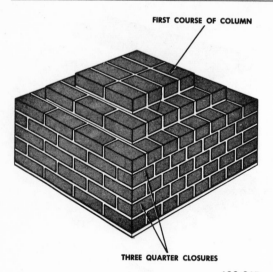

FIRST COURSE OF COLUMN

THREE QUARTER CLOSURES

133.307

Figure 7-67.—Column footing.

FOUNDATION

BRICK LAID WITHOUT MORTAR

133.308

Figure 7-68.—Determination of vertical brick joints and number of bricks in one course.

shallow furrow made in the mortar bed. Brick a (step 2, fig. 7-70) is then laid in the mortar bed and shoved down until the mortar joint is 1/2-inch thick. Brick b may now be shoved into place after mortar has been spread on its end. Excess mortar is removed and the joint checked for thickness. Bricks c, d, e, f, and g are laid in the same manner and checked to make them level and plumb. The level is checked by placing the plumb rule in the position indicated in step 2, figure 7-70. The brick are plumbed by using the plumb rule in a vertical position as shown in figure 7-71. This should be done in several places. As may be determined from 3, figure 7-70, seven bricks are required for the second

course. The remaining brick in the corner lead are laid in the manner described for the brick in the second course.

Since the portion of the wall between the leads is laid using the leads as a guide, the level of the courses in the lead must be checked continually, and after the first few courses the lead is plumbed. If the brickwork is not plumb, bricks must be moved in or out until the lead is accurately plumb. It is not good practice to move brick much once they are laid in mortar; therefore, care is taken to place the brick accurately at the start. Before the mortar has set, the joints are tooled or finished.

A corner lead at the opposite end of the wall is built in the same manner. It is essential that the level of the tops of corresponding courses be the same in each lead. That is, the top of the second course in one corner lead must be at the same height above the foundation as the second course in the other corner lead. A long 2- by 2-inch pole can be used to mark off the heights of the different courses above the foundation. This pole can be used to check the course height in the corner leads. The laying of leads should be closely supervised and only skilled Builders should be employed in this work.

With the corner leads at each end of the wall completed, the face tier of brick for the wall between the leads is laid. It is necessary to use a line, as shown in figure 7-72.

Knots are made in each end of the line to hold it within the slot of the line block as shown in figure 7-72. The line can be made taut by hooking one of the line blocks to each end of the wall.

The line is positioned 1/16 inch outside the wall face level with the top of the brick.

With the line in place, the first or header course is laid in place between the two corner leads. The brick is shoved into position so that its top edge is 1/16 inch behind the line. Do not crowd the line. If the corner leads are accurately built, the entire wall will be level and plumb. It is not necessary to use the level on the section of the wall between the leads; however, it is advisable to check it with the level at several points. For the next course, the line is moved to the top of the next mortar joint. The brick in the stretcher course should be laid as described previously. Finish the face joints before the mortar hardens.

When the face tier of brick for the wall between the leads has been laid up to, but not

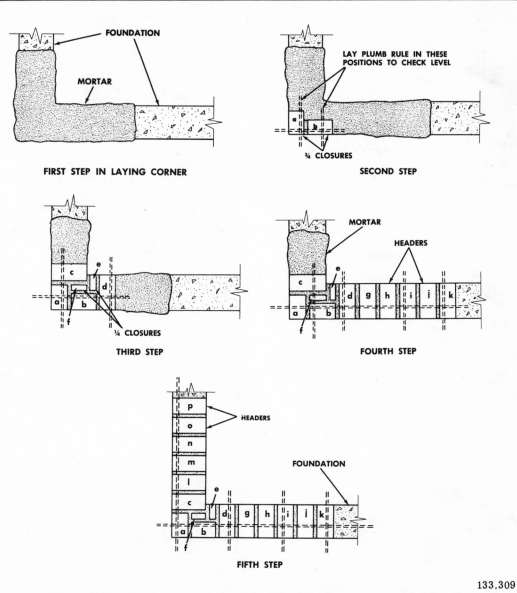

FIRST STEP IN LAYING CORNER

SECOND STEP

THIRD STEP

FOURTH STEP

FIFTH STEP

133.309

Figure 7-69.—First course of corner lead for 8-inch common bond brick wall.

including the second header course, normally six courses, the backup tier is laid. Procedure for laying backup brick has already been described. The backup brick for the corner leads are laid first and the remaining brick afterwards (fig. 7-73). The line need not be used for the backup brick in an 8-inch wall. When the backup brick have been laid up to the height

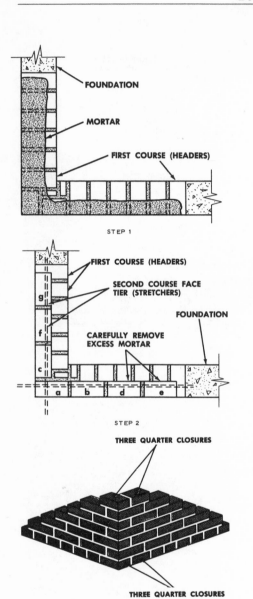

STEP 1

STEP 2

STEP 3

133.310
Figure 7-70.—Second course of corner
lead for 8-inch common bond brick wall.

133.311
Figure 7-71.—Plumbing a corner.

of the second header course, the second header
course is laid.

The wall for the entire building is built up to
a height including the second header course at
which time corner leads are continued six more
courses. The wall between the leads is constructed as before and the entire procedure repeated until the wall has been completed to the
required height.

Twelve-Inch Common Bond
Brick Wall

The 12-inch-thick common bond brick wall
is laid out as shown in 3, figure 7-74. Note that
the construction is similar to that for the 8-inch
wall with the exception that a third tier of brick
is used. The header course is laid (1, fig. 7-74)
first and the corner leads built. Two tiers of
backing brick are required instead of one. The
second course is shown in 2, figure 7-74 and
the third course in 3, figure 7-74. Two header
courses are required and they overlap as shown
in 1, figure 7-74. A line should be used for the
inside tier of backing brick for a 12-inch wall.

Protection of Brickwork
and Use of a Trig

The tops of all brick walls should be protected
each night from rain damage by placing boards

188

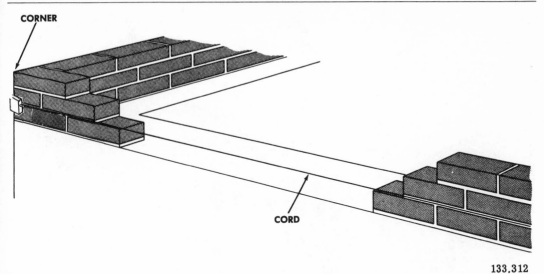

133.312

Figure 7-72.—Use of the line.

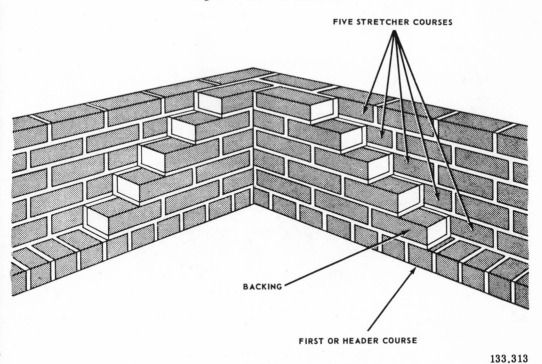

133.313

Figure 7-73.—Backing brick at the corner—8-inch common bond brick wall.

189

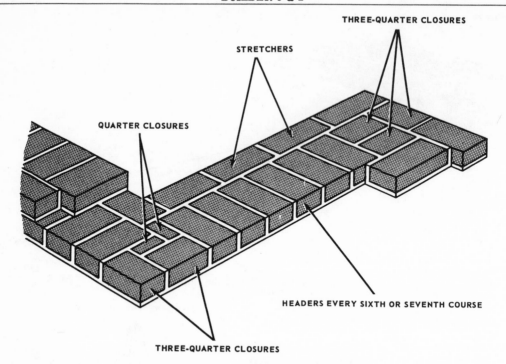

STEP 1 FIRST COURSE OF 12-INCH COMMON BOND WALL

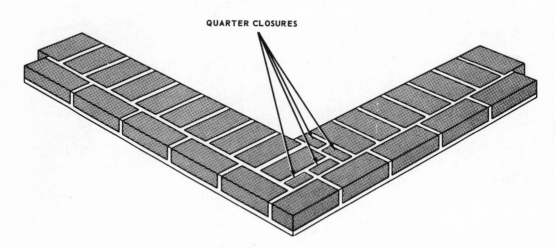

STEP 2 SECOND COURSE OF 12-INCH COMMON BOND WALL

45.484

Figure 7-74.—Twelve-inch common bond wall.

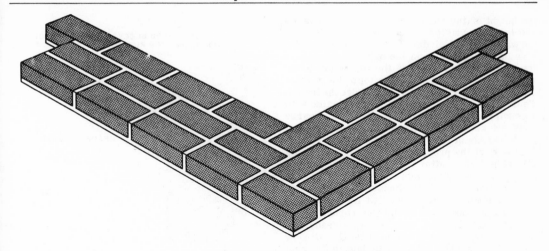

STEP 3 THIRD COURSE OF 12-INCH COMMON BOND WALL

45.484

Figure 7-74.—Twelve-inch common bond wall—continued.

or tarpaulins on top of the wall and setting loose bricks on them.

When a line is stretched on a long wall, a TRIG is used to prevent sagging and to keep it from being blown in or out from the face of the wall by the wind. The trig consists of a short piece of line looped around the main line and fastened to the top edge of a brick that has been previously laid in proper position. A lead between the corner leads must be erected in order to place the trig brick in its proper location.

Window and Door Openings

If windows are to be installed in the wall, openings are left for them as the bricklaying proceeds. The height to the top of one full course should be exactly the height of the window sill. When the distance from the foundation to the bottom of the window sill is known, the Builder can determine how many courses are required to bring the wall up to that height. If the sill is to be 4 feet 4 1/4 inches above the foundation and 1/2-inch mortar joints are to be used, 19 courses will be required. (Each brick plus one mortar joint is 2 1/4 + 1/2 = 2 3/4 inches. One course is thus 2 3/4 inches high. Four feet 4 1/4 inches divided by 2 3/4 is 19, the number of courses required.

With the brick laid up to sill height, the rowlock sill course is laid as shown in figure 7-75.

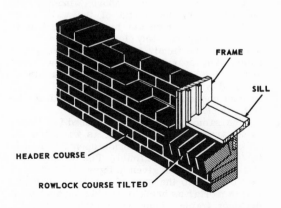

133.314

Figure 7-75.—Construction at a window opening.

The rowlock course is pitched downward. The slope is away from the window and the rowlock course normally takes up a vertical space equal to two courses of brick. The exterior surface of the joints between the brick in the rowlock course must be carefully finished to make them watertight.

The window frame is placed on the rowlock sill as soon as the mortar has set. The window frame must be temporarily braced until the brickwork has been laid up to about one-third

191

the height of the window frame. These braces are not removed for several days in order that the wall above the window frame will set properly. Now the Builder lays up the brick in the rest of the wall in such a way that the top of the brick in the course at the level of the top of the window frame is not more than 1/4 inch above the frame. To do this, he marks on the window frame with a pencil the top of each course. If the top course does not come to the proper level, he changes the thickness of the joints slightly until the top course is at the proper level. The corner leads should be laid up after the height of each course at the window is determined.

The mortar joint thickness for the corner leads is made the same as that determined at the window opening. With the corner leads erected, the line is installed as already described and is stretched across the window opening. The brick can now be laid in the rest of the wall. If the window openings have been planned properly, the brick in the face tier can be laid with a minimum of brick cutting.

LINTELS are placed above windows and doors to carry the weight of the wall above them. They rest on the brick course that is level or approximately level with the frame head, and are firmly bedded in mortar at the sides. Any space between the window frame and the lintel is closed with blocking and weather-stripped with bituminous materials. The wall is then continued above the window after the lintel is placed.

The same procedure can be used for laying brick around a door opening as was used for laying brick around a window opening, including placement of the lintel. The arrangement at a door opening is given in figure 7-76. Pieces of wood cut to the size of a half closure are laid in mortar as brick to provide for anchoring the door frame by means of screws or nails. These wood locks are placed at several points along the top and sides of the door opening to allow for plumbing the frame.

Lintels

The brickwork above openings in walls must be supported by lintels. Lintels can be made of steel, precast reinforced concrete beams, or wood. The use of wood should be avoided as much as possible. If reinforced brick masonry is employed, the brick above the wall opening can be supported by the proper installation of steel reinforcing bars. This will be discussed later. Figures 7-77 and 7-78 illustrate some

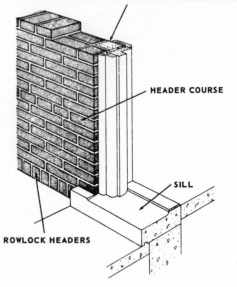

USE 5 WOOD BLOCKS ON EACH SIDE OF DOOR FRAME FOR PURPOSE OF SECURING FRAME

HEADER COURSE

SILL

ROWLOCK HEADERS

133.315

Figure 7-76.—Construction at a door opening.

of the methods of placing lintels for different wall thicknesses. The relative placement and position is determined both by wall thickness and the type of window being used.

Usually the size and type of lintels required are given on drawings for the structure. When not given, the size of double-angle lintels required for various width openings in an 8-inch and 12-inch wall can be selected from table 7-8. Wood lintels for various width openings are also given in table 7-8.

Installation of a lintel for an 8-inch wall is shown in figure 7-77. The thickness of the angle for a two-angle lintel should be 1/4 inch. This makes it possible for the two-angle legs that project up into the brick to fit exactly in the 1/2-inch joint between the face and backing-up ties of an 8-inch wall.

Corbeling

Corbeling consists of courses of brick set out beyond the face of the wall in order to form a self-supporting projection. This type of construction is shown in figure 7-79. The

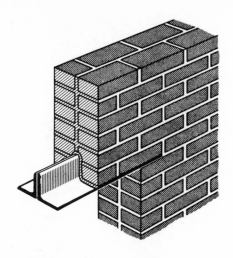

45.485
Figure 7-77.—Lintels for an 8-inch wall.

beyond the course below it and the total projection of the corbeling should not be more than the thickness of the wall.

Corbeling must be done carefully for the construction to have maximum strength. All mortar joints should be carefully made and completely filled with mortar. When the corbeled-out brick masonry is to withstand large loads, you should consult the design division of the operation department.

Brick Arches

If properly constructed, a brick arch can support a heavy load. The ability to support loads is derived primarily from its curved shape. Several arch shapes can be used; the circular and elliptical shapes are most common (fig. 7-80). The width of the mortar joint is less at the bottom of the brick than it is at the top, and it should not be thinner than 1/4 inch at any point. Arches made of brick must be constructed with full mortar joints. As laying progresses, care must be taken to see that the arch does not bulge out of position.

Table 7-8.—Lintel Sizes

Wall thickness	Span							
	3 feet		4 feet* steel angles	5 feet* steel angles	6 feet* steel angles	7 feet* steel angles	8 feet* steel angles
	Steel angles	Wood						
8"_____	2–3 x 3 x ¼	2 x 8 2–2 x 4	2–3 x 3 x ¼	2–3 x 3 x ¼	2–3½ x 3½ x ¼	2–3½ x 3½ x ¼	2–3½ x 3½ x ¼	
12"_____	2–3 x 3 x ¼	2 x 12 2–2 x 6	2–3 x 3 x ¼	2–3½ x 3½ x ¼	2–3½ x 3½ x ¼	2–4 x 4 x ¼	2–4 x 4 x 4¼	

*Wood lintels should not be used for spans over 3 feet since they burn out in case of fire and allow the brick to fall.

133.334

portion of a chimney that is exposed to the weather is frequently corbeled out and increased in thickness to improve its weathering resistance. Headers should also be used as much as possible in corbeling. It is usually necessary to use various-sized bats. The first projecting course may be a stretcher course if necessary. No course should extend out more than 2 inches

A brick arch is constructed on a temporary support that is left in position until the mortar has set. The temporary support is made of wood as shown in figure 7-81. The dimensions required are obtained from drawings. For arches up to 6 feet in span, 3/4-inch plywood should be used for temporary supports. Two pieces cut to the proper curved shape are made

193

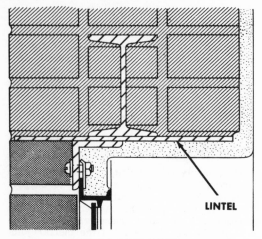

STEP 1 STEEL LINTEL

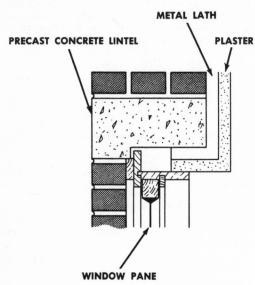

STEP 2 PRECAST CONCRETE LINTEL

45.486:.487
Figure 7-78.—Lintels for a 12-inch wall.

and nailed to 2 by 4's placed between them. This will provide a wide-enough surface to support the brick adequately.

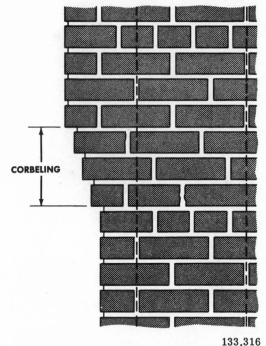

133.316
Figure 7-79.—Corbeled brick wall.

The temporary support should be held in position with wedges that can be driven out when the mortar has hardened enough for the arch to be self-supporting.

Construction of an arch is begun at the two ends or abutments of the arch. The brick is laid from each end toward the center or crown. The key or middle brick is the last to be placed. There should be an odd number of brick in order for the key or middle brick to come at the exact center of the arch. The arch should be laid out in such a way that no brick need be cut.

The best way to determine the number of brick required for an arch is to lay a temporary support on its side on level ground and set brick around it. Adjust the spacing until the key brick comes at the exact center of the arch. When this has been done, the position of the brick can be marked on the temporary support to be used as a guide when the arch is actually built.

194

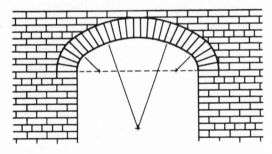

ELLIPTICAL ARCH

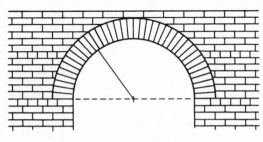

CIRCULAR ARCH

133.317

Figure 7-80.—Types of arches.

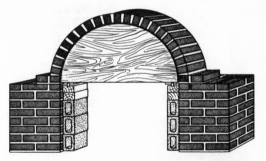

133.318

Figure 7-81.—Use of a templet in arch construction.

133.319

Figure 7-82.—Parging.

Watertight Walls

The water that passes through brick walls does not usually enter through the mortar or brick but through cracks between brick and mortar. Sometimes these cracks are formed because the bond between the brick and mortar is poor. They are more apt to occur in head joints than in bed joints. To prevent this, some brick must be wetted. If the position of the brick is changed after the mortar has begun to set, the bond between the brick and mortar will be destroyed and a crack will result. Shrinkage of the mortar is also frequently responsible for the formation of cracks.

Both the size and number of cracks between the mortar and the brick can be reduced if the exterior face of all the mortar joints is tooled to a concave finish. All head joints and bed joints must be completely filled with mortar if watertightness is to be obtained.

A procedure found effective in producing a leakproof wall is shown in figure 7-82. The back of the brick in the face tier is plastered with not less than 3/8 inch of rich cement mortar before the backing brick are laid. This is called PARGING or back plastering. Since parging should not be done over mortar protruding from the joints, all joints on the back of the face tier of bricks must be cut flush.

Membrane waterproofing, installed in the same way as specified for concrete walls, should be used if the wall is subject to considerable water pressure. The membrane, if properly installed, is able to adjust to any shrinkage or settlement without cracking. If the wall is to be subjected to considerable ground water or the surrounding soil is impervious, tile drains, or French drains if drainage tile is not available, should be constructed around the base of the wall (fig. 7-83).

For a foundation wall below ground level, two coats of bituminous mastic applied to the outside surface of the brick will yield satisfactory results. Asphalt or coal-tar pitch may be used and applied with mops.

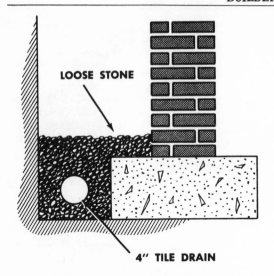

LOOSE STONE

4" TILE DRAIN

**WHEN TILE DRAIN IS OMITTED, THE
DRAIN IS CALLED A FRENCH DRAIN**

133.320
Figure 7-83.—Drain around foundation.

The watertightness of brick walls above
ground level is improved by the application of
transparent waterproof paints such as a water
solution of sodium silicate. Varnish is also effective. When used, these paints should be
applied as specified by the manufacturer. Certain white and colored waterproofing paints are
also available. In addition, good results have
been obtained by the use of high-quality oil
base paints.

Portland cement paint generally gives excellent results. The brick wall should be at least
30 days old before the portland cement paint is
applied and all efflorescence must be removed
from the surface to be painted. Manufacturer's
instructions for mixing and applying the paint
are to be followed. Surfaces must be damp
when the paint is applied, which is an advantage.
A water spray is the best means of wetting the
surface. Whitewash or calcimine type brushes
are used to apply the paint. Portland cement
paint can be applied with a spray gun but its
rain resistance will be reduced.

Fire-Resistant Brick

Fire brick are manufactured for such uses
as lining furnaces and incinerators. Their

purpose is to protect the supporting structure
or outer shell from intense heat. This outer
shell may consist of common brick or, in some
cases, steel, neither of which has good heat
resistance.

There are two types of fire-resistant brick:
FIREBRICKS are made from a special clay
known as fire clay. They will withstand high
temperatures and are heavier and usually
larger than common brick. The standard size
is 9 by 4 1/2 by 2 1/2 inches.

SILICA BRICK should be used if resistance
to acid gases is required. Silica brick should
not be used if it is to be alternately heated and
cooled. Most incinerators, therefore, should
be lined with fire brick rather than silica brick.

Thin joints are of the utmost importance in
laying fire brick. This is especially true when
the brick are exposed to high temperatures such
as those occurring in incinerators. The brick
should be kept in a dry place until the time they
are used.

The mortar to be used in laying fire brick
consists of fire clay mixed with water. The
consistency of the mortar should be that of thick
cream. Fire clay can be obtained by grinding
used fire brick.

The brick is dipped in the mortar in such a
way that all faces except the top face are
covered. The brick is then tapped firmly in
place with a bricklayer's hammer. The joint
between the brick should be as thin as possible
and the brick should fit tightly together. Any
cracks between the fire brick will allow heat to
penetrate to the outside shell of the incinerator
or furnace and damage it. The fire brick in one
course lap those in the course below by one-half
brick. The head joints are thus staggered in
the same way as they are staggered in the usual
type of brick construction.

Silica brick are laid without mortar. They
fit so closely that they fuse together at the
joints when subjected to high temperatures.
The head joints for silica brick are staggered,
as for fire brick.

Special Types of Walls

Many different types of walls may be built
of brick. The solid 8- and 12-inch walls in
common bond are the ones usually used for
solid wall construction in the United States.
The most important of the hollow walls are
the cavity wall and the rowlock type wall.

CAVITY WALLS provide a means of obtaining a watertight wall that may be plastered without the use of furring or lathing. From the outside they appear the same as solid walls without header courses (fig. 7-84). No headers are required because the two tiers of brick are held together by means of metal ties installed every sixth course and on 24-inch centers. To prevent waterflow to the inside tier, ties must be angled in a downward direction from the inside tier to the outside tier.

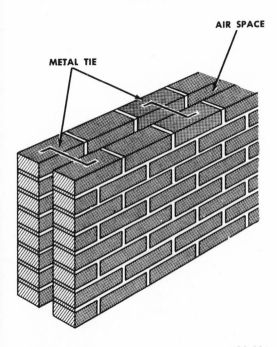

133.321
Figure 7-84.—Details for a cavity wall.

The 2-inch cavity between the two tiers of brick provides a space down which water that penetrates the outside tier may flow without passing through to the inside of the wall. The bottom of the cavity is above ground level and is drained by weep holes placed in the vertical joints between two bricks in the first course of the outer tier. These holes may be formed by leaving the mortar out of some of the vertical joints in the first course. The holes should be spaced at about 24-inch intervals. The air space also gives the wall better heat- and sound-insulating properties.

One type of ROWLOCK WALL is shown in figure 7-85. The face tier of this wall has the same appearance as a common bond wall with a full header course every seventh course. The backing tier is laid with the brick on edge. The face tier and backing tier are tied together by a header course as shown. A 2-inch space is provided between the two tiers of brick, as for a cavity wall.

An all-rowlock wall is constructed with brick in the face and backing tier both laid on edge. The header course would be installed at every fourth course: three rowlock courses to every header course. A rowlock wall is not as watertight as the cavity wall. Water is able to follow any crack present in the header course and pass through the wall to the inside surface.

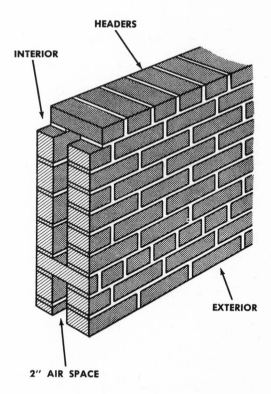

133.322
Figure 7-85.—Details of a rowlock backwall.

197

PARTITION WALLS that carry very little load can be made using one tier of brick only. This produces a wall 4 inches thick. A wall of this thickness is laid up without headers.

Brick are laid in cavity walls, and partition walls according to the procedure given for making bed joints, head joints, cross joints, and closures. The line is used the same as for a common bond wall. Corner leads for these walls are erected first and the wall between is built up afterward.

REINFORCED BRICK MASONRY

Because the strength of brick masonry in tension is low, as compared with its compressive strength, reinforcing steel is used when tensile stresses are to be resisted. In this respect, brick masonry and concrete construction are identical. The reinforcing steel is placed in the horizontal or vertical mortar joints. Reinforced brick masonry may be used for beams, columns, walls, and footings in the same manner as reinforced concrete is used. Structures built of reinforced brick masonry have successfully resisted the effect of earthquake shocks intense enough to damage unreinforced brick structures severely. The design of reinforced brick masonry structures is similar to the design of reinforced concrete structures.

Brick used for reinforced brick masonry is the same as that used for ordinary brick masonry. It should, however, have a compressive strength of at least 2,500 pounds per square inch.

The reinforcing steel is the same as the steel used to reinforce concrete and it is stored and fabricated in the same way. Hard-grade steel should not be used except in emergencies because many sharp bends are required in this type of construction.

Type N mortar is used because of its high strength.

Wire for tying reinforcing steel should be 16-gage soft annealed iron wire.

Construction Methods for Reinforced Brick Masonry

Bricklaying is the same as for normal brick masonry. Mortar joint thickness is 1/8 inch more than the diameter of the steel bar used for reinforcing. This will allow 1/16 inch of mortar between the surface of the brick and the bar. When large steel bars are used, the thickness of the mortar joint will exceed 1/2 inch.

All reinforcing steel must be firmly embedded in mortar.

Horizontal bars are laid in a bed of mortar and pushed down until in position. More mortar is spread on top of the rods and smoothed out until a bed joint of the proper thickness can be made. The next course of brick is then laid in this mortar bed according to the procedure outlined for laying brick without reinforcing steel.

Stirrups for most reinforced brick beams must be of the shape shown in figure 7-86 in order to place them in the mortar joints. The lower leg is placed under the horizontal bars and in contact with them. Note that this may require a thicker joint at this point.

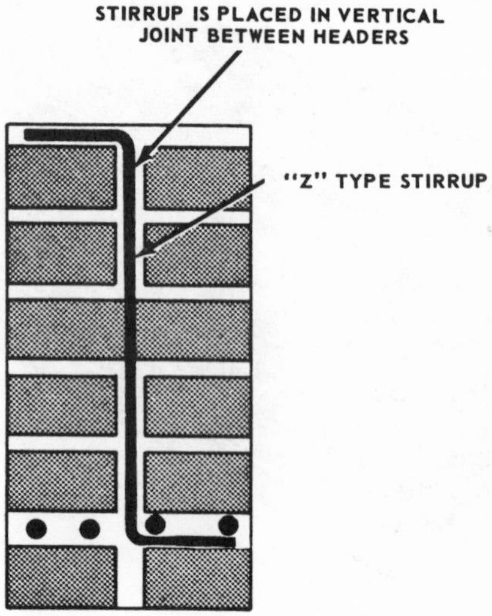

STIRRUP IS PLACED IN VERTICAL JOINT BETWEEN HEADERS

"Z" TYPE STIRRUP

133.323

Figure 7-86.—Reinforced brick masonry beam.

Vertical bars are placed in the vertical mortar joints. They are held in position by wood templets in which holes have been drilled at the proper bar spacing or by wiring to a horizontal bar. The brick is laid up around the vertical bars.

Horizontal and vertical bars need not be wired together as was recommended for reinforcing steel in concrete walls.

The minimum center-to-center spacing between parallel bars is 1 1/2 times the bar diameter.

Reinforced brick beams require form work for the same reason that reinforced concrete beams need form work. The form will consist only of a support for the bottom of the beam. No side form work is required. The form for the bottom is the same and is supported in the same way as recommended for concrete beams. No form work is required for walls, columns, or footings.

Where the beam joins a wall or another beam, the form should be cut 1/4 inch short and the gap filled with mortar to allow for swelling of the lumber and to permit easy removal of the forms. (At least 10 days should elapse before the bottom form work for beams is removed.)

Reinforced Brick Masonry Beams

The width and depth of beams depend upon brick dimensions, thickness of the mortar joints, and the load that the beam is required to support. Beam widths are usually the same as the wall thicknesses; that is, 4, 8, 12, and 16 inches. The depth should not exceed about three times the width.

The first course of brick is laid on the form with full head joints but without a bed joint (fig. 7-86).

A bed of mortar about 1/8-inch thicker than the diameter of the horizontal reinforcing bars is spread on the first course of brick and the bars embedded in it as already described.

If stirrups are required, the leg of the stirrup is slipped under the horizontal bars as shown in figure 7-86. Care must be taken to get the stirrup in the center of the vertical mortar joint in which it is to be placed.

After the stirrups and the horizontal bars are in the proper position, spread additional mortar on the bed joint if necessary, and smooth the surface of the mortar. The mortar bed is now ready for the remaining courses which are laid in the usual way.

All of the brick in one course are laid before any brick in the next course are placed. This is necessary to ensure a continuous bond between the mortar and steel bars. It is frequently necessary to have three or four Builders working on one beam in order to get the bed joint mortar for the entire course spread, reinforcing steel placed, and brick laid before the mortar sets up.

The proper placement of reinforcing steel in the brick wall above a window or door opening will serve the purpose of a lintel.

The steel bars should be 3/8 inch in diameter or less if it is necessary to maintain a 1/2-inch thick mortar joint. The bars should extend 15 inches into the brick wall on each side of the opening and should be placed in the first mortar joint above the opening and also in the fourth joint above the opening (fig. 7-87). The lintel acts as a beam and needs a bottom form. The number and size bars required for different width wall openings are as follows:

Width of wall opening in feet	Number and size of bars
6	2 1/4-inch diameter bars
9	3 1/4-inch diameter bars
12	3 3/8-inch diameter bars

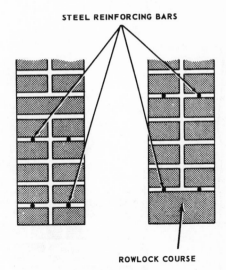

STEEL REINFORCING BARS

ROWLOCK COURSE

133.324

Figure 7-87.—Reinforced brick masonry lintels.

Reinforced Brick Masonry Foundations

In large footings, reinforcing steel is usually needed because of the tensile stresses that develop. As in all brick foundations, the first course of brick is laid in a bed of mortar about 1 inch thick that has been spread on the subgrade.

A typical wall footing is shown in figure 7-88. The dowels extend above the footing; their purpose is to tie the footing and brick wall together. The No. 3 bars shown running parallel to the direction of the wall are used to prevent the formation of cracks perpendicular to the wall.

Column footings are usually square or rectangular and are reinforced as shown in figure 7-89. The dowels are needed to anchor the column to the footing and to transfer stress from the column to the footing. Note that both layers of horizontal steel are placed in the same mortar joint. This is not necessary and, if large bars are used, one layer of steel should be placed in the second mortar joint above the bottom. If this is done, the spacing between the bars in the upper layer of steel must be reduced.

Reinforced Brick Masonry Columns and Walls

The load-carrying capacity of brick columns is increased when they are reinforced with steel bars. There should be at least 1 1/2 inches of mortar or brick covering the reinforcing bars and these bars should be held in place with 3/8-inch diameter steel hoops or ties as shown in figure 7-90. When possible, the hoops or ties should be circular rather than rectangular or square. The ends of the hoop or tie should be lap-welded together or bent around a reinforcing bar. Hoops should be installed at every course of brick.

After the footings are completed, the column reinforcing steel is tied to the dowels projecting from the footing. The required number of hoops is then slipped over the longitudinal reinforcing

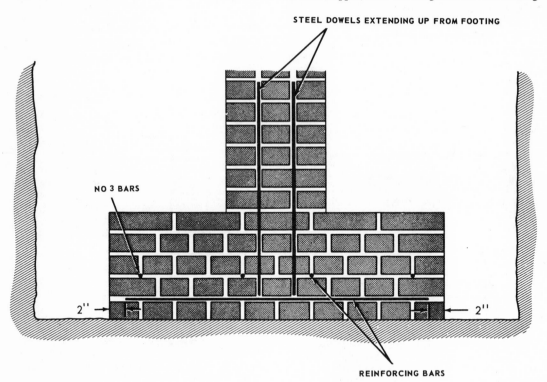

STEEL DOWELS EXTENDING UP FROM FOOTING

NO 3 BARS

2''   2''

REINFORCING BARS

133.325

Figure 7-88.—Reinforced masonry wall footing.

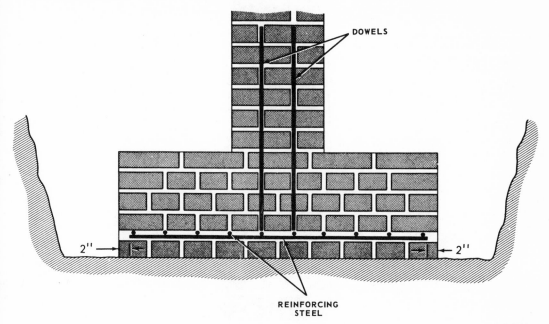

Figure 7-89.—Reinforced masonry column footing.

133.326

bars and temporarily fastened to these bars some distance above the level at which brick are being laid but within reach of the Builder laying brick. It is not necessary for the hoops to be held in position by wiring them to the longitudinal reinforcing. The tops of the longitudinal reinforcing bars are held in position by means of a wood templet or by securely tying them to a hoop placed near the top of the column.

The brick are laid as described previously. The hoops are placed in a full bed of mortar and the mortar smoothed out before the next course of brick is laid. Brick bats may be used in the core of the column or where it is inconvenient or impossible to use full-size brick. After all the brick in a course are laid, the core and all remaining space around the reinforcing bars is filled with mortar. Any bats required are then pushed into the mortar until completely embedded. The next mortar bed is now spread and the process repeated.

Reinforcing steel for walls consists of both horizontal and vertical bars and is placed as discussed previously. The vertical bars are wired to the dowels projecting up from the footing below and are placed in the mortar joint between tiers of brick. As the brick are laid, all space around the bars is filled with mortar. Otherwise, the wall is constructed as specified.

In the construction of corner leads, bars should be placed in the corner as shown in figure 7-91. The extension is 15 inches and the bar size should be the same as that used for horizontal bars in the rest of the wall. The horizontal bars in the remainder of the wall lap these corner bars by the same 15 inches. As for beams, all the brick in one course between corner leads are laid before any other brick are laid. This is necessary since the entire reinforcing bar must be embedded in mortar at the same time.

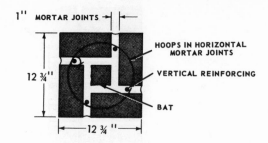

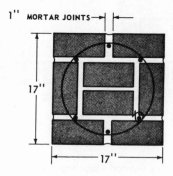

133.327

Figure 7-90.—Reinforced brick
masonry columns.

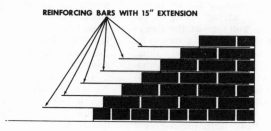

133.328

Figure 7-91.—Corner lead for reinforced
brick masonry wall.

CHAPTER 8
WOODWORKING: TOOLS, EQUIPMENT, AND FASTENINGS

The term WOODWORKING, as used as a subject-matter heading for this course, is intended to cover all types of wood fabrication and construction. In practice, however, the term is usually confined to shop work. Woodworking done in the field is generally called CARPENTRY, and carpentry itself is divided into ROUGH and FINISH carpentry. Rough carpentry includes the layout, cutting, and erection of formwork members and of such wooden structural members as plates, joists, studs, girders, bridging, bracing, and rafters. Since wall and roof sheathing and subflooring are considered to be structural elements, the layout, cutting, and erection of sheathing and subflooring members are also included under rough carpentry.

Finish carpentry includes the layout, cutting, and erection of siding, outside casings, cornice trim, corner boards, roofing, and the like (called EXTERIOR FINISH), and the layout, cutting, and erection of inside wall covering, finish flooring, stairs, moldings, and the like (called INTERIOR FINISH). The fitting and hanging of doors and of window sash, and the fabrication of the same if done in the field, are also phases of the interior finish carpentry.

Shop woodworking includes the manufacture and repair of furniture, cabinets, cases, and the fabrication of doors, window sash, stairway members, molding trim, and the like (called MILLWORK).

In civilian industry the several specialties included under the general heading of "woodworking" are usually distributed among several trades—meaning that in civilian industry the carpenter, joiner, cabinetmaker, and millworker are usually different individuals. The Navy Builder, however, must be at one and the same time a carpenter, joiner, cabinetmaker, and millworker. He is in short, a general woodworking CRAFTSMAN, and the first requirement for a craftsman is an ability to use the tools and equipment of the trade effectively and skillfully.

The large number and variety of woodworking tools discussed in the following sections are divided into HANDTOOLS and POWER TOOLS. The power tools are for the most part power-driven, sawing, boring, or shaving tools, equipped with devices for holding and/or guiding the work.

HANDTOOLS

After reading BASIC HANDTOOLS, NavPers 10085-A, you should be quite familiar with a variety of handtools. However, we believe that the fundamentals of using certain tools should be discussed further; therefore, we will stress the use of the framing square, and briefly mention several other handtools.

THE FRAMING SQUARE

The FRAMING SQUARE is one of the most generally used tools. The problems that can be solved with the square are so many and varied that books have been written on the square alone. Only a few of the more common uses of the square can be presented here; the Builder who desires to take full advantage of the square's capacities for solving a whole host of construction problems should obtain and study one of the books on the square.

The framing square consists of a wide and long member called the BLADE and a narrower and shorter member called the TONGUE, which forms a right angle with the blade. The FACE of the square is the side one sees when the square is held with the blade in the left hand, tongue in the right hand, heel pointed away from the body. The manufacturer's name is usually stamped on the face. The blade is 24 in. long and 2 in. wide and the tongue varies from 14 in. to 18 in. long and 1 1/2 in. wide, as measured from the outer corner, where the blade and the tongue meet. This corner is called the HEEL of the square.

The outer and inner edges of the tongue and the blade, on both face and back, are graduated

in inches. The first thing you must do is mem-
orize the manner in which the inch is subdivided
in the scales on the BACK of the square. In the
scales on the face, the inch is subdivided in the
regular units of carpenter's measure (eighths
or sixteenths of an inch). On the back of the
square, however, the outer edge of the blade
and outer edge of the tongue are graduated in
inches and TWELFTHS of inches; the inner
edge of the tongue is graduated in inches and
TENTHS of inches; and the inner edge of the
blade is graduated in inches and thirty-seconds
of inches on most squares.

Common uses of the twelfth and tenth scales
on the back of the framing square will be described later.

Basic Problems Solved
by the Framing Square

The framing square is used most frequently
to find the length of the hypotenuse (longest
side) of a right triangle when the lengths of the
other two sides are known. This is the basic
problem involved in, for example, determining
the length of a roof rafter, a brace, or any
other member which forms the hypotenuse of
an actual or an imaginary right triangle.

Figure 8-1 shows you how the framing
square is used to determine the length of the
hypotenuse of a right triangle with other sides
each 12 in. long. Plane a true, straight edge on
a board, and set the square on the board so as
to bring the 12-in. mark on the tongue and the
12-in. mark on the blade even with the edge of
the board. Draw the pencil marks shown in the
second view. The distance between these marks,
as measured along the edge of the board, is the
length of the hypotenuse of a right triangle with
other sides each 12 in. long. You'll find that the
distance, which is called the BRIDGE MEASURE,
measures just a shade under 17 in. To be exact, it is 16.97 in., as shown in the figure, but
for most practical Builder's purposes 16.97 in.
may be rounded off to 17 in.

Unit and Total Run and Rise

In figure 8-1 the problem could be solved by
a single set (called a CUT) of the framing square,
because the dimensions of the triangle in question lie within the dimensions of the square.
Now suppose that you are trying to find the
length of the hypotenuse of a right triangle with
the two known sides being 48 in. long each.

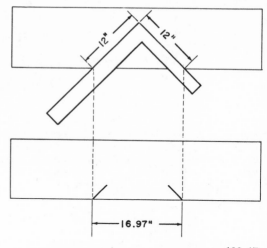

133.47
Figure 8-1.—Basic problem solved
by the framing square.

Let's assume that the member whose length
you are trying to determine is the brace shown
in figure 8-2. The TOTAL RUN of this brace is
48 in., and the TOTAL RISE is also 48 in.

To figure the length of the brace, you first
reduce the triangle in question to a similar
triangle which is within the dimensions of the
framing square. The length of the vertical
shorter side of this triangle is called the UNIT
OF RISE, and the length of the horizontal shorter
side is called the UNIT OF RUN. By a general
custom of the trade, unit of run is always taken
as 12 in., and measured on the tongue of the
framing square.

Now, if the total run is 48 in., the total rise
48 in., and the unit of run 12 in., what is the
unit of rise? Well, since the sides of similar
triangles are proportional, the unit of rise must
be the value of x in the proportional equation
48:48::12:x. In this case, then, the unit of rise
is obviously 12 in.

To get the length of the brace, you set the
framing square to the unit of run (12 in.) on the
tongue and to the unit of rise (also 12 in.) on the
blade as shown in figure 8-2, and then "step off"
this cut as many times as the unit of run goes
into the total run. In this case that is 48/12, or
4 times, as shown in the figure.

This problem involved a situation in which
the total run and total rise were the same, from

204

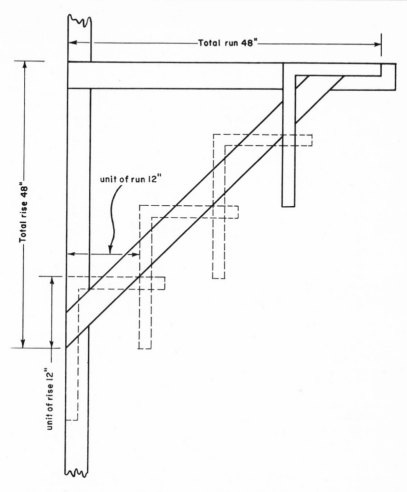

133.48

Figure 8-2.—"Stepping off" with the framing square.

which it followed that the unit of run and unit of rise were also the same. Suppose now that you want to know the length of a brace with a total run of 60 in. and a total rise of 72 in. Since the unit of run is 12 in., the unit of rise must be the value of x in the proportional equation 60:72::12:x. When you work this out, you will find that the unit of rise is 14.4 in. This is near enough to 14 3/8 in. to serve any practical purpose.

To lay out the full length of the brace, you set the square to the unit of rise (14 3/8 in.) and

the unit of run (12 in.), as shown in figure 8-3 and then "step off" this cut as many times as the unit of run goes into the total run (in this case 60/12, or 5 times).

Line Length

If you don't go through the procedure of "stepping off," you can figure the total length of the member in question by first determining the BRIDGE MEASURE. The line length is the length of the hypotenuse of a right triangle with

205

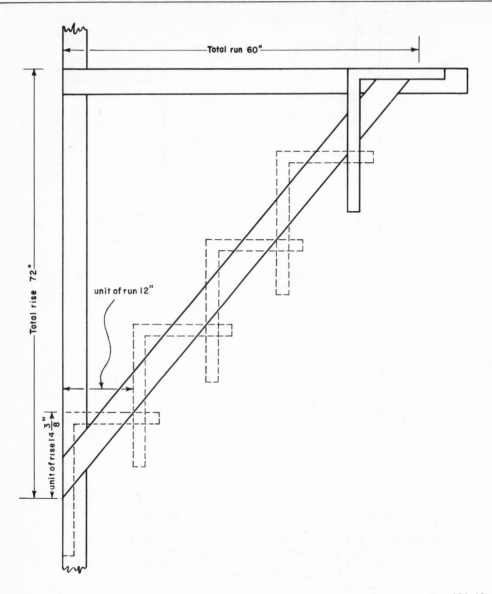

133.49

Figure 8-3.—Stepping off with the square when the unit of run and
unit of rise are different.

the other sides equal to the unit of run and the
unit of rise. Take the situation shown in figure
8-3, for example. The unit of run here is 12 in.,
and the unit of rise is 14 3/8 in. Set the square
to this cut as shown in figure 8-4, and mark the
edges of the board as shown. If you measure

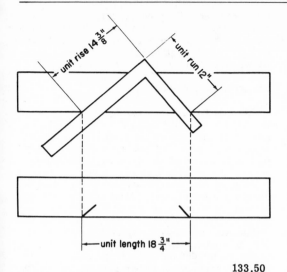

Figure 8-4.—Unit length.

133.50

the distance between the marks, you will find that it is 18 3/4 in.

To get the total length of the member, you simply multiply the bridge measure by the number of times that the unit of run goes into the total run. Since that is 5 in this case, the total length of the member is 18 3/4 x 5, or 93 3/4 in. Actually, the length of the hypotenuse of a right triangle with the other sides 60 and 72 in. long is between 93.72 in. and 93.73 in., but 93 3/4 in. is close enough for any practical purpose.

Once you have determined the total length of the member, all you need to do is measure it off and make the end cuts. To make these cuts at the proper angles, you simply set the square to the unit of run on the tongue and unit of rise on the blade and draw a line for the cut along the blade (lower end cut) or the tongue (upper end cut).

Using the Twelfths Scale

The graduations in inches and twelfths of inches which are located on the back of the square, along the outer edges of the blade and tongue, are called the TWELFTHS SCALE. The chief purpose of the twelfth scale is to provide various short cuts in problem-solving with the framing square. Since the scale is graduated in inches and twelfths of inches, dimensions in

feet and inches can be reduced to 1/12th of size by simply allowing each graduation on the twelfth scale to represent 1 in. For example: 2 6/12 in. on the twelfth scale may be taken to represent 2 ft 6 in.

A few examples will show you how the twelfth scale is used. Suppose you want to know the total length of a rafter with a total run of 10 ft and a total rise of 6 ft 5 in. Set the square on a board with the twelfth scale on the blade at 10 in. and the twelfth scale on the tongue at 6 5/12 in., and make the usual marks. If you measure the distance between the marks, you will find it to be 11 11/12 in. The total length of the rafter, then is 11 ft 11 in.

Suppose now that you know the unit of run, unit of rise, and total run of a rafter and you want to find the total rise and the total length. Let's say that unit of run and unit of rise are 12 in. and 8 in., respectively, and that total run is 8 ft 9 in. Set the square to the unit rise on the tongue and unit run on the blade, as shown in the first view of figure 8-5. Then slide the square to the right until the 8 9/12 in. mark on

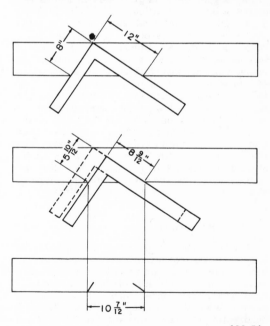

133.51

Figure 8-5.—Finding total rise and total length when unit of run, unit of rise, and total run are known.

the blade (representing the total run of 8 ft 9 in.) comes even with the edge of the board, as shown in the second view. The figure of 5 10/12 in. which is now indicated on the tongue is one-twelfth of the total rise. The total rise is therefore 5 ft 10 in. The distance between pencil marks (10 7/12 inches) drawn along the tongue and the blade is one twelfth of the total length. The total length is therefore 10 ft 7 in.

The twelfths scale may also be used to determine dimensions by inspection for proportional reductions or enlargements. Suppose, for example, that you have a panel 10 ft 9 in. long by 7 ft wide, and you want to cut a panel 7 ft long with the same proportions. Set the square as shown in figure 8-5, but with the blade at 10 9/12 in. and the tongue at 7 in. Then slide the blade to 7 in. and read the figure indicated on the tongue, which will be 4 7/12 in. The smaller panel, then, should be 4 ft 7 in. wide.

Using the Tenths Scale

The scale along the inner edge of the back of the tongue, which is graduated in inches and tenths of inches, is called the TENTHS SCALE. This scale can be used along with the scale along the inner edge of the back of the blade (which is graduated in inches and sixteenths of inches) to determine various proportions by inspection. Suppose that a crew can excavate 44 linear ft of trench in 8 hours. How many feet can they excavate in 3 1/4 hours? Set the square on a board with the tenth scale on the tongue at the 4.4-in. mark and the scale on the inner edge of the blade at the 8-in. mark. Then slide the blade down to the 3 1/4-in. mark. The reading on the tenth scale will now be 1.8 in. Since you took 4.4 to represent 44, 1.8 must represent 18, and the crew should therefore be able to excavate approximately 18 linear ft in 3 1/4 hours.

Using the Hundredths Scale

The hundredths scale is on the back of the tongue, in the corner of the square, near the brace table. This scale is called the hundredths scale because one inch is divided into one hundred parts. The longer lines indicate 25 hundredths while the next shorter lines indicate 5 hundredths, etc. By using dividers, a fraction of an inch can be easily obtained.

The inch is graduated in sixteenths, and located below the hundredths scale; therefore,

the conversion from hundredths to sixteenths can be made at a glance without the use of dividers. This can be a great help when determining rafter lengths, using the figures of the rafter tables where hundredths are given.

Using the Octagon Scale

The OCTAGON SCALE (sometimes called the EIGHT-SQUARE SCALE) is located in the middle of the face of the tongue. The octagon scale is used to lay out an octagon (8-sided figure) in a square of given even-inch dimensions. The procedure is as follows.

Suppose you want to cut an 8-in. octagonal piece for a stair newel. First square the stock to 8 in. by 8 in., square and smooth the end-section, and draw crossed center lines on the end-section as shown in figure 8-6. Then set a pair of dividers to the distance from the first to the eighth dot on the octagon scale, and lay off this distance on either side of the center lines on the 4 slanting sides of the octagon.

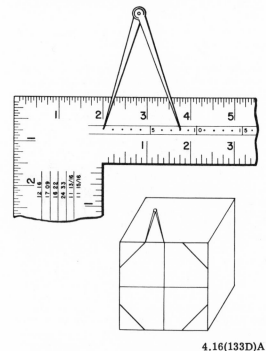

4.16(133D)A

Figure 8-6.—Using the octagon scale.

When you use the octagon scale, set one leg of the dividers on the first dot and the other leg on the dot whose number corresponds to the width in inches of the square from which you are cutting the piece. This distance amounts to one-half the length of a side of the octagon.

Using the Framing Tables on the Framing Square

There are three tables on the framing square, as follows: (1) the UNIT LENGTH RAFTER TABLE, located on the face of the blade, (2) the BRACE TABLE, located on the back of the tongue, and (3) the ESSEX BOARD MEASURE TABLE, located on the back of the blade. Before you can use the unit length rafter table, you must be familiar with the different types of rafters and with the methods of framing them. Consequently, the use of the unit length rafter table will be described in the later chapter entitled "Roof Framing" (ch. 11). The other two tables are used as follows.

Using the Brace Table

The brace table sets forth a series of equal runs and rises for every 3-unit interval from 24/24 to 60/60, together with the brace length, or length of the hypotenuse, for each given run and rise. The table can be used to determine by inspection the length of the hypotenuse of a right triangle with equal shorter sides of any length given in the table.

For example: in the segment of the brace table shown in figure 8-7, you can see that the length of the hypotenuse of a right triangle with two sides 24 units long is 33.94 units; with two sides 27 units long, 38.18 units; with two sides 30 units long, 42.43 units, and so on.

By applying simple arithmetic, you can use the brace table to determine the hypotenuse of a right triangle with equal sides of practically any even-unit length. Suppose, for example, that you want to know the length of the hypotenuse of a right triangle with two sides 8 in. long. The brace table shows that a right triangle with two sides 24 in. long has a hypotenuse 33.94 in. long. Since 8 amounts to 24/3, a right triangle with two shorter sides 8 in. long must have a hypotenuse 33.94/3, or 11.31 in. long.

Suppose you want to find the length of the hypotenuse of a right triangle with two sides 40 in. each. The sides of similar triangles are proportional, and any right triangle with two

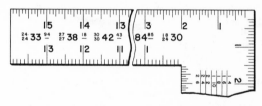

Figure 8-7.—Brace table.

equal sides is similar to any other right triangle with two equal sides. The brace table shows you that a right triangle with the two shorter sides being 30 in. each in length has a hypotenuse 42.43 in. long. The length of the hypotenuse of a right triangle with the two shorter sides being 40 in. each in length must be the value of x in the proportional equation 30:42.43::40:x, or 56.57 in.

Notice that the last item in the brace table (the one furthest to the right in fig. 8-7) gives you the hypotenuse of a right triangle with the other sides 18 and 24 units long respectively. The proportions 18:24:30 are those of the most common type of unequal-sided right triangle, which is called the "3-4-5" right triangle. Any triangle with sides in the proportions of 3:4:5 must be a right triangle.

Using the Essex Board Measure Table

Since the chief practical use of board measure is in connection with lumber costs, you may not have much use for the Essex board measure table. The table makes it possible for you to determine by inspection the board measure of a 1-in.-thick piece of given length and width. A segment of the table is shown in figure 8-8.

The inch graduations above the table (1, 2, 3, 4, and so on) represent the width in inches of the piece to be measured. The figures under

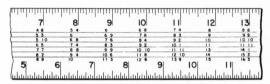

Figure 8-8.—Segment of Essex board measure table.

the 12-in. graduation (8, 9, 10, 11, 13, 14, and 15, arranged in column) represent lengths in feet. The figure 12 itself represents a 12-ft length. The column headed by the figure 12 is the starting point for all calculations.

To use the table, run down the figure-12 column to the figure that represents the length of the piece in feet. Then run horizontally to the figure which is directly below the inch mark that corresponds to the width of the stock in inches. The figure you find will be the number of board feet and twelfths of board feet in a 1-in.-thick piece of the given length and width.

For example: suppose you want to figure the board measure of a piece 10 ft long by 9 in. wide by 1 in. thick. Run down the column headed by the 12-in. graduation to 10, and then run horizontally to the left to the figure directly below the 9-in. graduation. You will find the figure to be 7.6 or 7 6/12 board feet.

What do you do if the piece is more than 1 in. thick? Obviously, all you have to do is multiply the result obtained for a 1-in. piece by the actual thickness of the piece in inches. For example: if the board described in the preceding paragraph were 5 in. thick instead of 1 in. thick, you would follow the procedure described and then multiply the result by 5.

The board measure scale can be read only for pieces from 8 to 15 feet in length, inclusive. If your piece is longer than 15 feet, you can proceed in one of two ways. If the length of the piece is evenly divisible by one of the tabulated lengths in the table, you can read for that length and multiply the result by the number of times that the tabulated length goes into the length of the piece. For example: suppose you want to find the number of board feet in a piece 33 ft long by 7 in. wide by 1 in. thick. Since 33 is evenly divisible by 11, go down the 12-in. column to 11 and then run left to the 7-in. column. The figure given there (which is 6 5/12 bd ft) is one-third of the number of bd ft in a piece 33 ft long by 7 in. wide by 1 in. thick. The total number of bd ft, then, is 6 5/12 x 3, or 19 3/12 bd ft.

If the length of the piece is not evenly divisible by one of the tabulated lengths, you can divide it into two tabulated lengths, read the table for these two, and add the results together. For example: suppose you want to find the board measure of a piece 25 ft long by 10 in. wide by 1 in. thick. This length can be divided into 10 ft and 15 ft. The table shows that the 10-ft length contains 8 4/12 bd ft and the 15-ft length 12 6/12 bd ft. The total length, then, contains 8 4/12 plus 12 6/12, or 20 10/12 bd ft.

MITER BOX

A MITER BOX permits sawing a piece of stock to a given angle without laying out a line. Figure 8-9 shows a common type of wooden 45° miter box. Stock can be cut at 45° by placing the saw in cuts M-S and L-F, or at 90° by placing the saw in cuts A-B. The STEEL MITER BOX shown in figure 8-10 can be set to cut stock at any angle.

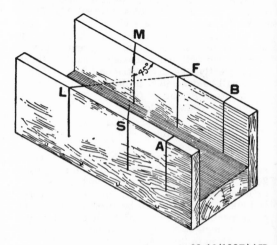

68.10(133D)AX
Figure 8-9.—Wooden 45° miter box.

LEVELS

The LINE level (fig. 8-11) consists of a bubble tube set into a metal case with a hook at each end to permit it to be hung on a line or cord.

The line level is used to test whether a line or cord is level. It is particularly useful when the distance between two points to be checked for level is too long to permit the use of a board and the carpenter's level. However, the line level will show a disadvantage at a long distance because the line has a tendency to sag. To use the level—stretch a cord between the two points which are to be checked for level. Hang the line level on the cord and see whether the bubble is in the middle of the tube. If it is not, raise the end of the cord which is toward

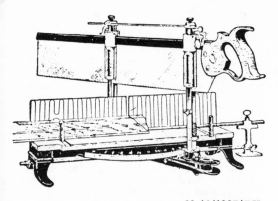

68.10(133D)BX
Figure 8-10.—Steel miter box.

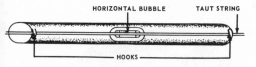

29.14
Figure 8-11.—Line level.

the lower end of the bubble until the bubble rests in the middle of the tube. Unhook the level and turn it end for end, hang it on the cord, and retest. Continue testing until the bubble rests in the same relative position in its tube when the level is turned end for end. Remember, to make the bubble rise in the tube, lift that end of the cord which is toward the lower end of the bubble.

The line level is a delicate instrument; therefore, it must be kept in a box when not in use, to protect the bubble tube from being broken and the hooks from being bent. Never clean the level with water or any liquid because condensation will appear. The CARPENTER's level (fig. 8-12) is usually a 24-inch wood block with true-surface edges. There are two bubble tubes in it. One is in the middle of one of the long edges. The other is at right angles to this, and parallel to the end of the level.

Bubble tubes are glass tubes nearly filled with alcohol. They are slightly curved. As a bubble of air in such a tube will rise to the highest point, the bubble will take its place in the middle of the tube when the tube is in a horizontal position.

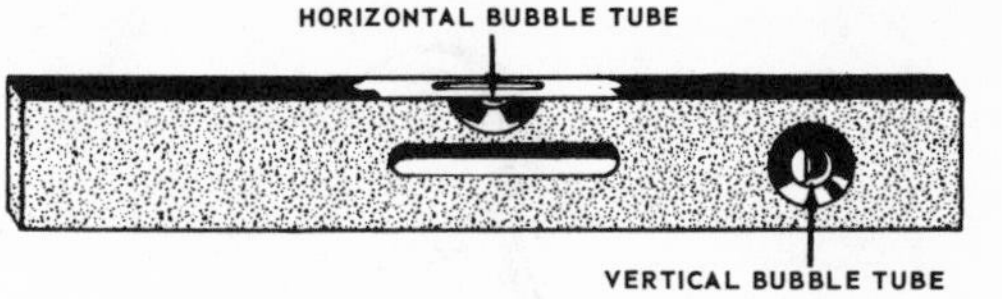

29.13
Figure 8-12.—Carpenter's level.

Scratch marks at equal distances from the middle of the tube mark the proper position of the bubble when the surface on which the tube rests is level.

The carpenter's level is used to determine whether a surface is level. "Level" usually describes a horizontal surface which, throughout its extent, lies on a line corresponding to that of the horizon. "Plumb" means vertical, or at right angles to "level."

To test for levelness of a surface, lay the carpenter's level on the surface and see where the bubble comes to rest. If the surface is level and the level is in adjustment, it will come to rest exactly between the two scratch marks mentioned above. Turn the level end for end and recheck. The bubble should come to rest in the same place. If it does not, raise the end of the surface being tested which is toward the low end of the tube until it checks level.

To check for plumb, set the long side of the carpenter's level against the upright to be tested and use the bubble which is set in the end in the same way as described above. Turn the level end for end to ensure accuracy, as mentioned above.

SCRATCH AWL

Lines for cuts may be drawn on stock with a sharp pencil, tilted to bring the pencil point close to the straightedge. However, a more accurate location of the line will be obtained if you scribe the stock with a SCRATCH AWL like the one shown in figure 8-13.

MULTIPLE FOLDING RULE

The multiple folding rule (fig. 8-14) is 6 feet long. The sections are so hinged that it is 6 inches from the center of one hinge joint to the center of the next, which makes the sections roughly 8 inches in length. It is graduated in sixteenths of an inch.

211

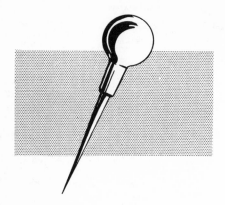

133.53
Figure 8-13.—Scratch awl.

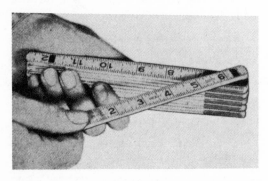

4.16(133)F
Figure 8-14.—Multiple folding rule.

Whenever using the folding rule, hold the rule in one hand and unfold the sections one by one with the other hand as illustrated in figure 8-14 until the rule is longer than the measurement to be taken.

Place the rule flat against the surface to be measured, and parallel to one edge.

Place the end of the rule at the starting point of the measurement.

Note the graduation which lines up with the point to which the measurement is being made.

Always remember that the folding rule can be easily bent or broken if used carelessly, particularly when it is being opened. Open it as illustrated in figure 8-14. Close the rule and keep it in your pocket or toolbox when not in use. Do not leave it lying around the workbench where it may be damaged.

TAPE

The tape (fig. 8-15) is a ribbon, 3/8 inch in width and ranges from 6 to 100 feet in length. It is graduated in feet, inches and fractions of an inch down to 1/8 inch. One end of the tape is fastened to a reel which is housed in a leather-covered metal box provided with a slot through which the other end of the tape protrudes. This end has a metal ring attached to it. The ring will not pass through the slot in the case; thus it forms a handle by which the tape may be drawn from the case. Zero on the tape is at the inside of the end of the ring. This makes it possible to hook the ring over a nail or other projection while measuring with the tape, making it unnecessary to have another man hold the end in position. A folding crank is provided on the reel, by which the tape can be returned to the case after use.

29.250(133F)
Figure 8-15.—Steel tape.

To measure with the tape, hold the ring end at the starting point, either by slipping it over a nail or by other means. Walk in the direction to be measured, letting the tape be pulled from the case as you walk. Stretch the slack out of the tape, making sure it is parallel to the surface or edge to be measured. Read the graduation which falls at the end of the distance to be measured.

Reel the tape back into its case whenever it is not actually being used, by turning the crank on the case in a clockwise direction. Do not permit the tape to be kinked. It is easily kinked by being used for measuring around corners or by permitting a vehicle to run over it. Keep the tape lightly oiled. If it gets wet or damp by being used in dew-covered grass or in the rain, wipe it thoroughly dry and oil it before returning it to its case.

CHALK LINE

Long straight lines between distant points on surfaces are marked by snapping a CHALK LINE as shown in figure 8-16. The line is first chalked by holding the chalk in the hand and drawing the line across it several times. It is then stretched between the points and snapped as shown. For an accurate snap, never snap the chalk line over a 20 foot distance.

Handtools not mentioned in this chapter are explained in Basic Handtools, NavPers 10085-A.

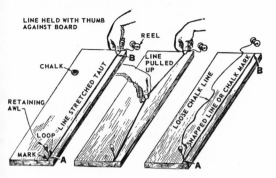

133.54X

Figure 8-16.—Snapping a chalk line.

FORSTNER BIT

The forstner bit does not have a feed screw but must be fed by pushing while turning. The rim projects slightly and prevents the bit from creeping when used. There is no tendency to split the wood as is often the case with screw feed bits. Forstner bits, because of the absence of a feed screw, will bore holes almost through a board without defacing the opposite side of the board. The size markings are the same as auger bits.

DRAWKNIFE

The DRAWKNIFE (fig. 8-17) is a two-hand cutter like the spokeshave; it is also pulled toward the operator in cutting. The blade has a single-bevel edge, like that of a plane iron, chisel, or spokeshave. The drawknife is used principally for rough-shaping cylindrical timbers, but it is also useful for removing a heavy

edge-cut prior to finish planing. Grinding and whetting procedures are about the same as they are for a plane iron, chisel, or spokeshave. The width of the bevel should be about twice the thickness of the blade.

133.59

Figure 8-17.—Drawknife.

HANDSAWS

Saws are tools used for cutting wood or metal. The handsaw consists of a steel blade with a handle at one end. Except on the hacksaw, the blade is narrower at the end opposite the handle. This end of the blade is called the "point" or "toe." The end of the blade nearest the handle is called the "heel" (fig. 8-18). One edge of the blade has teeth which act as two rows of cutters. When the saw is used, these teeth cut two parallel grooves close together. The chips (called "sawdust") are pushed out from between the grooves (the "kerf" (fig. 8-19)) by the beveled part of the teeth. The teeth are bent alternately to one side or the other, to make the kerf wider than the thickness of the blade. This bending is called the "set" of the teeth (figs. 8-19, 8-20, and 8-21). The number of teeth per inch, the size and shape of the teeth, and the amount of set depends on the use to be made of the saw and the material to be cut. Saws, except the hacksaw, are described by the number of tooth points per inch. There is always one more point than there are teeth

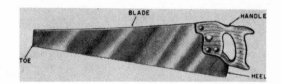

29.15(44)

Figure 8-18.—Crosscut handsaw.

213

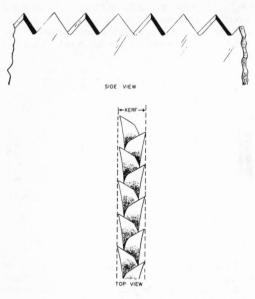

SIDE VIEW

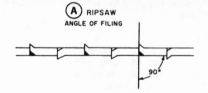

(A) RIPSAW
ANGLE OF FILING

90°

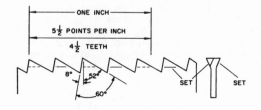

ONE INCH
5½ POINTS PER INCH
4½ TEETH
8° 52°
60°
SET   SET

29.15A(44)

Figure 8-19.—Crosscut saw teeth.

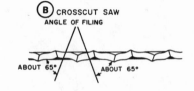

(B) CROSSCUT SAW
ANGLE OF FILING

ABOUT 65°   ABOUT 65°

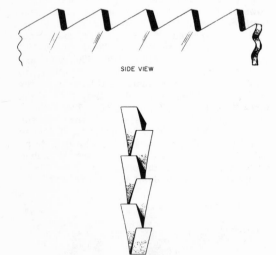

SIDE VIEW

TOP VIEW

29.15A(133F)A

Figure 8-20.—Ripsaw teeth.

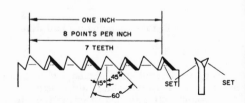

ONE INCH
8 POINTS PER INCH
7 TEETH
15° 45°
60°
SET   SET

29.15A(133F)B

Figure 8-21.—Angles of saw teeth.

per inch (fig. 8-21). A number stamped near the handle gives the number of points of the saw.

Types

The CROSSCUT saw is used for cutting across the grain of wood. It has 8 or more points, and the points are sharpened at a bevel so that they are like the ends of knife blades (fig. 8-19). A crosscut saw with coarse teeth and a wide set is needed for cutting green, unseasoned wood. A fine toothed saw does more accurate cutting, and is best for dry, seasoned wood.

The RIPSAW is designed for cutting with the grain of the wood. The teeth, unlike those of the crosscut saw, are sharpened straight across the front edge, which is nearly vertical, or at right angles to the edge of the blade (fig. 8-20). Thus the teeth of the ripsaw are like two rows of chisels in their action. The ripsaw in the Builder tool set has 5 1/2 points. Figure 8-21 shows angles of saw teeth.

The NESTED saws (fig. 8-22) consist of a handle which is common to three blades which are a keyhole saw, a compass saw, and a plumber's saw. The handle is of wood and is shaped somewhat like a pistol grip. Each of the blades has a slot in the heel, by which it is fastened to the handle. The handle has a thumbnut which is tightened to hold the blade securely in place. The KEYHOLE saw blade is much narrower than that of the compass saw. The point is narrow enough to enter a 1/4-inch hole. It is commonly used for cutting keyholes in fitting locks in doors, and for smaller types of work. Like the compass saw, it cuts a wider kerf than either the crosscut or the ripsaw, in order that the blade may turn in making curved cuts.

① KEYHOLE SAW
② COMPASS SAW
③ PLUMBERS SAW

HANDLE

29.22(133F)A

Figure 8-22.—Nested saws.

The COMPASS saw blade is designed for sawing curves. It is also used for starting cuts to be completed by larger saws, particularly in interior cuts. The blade is tapered to a point, and the teeth are filed in such a manner that the saw may be used either for crosscutting or for ripping. The kerf left by this saw is wider than that of either the crosscut or the ripsaw, in order to provide freedom for the blade to turn when cutting curves. The PLUMBER's saw blade is a heavy blade with fine teeth, designed for cutting nails or soft metals. The blade is thick enough to permit a woodcutting saw to pass freely through the cut it makes in a nail.

The HACKSAW (fig. 8-23) is a saw designed for cutting metal. It consists of a blade and a frame which has a handle at one end. The frame can be adjusted to hold various blade lengths at various angles. The blades have holes in each end, and are mounted on the frame by means of pins attached to the frame. The blades are of high grade tool steel, and are of two general types: "hard," which means the entire blade has been hardened in tempering, and "flexible," which means that only the teeth have been hardened. The blades furnished with the Builder tool set should be of the "hard" type, with a "pitch" (the number of teeth per inch) of 18. This type of blade is best for brass, tool steel, cast iron, and heavy stock, and is referred to as a "general purpose" blade.

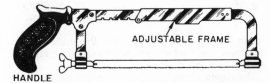

ADJUSTABLE FRAME

HANDLE

1.19(133F)A

Figure 8-23.—Hacksaw.

Uses

In sawing with either the crosscut (fig. 8-24) or the ripsaw, first draw a guideline for the saw to follow. Grasp the saw with the right hand on the handle. Grasp the wood with the left hand (and kneel on it with one knee, if possible) to hold it securely. Guide the saw with the left thumb by resting it against the blade above the line of teeth. Keep your right shoulder directly in front of the cut to be made. This will ensure that the saw is sawing in a plane perpendicular to the surface of the wood.

Rest the teeth of the saw against the edge of the wood, with the blade on the waste side of the guideline. Start the cut by drawing the saw toward you to make an initial groove to keep the saw in place. Hold your saw lightly. Do not force it into the wood, but simply draw it back and forth, using a long stroke. If the saw tends to run off the line, or the cut is not perpendicular to the work, slightly twist or bend the blade back into place. Test a portion of the blade occasionally with a try square to ensure that the cut is being made perpendicular to the surface of the wood. The crosscut saw should

215

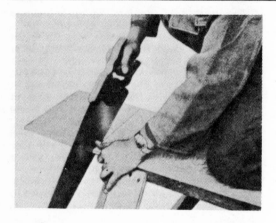

29.15(133F)C
Figure 8-24.—Using the crosscut handsaw.

make an angle of 45° between the edge of the
saw and the surface of the wood. The ripsaw
should be used at an angle of 60°.

In ripping long boards, a wooden wedge may
be inserted into the cut to spread it apart and
keep the saw from binding as shown in figure
8-25.

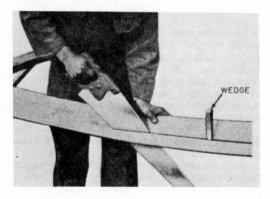

29.15(133F)D
Figure 8-25.—Using a wedge
to spread the cut.

In using the compass saw or the keyhole saw,
first bore a hole with an auger bit (fig. 8-26).
Insert the compass or keyhole saw into the hole
and start to cut (fig. 8-26) working slowly and
carefully, with a minimum of pressure. These
narrow-bladed saws are easily bent. When the

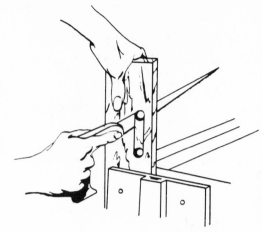

29.22(133F)B
Figure 8-26.—Using the keyhole or
compass saw.

cut is long enough to permit it, remove the
compass saw or keyhole saw and finish the cut
with the regular crosscut or ripsaw.

The plumber's saw is used to cut through
any nail encountered while sawing. The cut is
then continued with the regular wood saw.

In using the hacksaw, insert the blade with
the teeth pointing forward, away from the handle. Start your cut at a slight angle with a flat
surface, and guide the blade with the left thumb
until the cut is deep enough to allow use of both
hands. Avoid starting a cut on a sharp corner
as shown in figure 8-27.

An old blade will always make a narrower
kerf than a new blade. Therefore, if a blade
breaks before a cut is finished, it is better to
start a new cut in line with the old cut, or work
the blade into the cut with extreme care to prevent breaking. When cutting well away from
the edge of a piece of metal, the blade may be
turned in the frame as shown in figure 8-28.

Maintenance and Care

Care must be taken that the saw is not
kinked. If the saw binds in the cut, and pressure is then applied to force it through the
wood, a kink is almost certain to result. A
kinked saw is useless. Make certain that nails,
spikes, and other foreign objects are removed
from the wood before it is sawed. When not in

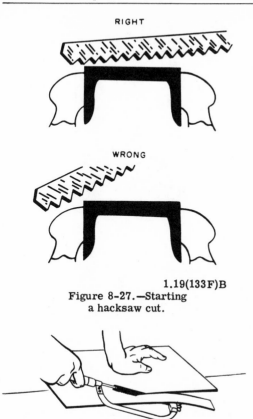

RIGHT

WRONG

1.19(133F)B
Figure 8-27.—Starting
a hacksaw cut.

1.19(133F)C
Figure 8-28.—Cutting deep with a hacksaw.

use, saws should be oiled and kept in a toolbox or in the rack. Saws rust easily, and a rusty saw will bind in the cut. Figure 8-29 illustrates some of the right and wrong ways of caring for saws.

Safety Precautions

Make sure that, if the saw slips from the work, it will not cut your hands or other portions of your body. Lay the saw down carefully when not in use, in such a position that no one can brush against the teeth and cut himself.

SAW-SHARPENING EQUIPMENT

The saw vise (A, fig. 8-30) is a special vise or clamp with long jaws. It has a handle on the front which only needs pulling away from the vise in order to open the jaws. Closing the handle puts pressure on the jaws of the vise by means of a cam, so that the blade of the saw being filed will be held securely.

The vise is held to the workbench by means of a clamp which has a turnscrew to hold it securely to the bench, and a wing nut which will permit the vise to be set at various angles to the clamp (A, fig. 8-30).

The file holder consists of a wooden handle to which is attached an adjustable frame for holding a triangular file. A pair of clamping screws on the file holder fastens the frame to the jaws of the vise. It can be adjusted so as to hold the file at any desired angle to the teeth being filed. A clamp on the top of the frame permits the file to be held at any position along the blade (A, fig. 8-30).

The saw set is a tool which, by means of a plunger and anvil, bends the teeth of the saw outward, so as to make the kerf wider than the thickness of the blade of the saw (B, fig. 8-30).

The reconditioning kit for large crosscut saws consists of a jointer, which is a file holder by which a flat or mill file can be held and guided while jointing the saw; two gages, one for the raker tooth and one for checking the set of the teeth; and a setting block (frequently called a "stumping tool").

Uses

There are five basic steps involved in the sharpening of a saw: Jointing, shaping, setting, filing, and dressing.

JOINTING is always the first step. Its purpose is to make all the teeth the same height. Place the saw in the vise, and, with a flat file held in the jointing tool, file lengthwise from heel to toe of the saw until a flat top has been filed on the tip of each tooth (fig. 8-31). On the large crosscut saws, the raker teeth are filed about 1/64th inch shorter than the cutting teeth.

SHAPING is done only when the teeth are unevenly spaced or shaped. To shape, file the teeth with a tapered file to the correct uniform size and shape. The gullets must be of equal depth. For the crosscut handsaw, the front of the tooth should be filed with an angle of 15° from the vertical, while the back slope should be 45° with the vertical (B, fig. 8-21). Disregard the bevel of the teeth, and file straight across at right angles to the blade with the file well down in the gullet while shaping. If the

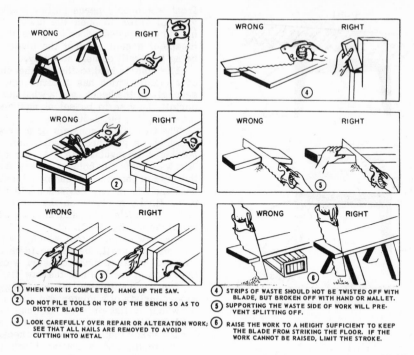

1 WHEN WORK IS COMPLETED, HANG UP THE SAW.

2 DO NOT PILE TOOLS ON TOP OF THE BENCH SO AS TO DISTORT BLADE

3 LOOK CAREFULLY OVER REPAIR OR ALTERATION WORK; SEE THAT ALL NAILS ARE REMOVED TO AVOID CUTTING INTO METAL

4 STRIPS OF WASTE SHOULD NOT BE TWISTED OFF WITH BLADE, BUT BROKEN OFF WITH HAND OR MALLET.

5 SUPPORTING THE WASTE SIDE OF WORK WILL PREVENT SPLITTING OFF.

6 RAISE THE WORK TO A HEIGHT SUFFICIENT TO KEEP THE BLADE FROM STRIKING THE FLOOR. IF THE WORK CANNOT BE RAISED, LIMIT THE STROKE.

44.14

Figure 8-29.—Care of saws.

teeth are of unequal size, press the file against the teeth with the largest flat tops until the center of the flat tops made by jointing is reached. Then move the file to the next gullet and file until the rest of the flat top disappears and the tooth has been brought to a point. Do not bevel the teeth while jointing. The teeth are now ready for setting.

In SETTING, particular care must be taken to see that the set is regular. It must be the same width for the entire length of the blade and the same width on both sides of the blade. The depth should never be more than half the depth of the tooth. If the set is made deeper, it may spring, crimp, crack the blade, or break out the teeth.

To set the handsaw, the saw set is placed over the blade so that the guides are over the teeth with the anvil behind the tooth to be set (D, fig. 8-32). The anvil, with its bevel at the top, is held in the frame by means of the set screw. The handles are now pressed together.

The plunger will press the tooth against the anvil and bend it to the angle of the bevel of the anvil. Each tooth is set in this manner, alternating to either side of the blade.

To FILE the handsaw (fig. 8-33), place the saw in the vise with the handle to the left. Begin to file at the heel. Adjust the file holder so that the file is held at the proper angle (fig. 8-21) and the file is between two teeth. File both teeth at once with one or more strokes of the file. Work down the whole saw, shifting the file by means of the clamp on the top of the file holder. Then turn the saw around so that the handle is to the right, readjust the file holder, and work down the entire length of the saw again. In filing the ripsaw, in addition to adjusting the saw for the angles shown in figure 8-21, lower the file handle about 2 inches to give a bevel on the top of these teeth which lean away from you.

DRESSING of the saw is necessary only when there are burrs left on the side of the teeth by

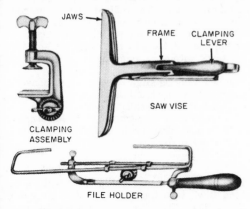

A VISE, CLAMPING ASSEMBLY AND FILE HOLDER

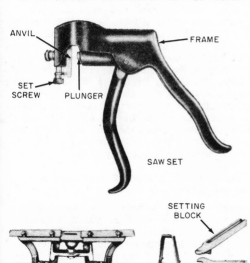

B SAW SET AND RECONDITIONING KIT

133.335

Figure 8-30.—Saw sharpening equipment.

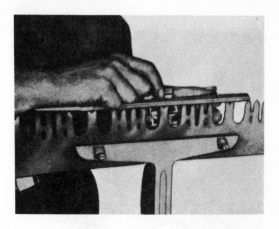

133.336

Figure 8-31.—Jointing.

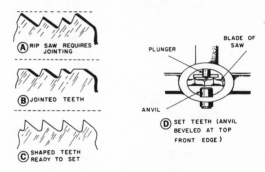

133.337

Figure 8-32.—Jointed and shaped teeth,
and use of the saw set.

filing. These burrs cause the saw to work in a ragged fashion. They are removed by laying the saw on a flat surface and running an oilstone or fine file lightly across the side of the teeth.

Safety Precautions

Make sure both rows of teeth are of the same length. If they are not, the saw will curve as it cuts.

Set the teeth before filing, to avoid injury to the cutting edges.

Never make the depth of the set more than half that of the tooth itself.

NAIL SET

A NAIL SET (fig. 8-34) is used to SET (meaning to countersink slightly below the surface)

133.338

Figure 8-33.—Filing the handsaw.

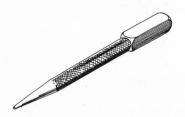

1.18

Figure 8-34.—Nail set.

the heads of nails in finish carpentry. The purpose of setting is to improve the appearance of the work by concealing the nail heads. A nail is set by placing the tip of the nail set on the head of the nail and striking the set a blow or two with the hammer. The small surface hole above the head is usually plugged with putty.

CLAW HAMMER

The carpenter's curved-claw nail hammer (A, fig. 8-35) is a steel-headed, wooden-handled tool used for driving nails, wedges, and dowels. The "claw," which is at one end of the head, is a two-pronged arch used to pull nails out of wood. The other parts of the head are the eye and face.

The face may be flat, in which case it is called a plain face. The plain-faced hammer is easier for the beginner to learn to drive nails with, but with this hammer it is difficult to drive the head of the nail flush with the surface of the work without leaving hammer marks on the surface.

The face may be slightly rounded, or convex, in which case it is called bell-faced. The bell-faced hammer is generally used in rough work. When handled by an expert, it can drive the nail-head flush with the surface of the work without damaging the surface.

Uses

To use the hammer, grasp the handle with the end flush with the lower edge of the palm (B, fig. 8-35). Keep the wrist limber and relaxed. Grasp the nail with the thumb and forefinger of the other hand and place the point at the exact spot where it is to be driven. Unless the nail is to be purposely driven at an angle, it should be perpendicular to the surface of the work. Strike the nailhead squarely (B, fig. 8-35) keeping the hand level with the head of the nail. To drive, first rest the face of the hammer on the head of the nail, then raise the hammer slightly and give the nail a few light taps to start it and to fix the aim. Then take the fingers away from the nail and drive the nail with firm blows with the center of the hammer face. The wrong way to drive a nail is shown in C, figure 8-35.

The nail can be started with one hand in either of the following ways:

Insert the nail between the claws of the hammer, with the head of the nail resting against the head of the hammer (D, fig. 8-35). Drive the nail slightly into the wood, then release it from the claw and finish driving in the usual manner.

Rest head of the nail against the side of the hammer and steady it in position with the fingers, as shown in E, figure 8-35. Start the nail with a sharp tap of the hammer held in this manner; then finish driving in the usual manner.

To pull nails, slide the claw of the hammer under the nailhead. Pull back on the handle until the handle is nearly vertical; then slip a block of wood under the head of the hammer and pull the nail completely free (fig. 8-36). The claw hammer should not be used for pulling nails larger than 8d. For larger sizes, use a wrecking bar.

Maintenance and Care

Hammer handles, when broken or loose, should be replaced or tightened. If the handle is loose, set it by striking the end of the handle with a mallet, and drive the wedges back into the handle. Wedges may be of either metal or straight-grained hard wood. Nails or screws should not be used. If the handle is broken, remove it, seat a new handle, and replace the wedges. If it is difficult to remove the old handle, saw it off close to the head and drive it through the larger end of the eye. The wedges should be saved and reused.

The face should be kept clean and smooth. This usually can be done by rubbing it with emery cloth. If it becomes necessary to grind the face to restore it because it is in very bad condition, take notice if it is a bell or plain face, and then grind it to the proper shape. Dip the head in water often to prevent burning and loss of temper while grinding. Do not grind the face oftener, nor remove more material, than necessary to restore the face.

Safety Precautions

The following safety precautions apply generally to all driving tools:

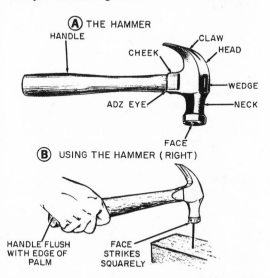

Figure 8-35.—The carpenter's curved-claw nail hammer.

5.5(133F)A

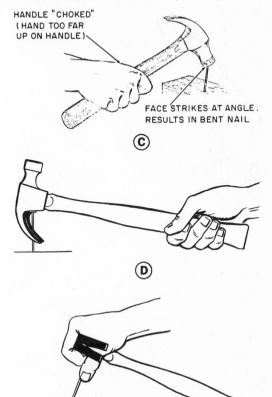

Figure 8-35.—The carpenter's curved-claw nail hammer.—continued.

5.5(133F)B

Check to see that the handle is tight before using the hammer.

Rest the face of the hammer on the work before striking, to get the FEEL or AIM.

Grasp the handle firmly, with the hand near the extreme end of the handle.

Strike squarely, but lightly, until the nail or tool to be driven is set.

Get the fingers of the other hand out of the way before striking with force.

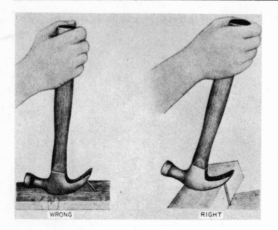

5.5(29C)

Figure 8-36.—Pulling nails with
the claw hammer.

Make sure the face strikes squarely, to
prevent damage to the work and to prevent the
nail or tool from flying or becoming bent.

PLASTIC FACED HAMMER

The plastic faced hammer (fig. 8-37) has a
metal head on a wooden handle, with replace-
able plastic faces which can be screwed onto
the ends of the head.

The plastic faced hammer is used for striking chisels and other tools which would be
damaged by a metal hammer (fig. 8-38).

The plastic faces, being of a soft material,
may be easily damaged in use. The faces may
be restored by rasping off the damaged surface

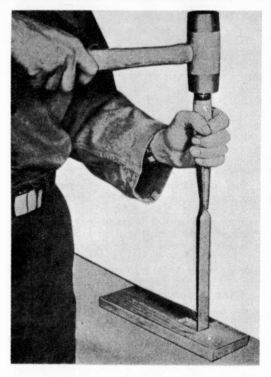

133.339

Figure 8-38.—Cutting a socket.

with a wood rasp, then smoothing with a file
and sandpaper. Care should be taken to remove
the same amount from each end of the head, to
maintain the proper balance of the hammer.
When the faces are too badly scarred for repair,
they should be unscrewed from the head and
new ones inserted.

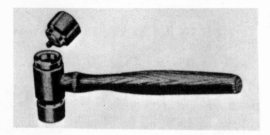

5.5(133F)

Figure 8-37.—Plastic faced hammer.

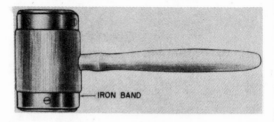

44.2

Figure 8-39.—Wooden mallet.

WOOD MALLET

The wood mallet (fig. 8-39) has a head 5 inches long and 3 inches in diameter, with two flat, circular faces reinforced by iron bands. It is set on a wooden handle.

Uses

The mallet is used for driving wooden stakes, or for smoothing out dents in sheet metal, or for turning thin metal edges without cutting the metal surface. It is also used for driving the framing chisel, in place of the plastic-faced hammer.

Maintenance and Care

The mallet is never used to drive spikes or any other sharp-headed object of metal.

Mallets should be stored out of direct sunlight or away from heat pipes, since excessive drying will cause cracking and splitting.

When the edges of the faces become mushroomed, the iron band should be removed and the faces restored by sawing off a thin section. The edges are then dressed with a wood rasp, and the iron bands replaced.

Handles are replaced in the same manner as described previously.

EQUIPMENT FOR HOLDING WORK

A woodworking BENCH VISE, designed for holding work for planing, sawing, or chiseling on the bench is shown in figure 8-40. Turning the SCREW by means of the HANDLE causes the MOVABLE JAW on the vise to move in or out on the SLIDE BARS (sometimes called the GUIDE BARS). On a vise with a CONTINUOUS SCREW the movable jaw must be threaded all the way. On a vise with an INTERRUPTED SCREW (which is called a QUICK-ACTING vise) the movable jaw can be moved rapidly in or out when the screw is in a certain position. When the jaw is in the desired position against the work, the quick-acting vise can be tightened by a partial turn of the handle.

Most woodworking vises are equipped with a DOG as shown in the figure. The dog, which can be raised as shown or lowered flush with the top of the vise, is used in conjunction with a BENCH STOP to hold work which is too wide for the maximum span of the vise.

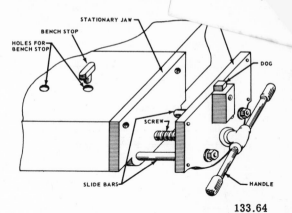

133.64

Figure 8-40.—Woodworking bench vise.

Sometimes a bench is equipped with two vises, so that long work can be held at both ends. When this is the case, the principal vise is called the SIDE VISE and the auxiliary vise the TAIL VISE.

A BENCH HOOK (fig. 8-41) is a device for holding work for backsawing.

The SAWHORSE might be called the carpenter's portable work bench and scaffold. If you don't already have a good sawhorse you will have to make one, and the layout part of the job will give you an idea of the practical use you can make of the framing square. A working drawing for a good, sturdy sawhorse is shown

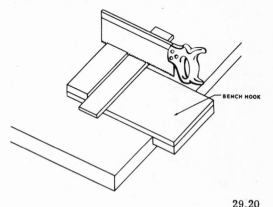

29.20

Figure 8-41.—Bench hook.

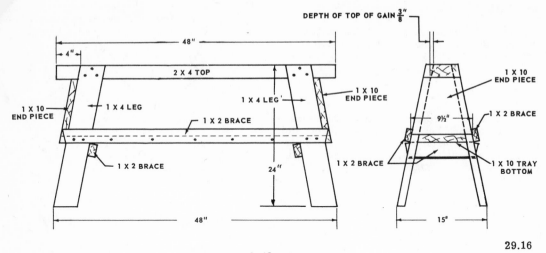

DEPTH OF TOP OF GAIN $\frac{3}{8}$"

48"

4"

2 X 4 TOP

1 X 10
END PIECE

1 X 10
END PIECE

1 X 4 LEG

1 X 4 LEG

1 X 2 BRACE

1 X 10
END PIECE

9½"

1 X 2 BRACE

1 X 2 BRACE

24"

1 X 2 BRACE

1 X 10 TRAY
BOTTOM

48"

15"

29.16

Figure 8-42.—Sawhorse.

in figure 8-42. A few pointers on the layout part of the job are as follows:

The first layout problem is laying off the end cuts for the legs. If you think about it for a moment while examining the drawing, you will see that there is a right triangle involved here, with a total rise of 24 in. (vertical height of the sawhorse) and a total run of 4 in. (amount that the top of the leg is set away from the end of the top). To get the correct end cuts, then, you set the square to 4 in. on the tongue and 24 in. on the blade, as shown in figure 8-43. How long a piece will you need to start with? Well, if you measure the hypotenuse, as shown in the figure, you will find that the length of the finished piece will be a little more than 24 1/4 in. Better start with a piece about 26 in. long.

Mark the left-hand end-cut along the tongue, and mark the point where the end of the blade contacts the edge of the piece at the opposite end. Then turn the square over and end for end and mark the opposite end-cut as shown. Saw off the ends and use the piece as a pattern for laying out the end-cuts on the other three legs.

Next problem is to lay off the SIDE CUTS on the legs. Once again there is a right triangle involved, and once again the total rise is 24 in. (vertical height of the sawhorse). The total run is a little harder to figure. If you study figure 8-42 closely, you will see that the total run

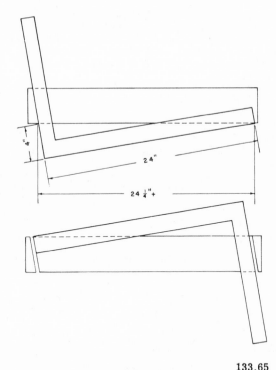

4"

24"

24 ¼"+

133.65

Figure 8-43.—Laying off end cuts for legs.

224

must amount to one-half the span of the legs (15 in. divided by 2, or 7 1/2 in.) minus the horizontal thickness of the leg (you can call that 3/4 in.), and minus one-half the ACTUAL width of the top (a 2 x 4 is usually only about 3 3/4 in. wide, and half of that is 1 7/8 in.), less the depth of the top of the gain, which is shown in the drawing to be 3/8 in.

If you can't quite see why this is so, study the simplified drawing in figure 8-44 where the basic triangle you are solving is shaded in. If you work out the arithmetic in the previous paragraph, you will find that the total run is 5 1/4 in. To lay off the side cuts for the legs, then, you set the square to 5 1/4 in. on the tongue and 24 in. on the blade, on the edge of a leg, as shown in figure 8-45. Mark a line along the tongue, carry the line across the face of the piece, parallel to the line of the end-cut, and bevel the end down to the line with a plane.

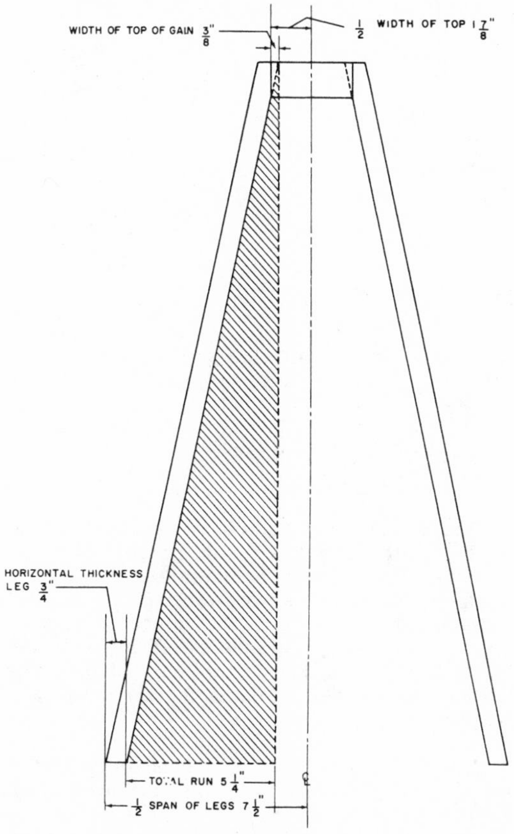

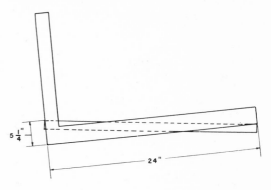

133.67

Figure 8-45.—Laying off side cuts for legs.

To lay out the gain on the side of the top, first set the top of a leg in place against the side, 4 in. from the end, as shown in figure 8-46, top view, and draw the lines for the sides of the gain. Then use the marking gage to score a line 3/8 in. from the edge of the top, and chisel out the gain as indicated in the lower view.

The set of the framing square for the edges of the 1 x 10 end piece is the same as the set for the side cuts of the legs; a study of figure 8-44 will show you why. Select a piece that is ACTUALLY 10 in. wide, and lay off the line for one of the edges as shown in figure 8-47. Since you won't be able to end-for-end the square to get the line for the other edge in this case, the best way to lay that line off is to set the T-bevel to the other line, measure off the prescribed 9 1/2 in. along the bottom, reverse the T-bevel, set it to the mark, and lay off the line as indicated in figure 8-47.

The set of the framing square for the edge cuts for the 1 x 10 tray is also 5 1/2 in. on the tongue and 24 in. on the blade, but the best way to fit the tray is to set it in place and mark it after the top, legs, and end pieces have been assembled. Use 8-penny coated nails to nail the pieces together.

WIDTH OF TOP OF GAIN 3/8"   1/2   WIDTH OF TOP 1 7/8"

HORIZONTAL THICKNESS LEG 3/4"

TOTAL RUN 5 1/4"
1/2 SPAN OF LEGS 7 1/2"

133.66

Figure 8-44.—Basic triangle for end cuts for legs.

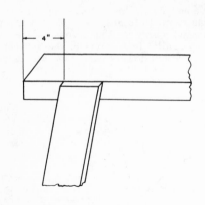

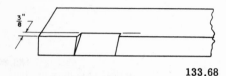

133.68

Figure 8-46.—Laying out
the gains for the legs.

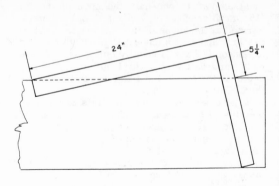

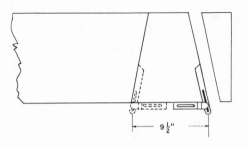

133.69

Figure 8-47.—Laying off
the 1 x 10 end piece.

CLAMPS

Two types of CLAMPS are used by the wood-worker in a large variety of ways; perhaps the most common use is clamping pieces together for gluing. The wooden HANDSCREW is relatively limited with regard to both scope and pressure. The STEEL BAR clamp applies a very strong pressure and can be set (by moving the ADJUSTABLE HEAD outward) to a very wide scope.

A handscrew is shown in figure 8-48; a steel bar clamp in figure 8-49. The size of a hand-screw is designated by the length of the jaw in inches; sizes range from 6-in. to 18-in. The size of a steel bar clamp is designated by the length of the bar in feet; sizes range from 2-ft to 8-ft.

A metal C-CLAMP is also shown in figure 8-48. When one of these is used for wood, the wood must be protected against damage from the metal jaw and the screw swivel on the clamp. C-clamps are designed chiefly for clamping metal. Size is designated by the max-imum scope between the screw swivel and the jaw.

CARE AND MAINTENANCE
OF HOLDING TOOLS

The screws and slide bars on vises snould be lubricated regularly with preservative lubricating oil. Never hammer the jaws of a vise, and never use a woodworking vise to hold a metal article. Never use a piece of pipe or similar device to increase the leverage of the handle. There is danger, not only of breaking the handle, but also of damaging the screw and the jaws.

Always keep the jaws on a handscrew parallel to each other. Tightening the handscrew with the jaws cocked will bend the spindles and damage the jaws. NEVER use anything but the hands to tighten the spindles. Keep the jaws well varnished to protect the wood.

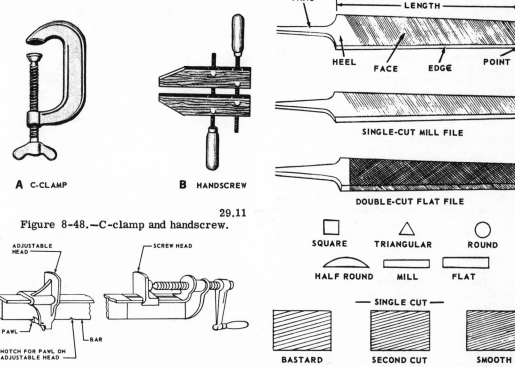

A C-CLAMP   **B** HANDSCREW

29.11

Figure 8-48.—C-clamp and handscrew.

133.70

Figure 8-49.—Steel bar clamp.

ABRASIVE TOOLS AND EQUIPMENT

The abrasive tools and equipment, discussed in the following sections, are designed to help the Builder in working with metal, wood, plastic, and other materials. If further information is needed concerning the abrasive tools and equipment, it can be obtained from Basic Handtools, NavPers 10085-A.

RASPS AND FILES

RASPS and FILES should be used for wood shaping only when the use of proper paring or shaving tools is impossible.

Files are classified according to the shape of their cross section and the manner in which the teeth are cut, as shown in figure 8-50. The teeth on a rasp consist of triangular projections. Most rasps are half-round in cross-section. Since a rasp cuts wood much faster

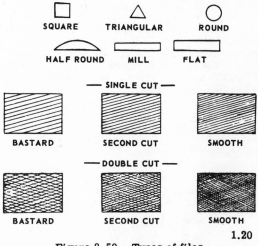

SINGLE-CUT MILL FILE

DOUBLE-CUT FLAT FILE

SQUARE   TRIANGULAR   ROUND

HALF ROUND   MILL   FLAT

— SINGLE CUT —

BASTARD   SECOND CUT   SMOOTH

— DOUBLE CUT —

BASTARD   SECOND CUT   SMOOTH

1.20

Figure 8-50.—Types of files.

than a file, and leaves a much coarser surface, rough shaping is usually done with the rasp and final smoothing with the file.

Most rasps and files have the tang type of handle attachment. ALWAYS PUT ON A HANDLE BEFORE USING THE TOOL, to avoid the possibility of puncturing the hand on the tang. If you have to use a handle with a hole too small for the tang, heat the same size tang on an old file red hot, and use it to burn out the hole to the proper size. Before you put the handle on, wet the tang. To seat the tang firmly in the handle, tap the butt of the handle on a hard surface. DO NOT HAMMER THE FILE INTO THE HANDLE.

Files and rasps are extremely brittle, and they must never be cleaned by striking against the vise or any other object. Brush filings from between the teeth with a wire brush, pushed in a direction parallel to the line of the teeth. Dislodge any particles that stick with a pointed piece of some soft metal, such as brass or copper. Use a soft metal to avoid damaging the teeth.

ABRASIVE GRINDERS

A GRINDSTONE is an abrasive wheel made of natural stone—usually sandstone. A GRINDING WHEEL is an abrasive wheel made of some synthetic abrasive material, such as emery or corundum. Most modern wheels are synthetic wheels which are usually called GRINDERS.

Grinders vary in design and construction from the small hand-driven DRY grinder shown in figure 8-51 to the ball-bearing motor-driven, multi-wheel OILSTONE grinder shown in figure 8-52. The grinder in figure 8-52 has two large CUPPED oilstone wheels, one coarse and the other fine, for grinding plane irons and chisels. A drip-spout on each wheel drips oil into the cup of the wheel and thus keeps the wheel properly oiled. The tool rest can be adjusted both vertically and horizontally to get just the right bevel angle on a tool. The tool holder slides

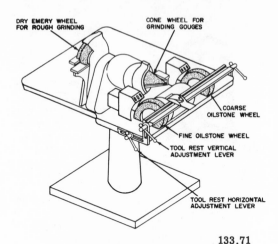

133.71

Figure 8-52.—Power-driven oilstone grinder.

back and forth in a groove on the tool rest, so that the tool which is being sharpened remains in correct position with respect to the face of the wheel. Besides the oilstone wheels, the grinder has a DRY WHEEL for rough grinding and a CONE WHEEL for grinding inside-bevel gouges.

OILSTONE

The flat, rectangular WHETSTONE, more commonly called an OILSTONE, is used for final whetting of ground tools, or for touching up the edge on a tool which is not dull enough to require grinding. Oilstones made of natural stone have unusually fine grains and are unsurpassed for putting razor edges on fine tools. Natural-stone oilstones are expensive, however, and most oilstones in general use are synthetic stones, made of silicone carbide or aluminum oxide.

CARE AND MAINTENANCE OF ABRASIVE EQUIPMENT

Abrasive wheels and oilstones are very easily broken or cracked, and must be handled and stowed with the greatest care. A wheel should be given a regular RING TEST for cracks. Tap the wheel with a rubber-faced hammer or mallet. A ringing sound indicates a sound wheel.

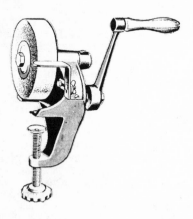

44.34

Figure 8-51.—Hand-driven dry grinder.

A dull thudding sound indicates a cracked wheel. NEVER USE A CRACKED WHEEL.

When you are installing a new wheel, NEVER force the wheel onto the spindle. The wheel must slide easily with about 0.003 to 0.005 in. clearance. If it doesn't, IT IS NOT THE RIGHT SIZE FOR THE SPINDLE. (Always check the grinder wheel for the proper rpm.)

Tighten the spindle nut just enough to set the flanges firmly against the wheel. Overtightening may crack the wheel. After installing, GET YOURSELF AND EVERYBODY ELSE OUT OF THE LINE OF THE WHEEL, turn the power on, and keep clear until the grinder has run long enough to indicate that the wheel is not going to fly apart.

If a wheel GLAZES rapidly, decrease the speed of the grinder or put on a softer wheel. If a wheel LOADS rapidly (LOADING means the clogging of surface pores with the material being ground), increase the speed of the grinder or put on a softer wheel.

A glazed or loaded wheel should be DRESSED, and a wheel which has become out-of-round or irregular on the surface must be TRUED. The same procedure is used to cure both conditions; it is called DRESSING, and it is done with a WHEEL DRESSER. CUTTER and TUBE type dressers are shown in figure 8-53. A DIAMOND wheel dresser (which is the most effective) is shown in figure 8-54.

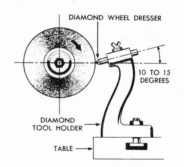

28.63(133E)B
Figure 8-54.—Diamond wheel dresser.

28.63(28C)
Figure 8-55.—Dressing with a cutter type dresser.

figure. The tube type dresser is held flat on the tool rest, as shown in figure 8-56.

Start the wheel and slowly press the dresser against the face until you feel the dresser start to "bite."

Move the dresser from side to side and gradually press it forward until you feel it "bite" all the way across the face of the wheel.

Do not grind against the sides or corners of a wheel unless it is absolutely impossible to do the grinding job on the face.

A grinding wheel will gradually wear down, or will gradually be dressed down, to a diameter which is much smaller than the original diameter. As the wheel becomes smaller, the speed of the grinder should be increased to allow for the reduced speed of travel of the smaller grinding face. If the same speed is maintained for the smaller wheel, the wheel will "act soft," and it will also wear down too rapidly.

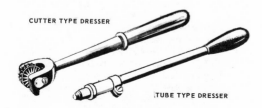

28.63(133E)A
Figure 8-53.—Cutter and tube type wheel dressers.

The procedure for dressing a wheel is as follows:

Adjust the tool rest to permit the wheel dresser to contact the centerline of the wheel, as shown in figure 8-55. The cutter type dresser is held with the lug on the cutter against the front edge of the tool rest, as shown in the

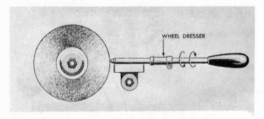

28.63(133E)D
Figure 8-56.—Dressing with a
tube type dresser.

A new oilstone should be soaked in engine oil before it is used for whetting. To prevent glazing, oil should always be applied when the stone is used for whetting. The stone should be wiped clean with cloth or cotton waste after each use. A glazed or "gummed up" stone should be washed with dry-cleaning solvent or aqua ammonia. If the stone cannot be thoroughly cleaned in this manner, it should be scored with aluminum oxide abrasive cloth or flint sandpaper.

For whetting plane irons, chisels, and the like, the faces of an oilstone must be perfectly flat. An uneven face can be trued up on the side of an old grinding wheel, or by rubbing on a piece of moistened waterproof artificial abrasive paper laid on a flat, true, hard surface.

The fragments of a broken oilstone can be rejoined as follows:

Bake all the oil out of the stone by heating the fragments on a hot plate.

Scrub the fragments thoroughly with dry-cleaning solvent or aqua ammonia.

Dust the broken edges thickly with flake or ground orange shellac. Work the shellac carefully into all recesses.

Reheat the fragments to melt the shellac, join them together, and clamp them securely in a handscrew.

If shellac is not available, cut a recess in a wooden block to mount the fragments. Make the recess a shade smaller than the length and width of the stone, and make it one-half as deep as the stone is thick. Assemble the fragments and tap them into the recess with the mallet.

Keep oilstones away from heat and store them in a cool place. Heat causes the oil in a stone to form a gummy residue on the surface.

POWER TOOLS

Your duties as a Builder will also involve developing and improving your skills and techniques whenever working with power tools. Therefore, along with naming and identifying the various equipment located in a Builder shop, we will provide a brief introduction concerning the operating features of each piece of equipment.

SAWS

Mechanical woodworking saws range in size and power from small shop jig-saws to huge bandsaws used in West Coast sawmills to saw redwood trees into lumber. Mechanical saws for sawmill work are beyond the scope of this chapter. Of the types of mechanical saws, the various members of the CIRCULAR SAW family are the most widely used.

A CIRCULAR SAW has a blade which is mounted on, and spun by, a shaft called an ARBOR. Most modern saws have what is called a MOTOR-ON-ARBOR drive, meaning that the arbor and the motor shaft are one and the same member.

Like a handsaw, a circular saw blade may be a crosscut saw (usually called a CUTOFF saw blade in the case of a circular saw) or a ripsaw. The teeth of these saw blades are similar to those on the corresponding handsaws, and they cut on the same principle. A third type of circular saw blade called a COMBINATION or MITER saw blade, may be used for either crosscutting or ripping.

A TILT-ARBOR BENCH saw is shown in figure 8-57. This saw is called a tilt-arbor saw because the saw blade can be tilted for cutting bevels and the like, by tilting the arbor. In the earlier types of bench saws the saw blade remained stationary and the table was tilted. A canted (tilted) saw table is hazardous in many ways, however, and most modern bench saws are of the tilt-arbor type.

For ripping stock, the CUTOFF GAGES are removed and the RIPPING FENCE is set a distance away from the saw which is equal to the desired width of the piece to be ripped off. The piece is placed with one edge against the fence, and fed through with the fence as a guide.

For cutting stock off square, the cutoff gage is set at 90° to the line of the saw, and the ripping fence is set to the outside edge of the table, away from the stock to be cut. The piece

29.136(29C)
Figure 8-57.—Tilt-arbor bench saw.

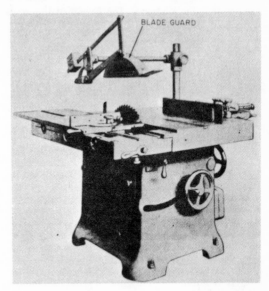

29.136(133D)
Figure 8-58.—Tilt-arbor bench saw
with sliding table section.

is then placed with one edge against the cutoff gage, held firmly, and fed through by pushing the gage along its slot.

The procedure for cutting stock off at an angle other than 90° (called MITER CUTTING) is similar, except that the cutoff gage is set to bring the piece to the desired angle with the line of the saw.

For ordinary ripping or cutting off, the distance the saw blade should extend above the table top is 1/8 in. plus the thickness of the piece to be sawed. The vertical position of the saw is controlled by the DEPTH OF CUT HANDWHEEL shown in figure 8-57. The angle of the saw blade is controlled by the TILT HANDWHEEL. THE GUARD MUST BE KEPT IN PLACE EXCEPT WHEN ITS REMOVAL IS ABSOLUTELY UNAVOIDABLE. Blade guards are shown in figures 8-57 and 8-58.

The slot in the table through which the saw blade extends is called the THROAT. The throat is contained in a small, removable section of the table called the THROAT PLATE. The throat plate is removed when it is necessary to insert a wrench to remove the saw blade. The blade is held on the arbor by a nut called the ARBOR NUT. A saw is usually equipped with several throat plates, containing throats of various widths. A wider throat is required when a DADO HEAD is used on the saw. A dado head consists of two outside

GROOVING SAWS (which are much like combination saws) and as many intermediate chisel-type CUTTERS (called chippers) as are required to make up the designated width of the groove or dado. Grooving saws are usually 1/8 in. thick; consequently, one grooving saw will cut a 1/8-in. groove, and the two, used together, will cut a 1/4-in. groove. Intermediate cutters come in various thicknesses.

A more elaborate type of tilt-arbor bench saw is shown in figure 8-58. In this type the table contains a sliding section which itself consists of two parts. The sliding section can be pulled outward (at right angles to the line of the saw) for changing saw blades, for widening the throat, and for making long cutoffs. The upper part of the sliding section can be slid past the saw, as shown in figure 8-58. A piece being cut off is fed through the saw by placing it against the cutoff gage and then pushing the whole upper part of the sliding section past the saw.

Circular Saw Safety

All equipment should be operated with special care, but here are some operating precautions especially for the circular saw.

Do not use a ripsaw for crosscutting or a cross-cut saw for ripping. Cross-cut saws can be used for ripping but they are not intended for such work and should not be so used.

See that the saw is in good condition before starting to use it. This means sharp, unbroken, and free from cracks. The blade should be changed if dull, cracked, chipped, or warped.

Be sure the saw is set at proper height above the table to cut through the wood.

Avoid "kickbacks" by standing to one side of the saw—not in line with it.

Always use a push stick to push short narrow pieces between the saw and the gage.

Keep material of any kind from accumulating on the saw table and in the immediate working area.

NEVER reach over the saw to obtain material from the other side.

When cutting, do not feed wood into the saw faster than the saw will cut freely and cleanly.

Never leave the sawing machine unattended with the power turned on.

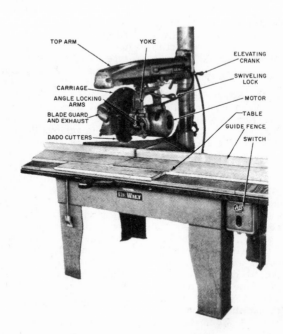

44.62(133E)A

Figure 8-59.—A radial arm saw.

Radial Arm Saw

A RADIAL arm saw is shown in figure 8-59. The motor and arbor are pivoted in a YOKE which can be swung in any direction. The yoke slides back and forth on an ARM (or OVERARM) which can also be swung in any direction. These arrangements make the radial saw adaptable to almost any conceivable type of saw cutting, as indicated in figure 8-60. Equipped with a grooving head, the saw can be used for grooving (fig. 8-61) and RABBETING (fig. 8-62). Equipped with a SHAPER HEAD, it can be used as a SHAPER (fig. 8-63). Equipped with a ROUTER BIT, it can be used for ROUTING (fig. 8-64). In short, the radial saw is just about the most versatile power tool in the shop.

Radial Arm Saw Safety

Make sure the saw blade is mounted on the arbor so that the teeth of the saw point toward the operator.

When crosscutting stock, make sure the stock is flat on the table and that the back edge of the stock is held firmly against the fence.

Always make sure that the saw is back as far as it will go before starting to use it for crosscutting work.

CROSSCUTTING WITH OVERARM SAW

RIPPING

COMPOUND MITER CUTTING

MITER CUTTING

ANGLE CUT-OFF

BEVEL RIPPING

44.62(133E)B

Figure 8-60.—Saw cutting with the radial arm saw.

44.62(133E)C
Figure 8-61.—Grooving with
the radial arm saw.

44.62(133E)D
Figure 8-62.—Rabbeting with the
radial arm saw.

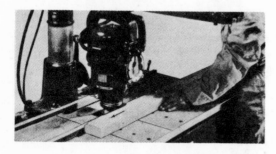

44.62(133E)E
Figure 8-63.—Shaping with the
radial arm saw.

When crosscutting long stock, make sure the ends are supported at the same level as the table.

Always keep the saw guards in place.

Adjust the saw for the correct depth, before starting the saw.

44.62(133E)F
Figure 8-64.—Routing with
the radial arm saw.

Never use a dull saw. Pinching or binding indicates a dull saw.

Make sure the anti-kickback guard is properly adjusted, whenever ripping stock.

Never rip stock without the stock having a straight edge.

Always feed the stock to be ripped against the rotation of the saw blade.

Never make any adjustments while the motor is turning.

Always remember that the radial arm saw cuts on the "pull" stroke.

Portable Circular Saw

The PORTABLE ELECTRIC circular saw is used chiefly as a great labor-saver in sawing wood framing members on the job. The saw shown in figure 8-65 can be set to cut a piece off square (as it is set in the figure) or to cut it off at any bevel angle up to 45°. To make an accurate ripping cut the RIPPING GUIDE is set a distance away from the saw equal to the width of the strip to be ripped off, and placed against the edge of the piece as a guide for the saw. For cutting off, the ripping guide is turned upside-down, so that it will be out of the way.

The portable saw shown in figure 8-66 is being placed in the system because it seems to offer more advantages. The advantages readily detected about this portable saw are: (1) the arbor can be locked whenever the blade is being changed and (2) the blade is on the opposite side to offer better visibility of the line to be cut. However, both saws are operated, basically, in the same manner.

The size of a portable circular saw is designated by the maximum diameter of the blade in inches it will support within its guard.

29.133(133C)
Figure 8-65.—Portable electric
circular saw.

Portable Circular Saw Safety

All portable, power-driven saws should be equipped with guards which will automatically adjust themselves to the work when in use, so that none of the teeth protrude above the work. The guard over the blade should be adjusted so that it slides out of its recess and covers the blade to the depth of the teeth when the saw is lifted off the work.

Goggles or face shields should be worn while using the saw and while cleaning up debris afterward.

Saws are to be grasped with both hands and held firmly against the work. Care should be taken that the saw does not break away, thereby causing injury.

The blade should be inspected at frequent intervals and always after it has locked, pinched, or burned. The electrical connection should be broken before this examination.

The saw motor should not be overloaded by pushing too hard or cutting stock that is too heavy.

Before using the saw, the material to be cut should be carefully examined and freed of nails or other metal substances. Cutting into or through knots should be avoided as far as possible.

The electric plug should be pulled before any adjustments or repairs are made to the saw. This includes changing the blade.

Bandsaw

While the bandsaw is designed primarily for making curved cuts, it can also be used for straight cutting. Unlike the circular saws, the band saw is frequently used for freehand cutting.

The bandsaw has two large wheels on which a continuous narrow saw blade or BAND turns, just as a belt is turned on pulleys. The LOWER WHEEL located below the WORKING TABLE is connected to the motor directly or by means of pulleys or gears and serves as the driver pulley. The UPPER WHEEL is the driven pulley.

The saw blade is guided and kept in line by two sets of BLADE GUIDES, one fixed set below the table and one set above with a vertical sliding adjustment. The alignment of the blade is adjusted by a mechanism on the back side of the upper wheel. TENSIONING of the blade—tightening and loosening—is provided by another adjustment located just back of the upper wheel.

Cutoff gages and ripping fences are sometimes provided for use with bandsaws, but you'll do most of your work freehand with the table clear. With this type of saw it is difficult to make accurate cuts when gages or fences are used.

The size of a bandsaw is designated by the diameter of the wheels. Common sizes are 14- (fig. 8-67), 16-, 18-, 20-, 30-, 36-, 42-, and 48-inch machines. The 14-inch size is the smallest practical bandsaw. With the exception of capacity, all bandsaws are much alike as regards maintenance, operation, and adjustment.

Blades or bands for bandsaws are designated by POINTS (tooth points per inch), THICKNESS (gage), and WIDTH. The required length of a blade is found by adding the circumference of one wheel to twice the distance between the wheel centers. Length can vary within a limit of twice the tension adjustment range. Blades are set and filed much the same as with a hand ripsaw.

Bandsaw Safety

Here are some safety pointers to keep in mind when you are operating a bandsaw. Keep your fingers away from the moving blade. Keep the table clear of stock and scraps so your work won't catch as you push it along. Keep the

235

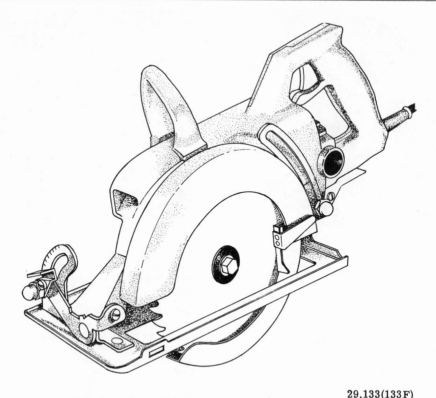

29.133(133F)

Figure 8-66.—Worm gear-driven portable electric circular saw.

upper guide just above the work, not excessively high. Do not stand to the right of the machine while it is running and do not lean on the table at any time.

Bandsaw wheels should be tested by experienced men at least once a week with a small machinist's hammer to detect cracks or loose spokes. The sound of a cracked or broken wheel is dull and flat.

Cracked blades should not be used. If a blade develops a "click" as it passes through the work, the operator should shut off the power as the click is a signal that the blade is cracked and may be ready to break. After the saw blade has stopped moving, it should be replaced with one in proper condition.

If the saw blade breaks the operator should shut off the power, and not attempt to remove any part of the saw blade until the machine is completely stopped.

If the work binds or pinches on the blade, the operator should never attempt to back the work away from the blade while the saw is in motion since this may break the blade. He should always see that the blade is working relatively freely through the cut.

A bandsaw should not be operated in a location where the temperature is below 45 degrees Fahrenheit as it may break when the machine is started.

Using a small saw for large work or forcing a wide saw on a small radius is bad practice. The saw blade should in all cases be as wide as the nature of the work will permit.

Bandsaws should not be stopped by thrusting a piece of wood against the cutting edge or side of the bandsaw blade immediately after the power has been shut off because the blade may break. Bandsaws 36 inches and larger should have a hand or foot brake.

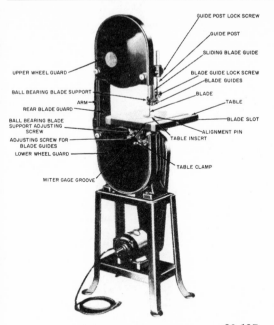

GUIDE POST LOCK SCREW

GUIDE POST

SLIDING BLADE GUIDE

UPPER WHEEL GUARD

BALL BEARING BLADE SUPPORT

ARM

REAR BLADE GUARD

BALL BEARING BLADE
SUPPORT ADJUSTING
SCREW

ADJUSTING SCREW FOR
BLADE GUIDES

LOWER WHEEL GUARD

MITER GAGE GROOVE

BLADE GUIDE LOCK SCREW
BLADE GUIDES

BLADE

TABLE

BLADE SLOT

ALIGNMENT PIN
TABLE INSERT

TABLE CLAMP

29.137

Figure 8-67.—Bandsaw.

Particular care should be taken when sharpening or brazing a bandsaw blade to see that the blade is not overheated and that the brazed joints are thoroughly united and are finished to the same thickness as the rest of the blade. IT IS RECOMMENDED THAT ALL BANDSAW BLADES BE BUTT WELDED WHERE POSSIBLE, AS THIS METHOD IS MUCH SUPERIOR TO THE OLD STYLE OF BRAZING.

Jigsaw

A JIGSAW performs about the same function as a bandsaw, but is usually capable of cutting more intricate curves. Instead of a flexible band-type blade, the jigsaw has a short, straight rigid blade which is rapidly oscillated vertically by the power mechanism.

Portable Field Saw

There are several types of portable units used at remote bases during peacetime. This is stated because at large, more permanent activities, there will be various shops fully equipped. Therefore, we will only be concerned

115.208

Figure 8-68.—Woodworking
trailer mounted shop.

with the portable field saw unit, which can be seen in figure 8-68. The unit illustrated is portable and self-contained for field construction.

Care and Maintenance
of Power Saws

The most important factors in the care and maintenance of a mechanical saw are the proper lubrication of all moving parts and the proper conditioning of the saw blade. A saw blade which is dull, or one in which the teeth are incorrectly shaped or improperly set, will "labor" in the wood. This in turn will place an excessive strain on the driving mechanism. The correct shapes of ripsaw and cutoff saw teeth are shown in figure 8-69. In a combination saw the RIP or RAKER teeth are shaped like ripsaw teeth and the CROSSCUT teeth like cutoff saw teeth, as shown in figure 8-70. As is the case with handsaws, the front and backslope of a circular ripsaw tooth are filed square across, while the front and backslope of a circular cutoff saw are beveled as shown in figure 8-69.

Complete reconditioning of a circular saw consists of (1) JOINTING, (2) GUMMING, (3) SETTING, and (4) SHARPENING, as follows:

JOINTING is done when wear and repeated sharpenings have caused the points on the saw to become out of round. The procedure for jointing is as follows:

PUT ON GOGGLES. Remove all sawdust from working area. Install blade in reverse

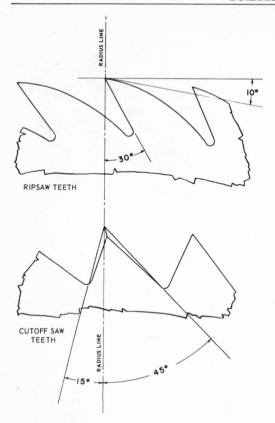

RIPSAW TEETH

CUTOFF SAW TEETH

29.15(44)A

Figure 8-69.—Correct shapes of circular ripsaw and cutoff saw teeth.

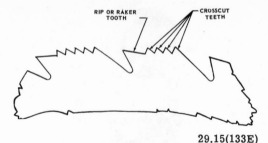

29.15(133E)

Figure 8-70.—Teeth on a combination saw.

the correct angle for the top of the backslope (15°, as shown in fig. 8-69), and free-hand in the gullet until it looks about right. Draw a circle (the GUM LINE shown in fig. 8-71) through the bottom of the gullet and all the way around the saw, to indicate the correct gullet depths of all the teeth.

A cutoff saw is marked for gumming as shown in figure 8-72. Draw two circles on the saw, one with a diameter equal to one-quarter of that of the saw, the other with a diameter equal to three-quarters of that of the saw. A tangent drawn from the smaller circle to the point of each tooth gives the line of the front of

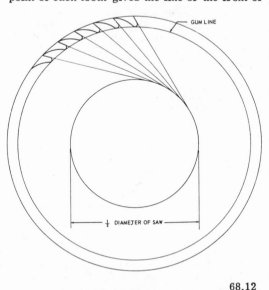

68.12

Figure 8-71.—Laying out a circular ripsaw for gumming.

order. Crank blade below table surface. Place and secure stone over blade. Start the saw and crank blade into stone slowly. When each tooth shows a bright spot the jointing process has been completed.

GUMMING is done when wear and repeated sharpenings have caused the gullets to become too shallow. It is very similar to the handsaw procedure called SHAPING. The first step in gumming is to lay out the shapes of several teeth on the saw as shown in figure 8-71 and 8-72. For a ripsaw (fig. 8-71), draw a circle on the saw with a diameter equal to one-half that of the saw, and draw a line from each point tangent to the circle. This line indicates the correct angle for the front of the tooth. Lay off

238

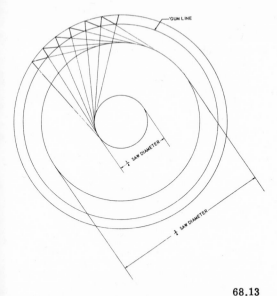

68.13

Figure 8-72.—Laying out a circular
cutoff saw for gumming.

103.31

Figure 8-73.—Circular saw sharpener
and gummer.

the tooth; a tangent drawn from the larger circle to the point of a tooth gives the line of the backslope of the tooth. Make the gum line circle large enough to run a little above the points of intersection of fronts and backslopes, to allow for a slight rounding of the gullet. A gullet which is filed to a corner has a tendency to crack at the corner.

A ripsaw may be gummed with a hand file of suitable shape or with a SAW SHARPENER AND GUMMER like the one shown in figure 8-73. The procedure with the saw sharpener and gummer is as follows:

Place the saw blade in the gumming machine and adjust so that the face of the grinding wheel is exactly in line with the correct line of the front of a tooth.

Bring the wheel into light contact with the front of the tooth, and then grind the gullet down to the gum line.

File down the backslope to the correct angle and shape by hand.

A cutoff saw may be gummed with a hand file of suitable shape or with the SAW FILING MACHINE shown in figure 8-74. This machine is a mechanical filer which works a file with a cross-section of the same shape as that of the

gullet. The machine is used in just about the same manner as the saw sharpener and gummer, with the exception of the fact that it files the front of one tooth and the backslope of the tooth next ahead in a single operation.

A circular saw is set in a SAW SETTING MACHINE. The ARBOR is set to the radius of the saw and the ANVIL is set to produce the desired amount of set on a tooth. Procedure for setting is as follows:

Move a tooth which is already bent downward onto the anvil.

Strike the anvil a single blow with a medium-weight BALL-PEEN hammer, held so as to bring the face of the hammer flush on the anvil.

Repeat on every other tooth all the way around.

Turn the saw over and perform the same operation on the teeth bent the other way.

SHARPENING may be done with a hand file of suitable shape, or with the SAW SHARPENER AND GUMMER (ripsaw) or the SAW FILING MACHINE (cutoff saw) already mentioned. For the ripsaw the machine must be set, or the file must be held, so as to grind or file the fronts of the teeth at 90° to the line of the saw. For the cutoff saw the machine must be set, or the file must be held, so as to file the front of one tooth and the backslope of the tooth next ahead at the correct bevel angle, which is about 45°

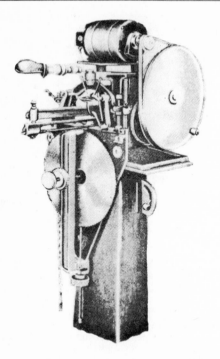

103.32
Figure 8-74.—Saw filing machine.

to the line of the saw. Procedure for sharpening is as follows:

Set the machine to the correct front angle and correct crosswise angle (90° for a ripsaw, 45° for a cutoff saw).

Grind or file the front of each tooth that is SET TOWARD THE MACHINE.

Reverse the saw blade and grind or file the fronts of the remaining teeth.

For the combination or miter saw, the reconditioning procedures are those of the ripsaw for the rip or raker teeth and those of the cutoff saw for the crosscut teeth. The points of the rip teeth should be slightly lower than the points of the cutoff teeth to get a smooth-cutting saw. To test the saw for this factor, make a shallow cut in a piece of waste wood. If the bottom of the cut is perfectly flat, the points of the rip teeth are higher than the points of the crosscut teeth. If two sharp lines are scored on either side of the bottom of the cut, the points of the crosscut teeth are higher than the points of the rip teeth, as they should be.

BANDSAW teeth are shaped like the teeth in a hand ripsaw, which means that their fronts are filed at 90° to the line of the saw. Reconditioning procedures are the same as they are for a hand ripsaw, except that very narrow bandsaws with very small teeth must usually be set and sharpened by special machines.

SHAVING TOOLS

To get the smooth surface or edge, desired, on certain materials, various operations must be performed with shaving tools; therefore, the following sections are provided to aid you in conducting these operations safely.

Jointer

THE JOINTER is a machine for power-planing stock on faces, edges, and ends. The planing is done by a revolving CUTTERHEAD, equipped with two or more KNIVES as shown in figure 8-75. Setting up on the SET SCREWS forces the THROAT PIECE against the knife for holding the knife in position. Loosening the set screws releases the knife for removal. The size of a jointer is designated by the width in inches of the cutterhead; sizes range from 4-in. to 36-in. A 6-in. jointer is shown in figure 8-76.

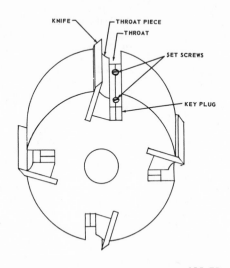

133.73
Figure 8-75.—Four-knife cutterhead for a jointer.

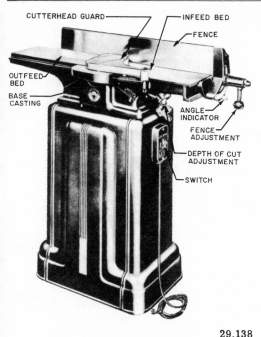

CUTTERHEAD GUARD

INFEED BED

FENCE

OUTFEED BED

BASE CASTING

ANGLE INDICATOR

FENCE ADJUSTMENT

DEPTH OF CUT ADJUSTMENT

SWITCH

29.138

Figure 8-76.—Six-inch jointer.

The principle on which the jointer functions is illustrated in figure 8-77. The TABLE consists of two parts on either side of the cutterhead. The stock is started on the INFEED TABLE and fed past the cutterhead onto the OUTFEED TABLE. The surface of the outfeed table must be exactly level with the highest point reached by the knife edges. The surface

of the infeed table is depressed below the surface of the outfeed table, an amount equal to the desired depth of cut. The usual depth of cut is about 1/16 to 1/8 in.

The level of the outfeed table must be frequently checked to ensure that the surface is exactly even with the highest point reached by the knife edges. If the outfeed table is too high, the cut will become progressively more shallow as the piece is fed through. If the outfeed table is too low, the piece will drop downward as its end leaves the infeed table, and the cut for the last inch or so will be too deep.

The outfeed table can be set to correct height as follows:

Feed a piece of waste stock past the cutterhead until a few inches of it lie on the outfeed table. Then stop the machine and look under the outfeed end of the piece. If the outfeed table is too low, there will be a space between the surface of the table and the lower face of the piece. Raise the outfeed table until this space is eliminated. If no space appears, lower the outfeed table until a space does appear. Now run the stock back through the machine. If there is still a space then raise the table just enough to eliminate it.

Note that the cutterhead cuts toward the infeed table; therefore, in order to cut with the grain, you must place the piece with the grain running toward the infeed table. A piece is EDGED by feeding it through on edge with one of the faces held against the FENCE. A piece is SURFACED by feeding it through flat with one of the edges against the fence. This operation however should if possible be limited to straightening the face of the stock. The fence

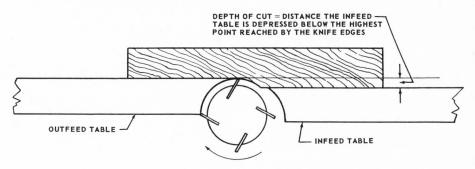

DEPTH OF CUT = DISTANCE THE INFEED TABLE IS DEPRESSED BELOW THE HIGHEST POINT REACHED BY THE KNIFE EDGES

OUTFEED TABLE

INFEED TABLE

133.74

Figure 8-77.—Principle of operation of the jointer.

can be set at 90° to produce squared faces and edges, or at any desired angle to produce beveled edges or ends.

Jointer Safety

Only sharp and evenly balanced knives should be used in a jointer cutting head.

The knives must not be set to take too heavy a cut, as a kickback is almost certain to result especially if there is a knot or change of grain in the stock.

The knives must be securely fastened after the machine has been standing in a cold building over the weekend.

When pieces shorter than 18 inches are machined, a push block should be used.

Each hand-fed jointer should be equipped with a cylindrical cutting head, the throat of which should not exceed 7/16 inch in depth nor 5/8 inch in width. It is strongly recommended that no cylinder be used in which the throat exceeds 3/8 inch in depth or 1/2 inch in width.

Each hand-fed jointer should have an automatic guard which will cover all the sections of the head on the working side of the fence or gage. The guard should automatically adjust horizontally for edge jointing and vertically for surface work, and should remain in contact with the material at all times.

Surfacer

A SINGLE SURFACER (also called a SINGLE PLANER) is shown in figure 8-78. This machine surfaces stock on one face (the upper face) only; double surfacers, which surface both faces at the same time, are used only in large planing mills.

The surfacer cuts with a cutterhead like the one on the jointer, but on the single surfacer the cutterhead is located above instead of below driven rollers, and the part adjacent to the cutterhead is pressed down against the FEED BED by a couple of members called the CHIP BREAKER (just ahead of the cutterhead) and the PRESSURE BAR (just behind the cutterhead). The pressure bar temporarily straightens out any warp a piece may have; in effect, a piece that goes into the surfacer warped will come out still warped. This is not a defect in the machine; the surfacer is designed for surfacing only, not for truing warped stock. If true, plane surfaces are desired, one face of the stock (the face which goes down in the

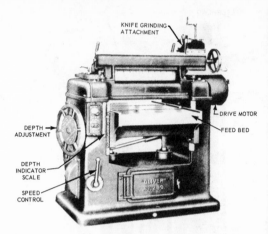

29.135

Figure 8-78.—Single surfacer.

surfacer) must be trued on the jointer before the piece is fed through the surfacer. If the face that goes down in the surfacer is true, the surfacer will plane the other face true.

Surfacer Safety

Each surfacing machine should have all cutting heads, covered by a metal guard. If such guard is constructed of sheet metal, the material used should not be less than 1/16 inch in thickness; and if cast iron is used, it should not be less than 3/16 inch in thickness.

Where an exhaust system is used, the guards should form part or all of the exhaust hood and should be constructed of metal of a thickness not less than the above.

Feed rolls should be guarded by a hood or a semicylindrical guard to prevent the hands of the operator from coming in contact with the in-running rolls at any point. The guard should be fastened to the frame carrying the rolls so as to remain in adjustment for any thickness of the stock.

Sectional feed rolls should be provided for surfacers. Where solid feed rolls are used, the sectional finger devices should be used to prevent kickbacks.

Shaper

The SHAPER is designed primarily for edging curved stock and for cutting ornamental

133.75

Figure 8-79.—Wood shaper.

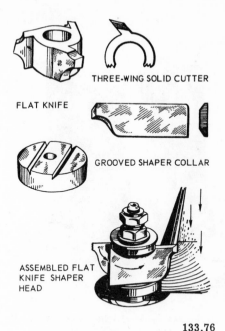

THREE-WING SOLID CUTTER

FLAT KNIFE

GROOVED SHAPER COLLAR

ASSEMBLED FLAT
KNIFE SHAPER
HEAD

133.76

Figure 8-80.—Three-wing cutter
and flat knives for a shaper.

edges, as on moldings; but it can also be used for rabbeting, grooving, FLUTING, and BEADING. A FLUTE is a straight groove with a curved rather than a rectangular cross-section. A BEAD might be called the reverse of a flute. A shaper is shown in figure 8-79.

The flat cutter or knives on a shaper are mounted on a vertical SPINDLE and held in place by a hexagonal SPINDLE NUT. A grooved COLLAR is placed below and above the cutter or knives to receive the edge of the knives. Ball bearing collars are available for use as guides on irregular work where the fence isn't used. The part of the edge that is to remain uncut runs against the ball bearing collar, as shown in the bottom view of figure 8-80. A THREE WING CUTTER fits over the spindle as shown in the upper view of figure 8-80. FLAT KNIFE cutters are assembled in pairs between collars. Both cutters and knives come with cutting edges in a great variety of shapes. BLANK flat knives are available which may be ground to any desired shape of cutting edge. This is done only by experienced personnel.

For shaping the side edges on a rectangular piece, a light-duty shaper has an ADJUSTABLE FENCE like the one shown on the shaper in figure 8-81. For shaping the end-edges on a rectangular piece, a machine of this type has a SLIDING FENCE, similar to the cutoff gage on a circular saw. The sliding fence slides in the groove shown in the table top.

On larger machines the fence consists of a board straightedge, clamped to the table with a handscrew as shown in figure 8-82. A semicircular opening is sawed in the edge of the straightedge to accommodate the spindle and the cutters or knives. Whenever possible, a guard of the type shown in the figure should be placed over the spindle.

For shaping curved edges there are usually a couple of holes in the table, one on either side of the spindle, in which vertical STARTER PINS can be inserted. When a curved edge is being shaped, the piece is guided by and steadied against the starter pin and the ball bearing collar on the spindle.

Like the jointer and surfacer, the shaper cuts toward the infeed side of the spindle, which is against the rotation of the spindle. Stock should therefore be placed with grain running toward the infeed side.

68.27

Figure 8-81.—Light-duty shaper
with adjustable fence.

Shaper Safety

Make sure the knives are sharp and are well secured.

If curved or irregularly-shaped edges are to be shaped, place the stock in position and check to see that the collar will rub against part of the edge which should not be removed.

Whenever the straight fence cannot be used, always use a starting pin in the table top.

Never make extremely deep cuts.

Make sure the shaper knives rotate toward the work.

Whenever possible, always use a guard, pressure bar, holddown, or holding jig.

If possible, place the cutter on the shaper spindle so that the cutting will be done on the lower side of the stock.

Do not attempt to shape small pieces of wood.

Check all adjustments before turning on the power.

"The spindle shaper is probably one of the most DANGEROUS machines used in the shop. Use extreme caution at all times."

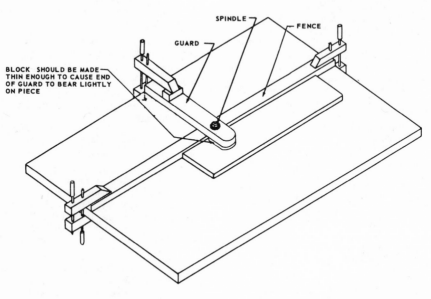

133.77

Figure 8-82.—Shaper table, showing straightedge fence and guard.

Care and Maintenance
of Power Shaving Tools

The two most important factors in the care and maintenance of a jointer, surfacer, or shaper are the proper lubrication of all moving parts and the proper sharpening and adjustment of the knives and/or cutters. Dull knives and cutters deteriorate the machinery by causing it to "labor," and to "chatter" or vibrate. Besides, a dull knife or cutter on a power shaving machine is a very dangerous hazard. A dull knife or cutter tends to "catch" in the wood, and since the machine is cutting toward the operator the result of a catch is a violent throw-back of the stock toward the operator. The piece may strike the operator, but more serious than this is the fact that the operator's hands, when the piece is torn out of them, may be driven against the knives or the cutters.

The best way to sharpen the knives on a jointer or surfacer is with a KNIFE GRINDING ATTACHMENT like the one shown on the surfacer in figure 8-78. With one of these devices the knives can be sharpened without removing them from the cutterhead. The knife grinding attachment consists of a small motor-driven grinding wheel, mounted in a SADDLE which can be cranked back and forth on a steel bar called a BRIDGE. The bridge can be mounted over the cutterhead by means of a couple of BRIDGE BRACKETS. The general procedure for sharpening with a knife-grinding attachment is as follows:

Open the starting switch on the machine and lock it open. If the power line has a main switch which can be opened, open that switch as well.

Revolve the cutterhead by hand until a knife is in a position where the cutterhead LOCKING PIN can be put on. The locking pin holds the uppermost knife in correct grinding position.

Loosen the set screws until they are holding the knife only lightly, and move the knife up about 1/12 in. The best way to do this and still keep the knife level is to use a THREE-PRONGED KNIFE GAGE. This device has two prongs which fit against the cutterhead on either side of the knife, and a third prong in the center which can be set to any desired amount of protrusion of the knife edge. When the knife has been set at the desired height, tighten the set screws.

Adjust the knife edges of the other knives to the same height.

Set the grinding attachment in place, bring the grinder down to contact the bevel on the first knife, and crank the grinder back and forth over the knife several times. Take a light cut, and crank fast enough to keep the knife from overheating. Repeat on the other two knives.

When the first knife is again under the grinder, lower the grinder slightly and repeat the above procedure on all three knives. Repeat this whole process, lowering the grinder a little every time you get back to the first knife, until all nicks have been ground away and there is a perfect bevel on every knife in the cutterhead.

The next step is JOINTING the knives, which means, as in the case of a circular saw, ensuring that the knife edges form a perfect circle as the cutterhead revolves. Remove the motor from the saddle and install a JOINTING ATTACHMENT. A jointing attachment is a device with a fine whetstone attached to its lower end; the whetstone can be set so that it barely touches the knife edges. Set it so, revolving the cutterhead by hand to ensure that there is the barest contact and no more.

Start the machine and crank the jointing attachment back and forth several times over the revolving knives. Stop the machine and examine the knife edges. If they have not all been slightly touched, lower the stone just a little and repeat the process until every knife edge has been touched.

In the absence of a knife grinding attachment, the knives must be removed from the cutterhead and ground on an oilstone grinder or in some other manner.

To readjust the knives in the cutterhead of a jointer, place a builder's level or a wooden straightedge on the outfeed table and line the highest point reached by each knife edge with the lower edge of the straightedge as follows. Place the knife in the cutterhead and set the set screws up lightly. Place the straightedge over one end of the knife and raise or lower the knife until the edge barely contacts the straightedge when the cutterhead is rotated by hand. Move the straightedge to the other end of the knife and repeat the same procedure. Tighten the setscrews and make a final check for correct height at both ends of the knife. Repeat the same procedure with the remaining knives.

A flat shaper knife with a straight cutting edge is ground and whetted like a plane iron or a chisel. As is the case with a jointer or surfacer, the knives in a shaper must be exactly equal in size and weight. Three-way cutters and knives with curved edges must be sharpened "free-hand" with a small portable grinding wheel, called a "grinding pencil." The greatest care must be taken to keep pairs of knives and the cutting extensions in a three-way cutter exactly alike in size, weight, and shape.

DRILL PRESS

Except in heavy timber construction (which is described in ch. 16), portable ELECTRIC DRILLS are not used much in woodworking. Many woodworking and carpenter shops have a stationary drill, however, which is usually called a DRILL PRESS (see fig. 8-83). Besides boring, the drill press (equipped with a ROUTER BIT like the one shown on the radial saw in fig. 8-64) is used for ROUTING, and also (equipped with a SHAPER HEAD and shaper knives or cutters) for shaping.

When it is used for boring, a portable or stationary power-driven drill always uses a twist drill, never an auger bit. The most important care and maintenance factors are proper lubrication of moving parts and the use of properly conditioned twist drills.

THE LATHE

The LATHE is without question the oldest of all woodworking machines. In its early form, it consisted of two holding centers with the suspended stock being rotated by an endless rope belt. It was operated by having one person pull on the rope hand-over-hand while the cutting was done by a second person holding crude hand lathe tools on an improvised beam rest.

The actual operations of woodturning performed on a modern lathe are still done to a great degree with woodturner's handtools. However, machine lathe work is coming more and more into use with the introduction of newly designed lathes for that purpose.

The lathe is used in turning or shaping round billets, drums, disks, and any object that requires a true diameter. The size of a lathe is determined by the maximum diameter of the work it can swing over its bed. There are various sizes and types of wood lathes, ranging from very small sizes for delicate work to large surface or "bull lathes" that can swing jobs 15 feet in diameter.

Figure 8-84 illustrates a type of lathe that you may find in your shop. It is made in three

11.10X
Figure 8-83.—Drill press.

sizes to swing 16-, 20-, and 24-inch diameter stock. The lathe has four major parts: (1) bed, (2) headstock, (3) tailstock, and (4) toolrest.

The lathe shown in figure 8-84 has a bed of iron. It can be obtained in any other length desired. The bed is a broad flat surface that supports the other parts of the machine.

The headstock is mounted on the left end of the lathe bed. All power for the lathe is transmitted through the headstock. It has a fully enclosed motor that will give a variable-spindle speed (from 600 to 3600 rpm). The spindle is threaded at the front end to receive the

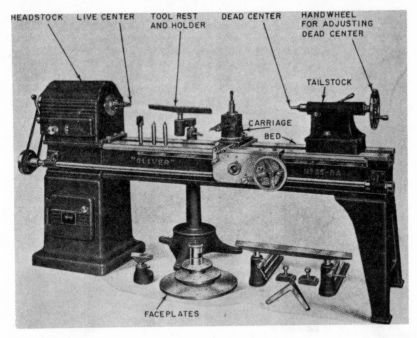

HEADSTOCK   LIVE CENTER   TOOL REST AND HOLDER   DEAD CENTER   HAND WHEEL FOR ADJUSTING DEAD CENTER

TAILSTOCK

CARRIAGE
BED

FACEPLATES

28.69X

Figure 8-84.—A woodturning lathe with accessories.

faceplates. A faceplate attachment to the motor spindle is furnished to hold or mount small jobs having large diameters. There is also a flange on the rear end of the spindle to receive large faceplates, which are held securely by four stud bolts.

The tailstock is located on the right end of the lathe and is movable along the length of the bed. It supports one end of the work while the other end is being turned by the headstock spur. The tail center may be removed from the stock simply by backing the screw. The shank is tapered to automatically center the point.

Most large sizes of lathes are provided with a power-feeding carriage. A cone-pulley bolt arrangement provides power from the motor, and ways are cast to the side of the bed for sliding the carriage back and forth. All machines have a metal bar that may be attached to the bed of the lathe between the operator and the work. This serves as a handtool rest and provides support for the operator in guiding tools along the work. It may be of any size and is adjustable to any desired position.

In lathe work, wood is rotated against the special cutting tools illustrated in figure 8-85. The special lathe tools include turning gouges; skew chisels; parting tools; round-nose, square-nose, and spear-point chisels; toothing irons; and auxiliary aids such as calipers, dividers, and templates.

Turning gouges are used chiefly to rough out nearly all shapes in spindle turning. The gouge sizes vary from 1/8 inch to 2 or more inches, with 1/4-, 3/4-, and 1-inch sizes being most common.

Skew chisels are used for smoothing cuts to finish a surface, turning beads, trimming ends or shoulders, and for making V-cuts. They are made in sizes from 1/8 inch to 2 1/2 inches in width and in pairs, right-handed and left-handed.

Parting tools are used to cut recesses or grooves with straight sides and a flat bottom and also to cut off finished work from the faceplate. These tools are available in sizes ranging from 1/8 to 3/4 inch.

Scraping tools of various shapes are used for the most accurate turning work, especially

247

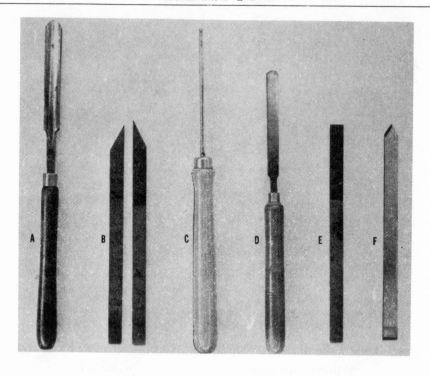

A. Turning gouge
B. Skew chisels
C. Parting tool

D. Round-nose chisel
E. Square-nose chisel
F. Spear-point chisel

28.66

Figure 8-85.—Lathe cutting tools.

for most faceplate turning. A few of the more commonly used shapes are illustrated in parts D, E, and F of figure 8-85. The chisels shown in B, E, and F are actually old jointer blades which have been ground to the required shape; the wood handles for these homemade chisels are not shown in the illustration.

A toothing iron is basically a square-nose turning chisel with a series of parallel grooves cut into the top surface of the iron. (See fig. 8-86.) These turning tools are used for rough turning of segment work mounted on a faceplate. The points of the toothing iron created by the parallel grooves serve as a series of spear-point chisels; therefore, the tool is not likely to catch and dig into the work like a square-nose turning chisel. The toothing iron is made with

coarse, medium, and fine parallel grooves and varies from 1/2 inch to 2 inches in width.

Lathe turning may be divided into two categories: center-to-center turning (also called between turning and spindle turning) and faceplate turning.

Being aware of the many dangers when using a lathe, you should follow and insist upon strict adherence to the following safety rules:

DETAIL "A"

68.16

Figure 8-86.—Toothing iron lathe tool.

Use the toolrest as much as possible.

Adjust and set the compound or the toolrest for the start of the cut before turning the switch on.

Take very light cuts, especially when using handtools.

Never attempt to use calipers on interrupted surfaces while the work is in motion.

METHODS OF FASTENING

The following sections will discuss the various devices used for fastening wood during construction.

The fastening devices most commonly used are usually made of metal; and they are classified accordingly such as: nails, screws, bolts, driftpins, corrugated fasteners, and timber connectors. Each type mentioned above will be explained in the following sections except timber connectors. Timber connectors will be discussed in a later chapter.

NAILS

The standard nail used by the Builder is the wire nail, so called because it is made from steel wire. There are many types of nails, all of which are classified according to use and form. The wire nail is round-shafted, straight, pointed, and may vary in size, weight, size and shape of head, type of point, and finish. All normal requirements of construction and framing are filled by one of the nail types below. There are a few general rules to be followed in the use of nails in building. A nail, whatever the type, should be at least three times as long as the thickness of wood it is intended to hold. Two-thirds of the length of the nail is driven into the second piece for proper anchorage while one-third provides the necessary anchorage of the piece being fastened. Nails should be driven at an angle slightly toward each other and should be carefully placed to provide the greatest holding power. Nails driven with the grain do not hold as well as nails driven across the grain. A few nails of proper type and size, properly placed and properly driven, will hold better than a great many driven close together. Nails can generally be considered the cheapest and easiest fasteners to be applied. In terms of holding power alone, nails provide the least; screws of comparable size provide more, and bolts provide the greatest amount.

COMMON WIRE NAILS and box nails are the same except that the wire sizes are one or two numbers smaller for a given length of the box nail than they are for the common nail. The common wire nail (A, fig. 8-87) is used for housing-construction framing. The common wire nail and the box nail are generally used for structural construction.

The FINISHING NAIL (B, fig. 8-87) is made from finer wire and has a smaller head than the common nail. It may be set below the surface of the wood into which it is driven and will leave only a small hole easily puttied up. It is generally used for interior or exterior finishing work and is used for finished carpentry and cabinetmaking.

The DUPLEX NAIL (C, fig. 8-87) is made with what may appear to be two heads. The lower head, or shoulder, is provided so that the nail may be driven securely home to give maximum holding power while the upper head projects above the surface of the wood to make its withdrawal simple. The reason for this design is that the duplex nail is not meant to be permanent. It is used in the construction of temporary structures such as scaffolding and staging and is classified for temporary construction.

ROOFING NAILS (D, fig. 8-87) are round-shafted, diamond-pointed, galvanized nails of relatively short length and comparatively large heads. They are designed for fastening flexible roofing materials and for resisting continuous exposure to weather. Several general rules apply to the use of roofing nails, especially their use with asphalt shingles. If shingles or roll roofing is being applied over old roofing, the roofing nails selected must be of sufficient length to go through the old material and secure the new. Asphalt roofing material is fastened with corrosion resistant nails, never with plain nails. Nailing is begun in the center of the shingle, just above the cutouts or slots, to avoid buckling.

Nail sizes are designated by the use of the term penny. This term designates the length of the nail (1 penny, 2 penny, etc.), which is the same for all types. The approximate number of nails per pound, varies according to the type and size. The wire gage number varies according to type. Figure 8-87 provides the information implicit in the term penny for each of the type of nails referenced to in this section. The d adjacent to the numbers in the Size column is the accepted abbreviation of the word penny as used in nail sizing and should be read

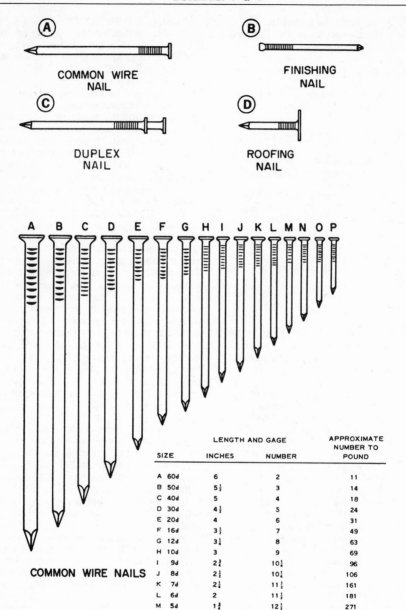

| SIZE | LENGTH AND GAGE | | APPROXIMATE NUMBER TO POUND |
	INCHES	NUMBER	
A 60d	6	2	11
B 50d	5½	3	14
C 40d	5	4	18
D 30d	4½	5	24
E 20d	4	6	31
F 16d	3½	7	49
G 12d	3¼	8	63
H 10d	3	9	69
I 9d	2¾	10¼	96
J 8d	2½	10¼	106
K 7d	2¼	11½	161
L 6d	2	11½	181
M 5d	1¾	12½	271
N 4d	1½	12½	316
O 3d	1¼	14	568
P 2d	1	15	876

29.121

Figure 8-87.—Types of nails and nail sizes.

2 penny, 3 penny, etc. Table 8-1 gives the general size and type of nail preferable for specific applications.

SCREWS

The use of screws, rather than nails, as fasteners may be dictated by a number of factors. These may include the type of material to be fastened, the requirement for greater holding power than could be obtained by the use of nails, the finished appearance desired, and the fact that the number of fasteners that can be used is limited. The use of screws, rather than nails, is more expensive in terms of time and money but is often necessary to meet requirements for superior results. The main advantages of screws are—they provide more holding power; can be easily tightened to draw the items being fastened securely together; are neater in appearance if properly driven; and may be withdrawn without damaging the material. The common wood screw is usually made of unhardened steel, stainless steel, aluminum, or brass. The steel may be bright finished or blued, or zinc, cadmium, or chrome plated. Wood screws are threaded from a gimlet point for approximately 2/3 of the length of the screw and are provided with a slotted head designed to be driven by an inserted driver.

WOOD screws as shown in figure 8-88 are designated according to head style. The most common types are: flathead, ovalhead, and roundhead, both in slotted and phillips heads. To prepare wood for receiving the screws, bore a pilot hole the diameter of the screw to be used in the piece of wood that is to be fastened (fig. 8-89). Then bore a smaller, starter hole in the piece of wood that is to act as anchor or hold the threads of the screw. The starter hole is drilled with a diameter less than that of the screw threads and to a depth 1/2 or 2/3 the length of the threads to be anchored. The purpose of this careful preparation is to assure accuracy in the placement of the screws, to reduce the possibility of splitting the wood, and to reduce the time and effort required to drive the screw. Properly set slotted and phillips

Table 8-1.—Size, Type, and Use of Nails

Size	Lgth (in.)[1]	Diam (in.)	Remarks	Where used
2d	1	.072	Small head	Finish work, shop work.
2d	1	.072	Large flathead	Small timber, wood shingles, lathes.
3d	1¼	.08	Small head	Finish work, shop work.
3d	1¼	.08	Large flathead	Small timber, wood shingles, lathes.
4d	1½	.098	Small head	Finish work, shop work.
4d	1½	.098	Large flathead	Small timber, lathes, shop work.
5d	1¾	.098	Small head	Finish work, shop work.
5d	1¾	.098	Large flathead	Small timber, lathes, shop work.
6d	2	.113	Small head	Finish work, casing, stops, etc., shop work.
6d	2	.113	Large flathead	Small timber, siding, sheathing, etc., shop work.
7d	2¼	.113	Small head	Casing, base, ceiling, stops, etc.
7d	2¼	.113	Large flathead	Sheathing, siding, subflooring, light framing.
8d	2½	.131	Small head	Casing, base, ceiling, wainscot, etc., shop work.
8d	2½	.131	Large flathead	Sheathing, siding, subflooring, light framing, shop work.
8d	1¼	.131	Extra-large flathead	Roll roofing, composition shingles.
9d	2¾	.131	Small head	Casing, base, ceiling, etc.
9d	2¾	.131	Large flathead	Sheathing, siding, subflooring, framing, shop work.
10d	3	.148	Small head	Casing, base, ceiling, etc., shop work.
10d	3	.148	Large flathead	Sheathing, siding, subflooring, framing, shop work.
12d	3¼	.148	Large flathead	Sheathing, subflooring, framing.
16d	3½	.162	Large flathead	Framing, bridges, etc.
20d	4	.192	Large flathead	Framing, bridges, etc.
30d	4½	.207	Large flathead	Heavy framing, bridges, etc.
40d	5	.225	Large flathead	Heavy framing, bridges, etc.
50d	5½	.244	Large flathead	Extra-heavy framing, bridges, etc.
60d	6	.262	Large flathead	Extra-heavy framing, bridges, etc.

[1] This chart applies to wire nails, although it may be used to determine the length of cut nails.

133.341

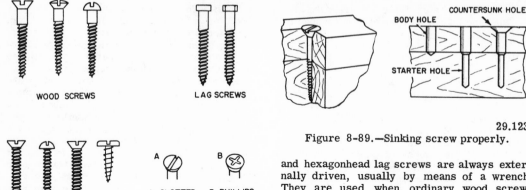

WOOD SCREWS LAG SCREWS

METAL SCREWS

A. SLOTTED HEAD   B. PHILLIPS HEAD

29.123

Figure 8-88.—Types of screws.

29.123

Figure 8-89.—Sinking screw properly.

flathead and ovalhead screws are countersunk sufficiently to permit a covering material to be used to cover the head. Slotted roundhead and phillips roundhead screws are not countersunk, but are driven so that the head is firmly flush with the surface of the wood. The slot of the roundhead screw is left parallel with the grain of the wood.

The proper name for LAG screws (fig. 8-88) is lag bolt, wood screw type. These screws are often required in construction building. They are longer and much heavier than the common wood screw and have coarser threads which extend from a cone or gimlet point slightly more than half the length of the screw. Squarehead

and hexagonhead lag screws are always externally driven, usually by means of a wrench. They are used when ordinary wood screws would be too short or too light and spikes would not be strong enough. For sizes of lag screws, see table 8-2. Combined with expansion anchors, they are used to frame timbers to existing masonry.

Expansion shields, or expansion anchors as they are sometimes called, are used for inserting a predrilled hole, usually in masonry, to provide a gripping base or anchor for a screw, bolt, or nail intended to fasten an item to the surface in which the hole was bored. The shield may be obtained separately or may include the screw, bolt, or nail. After the expansion shield is inserted in the predrilled hole, the fastener is driven into the hole in the shield, expanding the shield and wedging it firmly against the surface of the hole.

For the assembly of metal parts, SHEET METAL screws are used. These screws are made regularly in steel and brass with four types of heads: flat, round, oval, and fillister, as shown in that order in figure 8-88.

Table 8-2.—Lag Screws

Lengths (inches)	1/4	Diameters (inches)		
		3/8, 7/16, 1/2	5/8, 3/4	7/8, 1
1	x	x	----------	----------
1½	x	x	x	----------
2, 2½, 3, 3½, etc., 7½, 8 to 10	x	x	x	x
11 to 12	----------	x	x	x
13 to 16	----------	----------	x	x

133.342

Wood screws come in sizes which vary from 1/4 inch to 6 inches. Screws up to 1 inch in length increase by eighths, screws from 1 to 3 inches increase by quarters, and screws from 3 to 6 inches increase by half-inches. Screws vary in length and size of shaft. Each length is made in a number of shaft sizes specified by an arbitrary number that represents no particular measurement but indicates relative di ʼrences in the diameter of the screws. Prope nomenclature of a screw as illustrated in figure 8-90, includes the type, material, finish, length, and screw size number which indicates the wire gage of the body, drill or bit size for the body hole, and drill or bit size for the starter hole. Tables 8-3 and 8-4 provide size, length, gage, and applicable drill and auger bit sizes for screws; table 8-2 gives lengths and diameters of lag screws.

BOLTS

Bolts are used in construction when great strength is required or when the work under construction must be frequently disassembled.

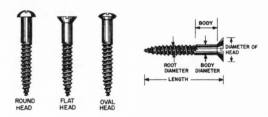

29.123

Figure 8-90.—Types of wood screws and nomenclature.

Their use usually implies the use of nuts for fastening and sometimes the use of washers to protect the surface of the material they are used to fasten. Bolts are selected for application to specific requirements in terms of length, diameter, threads, style of head, and type. Proper selection of head style and type of bolt will result in good appearance as well as good construction. The use of washers between the nut and a wood surface or between both the nut and the head and their opposing surfaces will

Table 8-3.—Screw Sizes and Dimensions.

Length (in.)	Size numbers																							
	0	1	2	3	4	5	6	7	8	9	10	11	12	13	14	15	16	17	18	20	22	24
1/4	x	x	x	x																		
3/8	x	x	x	x	x	x	x	x	x	x												
1/2		x	x	x	x	x	x	x	x	x	x	x	x									
5/8		x	x	x	x	x	x	x	x	x	x	x			x							
3/4			x	x	x	x	x	x	x	x	x	x			x		x					
7/8			x	x	x	x	x	x	x	x	x	x			x		x					
1				x	x	x	x	x	x	x	x	x			x		x		x	x		
1 1/4					x	x	x	x	x	x	x	x			x		x		x	x		x
1 1/2					x	x	x	x	x	x	x	x			x		x		x	x		x
1 3/4					x	x	x	x	x	x	x	x			x		x		x	x		x
2					x	x	x	x	x	x	x	x			x		x		x	x		x
2 1/4					x	x	x	x	x	x	x	x			x		x		x	x		x
2 1/2					x	x	x	x	x	x	x	x			x		x		x	x		x
2 3/4						x	x	x	x	x	x	x			x		x		x	x		x
3						x	x	x	x	x	x	x			x		x		x	x		x
3 1/2							x	x	x	x	x				x		x		x	x		x
4							x	x	x	x	x				x		x		x	x		x
4 1/2											x				x		x		x	x		x
5											x				x		x		x	x		x
6															x		x		x	x		x
Threads per inch	32	28	26	24	22	20	18	16	15	14	13	12	11		10		9		8	8		7
Diameter of screw (in.)	.060	.073	.086	.099	.112	.125	.138	.151	.164	.177	.190	.203	.216		.242		.268		.294	.320		.372

133.343

Table 8-4.—Drill and Auger Bit Sizes for Wood Screws

Screw size No.		1	2	3	4	5	6	7	8	9	10	12	14	16	18
Nominal screw		.073	.086	.099	.112	.125	.138	.151	.164	.177	.190	.216	.242	.268	.294
Body diameter		$\frac{5}{64}$	$\frac{3}{32}$	$\frac{3}{32}$	$\frac{7}{64}$	$\frac{1}{8}$	$\frac{9}{64}$	$\frac{5}{32}$	$\frac{11}{64}$	$\frac{11}{64}$	$\frac{3}{16}$	$\frac{7}{32}$	$\frac{15}{64}$	$\frac{17}{64}$	$\frac{19}{64}$
Pilot hole	Drill size	$\frac{5}{64}$	$\frac{3}{32}$	$\frac{7}{64}$	$\frac{7}{64}$	$\frac{1}{8}$	$\frac{9}{64}$	$\frac{5}{32}$	$\frac{11}{64}$	$\frac{3}{16}$	$\frac{3}{16}$	$\frac{7}{32}$	$\frac{1}{4}$	$\frac{17}{64}$	$\frac{19}{64}$
	Bit size	-----	-----	-----	-----	-----	-----	-----	-----	-----	-----	4	4	5	5
Starter hole	Drill size	------	$\frac{1}{16}$	$\frac{1}{16}$	$\frac{5}{64}$	$\frac{5}{64}$	$\frac{3}{32}$	$\frac{7}{64}$	$\frac{7}{64}$	$\frac{1}{8}$	$\frac{1}{8}$	$\frac{9}{64}$	$\frac{5}{32}$	$\frac{3}{16}$	$\frac{13}{64}$
	Bit size	-----	-----	-----	-----	-----	-----	-----	-----	-----	-----	-----	-----	-----	4

133.344

avoid marring the surfaces and permit additional torque in tightening.

CARRIAGE bolts fall into three categories: square neck (fig. 8-91) bolt, finned neck bolt, and ribbed neck bolt. These bolts have round-heads that are not designed to be driven. They are threaded only part of the way up the shaft; usually the threads are two to four times the diameter of the bolt in length. In each type of carriage bolt, the upper part of the shank, immediately below the head, is designed to grip the material in which the bolt is inserted and keep the bolt from turning when a nut is tightened down on it or removed. The finned type is designed with two or more fins extending from the head to the shank. The ribbed type is designed with longitudinal ribs, splines, or serrations on all or part of a shoulder located immediately beneath the head. Holes bored to receive carriage bolts are bored to be a tight fit for the body of the bolt and counterbored to permit the head of the bolt to fit flush with, or below the surface of, the material being fastened. The bolt is then driven through the hole with a hammer. Carriage bolts are chiefly for wood-to-wood application but may also be used for wood-to-metal applications. If used for wood-to-metal application, the head should be fitted to the wood item. Metal surfaces are sometimes predrilled and countersunk to permit the use of carriage bolts metal-to-metal. Carriage bolts can be obtained from 1/4 inch to 1 inch in diameter, and from 3/4 inch to 20 inches long (table 8-5). A common flat washer

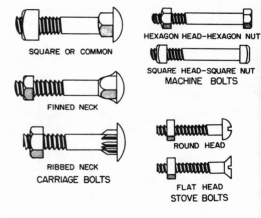

Figure 8-91.—Types of bolts.

29.124

should be used with carriage bolts between the nut and the wood surface.

Table 8-5.—Carriage Bolts

Lengths (inches)	Diameters (inches)			
	³⁄₁₆, ¼, ⁵⁄₁₆, ³⁄₈	⁷⁄₁₆, ½	⁹⁄₁₆, ⁵⁄₈	¾
¾ ----------------------------	x	----------	----------	----------
1 ----------------------------	x	x	----------	----------
1¼ ----------------------------	x	x	x	----------
1½, 2, 2½, etc., 9½, 10 to 20_	x	x	x	x

133.345

MACHINE bolts (fig. 8-91) are made with cut National Fine or National Coarse threads extending in length from twice the diameter of the bolt plus 1/4 inch (for bolts less than 6 inches in length), to twice the diameter of the bolt plus 1/2 inch (for bolts over 6 inches in length). They are precision made and generally applied metal-to-metal where close tolerance is desirable. The head may be square, hexagon, rounded, or flat countersunk. The nut usually corresponds in shape to the head of the bolt with which it is used. Machine bolts are externally driven only. Selection of the proper machine bolt is made on the basis of head style, length, diameter, number of threads per inch, and coarseness of thread. The hole through which the bolt is to pass is bored to the same diameter as the bolt. Machine bolts are made in diameters from 1/4 inch to 3 inches and may be obtained in any length desired (table 8-6).

STOVE bolts (fig. 8-91) are less precisely made than machine bolts. They are made with either flat or round slotted heads and may have threads extending over the full length of the body, over part of the body, or over most of the body. They are generally used with square nuts and applied metal-to-metal, wood-to-wood, or wood-to-metal. If flatheaded, they are countersunk; if roundheaded, they are drawn flush to the surface.

An EXPANSION bolt (fig. 8-91) is a bolt used in conjunction with an expansion shield to provide anchorage in substances in which a threaded fastener alone is useless. The shield, or expansion anchor, inserted in a predrilled hole expands when the bolt is driven into it and becomes wedged firmly in the hole, providing a secure base for the grip of the fastener.

DRIFTPINS are long, heavy, threadless bolts used to hold heavy pieces of timber together

Table 8-6.—Screw, Cap (Machine Bolts)

Lengths (inches)	Diameters (inches)					
	¼, ³⁄₈	⁷⁄₁₆	½, ⁹⁄₁₆, ⁵⁄₈	¾, ⅞, 1	1⅛, 1¼	
¾ ---------------	x	----------	----------	----------	----------	
1, 1¼ ------------	x	x	x	----------	----------	
1½, 2, 2½----------	x	x	x	x	----------	
3, 3½, 4, 4½, etc., 9½, 10 to 20.	x	x	x	x	x	
21 to 25-----------	----------	----------	x	x	x	
26 to 39-----------	----------	----------	----------	x	x	

133.346

255

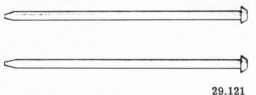

29.121

Figure 8-92.—Driftpins (driftbolts).

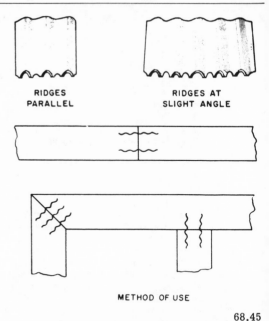

RIDGES
PARALLEL

RIDGES AT
SLIGHT ANGLE

METHOD OF USE

68.45

Figure 8-93.—Corrugated fasteners
and their uses.

(fig. 8-92). The term "driftpin" is almost universally used in practice. However, for supply purposes the correct designation is "driftbolt."

Driftpins have heads and they vary in diameter from 1/2 to 1 inch, and in length from 18 to 26 inches.

To use the driftpin, a hole slightly smaller than the diameter of the pin is made in the timber. The pin is driven into the hole and is held in place by the compression action of the wood fibers.

The CORRUGATED FASTENER is one of the many means by which joints and splices are fastened in small timber and boards. It is used particularly in the miter joint. Corrugated fasteners are made of sheet metal of 18 to 22 gage with alternate ridges and grooves; the ridges vary from 3/16 to 5/16 inch, center to center. One end is cut square; the other end is sharpened with beveled edges. There are two types of corrugated fasteners: One with the ridges running parallel (fig. 8-93); the other with ridges running at a slight angle to one another (fig. 8-93). The latter type has a tendency to compress the material since the ridges and grooves are closer at the top than at the bottom. These fasteners are made in several different lengths and widths. The width varies from 5/8 to 1 1/8 inches, while the length varies from 1/4 to 3/4 inch. The fasteners also are made with different numbers of ridges, ranging from three to six ridges per fastener. Corrugated fasteners are used in a number of ways; to fasten parallel boards together, as in fastening tabletops; to make any type of joint; and as a substitute for nails where nails may split the timber. The fasteners have a greater holding power than nails in small timber. The proper method of using the fasteners is also shown in figure 8-93.

GLUE

One of the oldest materials used for fastening is glue. In museums you will find furniture which was assembled with glue hundreds of years ago. It is still in good condition. Good glue applied properly will form a joint which is stronger than the wood itself.

There are several classes of glue. Probably the best one for joint work and furniture construction is ANIMAL glue. It may be obtained commercially in a variety of forms—liquid, ground, chipped, flaked, powdered, or formed into sticks. The best grades of animal glue are made from hides. Some of the best bone glues, however, may give as good results as the low grades of hide glue.

FISH glue is a good all-around wood shop glue, but it is not as strong as animal glue. It is usually made in liquid form, and it has a disagreeable odor.

VEGETABLE glue is manufactured by a secret process for use in some veneering work. It is NOT a satisfactory glue for wood joints.

CASEIN glue is made from milk in powdered form. The best grades of casein glue are water-resistant and are, therefore, excellent for forming waterproof joints. Casein glue, however, doesn't adhere well to oak. To join oak surfaces with it, coat the wood with a

10-percent solution of caustic soda and allow it to dry. Then apply the casein glue to form a strong joint.

BLOOD ALBUMIN glue is also practically waterproof, but to use it, you need very expensive equipment. It is, therefore, not often used.

PLASTIC RESIN glue may be procured in either liquid or powder form. It is durable and water resistant, but like casein glue, it doesn't adhere too well to oak. Plastic resin glue is used in the manufacture of balsa wood and plywood life floats.

Each type of glue must be prepared and used in a special manner if you are to get the strongest possible joint. Instructions are always found on the label of the container. Study these carefully before you attempt to use the glue. There are also certain general principles which you should follow when you apply any glue.

A lot depends on the wood itself. Dry wood makes stronger joints than wood which is not well seasoned. This is easy to understand if you'll remember that water in the wood will decrease the amount of glue which can be absorbed.

POWDER ACTUATED TOOLS

A number of different kinds of tools which utilize explosive charges to drive fastening devices are widely used. These tools are sometimes called stud guns, stud-type cartridge guns, builder's guns, or powder-actuated guns. Among the number of different tools, there are two basic types in use by the Navy. One type (fig. 8-94) is a high-velocity device in which the fastener is shot down the barrel of the tool by a relatively powerful powder charge. Another type (fig. 8-95) is a power-assisted hammer-drive tool operating on the low-velocity

133.78(127E)
Figure 8-94.—Power-mate stud driver.

principle. The manufacturers of the different types of tools provide detailed instructions for the safe and effective use of their products so follow their instructions closely at all times.

The powder-actuated tool shown in figure 8-94 may be new to you, because it has not been in the system as long as the one shown in figure 8-95. The powder-actuated tool in figure 8-94 covers the complete range of powder-actuated fastening, providing light, medium- and heavy-duty anchoring of 1/4" and 3/8" headed pins and threaded studs in masonry and steel. (See figure 8-96 and 8-97 for the proper pins and studs.) The barrel on this type powder-actuated tool can be changed in a matter of seconds, so as to adapt the tool to either of the kits described in figure 8-98. This can be a difficult and dangerous tool to use so be sure to study the manufacturer's manual beforehand.

The power assisted stud driver shown in figure 8-95 may be used either with or without the powder charge. When the powder charge is used, it acts as a booster for a hammer blow. Without a powder charge, the device may be used as an ordinary hammer-drive tool. The stud, shown in the lower part of figure 8-95 is seated, guided, and controlled in the recessed

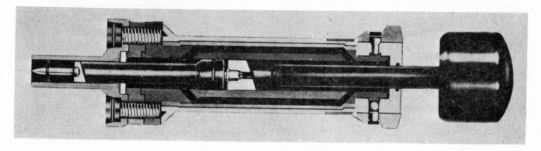

133.78X
Figure 8-95.—Cutaway view of power assisted stud driver.

257

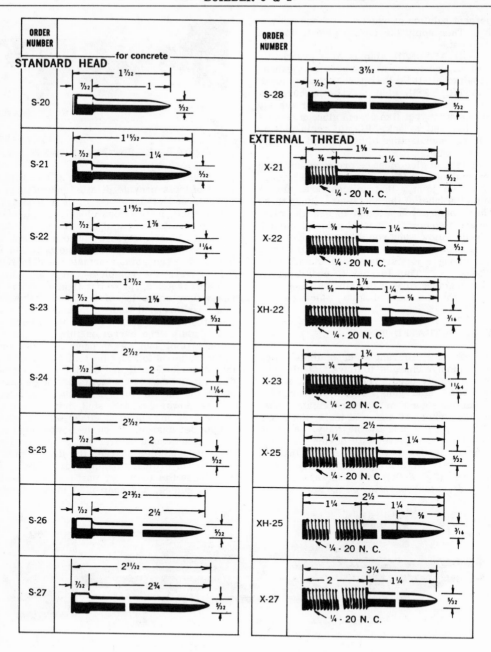

Figure 8-96.—1/4" headed pins and threaded studs.

29.121.1

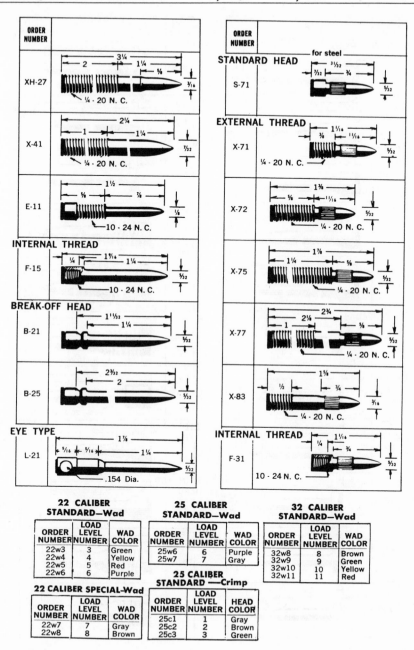

29.121.2

Figure 8-96.—1/4" headed pins and threaded studs—continued.

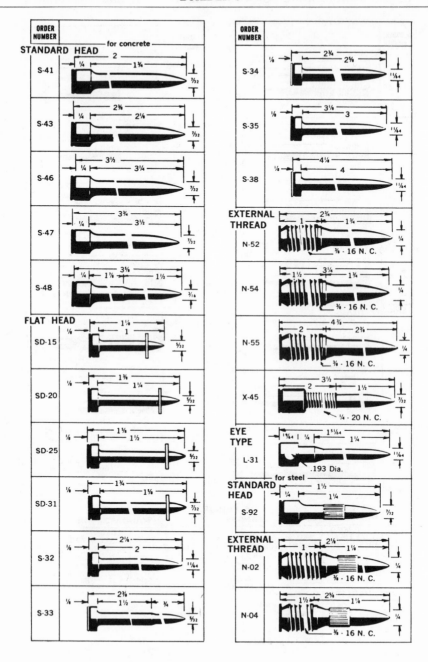

29.121.3

Figure 8-97.—3/8" headed pins and threaded studs.

K-1 CAPTIVE STUD KIT   K-2 LIGHT DUTY KIT

K-3 MEDIUM DUTY KIT   K-4 MEDIUM & HEAVY DUTY KIT

133.340.1

Figure 8-98.—Stud driver kits.

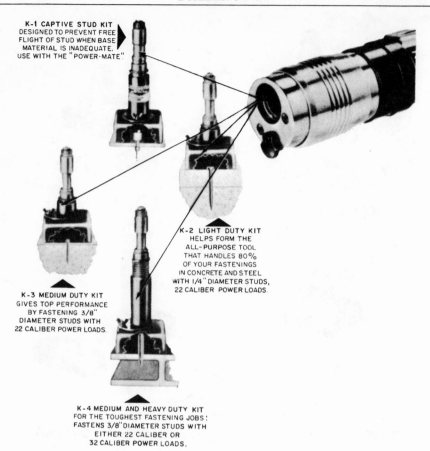

K-1 CAPTIVE STUD KIT
DESIGNED TO PREVENT FREE
FLIGHT OF STUD WHEN BASE
MATERIAL IS INADEQUATE.
USE WITH THE "POWER-MATE"

K-2 LIGHT DUTY KIT
HELPS FORM THE
ALL-PURPOSE TOOL
THAT HANDLES 80%
OF YOUR FASTENINGS
IN CONCRETE AND STEEL
WITH 1/4" DIAMETER STUDS,
22 CALIBER POWER LOADS.

K-3 MEDIUM DUTY KIT
GIVES TOP PERFORMANCE
BY FASTENING 3/8"
DIAMETER STUDS WITH
22 CALIBER POWER LOADS.

K-4 MEDIUM AND HEAVY DUTY KIT
FOR THE TOUGHEST FASTENING JOBS:
FASTENS 3/8" DIAMETER STUDS WITH
EITHER 22 CALIBER OR
32 CALIBER POWER LOADS.

133.340.2

Figure 8-98.—Stud driver kits—continued.

piston. The rim-fire booster blank, which contains a small slow-burning charge of powder, is seated backwards above the piston and below the ram, which is hit with the hammer. Rather than shooting the stud at high velocity, the captive, heavy-mass piston pushes the stud into the work at a relatively low velocity. The piston guides the head of the fastener from the start to the finish of driving. A washer or guide disc near the end of the pin or stud guides the fastener during operation. Since the piston is captive, no energy is imparted to the fastener after the piston stops travelling. The depth of penetration varies with the type of piston and fastener used. Over-penetration is prevented by the positive control of the fastener exercised by the piston and guide disc. The hazards inherent in using the high-velocity gun are eliminated by the use of this type of tool; special shields or protective devices are not generally considered necessary.

The power-assisted hammer-drive tool seems to be highly popular because it may be used in any position: on the deck, on the wall, in the overhead. It may be used to fasten almost any type of construction material to any other type. Figure 8-99 shows a wood-to-metal connection.

Figure 8-100 shows a metal-to-concrete connection.

Figure 8-101 shows some of the other types of widely used pins and studs. The tool illustrated in figure 8-95 will accommodate fasteners of up to 4-inch overall length. For most jobs you will need two pistons: one for pins and one for studs. However, if you have studs with two different thread lengths (such as shown in figure 8-101), you will need a separate piston for each thread length. There are many other types of fasteners for special requirements. They may be used in the hammer-drive tool if you order the special piston that is needed for the fastener.

Safety is a very important factor in the use of power actuated tools. In the Navy, and in many civilian jurisdictions, special authorization or licensing is required before you are permitted to use most types of stud guns. Never attempt to use one of these tools without proper authorization and instruction. Be sure you follow the manufacturer's instructions. Never use the powder charge in an explosive atmosphere. Lastly, remove any defective tools or parts from service immediately.

Figures 8-99 through
8-101 follow

133.79X

Figure 8-99.—Toenailing wood
to hollow metal decking.

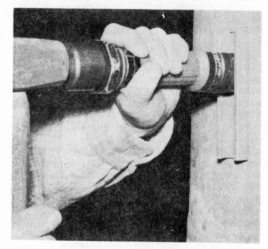

133.81X

Figure 8-100.—Fastening channel
to concrete.

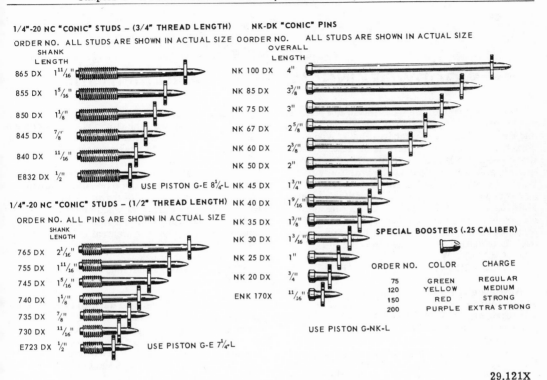

1/4"-20 NC "CONIC" STUDS – (3/4" THREAD LENGTH)

ORDER NO. ALL STUDS ARE SHOWN IN ACTUAL SIZE

SHANK
LENGTH

865 DX	$1\frac{11}{16}$"
855 DX	$1\frac{5}{16}$"
850 DX	$1\frac{1}{8}$"
845 DX	$\frac{7}{8}$"
840 DX	$\frac{11}{16}$"
E832 DX	$\frac{1}{2}$"

USE PISTON G-E $8\frac{1}{4}$-L

1/4"-20 NC "CONIC" STUDS – (1/2" THREAD LENGTH)

ORDER NO. ALL PINS ARE SHOWN IN ACTUAL SIZE

SHANK
LENGTH

765 DX	$2\frac{1}{16}$"
755 DX	$1\frac{11}{16}$"
745 DX	$1\frac{5}{16}$"
740 DX	$1\frac{1}{8}$"
735 DX	$\frac{7}{8}$"
730 DX	$\frac{11}{16}$"
E723 DX	$\frac{1}{2}$"

USE PISTON G-E $7\frac{1}{4}$-L

NK-DK "CONIC" PINS

OORDER NO. ALL STUDS ARE SHOWN IN ACTUAL SIZE

OVERALL
LENGTH

NK 100 DX	4"
NK 85 DX	$3\frac{3}{8}$"
NK 75 DX	3"
NK 67 DX	$2\frac{5}{8}$"
NK 60 DX	$2\frac{3}{8}$"
NK 50 DX	2"
NK 45 DX	$1\frac{3}{4}$"
NK 40 DX	$1\frac{9}{16}$"
NK 35 DX	$1\frac{3}{8}$"
NK 30 DX	$1\frac{3}{16}$"
NK 25 DX	1"
NK 20 DX	$\frac{3}{4}$"
ENK 170X	$\frac{11}{16}$"

USE PISTON G-NK-L

SPECIAL BOOSTERS (.25 CALIBER)

ORDER NO.	COLOR	CHARGE
75	GREEN	REGULAR
120	YELLOW	MEDIUM
150	RED	STRONG
200	PURPLE	EXTRA STRONG

29.121X

Figure 8-101.—Studs and pins.

CHAPTER 9

WOODWORKING: MATERIALS AND METHODS

The wood you will be handling in the Navy is ready to use—it's practically all sawed, dried, and dressed before you get it. But if you know something about wood you will be able to use it more intelligently and economically. Therefore, this chapter will deal primarily with the various types of wood used by the Navy.

Before proceeding with a discussion of materials used by the SEABEES, it may be helpful for you to review the sources, uses, and characteristics of the various types of common woods. Such information is provided in table 9-1.

TREE GROWTH AND STRUCTURE

Any piece of wood is made up of a number of small cells as shown in figure 9-1. The size and arrangement of the cells determine the grain of the wood and many of its properties. Examine a freshly cut tree stump—you'll see that the millions of small cells are arranged in circular rings around the pith or center of the tree (fig. 9-2). These rings are caused by a difference in the rate of growth of the tree during the various seasons of the year. In spring a tree grows rapidly and builds up a thick layer of comparatively soft, large cells which appear in the cross section of the trunk as the light colored annual rings.

As the weather becomes warmer during the early summer, the rate of growth slows and the summer growth forms cells that are more closely packed. These pairs of concentric springwood and summerwood rows form the annual rings which can be counted to find out the age of the tree. Because of climatic conditions, some trees, such as oak and walnut, have more distinctive rings than maple and birch. White pine is so uniform that you can hardly distinguish the rings, while many other softwoods have a very pronounced contrast between summerwood and springwood; this makes it easy to distinguish the rings.

The SAPWOOD of a tree is the outer section of the tree between the HEARTWOOD (darker center wood) and the BARK. The sapwood is lighter in color than the heartwood but, as it

gradually changes to heartwood on the inside, and as new layers are formed, it becomes darker. Depending upon the type of tree, it requires from 9 to 36 years to transform sapwood into heartwood.

The CAMBIUM LAYER, the boundary between the sapwood and the bark, is the thin layer where new sapwood cells form. MEDULLARY RAYS are radial lines of wood cells consisting of threads of pith which serve as lines of communication between the central cylinder of the tree and the cambium layer. They are especially prominent in oak.

When a tree is sawed lengthwise, the annual ring forms a pattern, called the GRAIN of the wood.

A number of terms are used to describe the various grain conditions. If the cells which form the grain are closely packed and small, the wood is said to be fine grained or close grained. Maple and birch are excellent examples of this type of wood. If the cells are large, open, and porous, the wood is coarse grained or open grained as in oak, walnut, and mahogany. Furniture made of open-grained woods requires the use of woodfiller to close the pores and provide a smooth outside finish.

When the wood cells and fibers are comparatively straight and parallel to the trunk of the tree, the wood is said to be straight grained. If the grain is crooked, slanting, or twisted, it is said to be cross grained. It is the arrangement, direction, size, and color of the wood cells that give the grain of each wood its characteristic appearance.

CUTTING AND SEASONING OF LUMBER

In a large lumber mill, such as is found in the Pacific Northwest, logs are usually processed into lumber with huge band or circular saws. There are two methods of sawing up logs, slash cutting and rift cutting (fig. 9-3). Slash cutting is accomplished by a series of cuts parallel to the side of the log. If hardwoods are being cut, the process is known as

Table 9-1.—Common Woods

Type	Sources	Uses	Characteristics
Ash	East of Rockies . .	Oars, boat thwarts, benches, gratings, hammer handles, cabinets, ball bats, wagon construction farm implements.	Strong, heavy, hard, tough, elastic, close straight grain, shrinks very little, takes excellent finish, lasts well.
Balsa	Ecuador.	Rafts, food boxes, linings of refrigerators, life preservers, loud speakers, sound-proofing, air-conditioning devices, model airplane construction.	Lightest of all woods, very soft, strong for its weight, good heat insulating qualities, odorless.
Basswood .	Eastern half of U.S. with exception of coastal regions.	Low-grade furniture, cheaply constructed buildings, interior finish, shelving, drawers, boxes, drainboards, woodenware, novelties, excelsior, general millwork.	Soft, very light, weak, brittle, not durable, shrinks considerably, inferior to poplar, but very uniform, works easily, takes screws and nails well and does not twist or warp.
Beech. . . .	East of Mississippi, Southeastern Canada.	Cabinetwork, imitation mahogany furniture, wood dowels, capping, boat trim, interior finish, tool handles, turnery, shoe lasts, carving, flooring.	Similar to birch but not so durable when exposed to weather, shrinks and checks considerably, close grain, light or dark red color.
Birch	East of Mississippi River and North of Gulf Coast States, Southeast Canada, Newfoundland.	Cabinetwork, imitation mahogany furniture, wood dowels, capping, boat trim, interior finish, tool handles, turnery, carving.	Hard, durable, fine grain, even texture, heavy, stiff, strong, tough, takes high polish, works easily, forms excellent base for white enamel finish, but not durable when exposed. Heartwood is light to dark reddish brown in color.
Butternut .	Southern Canada, Minnesota, Eastern U. S. as far south as Alabama and Florida.	Toys, altars, woodenware, millwork, interior trim, furniture, boats, scientific instruments.	Very much like walnut in color but softer, not so soft as white pine and basswood, easy to work, coarse grained, fairly strong.

103.127.1

Table 9-1.—Common Woods—continued

Type	Sources	Uses	Characteristics
Cypress....	Maryland to Texas, along Mississippi valley to Illinois.	Small boat planking, siding, shingles, sash, doors, tanks, silos, railway ties.	Many characteristics similar to white cedar. Water resistant qualities make it excellent for use as boat planking.
Douglas Fir..	Pacific Coast, British Columbia.	Deck planking on large ships, shores, strongbacks, plugs, filling pieces and bulkheads of small boats, building construction, dimension timber, plywood.	Excellent structural lumber, strong, easy to work, clear straight grained, soft, but brittle. Heartwood is durable in contact with ground, best structural timber of northwest.
Elm.......	States east of Colorado.	Agricultural implements, wheel-stock, boats, furniture, crossties, posts, poles.	Slippery, heavy, hard, tough, durable, difficult to split, not resistant to decay.
Hickory.....	Arkansas, Tennessee, Ohio, Kentucky.	Tools, handles, wagon stock, hoops, baskets, vehicles, wagon spokes.	Very heavy, hard, stronger and tougher than other native woods, but checks, shrinks, difficult to work, subject to decay and insect attack.
Lignum Vitae.....	Central America.	Block sheaves and pulleys, waterexposed shaft bearings of small boats and ships, tool handles, small turned articles, and mallet heads.	Dark greenish brown, unusually hard, close grained, very heavy, resinous, difficult to split and work, has soapy feeling.
Live Oak ...	Southern Atlantic and Gulf Coasts of U.S., Oregon, California.	Implements, wagons, ship building.	Very heavy, hard, tough, strong, durable, difficult to work, light brown or yellow sap wood nearly white.
Mahogany ...	Honduras, Mexico, Central America, Florida, West Indies, Central Africa, other tropical sections.	Furniture, boats, decks, fixtures, interior trim in expensive homes, musical instruments.	Brown to red color, one of most useful of cabinet woods, hard, durable, does not split badly, open grained, takes beautiful finish when grain is filled but checks, swells, shrinks, warps slightly.

103.127.2

Table 9-1.—Common Woods—continued

Type	Sources	Uses	Characteristics
Maple.	All states east of Colorado, Southern Canada.	Excellent furniture, high-grade floors, tool handles, ship construction crossties, counter tops, bowling pins.	Fine grained, grain often curly or "Bird's Eyes," heavy, tough, hard, strong, rather easy to work, but not durable. Heartwood is light brown, sap wood is nearly white.
Norway Pine	States bordering Great Lakes.	Dimension timber, masts, spars, piling, interior trim.	Light, fairly hard, strong, not durable in contact with ground.
Philippine Mahogany. .	Philippine Islands	Pleasure boats, medium-grade furniture, interior trim.	Not a true mahogany, shrinks, expands, splits, warps, but available in long, wide, clear boards.
Poplar	Virginias, Tennessee, Kentucky, Mississippi Valley.	Low-grade furniture cheaply constructed buildings, interior finish, shelving, drawers, boxes.	Soft, cheap, obtainable in wide boards, warps, shrinks, rots easily, light, brittle, weak, but works easily and holds nails well, fine-textured.
Red Cedar. .	East of Colorado and north of Florida.	Mothproof chests, lining for linen closets, sills, and other uses similar to white cedar.	Very light, soft, weak, brittle, low shrinkage, great durability, fragrant scent, generally knotty, beautiful when finished in natural color, easily worked.
Red Oak. . .	Virginias, Tennessee, Arkansas, Kentucky, Ohio, Missouri, Maryland.	Interior finish, furniture, cabinets, millwork, crossties when preserved.	Tends to warp, coarse grain, does not last well when exposed to weather, porous, easily impregnated with preservative, heavy, tough, strong.
Redwood . .	California.	General construction, tanks, paneling.	Inferior to yellow pine and fir in strength, shrinks and splits little, extremely soft, light, straight grained, very durable, exceptionally decay resistant.

103.127.3

Table 9-1.—Common Woods—continued

Type	Sources	Uses	Characteristics
Spruce	New York, New England, West Virginia, Central Canada, Great Lakes States, Idaho, Washington, Oregon.	Railway ties, resonance wood, piles, airplanes, oars, masts, spars, baskets.	Light, soft, low strength, fair durability, close grain, yellowish, sap wood indistinct.
Sugar Pine	California, Oregon.	Same as white pine.	Very light, soft, resembles white pine.
Teak	India, Burma, Siam, Java.	Deck planking, shaft logs for small boats.	Light brown color, strong, easily worked, durable, resistant to damage by moisture.
Walnut	Eastern half of U.S. except Southern Atlantic and Gulf Coasts, some in New Mexico, Arizona, California.	Expensive furniture, cabinets, interior woodwork, gun stocks, tool handles, airplane propellers, fine boats, musical instruments.	Fine cabinet wood, coarse grained but takes beautiful finish when pores closed with woodfiller, medium weight, hard, strong, easily worked, dark chocolate color, does not warp or check, brittle.
White Cedar. . . .	Eastern Coast of U.S., and around Great Lakes.	Boat planking, railroad ties, shingles, siding, posts, poles.	Soft, light weight, close grained, exceptionally durable when exposed to water, not strong enough for building construction, brittle, low shrinkage, fragment, generally knotty.
White Oak . .	Virginias, Tennessee, Arkansas, Kentucky, Ohio, Missouri, Maryland, Indiana.	Boat and ship stems, sternposts, knees, sheer strakes, fenders, capping, transoms, shaft logs, framing for buildings, strong furniture, tool handles, crossties, agricultural implements, fence posts.	Heavy, hard, strong, medium coarse grain, tough, dense, most durable of hardwoods, elastic, rather easy to work, but shrinks and likely to check. Light brownish grey in color with reddish tinge, medullary rays are large and outstanding and present beautiful figures when quarter sawed, receives high polish.

103.127.4

Table 9-1.—Common Woods—continued

Type	Sources	Uses	Characteristics
White Pine.	Minnesota, Wisconsin, Maine, Michigan, Idaho, Montana, Washington, Oregon, California	Patterns, any interior job or exterior job that doesn't require maximum strength, window sash, interior trim, millwork, cabinets, cornices.	Easy to work, fine grain, free of knots, takes excellent finish, durable when exposed to water, expands when wet, shrinks when dry, soft, white, nails without splitting, not very strong, straight grained.
Yellow Pine.	Virginia to Texas.	Most important lumber for heavy construction and exterior work, keelsons, risings, filling pieces, clamps, floors, bulkheads of small boats, shores, wedges, plugs, strongbacks, staging, joists, posts, piling, ties, paving blocks.	Hard, strong, heartwood is durable in the ground, grain varies, heavy, tough, reddish brown in color, resinous, medullary rays well marked.

103.127.5

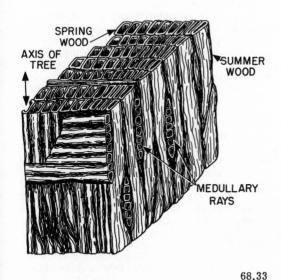

SPRING WOOD

AXIS OF TREE

SUMMER WOOD

MEDULLARY RAYS

68.33

Figure 9-1.—Structure of wood.

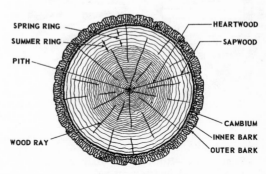

SPRING RING

SUMMER RING

PITH

WOOD RAY

HEARTWOOD

SAPWOOD

CAMBIUM

INNER BARK

OUTER BARK

29.115

Figure 9-2.—Cross section of a tree.

plain sawing. If softwoods are being cut, the process is referred to as flat-grain sawing.

Lumber that is specially cut to provide edge grain on both faces is said to be rift cut. If hardwood is being cut, the lumber is said to be quartersawed (fig. 9-4). If softwood is being sawed, it is called edge grain lumber. Incidentally, if an entire log is slash cut, several boards from near the center of the log will actually be rift cut.

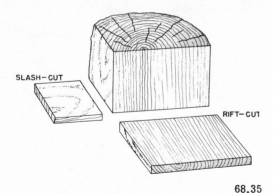

68.35

Figure 9-3.—Slash and rift cutting.

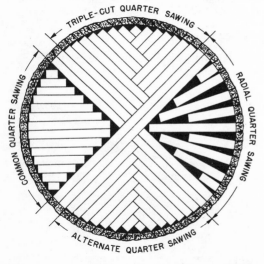

68.34

Figure 9-4.—Rift cutting: four methods
of quartersawing.

Slash-cut lumber is usually cheaper than rift-cut lumber because it takes less time to slash-cut a log, and there is less waste. Circular or oval knots appearing in slash-cut boards affect the strength and surface appearance much less than do spike knots which may appear in rift-cut boards. If, however, a log is sawed to produce all slash-cut lumber, more boards will contain knots than would be the case if the log were sawed to produce the maximum amount of rift-cut material. Another advantage of slash cutting is that shakes and pitch pockets when present will extend through fewer boards.

For Navy decking and for all kinds of flooring, rift-cut lumber is preferred because it offers more resistance to wear than does slash-cut lumber. Rift-cut lumber also shrinks and swells less in width. Another advantage of rift-cut lumber as compared with slash-cut lumber is that it twists and cups less and splits less when used. Rift-cut lumber usually holds paint better.

After being sawed, lumber must be thoroughly dried before it is suitable for most uses. The old method—and one still preferred for some uses—was merely to air-dry the lumber in a shed or stack it in the open. This method requires considerable time-up to 7 years for some of the hardwoods.

A faster method is known as kiln-drying. The wood is placed in a tight enclosure called the kiln and dried with heat supplied by artificial means. The length of time required for drying varies from 2 or 3 days to several weeks, depending on the kind of wood, its dimensions, and the method of drying. In most cases, a combination of drying methods is used—the wood is air-dried from 6 months to a year and then finished off in a kiln.

Lumber is considered dry enough for most uses when the moisture content has been reduced to about 12 or 15 percent. As a user of lumber you will soon learn to judge the dryness of wood by color, weight, smell, feel, and by a visual examination of shavings and chips.

Briefly, seasoning of lumber is accomplished by removing the moisture from the millions of small and large cells of which wood is composed. Moisture (water or sap) occurs in two separate forms; FREE WATER and EMBEDDED WATER. Free water is the amount of moisture the individual cells contain. Embedded water is the moisture absorbed by the cell walls. During drying or seasoning, the free water in the individual cells evaporates until a minimum amount of moisture is left. The point at which this minimum moisture remains is called the FIBER SATURATION POINT. The moisture content of this point varies from 25 to 30 percent. Below the fiber saturation point, the embedded water is extracted from the porous cell walls; this process causes a reduction of the thickness of the walls. Wood shrinks across the grain when the moisture content is lowered below the fiber saturation point. SHRINKING and SWELLING of the wood cells caused by varying amounts of moisture change

272

the size of the cells. Therefore, the LOWER-ING or RAISING of the moisture content causes lumber to shrink or swell.

The loss of moisture during seasoning causes wood to be: harder; stronger; stiffer; and lighter in weight.

CLASSIFICATION OF LUMBER

Lumber is classified into three major use categories as follows:

Yard lumber grades for general building purposes where the piece is to be used as a whole.

Factory and shop lumber grades where the lumber is to be cut-up in further manufacture.

Structural material of relatively large dimension where the piece is to be used as a whole and where strength factors are definitely appraised independently of appearance factors.

An IMPORTANT EXCEPTION to this generally applicable classification according to uses is that boxes and containers are produced largely from the yard lumber grades rather than factory grades, because for this purpose clear pieces are not normally required.

SIZE OF LUMBER

The NOMINAL cross section dimensions of a piece of lumber (2 x 4, 1 x 2, 8 x 10, etc.) are always larger than the actual DRESSED dimensions. Dressed lumber is lumber which has been SURFACED (planed smooth) on two or on all four sides. Lumber which has been surfaced on two sides is designated as S2S (surfaced two sides); lumber which has been surfaced on all four sides is designated as S4S (surfaced 4 sides). Most lumber used in general construction is S4S. The nominal sizes and the actual dressed (S4S) dimensions of some common sizes of boards follow:

Nominal size	Dressed dimensions
1 x 6	25/32 x 5 5/8
1 x 8	25/32 x 7 1/2
1 x 10	25/32 x 9 1/2

The nominal sizes and the actual dressed (S4S) dimensions of some common sizes of dimension lumber are as follows:

Nominal size	Dressed dimensions
2 x 2	1 5/8 x 1 5/8
2 x 4	1 5/8 x 3 5/8

Nominal size	Dressed dimensions
2 x 6	1 5/8 x 5 5/8
2 x 8	1 5/8 x 7 1/2
2 x 10	1 5/8 x 9 1/2
2 x 12	1 5/8 x 11 1/2
4 x 4	3 5/8 x 3 5/8

All softwood framing lumber, and most other softwood lumber, is cut to even-numbered-feet lengths, such as 10 ft, 12 ft, 14 ft, and so on. Hardwood is sometimes cut to odd-numbered as well as even-numbered-feet lengths.

BOARD MEASURE

BOARD MEASURE is a method of measuring lumber in which the basic unit is an abstract volume 1 ft long by 1 ft wide by 1 in. thick. This abstract volume or unit is called a BOARD FOOT.

There are several formulas for calculating the number of board feet in a piece of given dimensions. Since lumber dimensions are most frequently indicated by width and thickness in inches and length in feet, the following formula is probably the most practical.

$$\frac{\text{Thickness in in. x width in in. x length in ft.}}{12}$$

= board feet

Suppose you are calculating the number of board feet in a 14-ft length of 2 x 4. Applying the formula, you get:

$$\frac{\overset{1}{\cancel{2}} \times \overset{2}{\cancel{4}} \times 14}{\underset{\underset{3}{\cancel{6}}}{\cancel{12}}} = \frac{28}{3} = 9\ 1/3 \text{ bd ft}$$

The chief practical use of board measure is in cost calculations, since lumber is brought and sold by the board foot. Any lumber less than 1 in. thick is presumed to be 1 in. thick for board measure purposes. Board measure is calculated on the basis of the NOMINAL, not the ACTUAL, dimensions of lumber. As explained above the actual size of a piece of dimension lumber (such as a 2 x 4, for example) is usually less than the nominal size.

DEFECTS AND BLEMISHES

A DEFECT in lumber is any flaw which tends to affect the strength, durability, or utility value of the lumber. A BLEMISH is a flaw which mars the appearance of the lumber only. A blemish which affects the utility value of the lumber (such as a blemish in wood intended for fine cabinet work) is also a defect.

Common defects and blemishes are as follows:

A BARK POCKET is a patch of bark over which the tree has grown, and which it has entirely or almost entirely enclosed.

A CHECK is a separation along the lengthwise grain, caused by too rapid or nonuniform drying.

CROSS-GRAINED lumber is lumber in which the grain does not parallel the lengthwise axis of the piece, or in which the grain spirals around the lengthwise axis.

DECAY is deterioration caused by various kinds of fungi.

A KNOT is the root section of a branch. It may appear on a surface in cross section or in lengthwise section. A knot which appears in lengthwise section is a SPIKE KNOT, a spike knot is always a defect. A LOOSE knot of the cross-section type is also a defect. A TIGHT knot of this type may be a defect if it mars the appearance of wood intended for fine cabinet work or the like; otherwise it is usually considered to be only a blemish.

A PITCH POCKET is a deposit of solid or liquid pitch, enclosed in the wood.

A SHAKE is a separation along the lengthwise grain. It is not the same as a CHECK because it already exists when the tree is cut, while a check develops as the cut lumber dries. HEART SHAKE moves outward from the center of the tree; WIND SHAKE follows the circular lines of the annual rings. Heart shake is caused by decay at the center of the trunk. The cause of wind shake is not definitely known.

BLUE STAIN is a blemish caused by a mold fungus. It does not weaken the wood.

WANE is a term applied to any edge or corner defect which causes that particular part of a board or timber to be less than its full-size dimensions.

WARP is a general term applied to the various types of shrinkage distortions which were previously described.

GRADING LUMBER

Lumber is graded for quality in accordance with American Lumber Standards set by the National Bureau of Standards for the U.S. Department of Commerce. The major quality grades, in descending order of quality, are SELECT LUMBER, and COMMON LUMBER. Each of these grades has subdivisions in descending order of quality as follows:

GRADE A lumber is select lumber which is practically free of defects and blemishes.

GRADE B lumber is select lumber which contains a few minor blemishes.

GRADE C lumber is finish item lumber which contains more numerous and more significant blemishes than grade B. All of these must be capable of being easily and thoroughly concealed with paint.

GRADE D lumber is finish item lumber which contains more numerous and more significant blemishes than grade C, but which is still capable of presenting a satisfactory appearance when painted.

NO. 1 COMMON lumber is sound, tightknotted stock, containing only a few minor defects. It must be suitable for use as watertight lumber.

NO. 2 COMMON lumber contains a limited number of significant defects, but no knot holes or other serious defects. It must be suitable for use as graintight lumber.

NO. 3 COMMON lumber contains a few defects which are larger and coarser than those in No. 2 Common; occasional knot holes, for example.

NO. 4 COMMON lumber is low-quality material, containing serious defects like knot holes, checks, shakes, and decay.

NO. 5 COMMON is capable only of holding together under ordinary handling.

The grades of construction, standard, utility, and economy are used in some associations.

All species are covered by the grading rules and size standards of some association or grading bureau. In the case of softwood lumber standards are set by a regional manufacturer's association; in the case of hardwood lumber there is but one national association. In a few cases, a softwood species growing in more than one region is graded under rules of two different associations. There is great advantage to the purchaser, whether large or small, to buy according to these association grades rather than to attempt to buy according to his own individual specifications unless the requirements are actually very unusual. Occasionally a departure from the standard grade provision is necessary to cover unusual requirements. This is best handled as an exception to a standard grade rather than as an entirely special grade.

HANDLING AND STORAGE OF LUMBER

The advances made in the mechanized handling of lumber have to a great extent changed storage and handling methods. The development of handling equipment, such as forklift and straddle trucks or carriers, that can be used to pile, unpile, and transport lumber has brought about revolutionary changes in storage and handling practices; the most notable being the handling of lumber in packages (drafts). Regardless of whether lumber is handled by mechanized equipment or by manual labor, the objectives of storage and handling are unchanged.

The objective of lumber storage is to maintain the lumber at or bring it to a moisture content suitable for its end use with a minimum of deterioration. The objective of lumber handling is to load, transport, unload, pile, and unpile lumber economically and without damage. Both of these objectives are obtained easily if good handling and storage practices are followed. Adequate protection of lumber in storage will help prevent attack by fungi, insects, and changes in moisture content that will result in checking, warping, and stain in lumber and make it unsuitable for the intended use.

Available space limits the location of the storage yard, but it is preferably near the spot where the lumber is received, or used. The best location is on high ground that is level, well-drained, and remote from water bodies or wind-obstructing objects, such as tall trees or buildings. A low site is likely to be sheltered from the full sweep of the winds and to be damp, conditions that may retard drying and expose the lumber to stain and decay.

LAMINATED LUMBER AND PLYWOOD

Laminated lumber is made up of layers of wood that are glued face-to-face with the grain of adjacent layers parallel (fig. 9-5). The component parts which are glued together to make laminated lumber may be thin sliced sheets of veneer or they may be sawed boards. Plywood frequently alternates grain to give the member the quality of nonsplitting and stability. (Note: Plywood alternates grain each ply and laminated wood never alternates grain.)

One advantage of laminated wood is that it can be made up in unlimited thicknesses. Also, by staggering the ends of individual layers it is possible to secure members that are much longer than solid timbers.

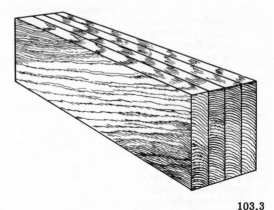

103.3

Figure 9-5.—Laminated lumber.

Plywood (fig. 9-6) is made up of thin layers of wood that are glued face-to-face at right angles to one another. It always has an odd number of plies—veneered stock for use in the manufacture of furniture usually having five layers. A thick layer, called the core, is in the center. The layers glued on with their grain running across that of the faces are called cross bands. The surface layers or faces are placed so that their grain runs parallel to the long direction of the panel.

29.117X

Figure 9-6.—Plywood.

Ordinarily 1/4-in. and 1/8-in. plywood (fir) has only 3 plies. Thicker plywood may have as many as 15 plies—but always an odd number. The standard size of plywood sheets is 4 feet wide by 6 to 12 feet long, though smaller and larger sizes are available. Because of the cross-grain effect, it is almost impossible to split plywood, and shrinking and swelling are negligible.

The development of special glues and other bonding materials has made possible a type of plywood highly resistant to water. It was widely used during World War II, and is still used extensively in the Navy.

GRADES OF PLYWOOD

There are two types of plywood—interior and exterior. Most plywood produced is of the interior type. Although it can stand an occasional wetting and subsequent normal drying without losing its original form and strength, interior plywood is unreliable in wet places. Exterior type plywood will retain its original form and strength when repeatedly wet and dried and otherwise subjected to the elements. It is suitable for permanent exterior use. Most plywood is branded or stamped on the edge with the symbol "EXT." or "INTERIOR" (INT). In addition, other markings carrying more complete information are stamped on the back of the plywood sheet. A typical Douglas fir back stamp, with all symbols explained, is shown in figure 9-7.

Plywood is graded by the quality of the face veneers, with A being the best and D the poorest (fig. 9-7). The grading is based upon the number of defects such as knotholes, pitch pockets, and splits, and the presence of streaks, discolorations, sapwood, shims, and patches in each face of the panel. Plywood also comes with resin-impregnated fiber faces which provide better painting surfaces and better wearing qualities.

PLYWOOD STORAGE

Because of the conditions of its manufacture, plywood can generally be assumed to be dry when received. It should therefore be stored in a closed shed. For long storage in winter or the rainy season, a heated storage building is recommended.

Plywood is commonly solid piled. Under humid conditions, there is some tendency for edges to swell because of exposed end grain, and this swelling causes dishing, especially in the upper panels of high piles. Dishing can be minimized by placing strips in the pile at intervals. Enough strips should be used so that plywood will not bend between them. Dry 1-inch strips are suitable for supporting plywood.

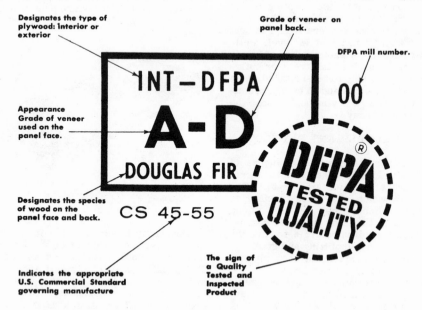

103.5X

Figure 9-7.—Typical Douglas fir back stamp.

Plywood reusable concrete forms should be stacked flat on dry, level platforms after use. Wet faces should be separated with strips to permit drying. If unused for long periods, forms should be stored indoors after being cleaned and dried. Before reuse, the faces should be oiled with standard wood form oil or pale oil. Newly cut edges should be sealed with white lead and oil or some other sealer.

WALLBOARD

According to Webster, wallboard is considered as any boarding designed to be used against a wall; or an artificial board of wood fiber (or the like) made in large sheets and used for the interior sheathing of the walls of rooms. Therefore, for a discussion concerning wallboard, this section will begin by discussing fiberboard.

FIBERBOARD

Fiberboard conforming to Federal Specification LLL-F-321 is made of wood or vegetable fiber, and is compressed to form sheets or boards. It is available in sizes from 1/2 in. to 1 in. in thickness, 2 to 4 ft in width, and 8 ft to 12 ft in length. The boards are comparatively soft and provide good insulation and sound absorbing qualities. Fiberboard usually has a rough surface, but is also available with finished surfaces.

GYPSUM WALLBOARD

Gypsum wallboard conforming to Federal Specification SS-W-0051 is composed of gypsum between two layers of heavy paper. The most common sizes are 1/4 in., 3/8 in., 1/2 in., and 5/8 in. Heavier gypsum wallboard is also available. The width is 4 ft and the lengths vary from 8 to 12 ft.

Some types have unfinished surfaces, while others have finishes which represent wood grain or tile. The joints of the unfinished type may be covered with strips to form panels. Another commonly used type of board has depressed or tapered edges. The joints are filled with a special cement and tape, so that the wall can be painted, and the joints will not show.

HARDBOARD

Hardboard is known by several trade names. They are all made by separating and treating wood fibers which are then subjected to heat and heavy pressure. Hardboard is available in thickness from 1/16 in. to 5/16 in. The most common size of sheet is 4 ft x 8 ft. but other sizes are available. The finish may be obtained in a plain smooth surface or in any of a number of glossy finishes, some of which imitate tile or stone. Structural type hardboard used in the Navy conforms to Federal Specification LLL-H-35. Where moisture resistance or extra strength is required, Class B treated hardboard should be used, otherwise Class A is satisfactory (see Federal Specification LLL-H-35).

PLYWOOD

Plywood for interior walls is made in the same manner and comes in the same sizes as plywood for other purposes. Plywood may be purchased with both sides good (G2S) or good on one side (G1S). It may be obtained with faces of walnut, mahogany, gum or other decorative woods. Single veneers or thin two-ply panels may be obtained to bend around curved surfaces.

WOODWORKING METHODS

The following sections will explain some of the methods used in woodworking, by explaining the procedures involved in developing various woodworking joints.

PLANING AND SQUARING TO DIMENSIONS

Planing and squaring a small board to dimensions is what you might call the first lesson in woodworking; like a good many other things, it looks easy until you try it. The six major steps in the process are illustrated and described in figure 9-8. You should practice them until you can get a smooth, square board with a minimum of planing.

JOINTS AND JOINING

The basic skill in woodworking is the art of JOINING pieces of wood to form tight, strong, well-made JOINTS. Simple joints like the BUTT (figs. 9-9 and 9-10), the LAP joints (fig. 9-11), and the MITER joints (fig. 9-12) are used mostly in rough or finish carpentry, though they may also be used occasionally in millwork and furniture making. More complex joints like the RABBET joints (fig. 9-13), the DADO and GAIN joints (fig. 9-14), the MORTISE-AND-TENON

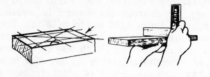

1. WORK FACE

PLANE ONE BROAD SURFACE SMOOTH AND STRAIGHT. TEST IT CROSSWISE, LENGTHWISE, AND FROM CORNER TO CORNER. MARK THE WORK FACE X.

4. SECOND END

MEASURE LENGTH AND SCRIBE AROUND THE STOCK A LINE SQUARE TO THE WORK EDGE AND WORK FACE. SAW OFF EXCESS STOCK NEAR THE LINE AND PLANE SMOOTH TO THE SCRIBED LINE. TEST THE SECOND END FROM BOTH THE WORK FACE AND THE WORK EDGE.

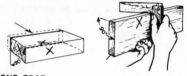

2. WORK EDGE

PLANE ONE EDGE SMOOTH, STRAIGHT AND SQUARE TO THE WORK FACE. TEST IT FROM THE WORK FACE. MARK THE WORK EDGE X.

5. SECOND EDGE

FROM THE WORK EDGE GAUGE A LINE FOR WIDTH ON BOTH FACES. PLANE SMOOTH, STRAIGHT, SQUARE AND TO THE GAUGE LINE. TEST THE SECOND EDGE FROM THE WORK FACE.

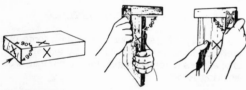

3. WORK END

PLANE ONE END SMOOTH AND SQUARE. TEST IT FROM THE WORK FACE AND WORK EDGE. MARK THE WORK END X.

6. SECOND FACE

FROM THE WORK FACE GAUGE A LINE FOR THICKNESS AROUND THE STOCK. PLANE THE STOCK TO THE GAUGE LINE. TEST THE SECOND FACE AS THE WORK FACE IS TESTED.

44.108

Figure 9-8.—Planing and squaring to dimensions.

and SLIP TENON joints (fig. 9-15), the BOX CORNER joint (fig. 9-16), and the DOVETAIL joints (fig. 9-17) are used mostly in furniture, cabinet, and mill work. Of the EDGE joints shown in figure 9-18, the DOWEL and SPLINE are used mainly in furniture and cabinet work, while the PLAIN BUTT and the TONGUE-AND-GROOVE, are used in practically all types of woodworking.

The joints used in rough and finish carpentry are for the most part simply nailed together. Nails in a 90-degree plain butt joint may be driven through the member abutted against and into the end of the abutting member, or they may be TOENAILED at an angle through the faces of the abutting member into the face of the member abutted against, as shown in figure 9-19. Studs and joists are usually toenailed to sole plates and sills.

The more complex furniture and cabinet-making joints are usually fastened with glue, with additional strength provided as necessary by dowels, splines, corrugated fasteners, slip feathers, keys, and other types of joint-fasteners. In the dado joint, the gain joint, the mortise-and-tenon joint, the box corner joint, and the dovetail joint, the interlocking character of the joint is an additional factor in fastening.

The two pieces which are to be joined together are called MEMBERS, and the two major steps in joining are the layout of the joint on the

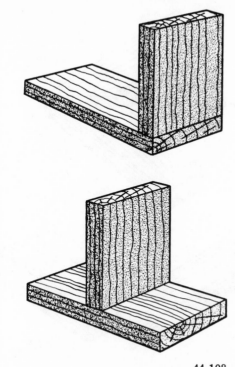

44.108

Figure 9-9.—90-degree plain butt joints.

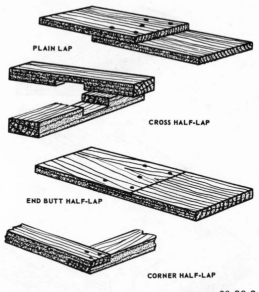

PLAIN LAP

CROSS HALF-LAP

END BUTT HALF-LAP

CORNER HALF-LAP

68.38.2

Figure 9-11.—Lap joints.

68.38.1

Figure 9-10.—End butt joint with fish plates.

ends, edges, or faces of the members, and the cutting of the members to the required shapes for joining.

The chief instruments for laying out joints are the try, miter, combination square, sliding T-bevel; the marking or mortising gage; and a scratch awl, sharp pencil; or knife for scoring lines. For cutting the more complex joints by hand, the backsaw, dovetail saw, and various chisels are essential, and the rabbet-and-fillister plane (for rabbet joints) and the router plane (for smoothing the bottoms of dados and gains) are very helpful.

With the possible exception of the dovetail joint, all the joints which have been mentioned can be cut either by hand or by machine. Whatever the method used, and whatever the type of joint, always remember the following important rule: To ensure a tight joint, always cut on the WASTE SIDE of the line, never on the line itself. Preliminary grooving ON THE WASTE SIDE of the line with a knife or chisel will help a backsaw to get a smooth start.

Half-Lap Joints

For half-lap joints the members to be joined are usually of the same thickness, and the following discussion is based on the assumption that this is the case. The method of laying out and cutting an end-butt half-lap or a corner half-lap is as follows: for the end butt half-lap, measure off the desired amount of lap from the end of each member and square a line all the way around at this point. For the corner half-lap, measure off the width of a member from the end of each member and square a line all the way around. These lines are called SHOULDER lines.

279

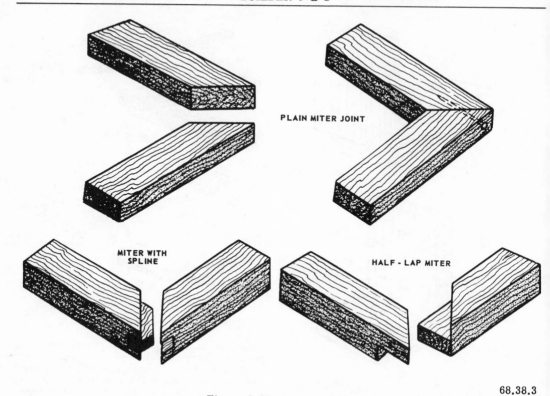

PLAIN MITER JOINT

MITER WITH SPLINE

HALF - LAP MITER

68.38.3

Figure 9-12.—Miter joints.

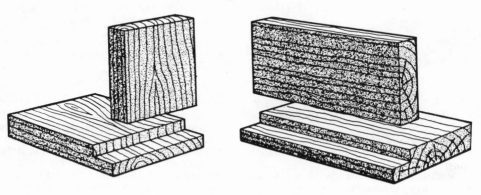

103.10

Figure 9-13.—Rabbet joints.

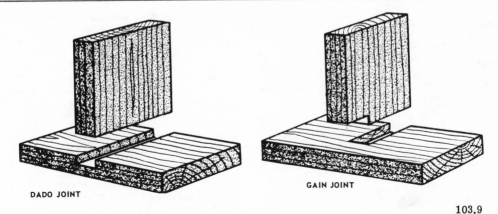

DADO JOINT

GAIN JOINT

103.9

Figure 9-14.—Dado and gain joints.

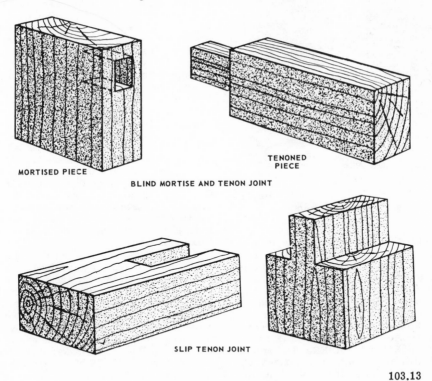

MORTISED PIECE

TENONED
PIECE

BLIND MORTISE AND TENON JOINT

SLIP TENON JOINT

103.13

Figure 9-15.—Mortise-and-tenon and slip-tenon joints.

281

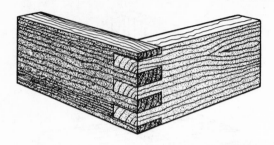

103.12

Figure 9-16.—Box corner joint.

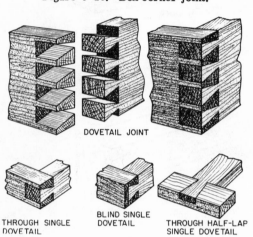

DOVETAIL JOINT

THROUGH SINGLE
DOVETAIL

BLIND SINGLE
DOVETAIL

THROUGH HALF-LAP
SINGLE DOVETAIL

103.11

Figure 9-17.—Dovetail joints.

Next, select the best wide surface of each member and place it upward. Call this surface the FACE of the member, call the opposite surface the BACK. Next set the marking gage to one-half the thickness and score a line (called the CHEEK LINE) on the edges and end of each member, from the shoulder line on one edge to the shoulder line on the opposite edge. BE SURE AND GAGE THE CHEEK LINE FROM THE FACE OF EACH MEMBER. The reason for this is that, if you gage from both faces, the faces will come flush after the joint is cut, regardless of whether or not the gage was set to exactly one-half the thickness. Too much waste cut from one member will be offset by less cut from the other. On the other hand, if you gage from the face of one member and the back of the other, and the gage happens to be set to more or less than one-half the thickness, the faces will be out of flush by the amount of the error. A rule of first importance for half-lap joints, then, is: ALWAYS GAGE THE CHEEK LINE FROM THE FACE OF THE MEMBER.

Next make the SHOULDER CUTS by sawing along the shoulder line down to the waste side of the cheek line, sawing from the BACK of the lapping member and from the FACE of the lapped member. Use a bench hook if possible; if not, clamp a piece of wood along the starting groove to steady the saw.

The CHEEK CUTS (sometimes called the SIDE CUTS) are made next, along the WASTE SIDE of the cheek line. Clamp the member in the vise so that it leans diagonally AWAY from you. With the member in this position you can see the end and the upper edge, and when the saw reaches the shoulder line on the upper edge, it will still be some distance away from the shoulder line on the edge you can't see. Reverse the member in the vise, and saw exactly to the shoulder line on that edge.

Completing the shoulder cut will detach the waste. When both shoulder cuts have been made, the members should fit together with faces, ends, and edges flush, or near enough to it to be brought flush by a little paring with the chisel.

A cross half-lap joint between members of equal cross-section dimensions is laid out and cut as follows: if the members are of the same length and they are to lap each other at the midpoint, place them face-to-face with ends flush, and square a center line all the way around. To test the accuracy of the center calculation, reverse one of the members end-for-end. If the center lines still meet, the center location is correct.

Lay off one-half the width of a member on either side of the center lines and square shoulder lines all the way around. Again check for accuracy by reversing a member end-for-end. If the shoulder lines meet, the layout is accurate. Next, gage one-half the thickness of a member FROM THE FACE OF EACH MEMBER and score cheek lines on the edges, between the shoulder lines. Next make the shoulder cuts, sawing from the BACK of the lapping member and from the FACE of the lapped member.

In this type of joint the waste must be chiseled out rather than sawed out. To make the work of chiseling easier, remove as much stock as possible with the saw first, by sawing a series of kerfs between the shoulder cuts.

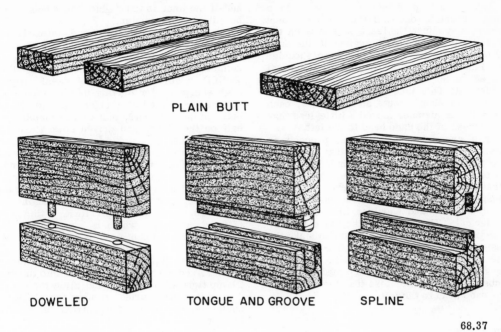

PLAIN BUTT

DOWELED   TONGUE AND GROOVE   SPLINE

68.37

Figure 9-18.—Edge joints.

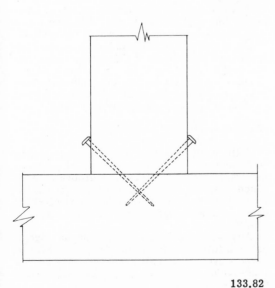

133.82

Figure 9-19.—Toenailing.

In chiseling, make a roughing cut first, down to just above the cheek line, with a firmer chisel and mallet, holding the chisel bevel down. Then finish off the bottom with a paring chisel, holding the chisel bevel up. For fine work, smooth the bottom with a router plane if you have one.

End butt half-lap and corner half-lap joints are known generally as END HALF-LAP, as distinguished from cross half-lap, joints. A third type of half-lap joint, much used in frame construction for tying partition plates to wall plates, is the so-called MIDDLE HALF-LAP joint, in which the end of one member is half-lapped to the other member at a point other than the end. In this joint the end of the lapping member is recessed as it would be for an end half-lap joint, while the lapped member is recessed as it would be for a cross half-lap joint.

End half-lap joints may be cut with the circular saw by the method described later for cutting tenons. Equipped with the dado head, the circular saw can be used to cut both end half-lap recesses and cross half-lap recesses. For an end half-lap recess, proceed as follows: set

283

the dado head to protrude above the table a distance equal to one-half the thickness of a member, and adjust the fence so that when the end of the member bears against it the dado head will cut on the waste side of the shoulder line. Place the member against the universal gage, set at 90° to the fence, and make the shoulder cut. Then take out the remaining waste by making as many recuts as necessary, each made with the member moved a little less than the thickness of the dado head to the left.

For a cross half-lap recess, proceed as follows: set the dado head so that its height above the table is equal to one-half the thickness of a member, and adjust the ripping fence so that when the end of the member is placed against it the dado head will cut on the waste side of the left-hand shoulder line. Make the shoulder cut. Then reverse the piece end for end and repeat the same procedure to make the opposite shoulder cut. Take out the remaining waste between the shoulder cuts by making as many recuts as necessary, each made with the member moved a little less than the thickness of the dado head to the left.

Miter Joints

A miter joint is made by MITERING (cutting at an angle) the ends or edges of the members which are to be joined together. The angle of the miter cut is one-half of the angle which will be formed by the joined members. In rectangular mirror frames, door casings, boxes, and the like, adjacent members form a 90° angle, and the correct angle for mitering is consequently one-half of 90°, or 45°. For members which will form an equal-sided figure with other than 4 sides (such as an octagon or a pentagon), the correct mitering angle can be found by dividing the number of sides the figure will have into 180 and subtracting the result from 90. For an octagon (8-sided figure), the mitering angle is 90 minus 180/8, or 67 1/2°. For a pentagon (5-sided figure) the angle is 90 minus 180/5, or 54°.

Members can be end-mitered to 45° in the wooden miter box and to any angle in the steel miter box (by setting the saw to the desired angle) or on the circular saw (by setting the universal gage to the desired angle). Members can be edge-mitered to any angle on the circular saw, by tilting the saw to the required angle. Sawed edges are unsuitable for gluing, however,

and if the joint is to be glued the edges should be mitered on a jointer.

Since abutting surfaces of end-mitered members do not hold well when they are merely glued, they must usually be reinforced. One type of reinforcement is the CORRUGATED FASTENER, a corrugated strip of metal with one edge sharpened for driving into the joint. The fastener is placed at a right angle to the line between the members, half on one member and half on the other, and driven down flush with the members.

The corrugated fastener mars the appearance of the surface into which it is driven, and it is therefore used only on the backs of picture frames and the like. A more satisfactory type of fastener for a joint between end-mitered members is the SLIP FEATHER, a thin piece of wood or veneer which is glued into a kerf cut in the thickness dimension of the joint. Saw about half-way through from the outer to the inner corner, apply glue to both sides of the slip feather, and push the slip feather into the kerf. Clamp tight with a clamp and allow the glue to dry. After it has dried, remove the clamp and chisel off the protruding portion of the slip feather.

A joint between edge-mitered members may be reinforced with a SPLINE, a thin piece of wood which extends across the joint into grooves cut in the abutting surfaces. A spline for a plain butt edge joint is shown in figure 9-12. The groove for a spline can be cut by hand, by laying out the outline of the groove, removing the major part of the waste by boring a series of holes with a bit of suitable size, and smoothing with a mortising chisel. The best way to cut a groove, however, is on the circular saw.

Grooved Joints

A GROOVE is a three-sided recess running with the grain. A similar recess running across the grain is called a DADO. A groove or dado which does not extend all the way across the piece is called a STOPPED groove or a STOPPED dado. A stopped dado is also known as a GAIN (fig. 9-14).

A two-sided recess running along an edge is called a RABBET (fig. 9-13). Dados, gains, and rabbets are not, strictly speaking, grooves, but joints which include them are generally called GROOVED joints.

Grooves on edges and grooves on faces of comparatively narrow stock can be cut by hand with the plow plane. The matching plane will cut a groove on the edge of one piece and a tongue to match it on the edge of another. A dado can be cut by hand with the backsaw and chisel, by the same method used to cut a cross half-lap joint by hand. Rabbets on short ends or edges can be sawed out by hand with the backsaw.

A long rabbet can be cut by hand with the rabbet-and-fillister plane as follows: first be sure that the side of the plane iron is exactly in line with the machined side of the plane; then set the width and depth gages to the desired width and depth of the rabbet. BE SURE TO MEASURE THE DEPTH FROM THE EDGE OF THE PLANE IRON, NOT FROM THE SOLE OF THE PLANE. If you measure from the sole of the plane, the rabbet will be too deep by the amount that the edge of the iron extends below the sole of the plane. Clamp the pieces in the vise, hold the plane exactly perpendicular, press the width gage against the face of the board, and plane down with even, careful strokes until the depth gage prevents any fruther planing.

A groove or dado can be cut on the circular saw as follows: lay out the groove or dado on the end wood (for a groove) or edge wood (for a dado) which will first contact the saw. Set the saw to the desired depth of the groove above the table, and set the fence at a distance from the saw which will cause the first cut to run on the waste side of the line that indicates the left side of the groove. Start the saw and bring the piece into light contact with it; then stop the saw and examine the layout to ensure that the cut will be on the waste side of the line. Readjust the fence if necessary. When the position of the fence is right, make the cut. Then reverse the piece and proceed to set and test as before for the cut on the opposite side of the groove. Then make as many recuts as are necessary to remove the waste stock between the side kerfs.

The procedure for grooving or dadoing with the dado head is about the same, except that in many cases the dado head can be built up so as to take out all the waste in a single cut. The two outside cutters alone will cut a groove 1/4 in. wide. Inside cutters vary in thickness from 1/16 to 1/4 in.

A stopped groove or stopped dado can be cut on the circular saw, using either a saw blade or a dado head, as follows: if the groove or dado is stopped at only one end, clamp a STOP BLOCK to the rear of the table in a position that will stop the piece from being fed any

further when the saw has reached the place where the groove or dado is supposed to stop. If the groove or dado is stopped at both ends, clamp a stop block to the rear of the table and a STARTING BLOCK to the front. The starting block should be placed so that the saw will contact the place where the groove is supposed to start when the infeed end of the piece is against the block. Start the cut by holding the piece above the saw, with the infeed end against the starting block and the edge against the fence. Then lower the piece gradually onto the saw, and feed it through to the stop block.

A rabbet can be cut on the circular saw as follows: the cut into the face of the piece is called the SHOULDER cut and the cut into the edge or end the CHEEK cut. To make the shoulder cut (which should be made first), set the saw to extend above the table a distance equal to the desired depth of the shoulder, and set the fence a distance away from the saw equal to the desired depth of the cheek. Be sure to measure this distance from a saw tooth SET TO THE LEFT, or AWAY FROM the ripping fence. If you measure it from a tooth set to the right, or toward the fence, the cheek will be too deep by an amount equal to the width of the saw kerf.

Make the shoulder cut first. Then place the face of the piece which was down for the shoulder cut against the fence and make the cheek cut. If the depth of the shoulder and the depth of the cheek are the same, the cheek cut will be made with the saw at the same height as for the shoulder cut. If the depth of the cheek is different, the height of the saw will have to be changed to conform before the cheek cut is made.

By using the dado head you can cut most ordinary rabbets in a single cut. First build up a dado head equal in thickness to the desired width of the cheek. Next set the head to protrude above the table a distance equal to the desired depth of the shoulder. Clamp a 1-in. board to the fence to serve as a guide for the piece, and set the fence so that the edge of the board barely contacts the right side of the dado head. Set the piece against the universal gage (set at 90°, of course), hold the edge or end to be rabbeted against the 1-in. board, and make the cut.

On some jointers a RABBETING STRIP on the outboard edge of the outfeed table can be depressed for rabbeting. The strip is outboard of the end of the cutterhead. To rabbet on a jointer of this type, you depress the infeed table and the rabbeting strip the depth of the rabbet below the outfeed table, and set the fence the width of the 'rabbet away from the outboard end of the cutterhead. When the piece is fed through the unrabbeted part feeds onto the rabbeting strip.

Some jointers are equipped with a RABBET-ING ARM. The rabbeting arm is bolted to the infeed table and moves up and down with it. To rabbet on a jointer of this type, you depress the infeed table the depth of the rabbet below the outfeed table and set the fence the width of the rabbet away from the outboard end of the cutter-head. The rabbeted part of the piece feeds onto the outfeed table, and the unrabbeted part feeds onto the section of the rabbeting arm that extends beyond the cutterhead.

Various combinations of the grooved joints are used in woodworking. The well-known TONGUE-AND-GROOVE joint is actually a combination of the groove and the rabbet, the tongued member simply being a member which is rabbeted on both faces. In some types of panel work the tongue is made by rabbeting only one face; a tongue of this kind is called a BAREFACED tongue. A joint often used in making boxes, drawers, cabinets and the like is the DADO AND RABBET joint shown in figure 9-20. As you can see, one of the members here is rabbeted on one face to form a bare-faced tongue.

Mortise-and-Tenon Joints

The MORTISE-AND-TENON joint is the most important and most frequently used of the joints used in furniture and cabinet work. In the BLIND mortise-and-tenon joint (fig. 9-15), the tenon does not penetrate all the way through the mortised member. A joint in which the tenon does penetrate all the way through is a THROUGH mortise-and-tenon joint. Besides the ordinary STUB joint (fig. 9-15 and the first view of fig. 9-21), there are HAUNCHED joints (second view of fig. 9-21) and TABLE-HAUNCHED joints (third view of fig. 9-21). Haunching and table-haunching increase the strength and rigidity of the joint.

The layout procedure for an ordinary stub mortise-and-tenon joint is as follows: MARK THE FACES OF THE MEMBERS PLAINLY. Lay off from the end of the tenon member the desired length of the tenon, and square the SHOULDER LINE all the way around. Then lay

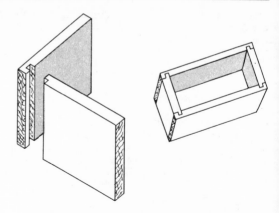

103.15
Figure 9-20.—Dado and rabbet joint.

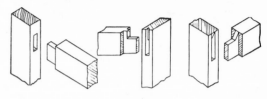

103.20
Figure 9-21.—Stub, haunched, and table-haunched mortise-and-tenon joints.

off the total width of the tenon member on the mortise member as shown in figure 9-22.

Determine the thickness of the tenon, which is usually between one-third and one-half of the thickness of the mortise member, and set the points on the mortising gage to this dimension. Adjust the block so that the points will score a double line on the center of the tenon member, as shown in figure 9-22. If the faces of the members are to be flush, use the same gage setting to score a double line on the mortise member, remembering to gage from the FACE of the member. If the face of the tenon member is to be set back from the face of the mortise member (as is often the case with table rails and the like), the mortising gage setting must be increased by the amount of the set-back. Remember, however, that the setting of the POINTS remains the same. Last, lay off from the end of the mortise member and from the appropriate edge of the tenon member the amount of end-stock which is to be left above the mortise, as indicated also in figure 9-22, and square lines as shown. For a

SLIP TENON joint like the one shown in figure 9-15 you wouldn't need this last phase of the layout.

Tenons can be cut by hand with the backsaw, by the same method previously described for cutting corner and end half-lap joints. Mortises can be cut by hand with the mortising chisel. As in the case of a spline groove cut by hand, you can remove the major part of the waste by boring a series of holes with a twist drill of diameter slightly smaller than the width of the mortise. For a blind mortise-and-tenon joint use a depth gage or a wooden block to prevent the drill from boring below the correct depth of the mortise.

Tenons can be cut with the circular saw as follows: to make the shoulder cuts, set the saw the depth of the shoulder above the table and set the ripping fence the length of the tenon away from the saw. Remember to measure from a saw-tooth SET TO THE LEFT.

Set the saw the depth of the cheek above the table, set the fence the width of the shoulder away from the saw, and make the cheek cuts. To maintain the stock upright, use a PUSH BOARD.

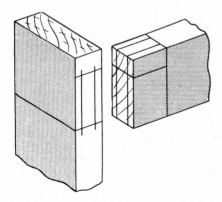

103.21

Figure 9-22.—Layout of stub mortise-and-tenon joint.

Tenons can be cut with the dado head by the same method previously described for cutting end half-lap joints. Mortises are cut mechanically on a HOLLOW-CHISEL MORTISING MACHINE like the one shown in figure 9-23. The cutting mechanism on this machine consists of a boring bit encased in a square, hollow steel

103.24

Figure 9-23.—Hollow-chisel mortising machine.

chisel. As the mechanism is pressed into the wood, the bit takes out most of the waste while the chisel pares the sides of the mortise square. Chisels come in various sizes, with corresponding sizes of bits to match.

The procedure for cutting a mortise on the machine is as follows: install a chisel and bit of the proper size, making sure that the rear edge of the chisel is exactly parallel to the fence on the machine. Place the piece to be mortised against the fence, clamp it to the table, and adjust the position of the table to bring one end of the mortise layout exactly under the chisel. Start the machine, and press down the foot pedal to make a cut to about one-half the depth of the mortise. If you go too deep on the first cut, the cutter may bind in the wood, causing overheating and making extraction difficult. Extract the cutter by releasing the foot pedal, move the table the required distance to the left by operating the large table lateral motion handwheel, and again cut to one-half the depth of the mortise. Continue this process to the end of the mortise; then work the other way, cutting, this time, to the full depth of the mortise.

In some mortise-and-tenon joints, such as those between rails and legs in tables, the tenon member is much thinner than the mortise member. Sometimes a member of this kind is too thin to shape in the customary manner, with shoulder cuts on both faces. When this is the case a BAREFACED mortise-and-tenon joint may be used. In a barefaced joint the tenon member is shoulder-cut on one side only. The cheek on the opposite side is simply a continuation of the face of the member.

Mortise-and-tenon joints are fastened with glue, and with additional fasteners as required. One or more wood or metal dowels may be driven through the joint. A through mortise-and-tenon joint may be fastened by sawing kerfs in the tenon and driving wedges into the kerfs after the joint is assembled, so as to jam the tenon tightly in the mortise. In a KEYED mortise-and-tenon joint the tenon extends some distance beyond the mortised member. The extending part contains a KEYWAY, into which a tapered KEY is driven. The key jams against the mortised member so as to hold the joint tightly together.

Dovetail Joints

The DOVETAIL joint (fig. 9-17) is the strongest of all the woodworking joints. It requires a good bit of labor, however, and is therefore used only for the finer grades of furniture and cabinet work, where it is used principally for joining sides and ends of drawers.

In the dovetail joint one or more PINS on the PIN MEMBER fit tightly into the openings between two or more TAILS (or, in the case of a single dovetail joint, between two HALF-TAILS) on the TAIL MEMBER. A joint containing only a single pin is called a SINGLE DOVETAIL JOINT; a joint containing two or more pins is called a MULTIPLE DOVETAIL JOINT. A joint in which the pins pass all the way through the tail member is a THROUGH dovetail joint. A joint in which they pass only part-way through is a BLIND dovetail joint.

About the simplest of the dovetail joints is the DOVETAIL HALF-LAP joint shown in figure 9-24. This joint is first laid out and cut like an ordinary end half-lap, after which the end of the lapping member is laid out for shaping into a dovetail as follows: set the sliding T-bevel

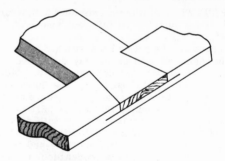

133.85

Figure 9-24.—Dovetail half-lap joint.

to 10°, which is the correct angle between the vertical axis and the sides of a dovetail pin or tail. You can set the sliding T-bevel with a protractor or with the protractor head on the combination square. If you don't have either of these, use the method shown in figure 9-25. Select a board with a straight edge, square a line across it, and lay of an interval of appropriate length, 6 times on the line as shown. From the sixth mark lay off the same interval perpendicularly to the right. A line drawn from this point to the starting point of the first line drawn will form a 10° angle with that line.

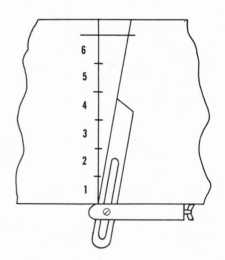

103.16

Figure 9-25.—Laying off 10° angle for dovetail joint.

Lay off this angle from the end corners of the lapping member to the shoulder line, as shown in figure 9-26, and saw out the waste as indicated. The lapping member now has a dovetail on it. Place this dovetail over the other member, in the position it is supposed to occupy, and score the outline of the recess. Then saw and chisel out the recess, remembering to saw on the WASTE side of the lines.

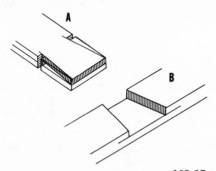

103.17

Figure 9-26.—Making a dovetail half-lap joint.

For a through multiple dovetail joint, the end of the tail member is laid out for cutting as shown in figure 9-27. A joint in which the pins and tails are the same size is the strongest type of dovetail, but for ease in cutting, the pins are usually made somewhat smaller than the tails, as shown. Determine the appropriate number of pins and the size you want to make each pin. Lay off a half-pin from each edge of the member, and then locate the center lines of the other pins at equal intervals across the end of the piece. Lay off the outlines of the pins at 10° to the center lines, as indicated. Then measure back from the end of the member a distance equal to the thickness of the tail member, and square a line all the way around. This line indicates the bottoms of the openings between the pins.

Cut out the pins by sawing on the waste sides of the lines and then chiseling out the waste. Chisel half-way through from one side, as shown in figure 9-28; then turn the member over and chisel through from the other side.

When you have finished cutting out the pins, lay the tail member flat and set the ends of the pins in exactly the position they are to occupy. Score the outlines of the pins, which will, of course, also be the outlines of the tails. Square

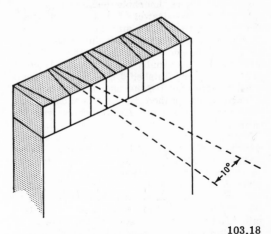

103.18

Figure 9-27.—Laying out pin member for through-multiple-dovetail joint.

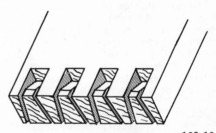

103.19

Figure 9-28.—Chiseling out waste in a through-multiple-dovetail joint.

lines across the end of the tail member, and saw and chisel out the waste between the tails just as you did the waste between the pins.

Box Corner Joints

With the exception of the obvious difference in the layout, the BOX CORNER JOINT (fig. 9-16) is made in just about the same manner as the through-multiple-dovetail joint.

SIMPLE DETAILS FOR
FABRICATING FURNITURE

The construction details for various kinds of furniture and cabinets are similar. Dressers, chests of drawers, kneehole desks and built-in-cabinets all have drawers for storage purposes and are constructed in a similar way.

A number of pieces of stock glued edge to edge should provide sufficient width for the CABINET SIDE. The sides usually range in width from 16 to 20 inches and finished 3/4 inch thick. Some constructions require the use of a square post in each corner of the case. If the square posts are used, they are usually connected with the rails.

Division rails and bearing rails are used to make up the DRAWER DIVISION FRAMES. These frames are usually made of stock 3/4 inch thick and 2 inches wide and fastened together at the corners with blind mortise and tenon joints. The frames are glued and checked to ensure they are square and the same size. Usually a gain is cut on the front edge of the frames, as shown in figure 9-29; and fitted and glued into the dadoes on the inside faces of the sides. The frames should be made 1/4 inch narrower than the sides when 1/4 inch plywood is used. This measurement will allow the plywood back to be glued and fastened into place. To keep dust and insects out of the case, a plywood panel can be installed in the lower frame.

The CABINET BASES should be similar to the other furniture located in the room. The bases usually vary from a straight mitered frame, legs, or a slanted base with hopper type joints.

The DRAWERS should have special attention so they will fit accurately. Drawers have been known to expand or shrink in the front, sides, and back; therefore, some allowance must be made accordingly. It will be helpful to you if you would remember WOOD SHRINKS OR EXPANDS MOSTLY ACROSS THE GRAIN AND VERY LITTLE LENGTHWISE OR WITH THE GRAIN. The height of the drawer opening should be 1/8 to 3/16 of an inch wider than the drawer sides and back. The edges and ends should be slightly beveled toward the back face and the drawer front fitted to the opening. (The lip type drawer may be fitted more loosely because the lip extension will cover the opening at the ends and top.)

There are several types of joints that can be used to join the drawer sides to the front and they are: plain rabbet joint; half blind dovetail; and the dado tongue and rabbet.

The bottom of the drawer is usually grooved into all four sides of the drawer and a plain grooved or dovetail center guide fastened to the bottom. After the drawer has been fitted into place and the front lined up with the front face of the case; the center guide is fastened permanently to the drawer rails, with screws. You may find it to be more convenient if you leave the back off the case until the drawer guides have been fastened to the drawer rails.

To minimize expansion and shrinkage of the wood, a sealer coat of finish should be applied, to the inside surfaces, of all cases, as well as drawers.

CONTOUR CUTTING

The term CONTOUR CUTTING refers to the cutting of ornamental face curves on stock which is to be used for molding or other trim. Most contour cutting is done on the shaper, equipped with a cutter or blades, or with a combination of cutters and/or blades, arranged to produce the desired contour.

The simple molding shapes are the QUARTER ROUND, the HALF ROUND, the SCOTIA or COVE, the CYMA RECTA, and the CYMA REVERSA (fig. 9-30). The quarter and half round form convex curves, the cove molding forms a concave curve, and the cyma moldings are combinations of convex and concave curves.

COPING JOINTS

Inside corner joints between molding trim members are usually made by butting the end of one member against the face of the other. Figure 9-31 shows the method of shaping the end of the abutting member to fit the face of the other member. First saw off the end of the abutting member square, as you would for an ordinary butt joint between ordinary flat-faced members. Then miter the end to 45° as shown in the first and second views of figure 9-31. Then set the coping saw at the top of the line of the miter cut, hold the saw at 90° to the lengthwise axis of the piece, and saw off the segment shown in the third view, following closely the face line left by the 45° miter cut. The end of the abutting member will then match the face of the other member as shown in the third view. A joint made in this manner is called a COPING JOINT.

WOODWORKING SAFETY

Practically everything used in woodworking is dangerous, much of it (such as the power woodworking equipment) very highly so. Yet

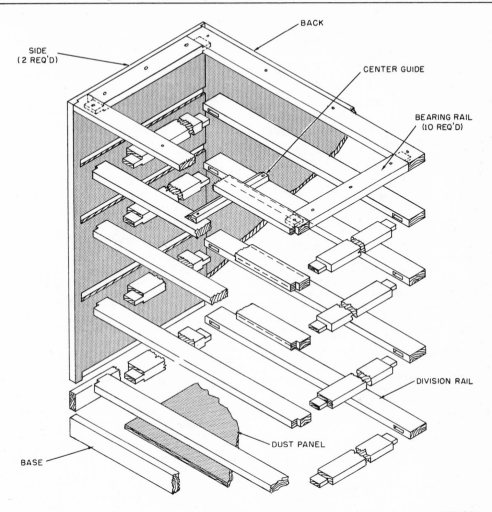

133.347

Figure 9-29.—Cabinet details.

the human factor remains by far the largest cause of woodworking accidents, those which are caused by inherent defects in equipment form only a small percentage of the total. Statistics show, also, that the average Navy woodworking casualty is not a beginner at the trade but a man with pretty long experience. A new man who hears the high-pitched scream of a circular saw for the first time is likely to be acutely conscious of the fact that the machine is dangerous.

Familiarity breeds contempt, however, and experienced men often take dangerous equipment too much for granted.

The vast majority of woodworking accidents could have been prevented by the observance of well-established safety rules. Some of these are rules of general application, others apply to specific tools and equipment. To be effective, these rules must be (a) KNOWN, and (b) OBSERVED. General rules are, or at least should

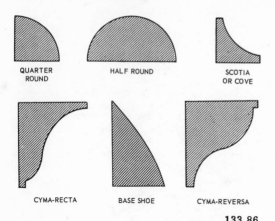

133.86

Figure 9-30.—Simple molding shapes.

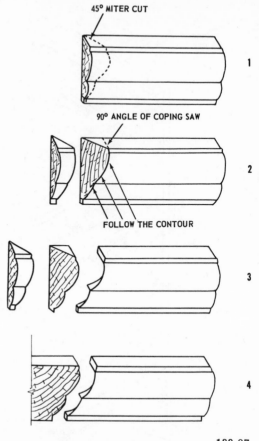

133.87

Figure 9-31.—Making a coping joint.

be, posted on bulletin boards and the like where everyone can see them. Rules applying to specific equipment should be posted somewhere near the equipment, or published in pamphlets and manuals which should be made available to men operating the equipment. DO NOT OPERATE A PIECE OF DANGEROUS EQUIPMENT UNTIL YOU KNOW THE SAFETY RULES WHICH APPLY TO IT. Once you know them OBSERVE THEM, unless a suspension (such as the necessary and unavoidable removal of a guard on a circular saw) is authorized by your superior.

GOOD HOUSEKEEPING AND SAFETY

"Good housekeeping" means "a proper place to stow everything, and everything not in use in it." The importance of good housekeeping as it applied to the protection and preservation of equipment was mentioned in the last chapter. Good housekeeping rules, however, are safety rules as well. If the rules for proper stowage are neglected, braces with bits in them (for example) may be left lying around where the bits may puncture people's skins. Loose articles, litter, and the like may be tripped over, and the person tripping over them may fall off a scaffold or against a spinning circular saw or cutterhead. Poor housekeeping also vastly increases the danger of fire, and seriously hampers the effectiveness of firefighting measures.

GENERAL SHOP SAFETY RULES

The posted or promulgated rules for the safe operation of all power equipment must be strictly followed, unless an unavoidable suspension of a rule is authorized by proper authority. The suspension must end as soon as the necessity for it has passed.

Loose garments, long sleeves, gloves, or neckties which might be snagged in moving machinery parts must not be worn by persons operating power machines. Long hair capable of being snagged must be cut shorter or confined under a hat or cap.

Goggles must always be worn during grinding, jointing, or any other procedure creating an eye hazard.

Before any machinery is operated, it must be determined whether all appropriate safety appliances are in place and in operating order.

A starting switch must never be closed to start a machine until it has been determined that the machine is in a condition to operate freely, with all locking devices released and all adjusting tools or instruments (such as saw arbor wrenches) removed.

Stock must never be fed into a machine's cutting mechanism until the operator has ascertained that the stock will pass through without meeting any obstruction.

Machines must always be stopped before any adjustments or measurements are made on the stock or the machine. When work is being done on or about the cutting mechanism (such as installing or removing jointer knives), not only the starter switch but also the power switch to the machine must be opened.

Whenever a guard or other safety device is removed (which is only when (a) unavoidable, and (b) authorized by superior authority), the device must be replaced as soon as the necessity for its removal has passed.

HANDS MUST BE KEPT AWAY FROM MOVING CUTTING MECHANISMS. They must also be kept out of any position in which they might drop on the cutting mechanism if the piece should happen to kick back.

In any situation in which a piece of stock might kick back, or in which a cut-off strip (such as a strip of waste cut off by a circular saw in rabbeting) might be thrown back, the operator must stand well aside from the probable line of flight.

An individual who is operating a power machine should be spoken to only when absolutely necessary. If the operator is feeding stock, his attention must not be distracted until after the piece has been fed through and recovery has been made.

Before proceeding into any dangerous situation, the basic general safety rule is: STOP, LOOK, AND THINK.

CHAPTER 10
FOUNDATION CONSTRUCTION AND FLOOR AND WALL FRAMING

The two major parts of a building are (1) the foundation, and (2) the part above the foundation, which is called the SUPERSTRUCTURE. A FRAME building is one in which the skeleton of the superstructure consists of a framework of wooden structural members. This framework is called the FRAMING of the building, and the framing is subdivided into FLOOR FRAMING, WALL FRAMING, and ROOF FRAMING. Floor framing consists for the most part of horizontal members called JOISTS, wall framing for the most part of vertical members called STUDS, and roof framing for the most part of inclined members called RAFTERS.

In the days when lumber and labor were plentiful and nails were scarce, it was the custom to use large-dimension timbers ("4-by," "6-by," "8-by," etc.) for framing members, and to join members together with mortise-and-tenon joints, fastened with wooden pins. As lumber and labor became more expensive, as nails became cheaper, and as the machinery for cutting lumber to smaller dimensions became more highly developed, the large-timber method of framing (called FULL framing) gradually went out of use. Newer methods, in which the framing members consist of small-dimension lumber (usually "2-by") fastened together with nails, are now used.

Of the newer framing methods, the most common is PLATFORM FRAMING (also called WESTERN and STORY-BY-STORY FRAMING). In platform framing there are separate studs for each floor, anchored on SOLE PLATES laid on the subflooring, as shown in figure 10-1.

FOUNDATIONS

Foundations vary according to their use, the bearing capacity of the soil, and the type of material available. The material may be cut stone, rock, brick, concrete, tile, or wood, depending upon the weight which the foundation is to support. Foundations may be classified as wall or column (pier) foundations.

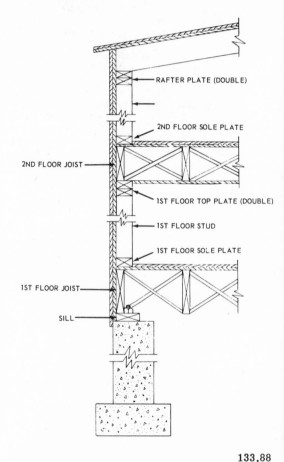

133.88

Figure 10-1.—Platform-frame wall section.

WALL foundations are built solid, the walls of the building being of continuous heavy construction for their total length. Solid walls are used when there are heavy loads to be carried or where the earth has low supporting strength.

294

These walls may be made of concrete, rock, brick, or cut stone, with a footing at the bottom (fig. 10-2). The rule of thumb for determining the width or depth of a footing for a foundation is as follows: Width = 2 times thickness of wall; thickness of footing = same as thickness of the wall. This rule of thumb is illustrated in figure 10-3. For complete information regarding the construction of concrete forms, see chapter 6. Because of the time, labor, and material required to build it, this type of wall will be used only when other types cannot be used. Steel rod reinforcements should be used in all concrete walls.

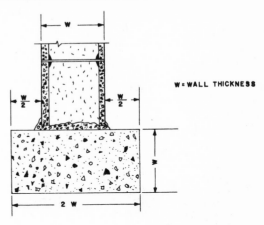

W = WALL THICKNESS

133.349

Figure 10-3.—Dimensions of masonry wall footings.

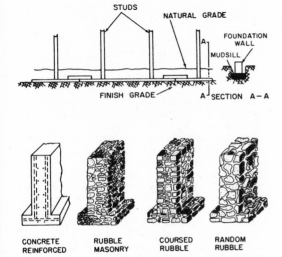

STUDS

NATURAL GRADE

FOUNDATION WALL

MUDSILL

FINISH GRADE

A — SECTION A—A

CONCRETE REINFORCED   RUBBLE MASONRY   COURSED RUBBLE   RANDOM RUBBLE

133.348

Figure 10-2.—Foundation walls.

Rubble stone masonry is used for walls both above and below ground and for bridge abutments. It is used when form lumber or masonry units are not available. Rubble masonry may be laid up with or without mortar; if strength and stability are desired, mortar must be used.

Coursed rubble is assembled of roughly squared stones in such a manner as to produce approximately continuous horizontal bed joints. For complete information regarding the use of rubble materials in masonry, see chapter 7.

Random rubble is the crudest of all types of stonework. Little attention is paid to laying the stone in courses. Each layer must contain bonding stones that extend through the wall. This produces a wall that is well tied together.

COLUMN or PIER foundations save time and labor. They may be constructed from masonry or wood. The piers or columns are spaced according to the weight to be carried. In most cases, the spacing is from 6 to 10 feet. Figure 10-4 shows the different types of piers with different types of footing. Wood piers are generally used since they are installed with the least time and labor. Where wood piers are used, braces are necessary (fig. 10-5).

SILL FRAMING

The work involved in sill construction is a very important one for the Builder. The foundation wall is the support upon which all structure rests. The sill is the foundation on which all framing structure rests and it is the real point of departure for actual building and joinery activities. The sills are the first part of the frame to be set in place. They rest either directly on the foundation piers or on the ground, and may extend all around the building; they are joined at the corners and spliced when necessary. Figure 10-6 shows some common types of sills. The type used depends upon the general type of construction used in the frame.

BOX sills are used often with the very common style platform framing, either with or without the sill plate. In this type of sill, the part that lies on the foundation wall or ground is called the sill plate. The sill is laid edgewise on the outside edge of the sill plate.

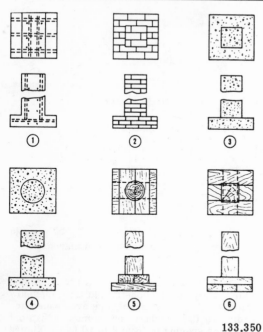

133.350

Figure 10-4.—Column and piers.

FLOOR FRAMING

The floors of a frame building are supported on a series of JOISTS. Depending upon the length of the SPAN (distance between the end-supports of the joists) and the expected size of the combined live and dead load on the floor, joists may run anywhere from 2 x 4 to 3 x 10 in size. The usual joist size for most ordinary frame construction is 2 x 10. The outside-wall ends of first-floor joists are toenailed to the sill.

In platform framing the outside-wall ends of upper-floor joists are anchored on the lower floor top plates. In most cases they butt against, and are nailed to, a HEADER JOIST, set flush with the outer edge of the plate. This will amount to a repeat of the box-sill framing arrangement used on the first floor.

FRAMING JOISTS TO GIRDERS

The distance between an opposing pair of outside walls is often too great to be spanned by a single joist. When two or more joists are required to cover the span, intermediate support for the inboard joist-ends is provided by one or more girders. First-floor girders are supported on piers or on basement columns; upper floor girders are supported on lower-floor columns. Girders may consist of wood, either solid or LAMINATED (built up of several wooden members spiked or bolted together), or they may consist of steel beams.

Figure 10-8 shows three common methods of framing inside ends of joists to wooden girders. In view A, figure 10-8, the joist ends are lapped on and toenailed to the girder, and spiked to each other. In view B, figure 10-8, the joist ends are notched so as to bear partly on the girder and partly on a LEDGER PLATE nailed to the side of the girder. Again the joists are toenailed to the girder and spiked to each other. Specifications usually require that joists not be notched to more than one-third of their depths. The JOIST HANGER (also called a STIRRUP) shown in view C, figure 10-8 is used when the nature of the construction requires that the upper and lower edges of the joists come flush with the top and bottom of the girder.

There are several ways of framing joists to a steel girder. One is by the use of joist hangers similar to those mentioned in the last section. In the absence of hangers, provision for nailing the joist ends can be made as shown in

There are two types of T-SILL construction; one commonly used in the South, or in dry, warm climates, and one commonly used in the East or less warm climates. Their construction is similar except that in the case of the Eastern T-sill the joists are nailed directly to the studs, as well as to the sills, and headers are used between the floor joists.

The sill shown in the lower portion of figure 10-6 is generally used in braced-framing construction. The floor joists are notched out and nailed directly to the sill and studs.

Where built-up sills are used the joints are staggered (fig. 10-7). The corner joints are made as shown in figure 10-7.

If piers are used in the foundation, heavier sills are used. These sills are of single heavy timbers or are built up of two or more pieces of timber. Where heavy timber or built-up type sills are used, the joints should occur over piers. The size of the sill depends upon the load to be carried and upon the spacing of the piers. The sill plates are laid directly on graded earth or on piers. Where earth floors are used, the studs are nailed directly to the sill plate.

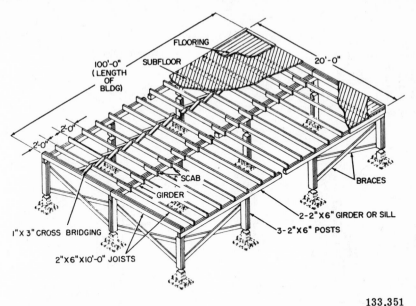

133.351

Figure 10-5.—Braced piers, sills, girders, and joist construction.

figure 10-9. In view A, figure 10-9, the joist ends are lapped on and toenailed to a 2 x 4, which is itself bolted to the upper FLANGE of an I-BEAM girder. The joists are also spiked to each other. In view B, figure 10-9, the ends of the joist are shaped to fit around the upper flange. The ends are butted to each other and each end is anchored on, and toenailed to, a 2 x 4 which is bolted to the WEB (vertical part) of the girder. The joist ends must be shaped so as to leave an allowance of about 3/8 in. (for 2 x 10 joists) above the top of the girder, as shown. This is a SHRINKAGE ALLOWANCE, so called because it allows the wood to shrink without causing the joist ends to split on the girder flange.

FRAMING AROUND FLOOR OPENINGS

Where a floor opening occurs (such as a stairway opening), the parts of the common joists which would extend across if there were no opening must be cut away. The segments remaining on either side of the opening are called CRIPPLE or TAIL joists. The wall-opening ends of cripples are framed against

HEADERS as shown in figure 10-10. Specifications usually require that headers be doubled—sometimes tripled.

Headers are framed between the full-length joists which lie on either side of the floor opening. These joists are called TRIMMERS, and they, too, are usually doubled or tripled. Headers up to 6 ft in length are fastened with 20-penny nails, driven through the trimmers into the ends of the headers. Headers more than 6 ft in length should be fastened with joint hangers.

FLOOR FRAMING UNDER PARTITION

A PARTITION is a wall other than one of the outside walls of the structure. An upper-story partition is not always supported by a partition located directly under it on the story below. When it is not, the floor must be strengthened to carry the load of the partition. For a partition running parallel to the lines of the joists, strengthening is accomplished by doubling the joist under the partition (fig. 10-11).

The joist is doubled by nailing two joists to a series of SOLID BRIDGES, usually placed from 14 to 20 in. O.C. The bridges must separate the joists by the width of the partition sole

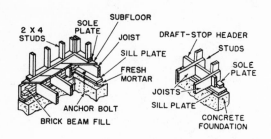

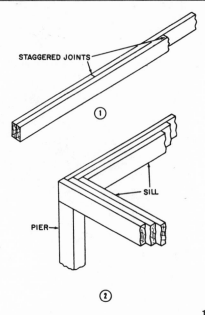

Figure 10-7.—Sill fabrication.

133.353

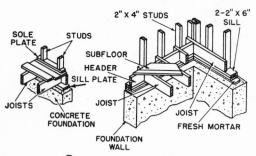

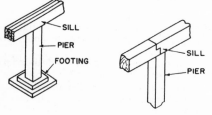

133.352

Figure 10-6.—Types of sills.

plate, to ensure that the upper edges of the joists will be available as nailing surfaces for the finish flooring. Sole plate stock, cut in lengths equal to the depth of the joist, is the best material to use for the bridging.

For a partition which runs across rather than parallel to the joists, every other joist in the floor (or every joist, if so specified) is doubled in the same manner.

BRIDGING

The system of bracing the joists to each other is called BRIDGING. The chief purpose of bridging is to hold the joists plumb and in correct alignment, but bridging also serves to distribute part of a concentrated heavy load (such as the weight of a piano) over several joists next to those directly under the load.

There are two types of bridging: CROSS bridging (view A, fig. 10-12) and SOLID bridging (view B, fig. 10-12). Cross bridging consists of pairs of STRUTS (common sizes of strut stock are 1 x 3, 1 x 4, 2 x 2, and 2 x 4), set diagonally between the joists. Solid bridging consists of pieces of joist-size stock set at right angles to the joists and can be staggered for easier installation.

Since cross bridging is more effective than solid bridging, cross bridging is the type most frequently used in modern construction. For joist spans of ordinary length, specifications usually require a row of cross bridging for every 5 to 8 ft of span. For unusually long spans, the maximum distance between rows of bridging is about 6 ft.

The required length of a cross-bridging strut and the required angle of cut for the ends may be figured as follows: select a piece of board equal in width to the ACTUAL depth of a joist, and 4 or 5 in. longer than the specified spacing of joists O.C. Square two lines across the board, separated from each other by a distance

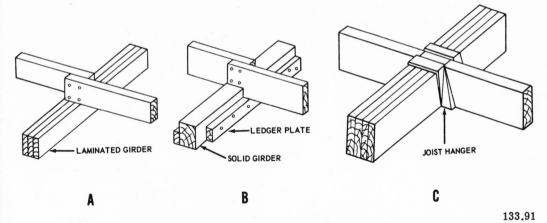

Figure 10-8.—Methods of framing joists to wooden girders.

133.91

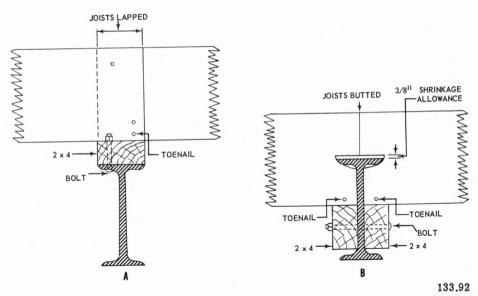

Figure 10-9.—Methods of framing joists to steel girders.

133.92

between the two joists. These two lines represent the opposing faces of two adjacent joists.

Next, sketch in the edge outline of one of the struts, as shown in figure 10-13, using the AC-TUAL thickness of the material. The measured length of this outline is the required length of a strut. To cut struts to this length and to the correct end-angle, proceed to make a miter box as follows:

First, edge-butt a length of 2 x 4 to a length of 2 x 6, as shown in the second and third views of figure 10-14. Then set the framing square on the layout as shown in the first view, with a convenient figure on the tongue intersected by the lower end of the strut outline. Note the figure that the outline intersects on the blade, as indicated. Set the framing square to this cut on the upper edge of the 2 x 6, as shown in

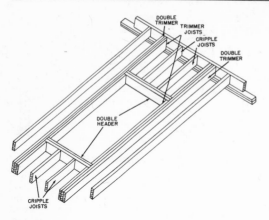

133.93

Figure 10-10.—Framing around floor opening.

the second view, and draw a line along the tongue.

A kerf sawed square from this line will guide the saw at the correct angle for making the end cuts. Measure off from the kerf the length of a strut, and nail a stop block to the miter box at

this point, as shown in the third view. Struts may now be sawed to correct length and correct angle by placing the strut stock on edge in the miter box with the end against the stop block.

The bridging is installed after the joists have been set in place, but before the subfloor is laid. At this time only the upper ends of the struts are nailed. The nailing of the lower ends is postponed until after the joists have adjusted to the weight of the subflooring.

SUBFLOORING

Since the subflooring helps to hold the joists plumb and rigid, it is considered to be a structural element and therefore a part of the framing. The specifications usually refer to the subflooring in language similar to the following:

Subfloors. Joists shall be floored with No. 2 common 6-in. sheathing, laid close and straight [or diagonal] and double-nailed at each joist crossing.

Unless otherwise specified, lumber for subflooring is usually square-edged. Unless boards are END-MATCHED (shaped on the ends to

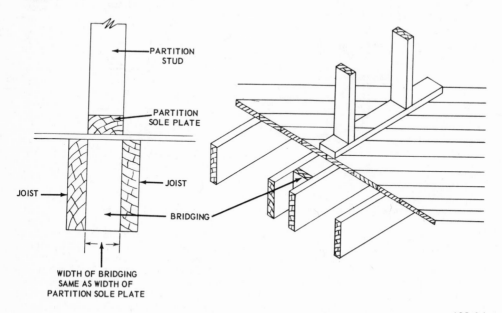

133.94

Figure 10-11.—Method of doubling joist under partition.

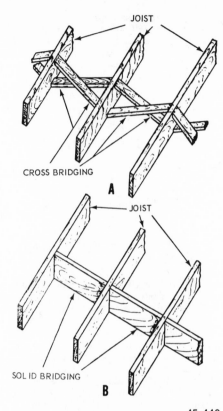

CROSS BRIDGING

A

SOLID BRIDGING

B

45.440

Figure 10-12.—Cross bridging and
solid bridging.

form tongue-and-groove end joints), they must
be cut so as to bring end joints over joists.

Wood flooring expands considerably when it
is wetted, and the subflooring may be wetted
repeatedly during construction operations. If
the flooring were laid so as to butt against the
inner faces of studs (for example), expansion of
the subflooring could push the studs out of line.
Besides the marginal expansion space, a space
of about 1/2 in. should be left between boards
at intervals of about 6 ft across the floor.

Straight-laid subflooring is laid at a 90°
angle to the lines of the joists; diagonal-laid
subflooring at a 45° angle. To ensure that the
lines of end joints will be parallel to the lines
of the joists, straight-laid boards must be cut

off square, and diagonal-laid boards mitered
to 45°.

Straight-laid subflooring is started at a wall
line; diagonal-laid subflooring at a corner. The
first board laid is called the STARTER BOARD.
The starter board for diagonal-laid subflooring
is a small piece shaped like a 45° triangle.

Subflooring is nailed down with two 8-penny
nails at each joist crossing—with 4 nails (2 in
each board) at every crossing where an end
joint between boards occurs.

WALL FRAMING

Wall framing (fig. 10-15) is composed of
regular studs, diagonal bracing, cripples, trimmers, headers, and fire blocks and is supported
by the floor sole plate. The vertical members
of the wall framing are the studs, which support
the top plates and all of the weight of the upper
part of the building or everything above the top
plate line. They provide the framework to which
the wall sheathing is nailed on the outside and
which supports the lath, plaster, and insulation
on the inside.

Walls and partitions which are classed as
framed constructions are composed of structural elements (fig. 10-16) are usually closely
spaced, slender, vertical members called studs.
These are arranged in a row with their ends
bearing on a long horizontal member called a
bottom plate or sole plate, and their tops capped
with another plate, called a top plate. Double
top plates are used in bearing walls and partitions. The bearing strength of stud walls is
determined by the strength of the studs.

CORNER POSTS

The studs used at the corners of the frame
construction are usually built up from three or
more ordinary studs to provide greater strength.
These built up assemblies are corner-partition-
posts. After the sill and first-floor joists are
in place, the sub-floor is placed to give a surface upon which to work. The corner posts are
set up, plumbed, and temporarily braced. The
corner posts may be made in several different
ways (fig. 10-17).

A corner post may consist of a 4 by 6 with a
2 by 4 nailed on the board side, flush with
one edge. This type corner is for a 4-inch
wall. Where walls are thicker, heavier timber is used.

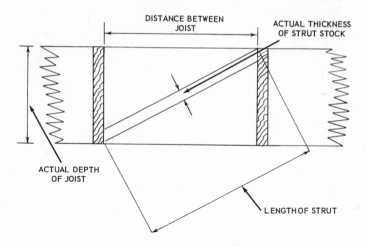

DISTANCE BETWEEN
JOIST

ACTUAL THICKNESS
OF STRUT STOCK

ACTUAL DEPTH
OF JOIST

LENGTH OF STRUT

133.95

Figure 10-13.—Layout for cross-bridging struts.

A 4 by 4 may be used with a 2 by 4 nailed to two of the adjoining sides.

Two 2 by 4's may be nailed together with blocks between and a 2 by 4 flush with one edge.

A 2 by 4 may be nailed to the edge of another 2 by 4, the edge of one flush with the side of the other. This type is used extensively where no inside finish is required.

Whenever a partition meets an outside wall, a stud wide enough to extend beyond the partition on both sides is used; this affords a solid nailing base for the inside wall finish. This type of stud is called a T-POST and is made in several different ways (fig. 10-18).

A 2 by 4 may be nailed and centered on the face side of a 4 by 6.

A 2 by 4 may be nailed and centered on two 4 by 4's nailed together.

Two 2 by 4's may be nailed together with a block between them and a 2 by 4 centered on the wide side.

A 2 by 4 may be nailed and centered on the face side of a 2 by 6, with a horizontal bridging nailed behind them to give support and stiffness.

Where a partition is finished on one side only, the PARTITION POST used consists of a simple stud, set in the outside wall, in line with

the side of the partition wall, and finished as stud A in 1, figure 10-19. These posts are nailed in place along with the corner post. The exact position of the partition walls must be determined before the posts are placed. Where the walls are more than 4 inches thick, wider timber is used. In special cases, for example where partition walls cross, a double T-post is used. This is made by using methods previously described and nailing another 2 by 4 to the opposite wide side, as shown in 2, 3, and 4, figure 10-19.

STUDS

After the posts, plates, and braces are in place, the studs are placed and nailed with two- 16- or 20-penny nails through the top plate. Before the studs are set in place, the window and door openings are laid out. Then the remaining or intermediate studs are laid out on the sole plates by measuring from one corner the distances the studs are to be set apart. Studs are normally spaced 12, 16, and 24 inches on centers, depending upon the type of building and the type of outside and inside finish. Where vertical siding is used, studs are set wider apart since the horizontal girts between them afford nailing surface.

When it is desirable to double the post of the door opening, first place the outside studs into position and nail them securely. Then cut short

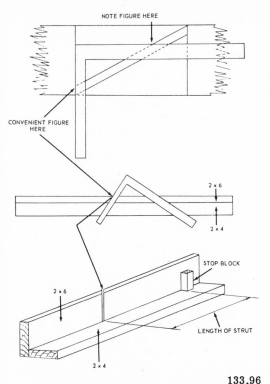

NOTE FIGURE HERE

CONVENIENT FIGURE
HERE

2 x 6

2 x 4

STOP BLOCK

2 x 6

LENGTH OF STRUT

2 x 4

133.96

Figure 10-14.—Making a miter box for
cutting cross-bridging struts.

studs, or FILLER STUDS, the size of the opening, and nail these to the inside face of the outside studs as shown in figure 10-15. In making a window opening, a bottom header must be framed; this header is either single or double. When it is doubled, the bottom piece is nailed to the opening studs at the proper height and the top piece of the bottom header is nailed in place flush with the bottom section. The door header is framed as shown in figure 10-15. The filler stud rests on the sole at the bottom.

TOP PLATE AND SOLE PLATE

The top plate serves two purposes—to tie the studding together at the top and form a finish for the walls; and to furnish a support for the lower ends of the rafters (fig. 10-15). The top plate serves as a connecting link between the wall and the roof, just as the sills and

girders are connecting links between the floors and the walls. The plate is made up of one or two pieces of timber of the same size as the studs. (In cases where the studs at the end of the building extend to the rafters, no plate is used at the end of the building.) When it is used on top of partition walls, it is sometimes called the cap. Where the plate is doubled, the first plate or bottom section is nailed with 16- or 20-penny nails to the top of the corner posts and to the studs; the connection at the corner is made as shown in 1, figure 10-20. After the single plate is nailed securely and the corner braces are nailed into place, the top part of the plate is then nailed to the bottom section by means of 16- or 20-penny nails either over each stud, or spaced with two nails every 2 feet. The edges of the top section should be flush with the bottom section and the corner joints lapped as shown in 1 and 2, figure 10-20.

All partition walls and outside walls are finished either with a 2 by 4 or with a piece of timber corresponding to the thickness of the wall; this timber is laid horizontally on the floor or joists. It carries the bottom end of the studs (fig. 10-15). This 2 by 4, or timber, is called the "sole" or "sole plate." The sole should be nailed with two 16- or 20-penny nails at each joist that it crosses. If it is laid lengthwise on top of a girder or joist, it should be nailed with two nails every 2 feet.

PARTITION

Partition walls are walls that divide the inside space of a building. These walls in most cases are framed as part of the building. In cases where floors are to be installed after the outside of the building is completed, the partition walls are left unframed. There are two types of partition walls: the bearing, and the nonbearing types. The bearing type supports ceiling joists. The nonbearing type supports only itself. This type may be put in at any time after the other framework is installed. Only one cap or plate is used. A sole plate should be used in every case, as it helps to distribute the load over a larger area. Partition walls are framed in the same manner as outside walls, and door openings are framed as outside openings. Where there are corners or where one partition wall joins another, corner posts or T-posts are used as in the outside walls; these posts provide nailing surfaces for the inside wall finish. Partition walls in a one-story

303

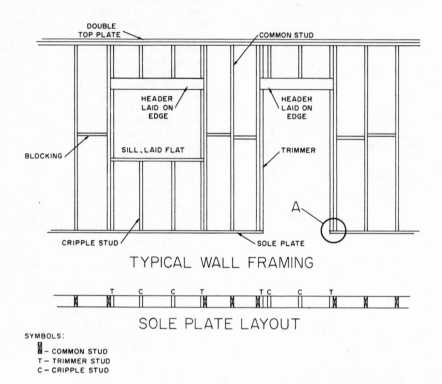

SYMBOLS:

◪ – COMMON STUD
T – TRIMMER STUD
C – CRIPPLE STUD

133.354

Figure 10-15.—Typical wall frame details.

building may or may not extend to the roof. The top of the studs has a plate when the wall does not extend to the roof; but when the wall extends to the roof, the studs are joined to the rafters.

BRACES

Bracing stiffens framed construction and helps it to resist winds, storm, twist, or strain stemming from any cause. Good bracing keeps corners square and plumb and prevents warping, sagging, and shifts resulting from lateral forces that would otherwise tend to distort the frame and cause badly fitting doors and windows and the cracking of plaster. There are three commonly used methods of bracing frame structures.

Let-in bracing (1, fig. 10-21). Let-in bracing is set into the edges of studs so as to be flush with the surface. The studs are always cut to let in the braces; the braces are never cut. Usually 1 by 4's or 1 by 6's are used, set diagonally from top plates to sole plates.

Cut-in bracing (2, fig. 10-21). Cut-in bracing is toenailed between studs. It usually consists of 2 by 4's cut at an angle to permit toenailing, inserted in diagonal progression between studs running up and down from corner posts to sill or plates.

Diagonal sheathing (3, fig. 10-21). The type of bracing with the highest strength is sheathing applied diagonally. Each board acts as a brace of the wall. If plywood sheathing 5/8-inch thick or more is used, other methods of bracing may be omitted.

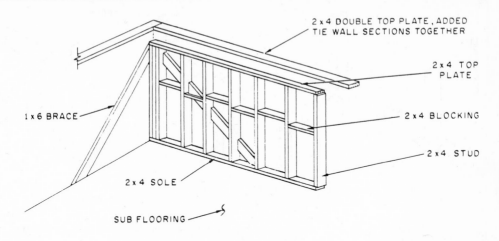

WALL SECTION INPLACE
WITH TEMPORARY BRACING

133.355

Figure 10-16.—Typical wall construction.

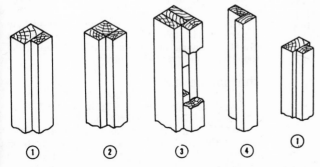

133.356

Figure 10-17.—Corner post construction.

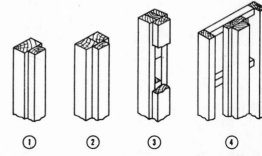

133.357

Figure 10-18.—T-post construction.

FRAMING LAYOUT AND ERECTION

Framing LAYOUT consists principally of laying out the various framing members for cutting to correct lengths, and marking the correct locations of members on other members to which they are to be joined.

SILL LAYOUT

The sill is normally the first member to be laid out. As indicated in figure 10-1, the edge of the sill is usually set back from the edge of the foundation a distance equal to the thickness of the sheathing. When this is the case, the length of sill stock required to cover a section of foundation wall is equal to the length of the wall section minus twice the amount of the set-back.

To make up this length you should select lengths of sill stock which will most conveniently and economically make up the total required length. Suppose, for example, that the section of wall calls for 33 ft of 2 x 8 sill stock

305

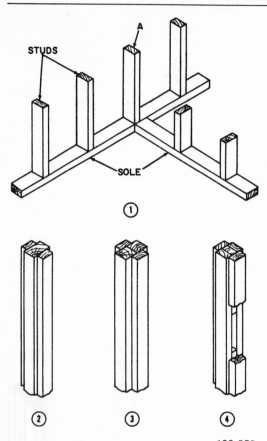

133.358

Figure 10-19.—Partition posts.

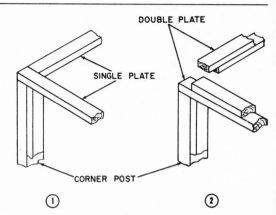

133.359

Figure 10-20.—Plate construction.

and you have 2 x 8 available in 18-ft, 16-ft, 14-ft, and 6-ft lengths. You could select two 18-ft pieces and cut 3 ft off one of them, or you could select two 14-ft pieces and a 6-ft piece and cut a foot off the 6-ft piece. In the first instance, however, you would have 3 ft of waste, while in the second you would have two joints in the sill. To minimize both waste and the number of joints, you should select one 18-ft and one 16-ft piece and cut a foot off one of them.

Once the required length has been made up, the next step is to lay out the locations of the bolt holes as follows: place each piece of sill stock on the foundation, inboard of the bolts, but otherwise in exactly the position it is to occupy, and square a line across the stock from

the center of each bolt. To lay out the bolt-hole center on each of these lines, measure the distance from the center OF EACH BOLT to the outer edge of the foundation; subtract the amount of the sill set-back from this distance, and lay off the remainder ON THE CORRESPONDING BOLT LINE, measuring from what is to be the outer edge of the sill.

The reason you must lay out each bolt hole separately is that the bolts may be set at slightly varying distances from the edge of the foundation and from each other.

SILL PLACEMENT

Bore the bolt holes with an auger bit 1/8 in. larger in diameter than the bolt diameter, to allow for making slight adjustments in the location of the sill. When all the holes have been bored, try the stock for the whole section on the bolts for a fit. If the fit is satisfactory, remove the pieces of stock and place a thin layer of mortar on top of the foundation. Replace the pieces and check the whole sill for line and level. Place small wedges, if necessary, to hold pieces level until the mortar sets. Then place the washers on the bolts, screw on the nuts, and bolt the sill down.

JOIST LAYOUT

A COMMON JOIST is a full-length joist, as distinguished from a cripple joist. The best way to lay out common joists for cutting is to figure the correct length of a common joist,

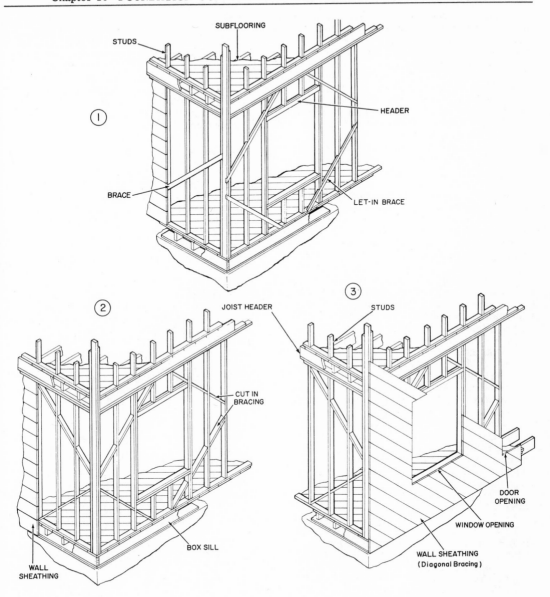

133.103

Figure 10-21.—Common types of bracing.

cut a piece of stock to this length, notch for identification, and use the piece as a PATTERN from which to cut the other common joists. The best way to lay out cripples for cutting is to postpone the cripple layout until after the headers have been placed; then measure the spaces which are to be spanned by the cripples.

In platform framing, the outer ends of the joists usually butt against a header joist which is set flush with the outer edge of the sill. In this case the length of a wall-to-wall common joist will be the distance between the outer edges of the sills, minus twice the thickness of a header joist.

The length of common joist required to cover a given span between an outside wall and a girder varies with the character of the wall framing and also with the manner in which the joists are framed to the girder. The length of common joist required to cover a given span between two girders varies with the manner in which the joists are framed to the girders. Joists which lap a girder with full bearing (meaning joists which extend all the way across the top of the girder) must obviously be longer than joists which butt each other on the top of a girder. Joists in hangers, which butt against the sides of a girder, are shorter than joists which butt each other on top of a girder.

The whole floor-framing situation, then, must be studied closely before a common joist pattern is cut. Whenever possible, the cutting of a pattern should be delayed until the sills, headers, and other supporting or abutting members are erected. The joist length can then be determined by measurements taken on the actual structure. Whenever possible, too, the common joist pattern should be tried on the actual structure for a fit before any joists are cut from it.

JOIST LOCATION LAYOUT

The location of a joist end is marked on a sill or a header joist by squaring a line across and drawing an X alongside it. The X indicates the side of the line on which the joist end-section is to be placed.

The location of one of the outside joists is marked first, and the locations of the others are then measured off from this one in accordance with the specified spacing of joists O.C.

Figure 10-22 shows the method of laying out joist locations on the header joists in a platform-frame box sill, in which the headers and outside

joists come flush with the outer edges of the sill.

Before you start laying out the joist locations you should study the floor framing plan to learn the locations of any double trimmers around floor openings. Locations of double trimmers are marked with two lines and two X's. The locations of cripples are marked the same as the locations of common joists, but with the word CRIP written in alongside.

JOIST ERECTION

The usual procedure for erecting joists is as follows: if there are any header joists, these joists are cut and erected first. As a general rule, the length of a platform-frame header is equal to the shortest distance between the outer edges of the sills. Header joists are toenailed to the sills with 16-penny nails spaced 16 in. O.C.

As soon as a common joist pattern has been laid out and cut as previously described, a CUTTING PARTY starts cutting common joists. As each joist is cut, a 2-man CARRYING PARTY carries it to its location and lays it flat across the span. A 2-man CONSTRUCTION PARTY (one man at each end of the span) erects the outside joists first. Each of these is toenailed down to the sill or plate with 16-penny nails spaced 16 in. O.C., and end-nailed through the headers with two 20-penny nails driven into each joist end. Incidentally, many joists have a slight curve to them, and the convex edge of a joist is called the CROWN. A joist should always be placed with the crown UP.

Next the joists lying between the outside joists are set on edge and the ends of each joist are toenailed down to the sill or plate with two 16-penny nails, one on each side of the joist. Only the inner trimmer of each pair of trimmers is erected at this time, and no cripples are cut at this time. After all the common joists, and the trimmers as mentioned, have been set on edge and toenailed, the joists are plumbed and temporarily braced as follows.

A temporary brace (usually a 1 x 6) is laid across the tops of the joists at the center of the span. The outer ends of this brace are tacked down to the outside joists with 8-penny nails, driven only part-way in to allow for extracting later when the brace is removed. Beginning with the joist next to an outside joist, the joists are plumbed consecutively, and as each joist is plumbed it is braced with an 8-penny nail, driven through the brace into the joist.

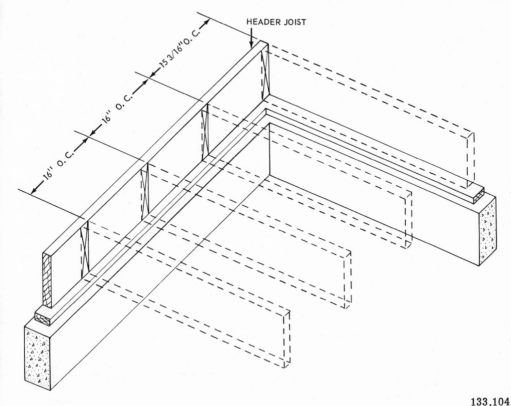

133.104

Figure 10-22.—Joist location layout—platform—frame box sill assembly
with header joists.

A joist that butts against a header is plumbed by lining up the joist end with the perpendicular location line on the header. When the joist is in plumb position, it is nailed at the ends with 20-penny nails, 2 to each end, driven through the header into the joist.

After all the common joists, plus the inside trimmers (if there are any), have been plumbed and braced, the framing around a floor opening (if there is one) is installed. First the locations of the headers are determined from a study of the floor framing plan. Next the length of a header is determined by measurement of the shortest distance between the inside trimmers. The four pieces of joist stock which will form the double headers are then cut to correct length, after which the outside header of each pair is set in place and fastened to the inside trimmers with 20-penny nails, three to each end, driven through the trimmers into the ends of the headers as shown in figure 10-23.

Once the outside headers are in place, the lengths of the cripple joists can be determined by simple measurement. The cripples are cut, set in place, plumbed, fastened at the outer ends like common joists, and fastened at the floor-opening ends with 20-penny nails, three to each cripple, driven through the outside headers into the ends of the cripples as shown in figure 10-24.

Next the inside headers are set in place, fastened to the outside headers with 16-penny nails spaced 6-in. O.C., and fastened to the inside trimmers with 20-penny nails, three to

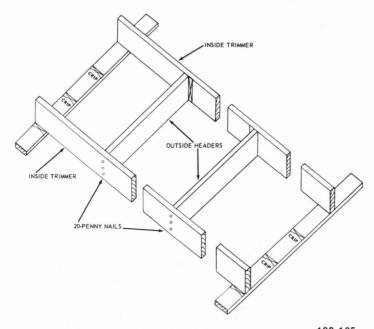

133.105

Figure 10-23.—First step in framing around floor opening.

each end, driven through the trimmers into the ends of the headers (fig. 10-25). Finally, the outside trimmers are set in place and nailed to the inside trimmers with 16-penny nails spaced 12 in. O.C., as shown in figure 10-26.

As soon as enough common joists have been erected, the installation of bridging begins. Cross-bridging struts are nailed (usually with 8-penny nails) at the top ends only at this time. Bottom ends will be nailed from below, after the joists have adjusted themselves to the weight of the subflooring. Remember the joist should be placed with the crown up, so that any settlement under the weight of the flooring will tend toward a level instead of toward a sag.

After the bridging is installed, the subflooring is laid as previously described. In the meantime, the layout and cutting of studs begins.

LAYING OUT STUDS FOR CUTTING

Before you can lay out any studs for cutting, you must calculate how long the studs must be. The best way to do this is to lay out to full scale on a piece of stud stock certain data obtained

from the wall sections and elevations, and then use the piece of stock as a pattern for cutting studs.

Next step is to lay out the segments of the gable-end studs which extend above the level of the top of the rafter plate. In order to do this, you must calculate the COMMON DIFFERENCE of gable-end studs as follows.

In figure 10-27 the line AC indicates the level of the side wall rafter plate, and line AB indicates the roof line of the building. Somewhere on the elevations you will find a small triangle like the one shown in the upper left of the figure. This is called the ROOF TRIANGLE, and it gives the proportion of run to rise in the roof. In this case this is also the proportion of run to rise between line AC and line AB, and the proportion is 8 inches of rise to every 12 inches of run.

The lines DE and FG represent the portions of two gable-end studs that extend above the level of the top of the side-wall rafter plate. You can calculate the length of DE as follows. Since the studs are spaced 16 in. O.C., the run of the right triangle AED is 16 in. The rise of

310

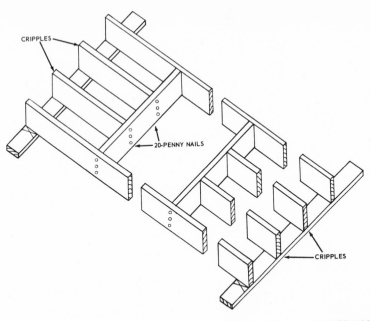

CRIPPLES

20-PENNY NAILS

CRIPPLES

133.106

Figure 10-24.—Second step in framing around floor opening.

this triangle is the length of the line DE. From the roof triangle you know that the rise of a similar triangle with a run of 12 in. is 8 in. If the rise of a right triangle with a run of 12 in. is 8 in., the rise of a similar right triangle with a run of 16 in. must be the value of x in the proportional equation 12:8::16:x, or 10 2/3 in. The length of DE, therefore, is 10 2/3 in. Rounded off to the nearest 1/16 in., this is 10 11/16 in. The common difference may also be found as follows. Multiply the cut of the roof, expressed as a fraction, by the spacing of the studs. Assume a roof cut of 8 in. and 12 in. and a stud spacing of 16 in. The common difference in the length of the gable stud is 16 in. x 8/12 in. = 10 2/3 in. Expressed as a formula, stud spacing x cut of the roof = common difference.

If the rise of a right triangle for 16 in. of run is 10 11/16 in., the rise for twice as much run, or 32 in., must be twice as much, or 2 x 10 11/16 in.; the rise for three times as much run must be 3 x 10 11/16; and so on. This means that, moving inboard from the rafter

plates, each gable-end stud is 10 11/16 in. longer than the preceding gable-end stud.

Knowing this, you can lay off the lengths of the gable-end studs by laying off 10 11/16 in. (which is called the COMMON DIFFERENCE of gable-end studs) progressively for each stud, from the shortest to the longest, in either side of the end wall. The top end cut of the gable stud is laid out by using the cut of the roof and marking on the rise side.

A pattern layout for platform-frame studs is shown in figure 10-28. Since the bottom of a platform-frame stud rests on the sole plate, which in turn rests on the subflooring, you should first lay off the vertical distance between the finish floors, MINUS the thickness of the sole plate, PLUS the thickness of the finish floor. This is distance 1 in figure 10-28; laying it off will give you the level of the upper finish floor. Lay off back from this level the combined thickness of the upper floor flooring, the depth of an upper floor joist, and the thickness of the top plate. You now have the length of a stud, as shown in the figure.

311

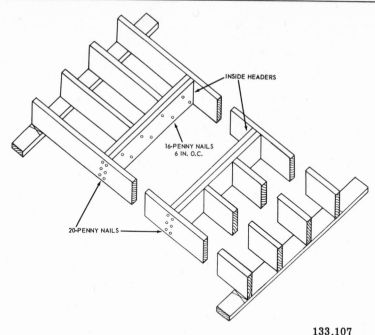

133.107

Figure 10-25.—Third step in framing around floor opening.

STUD LOCATION LAYOUT

Stud locations are marked on sole plates in the same manner as joist locations. The sole plate is marked first, as shown in figure 10-29. These marks are then transferred to the corresponding top plate or rafter plate, by "matching" the top plate or rafter plate against the marked sole plate and squaring the marks across.

The studs around wall openings require special treatment. First locate the center line of the opening by examining the floor plan. Let's say that the opening is a door, and that the plan shows that the center line of this door lies 7 ft 5 in. from one of the building corners. Measure this off and square a line across the sill or plate at this point. Next look on the door schedule and find the width of this door. Let's say that it is Door A, and you find that Door A is 3 ft wide. Lay off one-half of this, or 1 ft 6 in., on either side of the center line and square lines across.

FRAMING ALLOWANCE

These lines mark the boundaries of the FINISHED door opening. The trimmer studs on either side of the opening, however, must be located at the boundaries of the ROUGH opening. To get the width of the rough opening you add a FRAMING ALLOWANCE to the width of the finished opening. First, the width of the rough opening must exceed the width of the finished opening by the combined thicknesses of the SIDE JAMBS on the door, less the combined width of the rabbets if the door fits into rabbets cut in the side jambs.

Besides the allowance for the thickness of the jambs, you must make an additional FRAMING ALLOWANCE. As you will see later, the side jambs are wedged in place with wooden wedges, driven between the jambs and the trimmers. The usual wedging allowance is 1/2 in. on either side.

The width of the finished opening (which is the same as the width of the door) is the

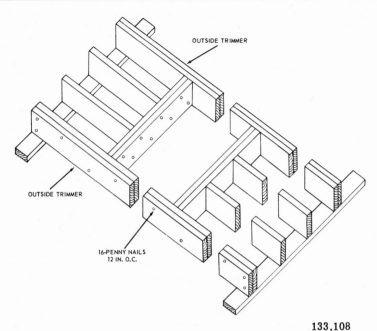

133.108

Figure 10-26.—Fourth step in framing around floor opening.

horizontal distance between the side jambs. The width of the rough opening is the same horizontal distance, plus the combined width of the jambs, plus the combined width of the wedging allowance.

To locate the trimmers, then, lay off, on either side of the center line, one-half the width of the door, plus the thickness of a side jamb (which should be measured on the actual stock), plus the wedging allowance (usually 1/2 in.). Mark the trimmer locations with the word TRIM, and postpone the cutting of the trimmers until after the header has been cut and set in place.

The header will be nailed between the first two full-length studs lying outside the boundaries of the finished opening. To locate the header at the right height you must add to the height of the door a framing allowance as follows. You must make allowance for the thickness of the head jamb, and also for the depth of the SIDE JAMB LUGS. The side jamb lugs are the portions of the side jambs which extend above the head jamb dadoes. Since you will be

measuring from the top of the subflooring and since the bottom of the door will have to clear the finish flooring, you must allow for the thickness of the finish flooring. If there is to be a threshold under the door, you must allow for the thickness of the threshold. If there will be no threshold, you must add a CLEARANCE ALLOWANCE which will permit the door to swing clear of any rugs or carpets. The usual clearance allowance is 5/8 in., which is also the usual thickness of a threshold. If the carpeting is to be extra thick, the clearance allowance may have to be more than 5/8 in.

The framing allowance for a window opening is calculated as follows: locate and mark the window center line and lay off on either side of the center line one-half the width of the window, as obtained from the window schedule. This will locate the limits of the finished window opening. The top header and subsill header will be set between the first two full-length studs lying outside these limits.

Further window-opening layout should be postponed until the subsill header has been set

313

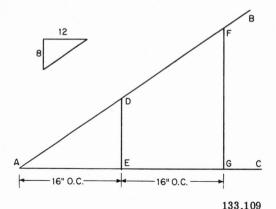

133.109

Figure 10-27.—Calculating common
difference of gable-end studs.

in place. The height of the subsill header is
obtained as follows: determine by examining
the appropriate elevation, the height of the top
of the window sill above the finish flooring.
Since you will be measuring from the subflooring, add the thickness of the finish flooring.
From this, subtract the thickness of the window
sill, plus the sill BEVEL ALLOWANCE, or
amount that the sill will be raised by tilting.
This is usually about 3/4". To sum up, the
height of the top of the subsill header above the
finish flooring will be the vertical distance

between the top of the window sill and the top of
the finish floor, MINUS the thickness of the
window sill, the sill bevel allowance (usually
3/4 in.), and the thickness of the finish flooring.

The next step is to locate the top header at
the proper height. On the elevation you will find
the vertical distance between the finished first
floor line and the bottom of the window head
jamb. Since you will measure this distance
from the top of the subfloor, add to it the thickness of the finish floor. Next add the thickness
of the head jamb plus the depth of the window
side jamb lugs, which are similar to those on a
door. The total will be the vertical distance
between the top of the subfloor and the bottom
of the top header.

When you have located the level of the bottom
of the top header, check the whole layout as
follows. You know that the height of the rough
opening should be the height of the window (as
given on the schedule) plus the total framing
allowance. Calculate the total framing allowance you have applied and add it to the window
height. The result should be the same as the
measured vertical distance between the top of
the subsill header and the bottom of the top
header. If it isn't, you have made a mistake
somewhere.

To locate the trimmers proceed as follows:
transfer the window center line to the subsill
header and lay off on either side of it one-half
the width of the window, as obtained from the
window schedule. For a window without sash

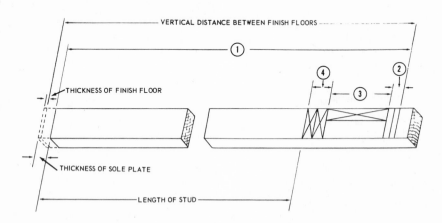

133.110

Figure 10-28.—Pattern layout for platform-frame studs.

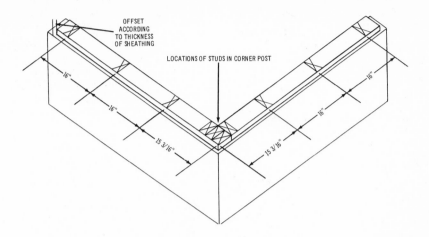

133.111

Figure 10-29.—Stud location layout.

pockets, add on either side a framing allowance consisting of the thickness of the side jamb plus a wedging allowance of 1/2 in. If the window is a double hung window with sash weights, add the thickness of the side jamb plus 2 in. for the width of the sash pocket. These terms are explained in chapter 13.

WALL FRAMING ERECTION

The steps in erecting a frame wall are to erect and plumb each of the corner posts as follows. Set the post in exact position on the plate, and toenail it down with 8-penny nails, 2 to each stud in the corner post. Attach temporary braces at the top, and nail couple of short blocks to the subflooring at the approximate points where the ends of the braces will be fastened. Set nails in the floor ends of the braces, ready to be driven into the blocks when the exact position of each end is found.

While one man applies and reads the level, another man should be ready to nail the brace to the block as soon as correct position is found. This man works the end of the brace back and forth, on signal from the man at the level, until he gets the word that the bubble is centered. He then nails the end of the brace to the block. When this procedure has been followed with both braces, the corner post will be plumb all around.

Erection of the section of wall lying between the corner posts may be either by the PIECE-BY-PIECE method or by the SECTION method. In the piece-by-piece method, the wall is erected a piece at a time, meaning that each of the studs is raised and toenailed in place separately, after which the top plate or rafter plate is nailed on. In the section method the entire wall section, with the exception usually of the framing around openings and the upper member of the top plate or rafter plate, is assembled lying flat on the subflooring. The section is then heaved up into place and fastened at the top and bottom. Nowadays the section method is used for almost all platform-frame walls.

The full-length studs are laid out adjacent to their location marks on the sole plate. As previously mentioned, the lower member of the top plate or rafter plate has already been matched against the sole plate, and marked with the corresponding stud locations. After the full-length studs have all been laid out flat, the lower member of the top plate or rafter plate is nailed to the tops of the studs with 16-penny nails, 2 to each stud, driven through the plate into the studs.

The wall section is then heaved up into place and temporarily braced. The bottoms of the braces are only tacked to the floor blocks at this time, so that their positions can be adjusted later when the wall is straightened. Each of the

315

studs is toenailed down to its mark on the sole plate with 8-penny nails, 2 to each side of a stud. An adjoining wall section is then erected in the same manner, after which the upper members of the top plates or rafter plates are nailed to the lower members with 10-penny nails spaced 16 in. O.C. End-laps between adjoining plates are nailed down with 16-penny nails, 2 to each lap.

When all four walls have been erected, each wall is straightened as follows. A guide line is stretched between the tops of the corner posts, and the bottoms of the temporary braces are released from the floor blocks. Beginning at one end of the wall, each brace is adjusted so as to bring the outer edge of the top plate in exact contact with the line. The bottom of the brace is then again nailed to the floor block.

The next step is to frame the rough openings. The procedure for this is much the same as it is for framing a floor opening. Trimmers are nailed to full-length studs, or to each other, with 10-penny nails spaced 16 in. O.C. Headers are nailed to full-length studs with 8-penny nails, 2 to each end of a header member, driven through the full-length studs into the ends of the headers. Double headers are nailed to each other with 10-penny nails spaced 16 in. O.C.

Next step is to cut gains for diagonal bracing (if any) in studs and plates. Lay out these gains by placing the 1 x 6 bracing material in position against the framing members and scoring the outline on each stud or plate. Nail bracing on with two 8-penny nails to each stud or plate crossing.

WALL SHEATHING

The inner layer of outside wall covering on a frame structure is called the SHEATHING (usually pronounced "SHEETING"); the outer layer is called the SIDING. The siding, because it is not a structural element, is considered a part of the exterior finish. The sheathing, because it strengthens and braces the wall framing, is considered a structural element and therefore a part of the framing.

TYPES OF SHEATHING

The four most common types of sheathing used on modern structures are WOOD, PLYWOOD, FIBERBOARD, and GYPSUM.

WOOD sheathing consists usually of 1 x 6 or 1 x 8 boards, but thicker and/or wider stock is sometimes used. Boards may be square-edged for ordinary edge-butt joining, or they may be SHIPLAP or TONGUE AND GROOVE (fig. 10-30). "Dressed-and matched" is simply a term which is used instead of "tongue-and-groove" with reference to sheathing, siding, or flooring.

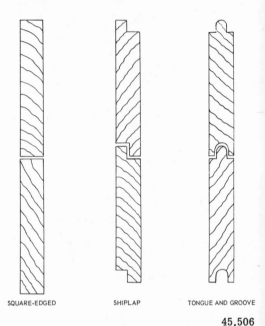

SQUARE-EDGED   SHIPLAP   TONGUE AND GROOVE

45.506

Figure 10-30.—Types of wood sheathing.

PLYWOOD sheathing is normally used in 4- by 8-ft sheets, which are usually applied VERTICALLY, or with the 8-ft dimension vertical. The type of plywood used is called SHEATHING GRADE; for studs spaced 16 in. O.C. the minimum thickness is 5/16 in.

FIBERBOARD (sometimes called INSULATION BOARD) is a synthetic material which may be coated or impregnated with asphalt to increase water resistance. Edges are usually shiplap or tongue and groove for joining. Thickness is normally 25/32 in.

GYPSUM sheathing consists of a treated gypsum filler faced on both sides with a lightweight paper. Sheets are usually dressed-and-matched, with V-shaped grooves and tongues.

APPLICATION OF SHEATHING

As soon as all the wall openings have been framed, the application of the sheathing begins. Wood wall sheathing can be obtained in almost all widths, lengths, and grades. Generally, widths are from 6 to 12 inches, with lengths selected for economical use. Almost all solid wood wall sheathing used is 13/16-inches thick and either square or matched edge. This material may be nailed on horizontally or diagonally (fig. 10-31). Diagonal application contributes much greater strength to the structure. Sheathing should be nailed on with three 8-penny common nails to each bearing if the pieces are over 6 inches wide. Wooden sheathing is laid on tight, with all joints made over the studs. If the sheathing is to be put on horizontally, it should be started at the foundation and worked toward the top. If it is to be put on diagonally, it should be started at the corners of the building and worked toward the center or middle of the building.

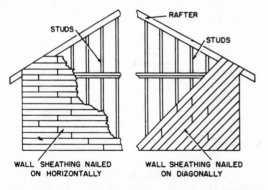

Figure 10-31.—Diagonal and horizontal wooden sheathing.

133.360

Plywood as a wall sheathing (fig. 10-32) is highly recommended by its size, weight, stability, and structural properties, plus the ease and rapidity of application. It adds considerably more strength to the frame than does diagonally applied wood boards. When plywood sheathing is used, corner bracing can be omitted. Large size panels effect a major saving in the time required for application and still provide a tight,

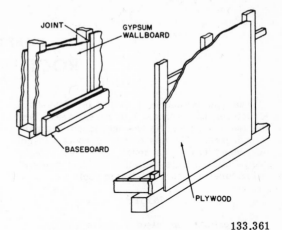

Figure 10-32.—Gypsum and plywood sheathing.

133.361

draft-free installation that contributes a high insulation value to the wall. Minimum thicknesses of plywood wall sheathing is 5/16-inch for 16-inch stud spacing and 3/8-inch for 24-inch stud spacing. The panels should be installed with the face grain parallel to the studs. However, a little more stiffness can be gained by installing them across the studs, but this requires more cutting and fitting. Use 6-penny common nails for 5/16-, 3/8-, and 1/2-inch panels and 8-penny common nails for 5/8- and 13/16-inch panels. Space the nails not more than 6 inches on center at the edges of the panels and not more than 12 inches on center elsewhere.

Fiberboard sheets are applied vertically or horizontally. The material is nailed on with 2-in. galvanized roofing nails. A nail should be started at least 3/8 in. away from the edge of a sheet.

Gypsum-board sheathing (fig. 10-32) is made by casting a gypsum core within a heavy water-resistant fibrous envelope. The long edges of the 4 by 8 foot boards are tongued and grooved. Each board is a full 1/2-inch thick. Its use is mostly with wood siding that can be nailed directly through the sheathing and into the studs. Gypsum sheathing is fireproof, water resistant, and windproof; does not warp nor absorb water: and does not require the use of building paper.

CHAPTER 11
ROOF FRAMING

The use of concrete walls in Navy-built structures has increased in recent years, and the use of frame walls has decreased to a certain degree. The use of frame roofs has not decreased nearly as much, however. Many Navy-built concrete-walled structures are still being covered with wood-frame roofs.

ROOFS

The primary object of a roof in any climate is to keep out the rain and the cold. The roof must be sloped so as to shed water. Where heavy snows cover the roofs for long periods of time, roofs must be constructed more rigidly to bear the extra weight. They must also be strong enough to withstand high winds. The most commonly used types of roof construction include the gable, the lean-to or shed, the hip, and the gable and valley.

The GABLE roof (fig. 11-1) has two roof slopes meeting at the center, or ridge, to form a gable. This form of roof is the one most commonly used by the Navy, since it is simple in design, economical to construct, and may be used on any type structure.

LEAN-TO or SHED ROOF (fig. 11-1), is a near-flat roof and is used where large buildings are framed under one roof, where hasty or temporary construction is needed, and where sheds or additions to buildings are erected. The pitch of the roof is in one direction only. The roof is held up by the walls or posts on four sides; one wall or the posts on one side are at a higher level than those on the opposite side.

The HIP roof (fig. 11-1) consists of four sides or slopes running toward the center of the building. Rafters at the corners extend diagonally to meet at the center, or ridge. Into these rafters, other rafters are framed.

GABLE and VALLEY roof is a combination of two gable roofs intersecting each other. The valley is that part where the two roofs meet, each roof slanting in a different direction. This type of roof is slightly complicated and requires much time and labor to construct.

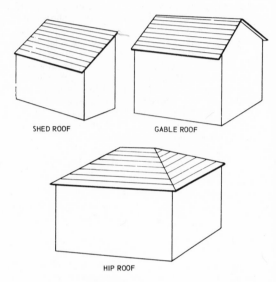

SHED ROOF   GABLE ROOF

HIP ROOF

45.449

Figure 11-1.—Most common types of pitched roofs.

TERMS USED IN ROOF CONSTRUCTION

The PITCH or "slope" of a roof is the angle which the roof surface makes with a horizontal plane. The surface may vary from absolutely flat to a steep slope. The usual way to express roof pitch is by means of numbers; for example, 8 and 12, 8 being the rise and 12 the run. On drawings, roof pitch is shown in figure 11-2.

The SPAN (part 1, fig. 11-3) of any roof is the shortest distance between the two opposite rafter seats. Seated in another way, it is the measurement between the outside plates, measured at right angles to the direction of the ridge of the building.

The TOTAL RISE (part 1, fig. 11-3) is the vertical distance from the plate to the top of the ridge.

The term "TOTAL RUN" (part 1, fig. 11-3) always refers to the level distance over which

318

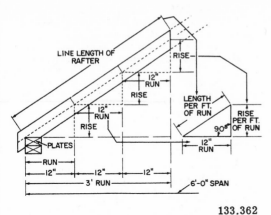

133.362

Figure 11-2.—Roof pitch.

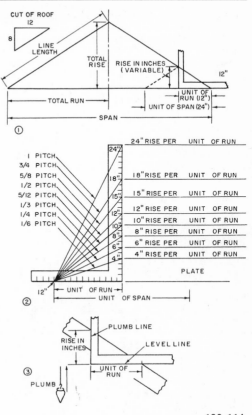

133.114

Figure 11-3.—Roof terms.

any rafter passes. For the ordinary rafter, this would be one-half the span distance.

The unit of measurement or unit of run, 1 foot or 12 inches is the same for the roof as for any other part of the building. By the use of this common unit of measurement, the framing square is employed in laying out large roofs (parts 1 and 2, fig. 11-3).

The rise in inches is the number of inches that a roof rises for every foot of run.

The cut of a roof is the rise in inches and the unit of run (12 inches) (part 2, fig. 11-3).

The "line length" as applied to roof framing is the hypotenuse of a triangle whose base is the total run and whose altitude is the total rise (part 1, fig. 11-3).

PLUMB and LEVEL LINES refer to the direction of a line on a rafter and not to any particular rafter cut. Any line that is vertical when the rafter is in its proper position is called a plumbline. Any line that is level when the rafter is in its proper position is called a level line (part 3, fig. 11-3).

RAFTERS

The pieces which make up the main body of the framework of all roofs are called rafters. They do for the roof what the joists do for the floor and what the studs do for the wall. Rafters are inclined members spaced from 16 to 48 inches apart which vary in size, depending on their length and the distance at which they are spaced. The tops of the inclined rafters are fastened in one of the various common ways

determined by the type of roof. The bottoms of the rafters rest on the plate member which provides a connecting link between wall and roof and is really a functional part of both. The structural relationship between rafters and wall is the same in all types of roofs. The rafters are not framed into the plate but are simply nailed to it, some being cut to fit the plate while others, in hasty construction, are merely laid on top of the plate and nailed in place. Rafters may extend a short distance beyond the wall to form the eaves and protect the sides of the building.

TERMS USED IN
CONNECTION WITH RAFTERS

Since rafters, with ridgeboards and plates, are the principal members of roof framing, it is important to understand the following terms that apply to them.

The COMMON rafters (part 1, fig. 11-4), extend from plate to ridgeboard at right angles to both.

HIP rafters (part 2, fig. 11-4), extend diagonally from the outside corners formed by perpendicular plates to the ridgeboard.

VALLEY rafters (part 3, fig. 11-4), extend from the plates to the ridgeboard along the lines where two roofs intersect.

JACK rafters never extend the full distance from plate to ridgeboard. Jack rafters are subdivided into the hip jacks (part 4, fig. 11-4), the lower ends of which rest on the plate and the upper ends against the hip rafter; valley

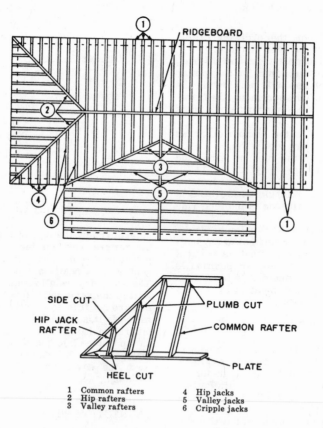

1	Common rafters	4	Hip jacks
2	Hip rafters	5	Valley jacks
3	Valley rafters	6	Cripple jacks

133.363

Figure 11-4.—Rafter terms.

jacks (part 5, fig. 11-4), the lower ends of which rest against the valley rafters and the upper ends against the ridgeboard; and cripple jacks (part 6, fig. 11-4), which are nailed between hip and valley rafters.

TOP or PLUMB CUT is the cut made at the end of the rafter to be placed against the ridge-board or, if the ridgeboard is omitted, against the opposite rafters.

SEAT, BOTTOM, or HEEL CUT is the cut made at the end of the rafter which is to rest on the plate.

SIDE or CHEEK CUT is a bevel cut on the side of a rafter to fit it against another frame member.

RAFTER LENGTH is the shortest distance between the outer edge of the plate and the center of the ridge line.

EAVE or TAIL is the portion of the rafter extending beyond the outer edge of the plate.

MEASURE LINE is an imaginary reference line laid out down the middle of the face of a rafter. If a portion of a roof is represented by a right triangle (fig. 11-5), the measure line will correspond to the hypotenuse, the rise to the leg, and the run to the base.

COMMON RAFTER LAYOUT

Rafters must be laid out and cut with slope, length, and overhang exactly right so that they will fit when placed in the position they are to occupy in the finished roof.

The Builder first determines the length of the rafter and the length of the piece of lumber from which the rafter may be cut. If he is working from a set of plans which includes a roof plan, the rafter lengths and the width of the building may be obtained from this plan. If no plans are available, the width of the building may be measured with a tape. To determine the rafter length, first find one-half of the distance between the outside plates. This distance is the horizontal distance which the rafter will cover. The amount of rise per foot has yet to be considered. If the building to be roofed is 20 feet wide, half the span will be 10 feet. For example, the rise per foot is to be 8 inches. To determine the approximate overall length of a rafter, measure on the steel carpenter square the distance between 8 on the tongue and 12 on the blade, because 8 is·the rise and 12 is the unit of run. This distance is 14 5/12 inches, and represents the line length of a rafter with a total run of 1 foot and a rise of 8 inches. Since

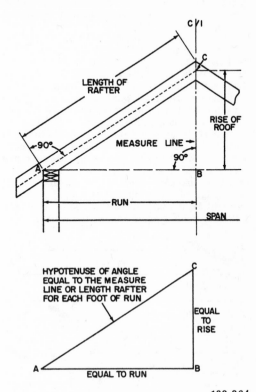

LENGTH OF RAFTER

RISE OF ROOF

MEASURE LINE

90°

RUN

SPAN

HYPOTENUSE OF ANGLE EQUAL TO THE MEASURE LINE OR LENGTH RAFTER FOR EACH FOOT OF RUN

EQUAL TO RISE

EQUAL TO RUN

133.364

Figure 11-5.—Measure line.

the run of the rafter is 10 feet, multiply 10 by the line length for 1 foot. The answer is 144 2/12 inches, or 12 feet and 1/6 inch. The amount of overhang, normally 1 foot, must be added if an overhang is to be used. This makes a total of 13 feet for the length of the rafter, but since 13 feet is an odd length for timber, a 14-foot timber is used.

After the length has been determined, the timber is laid on sawhorses, sometimes called "saw benches," with the crown or bow (if any) as the top side of the rafter. If possible, select a straight piece for the pattern rafter. If a straight piece is not available, have the crown toward the person laying off the rafter. Hold the square with the tongue in the right hand, the blade in the left, the heel away from the body, and place the square as near the upper end of the rafter as possible. In this case, the figure 8 on the tongue and 12 on the blade are placed along the edge of timber which is to be the top edge of the rafter as shown in view 1, figure 11-6. Mark along the tongue edge of the square, which will be the plumb cut at the ridge. Since the length of the rafter is known to be 12 feet and 1/6 inch, measure the distance from the top of the plumb cut and mark it on the timber. Hold the square in the same manner with the 8 mark on the tongue directly over the 12-foot and 1/6 inch mark. Mark along the tongue of the square to give the plumb cut for the seat (view 2, fig. 11-6). Next measure off, perpendicular to this mark, the length of overhang along the timber and make a plumb cut mark in the same manner, keeping the square on the same edge of the timber (view 3, fig. 11-6). This will be the tail cut of the rafter; often the tail cut is made square across the timber.

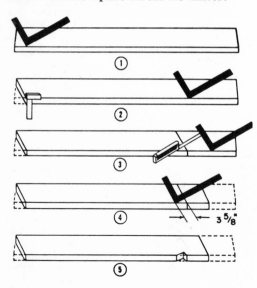

Figure 11-6.—Rafter layout—scale or measurement method.

133.365

The level cut or width of the seat is the width of the plate, measured perpendicular to the plumb cut, as shown in view 4, figure 11-6. Using the try square, square lines down on the sides from all level and plumb cut lines. Now the rafter is ready to be cut.

If a building is 20 feet 8 inches wide, the run of the rafter would be 10 feet 4 inches, or half the span. Instead of using the above method, the rafter length may be determined by "stepping it off" by successive steps with the square as shown in figure 11-7. Stake the same number of steps as there are feet in the run, which leaves 4 inches over a foot. This 4 inches is taken care of in the same manner as the full foot run; that is, with the square at the last step position, make a mark on the rafters at the 4-inch mark on the blade, then move the square along the rafter until the tongue rests at the 4-inch mark. With the square held for the same cut as before, make a mark along the tongue. This is the line length of the rafter. The seat-cut and hangover are made as described above. When laying off rafters by any method, be sure to recheck the work carefully. When two rafters have been cut, it is best to put them in place to see if they fit. Minor adjustments may be made at this time without serious damage or waste of material.

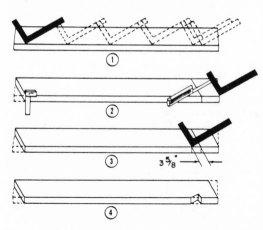

133.366

Figure 11-7.—Rafter layout—step-off method.

TABLE METHOD, USING RAFTER TABLE ON FRAMING SQUARE

The rafter table which is located on the blade gives both the line length of any pitch or rafter per foot of run and the line length of any hip or valley rafter per foot of run. The difference in length of the jack rafter spaced 16 or 24 inches (on center) is also shown in the table. Where the jack rafter, hip, or valley rafter requires side cuts, the cut is given in the table.

The table (fig. 11-8) appears on the face of the blade. It is used to determine the length of the common, valley, hip, and jack rafters, and the angles at which they must be cut to fit at the ridge and plate. To use the table, the Builder first must become familiar with it and know what each figure represents. The row of figures in the first line represents the length of common rafters per foot of run, as the title indicates at the lefthand end of the blade. Each set of figures under each inch division mark represents the length of rafter per foot of run with a rise corresponding to the number of inches over the number. For example, under the 16-inch mark appears the number 20.00 inches. This number equals the length of a rafter with a run of 12 inches and a rise of 16 inches, or, under the 13-inch mark appears the number 17.69 inches which is the rafter length for a 12-inch run and a 13-inch rise. The other five lines of figures in the table will not be discussed as they are seldom used.

out the rafters after the length has been determined was described above.

When the roof has an overhang the rafter is usually cut square to save time. When the roof has no overhang, the rafter cut is plumb, but no notch is cut in the rafter for a seat. The level cut is made long enough to extend across the plate and the wall sheathing. This type of rafter saves material, although little protection is given to the side wall.

BIRD'S MOUTH

A rafter with a projection has a notch in it called a BIRD'S MOUTH, as shown in figure 11-9. The plumb cut of the bird's mouth, which bears against the side of the rafter plate is called the HEEL cut; the level cut, which bears on the top of the rafter plate, is called the SEAT cut.

The size of the bird's mouth is usually stated in terms of the depth of the heel cut rather than in terms of the width of the seat cut. You lay out the bird's mouth in about the same way you lay out the seat on a rafter without a projection.

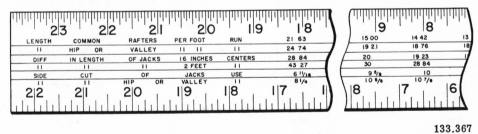

133.367

Figure 11-8.—Rafter table method.

To use the table for laying out rafters, the width of the building must first be known. Suppose the building is 20 feet 8 inches wide and the rise of the rafters is to be 8 inches per foot of run. The total run of the rafter will be 10 feet 4 inches. Look in the first line of figures, under the 8-inch mark appears the number 14.42, which is the length in inches of a rafter with a run of 1 foot and a rise of 8 inches. To find the line length of a rafter with a total run of 10 feet 4 inches, multiply 14.42 inches by 10 1/3 and divide by 12 so as to get the answer in feet. The 14.42 inches by 10 1/3 equals 149.007 inches, which is divided by 12 to equal 12 5/12 feet. Therefore 12 feet 5 inches is the line length of the rafter. The remaining procedure for laying

Measure off the depth of the heel on the heel plumb line, set the square as shown in figure 11-10, and draw the seat line along the blade. For the roof surface, ALL RAFTERS should be exact, therefore, the amount above the seat cut, rather than the bottom edge of the rafters, is the most important measurement. Suppose that on a hip roof, or an intersecting roof, the hips or valley rafters are 2 x 6 and the common rafters 2 x 4. The amount above the seat cut should be such as to adequately support the overhang of the roof, plus personnel working on the roof. The width of the seat cut is important as a bearing surface. The maximum width of the common rafter should not exceed the width of the plate.

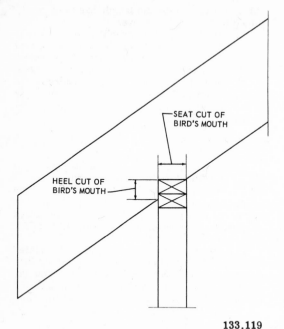

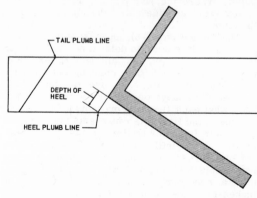

133.120

Figure 11-10.—Laying out a bird's mouth.

133.119

Figure 11-9.—Bird's mouth on a
rafter with projection.

HIP RAFTER LAYOUT

Most hip roofs are EQUAL-PITCH hip
roofs, in which the angle of slope on the roof
end or ends is the same as the angle of slope
on the sides. Unequal-pitch hip roofs do exist,
but they are quite rare, and they require special
layout methods. The UNIT LENGTH RAFTER
TABLE on the framing square applies only to
equal-pitch hip roofs.

In the following discussion of hip roof framing it will be assumed that in every case the
roof is an equal-pitch hip roof.

The length of a hip rafter, like the length of
a common rafter, is calculated on the basis of
bridge measure times the unit of run. Any of
the methods previously described for a common rafter may be used. Some of the basic
data for a hip rafter, however, are different.

Take a look at figure 11-11, which shows
part of a ROOF FRAMING DIAGRAM for an
EQUAL-PITCH hip roof. A roof framing diagram may be included among the working drawings; if it is not, you should lay one out for
yourself. Lay the building lines out to scale

first; you can find the span and the length of the
building on the working drawings. Then draw a
horizontal line along the center of the span.

In an equal-pitch hip roof framing diagram
the lines which indicate the hip rafters (FA,
GA, IB, and KB in fig. 11-11) forms 45° angles
with the building lines. Draw these lines in at
45°, as shown. The points where they meet the
center line are the THEORETICAL ends of the
ridge piece. The ridge-end common rafters
CA, DA, EA, HB, JB, and LB join the ridge
at the same points.

A line which indicates a rafter in the roof
framing diagram is equal in length (to scale, of
course) to the TOTAL RUN of the rafter it
represents. You can see from the diagram that
the total run of a hip rafter (represented by
lines FA, GA, IB, and KB) is the hypotenuse
of a right triangle with shorter sides each
equal to the total run of a common rafter. You
know the total run of a common rafter: it is
one-half the span, or one-half the width of the
building. Knowing this, you can find the total
run of a hip rafter by applying the Pythagorean
theorem.

Let us suppose, for example, that the span
of the building is 30 ft. Then one-half the span,
which is the same as the total run of a common
rafter, is 15 ft. By the Pythagorean theorem,
the total run of a hip rafter is the square root
of $(15^2 + 15^2)$, or 21.21 ft.

What is the total rise? Since a hip rafter
joins the ridge at the same height as a common
rafter, the total rise for a hip rafter is the
same as the total rise for a common rafter.

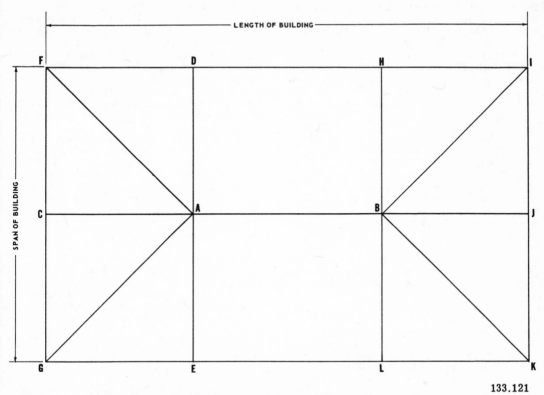

133.121

Figure 11-11.—Equal pitch hip roof framing diagram.

You know how to figure the total rise of a common rafter. Let us support that this roof has a unit run of 12 and a unit rise of 8. Since the total run of a common rafter in the roof is 15 ft, the total rise of a common rafter is the value of x in the proportional equation 12:8::15:x, or 10 ft.

Knowing the total run of the hip rafter (21.21 ft) and the total rise (10 ft), you can figure the line length by applying the Pythagorean theorem. The line length is the square root of $(21.21^2 + 10^2)$, or 23.44 ft, or about 23 ft 5 1/4 in.

To find the length of a hip rafter on the basis of bridge measure, you must first determine the bridge measure. As with a common rafter, the bridge measure of a hip rafter is the length of the hypotenuse of a triangle with shorter sides equal to the unit run and unit rise of the rafter. The unit rise of a hip rafter is always

the same as that of a common rafter, but THE UNIT RUN OF A HIP RAFTER IS DIFFERENT.

The unit run of a hip rafter in an equal-pitch hip roof is the hypotenuse of a right triangle with shorter sides each equal to the unit run of a common rafter. Since the unit run of a common rafter is 12, the unit run of a hip rafter is the square root of $(12^2 + 12^2)$, or 16.97.

If the unit run of the hip rafter is 16.97 and the unit rise (in this particular case) is 8, the unit length of the hip rafter must be the square root of $(16.97^2 + 8^2)$, or 18.76. This means that for every 16.07 units of run the rafter has 18.76 units of length. Since the total run of the rafter is 21.21 ft, the length of the rafter must be the value of x in the proportional equation 16.97:18.76::21.21:x, or 23.44 ft.

Like the unit length of a common rafter, the bridge measure of a hip rafter may be obtained

325

from the unit length rafter table on the framing square. If you turn back to figure 11-8, you will see that the second line in the table is headed "Length hip or valley rafters per foot run." This means "per foot run of A COMMON RAFTER IN THE SAME ROOF." Actually, the unit length given in the tables is the unit length for every 16.97 units of run OF THE HIP RAFTER ITSELF. If you run across to the unit length given under 8, you will find the same figure, 18.76 units, that you calculated above.

An easy way to calculate the length of an equal-pitch hip roof rafter is to multiply the bridge measure by the number of feet in the total run of a common rafter, which is the same as the number of feet in one-half of the span of the building. One-half of the span of the building in this case is 15 ft: the length of the hip rafter is therefore 18.76 x 15, or 281.40 in., which is 281.40/12, or 23.45 ft. Note that when you use this method you get a result in inches, which you must convert to feet. The slight difference of 0.01 ft between this result and the one previously obtained amounts to less than 1/8 in., and may be ignored.

You step off the length of an equal-pitch hip roof rafter just as you do the length of a common rafter, except for the fact that you set the square to a unit of run of 16.97 in. instead of to a unit of run of 12 in. Since 16.97 inches is the same as 16 in. and 15.52 sixteenths of an inch, setting the square to a unit of run of 17 in. is close enough for most practical purposes. Bear in mind that for any plumb cut line on an equal-pitch hip roof rafter you set the square to the unit rise of a common rafter and to a unit run of 17.

You step off the same number of times as there are feet in the total run of a common rafter in the same roof; only the size of each step is different. For every 12-in. step in a common rafter a hip rafter has a 17-in. step. In the roof on which we are working, the total run of a common rafter is exactly 15 ft; this means that you would step off the hip-rafter cut (17 in. and 8 in.) exactly 15 times.

Suppose, however, that there was an ODD UNIT in the common rafter total run. Assume, for example, that the total run of a common rafter is 15 ft 10 1/2 in. How would you make the odd fraction of a step on the hip rafter?

You remember that the unit run of a hip rafter is the hypotenuse of a right triangle with other sides each equal to the unit run of a common rafter. This being the case, the run of the

odd unit on the hip rafter must be the hypotenuse of a right triangle with other sides each equal to the odd unit of run of the common rafter, which in this case is 10 1/2 in. You can figure this by the Pythagorean theorem (square root of $(10.5^2 + 10.5^2)$), or you can set the square on a true edge to 10 1/2 in. on the tongue and 10 1/2 in. on the blade and measure the distance between the marks. It comes to 14.84 in., which rounded off to the nearest 1/16 in. equals 14 13/16 in.

To lay off the odd unit, set the tongue of the framing square to the plumb line for the last full step made and measure off 14 13/16 in. along the blade. Place the tongue of the square at the mark, set the square to the hip rafter plumb cut of 8 in. on the tongue and 17 in. on the blade, and draw the line length cut line.

Hip Rafter Shortening Allowance

As is the case with a common rafter, the line length of a hip rafter does not take into account the thickness of the ridge piece. The size of the ridge-end shortening allowance for a hip rafter depends upon the manner in which the ridge end of the hip rafter is joined to the other structural members. As shown in figure 11-12, the ridge end of the hip rafter may be framed against the ridge piece (view A, fig. 11-12) or against the ridge-end common rafters (view B, fig. 11-12). If the hip rafter is framed against the ridge piece, the shortening allowance is one-half of the 45° thickness of the ridge piece. The 45° thickness of stock is the length of a line laid at 45° across the thickness dimension of the stock. If the hip rafter is framed against the common rafters, the shortening allowance is one-half of the 45° thickness of a common rafter. To lay off the shortening allowance, set the tongue of the framing square to the line length ridge cut line, measure off the shortening allowance along the blade, set the square at the mark to the cut of the rafter (8 in. and 17 in.), and draw the actual ridge plumb cut line.

Hip Rafter Projection

A hip rafter projection, like a common rafter, is figured as a separate problem. The run of a hip rafter projection, however, is not the same as the run of a common rafter projection in the same roof. Figure 11-13 shows you why. The run of the hip rafter projection,

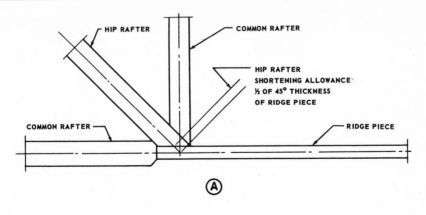

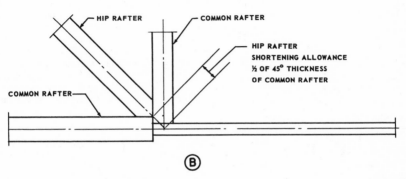

133.122

Figure 11-12.—Hip rafter shortening allowance.

as you can see, the hypotenuse of a right tri-angle with shorter sides each equal to the run of a common rafter projection. If the run of the common rafter overhang is 18 in., the run of the hip rafter is the square root of $(18^2 + 18^2)$, or 25.45 in. Since the rafter rises 8 units for every 17 units of run, the total rise of the projection is the value of x in the proportional equation 17:8::25.45:x, or 11.9 in. If the total run is 25.45 in. and the total rise 11.9 in., the length of the projection is the square root of $(25.45^2 + 11.9^2)$, or about 28 in.

Hip Rafter Side Cuts

Since a common rafter runs at 90° to the ridge, the ridge end of a common rafter is cut square, or at 90° to the lengthwise line of the

rafter. A hip rafter, however, joins the ridge, or the ridge ends of the common rafters, at an angle, and the ridge end of a hip rafter must therefore be cut to a corresponding angle, called a SIDE CUT. The angle of the side cut is more acute for a high unit rise than it is for a low one.

The angle of the side cut is laid out as shown in figure 11-14. Place the tongue of the framing square along the ridge cut line, as shown, and measure off one-half the thickness of the hip rafter along the blade. Shift the tongue to the mark, set the square to the cut of the rafter (17 in. and 8 in.), and draw the plumb line marked A in the figure. Then turn the rafter edge-up, draw an edge center line, and draw in the angle of the side cut as indicated in the lower view of figure 11-14. For a hip rafter

327

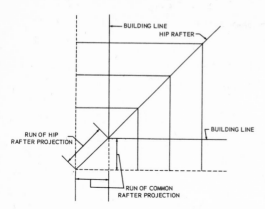

133.123

Figure 11-13.—Run of hip rafter projection.

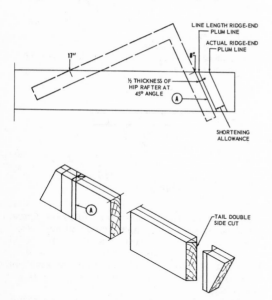

133.124

Figure 11-14.—Laying out hip rafter side cut.

which is to be framed against the ridge there will be only a single side cut, as indicated by the dotted line; for one which is to be framed against the ridge ends of the common rafters there will be a double side cut, as shown. The tail of the rafter must have a double side cut at the same angle, but in the reverse direction.

The angle of the side cut on a hip rafter may also be laid out by referring to the unit length rafter table on the framing square. If you turn back to figure 11-8, you will see that the bottom line in the table is headed "Side cut hip or valley use." If you follow this line over to the column headed by the figure 8 (for a unit rise of 8), you will find the figure 10 7/8. If you place the framing square face-up on the rafter edge, with the tongue on the ridge-end cut line, and set the square to a cut of 10 7/8 in. on the blade and 12 in. on the tongue, you can draw the correct side-cut angle along the tongue.

If the bird's mouth on a hip rafter had the same depth as the bird's mouth on a common rafter, the edges of the hip rafter would extend above the upper ends of the jack rafters as shown in figure 11-15. This can be corrected by either BACKING or DROPPING the hip rafter. Backing means to bevel the upper edge of the hip rafter. As shown in figure 11-15, the amount of backing is taken at the right angle to the roof surface, or the top edge of the hip rafter. Dropping means to deepen the bird's mouth so as to bring the top edge of the hip rafter down to the upper ends of the jacks. The amount of drop is taken on the heel plumb line.

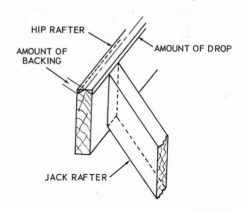

133.125

Figure 11-15.—Backing or dropping a hip rafter.

The amount of backing or drop required is calculated as shown in figure 11-16. Set the framing square to the cut of the rafter (8 in. and 17 in.) on the upper edge, and measure off one-half the thickness of the rafter from the edge along the blade. A line drawn through this

328

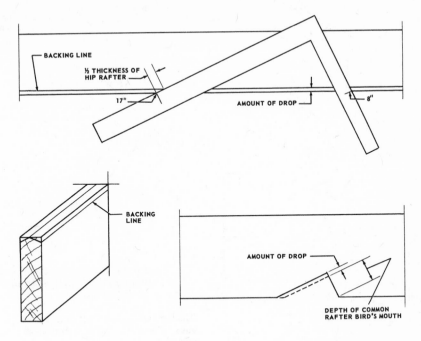

133.126

Figure 11-16.—Determining required amount of backing or drop.

mark, parallel to the edge, will indicate the bevel angle, as shown, if the rafter is to be backed. The perpendicular distance between the line and the edge of the rafter will be the amount of drop—meaning the amount that the depth of the hip rafter bird's mouth should exceed the depth of the common rafter bird's mouth.

VALLEY RAFTER LAYOUT

A valley rafter follows the line of intersection between a main roof surface and a gable-roof addition or a gable-roof dormer surface. Most roofs which contain valley rafters are EQUAL-PITCH roofs, in which the pitch of the addition or dormer roof is the same as the pitch of the main roof. There are UNEQUAL-PITCH valley-rafter roofs, but they are quite rare, and they require special framing methods. In the discussion of valley rafter layout it will be assumed that the roof is in every case an equal pitch roof, in which the unit of run and unit of rise of an addition or dormer common rafter is the same as the unit of run and unit of rise of a main roof common rafter. In an equal-pitch roof the valley rafters always run at 45° to the building lines and the ridge pieces.

Figure 11-17 shows an EQUAL-SPAN framing situation, in which the span of the addition is the same as the span of the main roof. Since the pitch of the addition roof is the same as the pitch of the main roof, equal spans bring the ridge pieces to equal heights.

If you look at the roof framing diagram in the figure, you will see that the total run of a valley rafter (indicated by AB and AD in the diagram) is the hypotenuse of a right triangle with shorter sides equal to the total run of a common rafter in the main roof. The unit run of a valley rafter is therefore 16.97, the same as the unit run for a hip rafter. It follows that figuring the length of an equal-span valley rafter is the same as figuring the length of an equal-pitch hip roof hip rafter.

329

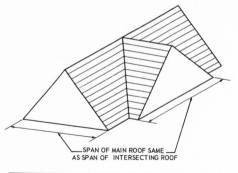

SPAN OF MAIN ROOF SAME
AS SPAN OF INTERSECTING ROOF

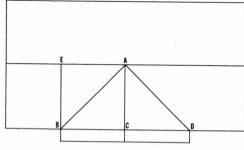

Figure 11-17.—Equal span main roof and
intersection roof.

133.127

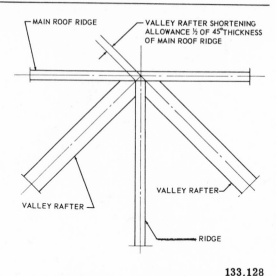

133.128

Figure 11-18.—Ridge-end shortening
allowance for equal span intersection valley rafter.

A valley rafter, however, does not require backing or dropping. The projection, if any, is figured just as it is for a hip rafter. Side cuts are laid out as they are for a hip rafter; the valley-rafter tail has a double side cut, like the hip-rafter tail, but in the reverse direction, since the tail cut on a valley rafter must form an inside rather than an outside corner. As indicated in figure 11-18 the ridge-end shortening allowance in this framing situation amounts to one-half of the 45° thickness of the ridge.

Figure 11-19 shows a framing situation in which the span of the addition is shorter than the span of the main roof. Since the pitch of the addition roof is the same as the pitch of the main roof, the shorter span of the addition brings the addition ridge down to a lower level than that of the main roof ridge.

There are two ways of framing an intersection of this type. By the method shown in figure 11-19, a full-length valley rafter (AD in the figure) is framed between the rafter plate and the ridge piece, and a shorter valley rafter

(CB in the figure) is then framed to the longer one. If you study the framing diagram you will see that the total run of the longer valley rafter is the hypotenuse of a right triangle with shorter sides each equal to the total run of a common rafter IN THE MAIN ROOF. The total run of the shorter valley rafter, on the other hand, is the hypotenuse of a right triangle with shorter sides each equal to the total run of a common rafter IN THE ADDITION. The total run of a common rafter in the main roof is equal to one-half the span of the main roof; the total run of a common rafter in the addition is equal to one-half the span OF THE ADDITION.

Knowing the total run of a valley rafter (or of any rafter, for that matter), you can always find the line length by applying the bridge measure times the total run. Suppose, for example, that the span of the addition in figure 11-19 is 30 ft, and that the unit rise of a common rafter in the addition is 9. The total run of the shorter valley rafter is the square root of $(15^2 + 15^2)$, or 21.21 ft. If you refer back to the unit length rafter table in figure 11-8, you will see that the bridge measure for a valley rafter in a roof with a common-rafter unit rise of 9 is 19.21. Since the unit run of a valley rafter is 16.97 and the total run of this rafter is 21.21 ft, the line length must be

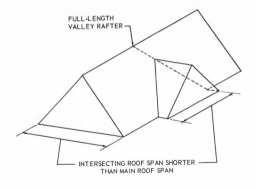

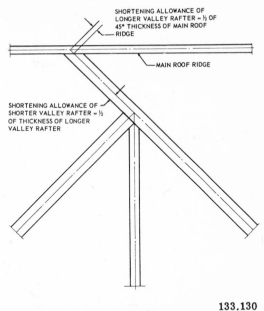

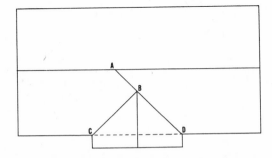

133.130

Figure 11-20.—Long and short valley rafter
shortening allowances.

133.129

Figure 11-19.—Equal-pitch but unequal
span framing situation.

the value of x in the proportional equation
16.97:19.21::21.21:x, or 24.01 ft.

An easier way to find the length of a valley
rafter is to simply multiply the bridge measure by the number of feet in one-half the span
OF THE ROOF TO WHICH THE VALLEY
RAFTER BELONGS. The length of the longer
valley rafter in figure 11-19, for example,
would be 19.21 times one-half the span OF
THE MAIN ROOF. The length of the shorter
valley rafter is 19.21 times one-half the span
OF THE ADDITION. Since one-half the span
of the addition is 15 ft, the length of the shorter
valley rafter is 15 x 19.21, or 288.15 in., which
is 288.15/12, or 24.01 ft. Note again that when
you use this method you get a result in inches,
which you must change to feet.

Figure 11-20 shows the long and short valley rafter shortening allowances. Note that the
long valley rafter has a single side cut for
framing to the main roof ridge piece, while the

short valley rafter is cut square for framing
to the addition ridge.

Figure 11-21 shows another method of framing an equal-pitch unequal-span addition. In
this method the inboard end of the addition
ridge is nailed to a piece which hangs from the
main roof ridge. As shown in the framing diagram, this method calls for two short valley
rafters, each of which extends from the rafter
plate to the addition ridge. The framing diagram shows that the total run of each of these
valley rafters is the hypotenuse of a right triangle with shorter sides, each equal to the total
run of a common rafter IN THE ADDITION.

As indicated in figure 11-22, the shortening
allowance of each of the short valley rafters is
one-half of the 45° thickness of the addition
ridge Each rafter is framed to the addition
ridge with a single side cut.

Figure 11-23 shows a method of framing a
gable dormer without side walls. The dormer
ridge is framed to a header set between a couple
of doubled main-roof common rafters. The
valley rafters are framed between this header
and a lower header. As indicated in the framing diagram, the total run of a valley rafter is

331

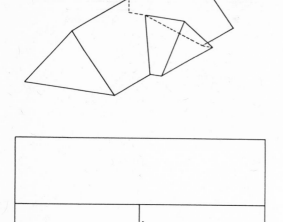

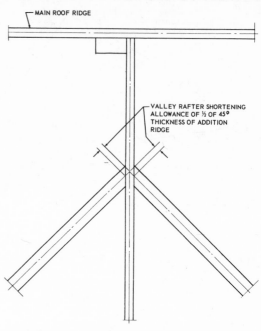

MAIN ROOF RIDGE

VALLEY RAFTER SHORTENING
ALLOWANCE OF ½ OF 45°
THICKNESS OF ADDITION
RIDGE

133.131

Figure 11-21.—Another method of framing
equal-pitch unequal span intersection.

133.132

Figure 11-22.—Shortening allowance of valley
rafters in suspended ridge method of intersection roof framing.

the hypotenuse of a right triangle with shorter
sides each equal to the total run of a common
rafter IN THE DORMER.

Figure 11-24 shows the arrangement and
names of framing members in this type of
dormer framing.

Figure 11-24 also shows that the upper
edges of the headers must be beveled to the cut
of the main roof. Figure 11-25 shows that in
this method of framing the shortening allowance for the upper end of a valley rafter is
one-half of the 45° thickness of the inside member in the upper doubled header. There is also
a shortening allowance for the lower end, consisting of one-half of the 45° thickness of the
inside member of the doubled common rafter.
The figure also shows that each valley rafter
has a double side cut at the upper end and a
double side cut at the lower end.

Figure 11-26 shows a method of framing a
gable dormer with side walls. As indicated in
the framing diagram, the total run of a valley

rafter is again the hypotenuse of a right triangle with shorter sides each equal to the run
of a common rafter IN THE DORMER. You
figure the lengths of the dormer corner posts
and side studs just as you do the lengths of
gable-end studs, and you lay off the lower-end
cut-off angle by setting the square to the cut
of the main roof.

Figure 11-27 shows the valley rafter shortening allowances for this method of framing a
dormer with side walls.

JACK RAFTER LAYOUT

A jack rafter is a part of a common rafter,
shortened for framing to a hip rafter, a valley
rafter, or both. This means that in an equal-
pitch framing situation the unit rise of a jack
rafter is always the same as the unit rise of a
common rafter.

A HIP JACK rafter is one which extends
from a hip rafter to a rafter plate. A VALLEY

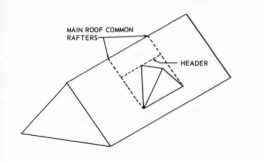

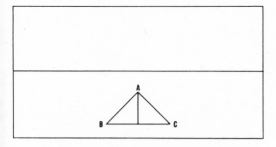

133.133

Figure 11-23.—Method of framing dormer
without sidewalls.

JACK rafter is one which extends from a valley
rafter to a ridge. A CRIPPLE JACK rafter is
one which does not contact either a rafter plate
or a ridge. A VALLEY CRIPPLE JACK is
one which extends between two valley rafters
in the long-and-short-valley-rafter method of
addition framing. A HIP-VALLEY CRIPPLE
JACK is one which extends from a hip rafter
to a valley rafter. All types of jacks except
cripple jacks are shown in figure 11-28. A
valley cripple jack and a couple of hip-valley
cripple jacks are shown in figure 11-29.

Lengths of Hip Jack Rafters

Figure 11-30 shows a roof framing diagram
for a series of hip jack rafters. The jacks are
always on the same spacing O.C. as the common rafters. Suppose that the spacing in this
instance is 16 in O.C. You can see that the
total run of the shortest jack is the hypotenuse
of a right triangle with shorter sides each
16 in. long. The total run of the shortest jack
is therefore the square root of $(16^2 + 16^2)$, or
22.62 in.

Suppose that a common rafter in this roof
has a unit rise of 8. The jacks, as you know,
have the same unit rise as a common rafter.
The unit length of a jack in this roof, then, is
the square root of $(12^2 + 8^2)$, or 14.42. This
means that a jack is 14.42 units long or every
12 units of run. The length of the shortest hip
jack in this roof is therefore the value of x in
the proportional equation 12:14.42::16:x, or
19.23 in.

This is always the length of the shortest hip
jack when the jacks are spaced 16 in O.C. and
the common rafter in the roof has a unit rise
of 8. It is also the COMMON DIFFERENCE
OF JACKS, meaning that the next hip jack will
be 2(19.23 in.) long, the next 3(19.23 in.) long,
and so on.

The common difference for hip jacks spaced
16 in. O.C., and also for hip jacks spaced 24 in.
O.C., is given in the unit length rafter table on
the framing square for unit rises ranging from
2 to 18 inclusive. Turn back to figure 11-8,
which shows a segment of the unit length rafter
table. Note the third line in the table, which
reads "Diff. in length of jacks 16 inches centers." If you follow this line over to the figure
under 8 (for a unit rise of 8), you will find the
same unit length (19.23 in.) that you worked out
above.

The best way to figure the length of a valley
jack or a cripple jack is to apply the bridge
measure to the total run. The bridge measure
of any jack is the same as the bridge measure
of a common rafter having the same unit of
rise as the jack. Suppose, for example, that
the jack has a unit rise of 8. In figure 11-8,
look along the line on the unit length rafter
tables headed "Length common rafters per foot
run" for the figure in the column under 8, and
you will find a unit length of 14.42. You should
know by this time how to apply this to the total
run of a jack to get the line length.

The best way to figure the total runs of
valley jacks and cripple jacks is to lay out a
framing diagram and study it to determine what
these runs must be. Figure 11-31 shows part
of a framing diagram for a main hip roof with
a long-and-short-valley-rafter gable addition.
By studying the diagram you can figure the
total runs of the valley jacks and cripple jacks
as follows:

The run of valley jack No. 1 is obviously the
same as the run of hip jack No. 8, which is the
run of the shortest hip jack. The length of

333

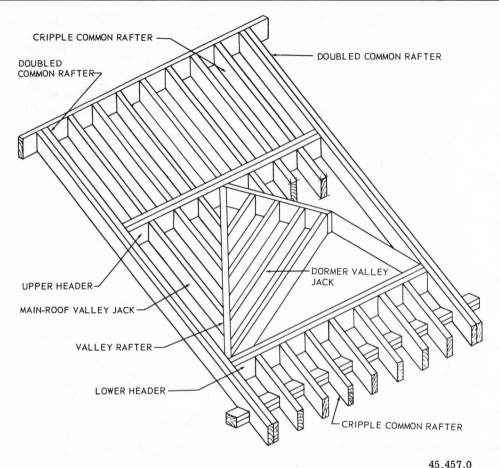

45.457.0

Figure 11-24.—Arrangement and names of framing members for
dormer without sidewall.

valley jack No. 1 is therefore equal to the common difference of jacks.

The run of valley jack No. 2 is the same as the run of hip jack No. 7, and the length is therefore twice the common difference of jacks.

The run of valley jack No. 3 is the same as the run of hip jack No. 6, and the length is therefore three times the common difference of jacks.

The run of hip-valley cripple No. 4, and also of hip-valley cripple No. 5, is the same as the run of valley jack No. 3.

The run of valley jack No. 9, and also of valley jack No. 10, is equal to the spacing of jacks O.C. Therefore, the length of one of these jacks is equal to the common difference of jacks.

The run of valley jacks Nos. 11 and 12 is twice the run of valley jacks Nos. 9 and 10, and the length of one of these jacks is therefore twice the common difference of jacks.

The run of valley cripple No. 13 is twice the spacing of jacks O.C., and the length is therefore twice the common difference of jacks.

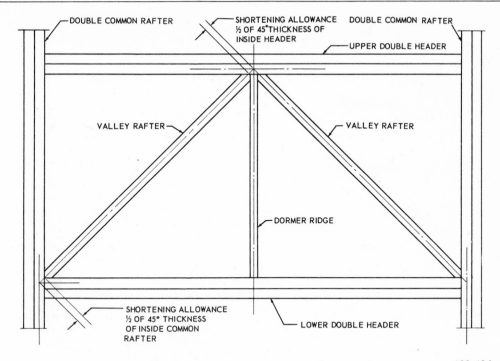

133.134

Figure 11-25.—Valley rafter shortening allowances for
dormer without sidewall.

The run of valley cripple No. 14 is twice the run of valley cripple No. 13, and the length is therefore 4 times the common difference of jacks.

Jack Rafter Shortening Allowances

A hip jack rafter has a shortening allowance at the upper end consisting of one-half of the 45° thickness of the hip rafter. A valley jack rafter has a shortening allowance at the upper end, consisting of one-half of the thickness of the ridge, and another at the lower end, consisting of one-half of the 45° thickness of the valley rafter. A hip-valley cripple has a shortening allowance at the upper end, consisting of one-half of the 45° thickness of the hip rafter, and another at the lower end, consisting of one-half of the 45° thickness of the valley rafter. A valley cripple has a shortening allowance at the upper end, consisting of one-half of the 45° thickness of the long valley rafter, and another at the lower end, consisting of one-half the 45° thickness of the short valley rafter.

Jack Rafter Side Cuts

The side cut on a jack rafter can be laid out by the method illustrated in figure 11-14 for laying out the side cut on a hip rafter. Another method is to use the fifth line of the unit length rafter table, which is headed "Side cut of jacks use" (fig. 11-8). If you follow that line over to the figure under 8 (for a unit rise of 8), you will see that the figure given is 10. To lay out the side cut on a jack, set the square face-up on the edge of the rafter to 12 in. on the tongue and 10 in. on the blade, and draw the side-cut line along the tongue.

Jack Rafter Bird's Mouth and Projection

A jack rafter is a shortened common rafter; consequently, the bird's mouth and projection

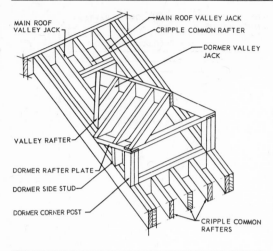

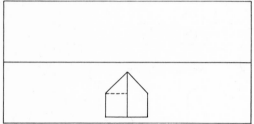

45.458

Figure 11-26.—Method of framing gable
dormer with sidewalls.

on a jack rafter are laid out just as they are
on a common rafter.

RIDGE LAYOUT

Laying out the ridge for a gable roof presents no particular problem, since the line
length of the ridge is equal to the length of the
building. The actual length would include any
overhang. For a hip main roof, however, the
ridge layout requires a certain amount of
calculation.

As previously mentioned, in an equal-pitch
hip roof the line length of the ridge amounts
to the length of the building minus twice the
total run of a main roof common rafter. The
ACTUAL length, however, depends upon the

way in which the hip rafters are framed to the
ridge.

As indicated in figure 11-32, the line length
ends of the ridge are at the points where the
ridge center line and the hip rafter center lines
cross. In figure 11-32 the hip rafter is framed
against the ridge; in this method of framing the
actual length of the ridge exceeds the line
length, at each end, by one-half of the thickness
of the ridge, plus one-half of the 45° thickness
of the hip rafter. In figure 11-32 the hip rafter
is framed between the common rafters; in this
method of framing the actual length of the ridge
exceeds the line length, at each end, by one-
half of the thickness of a common rafter.

Figure 11-33 shows that the length of the
ridge for an equal-span addition is equal to the
length of the addition rafter plate, plus one-half
the span of the building, minus the shortening
allowance at the main roof ridge; the shortening allowance amounts to one-half of the thickness of the main roof ridge. Figure 11-33
shows that the length of the ridge for an
unequal-span addition varies with the method of
framing the ridge. If the addition ridge is suspended from the main roof ridge, the length is
equal to the length of the addition rafter plate
plus one-half the span of the building. If the
addition ridge is framed by the long-and-short
valley rafter method, the length is equal to the
length of the addition rafter plate, plus one-half
of the span of the addition, minus a shortening
allowance consisting of one-half of the 45°
thickness of the long valley rafter. If the addition ridge is framed to a double header set between a couple of double main roof common
rafters, the length of the ridge is equal to the
length of the addition side-wall rafter plate,
plus one-half the span of the addition, minus a
shortening allowance consisting of one-half the
thickness of the inside member of the double
header.

Figure 11-34 shows that the length of the
ridge on a dormer without side walls is equal
to one-half of the span of the dormer, less a
shortening allowance consisting of one-half the
thickness of the inside member of the upper
double header. Figure 11-34 shows that the
length of the ridge on a dormer with side walls
amounts to the length of the dormer rafter
plate, plus one-half the span of the dormer,
minus a shortening allowance consisting of
one-half the thickness of the inside member of
the upper double header.

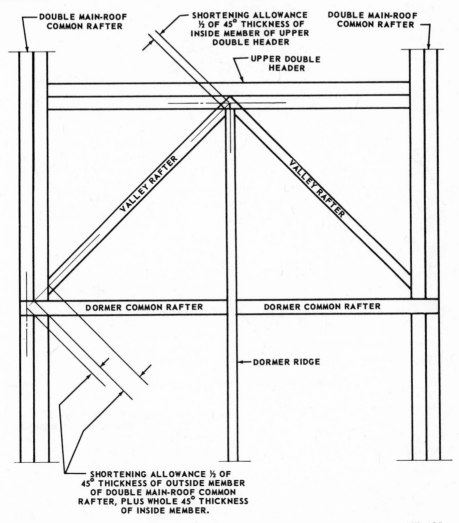

Figure 11-27.—Valley rafter shortening allowances for dormer with sidewall.

133.135

SHED ROOF FRAMING

As previously mentioned, a SHED or SINGLE-PITCH roof is essentially one-half of a gable or double-pitch roof. Like the full-length rafters in a gable roof, the full-length rafters in a shed roof are COMMON rafters. Note, however, that as shown in figure 11-35, the total run of a shed roof common rafter is equal to the span of the building MINUS THE WIDTH OF THE RAFTER PLATE ON THE HIGHER RAFTER-END WALL. Note also, that the run of the projection on the higher wall is measured from the INNER EDGE of the rafter plate. To this must be added the width of the plate and the length of the overhang at the top. Shed-roof common rafters are laid out like gable-roof common rafters. A shed-roof common rafter

337

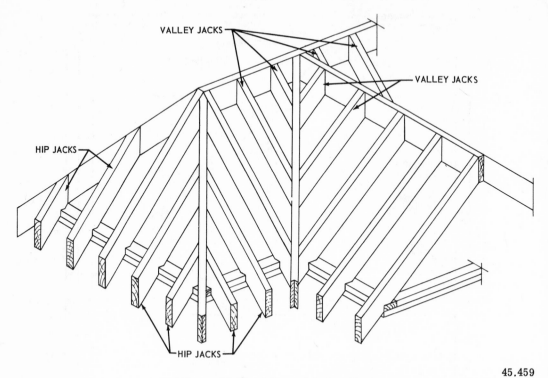

45.459

Figure 11-28.—Types of jack rafters.

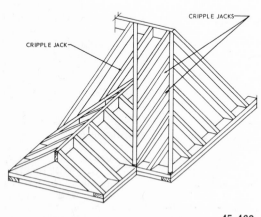

45.460

Figure 11-29.—Valley cripple jack and
hip-valley cripple jacks.

has two bird's mouths, but they are laid out just like the bird's mouth on a gable-roof common rafter.

Figure 11-35 also shows that the height of the higher rafter-end wall must exceed the height of the lower by an amount equal to the total rise of a common rafter.

Figure 11-36 shows a method of framing a shed dormer. There are 3 layout problems to be solved here, as follows: (1) determining the total run of a dormer rafter, (2) determining the angle of cut on the inboard ends of the dormer rafters, and (3) determining the lengths of the dormer side-wall studs.

To determine the total run of a dormer rafter you divide the height of the dormer end wall, in inches, by the difference between the unit rise of the dormer roof and the unit rise of the main roof. Take the dormer shown in figure 11-37, for example. The height of the

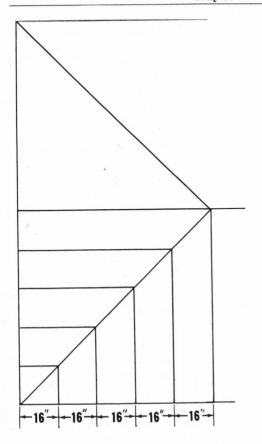

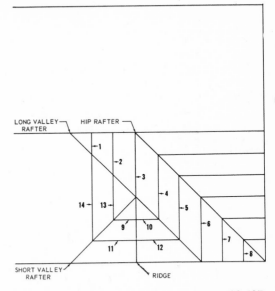

133.137

Figure 11-31.—Jack rafter framing diagram.

133.136

Figure 11-30.—Hip jack framing diagram.

dormer end-wall is 9 ft, or 108 in. The unit rise of the main roof is 8; the unit rise of the dormer roof is 2 1/2; the difference between them is 5 1/2. The total run of a dormer rafter is therefore 108 divided by 5 1/2, or 19.63 ft. Knowing the total run and the unit rise, you can figure the length of a dormer rafter by any of the methods already described.

As indicated in figure 11-37 the inboard ends of the dormer rafters must be cut to fit the slope of the main roof. To get the angle of this cut, set the square on the rafter to the cut of the main roof, as shown in the third view of figure 11-37; measure off the unit size of the dormer roof from the heel of the square along the tongue as indicated; make a mark at this point; and draw the cut-off line through this mark from the 12-in. mark.

You figure the lengths of the side-wall studs on a shed dormer as follows: in the roof shown in figure 11-37, a dormer rafter raises 2 1/2 units for every 12 units of run, and a main roof common rafter rises 8 units for every 12 units of run. If the studs were spaced 12 in. O.C., the length of the shortest stud (which is also the COMMON DIFFERENCE of studs) would be the difference between 8 and 2 1/2 in., or 5 1/2 in. This being the case, if the stud spacing is 16 in., the length of the shortest stud is the value of x in the proportional equation 12:5 1/2::16:x, or 7 5/16 in. The shortest stud, then, will be 7 5/16 in. long; the next stud will be 2(7 5/16)in. long, and so on. To get the lower-end cut-off angle for studs you set the square on the stud to the cut of the main roof; to get the upper-end cut-off angle you set it to the cut of the dormer roof.

RAFTER LOCATION LAYOUT

Rafter locations are laid out on plates, ridge and other rafters with the same lines and X's used to lay out stud and joist locations.

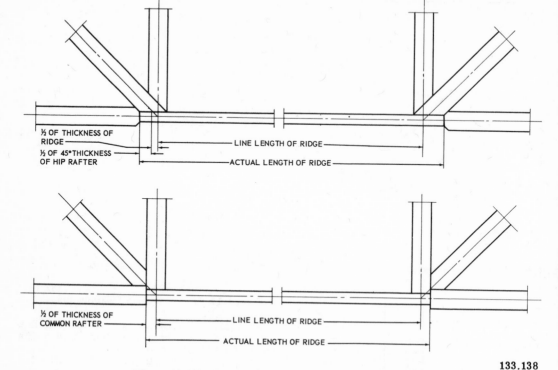

½ OF THICKNESS OF RIDGE

½ OF 45° THICKNESS OF HIP RAFTER

LINE LENGTH OF RIDGE

ACTUAL LENGTH OF RIDGE

½ OF THICKNESS OF COMMON RAFTER

LINE LENGTH OF RIDGE

ACTUAL LENGTH OF RIDGE

133.138

Figure 11-32.—Line and actual lengths of hip roof ridge.

For a gable roof the rafter locations are laid out on the rafter plates first, and the locations are then transferred to the ridge by matching the ridge against a rafter plate.

The rafter-plate locations of the ridge-end common rafters in an equal-pitch hip roof measure one-half of the span (or the run of a main-roof common rafter) away from the building corners. These locations, plus the rafter-plate locations of the rafters lying between the ridge-end common rafters, can be transferred to the ridge by matching the ridge against the rafter plates.

The locations of addition ridge and valley rafters can be determined as indicated in figure 11-38. In an equal-span situation (illustrated in parts 1 and 2, fig. 11-38) the valley rafter locations on the main roof ridge lie alongside the addition ridge location. In part 1 of figure 11-38 the distance between the end of the main roof ridge and the addition ridge location is equal to distance A plus distance B, distance B being one-half the span of the addition. In part 2 of figure 11-38 the distance between the line length end of the main roof ridge and the addition ridge location is the same as distance A. In both cases the line length of the addition ridge is equal to one-half the span of the addition plus the length of the addition side-wall rafter plate.

Part 3 of figure 11-38 shows an unequal-span situation. If framing is by the long-and-short valley rafter method, the distance from the end of the main roof ridge to the upper end of the longer valley rafter is equal to distance A plus distance B, distance B being one-half of the span of the main roof. The location of the inboard end of the shorter valley rafter on the longer valley rafter can be determined as follows: first calculate the unit length of the longer valley rafter, or obtain it from the unit-length rafter tables. Let us suppose that

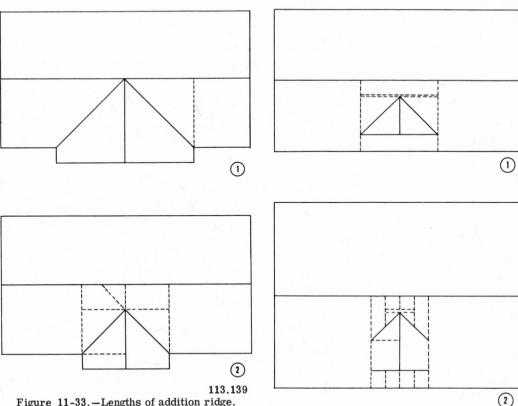

113.139

Figure 11-33.—Lengths of addition ridge.

133.140

Figure 11-34.—Lengths of dormer ridge.

the common-rafter unit rise is 8; in that case the unit length of a valley rafter is 18.76.

The total run of the longer valley rafter between the point where the shorter rafter ties in and the rafter plate is the hypotenuse of a right triangle with other sides each equal to one-half of the span of the addition. Suppose the addition is 20 ft wide; then the total run in question is the square root of $(10^2 + 10^2)$, or 14.14 ft.

You know that the valley rafter is 18.76 units long for every 16.97 units of run. The length of rafter for 14.14 ft of run must therefore be the value of x in the proportional equation 16.97:18.76::14.14:x, or 15.63 ft. The location mark for the inboard end of the shorter valley rafter on the longer valley rafter, then, will be 15.63 ft, or 15 ft 7 9/16 in., from the heel plumb cut line on the longer valley rafter. The length of the addition ridge will be equal

to one-half the span of the addition, plus the length of the addition side-wall rafter plate, minus a shortening allowance equal to one-half of the 45° thickness of the longer valley rafter.

If framing is by the suspended-ridge method, the distance between the suspension point on the main roof ridge and the end of the main roof ridge is equal to distance A plus distance C; distance C is one-half of the span of the addition. The distance between the point where the inboard ends of the valley rafters (both short in this method of framing) tie into the addition ridge and the out-board end of the ridge is equal to one-half the span of the addition plus the length of the addition side-wall rafter plate. The length of the addition ridge is equal to one-half of the span of the main roof

341

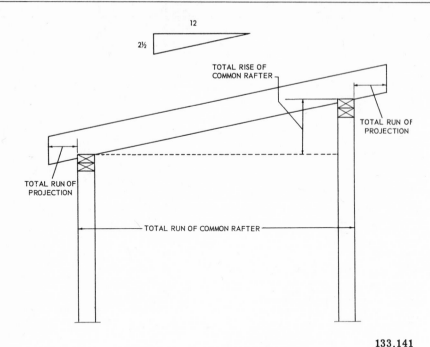

Figure 11-35.—Shed roof framing.

133.141

133.142

Figure 11-36.—Method of framing a
shed dormer.

plus the length of the addition side wall rafter
plate.

COLLAR TIE

Gable or double-pitch roof rafters are often
reinforced by horizontal members called collar
ties (fig. 11-39). In a finished attic the ties
may also function as ceiling joists.

To find the line length of a collar tie divide
the amount of drop of the tie in inches by the
unit of rise of the common rafter. This will
equal one-half the length of the tie in feet.
Double the result for actual length. The formula is: Drop in inches x 2 over unit of rise,
equals the length in feet.

The length of the collar tie depends on
whether the drop is measured to the top edge
or bottom edge of the collar tie (fig. 11-39).
The tie must fit the slope of the roof. To obtain this angle, use the framing square. Hold

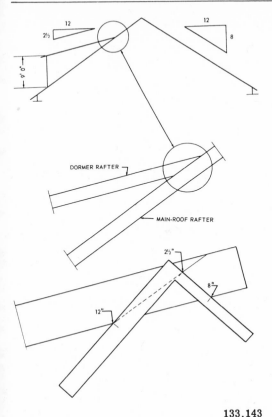

133.143

Figure 11-37.—Shed dormer framing
calculations.

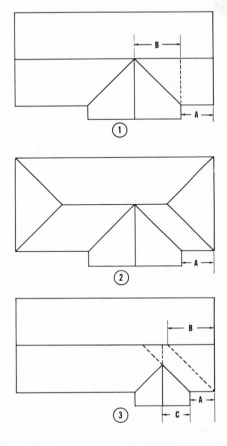

133.144

Figure 11-38.—Intersection ridge and
valley rafter location layout.

unit of run and unit of rise of the common
rafter. Mark and cut on unit of run side (fig.
11-40).

ROOF TRUSSES

Much modern roof framing is done with
ROOF TRUSSES like the one shown in figure
11-41. The principal parts of a truss are the
UPPER CHORD (consisting of the rafters), the
LOWER CHORD (corresponding to a ceiling
joist), and various diagonal and/or vertical
bracing and connecting members which are
known collectively as the WEB MEMBERS.

The truss shown in figure 11-41 is joined
at the corners with plywood GUSSETS. Other
methods of corner joining are by metal gussets
or by various types of notched joints, reinforced

with bolts. Construction information on trusses
is usually given in detail drawings.

ROOF FRAMING ERECTION

Roof framing should be done from a scaffold
with planking not less than 4 ft below the level
of the main roof ridge. The usual type of roof
scaffold consists of diagonally-braced 2-legged
horses, spaced about 10 ft apart and extending
the full length of the ridge.

If the building has an addition, as much as
possible of the main roof is framed before the
addition framing is started. Cripples and jack

343

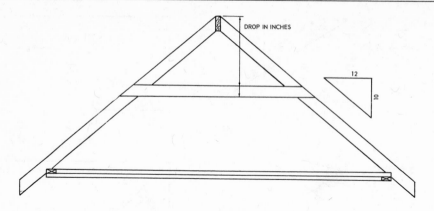

133.145

Figure 11-39.—Calculation for a collar tie.

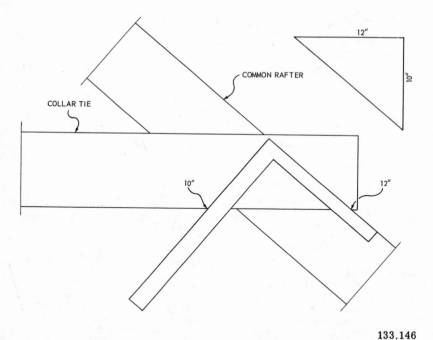

133.146

Figure 11-40.—Laying out end cut on a collar tie.

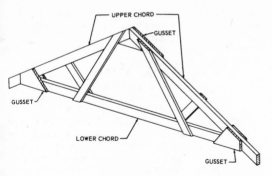

UPPER CHORD
GUSSET
GUSSET
LOWER CHORD
GUSSET

45.438

Figure 11-41.—Typical lightweight roof truss.

rafters are usually left out until after the headers, hip rafters, valley rafters, and ridges to which they will be framed have been installed.

For a gable roof the two pairs of gable-end rafters and the ridge are usually erected first. Two men, one at each end of the scaffold, hold the ridge in position, while a third man sets the gable-end rafters in place and toenails them at the rafter plate with 8-penny nails, one to each side of a rafter. Each man on the scaffold then end-nails the ridge to one of his rafters with two 10-penny nails, driven through the ridge into the end of the rafter; and toenails the other rafter to the ridge and to the first rafter with two 10-penny nails, one on each side of the rafter. Temporary braces like those for a wall should be set up at the ridge ends to hold the rafters approximately plumb, after which the rafters between the end-rafters should be erected. The braces should then be released, and the pair of rafters at one end should be plumbed with a plumb line, fastened to a stick extended from the end of the ridge. The braces should then be reset, and they should be left in place until enough sheathing has been installed to hold the rafters plumb. Collar ties, if any, are nailed to common rafters with 8-penny nails, 2 to each end of a tie. Ceiling-joist ends are nailed to adjacent rafters with 10-penny nails, 2 to each end.

On a hip roof the ridge-end common rafters and ridges are erected first, in about the same manner as for a gable roof, and the intermediate common rafters are then filled in. After that, the ridge-end common rafters extending

from the ridge ends to the mid-points on the end walls are erected. The hip rafters and hip jacks are installed next. The common rafters in a hip roof do not require plumbing; if the hip rafters are correctly cut, installing the hip rafters will bring the common rafters plumb. Hip rafters are toenailed to plate corners with 16-penny nails, 2 to each side. Hip jacks are toenailed to hip rafters with 10-penny nails, 3 to each jack.

For an addition or dormer the valley rafters are usually erected first. Valley rafters are toenailed to plates with 16-penny nails, 2 to each side. and to ridge pieces and headers with three 10-penny nails. Ridges and ridge-end common rafters are erected next, other addition common rafters next, and valley and cripple jacks last. A valley jack should be held in position for nailing as shown in figure 11-42. When properly nailed, the end of a straightedge laid along the top edge of the jack should contact the center line of the valley rafter as shown.

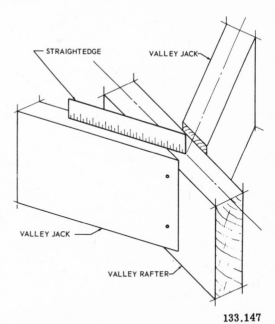

STRAIGHTEDGE   VALLEY JACK

VALLEY JACK

VALLEY RAFTER

133.147

Figure 11-42.—Correct position for nailing a valley jack rafter.

ROOF SHEATHING

The lower layer of roof covering is called the ROOF SHEATHING; the upper layer is called the ROOF COVERING or the ROOFING. The roof sheathing, like the wall sheathing and the subflooring, is a structural element and therefore a part of the framing. The roof covering or roofing is a part of the exterior finish. Roof sheathing, like wall sheathing and subflooring, may be laid either horizontally or diagonally. Horizontal sheathing may be either CLOSED sheathing (laid with no spaces between courses) or OPEN sheathing (laid with spaces between courses). Open sheathing is used for the most part only when the roof covering is to consist of wooden shingles. Closed sheathing is usually nominal 8-in. in width; it may consist of square-edged boards but may be dressed-and-matched or shiplap. Open sheathing usually consists of 1 x 3 or 1 x 4 strips, with spacing O.C. equal to the specified exposure of shingles TO THE WEATHER. An 18-in. shingle which is lapped 12 in. by the shingle above it is said to be laid 6 in. to the weather.

Sheathing should be nailed with two 8-penny nails to each rafter crossing. End-joint requirements are the same as those previously described for wall sheathing. The sheathing ends should be sawed flush with the outer face of the end-wall sheathing, unless a projection of the roof sheathing over the end-walls is called for. If such a projection is needed, projecting sheathing boards must be long enough to span at least 3 rafter spaces.

Plywood, usually in 8-ft x 4-ft sheets, laid horizontally, is frequently used for roof sheathing. Nailing requirements are the same as those previously described for 8-ft x 4-ft sheets of plywood wall sheathing.

CHAPTER 12
EXTERIOR FINISH

Chapter 10 and 11 have dealt with the FRAMING of a wood-frame structure, the framing consisting of (1) the main supporting framework of joists, studs, rafters, and other structural members; and (2) the subflooring and the wall and roof sheathing, which strengthen and brace the framing. These structural elements constitute the ROUGH CARPENTRY in the structure.

The remainder of the work on the structure consists of the construction and/or installation of nonstructural elements. This work is called the FINISH. Most of the finish involves items of essential practical usefulness, such as the door and window frames, the doors and windows themselves, the roof covering, and the stairs. Some of the finish, however, such as the casings on doors and windows and the moldings on cornices and on inside walls, is purely ornamental. The part of the finish which is purely ornamental is called TRIM.

The finish is divided into EXTERIOR FINISH and INTERIOR FINISH. The principal parts of the exterior finish are the CORNICES, the ROOF COVERING, ASBESTOS-CEMENT SIDING, INSULATION, and the OUTSIDE-WALL COVERING. The order in which these parts are erected may vary slightly, but since the roof covering must go on as soon as possible, the cornice work is usually the first item in the exterior finish.

CORNICE WORK

The rafter-end edges of a roof are called EAVES. A hip roof has rafter-end edges all the way around, and all four edges of a hip roof are therefore eaves. The rafter-end or sidewall edges of a gable roof are eaves; the gable-end or end-wall edges are called RAKES.

The exterior finish at and just below the eaves is called the CORNICE. Purely ornamental parts of a cornice (consisting mainly of molding) are called CORNICE TRIM. Exterior finish which runs up the rakes of a gable roof is called GABLE CORNICE TRIM. Besides the main roof, the additions and dormers (if any) also have cornices and cornice trim.

TYPES OF CORNICES

The type of cornice required for a particular structure is indicated on the wall sections, and there are usually cornice detail drawings as well. A roof with no rafter overhang usually has the SIMPLE cornice shown in figure 12-1. This cornice consists of a single strip called a FRIEZE, which is beveled on the upper edge to fit close under the overhang of the eaves, and rabbeted on the lower edge to overlap the upper edge of the top course of siding. If trim is used it usually consists of molding placed as shown in the figure. Molding trim in this position is called CROWN molding.

A roof with a rafter overhang may have an OPEN cornice or a CLOSED (also called a BOX) cornice. The simplest type of open cornice is shown in figure 12-2. Like the simple cornice, it consists only of a frieze, which in this case must be notched to fit around the rafters. If trim is used, it usually consists of molding cut to fit between the rafters as indicated. Molding trim in this position is called BED molding.

A closed or box cornice is shown in figure 12-3. In this type the rafter overhang is entirely boxed in by the roof covering, the fascia, and a bottom strip called a PLANCIER. The plancier is nailed to the lower edges of a series of horizontal members called LOOKOUTS, which are cut to fit between the rafter ends and the face of the sheathing. The frieze, if any, is set just below the lookouts. The trim, if any, is placed and named as shown in the figure.

The gable cornice trim on a gable-roof structure with a simple or an open cornice is made by carrying the frieze and the crown molding up the rakes as shown in figure 12-4. Molding trim along the rakes, however, is called RAKE molding.

Figure 12-5 shows gable-end-wall cornice work on a gable-roof structure with a closed cornice. As you can see, the crown molding and the fascia are carried up the rakes to form the gable cornice trim.

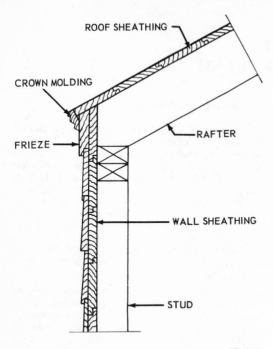

ROOF SHEATHING

CROWN MOLDING

FRIEZE

RAFTER

WALL SHEATHING

STUD

45.493

Figure 12-1.—Simple cornice.

CORNICE CONSTRUCTION

Most specifications call for BUILDING PA-PER between the sheathing and the siding. Building paper is impregnated with some waterproofing material such as asphalt or paraffin; it is used to make the walls water-tight and to keep out air and dust. It is usually applied horizontally, with a 2- to 4-in. overlap.

Before the cornice can be erected, the top course of building paper must be applied to the sheathing. For the open and closed cornice the paper must be cut to fit around the rafters.

Constructing a simple or an open cornice is simply a matter of laying out, beveling, rabbeting, notching (if required) and nailing on the frieze and the trim. Nails should be coated-casing, or finish; the size depends on the thickness of the piece being set in place. Carry a supply of 4-penny, 6-penny, and 8-penny nails, and drive nails in only part way until all the pieces of the cornice have been set in place. All joints should be planed smooth with a block plane and fitted together tightly. All members

must be mitered for joining on outside corners and mitered or coped for joining on inside corners.

The normal procedure for constructing a closed cornice is as follows:

1. Line up the tail plumb cuts and lower corners of the rafters by stretching a line and planing or sawing down any irregularities.
2. Lay out and cut the lookouts and nail them in place (if this was not done in the framing stage). Lookouts must be level, with bottom edges and outer ends in perfect alignment. Each lookout should be first nailed to the rafter and then toenailed against the ledger.
3. Lay out, cut, and rabbet the frieze, and nail it in place just below the lookouts.
4. Lay out and cut the plancier, and fit and nail it to the bottom edges of the lookouts.
5. Lay out, cut, and bevel the fascia, and nail it to the ends of the rafters and lookouts.
6. Lay out, cut, bevel (if necessary), and nail on the moldings.

ROOF COVERING

Roofs are covered with many different kinds of materials, such as slate, tile, wood shingles, asphalt, asbestos-cement, sheet metal, and BUILT-UP roofing. You are not likely to work with any specifications calling for slate, tile, sheet metal, or wood-shingle roofing. Built-up roofing is used mainly on flat or nearly flat roofs. On pitched-roof structures, asphalt and asbestos-cement are the types of roof covering most frequently used. For further details on roofing procedures, see NavFac Specification 7Yk—Roofing and Sheet Metal Work.

ASPHALT AND ASBESTOS-CEMENT ROOFING

Asphalt roofing comes in ROLLS (usually 36 in. wide, called ROLLED ROOFING), ROLLED STRIPS (usually 15 in. wide), FLAT STRIPS (usually 12 in. wide and 36 in. long), and as individual separate shingles. The type most commonly used is the flat strip, often called a STRIP SHINGLE.

A 12 x 36 SQUARE-BUTT strip shingle is shown in figure 12-6. This shingle should be laid 5 in. TO THE WEATHER, meaning that 7 in. of each course should be overlapped by the next higher course. The lower, exposed end of a shingle is called the BUTT; the shingle shown in figure 12-6 has a SQUARE BUTT,

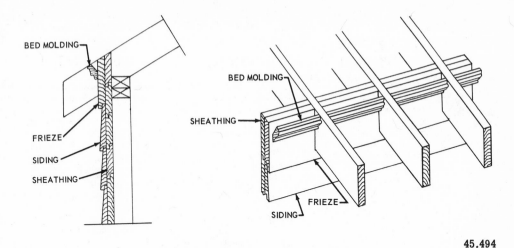

Figure 12-2.—Simplest type of open cornice.

45.494

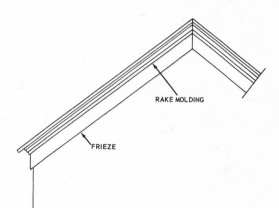

Figure 12-3.—Closed or box cornice.

133.148

Figure 12-4.—Gable cornice trim on gable-roof structure with simple cornice.

45.497

divided into 3 TABS. Various other butt shapes are manufactured.

Asbestos-cement roofing usually consists of individual shingles, 12 in. by 24 in. being the size most commonly used.

The first essential in covering a roof is to erect a scaffold extending to a height which will bring the eaves about waist-high to a man standing on the scaffold. Before any roof covering is applied, the roof sheathing must be swept clean and carefully inspected for irregularities, cracks, holes, or any other defects. No roofing should be applied unless the sheathing boards are absolutely dry. An UNDERLAY of ROOFING

FELT is first applied to the sheathing. Roofing felt usually comes in 3-ft-wide rolls, and it should be laid with a 4-in. lap as indicated.

Before work begins, bundles of shingles should be distributed along the scaffold. There are 27 strips in a bundle of 12 x 36 asphalt strip shingles, and 3 bundles will cover 100 sq ft. After the first course at the eaves (called the STARTER course) is laid by inverting the first course of shingles, you begin each course which follows by stretching

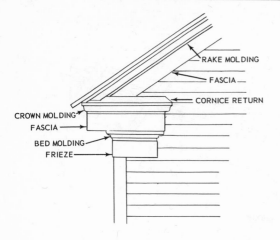

45.496.0

Figure 12-5.—Gable-end-wall cornice work on a gable-roof structure with a closed cornice.

An asbestos-cement roof is laid in about the same manner.

SHINGLES AT HIPS AND VALLEYS

One side of a hip or valley shingle must be cut at an angle to obtain an edge line which will match the line of the hip or valley rafter. One way to cut these shingles is to use a pattern made as follows:

Select a piece of 1 x 6 about 3 ft long. Determine the UNIT LENGTH of a common rafter in the roof (if you don't already know it); set the framing square back-up on the piece to the unit run of a common rafter on the tongue and the unit length of a common rafter on the blade, as shown in the top view of figure 12-8. Draw a line along the tongue; saw the piece along this line, and use it as a pattern to cut the shingles as shown in the bottom view of figure 12-8.

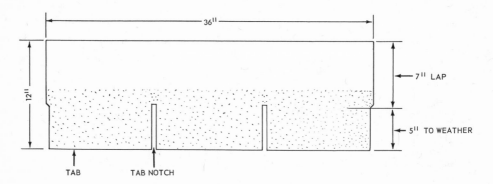

29.120

Figure 12-6.—A 12 x 36 square-butt asphalt strip shingle.

a guide line or snapping a chalk line from edge to edge to position the course.

Figure 12-7 shows the method of laying a 12 x 36 asphalt strip-shingle roof.

Strip shingles should be nailed with 1-in. copper or hot-dipped galvanized roofing nails, 2 to each tab; this means 6 nails to each full strip. Nails should be placed about 6 1/2 in. from the butt edges, to ensure that each nail will be covered by the next course, and driven through 2 courses. Placing a nail so that it will be covered by the next course is called BLIND NAILING.

FLASHING

Places especially liable to leakage in roofs and outside walls are made watertight by the installation of FLASHING. Flashing consists of sheets or strips of a watertight, rust-proof material (such as galvanized sheet or sheet copper alloy for valleys and felt for hips), installed so as to deflect water away from places that are liable to leakage. The places in a roof most liable to leakage are the lines along which adjoining roof surfaces intersect (such as the lines followed by ridge hips and valleys), and

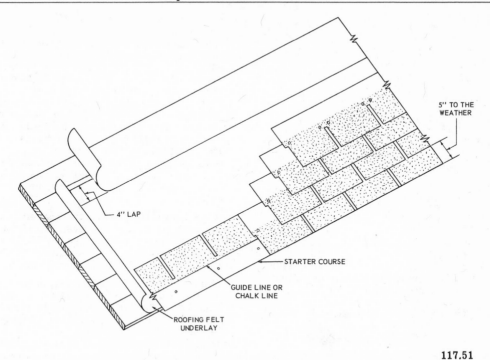

5" TO THE
WEATHER

4" LAP

STARTER COURSE

GUIDE LINE OR
CHALK LINE

ROOFING FELT
UNDERLAY

117.51

Figure 12-7.—Laying an asphalt shingle roof.

the lines of intersection between roof surfaces and the walls of dormers, chimneys and skylights.

Ridge lines and hip lines tend naturally to shed water, and these lines are therefore only moderately subject to leakage. A strip of felt paper, applied as shown in figure 12-9, usually makes a satisfactory flashing for a ridge or hip. The ridge or hip is then FINISHED. On an asphalt shingle roof a ridge or hip may be finished as shown in figure 12-9. A sufficient number of SQUARES are made by cutting shingles into thirds and the squares are then blind-nailed to the ridge or hip as shown.

Since water gathers in the valleys of a roof they are highly subject to leakage. Valley flashing varies with the manner in which the valley is to be finished. There are two common types of valley finish, known as the OPEN valley and the CLOSED valley.

In working with an open valley, always remember that the roof covering does not extend across the valley. The flashing consists of a prefabricated piece of galvanized iron, copper, or some similar metal, with a SPLASH RIB

or RIDGE down the center and a smaller CRIMP along each of the edges. The flashing is nailed down to the valley with nails driven in the edges, outside the crimps. Great care must be taken not to drive any nails through the flashing inside of the crimps. Puncturing the flashing inside the crimps is very likely to cause leaking.

In the closed valley the roof covering extends across the valley. Sheet metal flashing, cut into small sheets measuring about 18 in. x 10 in. and called SHINGLE TINS, is laid under each course of shingles, along the valley, as the course is laid. The first course of the double course at the eaves is laid, and the first sheet of flashing is placed on top of it. The second course is laid over the first course, and a sheet of flashing is then laid over this one so that the metal is partly covered by the next course. This procedure is continued all the way up the valley.

Shingle tins measuring about 5 in. x 7 in. are used in a similar manner to lay flashing up the side walls of dormers, chimneys, skylights, and the like. Each tin is bent at a right angle so that part of the tin extends up the side wall and the

351

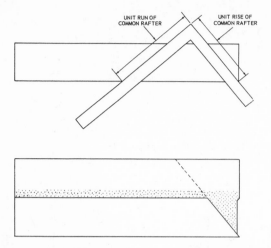

117.52

Figure 12-8.—Laying out pattern for cutting
hip and valley shingle.

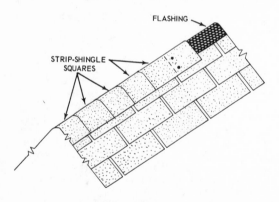

133.149

Figure 12-9.—Hip or ridge flashing and finish
on asphalt strip-shingle roof.

rest lies flat on the roof covering. Flashing of
this type is called SIDE FLASHING. In addition
to the side flashing, a dormer, chimney, or skylight has a strip of flashing called an APRON
along the bottom of the outer wall or face and a
chimney or skylight has a similar strip, called
the SADDLE flashing, along the bottom of the
inner wall or face.

BUILT-UP ROOFING

Built-up roofing consists of several layers
of tar-rag-felt, asphalt-rag-felt, or asphalt-
asbestos-felt set in a hot BINDER of melted
pitch or asphalt. A final layer of binder is
spread on top and sprinkled with a layer of
gravel, crushed stone, or slag. Built-up roofing
is confined to roofs which are no steeper than
about 4 in 12. On steeper roofs the binder tends
to work down and clog gutters and drains. Pitch
binder should not be used on a roof steeper than
3 in 12. Asphalt binder may be used on somewhat steeper roofs. For built-up roofing, roof
sheathing should be tight-laid and, preferably,
doubled.

Each layer of built-up roofing is called a PLY.
In a 5-ply roof the first two layers are laid without binder; these are called the DRY NAILERS.
Before they are nailed in place, a layer of building paper is tacked down to the roof sheathing.

Built-up roofing, like shingling, is started at
the eaves, so that strips will overlap in the direction of the watershed. Figure 12-10 shows the
manner of laying 32-in. material to obtain 5-ply
coverage at all points on the roof. Nailing must
be in accordance with a predetermined schedule,
designed to distribute the nails in successive
plys evenly among the nails already driven. The
roofing shown in figure 12-10 is laid as follows:

1. Lay the building paper with a 2-in. overlap
as shown. Spot-nail it down just enough to keep
it from blowing away.
2. Cut a 16-in. strip of saturated felt and lay
it along the eaves. Nail it down with nails
placed 1 in. from the back edge, spaced 12 in.
on centers.
3. Nail a full-width (32 in.) strip over the
first strip, in the same nailing schedule.
4. Nail the next full-width strip with the outer
edge 14 in. from the outer edges of the first two,
to obtain a 2-in. overlap over the edge of the
first strip laid. Continue laying full-width strips
with the same exposure (14 in.) until the opposite edge of the roof is reached. Finish off with
a half-strip along this edge. This completes
2-ply dry nailer.
5. The 3-ply starts with one-third of a strip,
covered by two-thirds of a strip and then by a
full strip, as shown. To obtain a 2-in. overlap
of the outer edge of the second full strip over
the inner edge of the first strip laid, the outer
edge of the second full strip must be 8 2/3 in.

352

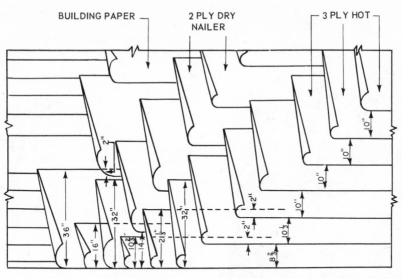

45.499

Figure 12-10.—Laying a 5-ply built-up roof.

from the outer edges of the first three strips laid. To maintain the same overlap, the outer edge of the third full strip must be 10 1/3 in. from the outer edge of the second full strip. Subsequent strips may be laid with an exposure of 10 in. Finish off at the opposite edge of the roof with a full strip, two-thirds of a strip, and one-third of a strip, to maintain 3 plys throughout.

The binder is melted and maintained at proper temperature in a pressure fuel kettle. The kettle must be set up and kept level. If it is not level it will heat unevenly, and this creates a hazard. The first duty of the kettle man is to inspect the kettle, especially to ensure that it is perfectly dry. Any accumulation of water inside will turn to steam when the kettle gets hot. This may cause the hot binder to bubble over, which creates a very serious fire hazard. Detailed procedure for lighting off operating, servicing, and maintaining the kettle is given in the manufacturer's manual.

The kettle man must maintain the binder at a steady temperature, as indicated by the temperature gage on the kettle. Correct temperature is designated in binder manufacturer's specifications; for asphalt it is about 400° F. The best way to keep an even temperature is to add material pro rata as melted material is tapped off. Pieces must not be thrown into the melted mass, but placed on the surface, pushed under slowly, and then released. If the material is not being steadily tapped off, it may eventually overheat, even with the burner flame at the lowest possible level. In that case, the burner should be withdrawn from the kettle and placed on the ground, to be re-inserted when the temperature falls. Prolonged overheating causes flashing and impairs the quality of the binder.

Asphalt or pitch must not be allowed to accumulate on the exterior of the kettle, because of the fire hazard. If the kettle catches fire, close the lid immediately, shut off the pressure and burner valves, and, if possible, remove the burner from the kettle. Never attempt to extinguish a kettle fire with water. Use sand, dirt, or a chemical fire extinguisher.

A hot roofing crew consists of a mop man as shown in figure 12-11 and as many felt layers, broomers, nailers, and carriers as the size of the roof requires. The mop man is in charge of the roofing crew. It is his important responsibility to mop on only binder which is at the proper temperature. Binder which is too hot will burn the felt, and the layer it makes will be too thin. A layer which is too thin will eventually crack,

133.151
Figure 12-11.—Applying built-up roofing.

and the felt may separate from the binder. Binder which is too cold goes on too thick, so that more material is used than is required.

The felt layer must get the felt down as soon as possible after the binder has been placed. If the interval between mopping and felt-laying is too long, the binder will cool to the point where it will not bond well with the felt. The felt layer should follow the mop man at an interval of not more than 3 feet. The broomer should follow immediately behind the felt layer, brooming out all air bubbles and imbedding the felt solidly in the binder.

Buckets of hot binder should never be filled more than three-fourths full, and they should never be carried at any speed faster than walking. Whenever possible, the mop man should work downwind from the felt layer and broomer, to reduce the danger of spattering. He must take every precaution against spattering at all times. He should LIFT his mop out of the bucket, not drag it across the rim. Dragging the mop in this manner may upset the bucket, and the hot binder may quickly spread to the feet, or, worse still, to the knees, of nearby members of the roofing crew.

OUTSIDE WALL COVERING

After the door and window frames, the outside-wall covering is the next major item in the exterior finish. On an all-wood structure the principal parts of the outside-wall covering are the WATER TABLE, the CORNER COVERING, and the SIDING, usually erected in that order.

WATER TABLE

The term water table may be applied to anything that is used to keep the water from running down the face of the foundation wall. A water table may also be used to form a starting point for the siding material and to improve the exterior appearance of the building. Figure 12-12 shows two common types of water tables.

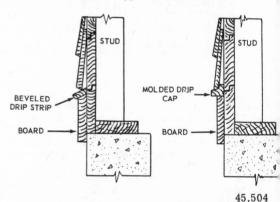

45.504
Figure 12-12.—Common types of water table.

In general, any type of assembled water table should be flashed with metal at the drip cap. There should be a quirk (curve) provided in the underside of the drip cap to prevent water from working into the joints of the assembled water table and causing decay.

CORNER COVERING

The outside corners of a wooden frame structure can be finished in several ways. Siding boards can be miter-joined at the corners. Shingles can be edge-lapped alternately, first from one side, then from the other. Ends of siding boards can be butted and the corner then covered with a metal cap. A type of corner finish which can be used with almost any kind of outside-wall covering is called a CORNER BOARD. This corner board can be applied to the corner, with the siding or shingles end-or edge-butted against the board.

A corner board usually consists of 2 pieces of 1 1/8-in. stock, one piece 3 in. wide, the other 4 in. wide if an edge-butt joint between boards is used. The boards, cut to a length which will extend from the top of the water table to the bottom of the frieze, are edge-butted and nailed together before they are nailed to the corner, a procedure which ensures a good tight joint. (See fig. 12-13.) A strip of building paper should be tacked over the corner before the corner board is nailed in position (always allow an overlap of paper to cover the subsequent crack formed where the ends of the siding butts against the cornerboard).

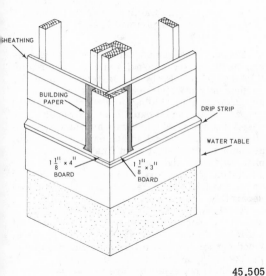

45.505

Figure 12-13.—Corner board.

SIDING

When the cornices, door and window frames, water table, and corner boards (if any) have been installed, the application of the siding begins. For wood siding the specifications usually contain such language as the following:

All exterior sheathing is to be covered with one layer of waterproof building paper before finished material is applied. Paper is to be placed horizontally with at least a 2-in. lap.

Care must be taken to ensure that the building paper overlaps the drip caps or drip strips on the water table, or the flashing on the table if there is any. As the application of either shingle or board siding begins at the water table, the first strip of paper is applied there. The next strip is not applied until the major part of the first strip has been covered with siding.

The type of siding to be used is indicated in the wall sections, and also, as a rule, in the specification, which may state something like the following:

Exterior walls to be covered with the best grade of clear vertical grain shingles laid 10 in. to the weather,
or:
Exterior walls to be covered with 1 x 8 clear cypress shiplap.

The first course of shingle siding is doubled, as in roof shingling, or even tripled. When the first course has been laid, a careful study of the rest of the wall should be made, with consideration given to the total height and the size and height of window openings. Theoretically, all courses should have the exposure specified. Actually, however, in order to make courses line up as nearly as possible with the top and bottom lines of door and window openings, slight adjustments in the amount of exposure are made. These must be evened out by distributing them over adjacent courses, so that the appearance of uniform exposure is maintained. When the heights of all the courses have been determined, they should be laid out on a story pole. Use the pole to mark the heights of courses at the ends of the wall, and use a straightedge or a chalk line between the marks to guide the course laying.

The same general procedure should be followed for bevel siding. Recommended minimum amounts of lap for this type of siding are as follows:

4-in. bevel siding . . . . 3/4 in.
5-in. bevel siding . . . . 7/8 in.
6-in. bevel siding . . . . 1 in.
8-in. bevel siding . . . . 1 1/4 in.
10-in. bevel siding . . . . 1 1/2 in.

In adjusting the exposures of courses, these minimums should be observed as closely as possible. Lay out a story pole for siding courses in the same manner as for shingle courses. Regular siding nails should be used: 6d for 1/2-in. siding, 8d for anything thicker. The lower edge of the first strip laid should be beveled to fit tightly on the drip strip or drip cap. End butt joints between strips should be broken by as many strips as possible, never by less than 2. Ends should be smoothed with a block plane after cutting, to ensure tight-fitting joints which will keep out wind, dust, and water.

Much wood siding used nowadays consists of large plywood panels. For this type of siding horizontal girts must be nailed between the studs along the lines where horizontal joints between panels will occur. Both the horizontal and the vertical joints between panels must be made weathertight. There are several methods of this. Horizontal joints may be protected by flashing laid on the girts and shaped so as to protrude through the joint and overhang the upper edge of the lower panel. Or the horizontal edges of the panels may be rabbeted so they will join together in an overlapping joint like that between strips of shiplap.

Vertical joints may be closed by nailing vertical battens over them; by leaving a slight space between the edges of panels, rabbeting the edges, and gluing in a spline; by a vertical joint sealed by calking compound. The best way to calk a vertical joint is to bevel the edges of the panels as shown in figure 12-14, so that a V-shaped reservoir for the compound is made when the edges are brought together.

Wood siding of all kinds has been to a large extent superseded by various kinds of COMPOSITION siding. Manufacturers of each type include complete instructions for its application with their product, and the only way to ensure satisfactory results is to follow these instructions closely.

ASBESTOS-CEMENT SIDING

Asbestos-cement siding, made principally of asbestos fiber and portland cement, is usually supplied in rectangular units with straight or wavy butt edges. Asbestos shingles are usually 12 by 24 inches, but other units may range from 9 to 16 inches in width and from 24 to 48 inches in length. Thickness ranges from 5/32 to 3/16 inch. The material is rigid, strong, fire-resistant, pestproof, and resists weathering. Colors are obtained by pigmentation or by embedding of colored mineral granules. The siding may be painted but does not require painting for preservation.

133.368
Figure 12-14.—Calking a vertical joint between plywood panels.

The only accessories furnished with asbestos-cement siding are face-nails and backer or joint flashing strips. Nails and fasteners must be permanently and effectively corrosion-resistant and nonstaining. Siding units are made with properly sized and located holes to receive exposed facenails, which serve as guides for the correct amount of headlap and exposure and unit alignment. Backer or joint flashing strips, asphalt saturated and coated, must always be applied back of each vertical joint between siding units. The following accessories will be procured separately.

Metal moldings and corner finishing trim should be noncorrodible, nonstaining, and of sufficient thickness and rigidity for the purpose. Wood corner finish and trim should be suitable in size and type for the job conditions.

Flashing materials for use around jambs and sills should be noncorrodible and nonstaining.

Calking compound should be nonshrinking.

Underlayment material or sheathing paper should be the "breather" type, previous to water vapor, such as No. 15 asphalt-saturated felt. Coal-tar-saturated felts should not be used because they may stain the siding.

Shingle backers are strips of rigid fiber insulating board not less than 5/16 inch thick and of convenient length. They must be made water-resistant by: impregnation or coating with asphalt or its equivalent.

Portable shingle-cutting machines may be used to cut, punch, and notch asbestos siding; they save time and labor and do a superior job.

The siding may be sawed with a hacksaw, or a power saw equipped with a fabric-reinforced flexible abrasive wheel or a carbide-tipped blade. Edges of the material may be dressed with a file. Holes may be drilled or punched with a special punching device mounted on the shingle cutter.

CARE OF MATERIAL

Asbestos-cement siding is a high-grade finish material and must be properly and carefully handled during transportation and application. It must be properly stored in the warehouse and on the job. While still in packages and until applied, asbestos-cement siding can be seriously harmed and discolored by moisture and dampness. KEEP IT DRY. Pile on a solid, flat, unbending platform raised at least 4 inches above-ground. Keep it completely covered and protected from the weather by a watertight and waterproof cover. Do not apply siding over wet sheathing or underlay, or during rain or snow storms. Do not permit water draining from uncovered sheathing or underlay materials to drain over asbestos-cement siding, or staining may result. Fiberboard, gypsum board, and plywood sheathing can be seriously harmed by the absorption of moisture during careless storage. Wet sheathing can seriously and permanently harm any siding material applied over it. Keep these materials completely protected from the weather by a waterproof covering until installed.

PREPARATION

Much time and expense can be saved by planning the job properly. Use safe scaffolding. Use competent and experienced mechanics. Make sure proper material storage facilities are on the job to protect the asbestos-cement siding from all hazards and damage.

Siding from different lots or factory runs may have slight and unavoidable differences in colors. All surfaces to which siding is applied should be supported adequately, be smooth, clean and dry, and provide an adequate nailing base and support. Provide a suitable sheathing or surface for the siding that will serve as an adequate nailing base, capable of developing the full holding power of nails or fasteners that must be used, and that is substantially level, plumb, and smooth. When men are working on a structure that has been or is being sided with asbestos-cement siding, they must be required to take adequate precautions not to damage, stain, or harm the exterior wall siding. This is especially important when painting or built-up roofing work is being done.

FLASHING AT OPENINGS AND CORNERS

Metal flashing should be applied properly at all door and window openings. (See fig. 12-15.)

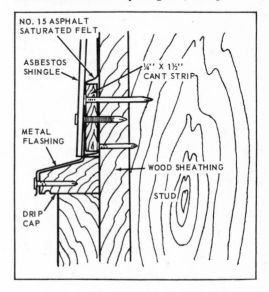

133.152

Figure 12-15.—Flashing cap mold on doors and windows.

Flash all outside corners and inside corners with a 12-inch-wide strip of underlay material centered in or around the corner when corner boards are used. (See fig. 12-16.)

In other corner treatments, carry the underlayment felt around the corner of each sidewall so that a double thickness of felt results over the corner, and use folded backer strips at each course of shingles at the corner. (See fig. 12-16.)

Asbestos-cement siding should be bedded in nonshrinking calking compound at all corners and wherever it butts against wooden trim, masonry, or other projections. Care must be taken in applying the compound to avoid smearing the face of the shingles. Avoid applying visible or exposed calking compound.

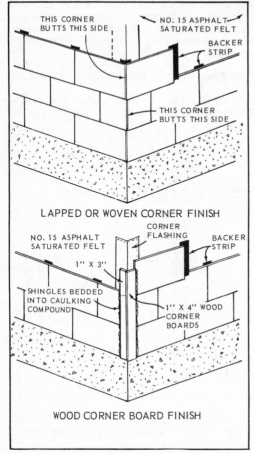

LAPPED OR WOVEN CORNER FINISH

WOOD CORNER BOARD FINISH

133.153

Figure 12-16.—Flashing corners.

CORNER FINISHING

Where wall surfaces join at inside corners, the courses of siding are generally butted, although metal molding or wood corner strip may be used. Outside corners can be handled by any one of the following methods.

For lapped adjoining courses at outside corners, temporarily place a whole shingle against each adjoining wall, so that they meet and join at the corner. Scribe and cut the adjoining vertical edges of the siding units at the proper angle to form a lapped or woven corner joint.

Corner joints should be lapped to the left and right in alternate courses. Courses on adjoining walls should meet and match at corners.

Wood corner boards are made of two pieces of nominal one inch lumber. A 1 by 3 member is nailed to the backside of the 1 by 4 member. This will form a face surface of equal dimension on each side of the corner. Corner boards, as well as all other exterior trim, should be face and back primed before assembly to the structure.

Several styles of nonstaining metal corner finish moldings are available. Apply as recommended by the manufacturer.

APPLICATION OF SIDING TO WALL

The following is based on applying 12- by 24-inch asbestos-cement siding over nominal 1 inch-thick wood lumber sheathing. For applying other sizes of siding, follow the manufacturer's recommendations. For application over nonlumber sheathing, including plywood, the following instructions may require modification as described in other applicable areas of this paragraph. Methods of applying asbestos-cement siding over nonlumber sheathing are detailed later in this paragraph. Very few buildings are true and parallel. Therefore, it is necessary to watch the relationship of the courses to the eave lines, and make sure adjustments as may be needed so that the final course is not too narrow or wedgeshaped. Some uniform adjustments of the exposure of each course may be necessary. Determine where the bottom edge of the first course is to be. Make sure that all courses meet and match at corners and are level all around the building. Determine the total number of courses to complete one wall and lay out the job so that top courses under the eaves will not be too narrow or wedgeshaped. Determine how all corners are to be finished and how openings and other places are to be flashed properly and trimmed. Remove all unnecessary projections from the wall. Snap a level chalkline all around the building to fix the location of the top edge of the first course of siding as shown in figure 12-17. The siding will overhang the bottom edge of the cant strip 1/4 inch to provide a drip edge. Snap additional horizontal chalklines to mark the top of the cant strip and each succeeding course. Space the lines the distance necessary to provide the required exposure for the type of asbestos-cement siding being used.

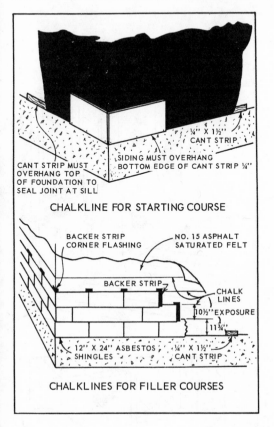

CHALKLINE FOR STARTING COURSE

BACKER STRIP
CORNER FLASHING

NO. 15 ASPHALT
SATURATED FELT

BACKER STRIP

CHALK
LINES

10½" EXPOSURE

11¾"

12" X 24" ASBESTOS
SHINGLES

¼" X 1½"
CANT STRIP

CHALKLINES FOR FILLER COURSES

133.154

Figure 12-17.—Use of chalklines.

CANT STRIP

Nail a 1/4- by 1-1/2-inch wood strip along the bottom edge of the sheathing so that it is level and overhangs the top of the foundation enough to seal the joint between the top of the foundation, the wood sill, and the bottom of the sheathing. This strip gives a necessary cant or pitch to the first course of shingles and should always be used.

FIRST AND ODD-NUMBERED COURSES

Start at the outside corner of the wall with a full-size siding unit. Make sure this unit is placed plumb and level, and aligned with the chalkline, because it guides the lay of all other

units. All siding units in this course must overhang the bottom edge of the cant strip 1/4 inch to provide a drip edge. Use the proper face nails supplied with the siding for the type of sheathing and application method being used. Drive nails snug but not too tight. Before driving the last nail at the right-hand end of the unit, insert a backer strip in place and secure it with the last nail. Backer strips must always be used and placed centered at the joint between siding units, and with the lower end overlapping the head of the cant strip or lower course. Continue to apply full-size siding units in the first course, with their top edges aligned with the chalkline. The last unit in a course or at an opening should not be less than 6 inches wide, and if a smaller space will remain to be filled, a few inches should be cut from the units applied earlier in the course. Punch any necessary facenail holes in short pieces of siding. Do not leave spaces between ends of units. Wedgeshaped spaces between the ends of siding units are proof of incorrect application. Butt units tightly together end to end.

SECOND AND SUCCEEDING EVEN-NUMBERED COURSES

When using 12- by 24-inch siding, succeeding courses should have their vertical joints break on "halves." Start the second course with a half unit. When using 32 inch-long units, break on "thirds." Start the second course of 48 inch-long units with a 2/3 unit. Some bundles of siding contain units shorter than full length to provide the necessary shorter pieces for starting courses. Starting at the left-hand corner with a partial unit, having its head edge aligned with the chalkline and its lower edge overlapping the head of the next lower course the correct distance to provide the necessary head-lap between courses, insert a nail in a face-nail hole, making sure the shank of the nail is resting on the top edge of the next lower course, thus establishing the proper amount of head-lap. Then nail in place, and continue to work with full size units.

INSULATION

Exterior wall insulation is normally installed at the time a building or structure is built, according to area climatic conditions and building occupancy. The economic feature of saving and equalizing heat and/or air conditioning is of primary importance. Insulation also serves a valuable purpose in moisture control, which prevents rot and fungus growth. In buildings and structures without adequate insulation, or where insulation has deteriorated or been displaced, it should be installed or replaced after a study of the best type and method of application for prevailing conditions. The fireproofing and verminproofing qualities of insulation should also be considered.

TYPES OF INSULATION

Roll or batt blankets may be used where access to the space between studs allows their placement and fastening. Loose material (pellets or wool) may be used where areas are accessible from a limited opening only, such as around windows and doors and in wall utility compartments. Other types of insulation include rigid and semirigid composition board, which is generally used around concrete slabs and as sheathing under the siding. Utility batts may be used where no vapor barrier is required or where a separate vapor barrier has been provided.

Roll or batt insulation is most satisfactorily placed when either the inside or outside surface of a building or structure is uncovered. Replacement of insulation should be considered when the outer face of a wall is resheathed or when an inner surface is replaced. When both wall faces are covered it is necessary to pour loose insulation from the top or force it in by compressed air from some opening in the wall. In any case, care should be exercised to fill all small crevices and to place material into confined spaces and around piping and wiring. The vapor barrier side of insulation should face toward the warm side of the wall. In placing any type or kind of insulation, follow the manufacturer's recommendations for proper thickness, form, and fastening. Figure 12-18 illustrates application of insulating batts, blankets, and utility batts to standard wood-constructed walls. Figure 12-19 shows methods of placing insulated material on masonry and metal sidewalls.

Batts and Blankets

In figure 12-18 the following steps are demonstrated for batts and blankets.

Cut insulation to stud height plus 3 inches for top and bottom nailing flanges. Foot and inch markings along the edge of the blanket simplify

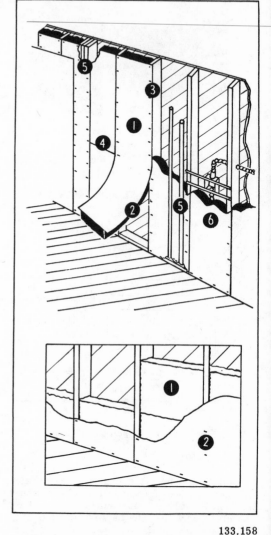

133.158
Figure 12-18.—Placing batts, blankets, and utility batts in exterior wood frame wall.

measuring. Insulation may also be applied from a roll and cut off at bottom to fit.

Fluff the blanket to full thickness, open the nailing flanges, and press back the insulation to leave an end nailing flange exposed. Make sure vapor barrier faces the building interior (warm-in-winter side).

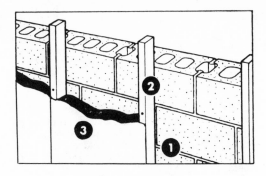

MASONRY SIDEWALLS

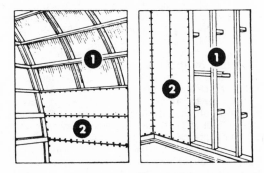

METAL SIDEWALLS

133.159

Figure 12-19.—Placing insulation inside masonry and metal sidewalls.

Start at the top of the stud space and work down if roll blankets are used. Batts can be installed from the floor up. Staple or nail flanges to the stud at 5- to 6-inch spacing.

Press insulation closely together at joints so that no voids are left. Make sure the vapor barrier is not broken by spaces at joints.

Insulate with special care on the cold side of pipes and drains. Compress insulation behind pipes where possible, or pack with utility batts or pouring wool.

Hand-pack narrow spaces with utility batts, pouring wool, or scraps from batts or blankets. Cut and apply the vapor barrier to provide vapor protection.

Utility Batts

In figure 12-19 the following steps are described for utility batts.

1. Stack 15- by 10-inch utility batts between studs. If the 15-inch dimension is placed horizontally, batts fit between studs placed 16 inches on center. With the 15-inch dimension vertical, 2 batts can be packed into the space between studs on 20-inch centers.

2. Tack the vapor barrier paper over the insulation to prevent condensation. For complete vapor protection, the vapor barrier must be continuous at joints.

Masonry Sidewalls

For masonry sidewalls, take the following steps (fig. 12-19):

1. Dampproof the inner face of the masonry with a vapor-porous material such as a water-emulsion asphalt or fibrated mastic.

2. Attach furring strips slightly thicker than normal to provide space for economy (1-1/2-inch) or medium (2-inch) roll blankets.

3. Apply roll or batt blankets to furring strips, following directions given for wood sidewalls.

Metal Sidewalls

For metal sidewalls, take the following steps (fig. 12-19):

1. Attach furring strips to purlins or grits of the metal building on a standard spacing to take roll blanket insulation.

2. Staple or nail roll blankets to furring strips. Make sure the vapor barrier is continuous to prevent condensation on steel sheets. Cover with the desired finish.

CHAPTER 13

INTERIOR FINISH

The interior finish consists mainly of the finish covering applied to the rough walls, ceilings, and floors. Other major interior finish items are the inside door frames, the doors, the window sash, and the stairs.

Interior-finish items whose function is principally ornamental are classified under the general heading of INTERIOR TRIM. Interior trim includes inside door and window casings, window stools and aprons, baseboards, and molding trim.

The usual order of construction for the interior finish is as follows:

1. Ceiling covering
2. Wall covering
3. Stairs
4. Window sash
5. Window inside casings, stools, and aprons
6. Finish flooring
7. Inside door frames and casings
8. Baseboards
9. Molding trim.

WALL AND CEILING COVERING

The two major types of wall and ceiling covering are PLASTER and DRY-WALL COVERING. Dry-wall covering is a general term applied to sheets or panels of wood, plywood, fiberboard, and the like.

PLASTER

A PLASTER wall and/or ceiling covering requires the construction of a PLASTER BASE, or surface on which the plaster can be spread and to which it will adhere. A surface of this kind was formerly constructed by nailing wooden LATHS (thin, narrow strips usually 48 in. long) to the edges of studs and joists, or to wooden FURRING STRIPS anchored to concrete or masonry walls. In modern construction, wooden lath has been almost entirely superseded by GYPSUM lath, FIBERBOARD lath and METAL lath.

Gypsum lath usually consists of 16 in. by 48 in. sheets of GYPSUM BOARD, either solid or perforated and usually squared-edged. It is applied horizontally to studs and at right angles to joists, and nailed to studs, joists, or furring strips with 1 1/8-in. flat-headed GYPSUM-LATH NAILS, 5 to each stud, joist or strip crossing.

Fiberboard lath consists of sheets of fiberboard, also usually 16 in. by 48 in. in size. It may be either square-edged or shiplap edged. It is applied in much the same manner as gypsum lath, except that 1 1/4-in. blued FIBERBOARD-LATH NAILS are used.

Metal lath consists of screen-like sheets of MESHED or RIBBED metal, usually 27 in. by 96 in. in size. To walls it is applied horizontally; to ceilings with the long dimension perpendicular to the line of the joists. It may be nailed to studs or to furring strips with regular metal-lath STAPLES, or with 8-penny nails driven part-way in and then hammered over. It may be similarly nailed to ceiling joists, or it may be tied up with wire ties to nails driven through the joists about 2 in. above the lower edges.

Before lath is applied to walls and ceilings, PLASTER GROUNDS are installed as called for in the working drawings. Plaster grounds are wood strips of the same thickness as the combined thickness of the lath and plaster. They are nailed to the framing members around doors and windows and to the studs along floor lines. They serve as a guide to the plasterers, to ensure that the plaster behind door casings, window casings, and baseboards will be of uniform and correct thickness. They also serve as nailing bases for the trim members mentioned.

Plastering is usually done in three coats, which form a combined thickness of about 5/8 in. The first coat is called the SCRATCH coat, because it is usually scored when partially set to improve the adhesion of the second coat. The second coat is called the BROWN coat, and the third the WHITE (also the SKIM or FINISH) coat. As gypsum or fiberboard lath provides the equivalent of a scratch coat, only the brown and finish coats of plaster are applied when these types of lath are used.

The basic ingredients for scratch-coat and brown-coat plaster are lime and sand. Proportions vary, but a scratch coat usually has about 1 part of lime to 2 parts of sand, by volume. The proportion of lime to sand in a brown coat is slightly smaller.

Plaster for an ordinary white coat usually consists of lime putty mixed with plaster-of-paris; a little marble dust may be included. Plaster for a high grade finish coat contains calcium sulphate instead of lime. KEENE's CEMENT is a well-known variety of calcium sulphate finish plaster. A very superior hard-finish coat can be obtained by mixing 4 parts of Keene's cement with 1 part of lime putty.

Manufacturers of plaster usually furnish instruction sheets which set forth the recommended ingredient proportions and methods of application for their products. Follow these instructions closely. The actual application of plaster, especially to ceilings, is a skill which can be acquired only through practice. Additional information on plaster work may be found in chapter 14.

DRY-WALL FINISH

DRY-WALL FINISH is a general term applied to sheets or panels of various materials used for inside-wall and ceiling covering. The most common dry-wall finishes are GYPSUM-BOARD, PLYWOOD, FIBERBOARD, and WOOD.

Gypsum Board

Gypsum board usually comes in a standard size of 4' by 8'. However, on notice it can be obtained in any length up to 16 ft. It can be applied to walls, either vertically or horizontally. A 4-ft wide sheet applied vertically to studs 16 in. O.C. will cover 3 stud spaces. Five-penny cement-coated nails should be used with 1/2-in.-thick gypsum, 4-penny nails with 3/8-in.-thick gypsum. Nails should be spaced 6 to 8 in. O.C. for walls and 5 to 7 in. O.C. for ceilings.

Nail heads should be driven about one-sixteenth inch below the face of the board; this set can be obtained by using a crowned hammer. The indentations around nails away from edges are concealed by applying JOINT CEMENT. The nail indentations along edges are concealed with a perforated fiber JOINT TAPE set in joint cement. Edges are slightly recessed to bring the tape flush with the faces. Besides concealing the nail indentations, the tape also conceals the joint.

The procedure for taping a joint is as follows:

1. Spread the joint cement along the joint with a 4- to 6-in. putty knife. Joint cement comes in powder form; the powder is mixed with water to about the consistency of putty.
2. Lay the tape against the joint and press it into the recess with the putty knife. Press until some of the joint cement is forced out through the holes in the tape.
3. Spread joint cement over the tape, and FEATHER (taper off) the outer edges.
4. Allow the cement to dry, then sand lightly. Apply a second coat, and again feather the edges.
5. Allow the cement to dry, and then sand the joint smooth.

For nail indentations away from edges, fill the indentations with cement, allow the cement to dry, and sand lightly. Apply another coat, allow to dry, and sand smooth.

Plywood

Plywood finish comes in sheets of various sizes which can be applied either vertically or horizontally. With horizontal application, lengths of stud stock called NAILERS are framed between the studs along the lines of horizontal joints. Panels can be nailed directly to studs and nailers, but a better method is to nail 2-in. furring strips to the studs and nailers and then glue and nail the panels to the strips. This method reduces joint movements caused by swelling or shrinking of the studs and nailers.

Joints between plywood panels can be finished in a variety of ways. For a tight butt joint, spread enough glue on the furring strip, stud, or nailer to provide a SQUEEZE of glue between the edges, allow the glue to dry, and then block-sand the joint smooth. Another smooth joint can be obtained by rabbeting the edges for shiplap. Edges of panels can be smoothed and the joints left open for ornamental effect; or the edges can be beveled to form a V-groove joint when brought together; or joints can be left open and then filled with glued-in wooden splines. Outside corners between panels can be miter-joined, or the right angle between square edges at outside corners can be filled with quarter-round molding. Inside corners can be butted or mitered.

One-half inch plywood finish is nailed on with 1 1/4 in. finish nails spaced 6 in. O.C.

Fiberboard

Fiberboard wall finish comes in 2 ft by 8 ft sheets which are applied horizontally. The long edges are usually rabbeted or tongue-and-grooved for joining. Fiberboard is nailed in place with finish nails, brads, or cadmium plated fiberboard nails. Use 1 1/2-nails for 1/2-inch thick boards and 2-inch nails for 1-inch thick boards.

Fiberboard in small squares or rectangles is called TILEBOARD and each piece of tileboard is called a TILE. Common sizes are 12 inches by 12 inches, 12 inches by 24 inches, 16 inches by 16 inches, and 16 inches by 32 inches. Tiles can be nailed to studs, joists, and furring strips; usually, however, they are glued to a continuous surface of wood or plasterboard with a special type of adhesive.

STAIRS

There are many different kinds of stairs, but all have two main parts in common: the TREADS people walk on, and the STRINGERS (also called STRINGS, HORSES, and CARRIAGES) which support the treads. A very simple type of stairway, consisting only of stringers and treads, is shown in the left-hand view of figure 13-1. Treads of the type shown here are called PLANK treads, and this simple type of stairway is called a CLEAT stairway, because of the cleats attached to the stringers to support the treads.

A more finished type of stairway has the treads mounted on two or more sawtooth-edged stringers, and includes RISERS, as shown in the right-hand view of figure 13-1. The stringers

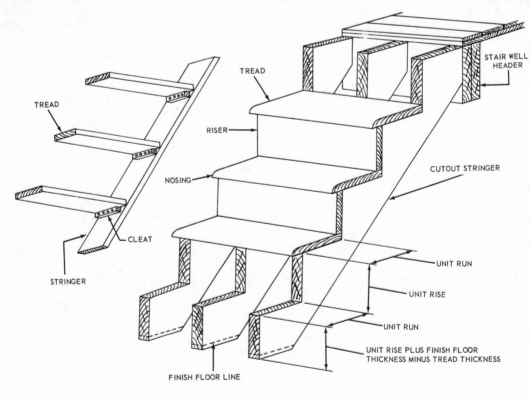

45.507

Figure 13-1.—Stairway nomenclature.

shown here are cut out of solid pieces of dimension lumber (usually 2 x 12), and are therefore called CUTOUT or SAWED stringers.

STAIRWAY LAYOUT

The first step in stairway layout is to determine the UNIT RISE and UNIT RUN shown in figure 13-1. The unit rise is calculated on the basis of the TOTAL RISE of the stairway, and the fact that the customary permissible unit rise for stairs is in the vicinity of 7 inches.

The total rise is the vertical distance between the lower finish floor level and the upper finish floor level. This may be shown in the elevations; however, since the actual vertical distance as constructed may vary slightly from what it should have been, and since it is the actual distance you are dealing with, the distance should be measured.

At the time the stairs are to be laid out, the subflooring is laid but the finish flooring isn't. If both the lower and the upper floor are to be covered with finish flooring of the same thickness, the measured vertical distance from lower subfloor surface to the upper subfloor surface will be the same as the eventual distance between the finish floor surfaces, and therefore equal to the total rise of the stairway. But if you are measuring up from a finish floor (such as a concrete basement floor, for instance), then you must add to the measured distance the thickness of the upper finish flooring to get the total rise of the stairway. If the upper and lower finish floors will be of different thicknesses, then you must add the difference in thickness to the measured distance between subfloor surfaces to get the total rise of the stairway. Use a straight piece of lumber plumbed in the stair opening with a spirit level, or a plumb bob and cord, to measure the vertical distance.

Assume that the total rise measures 8 ft 11 in., as shown in figure 13-2. Knowing this, you can determine the unit rise as follows. First, reduce the total rise to inches—in this case it comes to 107 in. Next, divide the total rise in inches by the average permissible unit rise, which is 7 in. The result, disregarding any fraction, is the number of RISERS the stairway will have—in this case it is 107/7, or 15. Now divide the total rise in inches by the number of risers—in this case, this is 107/15, which comes to 7.13 in., or, rounded off to the nearest 1/16 in., 7 1/8 in. This, then, is the unit rise, as shown in figure 13-2.

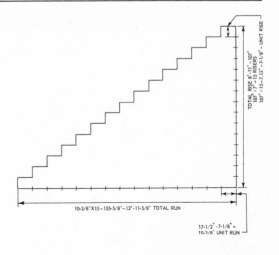

117.54

Figure 13-2.—Stairway layout computations.

The unit run is calculated on the basis of (1) the unit rise, and (2) a general architects' rule that the sum of the unit run and unit rise should be 17 1/2 in. In view of (2), if the unit rise is 7 1/8 in., the unit run is 17 1/2 in. minus 7 1/8 in., or 10 3/8 in.

You can now calculate the TOTAL RUN of the stairway. The total run is obviously equal to the product of the unit run times the total number of treads in the stairway. However, the total number of treads depends upon the manner in which the upper end of the stairway will be anchored to the header.

In figure 13-3, three methods of anchoring the upper end of a stairway are shown. In the first view there is a complete tread at the top of the stairway. This means that the number of complete treads will be the same as the number of risers. For the stairway shown in figure 13-1, there are 15 risers and 15 complete treads. Therefore, the total run of the stairway will be the product of the unit run times 15, or 10 3/8 in. x 15, or 155 5/8", or 12 ft 11 5/8 in., as shown.

In figure 13-3, second view, there is only part of a tread at the top of the stairway. If this method were used for the stairway shown in figure 13-2, the number of complete treads would be ONE LESS than the number of risers, or 14. The total run of the stairway would be the product of 14 x 10 3/8, PLUS THE RUN OF

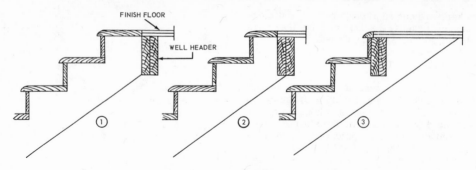

45.508

Figure 13-3.—Three methods of anchoring upper end of a stairway.

THE PARTIAL TREAD AT THE TOP. Suppose this run were 7 inches. Then the total run would be 14 x 10 3/8 + 7, or 152 1/4 in., or 12 ft 8 1/4 in.

In figure 13-3, third view, there is no tread at all at the top of the stairway; the upper finish flooring serves as the top tread. In this case the total number of complete treads is again 14, but since there is no additional partial tread, the total run of the stairway is 14 x 10 3/8, or 145 1/4 in., or 12 ft 1 1/4 in.

When you have calculated the total run of the stairway, drop a plumb bob from the well head to the floor below and measure off the total run from the plumb bob. This locates the anchoring point for the lower end of the stairway.

Cutout stringers for main stairways are usually made from 2 x 12 stock. The first question is: About how long a piece of stock will you need? Let's assume that you are to use the method of upper-end anchorage shown in the first view of figure 13-3 to lay out a stringer for the stairway shown in figure 13-2. This stairway has a total rise of 8 ft 11 in. and a total run of 12 ft 11 5/8 in. The stringer must be long enough to form the hypotenuse of a triangle with sides of those two lengths. For an approximate length estimate, call the sides 9 and 13 ft long. The length of the hypotenuse, then, will equal the square root of $9^2 + 13^2$, or the square root of 250, or about 15.8 ft, or about 15 ft 9 1/2 in.

Figure 13-4 shows the layout at the lower end of the stringer. Set the framing square to the unit run on the tongue and the unit rise on the blade, and draw the line AB. This line represents the bottom tread. Then draw AD perpendicular to AB, in length equal to the unit rise.

This line represents the bottom riser in the stairway. Now, you've probably noticed that, up to this point, the thickness of a tread in the stairway has been ignored. This thickness is now about to be accounted for, by making an allowance in the height of this first riser, a process which is called DROPPING THE STRINGER.

As you can see in figure 13-1, the unit rise is measured from the top of one tread to the top of the next for ALL RISERS EXCEPT THE BOTTOM ONE. For this one, the unit rise is measured FROM THE FINISHED FLOOR SURFACE TO THE SURFACE OF THE FIRST TREAD. If AD were cut to the unit rise, the actual rise of the first step would be the sum of the unit rise plus the thickness of a tread. Therefore, the length of AD is shortened by the thickness of a tread, as shown in figure 13-4— or by the thickness of a tread less the thickness of the finish flooring. The first is done if the stringer will rest on a finish floor, such as concrete basement floor. The second is done if the stringer will rest on subflooring.

When you have shortened AD to AE, as shown, draw EF parallel to AB. This line represents the bottom horizontal anchor-edge of the stringer. Then proceed to lay off the remaining risers and treads to the unit rise and unit run, until you have laid off 15 risers and 15 treads. Figure 13-5 shows the layout at the upper end of the stringer. The line AB represents the top—that is, the 15th—tread. BC, drawn perpendicular to AB, represents the upper vertical anchor-edge of the stringer, which will butt against the stairwell header.

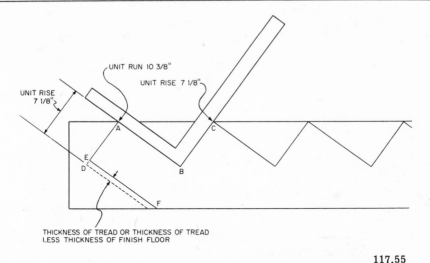

UNIT RUN IO 3/8"

UNIT RISE 7 1/8"

UNIT RISE 7 1/8"

THICKNESS OF TREAD OR THICKNESS OF TREAD
LESS THICKNESS OF FINISH FLOOR

117.55

Figure 13-4.—Layout of lower end of cutout stringer.

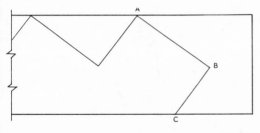

117.56

Figure 13-5.—Layout at upper end
of cutout stringer.

STAIRWAY CONSTRUCTION

We have been dealing with a common STRAIGHT-FLIGHT stairway, meaning one which follows the same direction throughout. When floor space is not extensive enough to permit construction of a straight-flight stairway, a CHANGE stairway is installed—meaning, one which changes direction one or more times. The most common types of these are 90-DEGREE change and 180-DEGREE change. These are usually PLATFORM stairways—that is, successive straight-flight lengths, connecting platforms at which the direction changes 90 degrees, or doubles back 180 degrees. Such

a stairway is laid out simply as a succession of straight-flight stairways.

The stairs in a structure are broadly divided into PRINCIPAL stairs and SERVICE stairs. Service stairs are porch, basement, and attic stairs. Some of these may be simple cleat stairways; others may be OPEN-RISER stairways. An open-riser stairway has treads anchored on cut-out stringers or stair-block stringers, but no risers. The lower ends of the stringers on porch, basement, and other stairs anchored on concrete are fastened with a KICK-PLATE like the one shown in figure 13-6.

A principal stairway is usually more finished in appearance. Rough cutout stringers are concealed by FINISH stringers like the one shown in figure 13-7. Treads and risers are often rabbet-joined as shown in figure 13-8. To prevent squeaking, triangular blocks may be glued into the joints, as shown in the same figure.

The vertical members which support a stairway handrail are called BALUSTERS. Figure 13-9 shows a method of joining balusters to treads. For this method, dowels shaped on the lower ends of the balusters are glued into holes bored in the treads.

Stringers should be toenailed to well headers with 10-penny nails, three to each side of the stringer. Those which face against trimmer joists should be nailed to the joist with at least three 16-penny nails apiece. At the bottom a

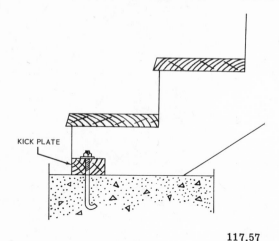

KICK PLATE

117.57

Figure 13-6.—Kick-plate for anchoring stairs to concrete.

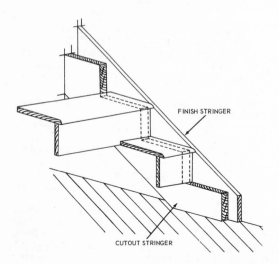

FINISH STRINGER

CUTOUT STRINGER

117.58

Figure 13-7.—Finish stringer.

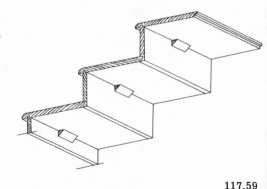

117.59

Figure 13-8.—Rabbet-joined treads and risers.

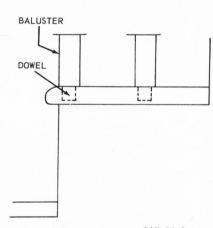

BALUSTER

DOWEL

117.60.1

Figure 13-9.—One method of joining a baluster to the tread.

WINDOW SASH

stringer should be toenailed with 10-penny nails, 4 to each side, driven into the subflooring and if possible into a joist below.

Treads and risers should be nailed to stringers with 6-penny, 8-penny, or 10-penny finish nails, depending on the thickness of the stock.

A window frame is built to the dimensions of the window, as given on the window schedule. To prevent the sash from binding in the frame, it is necessary to apply a CLEARANCE ALLOWANCE when laying out the sash. Sash for a double-hung window is made 1/8 in. narrower and 1/16 in. shorter than the finished opening size; sash for wooden casements is made 1/8 in. narrower and 1/32 in. shorter than the opening size. Wooden sash is usually made from 1 3/8-in.-thick stock.

368

INSTALLING WINDOW SASH

Casement sash is hung in about the same manner that a door is hung.

Double-hung sash consists of an upper and a lower sash, each of which can be slid up and down in a separate vertical runway. The upper sash slides in the outer runway, the lower sash in the inner runway. The inner side of the outer runway is formed by the parting stop, the outer side by the blind stop, or by a SIDE STOP nailed to the faces of the jambs. The outer side of the inner runway is formed by the parting stop, the inner side by a side stop nailed to the faces of the side jambs. All this is shown in figures 13-10 and 13-11.

The weight of a double-hung sash may be counterbalanced by a couple of SASH WEIGHTS,

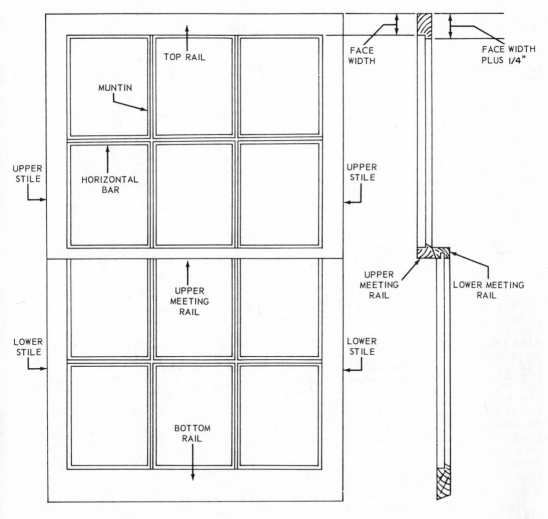

45.509

Figure 13-10.—Parts of a double-hung window sash.

369

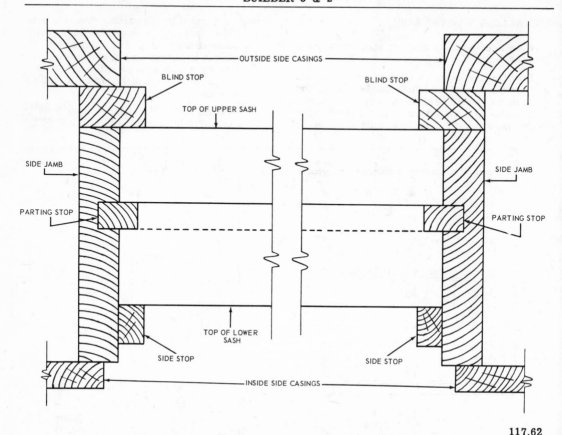

117.62

Figure 13-11.—Double-hung sash installed.

which hang in **PULLEY POCKETS** on either side of the frame, and which are connected to the tops of the upper and lower sash by lengths of SASH CORD running up and over pulleys at the top of the frame. SASH WEIGHTS HAVE BEEN LARGELY REPLACED, HOWEVER, BY VARIOUS SPRING DEVICES WHICH LIE INSIDE THE JAMBS AND DO NOT REQUIRE PULLEY POCKETS. For sash cord the outer edges of the stiles must be grooved about one-third of the way down from the top, and a hole must be cut at the end of each groove to contain a knot in the end of the cord. For some types of spring balances the stiles are not grooved; other types require a groove the full length of the stile.

Steps in fitting and hanging double-hung sash are as follows:

1. Try the upper sash in the frame for a fit; if necessary, plane down the stiles to get a clearance of 1/8 in.

2. Notch the ends of the meeting rails so the rails will fit around the parting stop as shown in figure 13-12. The depth of the notch is equal to the thickness of the parting stop, plus a 1/16-in. allowance for clearance. The width of the notch is the width of the parting stop, less depth of the parting stop groove, plus a 1/16-in. allowance for clearance.

3. Remove the parting stop from the jambs, set the upper sash in its runway, and replace the parting stop. Run the upper sash all the way up and fasten it there with a nail tacked into each of the side jambs.

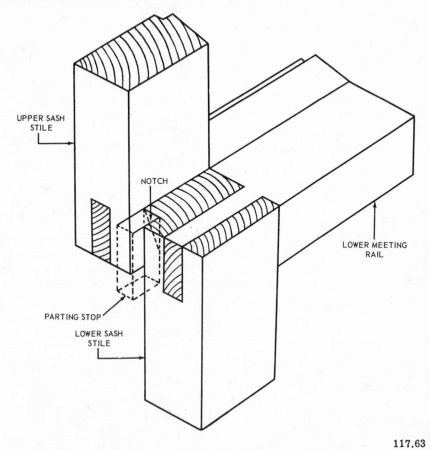

UPPER SASH
STILE

NOTCH

LOWER MEETING
RAIL

PARTING STOP

LOWER SASH
STILE

117.63

Figure 13-12.—Notching meeting rails for parting stop.

4. Try the lower sash for a fit, planing down the stiles as necessary.

5. Set the angle of the sill on the T-bevel by lining the handle of the bevel up with the parting stop and the blade with the sill. Lay off this angle on the bottom of the bottom rail and bevel the bottom of the rail to the angle.

6. Set the lower sash in its runway, all the way down, and measure the amount that the tops of the meeting rails are out of flush with each other. This is the amount that must be planed off the bottom rail to ensure that the meeting rails will be exactly flush when the window is closed. Plane down the bottom rail until the meeting rails come flush.

7. Remove the sash and the parting stop, and install or attach the counterbalance for the upper sash. Manufacturer's instructions for installing are usually included with SPRING BALANCES. To attach a sash weight, first run the end of the sash cord over the pulley into the sashweight pocket. Place the weight in the pocket and bend the cord to it with a round turn and two half-hitches through the eye of the weight. Set the sash in its runway, all the way down, and haul down on the sash cord until the weight is up to the pulley. Bring the cord against the stile, and cut it off about 4 in. below the hole at the end of the groove in the stile. This 4 in. is about the amount required to tie a figure-of-eight knot to set in the hole at the end of the groove.

371

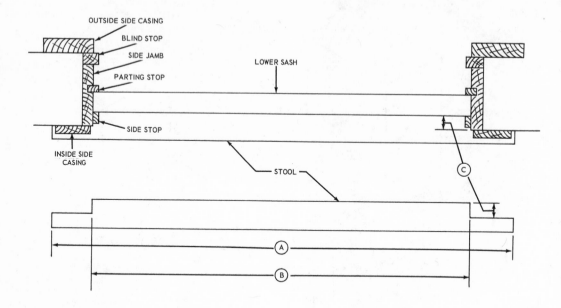

117.65

Figure 13-13.—Window stool layout.

When the counterbalances have all been prepared, set the upper sash in its runway, all the
way up, and nail the parting stop into its groove
with 8-penny finish nails spaced 12 in. O.C.

The side stop and the inside casings cannot
be installed until after the STOOL and APRON
have been installed. Figure 13-13 shows the
general layout of a window stool; whereas figure 13-14 shows the assembled window stool
and apron.

METAL WINDOWS

Either aluminum or steel windows will most
likely be installed in a permanent type of building. Information on construction requirements
and pointers on installing metal windows are
given below.

Regardless of the type of window used, it
should be of the size, combination, and type indicated or specified. Windows should be constructed to produce the results specified and
to assure a neat appearance. Permanent joints
should be formed by welding or by mechanical
fastenings, as specified for each type window.

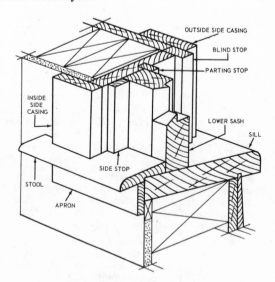

117.64

Figure 13-14.—Window stool
and apron.

Joints should be of sufficient strength to maintain the structural value of members connected. Welded joints should be solid, have excess metal removed, and be dressed smooth on exposed and contact surfaces. The dressing should be done so that no discoloration or roughness will show after finishing. Joints formed with mechanical fastenings should be closely fitted and made permanently watertight. Frames and sash, including ventilators, come assembled as a unit with hardware unattached.

Hardware should be of suitable design and should have sufficient strength to perform the function for which it is used. It should be attached securely to the windows with noncorrosive bolts or machine screws; sheet metal screws should not be used. Where fixed screens are specified, the hardware should be especially adapted to permit satisfactory operation of ventilators.

Make sure you exercise care in handling windows to avoid dropping them. In addition, store windows upright on pieces of lumber to keep them off the ground, and cover them thoroughly to protect them from the elements.

Windows should be installed and adjusted by experienced and qualified Builders. Aluminum windows in concrete or masonry walls should be set in prepared openings. Unless indicated or specified otherwise, all other windows should be built-in as the work progresses, or they should be installed without forcing into prepared openings. Windows should be set at the proper elevation, location, and reveal. They should be set plumb, square, level, and in alignment. They should also be braced, strutted, and stayed properly to prevent distortion and misalignment. Ventilators and operating parts should be protected against accumulation of cement, lime, and other building materials, by keeping ventilators tightly closed and wired fast to the frame. Screws or bolts in sill members, joints at mullions, and contacts of windows with sills, built-in fins, or subframes should be bedded in mastic sealant of a type recommended by the window manufacturer. Windows should be installed in a manner that will prevent entrance of water.

Ample provision should be made for securing units to each other, to masonry, or to other adjoining or adjacent construction. Windows that are to be installed in direct contact with masonry must have head and jamb members designed to enter into masonry not less than 7/16 inch. Where windows are set in prepared masonry openings, the necessary anchorage or fins should be placed during progress of wall construction. Anchors and fastenings should be built into, anchored, or bolted to the jambs of openings, and should be fastened securely to the windows or frames and to the adjoining construction. Unless indicated otherwise, anchors should be spaced not more than 18 inches apart on jambs and sills. Anchors and fastenings should have sufficient strength to hold the member firmly in position.

After windows have been installed and upon completion of glazing and painting, all ventilators and hardware should be adjusted to operate smoothly and to be weathertight when ventilators are closed and locked. Hardware and parts should be lubricated as necessary. Adjustments and tests should be as follows:

(a) Double-hung windows should have balances adjusted to proper tension, and guides waxed or lubricated.

(b) Casements equipped with rotary operators should be adjusted so that the top of the ventilator makes contact with the frame approximately 1/4 inch in advance of the bottom.

(c) Casements equipped with friction hinges, or friction holders, should be adjusted to proper tension.

(d) Projected sash should have arms or slides lubricated and adjusted to proper tension.

(e) Awning windows should have arms to ventilators adjusted so that the bottom edge of each ventilator makes continuous initial contact with frames when closed.

(f) Where windows are weatherstripped, the weatherstripping should make weathertight contact with frames when ventilators are closed and locked. The weatherstripping should not cause binding of sash, or prevent closing and locking of the ventilator.

After adjustment, all non-weatherstripped steel and aluminum windows, except security and commercial projected steel windows, should comply with prescribed feeler gage tests. Windows failing to comply with the tests should be removed and replaced with new windows, or should be corrected and restored to approved condition meeting the required tests. When ventilators are closed and locked, the metal-to-metal contacts between ventilators and their frames should conform to the following requirements:

Whenever conducting the feeler gage test on SIDE-HUNG VENTILATORS, the Builder should remember that it should not be possible to freely insert a steel feeler gage, 2 inches wide by 0.031 inch thick, at any point between the outside contacts of ventilator and frame; nor to freely insert a similar feeler gage, 0.020 inch thick, between more than 40 percent of such contacts.

Remember that for PROJECTED-OUT HORIZONTAL VENTILATORS, it should not be possible to freely insert a steel feeler gage, 2 inches wide by 0.031 inch thick, between the top rail inside contacts, or between the bottom and side rail outside contacts; nor to freely insert a similar feeler gage, 0.020 inch thick, between more than 40 percent of such contacts.

For PROJECTED-IN HORIZONTAL VENTILATORS, it should not be possible to freely insert a steel feeler gage, 2 inches wide by 0.031 inch thick, between the bottom rail outside contacts, or between the top and side rail inside contacts; nor to freely insert a similar feeler gage, 0.020 inch thick, between more than 40 percent of such contacts.

GLAZING

Glazing wood and metal sashes and doors consists of sash conditioning and placement of glass. Maintenance often involves only replacement of loose, deteriorated, or missing putty. When replacing glazing items in buildings and structures, use the same type materials as were used in the original work. Use replacement materials of improved quality only when justified by obvious inadequacy of the materials that have failed or by planned future utilization of the building or structure.

Wood sash may be glazed at the factory or on the job. In some instances it will reduce breakage and labor costs to have glazing done at the job site after sash is fitted. When a large number of stock-size wood sash are used, it is generally cheaper to have glazing done at the factory.

Steel sash are generally furnished open and glazing is performed on the job.

Cost of material varies with the size and kind of glass and whether glass is bedded in putty and face puttied, face puttied only, or set with wood or metal beads.

TYPES OF GLASS

Single strength glass is approximately 1/10 inch thick and used for small areas, never to exceed 400 square inches. Double strength glass is approximately .133 thick and is used where high wind resistance is necessary. Window glass comes in three grades, (AA) or superior grade, (A) or very good, and (B) for general or utility grade.

Heavy sheet glass comes in various thicknesses from 3/16 inch to 1/4 inch and in sheet sizes up to 76 inches x 120 inches. Sheet glass is sometimes used for windows but is usually used for greenhouses. It is slightly wavy and may cause a slight distortion of images viewed through it.

Plate glass is manufactured in a continuous ribbon and cut into large sheets. Plate glass is ground and polished for high quality. It comes in thicknesses from 1/8 inch to 1 1/4 inches and is usually used for large windows, such as store fronts.

Tempered glass is glass that has been reheated to just below its melting point and suddenly cooled by oil bath method.

By cooling against metallic surface. Tempered glass cannot be cut or drilled after tempering and must be ordered to exact size. It will withstand heavy impacts and great pressures but if tapped near edge, will disintegrate into small pieces.

Heat strengthened glass is made of polished plate or patterned glass and is reheated and cooled to strengthen it.

It is used in curtain wall design as spandrel glazing of multistoried buildings.

Patterned glass is a rolled flat glass with an impressioned design on one or both sides.

Wire glass is a regular rolled flat glass with either a hexagonal twisted or a diamond shaped welded continuous wire mesh as near as possible in the center of the sheet. The surface may be either patterned, figured or polished.

Heat absorbing glass is usually a heavy sheet glass, 1/8 inch or 1/4 inch thick, either a bluish or greenish color, has the ability to absorb the infra-red rays from the sun. More than 35 percent of the heat is excluded.

Insulating glass units are comprised of two or more sheets of glass separated by either 3/16 inch, 1/4 inch, or 1/2 inch air space. These units are factory sealed and the captive air is hydrated at atmospheric pressure. They are made of either window glass or polished plate glass. Special units may be obtained of varying combinations of heat absorbing, laminated patterned or tempered glass.

Glare reducing glass is available in double strength, in panes up to 60 inches x 80 inches, and 3/16 inch, 7/32 inch and 1/4 inch in panes up to 72 inches x 120 inches in size. It is light gray in color, gives clear vision and is also slightly heat absorbent. One-fourth inch glass will exclude about 21 percent of the sun's heat rays.

Laminated glass is comprised of two or more sheets of glass with one or more layers of transparent vinyl plastic sandwiched between the glass. An adhesive applied with heat and pressure cements the layers into one unit. The elasticity of the plastic cushions any blow against the glass, preventing sharp pieces from flying. There is also laminated glare reducing glass where the pigment in the vinyl plastic laminated provides the glare control quality.

SASH PREPARATION

Attach the sash to structure so it will withstand the design load and to comply with the specifications. Adjust, plumb and square the sash to within 1/8 inch of nominal dimensions on shop drawings. Remove all rivet, screw, bolt or nail heads, welding fillets and other projections from specified clearances. Seal all sash corners and fabrication intersections to make the sash watertight. Primer paint all sealing surfaces of wood sash and carbon steel sash. Use appropriate solvents to remove grease, lacquers and other organic protecting finishes from sealing surfaces of aluminum sash.

GLASS CUTTING

Insofar as possible, glass should be purchased and stocked in sizes that can be used without cutting. Glass of special sizes is cut in the shop. For glass sizes, measure all four sides of the sash and deduct 1/16 to 1/8 inch in the light size for irregularities in the sash. Minimum equipment required for glass cutting consists of a table, a common wood or metal T-square, and a glass cutter. The table should be about 4 feet square, with front and left-hand edges square. Mark off the surface of the table vertically and horizontally in inches. A thin coating of turpentine or kerosene on the glass line to be cut is helpful in lubricating the action of the cutter wheel. A sharp cutter must be carefully drawn only ONCE along the line of the desired cut. Additional strokes of the cutter may result in breakage.

Check dimensions related to sash openings to be sure that adequate clearances are maintained on all four sides of the perimeter. No attempt should be made to change the size of heat strengthened, tempered or doubled glazed units since any such effort will result in permanent damage. All heat absorbing glass must be clean cut. Nipping to remove flares or to reduce oversized dimensions of heat-absorbing glass is not permitted.

PREPARATION BEFORE GLAZING

Old wood sash. Clean all putty runs of broken glass fragments and glazier's points. Remove loose paint and putty by scraping. Wipe the surface clean with cloth saturated in mineral spirits or turpentine, prime the putty runs, and allow them to dry.

New wood sash. Remove dust, prime the putty runs, and allow them to dry. All new wood sash should be pressure treated for decay protection in accordance with Federal Specification TT-W-571.

Old metal sash. Remove loose paint or putty by scraping. Use steel wool or sandpaper to remove rust. Clean the surfaces thoroughly with a cloth saturated in mineral spirits or turpentine. Prime bare metal and allow it to dry thoroughly.

New metal sash. Wipe the sash thoroughly with a cloth saturated in mineral spirits or turpentine to remove dust, dirt, oil, or grease. Remove rust with steel wool or sandpaper. If the sash is not already factory primed, prime it with rust-inhibitive paint and allow it to dry thoroughly.

SETTING GLASS IN WOOD AND METAL SASH

Do not glaze or reglaze exterior sash when the temperature is 40 degrees F or lower unless absolutely necessary. Sash and door members must be thoroughly cleaned of dust with a brush or cloth dampened with turpentine or mineral spirits. Lay a continuous 1/6-inch-thick bed of putty or compound in the putty run (fig. 13-15). The glazed face can be recognized as the size on which the glass was cut. If the glass has a bowed surface, it should be set with the concave side in. Wire glass is set with the twist vertical. Press the glass firmly into place so that the bed putty will fill all irregularities.

When glazing wood sash, insert two glazier's points per side for small lights and about 8 inches apart on all sides for large lights. When glazing metal sash, use the wire clips or metal glazing beads.

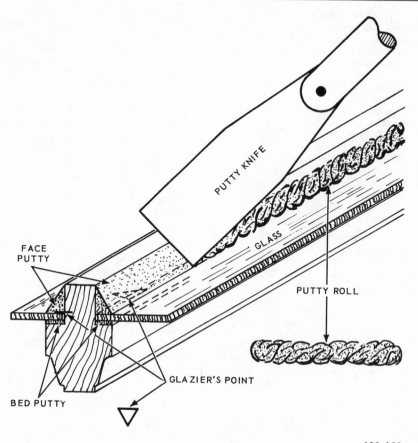

133.160

Figure 13-15.—Setting glass with glazier's points and putty.

After the glass has been bedded, lay a continuous bead of putty against the perimeter of the glass-face putty run. Press the putty with a putty knife or glazing tool with sufficient pressure to ensure its complete adhesion to the glass and sash. Finish with full, smooth, accurately formed bevels with clean cut miters. Trim up the bed putty on the reverse side of the glass. When glazing or reglazing interior sash and transoms, whether fixed or movable, and interior doors, use wood or metal glazing beads. Exterior doors and hinged transoms should have glass secured in place with inside wood or metal glazing beads bedded in putty. When setting wire glass for security purposes, set wood or metal glazing beads, secured with screws, on the side facing the area to be protected. Wood sash putty should be painted as soon as it has surface-hardened. Do not wait longer than 2 months after glazing. Metal sash, Type I, elastic compound, should be painted immediately after a firm skin forms on the surface. Depending on weather conditions, the time for skinning over may be 2 to 10 days. Type II, metal sash putty, can usually be painted within 2 weeks after placing. This putty should not be painted before it has hardened because early painting may retard the set.

Clean the glass on both sides after painting. A cloth moistened with mineral spirits will remove putty stains. Ammonia, acid solutions, or water containing caustic soaps must not be used.

When scrapers are used, care should be exercised to avoid breaking the paint seal at the putty edge.

Handling and cutting glass creates a serious cutting hazard. Appropriate gloves and other personal protective equipment must be provided and adequate procedures for the disposal of cuttings and broken glass established.

FINISH FLOORING

Before any finish flooring is laid the rough floor must be thoroughly cleaned. All plaster droppings must be removed, all protruding nailheads driven flush, and all irregularities planed down or otherwise smoothed. The rough floor should then be carefully inspected for any loose boards or other imperfections.

WOOD-STRIP FINISH FLOORING

Most wood-strip finish flooring is SIDE-MATCHED (tongue-and-grooved on the edges), and some is END-MATCHED (tongue-and-grooved on the ends) as well. Softwood flooring comes in face widths ranging from 2 1/4 to 5 in. The most widely used standard pattern of hardwood flooring has a face width of 2 1/4 in. Most wood-strip flooring is recessed on the lower face as shown in figures 13-16 and 13-17.

Wood subfloors are covered with building paper or with a layer of heavy felt before wood-strip finish flooring is applied. If the specifications call for furring strips between the subflooring and the finish flooring, the strips are nailed on top of the paper or felt. Furring strips are laid at right angles to the line of the finish flooring; they are usually spaced 12 or 16 in. O.C.

Wood-strip flooring is laid at right angles to the line of direction of the joists under the largest room on the floor. The first strip laid (which is called the STARTER strip) is laid parallel to and 5/8 in. away from the outer joist-end wall in the key room. This strip is placed with the side groove toward the wall, and face-nailed down with nails placed where they will be concealed by the SHOE MOLDING (molding placed in the angle between the baseboard and the floor) as shown in figure 13-16.

Subsequent strips are cut, fitted, and laid ahead of the nailing, about 6 or 8 courses (continuous wall-to-wall strips) at a time. A 3-man crew is convenient for wood-strip flooring, with one man cutting, the second fitting, and the third nailing. The cutter cuts strips of random

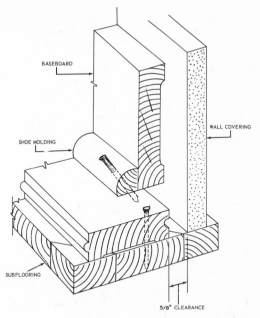

45.512

Figure 13-16.—Blind-nailing starter strip of wood finish flooring.

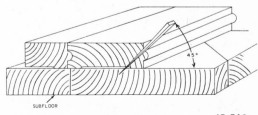

45.510

Figure 13-17.—Toenailing wood-strip flooring.

(various) lengths. The fitter lays out wall-to-wall strips, taking care to stagger end-joints in as uniform a manner as possible. The nailer drives strips up hard against previously nailed strips, using a piece of scrap flooring for the purpose, and then nails the strips down.

Courses which follow the starter course are toenailed down as shown in figure 13-17. Nails should be driven into joists, and it is a good idea to chalk-mark the lines of the joists on the building paper before the floor-laying is started. For 25/32-in.-thick flooring use 8-penny cut flooring nails; for 1/2-in.-thick flooring use 6-penny wire casing nails; for 3/8-in.-thick flooring use 4-penny wire casing nails. Drive each nail down to the point where another blow or two might cause the hammer to damage the edge of the strip; then use a nail set to drive the nail the rest of the way home. Best nailing procedure is to stand on the strip, with toes in line with the outer edge, and strike the nail from a stooping position which will bring the hammer head square against the nail.

Sanding

Power-operated sanding machines are the most satisfactory means of preparing wood floors for finishing. The operator should wear an approved respirator or dust mask while sanding. Abrasive paper, commonly called sandpaper, is made with paper of fabric backing. For machine use, a fabric-backed or fabric-reinforced paper backing is recommended. The mineral cutting agent glued to the face of the paper may be flint (Federal Specification P-P-105), garnet (Federal Specification P-P-121, waterproof), or silicon carbide (Federal Specification P-P-101, waterproof). Cutting surfaces are designated close coat (cutting grits covering the entire face) or open coat (grits covering about half the cutting surface). Opencoat paper is recommended for sanding over materials, such as paint and varnish, that tend to clog spaces between the grits. Flint papers are made in at least 12 grades: 5/0 (very fine), 4/0, 3/0, 2/0, 0, 1/2, 1, 1 1/2, 2, 2 1/2, 3, 3 1/2 (very coarse). Flint (sand) papers having glue binders must not be stored where they will be subject to oil, moisture, or extreme heat and cold. Brittle paper can be softened by dampening the backing. The following table is a guide to sandpaper selection for floor furnishing.

Grade	Type	Use
3 1/2	Open	Preliminary roughing off of stubborn varnish, shellac, floor oil, wax, and deep penetrating filler compounds. Not to be used for cutting into wood surfaces.

Grade	Type	Use
3	Open	Used in place of No. 3 1/2 for surfaces of less resistance; is preferred if it does the required work.
2 1/2	Open	Preliminary roughing off of floor finishes such as shellac, wax, floor oils, alcohol stains, and lacquered surfaces. Use as followup paper for floors roughed off with No. 3 1/2.
2	Close	Use instead of No. 2 and No. 2 1/2 open coat where surface permits cutting without gumming. Closed coat should be used in preference to open coat whenever practicable.
1 1/2	Close	Use as a first paper on all new floors.
1	Open	Use as a followup for No. 2 and No. 2 1/2 in all cases.
1	Close	Use the same as No. 1 open coat to provide a smooth floor finish.
1/2	Close	Use a final finish on most floor work.
1/0 & 2/0	Close	Use as a final finish on best hardwood floor work.
3/0 & 4/0	Close	Use for finishing fine woodwork, such as furniture, and for rubbing down paint and varnish finishes.

In exceptional cases, when old floor finishes cannot be removed by sanding or scraping with an abrasive, highly volatile liquids may be used. These liquids, as well as those used in floor finishing, include paint and varnish remover, varnish, liquid paint, and shellac, which have flashpoints as low as 40 degrees F. Finishing should be done only under expert supervision.

Sealing

Seal wood floor by sealing and waxing them in the following manner: Apply liberally a sealer of light varnish that conforms to Federal Specification TT-S-176. Spread or spray it along the grain of the wood. After the sealer has dried completely, buff the floor with a floor-polishing machine, using No. 1 steelwool pads. If portions of the floor look lusterless, dry, or dead after the buffing, continue sealing and polishing until the floor surface has a uniform appearance. Apply two thin coats of water emulsion wax that conforms to Federal Specification P-W-155. Buff the wax after each application has thoroughly dried.

RESILIENT FLOORING

In Navy construction, wood-strip flooring has been largely replaced by various types of RESILIENT flooring, most of which is applied in the form of 6 x 6-, 9 x 9-, or 12 x 12-in. squares called TILES. The types most frequently used are ASPHALT, VINYL, LINOLEUM, CORK, and RUBBER.

Manufacturers recommend that wood subfloors have an underlayment for resilient flooring, or that sheets of synthetic wood, such as plywood or tempered hardboard, be nailed over single subfloors. The subsurface must be carefully cleaned, smoothed, and inspected, and any cracks wider than 1/8 in. or holes larger than 1/4 in. must be filled. The subsurface is then covered with a felt backing, cemented down with adhesive. The tile is then laid on the felt.

Asphalt, and vinyl tile is set in an asphalt tile EMULSION, linoleum and cork tile in linoleum cement, and rubber tile in waterproof rubber cement. The manufacturer's instructions on proper methods of applying adhesive and laying tile are provided and should be carefully followed. All floors subjected to excessive moisture should be applied with a waterproof adhesive.

ASPHALT AND VINYL TILES

Asphalt tile is a blended composition of asphaltic and/or resinous binders, asbestos fibers, and inert fillers or pigments. It can be installed satisfactorily over concrete floors in direct contact with the ground without the need to completely waterproof the concrete slab. It is quiet and safe to walk on, durable, and resistant to abrasion from foot traffic and common abuses such as scuffing and cigarette burns. The tile is low in maintenance cost. Tiles are available in sizes of 4 by 4 inches, 9 by 9 inches, and 12 by 12 inches, in thicknesses of 1/8 and 3/16 inch. Tiles 9 by 9 inches are most commonly used in military construction.

Vinyl tiles are available in two types: vinyl asbestos tile, Federal Specification L-T-345, and flexible vinyl, Federal Specification L-F-450. Tiles are available in sizes of 6 by 6 inches, 9 by 9 inches, and 12 by 12 inches, and in thicknesses of 1/8 and 3/32 inch. Vinyl is also available in 54-inch sheets. Vinyl tile may be laid on a concrete floor in direct contact with the ground only if the slab is membrane-waterproofed. Vinyl tiles are durable and easy to keep clean. Vinyl plastic floorings have good resistance to abrasion, are impervious to water, and are outstanding in resistance to grease, oils, and alkalies.

Asphalt and vinyl tiles should be laid according to the manufacturer's recommendations, with or without lining felt as suitable for the application. Before the tile is laid, the floor area should be squared and the best method of laying the tile determined, depending on the shape of the room, location of fixed furnishings and equipment, and doorways. Tile should always be laid from the center of the room toward the walls so that border widths can be adjusted accordingly. Tiles should be stored for 24 hours before installation in a room heated to at least 70 degrees. Cold tiles may cause condensation on the underside and break down the cement bond. Cement should be spread at a uniform consistency ahead of the work and allowed to dry to a tacky state before tile is laid in it.

CERAMIC AND QUARRY FLOOR TILE

Ceramic floor tile is glazed or unglazed, manufactured in small square, hexagonal, rectangular, and circular shapes about 1/4 inch thick, and often arranged in mosaic patterns. The pieces are usually factory-assembled (face side up) on paper sheets in the required pattern, laid on a mortar setting bed, pressed firmly on the mortar, and tamped true and even with the finished floor line. Grout is then forced into the joints, filling them completely, and is finished flush and level with the floor line.

Quarry tile is usually unglazed and manufactured in square and rectangular shapes, ranging from 2 3/4 inches to 9 inches in width, from 2 3/4 inches to 12 inches in length, and of varying thicknesses. Tiles are laid individually on a mortar setting bed with joints about 1/2 inch wide.

In locations such as galleys and food preparation areas, where the floor is directly exposed to the effects of corrosion agents, use acid-resistant joint material to fill the joints. The acid-resistant mortars are proprietary products and should be mixed in accordance with the manufacturer's recommendations. They should be composed of powdered resin and liquid resin cement and be resistant to the effects of oils, fats, greases, organic and inorganic acids, salts, alkalies, and mineral solvents.

DOORS

Inside door frames are constructed in several ways. The interior type is constructed like the outside type except that no casing is used on inside door frames. Hinge blocks are nailed to the inside wall finish, where the hinges are to be placed, to provide a nailing surface for the hinge flush with the door. Both the outside and inside door frames may be modified to suit a climatic condition.

DOOR JAMBS

Door jambs (fig. 13-18) are the linings of the framing of door openings. Casings and stops are nailed to the door jambs and the door is hung from them. Inside jambs are made of 3/4-inch stock and outside jambs of 1 3/8-inch stock. The width of the stock will vary in accordance with the thickness of the walls. Inside jambs are built up with 3/8- by 1 3/8-inch stops nailed to the jamb, while outside jambs are usually rabbeted out to receive the door. Jambs are made and set in the following manner:

Regardless of how carefully rough openings are made, be sure to plumb the jambs and level the heads, when jambs are set.

Rough openings are usually made 2 1/2 inches larger in width and height than the size of the door to be hung. For example, a 2-foot 8-inch by 6-foot 8-inch door would need a rough opening of 2 feet 10 1/2 inches by 6 feet 10 1/2 inches. This extra space allows for the jambs, the wedging, and the clearance space for the door to swing.

Level the floor across the opening to determine any variation in floor heights at the point where the jambs rest on the floor.

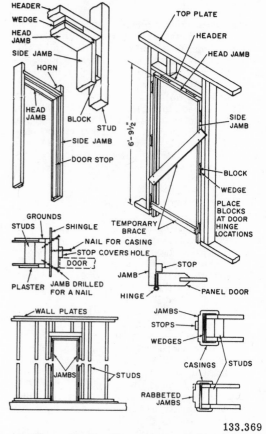

133.369

Figure 13-18.—Door jamb and door trim.

Now cut the head jamb with both ends square, having allowed width of the door plus the depth of both dadoes and a full 3/16 inch for door clearance.

From the lower edge of the dado, measure a distance equal to the height of the door plus the clearance wanted under it. Mark and cut square.

On the opposite jamb do the same, only make additions or subtractions for the variation in the floor, if any.

Now nail the jambs and jamb heads together with 8-penny common nails through the dado into the head jamb.

Set the jambs into the opening and place small blocks under each jamb on the subfloor just as thick as the finish floor will be. This is to allow the finish floor to go under.

Plumb the jambs and level the jamb head.

Wedge the sides with shingles between the jambs and the studs, to align, and then nail securely in place.

Take care not to wedge the jamb unevenly.

Use a straightedge 5 or 6 feet long inside the jambs to help prevent uneven wedging.

Check jambs and head carefully, because jambs placed out of plumb will have a tendency to swing the door open or shut, depending on the direction in which the jamb is out of plumb.

DOOR TRIM

Door trim material is nailed onto the jambs to provide a finish between the jambs and the plastered wall. It is frequently called "casing" (fig. 13-18). Sizes vary from 1/2 to 3/4 inches in thickness, and from 2 1/2 to 6 inches in width. Most trim has a concave back, to fit over uneven plaster. In mitered work, care must be taken to make all joints clean, square, neat, and well fitted. (If the trim is to be mitered at the top corners, a miter box, miter square, hammer nail set, and block plane will be needed.) Door openings are cased up in the following manner:

Leave a margin of 1/4-inch from the edge of the jamb to the casing all around.

Cut one of the side casings square and even at the bottom, with the bottom of the jamb.

Cut the top or mitered end next, allowing 1/4-inch extra length for the margin at the top.

Nail the casing onto the jamb and even with the 1/4-inch margin line, starting at the top and working toward the bottom.

Use 4-penny finish nails along the jamb side and 6-penny or 8-penny case nails along the outer edge of the casings.

The nails along the outer edge will need to be long enough to go through the casing and plaster and into the studs.

Set all nailheads about 1/8 inch below the surface of the wood with a nail set.

Now apply the casing for the other side and then the head casing.

FITTING A DOOR

If a number of doors are to be fitted and hung, a DOOR JACK like the one shown in figure 13-19 should be constructed, to hold doors upright for the planing of edges and the installation of HARDWARE (hinges, locks, knobs, and other metal fittings on a door or window).

NOTE: The edge of the door can be beveled to prevent binding and to give a tighter fit.

The first step in fitting a door is to determine from the floor plan which stile is the hinge stile and which the lock stile, and to mark both the stiles and the corresponding jambs accordingly. Next, carefully measure the height of the finished opening ON BOTH SIDE JAMBS and the width of the opening AT BOTH TOP AND BOTTOM. The finished opening should be perfectly rectangular; but IT MAY NOT BE. Your job now is to fit the door accurately to the opening, regardless of the shape of the opening.

A well-fitted door, when hung, should conform to the shape of the finished opening, less a clearance allowance of 1/16 in. at the sides and on top. For an interior door without sill or threshold there should be a bottom clearance above the finished floor of from 3/8 to 1/2 in. This clearance is required to ensure that the door will swing clear of carpeting; if the carpeting is to be extra-thick, the bottom clearance will have to be greater than 1/2 in. For a door with a sill and no threshold, the bottom clearance should be 1/16 in. above the sill. For a door with a threshold, the bottom clearance should be 1/16 above the threshold. The sill and threshold, if any, should be set in place before the door is hung.

Lay off the measured dimensions of the finished opening, less allowances, on the door. Check the door jambs for trueness, and if you find any irregularities, transfer them to the door lines. Place the door in the jack and plane the edges to the lines, setting the door in the opening frequently to check the fit.

HANGING A DOOR

You will be dealing mainly with doors equipped with SIDE hinges (hinges located on the edges of one stile or the other). There are various types of side hinges, but yours will be mostly LOOSE-PIN BUTT MORTISE hinges like the one shown in figure 13-20. A loose-pin butt hinge consists of two rectangular LEAVES, pivoted on a PIN which is called a LOOSE PIN because it can be removed by simple extraction. The hinge is called a MORTISE hinge because the leaves are MORTISED into gains cut in the hinge stile of the door and the hinge jamb of the door frame.

The first step in hanging a door is to lay out the locations of the hinges on the hinge stile and the hinge jamb. Set the door in the frame, and

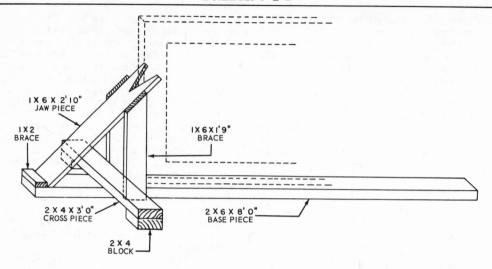

1 X 6 X 2' 10"
JAW PIECE

1 X 2
BRACE

1 X 6 X 1'9"
BRACE

2 X 4 X 3' 0"
CROSS PIECE

2 X 6 X 8' 0"
BASE PIECE

2 X 4
BLOCK

117.68

Figure 13-19.—Door jack.

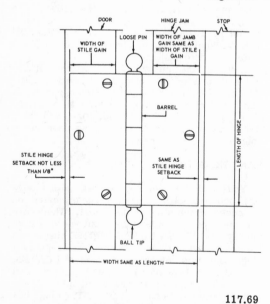

DOOR

HINGE JAM

STOP

WIDTH OF
STILE GAIN

LOOSE PIN

WIDTH OF JAMB
GAIN SAME AS
WIDTH OF STILE
GAIN

BARREL

STILE HINGE
SETBACK NOT LESS
THAN 1/8"

SAME AS
STILE HINGE
SETBACK

LENGTH OF HINGE

BALL TIP

WIDTH SAME AS LENGTH

117.69

Figure 13-20.—Loose-pin butt
mortise hinge.

force the hinge stile against the hinge jamb with
the wedge marked A in figure 13-21. Then insert a 4-penny finish nail between the top rail

and the head jamb, and force the top rail up
against the nail with the wedge marked B in the
figure. Since a 4-penny finish nail has a diameter of 1/16 in. (which is the standard top
clearance for a door), the door is now at the
correct height.

Exterior doors usually have 3 hinges, interior
doors, as a rule, only 2. The vertical distance
between the top of the door and the top of the
top hinge, and between the top of the finish floor
and the bottom of the bottom hinge, may be
specified. If not, the distances customarily
used are those shown in figure 13-21. The
middle hinge, if there is one, is usually located
midway between the other two.

The size of a loose-pin butt mortise hinge is
designated by the length (height) and by the combined width of the leaves in inches (height is
always given first). The width varies with the
requirements of setback, clearance, door thickness, etc., and is calculated individually for each
door. Doors 1 1/8 to 1 3/8 in. thick and up to
32-in. wide take a 3 1/2-in. hinge. Doors 1 1/8
to 1 3/8 in. thick and from 32 to 37-in. wide take
a 4-in. hinge. Doors more than 1 3/8 in. but
not more than 1 7/8 in. thick and up to 32-in.
wide take a 4 1/2 in. hinge; if more than 32 but
not more than 37-in. wide they take a 5-in.
hinge; if from 37 to 43-in. wide they take a 5-in.
EXTRA HEAVY hinge. Doors thicker than 1 7/8

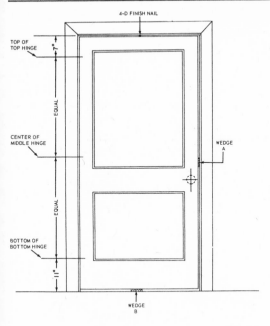

Figure 13-21.—Laying out hinge locations on a door.

117.70

in. and up to 43-in. wide take a 5-in. extra heavy hinge. Doors thicker than 1 7/8 in. and wider than 43-in. take a 6-in. extra heavy hinge.

Place the door in the door jack and lay off the outlines of the gains on the edge of the hinge stile, using a hinge leaf as a marker. The STILE HINGE SETBACK (shown in fig. 13-20) should be not less than 1/8-in. and is usually made about 1/4-in. Lay out gains of exactly the same size on the hinge jamb, and then chisel out the gains to a depth exactly equal to the thickness of a leaf.

Separate the leaves on the hinges by extracting the loose pins, and screw the leaves into the gains, taking care to ensure that the loose pin will be up when the door is hung in place. Hang the door in place, insert the loose pins, and check the clearances at the side jambs. If the clearance along the hinge jamb is too large (more than 1/16-in.) and that along the lock jamb too small (less than 1/16), remove the door, remove the hinge leaves from the gains, and slightly deepen the gains. If the clearance along the hinge jamb is too small and that along

the lock jamb too large, the gains are too deep. This can be corrected by shimming up the leaves with strips of cardboard placed in the gains.

INSTALLING A CYLINDER LOCK

The parts of an ordinary cylinder LOCK for a door are shown in figure 13-22. The procedure for installing a lock of this type is as follows:

Open the door to a convenient working position and check it in place with wedges under the bottom near the outer edge.

Measure up 36 in. from the floor (the usual knob height), and square a line across the face and edge of the lock stile.

Use the template that is usually supplied with cylinder lock; place the template on the face of the door (at proper height and alignment with layout lines) and mark the centers of holes to be drilled. (See fig. 13-23.)

Drill the holes through the face of the door and then the one through the edge to receive the latch bolt. It should be slightly deeper than the length of the bolt.

Cut a gain for the latch-bolt mounting plate, and install the latch unit.

Install interior and exterior knobs.

Find the position of the strike plate and install it in the jamb.

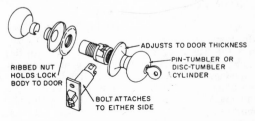

133.161

Figure 13-22.—Parts of a cylinder lock.

INTERIOR TRIM

The casing around the doors and windows, the baseboard with its base mold and shoe mold, the picture mold, chair rail, cornice mold, and panel mold are the various trim members used in finishing the interior of a building.

Various types of wood can be used for interior trim, such as birch, oak, mahogany, walnut, white and yellow pine, and other available woods.

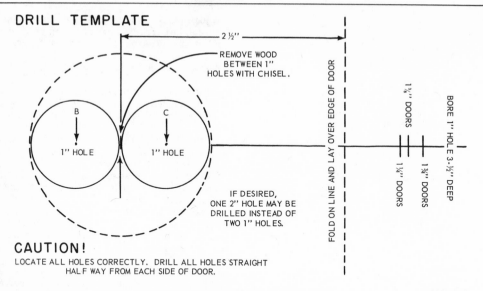

DRILL TEMPLATE

2½"

REMOVE WOOD BETWEEN 1" HOLES WITH CHISEL.

B
1" HOLE

C
1" HOLE

IF DESIRED, ONE 2" HOLE MAY BE DRILLED INSTEAD OF TWO 1" HOLES.

FOLD ON LINE AND LAY OVER EDGE OF DOOR

1⅜" DOORS

1¼" DOORS

1¾" DOORS

BORE 1" HOLE 3-½" DEEP

CAUTION!
LOCATE ALL HOLES CORRECTLY. DRILL ALL HOLES STRAIGHT HALF WAY FROM EACH SIDE OF DOOR.

133.162

Figure 13-23.—One type of template.

A close-grain wood should be used when the trim is to be painted. However, harder woods free from pitch will provide a better paint surface.

BASEBOARDS

A trim member called a BASEBOARD is usually installed on the line along which the walls join the floors. Baseboard is nailed to the studs with two 6-penny finish nails at each stud crossing. The first step in installing baseboard, therefore, is to locate all the studs in the wall and mark the locations on the floor with light pencil marks.

Baseboard is miter-joined at outside corners and butt-joined at inside corners. Where baseboards cannot be miter-joined or butt-joined at corners, they should be capped. Since the walls at corner baseboard locations may not be perfectly vertical, inside and outside corners should be joined as follows:

To butt-join a piece of baseboard to another piece already in place at an inside corner, set the piece to be joined in position on the floor, bring the end against or near the face of the other piece, and take off the line of the face with a scriber as shown in figure 13-24. Use the

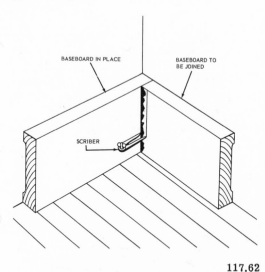

BASEBOARD IN PLACE

BASEBOARD TO BE JOINED

SCRIBER

117.62

Figure 13-24.—Butt-joining baseboard at an inside corner.

same procedure when butting ends of baseboard against the side casings of doors.

For miter-joining at an outside corner, proceed as shown in figure 13-25. First set a

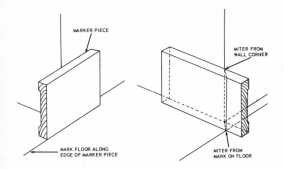

MARKER PIECE

MITER FROM
WALL CORNER

MARK FLOOR ALONG
EDGE OF MARKER PIECE

MITER FROM
MARK ON FLOOR

117.73

Figure 13-25.—Miter-joining baseboard
at an outside corner.

MARKER PIECE of baseboard across the wall corner, as shown in the left-hand view and mark the floor along the edge of the piece. Then set the piece to be mitered in place, and mark the point where the wall corner intersects the top edge and the point where the mark on the floor intersects the bottom edge. Lay 45 degree lines across the edge from these points (for a 90-degree corner), connect these lines with a line across the face, and miter to the lines as indicated.

The line along which the baseboard joins the floor is usually covered by a strip of quarter-round molding called a SHOE molding. The shoe molding should be nailed to the floor, as shown in figure 13-16, and not to the baseboard. If it is nailed to the baseboard and the floor should

happen to settle, a space will appear between the bottom of the shoe molding and the floor surface.

The upper edges of baseboards are sometimes trimmed with a strip of molding called a BASE CAP.

MISCELLANEOUS TRIM MEMBERS

The PICTURE MOLD is usually placed against the wall near the ceiling; however, at times you may prefer to lower it to 12 or 16 inches below the ceiling. CORNICE MOLD is usually a large cove mold fitted and nailed against both the wall and ceiling. The cornice mold of a room is sometimes ornamental and made up of several members. The CHAIR RAIL may be placed at various heights on the wall, usually around 48 inches up from the floor. The chair rail can be used to fasten fixtures. The PANEL MOLD is used to divide wall spaces into panels; this mold may be used horizontal or vertical. SHELF CLEATS make removal of shelves easier and they are very convenient for closets.

CASINGS and STOPS for doors and windows as well as STOOLS and APRONS, usually come in rough lengths. When this happens, it is a good plan to assort, select, and place the various members at each opening. When they come in random lengths, cut them to the rough lengths, and then assort them. Most base members and other moldings come in random lengths. Remember that the longest pieces should be reserved for the longest distances to be trimmed to avoid unsightly patching and piecing of trim.

CHAPTER 14
PLASTERING, STUCCOING AND TILE SETTING

PLASTER and STUCCO, like concrete, are construction materials which are applied in a plastic condition, and which harden in place after being applied. The fundamental difference between plaster and stucco is simply one of location; if the material is used internally it is called plaster; if it is used externally it is called stucco.

Again like concrete, the active ingredient in plaster is a CEMENTITIOUS material, or BINDER. If plaster is applied in more than one layer, the top layer is called the FINISH COAT and each of the lower layers is a BASE COAT. Plaster for a finish coat may consist of binder alone; however, most finish coat plaster and most base coat plaster contains AGGREGATE as well as binder. Plaster aggregate may consist of sand or one of several other materials. The aggregate in plaster, like the aggregate in concrete, provides additional bulk and stability.

You can see that plaster is to a large extent very much like concrete. The principal difference lies in the fact that concrete can, because of its high compressive strength, be used as a load-bearing structural material. The considerably lower strength of plaster has, up until now, confined its use principally to finish. However, experiments are being conducted with an eye to developing plasters with load-bearing strength.

A plaster mix, like a concrete mix, is made plastic for application by the addition of water to the dry ingredients. Again like concrete, it is a reaction of the binder to the water called HYDRATION that causes the mix to harden.

PLASTER INGREDIENTS

The binders most commonly used for plaster are GYPSUM, LIME, and PORTLAND CEMENT. Because gypsum plaster should not be exposed to free water or severe moisture conditions, it is usually confined to interior use. Lime and portland cement plaster may be used both internally and externally.

GYPSUM PLASTER

Gypsum is a naturally occurring sedimentary gray, white, or pink rock. The natural rock is crushed and then heated to high temperature, a process (known as CALCINING) which drives off about three-quarters of the WATER OF CRYSTALLIZATION which forms about 20 percent by weight of the rock in a natural state. The calcined material is then ground to a fine powder, to which certain ADDITIVES are added to control set, stabilization, and other physical or chemical characteristics.

For a type of gypsum plaster called KEENE'S CEMENT the crushed gypsum rock is heated until nearly all of the water of crystallization is driven off. To offset slow-setting caused by absence of so much WATER OF HYDRATION, an Englishman named Keene patented a process of adding alum as an accelerator. The resulting plaster, called Keene's cement, produces a very hard, fine-textured finish coat.

The removal of water of crystallization from natural gypsum is a DEHYDRATION process. In the course of setting, mixing water (water of hydration) added to the mix REHYDRATES with the gypsum, thus causing RECRYSTALLIZATION. Recrystallization causes the plaster to harden.

There are four common types of gypsum basecoat plasters, as follows:

GYPSUM NEAT plaster is gypsum plaster without aggregate, intended for mixing with aggregate on the job.

GYPSUM READY-MIXED plaster consists of gypsum and ordinary mineral aggregate; at the job it requires addition of only the water.

GYPSUM WOOD-FIBERED plaster consists of calcined gypsum combined with not less than 0.75 percent by weight of non-staining wood fibers. It may be used as is or mixed with 1 part sand to produce base coats of superior strength and hardness.

GYPSUM BOND plaster is so-called because it is designed to bond to properly prepared monolithic concrete. It consists essentially of calcined gypsum mixed with from 2 to 5 percent of lime by weight.

There are five common types of gypsum finish coat plasters, as follows:

READY-MIX GYPSUM FINISH plasters are designed for use over gypsum plaster basecoats. They consist of finely ground calcined gypsum, some with and others without aggregate. At the job they require addition of water only.

GYPSUM ACOUSTICAL plasters are designed to reduce sound reverberation.

GYPSUM GAUGING plasters contain LIME PUTTY, the inclusion of which provides certain setting properties, increases dimensional stability during drying, and provides initial surface hardness. Gauging plasters are obtainable as SLOW-SET, QUICK-SET, and SPECIAL HIGH STRENGTH.

GYPSUM MOLDING plaster is used primarily in casting and ornamental plaster work. It is available neat (that is, without admixtures) or with lime. As with portland cement mortar, the addition of lime to a plaster mix makes the mix more "buttery."

KEENE'S CEMENT is a fine, high density plaster capable of creating a highly polished surface. It is customarily used with lime putty, and with fine sand which provides crack-resistance.

LIME PLASTER

LIME is obtained principally from the burning (called calcining) of LIMESTONE, a very common mineral. During the calcining process certain chemical changes occur which transform the limestone into what is called QUICK-LIME. Quicklime which meets certain requirements is pulverized for building use; other quicklime is further processed into HYDRATED lime for building use.

Before being used for plastering, quicklime must be SLAKED. Slaking consists of adding the quicklime to water. Be careful when adding quicklime to water because of a chemical change that will occur. For example, always add quick-slaking lime to water; when escaping steam appears, the lime should be hoed and just enough lime added to stop the steaming. When mixing medium-slaking and slow-slaking limes, the water should be added to the lime. The slow-slaking lime must be mixed under an ideal temperature; thereby making it necessary to heat the water in cold weather. Magnesium lime is easily "drowned" so be careful when adding too much water to quick-slaking calcium lime. When too little water is added to either calcium or magnesium limes they can be "burned." Whenever lime is burned or drowned, a part of it is spoiled and it will not harden and the paste is not as viscous and plastic as it should be. The quicklime must be soaked for an extended period of as much as 21 days. The end-product is plastic LIME PUTTY.

Because of the delays involved in the slaking process, most building lime is hydrated lime. NORMAL hydrated lime is converted into lime putty by soaking for at least 16 hours. SPECIAL hydrated lime develops immediate plasticity when mixed with water and may be used right after mixing.

Like calcined gypsum, lime plaster tends to return to its original rock-like state after application.

For interior basecoat work, lime plaster has been largely supplanted by gypsum plaster. It is now used principally for interior finish coats. Because lime putty is the most plastic and workable of the cementitious materials used in plaster, it is often added to other less workable plaster materials to improve plasticity. For lime plaster, lime (in the form of either dry hydrate or lime putty) is mixed with sand, water, and a GAUGING MATERIAL. A gauging material is intended to produce early strength and to counteract shrinkage tendencies. The gauging material may be either GYPSUM GAUGING PLASTER or Keene's cement for interior work, or portland cement for exterior work.

PORTLAND CEMENT

Portland cement plaster is similar to the portland cement mortar used in masonry. It may contain cement, sand, and water only; however, lime, ground asbestos, or some other plasticizing material is usually added for "butteriness."

Portland cement plaster may be applied direct to exterior and interior masonry walls. Elsewhere it will be applied over metal lath. Never apply portland cement plaster over gypsum plasterboard or over gypsum tile. Portland cement plaster is recommended for use in plastering walls and ceilings of large walk-in refrigerators and cold storage spaces, basement spaces, toilets, showers, and similar areas where an extra hard or highly water-resistant surface is required.

AGGREGATE

The aggregates most commonly used in plaster are SAND, VERMICULITE, and PERLITE. Generally speaking, any sand retained on the No. 4 sieve is too coarse to use in plaster, and only a small percentage of the material (about 5 percent) should pass the No. 200 sieve.

Sand

Sand for plaster, like sand for concrete, must be free of more than a specified minimum of organic impurities and harmful chemicals. Certain tests for these impurities and chemicals are conducted by qualified personnel.

Proper aggregate gradation influences plaster strength and workability, and likewise has an effect on the tendency of the material to shrink or expand while setting. For sand intended for use in gypsum plaster, recommended gradation is as follows:

| Sieve Size | Percentage Retained by Weight | |
	Max	Min
No. 4	0	-
No. 8	5	0
No. 16	30	5
No. 30	65	30
No. 50	95	65
No. 100	100	90

For sand intended for use in exterior plaster, recommended gradation is as follows:

| Sieve Size | Percentage Retained by Weight | |
	Max	Min
No. 4	0	-
No. 8	10	0
No. 16	40	10
No. 30	65	30
No. 50	90	70
No. 100	100	95

Plaster strength is reduced if excessive fine aggregate material is present in a mix. The greater quantity of mixing water required raises the water:cement ratio, thereby reducing the dry set density. The cementitious material becomes overextended, because it must coat a relatively larger overall aggregate surface.

An excess of coarse adversely affects workability; the mix becomes "harsh working" and difficult to apply.

Plaster shrinkage during drying may be caused by an excess of either fine or coarse. Because an excess of fine increases the aggregate total surface area, a larger quantity of binder paste is needed to coat all particles. The mix becomes too rich in cementitious material, and it is the cementitious material which is unstable after application. The end-effect is much the same if there is too much coarse; in this case, there is not enough fine to fill the voids between coarse particles, and more cementitious material must be used to fill these voids. Again the result is a rich and relatively unstable material.

Vermiculite

VERMICULITE is a MICACEOUS mineral—meaning a mineral in which each particle is LAMINATED, or made up of adjoining layers. When vermiculite particles are exposed to intense heat, steam forms between the layers so as to force them apart; this causes each particle to increase from 6 to 20 times in volume. The expanded material is soft and pliable, with a color varying between silver and gold.

For ordinary plaster work, vermiculite is used only with gypsum plaster—therefore, in general, only for interior plastering. For acoustical plaster, vermiculite is combined with a special acoustical binder.

Expanded vermiculite is manufactured in five types (I, II, III, IV, and V) according to particle size. Only type III is used in plastering. It is the lightest of the standard plaster aggregates, weighing only from 6 to 10 lbs per cu ft. The approximate dry weight of a cu ft of 1:2 gypsum-vermiculite plaster is 50 to 55 lbs; the dry weight of a cu ft of comparable sanded plaster is 104 to 120 lbs.

For gypsum-vermiculite plaster the following gradation for the vermiculite is recommended:

Sieve Size	Percentage Retained by Volume	
	Max	Min
No. 4	0	-
No. 8	10	0
No. 16	75	40
No. 30	95	65
No. 50	98	75
No. 100	100	90

Perlite

Raw perlite is a volcanic glass which, when flash-roasted, expands to form frothy particles of irregular shape that contain countless minute air cells. Perlite ore is crushed and then heated to high temperature; as the particles soften, combined water turns to steam. This causes the particles to "pop," forming a frothy mass of glass bubbles 4 to 20 times the volume of the raw particle. The process is called EXPANDING; the color of expanded perlite ranges from pearly white to grayish white.

Perlite is used with calcined gypsum or portland cement for interior plastering; it is also used with special binders for acoustical plaster. The approximate dry weight of a cu ft of 1:2 gypsum-perlite plaster is 50 to 55 lbs, or about half the weight of a cu ft of sand-plaster.

For gypsum-perlite plaster the recommended gradation for the perlite is as follows:

Sieve Size	Percentage Retained by Volume	
	Max	Min
No. 4	0	-
No. 8	5	0
No. 16	60	10
No. 30	95	45
No. 50	98	75
No. 100	100	88

Other Aggregates

Although sand, vermiculite, and perlite constitute the great preponderance of plaster aggregate, certain other materials are used. Wood fiber may be added to neat gypsum plaster at the time of manufacture, to improve the working qualities of the gypsum. PUMICE is a naturally foamed volcanic glass similar to perlite, but heavier (28 to 32 lbs per cu ft, against 7.5 to 15 lbs for perlite). The weight differential gives perlite an economic advantage, and limits the use of pumice to localities near where it is produced.

WATER

The mixing water in plaster performs two functions. First, it transforms the dry ingredients into a plastic, workable mass; second, it combines mechanically and/or chemically with the binder to induce hardening. As is the case with concrete, there is a maximum quantity of water per unit of binder required for complete hydration, and an excess over this amount reduces the plaster strength below the maximum attainable.

However, in all plaster mixing more water is added than is necessary for complete hydration of the binder; the excess is necessary to bring the mix to workable consistency. The amount that must be added for workability depends on the character and age of the binder, the method of application, the drying conditions, and the tendency of the base to absorb water. A porous masonry base, for example, will draw a good deal of water out of a plaster mix. If this reduces the water content of the mix, below the maximum required for hydration, incomplete curing will result.

As a general rule, only the amount of water required to attain workability is added to a mix, and no more. The water should be clean and fresh, and it must contain no dissolved chemicals which might accelerate or retard the set. Water previously used to wash plastering tools should never be used for mixing plaster; such water may contain particles of set plaster which may accelerate setting. Stagnant water should be avoided, because such water may contain organic material which may retard setting and possibly cause staining.

PLASTER BASES

For plastering there must be a continuous surface to which the plaster can be applied and to which it will cling; such a surface is called a plaster BASE. A continuous concrete or masonry surface may serve as a base without the necessity for further treatment.

For plaster planes such as those defined by the inner edges of studs or the lower edges of

joists, however, base material must be installed to form a continuous surface which will
span the spaces between the structural members. Material of this kind is called LATH.
Lath formerly consisted of thin wooden strips
which were nailed at right angles to the studs
or joists. Narrow openings were left between
adjacent laths, through which the plaster penetrated to form a KEY which bonded the plaster
to the lath.

In modern plastering, wooden lath has been
almost entirely superseded by GYPSUM lath
and METAL lath.

GYPSUM LATH

Gypsum lath is made by sandwiching a core
of gypsum plaster between two sheets of a
fibrous, absorbent paper. For PLAIN (non-
perforated) gypsum lath, bond is effected by
absorption or suction of the face of the lath.
This absorption draws in some of the cementitious material in the plaster. As the plaster
sets, particles of this absorbed material interlock with nonabsorbed particles in the plaster.
For PERFORATED (punched with 3/4-in. holes
4 in. apart) gypsum plaster, suction bond is
supplemented by keys formed by plaster which
penetrates the holes.

Standard sheet size for gypsum lath is
16 in. x 48 in., except in the western U.S.,
where it is 16 1/5 in. x 48 in. LONG LENGTH
gypsum lath comes 16 or 24 in. wide and any
length up to 12 ft as ordered. Available thicknesses are 3/8 in. and 1/2 in. INSULATING
gypsum lath has aluminum foil bonded to the
back of the sheet; this material provides thermal insulation and also serves as a vapor
barrier.

Gypsum lath is nailed to studs, joists, or
furring strips with 1 1/8-in. to 1-1/4 in. flat-
headed GYPSUM LATH NAILS, 5 nails to each
stud, joist, or strip crossing. It may also be
attached with power-driven staples.

METAL LATH

Metal lath consists essentially of a metal
screen. Bond is created by keys formed by
plaster forced through the screen openings; as
the plaster hardens, it and the metal become
rigidly interlocked.

WIRE lath consists simply of wire screen,
formed by weaving or welding intersecting
wires together. SHEET metal lath consists of
sheet metal perforated with openings of various
shapes. EXPANDED metal lath is manufactured by first cutting staggered slits in a sheet
and then expanding (stretching) the sheet to
form the screen openings. RIB EXPANDED
metal lath contains V-shaped metal ribs for the
purpose of furring the lath out from the surface
to which it is attached. Ordinary unribbed expanded metal lath is called FLAT EXPANDED.

Types of Flat Expanded Lath

DIAMOND MESH lath, suitable for all types
of plastering, comes in 24-in. x 96-in. and
27-in. x 96- in. sheets.

SELF-FURRING DIAMOND MESH contains
DIMPLES which fur it out 1/4 in. from the surface to which it is attached. This lath may be
nailed to smooth concrete or masonry surfaces,
or wrapped around structural steel, without the
necessity for previous furring. It is widely
used for replastering old walls and ceilings
when the removal of the old plaster is not desired. Standard sizes are the same as for
diamond mesh.

PAPER-BACKED DIAMOND MESH is designed to receive plaster applied by machine.

STUCCO MESH has larger openings than
diamond mesh; it is intended primarily for exterior plastering.

Types of Rib Expanded Lath

FLAT rib lath has ribs 1/8 in. deep; THREE-
EIGHTHS INCH rib lath has ribs 3/8 in. deep;
and THREE-QUARTER INCH rib lath has ribs
3/4 in. deep. Standard sheet sizes for flat and
three-eighths are the same as for diamond
mesh. For three-quarter the widths are the
same, but lengths of 120 in. and 144 in. are
available besides 96 in.

Attachment of Metal Lath

Metal lath is nailed to vertical wooden supports (such as wall studs cr wall furring strips)
with 4d common nails. It is nailed to horizontal wooden supports (such as ceiling joists or
ceiling furring strips) with 1 1/2-in. barbed
roofing nails. It may also be attached to wooden
supports with power-driven staples. For attachment to metal supports, tie wires are used.

LATHING ACCESSORIES

LATHING ACCESSORIES consist of STRUC-
TURAL COMPONENTS and MISCELLANEOUS

ACCESSORIES. The principal use of structural components is in the construction of HOLLOW PARTITIONS. A hollow partition is one which contains no building framing members (such as studs and plates). Structural components are lathing accessories which take the place of the missing framing members in supporting the lath. They include prefabricated METAL STUDS and floor and ceiling RUNNER TRACKS. The runner tracks take the place of missing stud top and bottom plates; they usually consist of metal CHANNELS. Channels are also used for furring and bracing.

Miscellaneous accessories consist principally of various devices which are attached to the lath at corner and other locations, and which serve to define and reinforce corners, to provide dividing strips between plaster and the edges of baseboard or other trim, or to define plaster edges at unframed openings. CORNER BEADS are the most common miscellaneous accessories. Figure 14-1 shows a STANDARD FLANGE corner bead, in which the flanges are perforated metal. There are also EXPANDED FLANGE and WIDE FLANGE corner beads. CASING BEADS are similar devices for providing dividing strips between plaster edges and the edges of door and window casing. BASE BEADS (also called BASE SCREEDS) provide dividing strips between plaster edges and the edges of baseboards. All of these devices are attached to the lath before plaster is applied.

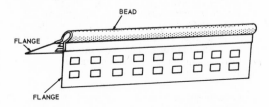

117.74

Figure 14-1.—Standard flange corner bead.

GROUNDS AND SCREEDS

GROUNDS are narrow strips of wood or metal that are placed around, and parallel to, the edges of surfaces and openings within the area to be plastered, principally to ensure that plaster will be applied to the correct thickness in locations where variations in thickness would be especially noticeable. The grounds are designed to be used as guides for the plastering straightedge when the final basecoat is brought to the required thickness and line. Such miscellaneous accessories as casing beads and base beads serve as grounds, in addition to providing dividing strips between plaster edges and the edges of trim.

Edges of door and window jambs are often used as grounds; however, it is not advisable to plaster directly to the wood in such cases. Contact between the dimensionally unstable wood and the more stable plaster produces differential movement (additionally complicated by the shock of opening and closing of door or window) which may damage plaster edges. If casing beads are not used, the plaster should be struck away from the wooden jamb after the surface has been leveled.

PLASTER SCREEDS are grounds consisting of narrow strips of plaster 4 to 6 in. wide, placed at intervals on large wall or ceiling areas. DOTS of plaster of the proper thickness are placed first, then connected by bands of the proper thickness. The spaces between the bands are then filled in, after the band (that is, the screeds) have hardened enough to support the plastering straightedge. Dampness will damage plaster; therefore, plaster should not be applied directly to exterior masonry walls. However, in such a case, it is advisable to fur the plaster at least 1 inch from the masonry.

MIXING PLASTER

Much plaster comes ready-mixed, requiring only the addition of enough water on the job to attain minimum required workability. For job-mixing, tables are available which give recommended ingredient proportions for gypsum, lime, lime-portland cement, and portland cement plaster for base coats on lath or on various types of concrete or masonry surfaces, and for finish coats of various types. This course can present recommended proportions for only the more common types of plastering situations. In the following sections, 1 part of cementitious material means 100 lbs (1 sack) gypsum, 100 lbs (2 sacks) hydrated lime, 1 cu ft lime putty, or 94 lbs (1 sack) portland cement. One part of aggregate means 100 lbs sand or 1 cu ft vermiculite or perlite. Vermiculite and perlite are not used with lime plaster; therefore, while aggregate parts given for gypsum or portland cement plaster may be presumed to refer to either sand or vermiculite/perlite, aggregate parts given for lime plaster mean sand only.

BASE COAT PROPORTIONS

TWO-COAT plaster work consists of a single base coat and a finish coat. THREE-COAT work consists of two base coats (the first called the SCRATCH coat, the second the BROWN coat) and a finish coat.

Portland cement plaster cannot be applied to a gypsum base. Lime plaster can in theory, but in practice only gypsum plaster is applied to gypsum lath as a base coat. For two-coat work on gypsum lath, the recommended base coat proportions for gypsum plaster are 1:2.5.

For two-coat work on a masonry (using this term to mean either monolithic concrete or masonry) base the recommended base coat proportions are as follows:

Gypsum plaster: 1:3
Lime plaster using hydrated lime: 1:7.5
Lime plaster using lime putty: 1:3.5

Portland cement plaster is not used for two-coat work, and two-coat work is not usually done on metal lath.

For three-coat work on gypsum lath the recommended base coat proportions for gypsum plaster are: scratch coat 1:2, brown coat 1:3; or both coats 1:2.5.

For three-coat work on metal lath the recommended base coat proportions are as follows:

Gypsum plaster: same as for three-coat work on gypsum lath
Lime plaster using hydrated lime: scratch 1:6.75, brown 1:9
Lime plaster using lime putty: scratch 1:3, brown 1:4
Portland cement plaster: both coats 1:3 to 1:5

For three-coat work on a masonry base the recommended base coat proportions are as follows:

Gypsum plaster: both coats 1:3
Portland cement plaster: both coats 1:3 to 1:5

Lime plaster is not usually used for three-coat work on a masonry base.

FINISH COAT PROPORTIONS

A lime finish may be applied over a lime, gypsum, or portland cement base coat; other finishes, however, should be applied only to basecoats containing the same cementitious material. A gypsum-vermiculite finish should be applied only to a gypsum-vermiculite base-coat.

Finish coat proportions vary according to whether the surface is to be finished with a TROWEL or with a FLOAT. These tools are described later. The trowel attains a smooth finish; the float attains a finish of a desired texture.

For a trowel-finish coat using gypsum plaster the recommended proportions are 200 lbs hydrated lime or 5 cu ft lime putty to 100 lbs gypsum gauging plaster.

For a trowel-finish coat using lime-Keene's cement plaster the recommended proportions are, for a medium-hard finish, 50 lbs hydrated lime or 100 lbs lime putty to 100 lbs Keene's cement. For a hard finish the recommended proportions are 25 lbs hydrated lime or 50 lbs lime putty to 100 lbs Keene's cement.

For a trowel-finish coat using lime-portland cement plaster the recommended proportions are 200 lbs hydrated lime or 5 cu ft lime putty to 94 lbs portland cement.

For a finish coat using portland cement-sand plaster the recommended ingredient proportions are 300 lbs sand to 94 lbs portland cement. This plaster may be either trowled or floated. Hydrated lime up to 10 percent by weight of the portland cement, or lime putty up to 25 percent of the volume of the portland cement, may be added as a plasticizer.

For a trowel-finish coat using gypsum gauging or gypsum neat plaster and vermiculite aggregate the recommended proportions are 1 cu ft vermiculite to 100 lbs plaster.

Recommended proportions for various types of float-finish coats are as follows:

Lime putty 2: Keene's cement 1.5: sand 4.5, by volume
Hydrated lime 1: gypsum gauging plaster 1.5: sand 2.3, by weight
Hydrated lime 2: portland cement 1: sand 2.5, by weight
Lime putty 1: sand 3, by volume
Gypsum neat plaster 1: sand 2, by weight

PLASTER QUANTITY ESTIMATES

The total volume of plaster required for a job is, of course, the product of the thickness of the plaster times the net area to be covered.

Plaster specifications state a minimum thickness, which the plasterer must not go under, and which he should likewise exceed as little as possible, because a tendency to cracking increases with thickness. Specified minimum thickness for gypsum plaster on metal lath, wire lath, masonry/concrete walls and masonry ceilings is usually 5/8 in.; on gypsum lath it is 1/2 in.; on monolithic concrete ceilings it is 3/8 in. For interior lime plaster on metal lath (3-coat work) the specified minimum thickness is usually 7/8 in.; for exterior lime plaster on metal lath it is 1 in. For lime plaster on interior masonry walls/ceilings the minimum thickness is 5/8 in.; for exterior lime plaster on masonry it is 3/4 in. For lime plaster on interior concrete ceilings the minimum thickness is 1/16 in. to 1/8 in.; on interior walls, 5/8 in. For lime plaster on exterior concrete the minimum thickness is 3/4 in. For portland cement plaster, either interior or exterior, recommended thicknesses are 3/8 in. for each base coat (3-coat work) and 1/8 in. for the finish coat.

The YIELD for a given quantity of plaster ingredients, like the yield for a given quantity of concrete ingredients, amounts to the sum of the ABSOLUTE VOLUMES of the ingredients. The absolute volumes of typical plaster ingredients are as follows:

100 lbs gypsum	0.69 cu ft
1 cu ft lime putty	0.26 cu ft
100 lbs hydrated lime	0.64 cu ft
100 lbs sand	0.61 cu ft
94 lbs portland cement	0.48 cu ft

This list indicates that (for example) 94 lbs of portland cement, which has a loose volume of 1 cu ft, has an absolute volume (that is, a solid or exclusive-of-air-voids volume) of only 0.48 cu ft. Therefore, 94 lbs of portland cement contributes a volume of only 0.48 cu ft to a plaster (or concrete) mix.

The absolute volume of the last ingredient— the water—is the same as its "loose" volume: 0.13 cu ft per gallon.

Determining Yield

Suppose now that you want to determine the yield of a plaster mix containing 1 part of gypsum plaster to 2.5 parts of sand. One part of gypsum plaster is 100 lbs, with an absolute volume of 0.69 cu ft. Two and five-tenths parts

of sand means 250 lbs of sand. Sand has an absolute v o l u m e of 0.61 cu ft per 100 lbs; therefore, the absolute volume of the sand is 2.5 x 0.61, or 1.52 cu ft.

The water will contribute 0.13 cu ft of volume to the mix for every gallon of water added. For approximate yield calculations, you can assume that 8 gals of water will be used for every 100 lbs of cementitious material. There are 100 lbs of gypsum plaster in question here, which means 8 gals of water. The water volume, then, will be 8 x 0.13, or 1.04 cu ft.

The yield for a 1-sack batch of this mix will be the sum of the absolute volumes, or 0.69 cu ft (for the gypsum) plus 1.52 cu ft (for the sand) plus 1.04 cu ft (for the water), or 3.25 cu ft.

Estimating Ingredient Quantities

Suppose that the plastering job is a wall with a net area of 160 sq ft, with a specified total plaster thickness of 5/8 in. and a finish coat thickness of 1/16 in. You are doing two-coat work (only a single base coat), and you want to estimate ingredient quantities for the base coat. The thickness of the base coat will be 5/8 in. minus 1/16 in., or 9/16 in., which equals about 0.046 ft. The volume of plaster required for the base coat, then, will be 160 x 0.046, or about 7.36 cu ft.

The yield for a 1-sack batch is 3.25 cu ft; therefore, the job calls for a batch with sacks to the number indicated by the value of x in the equation 1:3.25::x:7.36, or about 2.3 sacks. The number of parts of sand required equals the value of x in the equation 1:2.5::2.3:x, or 5.75 parts. There are 100 lbs of sand in a "part," and 100 lbs of gypsum in a sack. Therefore, for the base coat you will need 230 lbs of gypsum and 575 lbs of sand.

MIXING PLASTER BY HAND

Equipment for plaster mixing by hand consists of a flat, shallow-sided MIXING BOX and a hoe; the hoe usually has a perforated blade. Mixed plaster is transferred from the mixing box to a MORTAR BOARD, similar to the one used in bricklaying. Men applying plaster pick it up from the mortar board.

In hand mixing, the dry ingredients are first placed in the mixing box and thoroughly mixed until a uniform color is obtained. The pile is then coned up and troughed, and the water is mixed in much as it is in hand concrete mixing.

Mixing is continued until the materials have been thoroughly blended and proper consistency has been attained. With experience a man acquires a "feel" for proper consistency. Mixing should not be continued for more than 10 or 15 minutes after the materials have been thoroughly blended, because excessive agitation may hasten the rate of solution of the cementitious material and thereby cause accelerated set.

Finish-coat lime plaster is usually hand-mixed on a small 5 ft x 5 ft mortar board called a FINISHING BOARD. If the lime used is hydrated lime, it is first converted to lime putty by soaking in an equal amount of water for 16 hours. In mixing the plaster, the lime putty is first formed into a ring on the finishing board. Water is then poured into the ring, and the gypsum or Keene's cement is then sifted into the water to avoid lumping. The mix is allowed to stand for one minute, after which the materials are thoroughly blended. Sand, if it is to be used, is then added and mixed in.

MIXING PLASTER BY MACHINE

A plaster mixing machine (fig. 14-2) consists primarily of a metal DRUM containing MIXING BLADES, mounted on a chassis equipped with wheels for road towing. Mixing is accomplished either by rotation of the drum or by rotation of the blades inside the drum. Discharge into a wheelbarrow or other receptacle is usually accomplished by tilting the drum as shown in figure 14-2.

117.75
Figure 14-2.—Plaster mixing machine.

Steps in the machine mixing of gypsum plaster are as follows:

For job-mixed gypsum plaster:
1. Put in the approximate amount of water. Approximate water amounts for various gypsum-aggregate proportions and the common aggregates are as follows:

Aggregate	Gypsum-Aggregate Proportions		
	1:2	1:2.5	1:3
Sand	6.8 gals	7.4 gals	8.2 gals
Perlite	7.7 gals	8.5 gals	9.1 gals
Vermiculite	9.0 gals	10.0 gals	10.1 gals

2. If sand is used, add approximately one-half of the aggregate. If perlite or vermiculite is used, add all the aggregate.
3. Add all the cementitious material.
4. Add the remainder of the sand aggregate.
5. Mix to required consistency, adding more water IF NECESSARY.

For ready-mix gypsum plaster:
1. Put in the approximate amount of water, as prescribed by manufacturer's instructions printed on the sack.
2. Add the plaster.
3. Mix to the required consistency, adding water IF NECESSARY.

For machine mixing of lime and portland cement plaster, place the dry ingredients in the drum first and mix dry until a uniform color is attained. Then add the water and mix to the required consistency. Approximate water amount is 8 gals per 100 lbs cementitious material.

It is generally recommended that the mixer be allowed to run no longer than three minutes after all materials have been added.

APPLYING PLASTER

To attain complete structural integrity, a plaster layer must be uniform in thickness; also, a plane plaster surface must be flat enough to appear flat to the eye and to receive surface-applied materials (such as casings and other trim) without the appearance of noticeable spaces. Specified flatness tolerance is usually 1/8 in. in 10 ft.

PLASTERING TOOLS

Steel TROWELS are used to apply, spread, and smooth plaster. The shape and size of the blade of a trowel is determined by the purpose for which the tool is used and the manner of using it.

The four common types of plastering trowels are shown in figure 14-3. The RECTANGULAR TROWEL, with a blade approximately 4 1/2 in. wide by 11 in. long, serves as the principal conveyor and manipulator of plaster. The POINTING trowel, 2 in. wide by about 10 in. long, is designed for use in places where the rectangular trowel won't fit. The MARGIN trowel is another smaller trowel, similar to the pointing trowel, but with a square rather than a pointed end. The ANGLE trowel is used for finishing corner angles formed by adjoining right-angle plaster surfaces.

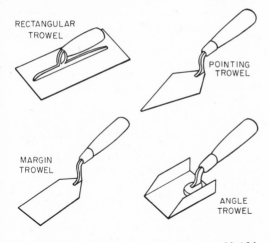

RECTANGULAR TROWEL

POINTING TROWEL

MARGIN TROWEL

ANGLE TROWEL

29.164

Figure 14-3.—Plastering trowels.

The HAWK (fig. 14-4) is a square lightweight sheet metal platform with a vertical central handle, used for carrying mortar from mortar board to the place where it is to be applied. The plaster is then removed from the hawk with the trowel. The size of a hawk varies from 10 in. square to 14 in. square.

The FLOAT is glided over the surface of the plaster, to fill voids and hollows or to level bumps left by previous operations, and to impart a texture to the surface. Common types of

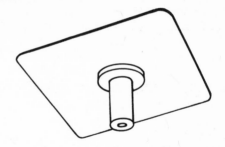

117.76

Figure 14-4.—Hawk.

floats are shown in figure 14-5. The WOOD float has a wood blade, the ANGLE float a stainless steel or aluminum blade. The SPONGE float is faced with foam rubber or plastic, intended to attain a certain surface texture. A CARPET float is similar to a sponge float, but faced with a layer of carpet material. A CORK float is faced with cork.

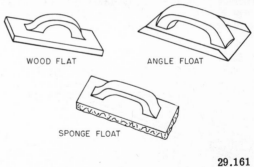

WOOD FLAT

ANGLE FLOAT

SPONGE FLOAT

29.161

Figure 14-5.—Plastering floats.

A float blade is 4 or 5 in. wide and about 10 in. long.

The ROD and STRAIGHTEDGE consists of a wood or lightweight metal blade 6 in. wide by from 4 to 8 ft long. This is the first tool used in leveling and straightening applied plaster between the grounds. A wood rod has a slot for a handle cut near the center of the blade. A metal rod usually has a shaped handle running the length of the blade. A wood rod is shown in figure 14-6.

The FEATHEREDGE (fig. 14-6) is similar to the rod, except that the blade tapers to a sharp edge. It is used to cut in corners and to

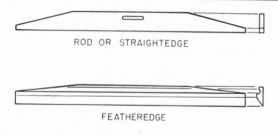

ROD OR STRAIGHTEDGE

FEATHEREDGE

117.77

Figure 14-6.—Rod or straightedge
and featheredge.

shape sharp, straight lines at corner lines of
intersection.

The DARBY (fig. 14-7) is, in effect, a float
with an extra-long (3 1/2 to 4 ft) blade, equipped
with handles for two-handed manipulation. It is
used for further straightening of the base coat
after rodding is completed; also to level plaster
screeds and to level finish coats. The blade of
the darby is held nearly flat against the plaster
surface, and in such a way that the line of the
edge makes an angle of about 45° with the line
of direction of the stroke.

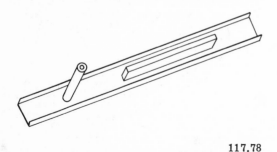

117.78

Figure 14-7.—Darby.

When a plaster surface is being leveled,
the leveling tool must move over the plaster
smoothly. If the surface is too dry, lubrication
must be provided by moistening. In base coat
operations this is accomplished by dashing or
brushing water on with a water-carrying brush
called a BROWNING brush. This is a fine-
bristled brush about 4 or 5 in. wide and 2 in.
thick, with bristles about 6 in. long. For finish
coat operations a FINISHING brush with softer,
more pliable bristles is used.

A MECHANICAL TROWEL (often called a
POWER TROWEL) is an electrically operated

rotating trowel which weighs about 6 lbs and
resembles a 6-bladed fan. There are usually
two sets of blades, one more flexible than the
other. The flexible set is used for preliminary
troweling, the stiffer set for final troweling.
Mechanical troweling can be done to within
1/2 in. of corner angles, leaving the angles to
be finished by angle troweling.

There are two types of PLASTERING MA-
CHINES. The WET MIX PUMP carries mixed
plaster from the mixing machine to a hose
nozzle. The DRY MIX machine carries dry ingredients to a mixing nozzle where water under
pressure combines with the mix and provides
spraying force. Most plastering machines are
of the wet mix pump variety.

A wet mix pump may be of the WORM
DRIVE, PISTON PUMP, or HAND HOPPER
type. In a worm drive machine mixed plaster
is fed into a hopper and forced through the hose
to the nozzle by the screw action of a rotor and
stator assembly in the neck of the machine. A
machine of this type has a hopper capacity of
from 3 to 5 cu ft, and can deliver from 0.5 to
2 cu ft of plaster per minute.

On a piston pump machine a hydraulic, air-
operated, or mechanically operated piston supplies the force for moving the wet plaster. On
a hand hopper machine the dry ingredients are
placed in a hand-held hopper just above the
nozzle. Hopper capacity is usually around
1/10 cu ft. These machines are used principally for applying finish plaster.

Machine application cuts down on the requirements for the use of the hawk and trowel
in initial plaster application; however, the use
of straightening and finishing hand tools remains about the same for machine-applied
plaster.

PLASTERING CREWS

A typical plastering crew for hand application consists of a crew chief, 2 to 4 plasterers,
and 2 to 4 TENDERS. The plasterers, under
the crew chief's supervision, set all levels and
lines and apply and finish the plaster. The
tenders mix the plaster, deliver it to the plasterers, construct scaffolds, handle materials,
and do cleanup tasks.

For machine application a typical crew consists of a NOZZLEMAN who applies the material, 2 or 3 plasterers leveling and finishing,
and 2 or 3 tenders.

APPLICATION OF PLASTER

Lack of uniformity in the thickness of a plaster coat detracts from the structural performance of the plaster, and the thinner the coat, the smaller the permissible variation from uniformity. Specifications usually require that plaster be finished "true and even, within 1/8 in. tolerance in 10 ft, without waves, cracks, or imperfections." The standard of 1/8 in. appears to be the closest practical tolerance to which a plasterer can work by the methods commonly in use.

The importance of adhering to the recommended minimum thickness for the plaster cannot be overstressed. A plaster wall becomes more rigid as thickness over the minimum recommended increases—which means in effect that the tendency to cracking increases as thickness increases. However, tests have shown that a reduction of thickness from a recommended minimum of 1/2 in. to 3/8 in., with certain plasters, decreases cracking resistance by as much as 60 percent, while reduction to 1/4 in. decreases it as much as 82 percent.

Base Coat Application

GYPSUM BASE COATS.—The sequence of operations in three-coat gypsum plastering is as follows:

1. Install the plaster base.
2. Attach the grounds.
3. Apply the scratch coat approximately 3/16 in. thick.
4. Before the scratch coat sets, RAKE and CROSS-RAKE. This procedure consists of scratching with a tool that leaves furrows approximately 1/8 in. deep, 1/8 in. wide, and 1/2 to 3/4 in. apart. The furrows are intended to improve the bond between the scratch coat and the brown coat.
5. Allow the scratch coat to set firm and hard.
6. Apply plaster screeds if required.
7. Apply the brown coat to the depth of the screeds.
8. Using the screeds as guides, straighten the surface with a rod.
9. Fill in any hollows and rod again.
10. Level and compact the surface with a darby; then rake and cross-rake to receive the finish coat.

11. Define angles sharply with angle float and featheredge, and trim back plaster around grounds so that finish coat can be applied flush with grounds.

The two-coat method is used with gypsum plaster over a gypsum lath or a masonry base. Steps are as follows:

1. Install the base if necessary.
2. Attach the grounds and apply plaster screeds if necessary.
3. Apply the first thickness, and double back immediately with a second thickness to the depth of the screeds; because of this procedure, two-coat work is frequently called DOUBLE-BACK.

The remaining steps are similar to the last four steps discussed in three-coat work.

LIME BASE COATS.—Steps for lime base coat work are similar to the steps for gypsum work, except that for lime an additional floating is required the day after the brown coat is applied. This extra floating is required to increase the density of the slab and to fill in any cracks which may have developed because of shrinkage of the plaster. A wood float with one or two nails protruding 1/8 in. from the sole (called a DEVIL'S float) is used for the purpose.

The sequence of steps for three-coat lime plaster work over various bases is as follows:

1. Install the base if necessary, and attach the grounds.
2. Apply the scratch coat with sufficient plaster and pressure to evenly cover the plaster base and (for metal lath) provide positive keying.
3. Allow the scratch coat to become hard, but not dry, and scratch with metal scratching tool.
4. Apply plaster screeds if necessary. For interior lime plaster on metal lath grounds and screeds are usually established to provide for 7/8 in. plaster from the face of the plaster base.
5. Allow the scratch coat to dry and then apply the brown coat to the depth of the grounds.
6. Rod and darby the surface to a true plane and straighten all angles. Cut the brown coat back 1/16 in. at grounds to allow the finish coat to be plastered flush with the grounds.
7. Allow the brown coat to dry for 24 hours; then float the surface with a devil's float.

The steps for two-coat lime plaster work, usually done on a masonry base, are as follows:

1. Apply grounds and screeds. For interior work, lime plaster on masonry thickness is usually 5/8 in.; for exterior work, 3/4 in.
2. Apply a thin coat of plaster to cover evenly and form good bond with the base.
3. Using plaster of the same mix, double back and bring the plaster out to the grounds.
4. Rod and darby the surface, straighten angles, and cut the plaster back at the grounds to allow for finish coat (usually 1/16 to 1/8 in. thick).
5. After approximately 24 hours, float with devil's float.

PORTLAND CEMENT BASE COATS.—Portland cement plaster is actually cement mortar, subject to the control procedures described in the chapter on concrete. It is usually applied in three coats, the steps being the same as those described for gypsum plaster. Minimum recommended thicknesses are usually scratch coat 3/8 in., brown coat 3/8 in., finish coat 1/8 in.

Portland cement plaster should be moist cured, like concrete. The best procedure is fog-spray curing. The scratch coat should be fog-spray cured for 48 hrs, then the brown coat for the same interval. The finish coat should not be applied for at least 7 days after the brown coat; for application, it, too, should be spray-cured for 48 hrs.

Finish Coat Application

Interior plaster may be finished by troweling, floating, or spraying. Troweling gets a smooth finish, floating or spraying a finish of a desired surface texture.

LIME PUTTY-GYPSUM TROWEL FINISH.— Finish plaster made of gypsum gauging plaster and lime putty (familiarly called WHITE COAT or PUTTY COAT) is the most widely used material for smooth finish coats. A putty coat is usually applied by a team of two or more men. Steps are as follows:

1. One man applies plaster at the angles.
2. Another man follows immediately, straightening the angles with a rod or featheredge.

3. The remaining surface is covered with a SKIM coat of plaster. Pressure on the trowel must be sufficient to force the material into the rough surface of the base coat, to ensure good bond.
4. The surface is immediately doubled back to bring the finish coat to final thickness.
5. All angles are floated, with additional plaster added if required to fill hollows.
6. The remaining surface is floated, and all hollows filled. This operation is called DRAWING UP; the hollows being filled are called CAT FACES.
7. The surface is allowed to DRAW for a few minutes. As the plaster begins to set, the surface water glaze disappears and the surface becomes dull. At this point, troweling should begin. The plasterer holds the water brush in one hand and the trowel in the other, so troweling can be done immediately after water is brushed on.
8. Water is brushed on lightly and the entire surface is rapidly troweled, with enough pressure fully to compact the finish coat. The troweling operation is repeated until the plaster has set.

The sequence of steps for trowel finishes for other types of finish plaster are about the same. Gypsum finish plaster requires less troweling than white coat plaster. Regular Keene's cement requires longer troweling, but quicksetting Keene's cement requires less. Preliminary finishing of portland cement-sand is done with a wood float, after which the steel trowel is used. To avoid excessive drawing of fines to the surface, troweling of portland cement-sand should be delayed as long as possible. For the same reason, the surface must not be troweled too long.

Steps in float finishing are about the same as those described for trowel finishing, except, of course, that the final finish is obtained with the float. A surface is usually floated twice; a rough floating with a wooden float first, then final floating with rubber or carpet float. The plasterer applies brush water with one hand while the float in his other hand moves in a circular motion immediately behind the brush.

A spray finish is machine-applied. The degree of coarseness of the surface texture is controlled by the air pressure at the nozzle, the distance the nozzle is held from the surface, and the composition of the plaster mix, particularly the aggregate. A spray finish is usually applied in two thin applications. After the first coat has been applied, all depressions, holes, or irregularities are touched up by hand to prevent their showing in the final coat.

Some special interior finish textures are obtained otherwise than by floating, or by procedures used in addition to floating. A few of these are as follows:

STIPPLED FINISH.—After the finish coat has been applied, additional plaster is daubed over the surface with a stippling brush.

SPONGE FINISH.—By pressing a sponge against the surface of the finish coat, a very soft, irregular texture can be obtained.

DASH COAT FINISH.—This texture is obtained by throwing plaster onto the surface from a brush. It produces a fairly coarse finish, which can be modified by brushing the plaster with water before it sets.

TRAVERTINE FINISH.—The plaster is jabbed at random with a whisk broom, wire brush, or other tool that will form a dimpled surface. As the plaster begins to set, it is troweled intermittently to form a pattern of rough and smooth areas.

PEBBLE DASH.—This is a rough finish obtained by throwing small pebbles or crushed stone against a newly plastered surface. If necessary, a trowel is used to press the stones lightly into the plaster.

CERAMIC WALL TILE

Some walls, especially in bathrooms, shower rooms, galleys, corridors, and the like, are entirely or partly covered with CERAMIC TILE. The type most commonly used is 3/8-in.-thick GLAZED INTERIOR tile, mostly in 4 1/4-in. or 6-in. squares. Margins, corners, and base lines are finished with TRIMMERS of various shapes. Available shapes and sizes of trimmers are shown on a TRIMMER CHART provided by the manufacturer.

Ceramic tile can be set in a bed of TILE MORTAR, or it can be set in a TILE ADHESIVE furnished by the manufacturer.

MORTAR APPLICATION

For mortar bed setting on a wall with wooden studs, a layer of waterproof paper is first tacked to the studs, and metal lath is then nailed on over the paper. The first coat of mortar applied on a wall for setting tile is a scratch coat and the second a float, leveling, or brown coat. A scratch coat for application as a foundation coat must be not less than 1/4 inch thick and composed of 1 part cement to 3 parts sand, with the addition of 10 percent hydrated lime by volume of the cement used. While still plastic, the scratch coat is deeply scored or scratched and cross-scratched. The scratch coat should be protected and kept reasonably moist during the seasoning period. All mortar for scratch and float coats should be used within 1 hour after mixing. The retempering of partially hardened mortar will not be permitted. The scratch coat should be applied not more than 48 hours, nor less than 24 hours, before starting the setting of tile.

The float coat should be composed of 1 part cement, 1 part of hydrated lime, and 3 1/2 parts sand. It should be brought flush with screeds or temporary guide strips, so placed as to give a true and even surface at the proper distance from the finished face of the tile.

Wall tile should be thoroughly soaked in clean water before it is set. It is set by troweling a skim coat of neat portland cement mortar on the float coat, or applying a skim coat to the back of each tile unit, and immediately floating the tile into place. Joints must be straight, level, perpendicular, and of even width not exceeding 1/16 inch. Wainscots are built of full courses, which may extend to a greater or lesser height, but in no case more than 1 1/2 inches difference than the specified or figured height. Vertical joints must be maintained plumb for the entire height of the tile work.

All joints in wall tile should be grouted full with a plastic mix of neat white cement or commercial tile grout immediately after a suitable area of the tile has been set. The joints should be tooled slightly concave and the excess mortar cut off and wiped from the face of tile. Any interstices or depressions in the mortar joints after the grout has been cleaned from the surface should be roughened at once and filled to the line of the cushion edge (if applicable) before the mortar begins to harden. Tile bases or coves should be solidly backed with mortar. All joints between wall tile and plumbing or other built-in fixtures should be made with a light-colored calking compound. Immediately after the grout has had its initial set, tile wall surfaces should be given a protective coat of noncorrosive soap or other approved protection.

Application of tile in existing construction. Wall tile installed over existing and patched or new plaster surfaces in an existing building are completed as described, except that such wall tile is applied by the adhesive method.

Where wall tile is to be installed in areas subject to intermittent or continual wetting, the wall areas should be primed as recommended by the manufacturer of the adhesive used.

ADHESIVE APPLICATION

Wall tile may be installed either by the floating method or by the buttering method. In the floating method, apply the adhesive uniformly over the prepared wall surface, using quantities recommended by the adhesive manufacturer. Use a notched trowel held at the proper angle to ensure a uniformly spread coating of the proper thickness. Touch up thin or bare spots by an additional coating of adhesive. The area coated at one time should not be any larger than that recommended by the manufacturer of the adhesive. In the buttering method, daub the adhesive on the back of each tile in such amount that the adhesive, when compressed, will form a coating not less than 1/16 inch thick over 60 percent of the back of each tile.

SETTING TILE

Joints must be straight, level, plumb, and of even width not exceeding 1/16 inch. When the floating method is used, one edge of the tile is pressed firmly into the wet adhesive, the tile snapped into place in a manner to force out all air, then aligned by using a slight twisting movement. Tile should not be shoved into place. Joints must be cleaned of any excess adhesive to provide for a satisfactory grouting job. When the buttering method is used, tile is pressed firmly into place, using a "squeegee" motion to spread the daubs of adhesive. After the adhesive partially sets, but before it is completely dry, all tiles must be realigned so that faces are in same plane and joints are of proper width, with vertical joints plumb and horizontal joints level.

Wainscots are built of full courses to a uniform height. The wainscots height may be adjusted somewhat to accommodate full courses, but the adjustment should not exceed or be less than 1 1/2 inches from the top.

The adhesive should be allowed to set for 24 hours before grouting is done. Joints must be cleaned of dust, dirt, and excessive adhesive, and should be thoroughly soaked with clean water before grouting. A grout consisting of portland cement, lime, and sand, or an approved ready-mix grout may be used, but the grout should be water resistant and nonstaining.

Nonstaining calking compound should be used at all joints between built-in fixtures and tilework, and at the top of ceramic tile bases, to ensure complete waterproofing. Internal corners should be calked before corner bead is applied.

Cracked and broken tile should be replaced promptly to protect the edges of adjacent tile and to maintain waterproofing and appearance. Timely pointing of displaced joint material and spalled areas in joints is necessary to keep tiles in place.

Newly tiled surfaces should be cleaned to remove job marks and dirt. Cleaning should be done according to the tile manufacturer's recommendations to avoid damage to the glazed surfaces.

MODULAR LAYOUT OF TILE

The required number of acoustical or ceramic tiles required to cover a given area is estimated just as it is for floor tiles. For acoustical tile, a 2-man crew pattern is best, one man applying cement to the tile and moving and tending the platform, the other placing the tiles on the ceiling. The norm is an average of 250 12" x 12" tiles placed per man-day.

For ceramic tile a 2-man crew pattern is usually best, one man setting tile and the other mixing mortar, making cuts, grouting joints, and cleaning tile. The ideal construction norm is 20 4 1/4" x 4 1/4" x 3/8" units per man-hour, or about 200 units or 20 square feet per manday and this includes the scratch coat, the brown coat, and the smooth coat of plaster.

GENERAL HINTS ON STUCCOING

Stucco is the term applied to plaster whenever it is applied on the exterior of a building or structure. Stucco can be applied over wood frames or masonry structures. The material is a combination of cement or masonry cement, sand and water, and frequently a plasticizing material. Color pigments are also often used in the finish coat, which is usually a factory prepared mix. The end product has all the desirable properties of concrete. It is hard, strong, fire resistant, weather resistant, does not deteriorate after repeated wetting and drying, resists rot and fungus, and retains colors.

The material used in a stucco mix should be free of contaminants and unsound particles. Type I normal portland cement is generally used for stucco, although type II, type III, and air-entraining may be used. The plasticizing material added to the mix is hydrated lime and asbestos fibers. Mixing water should be clean. The aggregate used in cement stucco can greatly affect the quality and performance of the finished product. It should be well graded, clean, and free from loam, clay or vegetable matter, since these foreign materials prevent the cement paste from properly binding the aggregate particles together. The project specification should be followed as to the type of cement, lime, and aggregate to be used.

Metal reinforcement should be used whenever stucco is applied on the following: wood frame, steel frame, flashing, masonry or any surfaces not providing a good bond.

Stucco may be applied directly on masonry. The rough-floated base coat is approximately 3/8 inch thick. The finish coat is approximately 1/4 inch thick (see fig. 14-8). On open frame construction nails are driven 1/2 the length into the wood. Spacing should be 5 to 6 inches on center from the bottom. Nails should be placed at all corners and openings throughout the entire structure on the exterior, see figure 14-9. The next step is to place wire on

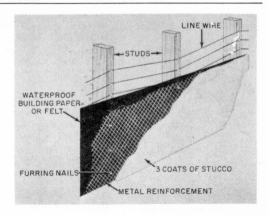

133.156

Figure 14-9.—Open frame construction.

the nails; this is called installing the line wire. Next, a layer of waterproof paper is applied over the line wire. Laps should be 3 to 4 inches and nailed with roofing nails. Next, install wire mesh (stucco netting) used as the reinforcement for the stucco. Furring nails are used to hold the wire away from the paper to a thickness of 3/8 of an inch. See figure 14-10. Stucco or sheathed form construction is the same as an open frame, except no line wire is required. The open and sheathed frame construction requires three coats of 3/8-inch scratch coat horizontally scored or scratched, a 3/8-inch brown coat, and a 1/8-inch finish coat.

PREPARATION OF BASE AND APPLICATION OF STUCCO

Stucco should be applied in three coats. The first coat is called the "scratch" coat; the second the "brown" coat; and the final coat the "finish" coat. However, on masonry where no reinforcement is used, two coats may be sufficient. Start at the top and work down the wall. This will eliminate the ball of mortar from falling on the completed work. The first "scratch" coat should be pushed through the mesh to ensure that the metal reinforcement is completely embedded for mechanical bond. The second or brown coat should be applied as soon as the scratch coat has set up enough to carry the weight of both coats (usually about 4 or 5 hours). The brown coat should be moist-cured for about 48 hours and then allowed to dry for about

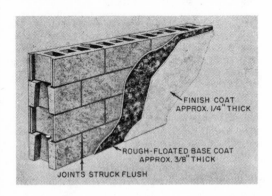

133.155

Figure 14-8.—Masonry (2 coat work directly applied).

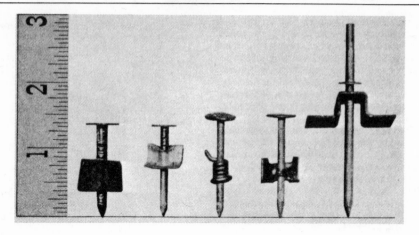

29.121

Figure 14-10.—Several types of furring nails.

5 days. Just prior to the application of the finish coat, the brown coat should be uniformally dampened. The third or finish coat is frequently pigmented to obtain decorative colors. Although the colors may be job mixed, a factory-prepared mix is recommended. The finish coat may be applied by hand or machine. Stucco finishes are obtainable in an unlimited variety of textures, patterns, and colors.

Before the various coats of stucco can be applied, the surfaces have to be prepared properly. Roughen the surfaces of masonry units enough to provide good mechanical key and clean off paint, oil, dust, soot, or any other material which may prevent a tight bond. Joints may be struck off flush or slightly raked. Old walls softened and disintegrated by weather action, surfaces that cannot be cleaned thoroughly (painted brick-work, etc.), and all masonry chimneys should be covered with galvanized metal reinforcement before applying the stucco. When masonry surfaces are not rough enough to provide good mechanical key, one or more of the following actions may be taken.

Old cast-in-place concrete or other masonry may be roughened with bush hammers or other suitable hand tools. Roughen at least 70 percent of the surface, with the hammer marks uniformly distributed. Wash the roughened surface free of chips and dust. Let the wall dry thoroughly.

Concrete surfaces may be roughened with an acid wash. Use a solution of one part of muriatic acid to six parts of water. First wet the wall so that the acid will act on the surface only. More than one application may be necessary. After the acid treatment, wash the wall thoroughly to remove all acid. Allow the washed wall to dry thoroughly.

Rapid roughing of masonry surfaces may be accomplished by use of a power driven machine equipped with a cylindrical cage fitted with a series of hardened steel cutters (fig. 14-11). The cutters are so mounted as to provide a flailing action which results in a scored pattern. After roughing, wash the wall clean of all chips and dust and let it dry.

Suction is absolutely necessary in order to attain a proper bond of stucco on concrete and masonry surfaces. It is also necessary in first and second coats so that the following coats will bond properly. Uniform suction helps to obtain a uniform color. If one part of the wall draws more moisture from the stucco than another, the finish coat may be spotty. Obtain uniform suction by dampening the wall evenly, but not soaking, before applying the stucco. The same applies to the scratch and brown coats. If the surface becomes dry in spots, dampen those areas again to restore suction. Use a fog spray for dampening.

When the masonry surface is not rough enough to ensure adequate bond for a trowel applied scratch coat, use the dash method. Acid treated surfaces usually require a dashed scratch coat. Dashing on the scratch coat aids

402

133.370

Figure 14-11.—Power driven
roughing machine.

Variations in the amount of mixing water.

Use of additional water to retemper mortar.

Corrosion and rust of flashings or other metal attachments, and failure to provide drips and washes on sills and projecting trim, often cause surface stains.

CONTROL JOINTS

Cracks can develop in stucco through many causes or combinations of causes, such as foundation settlement, shrinkage, and building movement. It is difficult to prevent cracking, but this can be largely controlled by dividing the area into rectangular panels every 20 feet by means of metal control joints. See figure 14-12. The control joint is also used where frame construction joins masonry construction.

133.157

Figure 14-12.—Control joint.

Grounds are wood strips of uniform thickness installed around all openings and other places where trim is required. They serve as a guide in bringing the stucco to a uniform thickness. Temporary wood grounds are often used in gaging the thickness of scratch and brown coats of stucco.

STUCCO SAFETY

The observance of safety rules in plastering or stuccoing cannot be over emphasized. So to help prevent accidents and harm to yourself, we strongly suggest that you observe these following safety hints.

All material in bags or bundles should be stacked, blocked, interlocked, and limited in height so that the pile is stable and secure against sliding or collapsing.

Material stored inside a building under construction should be placed not less than 6 feet from hoistways or other inside floor openings.

in getting a good bond by excluding air which might get trapped behind a trowel applied coat. Apply the dash coat with a fiber brush or whisk broom, using a strong whipping motion at right angles to the wall. A cement gun or other machine which can apply the dash coat with considerable force will produce a suitable bond. Keep the dash coat damp for at least two days immediately following its application and then allow it to dry.

Protect the finish coat against exposure to sun and wind for at least six days after application. During this time, keep the stucco moist by frequent fog-spraying.

There may be times, when the finish is not what you had expected. To help you understand the reasons for discoloration and stains in stucco, we will provide some reasons. Some of the common reasons for discoloration and stains are—

Failure to have uniform suction in either of the base coats.

Improper mixing of the finish coat materials.

Changes in materials or proportions during progress of the work.

When material is placed or encroaches upon passageways, it should be located so as to present the least possible hazard.

Bags of cement and lime should not be stacked more than 10 bags high without set-back, unless restrained by walls of appropriate strength.

The outside row of bags should be placed with the mouths of the bags facing the center of the stack.

During unstacking, keep the entire top of the stack nearly level and maintain the necessary set-backs.

Handle paper sacks with care to prevent breaking and showering men with cement and dust.

Store lime and cement on off-the-floor platforms in dry spaces. Lime must be kept dry to prevent possible premature slaking which could cause fire.

Wear heavy gloves when handling metal lath.

Wear goggles for eye protection when handling cement and lime.

Wear shirts with closed neck and wrist bands and be sure that exposed parts of the body do not come in direct contact with lime.

Avoid wearing clothing which has become stiff and hard with cement or lime, since such clothing irritates the skin and may cause infection.

Wear goggles, gloves, and other protective clothing and equipment when handling muriatic acid.

Practice personal cleanliness and frequent washing, which are effective preventive of skin ailments.

CHAPTER 15
FIELD STRUCTURES

By using a variety of prefabricated field-type structures, a Construction Battalion (temporary) is able to set up living quarters, latrines, storage spaces, and other essential accommodations in a very short time. With team work the assembly and erection of prefabricated structures is simple and fast.

BASIC ERECTION PROCEDURES

The component parts of a prefabricated structure are shipped K.D. (knocked down). A manufacturer's instruction manual, containing working drawings and detailed instructions as to how the parts should be assembled, accompanies the shipment. These directions vary, of course, with different types of structures, but there are certain basic erection procedures which should be followed in all cases.

IMPORTANCE OF FOUNDATIONS

In addition to the usual reasons for stressing the importance of a square and level foundation, there is an additional reason peculiar to the erection of a prefabricated structure. Prefabricated parts are designed to fit together without forcing. If the foundation is even slightly out of square and/or level, many of the parts will not fit together as designed.

PREPLANNING

A preplan of the erection procedures, based upon a study of the working drawings and of the manufacturer's instructions, should be made in advance. Consideration should be given to the manpower, equipment, rigging, and tools that will be required, and everything necessary in this line should be procured. Consider the possibility of using jigs or templates for assembling parts of similar trusses, frames, and the like; construct jigs or templates if their use is feasible and advantageous.

The working drawings will show that certain items are not prefabricated and included in the shipment, but must be constructed in the field.

Plans must be made in advance for the procurement of necessary materials for these items, and for the construction of the items as and when required. Foundations, for example, are often designated as "to be constructed in the field."

Preplanning should also include the establishment of the most logical and expeditious order of construction sequences.

UNPACKAGING AND DISTRIBUTION OF PARTS

Parts are assembled for shipment in various kinds of groups, bundles, and containers, which are called PACKAGES. When the shipment arrives at the site, packages should be arranged in storage areas so as to be available in the order indicated by the pre-established order of erection sequences.

As unpackaging proceeds, check the parts against the bill of materials to ensure that all parts have been included in the shipment. If any part is missing, report this fact at once, so that steps can be taken immediately to remedy the situation. Examine all parts closely for damage or defects, and promptly report any damage or defect noted.

As parts are unpackaged, mark their order of erection, if necessary, and then distribute them to positions indicated by the working drawings and/or the order of construction sequences. Whenever possible, make a precheck to ensure that adjoining parts will fit together accurately when erected.

Remember that prefabricated parts are designed to fit together WITHOUT FORCING. If they will not do so, one of the following conditions could be the cause: (1) foundation is not right, (2) one of the parts is the wrong part, or (3) one of the parts was not constructed correctly.

THE QUONSET HUT

The Quonset hut, developed during World War II at Quonset Point, Rhode Island (thus the name Quonset hut) has been used extensively over the past 25 years at advanced bases for almost any purpose imaginable—from the housing of men to the storing of supplies and equipment. Its use, however, is being discontinued (upon depletion from storage depot stock). Therefore, as a Builder, you probably will not have the opportunity of completely erecting a Quonset hut. The Quonset hut is being replaced by a similar type of prefabricated structure which is a rigid frame, 20' x 48', straight-walled building. Information on erecting the rigid frame building is given later in this chapter.

Many of the Quonset huts erected in World War II, the Korean Conflict and, more recently, in South-East-Asia may still be in use. In that case you may be assigned to areas where you will have to repair and maintain existing Quonset

huts. The following information is intended as guidelines if such a need arises.

The basic Quonset hut built by the Builder is a prefabricated 20' x 48', steel arch-rib building. It can be erected on metal joists and sills provided, or on a poured concrete slab. Basically, the building consists of a series of steel arch ribs spaced 4' - 0'' on center. These are connected on each side at the base to steel channels which in turn are bolted to the slab or screwed to the floor assembly. Notice in figure 15-1, that three metal purlins at the top provide longitudinal support and proper spacing. The entire exterior is covered with corrugated sheet metal as shown in figures 15-2, and 15-3. Notice that the roof is covered with formed curved roofing metal sheets. Since these type sheets are often hard to replace, care should be taken when making repairs to any section of the hut.

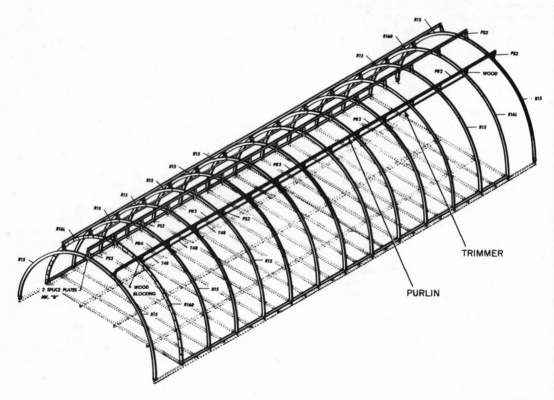

133.169X

Figure 15-1.—Complete framing.

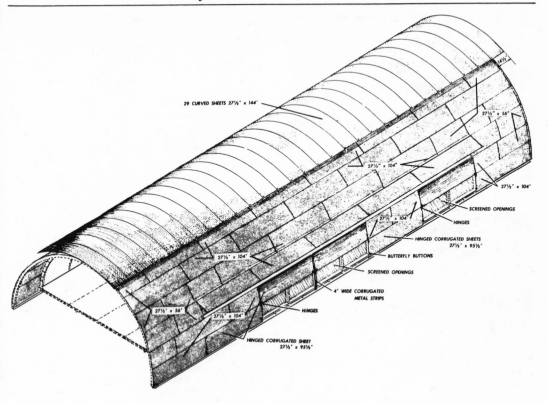

29 CURVED SHEETS 27½" x 144"

14½"

27½" x 56"

27½" x 104"

27½" x 104"

SCREENED OPENINGS

27½" x 104"

HINGES

27½" x 104"

HINGED CORRUGATED SHEETS
27½" x 95½"

BUTTERFLY BUTTONS

SCREENED OPENINGS

4" WIDE CORRUGATED
METAL STRIPS

27½" x 104"

HINGES

27½" x 56"

27½" x 104"

HINGED CORRUGATED SHEET
27½" x 95½"

133.180X

Figure 15-2.—Layout of corrugated sheets.

The endwalls which come with the building consist of steel studs, precut corrugated sheet metal siding, one door, two windows, and a louver. However, for the larger size Quonset hut (40' x 100') which is used for maintenance, storage of materials, and so forth, the endwalls consist of large metal pre-hung sliding doors allowing for the movement, in or out, of material and/or equipment. Many of these type buildings in tropical areas may have had one of the metal endwalls removed and replaced with a concrete block wall as protection against typhoons or hurricanes.

Any major repair work needed for the exterior of these buildings may consist of replacing the corrugated metal, caulking around seams, openings, and applying heat-reflective or other preservative type paint.

The interior walls are covered with precut, fiber-wallboard panels, thus covering the insulating material which has been placed between each 4-foot frame. The horizontal joints are held in metal splines and vertical joints are covered with fiber-board battens. (See figures 15-4, 15-5 and 15-6.) Again, much of the interior repair work consists of removing old panels and insulating material when needed. Interior panels may be replaced by 1/4-inch plywood or 1/8-inch tempered masonite or other suitable material. If plywood is used, additional wooden nailers must be installed prior to nailing on the plywood.

In the event it is ever necessary to erect a Quonset hut, complete manufacturer's erection instructions are included in each component package and should be followed carefully.

4" MULLION SHEET

INSTALLING SHEETS

133.182X

Figure 15-3.—Installing sheets.

Ensure that floor assemblies or slabs are square and level before erecting.

THE RIGID FRAME 20' x 48' STRAIGHT WALL BUILDING

The rigid frame, 20' x 48', straight wall building, being used by the SEABEES, is called the "Butlerhut." The Butlerhut is replacing the Quonset hut at most advanced bases. Like the Quonset hut this building is prefabricated and shipped in compact crates, ready for erection. Each component comes equipped with basic tools and a manual for erection purposes. It is extremely important that the manual be consulted from time to time; because you can very easily install a part wrong.

The 20' x 48' rigid frame building is designed to be erected with basic handtools and a minimum number of men. The erection manual suggests that the Butlerhut can be erected by seven persons. However, for military construction two team/work crews are recommended with an E-6 supervisor. The Butlerhut is designed to be erected on a floor system with piers, concrete blocks, or a concrete slab.

Whenever one rigid frame building has been completed it can easily be expanded to provide additional space. If desired, buildings can be erected end to end as in figure 15-7 or side by side "in multiple." As this type building utilizes only bolted connections, it can be disassembled easily, moved to a new location, and erected again without waste or damage.

PRE-ERECTION WORK

A lot of preliminary work is necessary before the actual erection of the Butlerhut can begin. After the building site is selected, the foundation is outlined by Engineering Aids and leveled by Equipment Operators. Batter boards are set up at each corner, where the foundation is to be located. Forms for the concrete piers must be set and then the concrete placed.

Before concrete for the foundation piers can be poured, templates for the anchor bolts are placed on the forms, and anchor bolts are inserted in the holes. The threads of the bolts are greased and nuts are placed on them to protect the threads from the concrete. After a last minute check to ensure that all forms are level and anchor bolts properly aligned, concrete is placed in the forms and carefully worked around the bolts so that they remain vertical and true.

While the foundation is being prepared, your job supervisor will probably assign work crews to perform various kinds of preliminary work; such as, uncrate material and check it off on the shipping list, bolt up rigid frame assemblies, assemble door leaves, and to glaze windows. If all preliminary work is properly done, then assembly and erection of the entire building is very likely to be completed in the shortest amount of time.

All material except paneling should be uncrated and laid out in an orderly manner so that parts can be easily found. Do not uncrate panels until you are ready to install them. In opening the crates, exercise care so as not to cause undue damage to the lumber. This is important since the lumber can be used for scaffolding, props, and sawhorses.

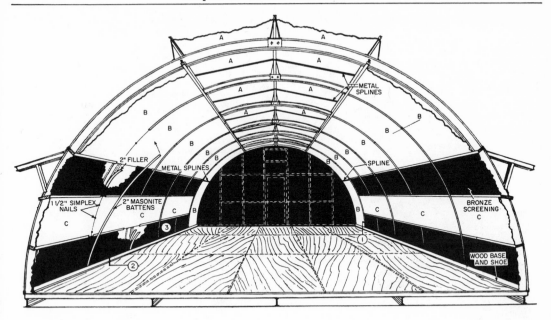

133.176X

Figure 15-4.—Cut away view.

After the building foundation has been pre-pared, where practicable, building materials should be placed in and around the building site near the place where they will be used, similar to the layouts shown in figure 15-8. This ar-rangement offers the greatest convenience and accessibility during assembly.

Girts, purlins, eave struts, and brace rods should be equally divided along each side of the foundation. Panels and miscellaneous parts, which will not be used immediately, should be placed on each side of the foundation on boards and covered with tarpaulins or similar covering until needed. Parts making up the rigid frame assemblies are laid out ready for assembly and in position for raising.

Care should always be exercised in unloading materials. Remember that damaged parts can cause delay in getting the job done in the short-est possible time. To avoid damage, lower the materials to the ground—do not drop them.

Figure 15-9 will help you identify the various structural members of the Butlerhut and their location. Each part serves a specific purpose and must be installed in the location called for

to ensure a sound structure. NEVER OMIT ANY PART CALLED FOR ON THE DETAILED ERECTION DRAWINGS. Each of the members, parts, and accessories of the building is labeled by stencil, so that it is not necessary to guess which part goes where. Refer to the erection plans and find the particular members you need as you work.

High strength steel bolts are used at rigid frame connections—roof beam splice and roof beam to column. Note that these high strength bolts are identified by a "Y" embossing on the head, as shown in figure 15-10. It is important that all high strength steel bolts and nuts be tightened to give at least the required minimum bolt tension values. The bolts may be tightened with a torque wrench, an impact wrench, or an open-end wrench as in figure 15-10.

FLOOR MATERIAL AND ERECTION
PROCEDURES

The floor system material, as it is uncrated, should be placed around the building site near the location where it will be used. Open all

409

133.178X

Figure 15-5.—Installing insulation.

crates carefully and save the lumber for other use.

The side and center stringers should be positioned on the PIER anchor bolts, and secured in place with a 1/2 inch nut and flat washer. The top flange of the side stringers must face to the outside of the building.

Start installing FLOOR JOISTS at one end of the building as shown in figure 15-11 and assemble the appropriate joist clips to both ends of the floor joists. The floor joists are placed 2 ft on center; the top flange of the starting joist, with the 5/16-inch diameter holes, is placed 2' on center and must face toward the outside of the building. The intermediate joists are set with the top flange in the same direction as the starting joist maintaining 2 ft center-to-center of joists. The last joist is turned so that the 5/16 inch holes will face the outside of the building. Braces are installed, and the floor is checked for squareness and proper alignment. When the squareness and alignment has been proven correct, tighten all connections.

The plywood DECK comes in 4' x 8' sheets of 1/2 inch plywood with steel splines for all longitudinal joints of the plywood. Layout the plywood carefully, making sure that:

The joists are properly positioned at the joints.

The end joints are tight.

The sides are firmly nested into the steel splines.

The flooring is started at the center joist by placing a 4' x 8' sheet in such a position that the 8' side extends 3 1/4 inches FROM THE WEB of the side stringer. If done properly, the 4' side should line up with the center line of the holes in the center joist.

NOTE: It is necessary to cut out the plywood for the column bearing plates at each frame column.

BASIC STRUCTURAL ERECTION

After the floor system or concrete slab has been prepared, the next step is to uncrate and layout the structural parts as shown in figure 15-8(B). The structural parts should be laid out as follows:

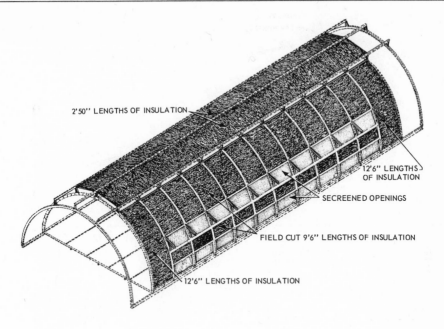

2'50" LENGTHS OF INSULATION

12'6" LENGTHS OF INSULATION

SECREENED OPENINGS

FIELD CUT 9'6" LENGTHS OF INSULATION

12'6" LENGTHS OF INSULATION

133.179X

Figure 15-6.—Insulation in place.

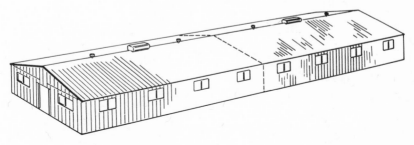

133.371X

Figure 15-7.—20' x 48' rigid frame Butlerhut.

Parts making up the frame assembly should be laid out ready for assembly and in a position for raising.

Girts, purlins, and base angles should be divided (equally) along each side of the foundation.

Endwall parts should be divided (equally) between the two ends.

All miscellaneous parts should be centrally located.

Panels and other parts which are not used immediately should be placed on boards and covered with a tarpaulin.

Layout the column and roof beams for assembly using the crate lumber to block up the frames. The center frame is to be erected first. ("A" frame props are handy devices to have around when erecting the frame.) Use just enough high strength bolts to bring the frame

411

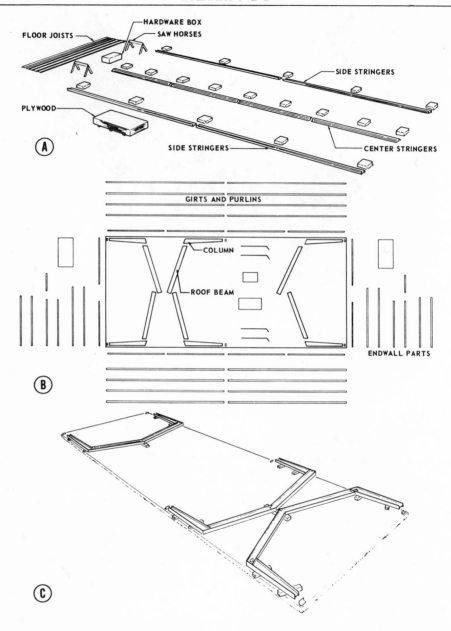

133.372X

Figure 15-8.—Building material layouts.

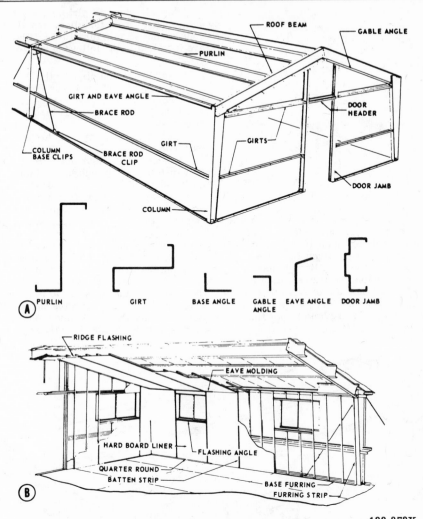

Figure 15-9.—Identification of structural members and liner panels.

members together. Install the remaining bolts to acquire the proper tightness.

Galvanize machine bolts (3/8" x 1") should be used to assemble the girt and purlin clips to the frame. Bear in mind that the end frames have girt and purlin clips on one side ONLY; while the center frame has grit and purlin clips on each side of the frame.

The eave girts are to be attached to the eave angles with 5/16 inch left hand nuts and shoulder bolts as shown in figure 15-12. You will need two eave angles for each eave girt. In fastening these together remember that the shortest section eave angle is always fastened to the left hand of the eave girt; whereas the longer section of the eave angle is fastened to the right hand of the eave girt.

Use galvanized machine bolts (3/8" x 1") to attach the gable angles and door jambs top clips to the bottom flange of the end frame roof beams.

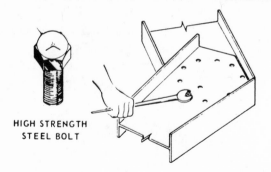

127.125(133F)X
Figure 15-10.—High strength steel bolt.

To erect the frame, place the "A" frames where they will be used. (One 8-foot frame at each side of the building and a 10-foot frame in the center of the building.) Prop the frame on two sawhorses, and attach tag lines to assist in raising the ridge. Raise the frame and brace it up with the "A" frames as shown in figure 15-13. The end frames are erected in a similar manner, except they are held in position by installing purlins and girts.

After all sidewall girts, eave girts and base angles have been installed, install the brace rods as shown in figure 15-14. The brace rods are installed in the following manner:

Attach brace rod clips to the floor.

Insert the end of the brace rod down through the hole in the sidewall girt. Connect the top end through the eave girt and the eave girt clip.

Connect the bottom end through the clip on the floor.

As soon as the four brace rods are in position, use them to plumb the building. To plumb the rigid frame, tighten or loosen the rod nuts at the brace rod clips to adjust the column to plumb condition. Do not forget, when you tighten one side, the other side must be loosened.

To make sure you are installing the endwall members correctly snap a chalk line across the building using one edge of the columns for positioning the line. Mark the center of the building on this line. Now drop a plumb bob from the center of the joint of the roof beams at the ridge, with the line over the same side of the roof beam as the chalk line. Adjust the frame so the plumb bob is directly over the center

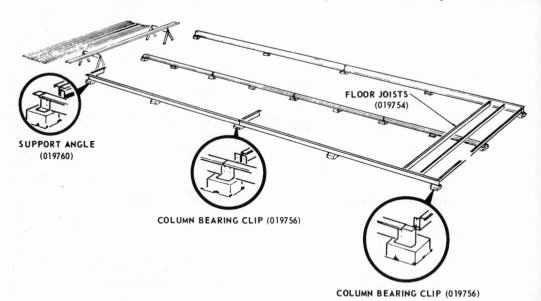

133.374X
Figure 15-11.—Layout of the floor system for the 20' x 48' Butlerhut.

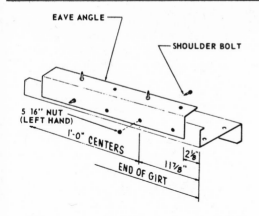

133.375X

Figure 15-12.—Attaching eave angle to girt.

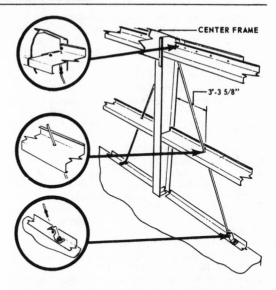

133.377X

Figure 15-14.—Installing brace rods.

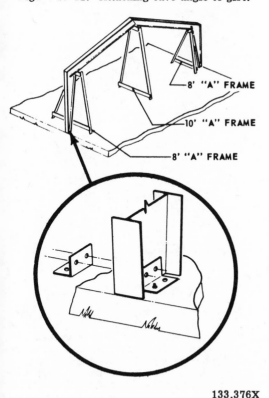

133.376X

Figure 15-13.—Frame erection with
"A" frame props.

mark, and then, brace the roof beam in this position until the roof panels are in place.

The next operation is to uncrate exterior PANELS and distribute them near where they will be used. First, separate and place panels for each endwall. Place full length wall panels at each corner. Centrally locate lower and upper sidewall panels, above and below window panels, along each side of the building. Place roof and ridge panels in stacks of eight each on the floor. Remember, make all joints properly; tighten all fasteners; use metal backed neoprene washers with all roof fasteners and with all shoulder bolts in the sidewalls; and apply BLACK MASTIC properly to all roof panel side and end laps.

Start paneling the ENDWALL at one corner and work across to the other corner. Install the corner panel, locating the bottom of the panel over the first two shoulder bolts in the base angle. Use a level to plumb this panel with the other shoulder bolts located at the center of the corrugations. Locate the "below window panel" over the base angle shoulder bolts, and impale over the shoulder bolts. Remove the panel and reinstall it so it underlaps the first panel by pulling out on the edge corrugation of the first panel.

Follow the same general instructions for paneling and installing windows as were given for the endwall. However, be sure that the girts are in a straight line before impaling panels onto shoulder bolts. It is very important to block the girts in a straight line with crating lumber cut to the correct length. The drawings should be checked for proper location of shoulder bolts. The first shoulder bolt should be 12 inches from the center of the column, then 12 inches on center.

Recheck the center frame for plumbness. Adjust brace rods to plumb as required. Check drawing for locations of base angles.

The upperwall panels must lap over the lower wall panels for weathertightness. Remember—metal backed neoprene washers and #10 hex nuts are used on all shoulder bolts; machine screws (1/4" x 3/4") are used for panel to panel connections at sidelaps.

Since the ROOF PANELS are factory punched for panel to purlin connecting, it is important that the purlins be accurately aligned. Spacer boards constructed from crating lumber can be used as in figure 15-15 to align purlins. Move the spacer boards ahead to the next bay as the paneling progresses. Before you actually start paneling the roof, place the spacer board over the shoulder bolts, and insert nails in the 5/16 inch holes in the ridge purlins.

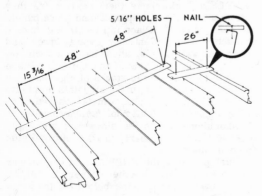

133.378X

Figure 15-15.—Aligning purlins with spacer board.

The roof paneling operation should start at one end of the building. Place the panels so the holes in the corrugation line up with the shoulder bolts in the roof beam, eave angles and ridge purlins; install one eave panel to each side of the building. The eave panels should be installed one row ahead of the ridge panels. (See figure 15-16.) (Before preceding with the work, make sure you are applying enough black mastic.) Roof paneling should continue in this order to ensure a weathertight joint at the corner laps. However, you should keep in check with the drawings for location and installation of the smoke stacks and ridge ventilation.

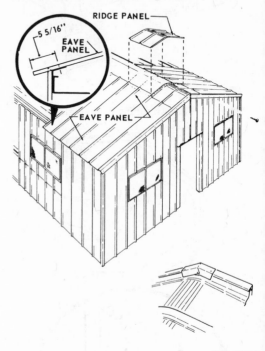

133.379X

Figure 15-16.—Installing ridge and eave panel.

DOORS

The doors to the Butlerhut can be hung anytime after the endwall structurals are completed. But, they MUST be hung prior to installing the interior lining. A helpful hint is to hang the doors before installing the exterior endwall paneling, this way adjustments on the door frame can be made easier.

Hinges are factory welded to the door jamb and the entrance door is supposed to swing to the INSIDE of the building. Remove the hinge leaf from the door jamb and attach it to the door with (#10 x 1 inch) flat head wood screws. Hang the door and make adjustments to get the proper clearances at the top and sides of the door. Install the lockset in the door and attach the face plate to the door with (#8 x 3/4 inch) flat head wood screws. Attach the strike plate to the door jamb with (#8 x 1/2 inch) flat head machine screws.

Hinges are also factory welded to the screen doors and screen doors swing to the OUTSIDE of the building. The method used in hanging the screen door is similar to hanging the entrance door. However, a spring is needed to hold the screen door closed.

LINER PANELS

There are three basic application operations used when installing liner panels. These operations consist of installing furring strips, hardboard panels, trim and battens. Figure 15-9(B) shows the various liner panel parts.

Endwalls

To begin the various operations, precut the liner panels according to the cutting diagrams. The hardboard must be installed with the smooth surface exposed and with an 1/8 inch gap between panels; as shown in figure 15-17. A scrap piece of hardboard or batten can be used as a shim to maintain the proper gap.

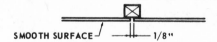

SMOOTH SURFACE — 1/8"

133.380X
Figure 15-17.—Installation of hardboard.

Nail the base furring to the floor, 3 inches from each end and on 2' 8" centers, with the inside edge 7 3/8 inches inside the building structural line. This is shown in figure 15-18. When the base furring is to be used on a wood floor use 8d box nails; and use (#9 x 1 1/4 inch) concrete nails with a concrete floor. Drill the 2 x 2's and girts with a #24 or 5/32 inch drill so that furring can be attached to the sidewall and eave girt with (#10 x 2 inch) pan head sheet metal screws. Attach the hardboard to the furring strips with 1 1/4 inch aluminum shingle nails, on 4 inch centers at sides and ends; on

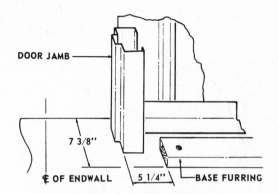

DOOR JAMB

7 3/8"

℄ OF ENDWALL   5 1/4"   BASE FURRING

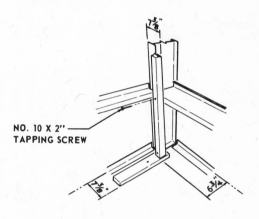

NO. 10 X 2"
TAPPING SCREW

7 3/8"   6 1/4"

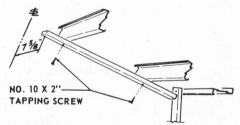

7 3/8"

NO. 10 X 2"
TAPPING SCREW

133.381X
Figure 15-18.—Installing furring for the endwall liners.

8 inch centers at intermediate furring. See figure 15-19.

The vertical furring should be installed immediately after the base, corner, and gable furring are in place. See figure 15-20. The center line of the furring on each side of the

417

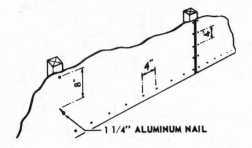

1 1/4" ALUMINUM NAIL

133.382X

Figure 15-19.—Nailing pattern for attaching hardboard to furring.

window should be in line with the center line of the endwall panel corrugations. After the

endwall furring is in place the hardboard liner should be installed. After all endwall hardboard has been installed, install door side and top flashing. Attach flashing (fig. 15-21) to furring with 4d aluminum nails and to door frame with #10 x 1/2 inch sheet metal screws.

Sidewalls

Upon completion of installing the endwall liner; the furring for the sidewall and ceiling should be installed. The base furring should be cut in such a way that the end will just clear the inside flange of the center frame column. The furring is nailed in the same manner as the endwalls.

Now that you have the furring in place, the hardboard liner can be installed. Install top and bottom hardboard flashings as shown in

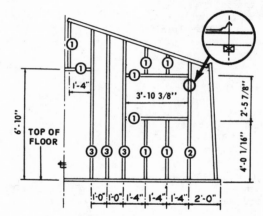

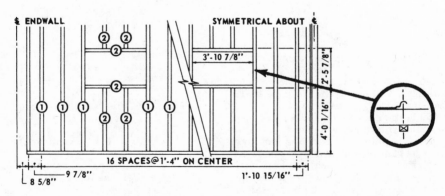

133.383X

Figure 15-20.—Placement of furring for liners.

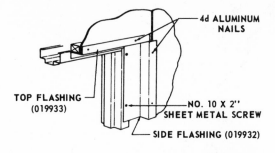

133.384X

Figure 15-21.—Side and top flashing
for doors.

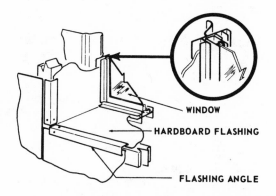

133.385X

Figure 15-22.—Top and bottom
hardboard flashing.

figure 15-22. Insert outside edge into retaining
grooves in the window. Nail metal flashing
angle and hardboard to horizontal furring with
4d aluminum nails 1 foot 8 inches on center.
Install side hardboard flashings and metal
flashing angles using the same procedure discussed above.

Ceiling

The ceiling furring is to be installed in the
vicinity of the sidewall furring. Whenever all
the ceiling furring has been installed, the hardboard liner can be installed. REMEMBER THE
1/8 INCH GAP BETWEEN PANELS.
The smoke stack assembly is to be attached
to the blocking and furring with 4d aluminum
nails.

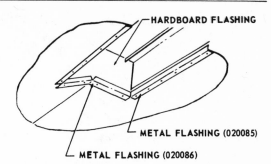

133.386X

Figure 15-23.—Metal ventilator flashing.

Hand trim hardboard flashings, for ends of
ventilator opening, and attach metal ventilator
flashings as shown in figure 15-23.

Install eave molding with the beveled edge
against the ceiling panels and attach each side-
wall furring strip with 4d aluminum nails. Use
quarter round molding to trim ceiling to endwall, endwall to sidewall, and walls to floor,
and use metal ridge flashings as shown in figure
15-24 to trim ridge of ceiling liner. It can be
attached to the ceiling furring with 4d aluminum
nails. Check the drawings to make sure you
are installing it right. Now, cut battens to the
required length and attach them to the furring
with 4d aluminum nails, 8 inches on center.

See figure 15-25.

GENERAL NOTES: Bolts, nuts and miscellaneous fasteners have been furnished in quantities greater than actual requirements. Care
should be exercised when using these fasteners
to prevent scattering on the ground. Empty
your pockets each evening of fasteners and
small parts before leaving the erection site.

An excessive amount of BLACK MASTIC is
also furnished with each Butlerhut; therefore,
reasonable care in its application to roof panels
and roof accessories will ensure an adequate
supply.

Crating lumber can also be used to construct
an entrance platform and stairs at each end of
the Butlerhut as shown in figure 15-26.

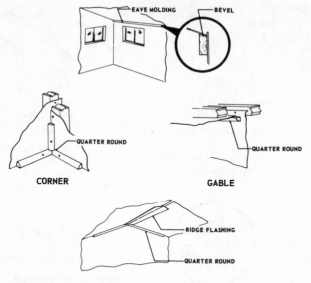

133.387X

Figure 15-24.—Interior trim.

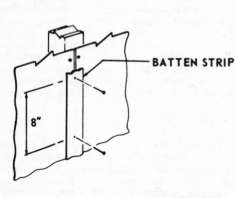

133.388X
Figure 15-25.—Batten strip.

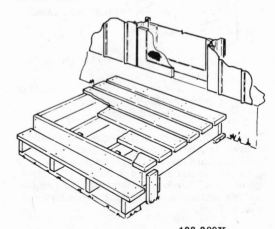

133.389X
Figure 15-26.—Crate platform.

WOOD-FRAME TENTS

Figure 15-27 shows working drawings for framing and flooring of a 16' by 32' wood-frame tent. Tents of this type are used for temporary housing, storage, shower, washrooms, latrines, and utility spaces at an advanced base. Tent flooring consisting of floor joists (16' lengths of 2 x 4), and flooring (4' by 8' sheets of 1/2" plywood) is prefabricated. Supports for the flooring (doubled 2 x 4 posts anchored on 2 x 12 x 12 footings), the wall framing members (2 x 4 studs spaced 4' O.C.), the roof framing members (2 x 4 rafters spaced 4' O.C.), the plates (2 x 4's), and the bracing members (1 x 6's) are procured in the field.

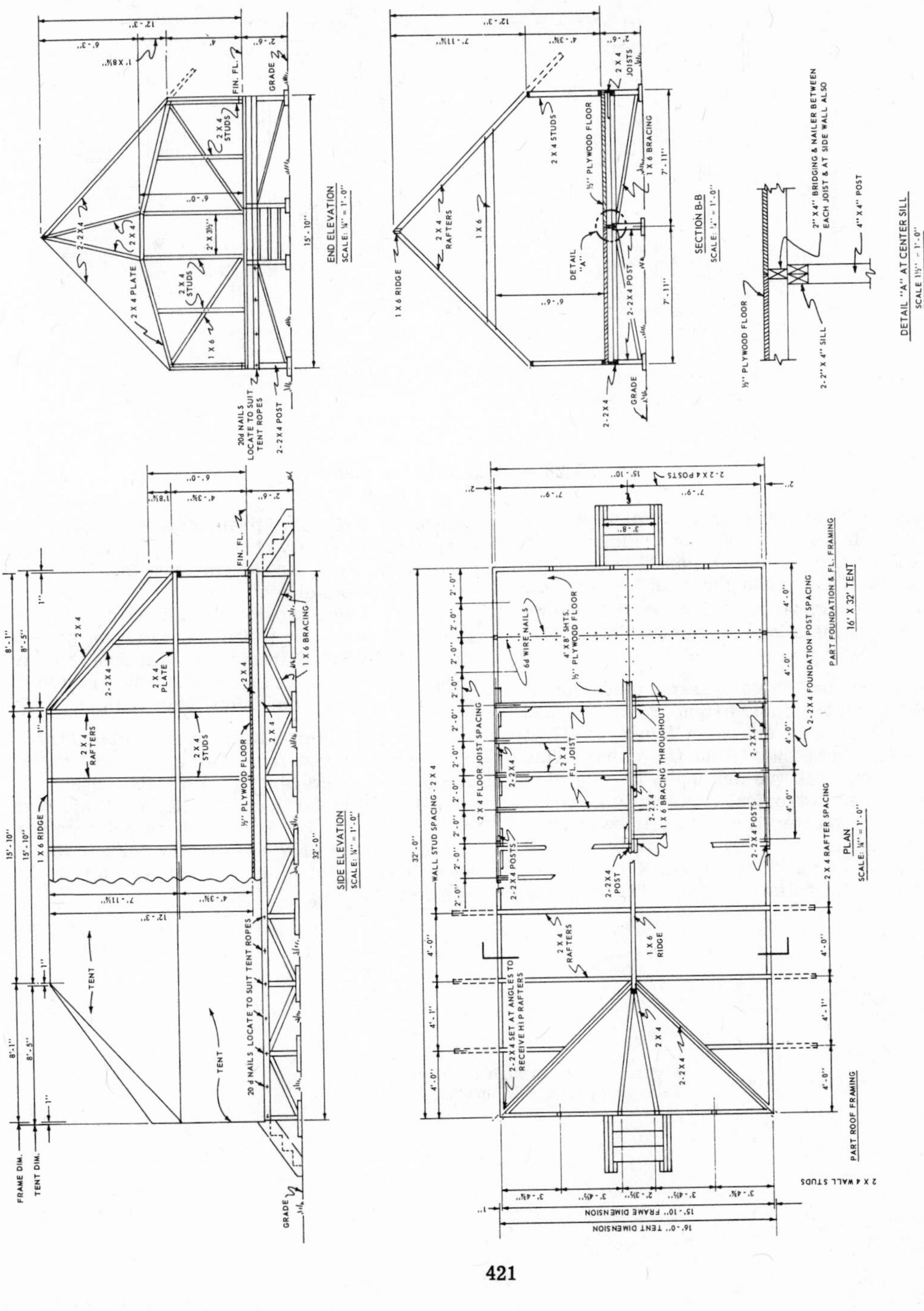

Figure 15-27.—Framing and flooring plans for 16 ft by 32 ft wood-frame tent.

421

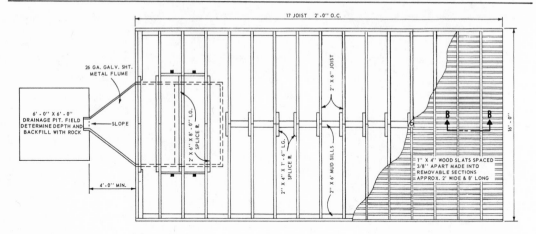

133.185

Figure 15-28.—Floor framing plan.

Figure 15-28 shows a floor framing plan for a field type shower and washroom. Figure 15-29 shows a floor and equipment plan. Figure 15-30 shows a section through the framing for field type shower and washroom. Figure 15-31 shows the flooring consisting of removable panels.

When the 16' by 32' wood-frame tent is modified with a metal roof, extended rafters and screened in areas as shown in figure 15-32, it is called a South East Asia (SEA) hut. This South East Asia hut was originally developed in Vietnam for use in tropical areas by U.S. troops for berthing; however, it can readily be adapted for other use such as a galley or mess hall. It is also known as the STRONGBACK because of the roof and sidewalls material. The SEA hut is usually a standard prefabricated unit but the design can be easily changed, to fit the existing conditions, such as lengthening the floor or making the roof higher.

The SEA hut should be built on a concrete slab when possible; because it has been proven that a 16' by 32' concrete slab 4 inches thick is cheaper to construct than a floor constructed of wood having the same width and length.

As stated before, basically all field structures are derived from the 16' by 32' wood-frame tent; however, if more tent space is needed a 40' by 80' tent is available. This tent is easy to assemble because it is put together without a floor. No matter how easy it might seem to assemble this tent, always follow the instructions.

Figures 15-29 through 15-32 are on the following pages, 423 through 425

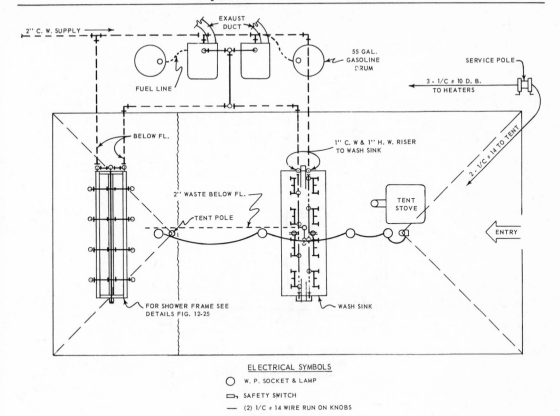

2'' C. W. SUPPLY

EXAUST DUCT

FUEL LINE

55 GAL. GASOLINE DRUM

SERVICE POLE

3 - 1/C # 10 D. B. TO HEATERS

2 - 1/C # 14 TO TENT

BELOW FL.

1'' C. W & 1'' H. W. RISER TO WASH SINK

2'' WASTE BELOW FL.

TENT POLE

TENT STOVE

ENTRY

FOR SHOWER FRAME SEE DETAILS FIG. 12-25

WASH SINK

ELECTRICAL SYMBOLS

○   W. P. SOCKET & LAMP

⊐╮ SAFETY SWITCH

—   (2) 1/C # 14 WIRE RUN ON KNOBS

▭   TOGGLE SWITCH

⊖   DUPLEX RECEPTACLE

133.186

Figure 15-29.—Equipment plan.

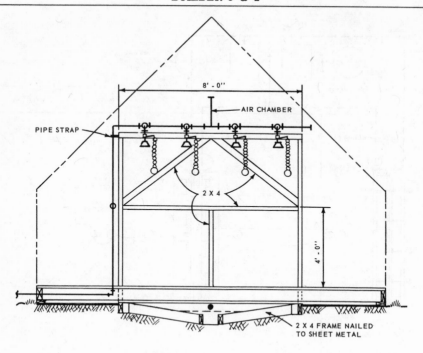

133.187

Figure 15-30.—Section through framing.

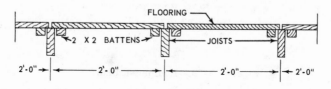

133.188

Figure 15-31.—Section through floor panels for
field-type shower.

133.390

Figure 15-32.—Completed SEA huts.

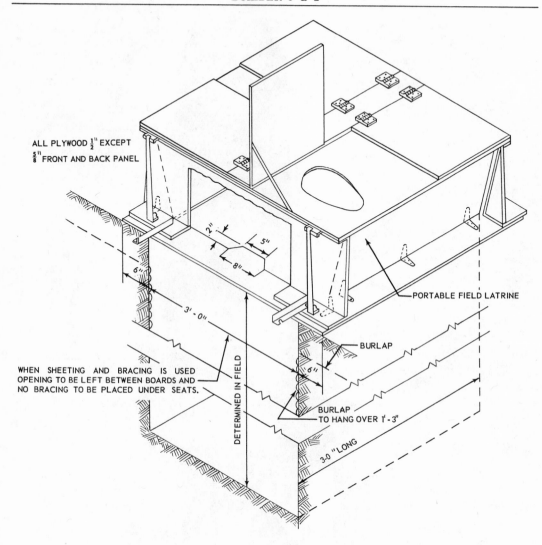

ALL PLYWOOD $\frac{1}{2}''$ EXCEPT
$\frac{5}{8}''$ FRONT AND BACK PANEL

PORTABLE FIELD LATRINE

2"

5"

8"

6"

3' - 0"

DETERMINED IN FIELD

WHEN SHEETING AND BRACING IS USED
OPENING TO BE LEFT BETWEEN BOARDS AND
NO BRACING TO BE PLACED UNDER SEATS.

BURLAP

6"

BURLAP
TO HANG OVER 1' - 3'

3-0 " LONG

133.189

Figure 15-33.—Prefabricated 4-seat latrine box.

FIELD-TYPE LATRINES

The 16' by 32' wood-frame tent is used to house the standard portable FIELD-TYPE LATRINE. The central unit in the latrine is the prefabricated 4-seat LATRINE BOX shown in figure 15-33. The box can be collapsed for shipment as shown in figure 15-34.

A plan view of an 8-seat field-type latrine is shown in figure 15-35. Two 4-seat boxes are placed so as to straddle a 3' by 7' pit. After the pit is dug, and before the boxes are placed,

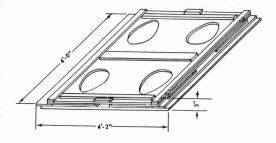

Figure 15-34.—Latrine box collapsed for shipment.

133.190

a 4' wide margin around the pit is excavated to a depth of 6", as shown in figure 15-36. A layer of oil-soaked burlap is laid in this excavation, after which the excavated earth is soaked with oil, replaced, and tamped down, to keep surface water out.

Two 4' 6" trough-type urinals are furnished with the 8-seat latrine. Each is mounted in a frame constructed as shown in figure 15-37. A 2" urinal drain pipe leads from the down pipe on each urinal to a 6' by 6' urinal SEEPAGE PIT, located as shown in figure 15-35. The

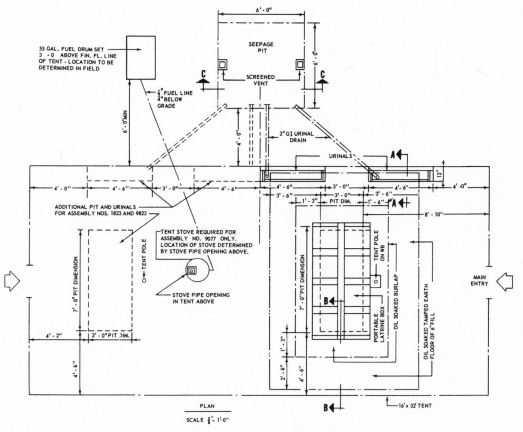

133.191

Figure 15-35.—Plan view of 8-seat field-type latrine.

427

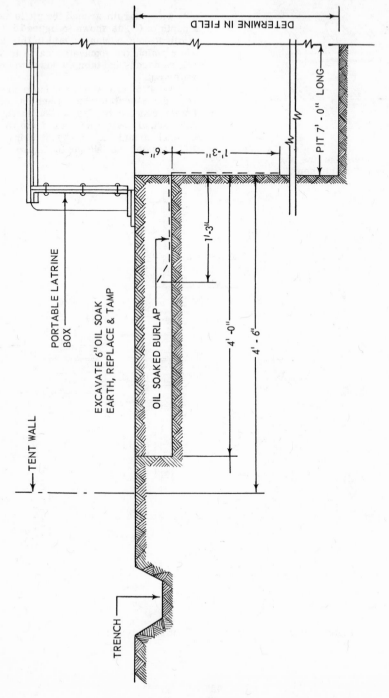

133.192

Figure 15-36.—Margin of oil-soaked earth around latrine boxes.

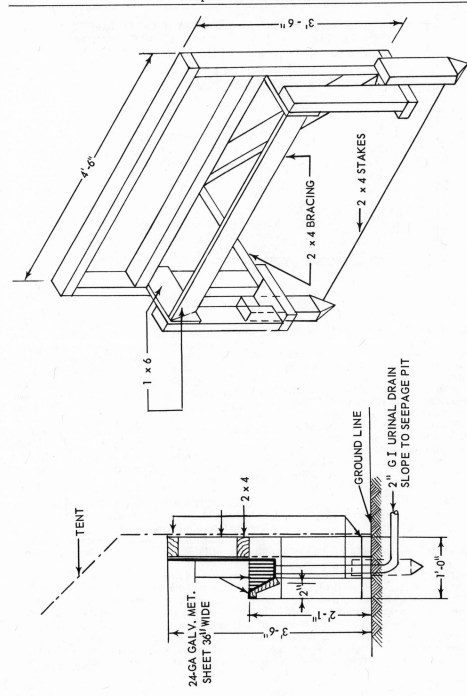

133.193

Figure 15-37.—Frame for urinal trough.

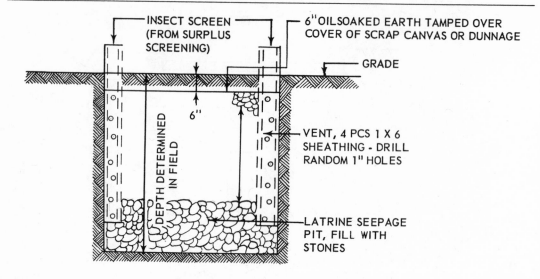

Figure 15-38.—Urinal seepage pit.

133.94

seepage pit is constructed as shown in figure 15-38.

As indicated in figure 15-35, the 8-seat field-type latrine can be expanded to a 16-seat field-type latrine.

A complete plan view of a 4-hole burn out field-type latrine is shown in figure 15-39. This type latrine is used at most advance or temporary bases. The burn out latrine is kept in an orderly condition (daily) by the camp maintenance personnel or the assigned sanitation crew. There are two easy ways of maintaining this type latrine and they are: by spreading lime over the waste material; or by using diesel fuel to burn the waste material.

THE HILLSIDE INCINERATOR AND BURNING PIT

There are several methods used for disposing of refuse. But, the two methods usually used by the SEABEES would be either the hillside incinerator or the burning pit method.

The HILLSIDE method of incineration (fig. 15-40) has proved simple and satisfactory. A trench about 2' wide, 3' deep and 6' or more long is excavated in a steep hillside or bank. At the foot of this trench, a soakage pit is excavated and the bottom of the trench and the soakage pit are filled with stone. The trench is covered with sheets of corrugated iron or other metal to assist in creating a draft when the wood or rubbish fire is built over the soakage pit. Garbage or other waste is dumped at the top of the trench and is stoked gradually down the rock bottom of the trench. Liquids drain down into the rocks in the trench and pit where they soak into the ground or are evaporated. The hot rocks and combustible gases dry the garbage as it progresses downward into the fire. This mode of disposal has the following advantages:

SIMPLICITY. One man can effectively and efficiently dispose of the excremental and garbage refuse of 5000 persons.

AVAILABILITY. Most terrain contains a sloping hillside or a small embankment that may be utilized.

It requires a minimum amount of fuel.

A large surface area of liquid is exposed to heat, thus facilitating evaporation. The hillside incinerator will prove most useful where there is a large mass of wet garbage to dispose of and where night soil must be burned.

Supervision is necessary to prevent the fire from going out and to stir up the garbage and

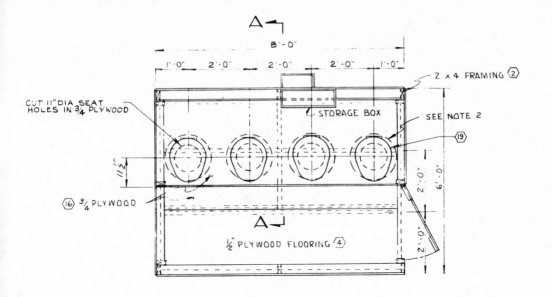

PLAN VIEW

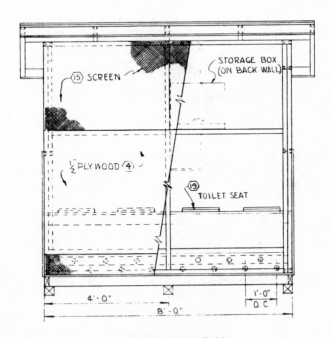

FRONT ELEVATION

Figure 15-39.—Burn out type, 4-hole latrine.

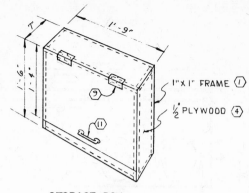

STORAGE BOX
NO SCALE

1"x1" FRAME ①

½" PLYWOOD ④

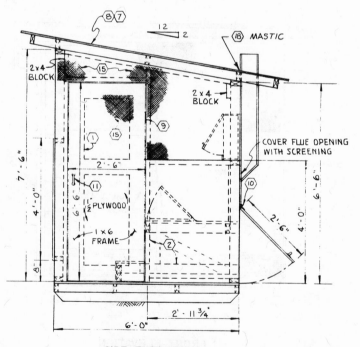

19

3'-1"

1'-1"

½ PLYWOOD BACK PANEL

CENTER STUD

ALL FRAMES 2x4

16 ¾ PLYWOOD

PLYWOOD GUSSETS

11

FLOOR

TO ALLOW FOR VENTILATION CUT 2" DIA HOLES THIS AREA 1'-0" O.C. & COVER WITH SCREEN

COVER END OF STEP WITH PLYWOOD

SECTION A-A

8 7

12
2

18 MASTIC

2x4 BLOCK

15

2x4 BLOCK

15

9

COVER FLUE OPENING WITH SCREENING

7'-6"

6'-6"

①

2'-6"

4'-0"

4'-0"

11

½ PLYWOOD

10

2'-6"

1x6 FRAME

2

8"

2'-11¾"

6'-0"

SIDE ELEVATION
OPP SIDE W/O DOOR

Figure 15-39.—Burn out type, 4-hole latrine.

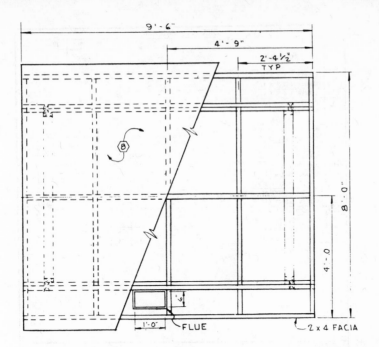

ROOF FRAME DETAIL

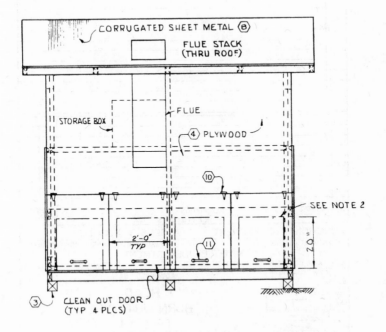

REAR ELEVATION

Figure 15-39.—Burn out type, 4-hole latrine.

BILL OF MATERIAL

ITEM	DESCRIPTION	UNIT	ASSEMBLY	QUAN.	ZONE
	HEAD, FOUR HOLE		1156		
1	LUMBER 1 X 6 X 16'	BF		25	
2	LUMBER 2 X 4 X 12'	BF		480	
3	LUMBER 4 X 4 X 12'	BF		32	
4	PLYWOOD 1/2 X 48 X 96	SH		10	
5	NAILS 8D COMM	LB		10	
6	NAILS 16D COMM	LB		5	
7	NAILS W/NEOP WASHER 5 LB	PG		1	
8	CORR SHT MTL 27 1/2 X 96"	SH		5	
9	HINGE BUTT 3 1/2"	PR		2	
10	HINGE TEE 3"	PR		8	
11	DOOR PULL	EA		6	
12	SPRING DOOR 9"	EA		1	
13	STAPLE TACKER, 3/8	BX		1	
14	PLASTIC CEMENT 50 LB DR	DR		1	
15	SCREEN INSECT 48"	YD		20	
16	PLYWOOD 3/4 X 48 X 96	EA		1	
17	STEEL BAR REINF 3/8	FT		6	
18	CALKING COMPOUND	CN		1	
19	SEAT, WATER CLOSET	EA		4	

NOTES:

1 HEX SYMBOL ON BILL OF MATERIAL IDENTIFIES ITEM SHOWN ON DRAWING.

2 CUT SURPLUS DRUMS 18" HIGH AND WELD HANDLES USING ITEM 17.

3 DRAWING DEVELOPED PER INFORMATION 3RD NCB DRAWING 67-STD-D-6001.

SYM	DESCRIPTION	BY	DATE	APPD
	REVISIONS			

FUNCTIONAL COMPONENT   **ASSEMBLY NO. 1156**

DEPARTMENT OF THE NAVY   NAVAL FACILITIES ENGINEERING COMMAND

MATERIEL DEPARTMENT

U. S. NAVAL CONSTRUCTION BATTALION CENTER   PORT HUENEME, CALIFORNIA

	ARCH	ELEC	MECH	ADVANCED BASE
DSGN	R.G.			
DRW	B J HEINAUER 9-11-68			**HEAD**
CHK	J.E.			**BURN OUT TYPE**
PROJ DIR				FOUR HOLE

DRFTG SECT HD

DSGN SECT HD

ENGRG BR MGR

DIV DIR   APPROVED

FOR COMMANDER NAVFAC   DATE

SATISFACTORY TO

SCALE 3/4" = 1'-0"   SK. NO. 68 232

DATE ____ BY ____

SH. ____ OF ____

NAVFAC DRAWING NO.   **1109837**

Figure 15-39.—Burn out type, 4-hole latrine.

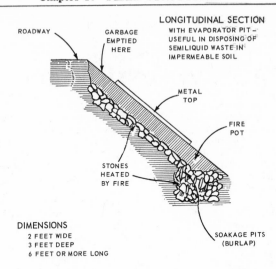

LONGITUDINAL SECTION
WITH EVAPORATOR PIT—
USEFUL IN DISPOSING OF
SEMILIQUID WASTE IN
IMPERMEABLE SOIL

ROADWAY

GARBAGE
EMPTIED
HERE

METAL
TOP

FIRE
POT

STONES
HEATED
BY FIRE

DIMENSIONS
2 FEET WIDE
3 FEET DEEP
6 FEET OR MORE LONG

SOAKAGE PITS
(BURLAP)

133.95

Figure 15-40.—Hillside incinerator.

refuse in order that the incinerator may function efficiently.

The BURNING PIT is the other disposal method used at installations where the production of large quantities of scrap lumber, crating, rubbish, and industrial waste is common. (The type of waste material that has to be disposed of is a determining factor in deciding on a disposal.) Under certain circumstances the burning pit may be better than the hillside incinerator, even though it requires a supplementary dump. The construction and operating of a burning pit should be approved by everyone, because of the hazards involved. The pit should

be located so that resulting smoke, fumes, odors, and blowing ashes will not interfere with any operations or the health and well being of your fellow SEABEES.

The waste material should be unloaded into one pit at a time. Trucks should NEVER be backed up to a burning pit. Waste material should be fired in the late afternoon to burn the greatest accumulation at one time, and also at noon if the quantity of waste requires two firings. The pit should be cleaned out weekly, and ashes, metal, and other noncombustible materials placed on a regulated dump or covered. Unburned garbage should be placed on top of the next fire to complete burning.

CHAPTER 16
HEAVY CONSTRUCTION

Construction which involves the use of heavy, large-dimension structural members is called HEAVY construction. Trestles and waterfront structures are typical examples. Heavy construction is done with steel, timber and concrete; as a Builder you will be concerned chiefly with timber and concrete.

TOOLS, EQUIPMENT, AND FASTENINGS

The tools used in concrete construction are about the same, regardless of whether the construction is heavy or light. Heavy timber construction, however, requires the use of certain tools, equipment, and fastenings which are not commonly used in ordinary rough and finish carpentry.

POWER CUTTING AND BORING TOOLS

Rough-cutting of large timbers may be done with portable power-driven CHAIN saws like the one shown in figure 16-1. Chain saws are made with blades as long as 84 in.; the most common blade sizes, however, are 24 in. and 36 in. A chain saw may be gasoline-driven or compressed air-driven (pneumatic); the one shown in figure 16-1 is gasoline-driven. Complete instructions for the operation and maintenance of the saw (including the conditioning of the blade) are contained in the manufacturer's manual.

Timbers up to about 4 in. thick are roughcut with portable power-driven CIRCULAR saws like the one shown in figure 16-2. A saw of this type may be either electric or pneumatic; the one shown in the figure is pneumatic. Conditioning procedures for a circular saw blade are described in chapter 9. Complete instructions for the operation and maintenance of a portable power-driven circular saw mechanism are contained in the manufacturer's manual.

The pneumatic reversible wood drill (fig. 16-3) is a heavy duty low speed machine

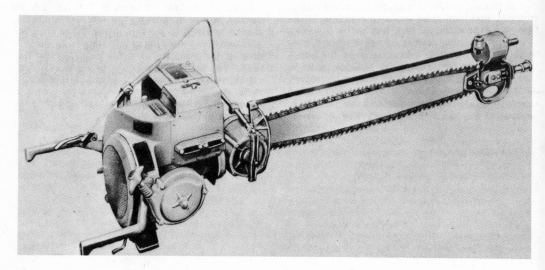

29.132

Figure 16-1.—Gasoline powered chain saw.

29.133

Figure 16-2.—Pneumatic circular saw.

29.134

Figure 16-3.—Pneumatic power-driven wood borer.

designed to drive ship auger type drills. It is used extensively in trestle bridge and other timber construction work where it is necessary to drill holes for bolts or pins. The drill body houses a four-vane rotary type pneumatic motor, a gear train for reducing the motor speed to a chuck speed of about 800 revolutions per minute, and an oil reservoir. A chuck is provided for 1/2-inch diameter drill bit shanks and a large "Allen" type setscrew holds the shank in place. The shaft on which the chuck is mounted, is drilled so the shank will extend into the base of the grip handle. A slot in the base of this handle provides for insertion of a wedge against the end of the bit to loosen it if it is jammed in the chuck. Three handles are provided on this drill. A fixed handle is mounted directly opposite the chuck, a grip handle extends opposite the throttle handle. The air line is attached to the end of the throttle handle.

Drill bits of the ship auger type are issued in 1- and 3-foot lengths, in diameter sizes of 7/16-inch, 3/4-inch, 1-inch, and 2-inch.

Improper use of the augers causes most of the maintenance problem with the wood drill. The auger frequently becomes stuck in the chuck. It should be removed by using the ejector but operators often try to knock it out with a hammer. This results in damage to the chuck or auger or both.

Accessories Used with Pneumatic Tools

The AIR LINE OILER is a reservoir of either a pint or a quart capacity which is placed in the air line directly in front of the air tool for the purpose of lubricating the tool. As the air passes through the oiler, it picks up oil which is carried into the tool. The amount of oil entering the air stream is controlled by an adjustable needle. Oilers occur in both direction and non-direction types. The directional oiler can be identified by an arrow on the outside shell. The arrow should be pointed in the direction of the air flow when connected in the line.

An air line HOSE is a rubber covered pressure type hose used for transmitting the compressed air. Hose with 3/4-inch inside diameter is used with the hand operated tools and a 1 1/4-inch hose is used with the drifter drill. Hose is usually furnished in 50-foot lengths equipped with quick acting couplings for attaching to tools, the compressor, or to other lengths of hose.

433

A LEADER hose is an oil resistant neoprene rubber hose with end attachments used between the air line oiler and an air tool. Leader hose sections are usually furnished in 12 1/2- or 25-foot lengths.

Cutting Tools—Hand

The ONE-MAN CROSSCUT SAW and the TWO-MAN CROSSCUT SAW (fig. 16-4) are preferred to the power saws for making accurate finish cuts and for small framing jobs. The so-called one-man saw can be and usually is operated by two men, by means of the additional handle shown, which can be attached to the blank end of the saw.

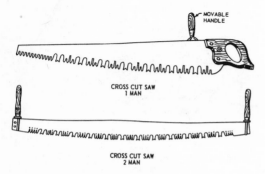

CROSS CUT SAW
1 MAN

CROSS CUT SAW
2 MAN

44.13

Figure 16-4.—One-man and two-man crosscut saws.

The teeth on one of these saws consist of a number of CUTTING teeth, usually 4, alternated with single RAKER teeth. The cutting teeth score parallel grooves in the bottom of the kerf; the raker teeth chisel out the waste between the grooves. The points of the cutting teeth should therefore extend slightly beyond those of the raker teeth. The cutting teeth are conditioned like the teeth on a crosscut handsaw. The raker teeth are conditioned like the teeth on a rip handsaw, except that the raker teeth on a one-man or two-man crosscut saw are not set.

Chopping Tools

Figure 16-5 shows an ADZ, various types of AXES, and a HALF-HATCHET (commonly called just a HATCHET). In heavy timber construction the adz is used chiefly for hewing plane surfaces

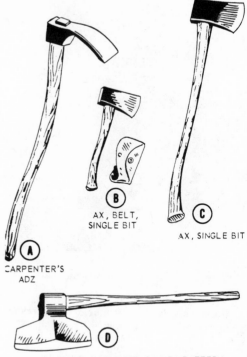

B — AX, BELT, SINGLE BIT

C — AX, SINGLE BIT

A — CARPENTER'S ADZ

D — AX, BROAD SINGLE BIT, CANADA PATTERN

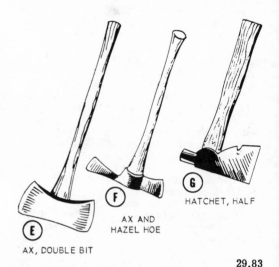

E — AX, DOUBLE BIT

F — AX AND HAZEL HOE

G — HATCHET, HALF

29.83

Figure 16-5.—Chopping tools.

29.84

Figure 16-6.—Using the adz and the ax.

as shown in figure 16-6. It has a straight blade with a single bevel on the under side. The blade of a CARPENTER'S adz is 4 in. wide, the blade of a RAILROAD adz is 5 in. wide. In using the adz, short, choppy strokes are better than long ones. Take great care to keep the work clear of chips which might deflect the blade. The adz cuts toward the person using it, and is therefore a very dangerous tool. Therefore, if much work is to be done with the adz, the Builder should wear skim guards.

In heavy timber construction the AX is used chiefly for notching and for general hewing and shaping, as shown in figure 16-6. Of the various axes shown in figure 16-5, the SINGLE-BIT ax is the one most frequently used. The head of this ax, which weighs about 4 lbs, has a curved edge which is beveled on both sides.

Care and Maintenance of
Chopping Tools

Chopping tools are sharpened as shown in Basic Handtools, NavPers 10085-A. Handles on chopping tools must be inspected constantly to ensure that they are tight and not split or broken.

If a handle is found to be loose, reseat it solidly in the EYE (hole through the head) of the tool, by striking the end of the handle with a mallet and then driving the wedges in solidly. If the wedges do not spread the handle enough to tighten it, add another wedge. If this is not possible, remove the original wedge and insert a larger wedge.

Procedure for replacing a defective handle on a chopping tool is the same as that described in chapter 9 for a percussion tool. Chopping tools, like any other edged tools, must be stowed in the manner which will best protect their edges. For short-term storage, the heads should be cleaned and coated with light oil. For long-term storage the heads should be cleaned and coated with a rust-preventive.

Sledges and Mauls

The DOUBLE-FACE SLEDGE (fig. 16-7) is the percussion tool most frequently used in heavy timber construction. A sledge is designated as to size by the weight of the head in pounds, and by the additional designation of SHORT-HANDLED or LONG-HANDLED. Common weights of heads are 6, 8, 12, 14, and 16 lbs. Sledges are used for percussion requirements ranging from the driving of spikes and drift bolts (done with a short-handled lightweight sledge) up to the DRIFTING (pounding into place of heavy timbers (done with a long-handled, heavyweight sledge)).

45.36

Figure 16-7.—Double-face sledge.

When it is used for drifting timbers, the steel sledge is likely to mark up the wood. The reinforced-head double-face wood MAUL shown in figure 16-8 can be used for drifting without this disadvantage. Wood mauls come with heads ranging from 15 to 25 lbs in weight; the usual head size is 8 in. diameter by 10 in. long. Handles run from 30 to 36 in. in length. Besides drifting, the maul is also for driving wooden

44.2(133C)

Figure 16-8.—Reinforced-head double-face wood maul.

stakes and posts. It is NEVER used for driving metal.

If the faces of a sledge become rounded or damaged in use, they must be reground square. Do not use a sledge with rounded faces; it may glance off the object you are striking and injure you or somebody else. Dip the head of the sledge in water frequently during grinding, to prevent overheating, and take an equal amount off each face to preserve the balance of the sledge.

The procedure with regard to handles is the same as it is for chopping tools. Stowage procedures are likewise the same, with the addition of the fact that wood mauls should not be stowed in hot sunlight or near hot water pipes or other sources of heat. Excessive heat may dry out the head of a wood maul enough to cause checking.

Handling Equipment

The principal devices for handling heavy timbers by hand are shown in figure 16-9. The CANT HOOK and the PEAVY are used to roll, turn, and sometime carry large timbers—especially cylindrical timbers. The only essential difference between the two is that the cant hook has a blunt end and the peavy a pike point. The TIMBER CARRIER is a pair of tongs which grasp timber when the handles are lifted by a couple of men. Two cant hooks or two peavys, with handles located on opposite sides of the timber, can do the same job but should not be used when a carrier is around. HOOK, when hung on the hook of a crane or tackle, functions in the same manner for hoisting timbers. The LUMBER BUGGY is a two-wheeled pushcart for carrying timbers over short distances. The LOAD BINDER is a device for binding timbers carried on the buggy. A length of chain is passed around the load and hung off on the hooks of the binder. When the lever on the binder is brought down, the chain tightens up around the load.

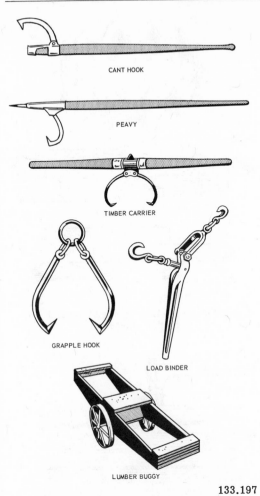

CANT HOOK

PEAVY

TIMBER CARRIER

GRAPPLE HOOK

LOAD BINDER

LUMBER BUGGY

133.197

Figure 16-9.—Timber handling tools
and equipment.

Timber Fastenings

The BOLTS used to fasten heavy timbers usually come in 1/2-in., 3/4-in., and 1-in. diameters, with square heads and square nuts. Round steel washers are placed under the heads and the nuts, and a bolt should be tightened until the washers bite well into the wood, to compensate for future shrinkage. Bolts should be spaced not less than 9 in. O.C. Edge distance

should be not less than 2 1/2 in., and end distance not less than 7-in.

End-butt joints are customarily fastened with DRIFT BOLTS (often called DRIFT PINS). A drift bolt is a long, threadless bolt which is driven into a hole bored through the member butted against and into the end of the abutting member. The bored hole is made slightly smaller than the bolt diameter and about 3 in. shorter than the bolt length. Drift bolt diameters run from 1/2 in. to 1 in., lengths from 18 in. to 26 in.

End-butt joints are also fastened with SCABS, a scab being a short length of timber, spiked or bolted to the adjoining members at the joint as shown in figure 16-10.

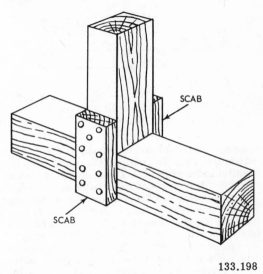

SCAB

SCAB

133.198

Figure 16-10.—Scabs.

Timber Connectors

TIMBER CONNECTOR is a general term applied to a variety of devices used to increase the strength and rigidity of bolted laps joints between heavy timbers. The SPLIT RING is used as shown in figure 16-11. It is embedded in circular grooves, cut with a special type of bit in the faces of the timbers which are to be joined. Split rings come with 2 1/4-in., 4-in., 6-in., and 8-in. diameters. The 2 1/2-in. ring takes a 1/2-in. bolt, the others a 3/4-in. bolt. If more than one ring is used at a joint, minimum

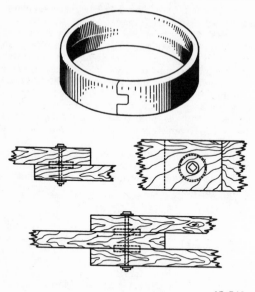

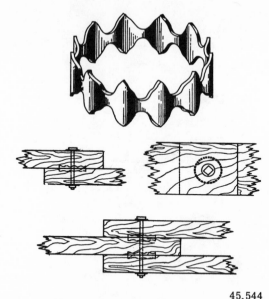

45.543

Figure 16-11.—Split ring and
split ring joint.

45.544

Figure 16-12.—Toothed ring and
toothed ring joint.

spacings center-to-center should be 2 1/2 ring diameters when the pull on the joint will be parallel to the grain, 1 1/2 ring diameters when the pull will be perpendicular to the grain. Edge distance, measured from the center of the ring to the edge of the member, should be not less than 1/2 the ring diameter plus 1 in. End distance, measured from the center of the ring to the end of the member, should be not less than 7 in. When more than one ring is used, minimum spacing between centers should be 9 in.

The TOOTHED RING (fig. 16-12) functions in much the same manner as the split ring, but can be embedded without the necessity for cutting grooves in the members. The toothed ring is embedded by pressure produced by tightening a bolt of high tensile strength, as shown in figure 16-13. The hole for this bolt is made 1/16 in. larger than the bolt diameter, so that the bolt may be easily extracted after the ring is embedded. It is then replaced by an ordinary steel bolt.

Toothed rings come with 2-in., 2 5/8-in., 3 3/8-in., and 4-in. diameters. The 2-in. ring takes a 1/2-in. bolt, the 2 5/8-in. ring a 5/8-in. bolt, and the others a 3/4-in. bolt. Spacings

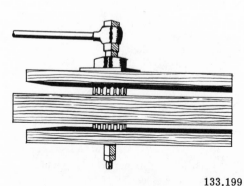

133.199

Figure 16-13.—Embedding toothed rings.

and edge and end distances are the same as they are for split rings.

The SPIKE GRID is used as shown in figure 16-14. A spike grid may be FLAT (for joining two flat surfaces), SINGLE-CURVED (for joining a flat and a curved surface), or DOUBLE-CURVED (for joining two curved surfaces). A spike grid is embedded in the same manner as a toothed ring.

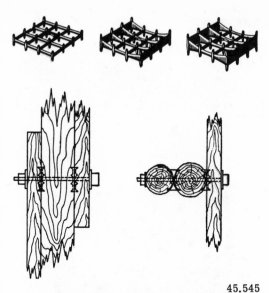

45.545

Figure 16-14.—Spike grid joints.

PRESSURE MACHINERY SAFETY

The air compressor, supplemented by a variety of pneumatic accessories, is an efficient and versatile tool during almost all stages of military construction. Compressed air is used extensively in military operations for such jobs as sawing, drilling, spraying, inflating, and operating a wide variety of available pneumatic tools. Energy is imparted to air by a compressor. The compressed air is transmitted through a pipe or hose to the operating tool where a portion of the energy is converted into rotary or reciprocating motion, thus operating the tool.

Various safety factors concerning compressors, tanks, piping systems, and compressed air are discussed in the following sections.

All compressed air receiving tanks should be installed in a cool, dry location and positioned so that they may be inspected on all sides with ease. Receiving tanks should be equipped with pressure activated relief valves that are maintained in a constant state of good repair. The relief valves should be adjusted to vent compressed air at pressures 20 percent lower than the maximum rated working pressures of the receiving tank.

All power sources for compressors should be of a constant speed type either by design or by the addition of speed regulating devices. These devices should act independently of the onloader compressor. Each air compressor should also be equipped with an automatic mechanism so arranged that the compressor will automatically stop its operation before the discharge pressure exceeds the maximum allowable pressure on the weakest portion of the system to which the compressor is connected. This automatic mechanism should be so designed and built that its failure will not cause the compressor to continue to operate.

All compressed air receiving tanks should be drained of water not less than once a day. If in constant use, the tank should be drained as often as humidity conditions require. There should be a preventive maintenance schedule in effect.

All compressors should be operated at the minimum pressure needed to perform the desired function. Compressed air systems supplied by a single compressor should have pressure regulating devices installed in the system in such a manner that the following working pressures are not exceeded at the point of application:

Tire inflation . . . . . 110 pounds per square
      inch
Work bench . . . . 30 pounds per square
      inch
Machinery . . . . Pressure established
      by manufacturer.

There should be no smoking in the vicinity of any TANK in which flammable material is stored. Fluids should not be mixed in tanks.

All tank vents and other fittings should be inspected periodically. All defects noted in these inspections should be reported and repaired at once. No one should enter any tank until it is declared gas-free; however in case of emergency, you may enter with the necessary protective devices.

Tanks previously containing inflammable fluids, which are put out of service, should either be dismantled and the sections stored or should be filled with water and secured.

All PIPING SYSTEMS should be stripe-painted in accordance with Standard Navy Color Code for Piping Systems. No pipe system should be operated at pressure exceeding its rated capacity.

All systems should be inspected periodically, and all noted defects corrected. All leaks noted in any pipe line system should be reported, and repaired as soon as possible. Valves, couplings, and other fittings should be matched as to size, pressure capacity, etc., within the entire system.

All pipeline systems should be tested periodically by making a valve-to-valve pressure drop test. All pressure gages and pressure regulating devices used in conjunction with compressed air should be tested at frequent intervals. All defective devices so found should be repaired or discarded at once.

All piping, hoses, couplings, etc., used in compressed air systems should conform to standards for Pressure Piping Systems in all respects. No compressed air hose should be kinked to control air. Turn off base valve.

COMPRESSED AIR should be used only as a power supply for tools and equipment which are of proper design and with approved safety devices.

No person should turn compressed air on himself or any other person for any purpose whatsoever.

Compressed air will not be used for drying bearings or cleaning floors, benches, machinery, tools, or equipment unless specifically authorized by the petty officer in charge. Any area where compressed air is admitted into the atmosphere directly from an air hose is considered an eye hazardous area and suitable eyewear will be worn by all personnel so exposed.

Strict disciplinary action should be taken against personnel who violate or fail to observe the safety rules.

TRESTLES

A TRESTLE is a braced framework of timbers, piles, or steelwork built to carry a roadway across a depression, such as a gully, a canyon, or the valley of a stream. The two main subdivisions of a trestle are the SUBSTRUCTURE, consisting of the supporting members, and the SUPERSTRUCTURE, consisting of the DECKING and the STRINGERS (also called GIRDERS) on which the decking is laid.

The substructure of a timber trestle consists of a series of transverse frameworks called BENTS. TRESTLE bents are used on solid, dry ground, or on solid bottom in shallow water. PILE bents are used in soft or marshy ground, or in water so deep, or where the

current is so swift, as to make the use of trestle bents impossible.

PARTS OF A TRESTLE BENT

A trestle bent may be a SINGLE-STORY bent or a MULTI-STORY bent. The parts of a single story bent are shown in figure 16-15. A 2-story bent is shown in the left-hand view of figure 16-16.

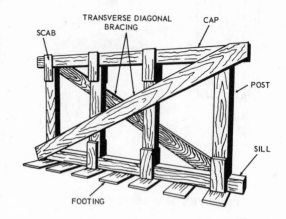

45.523

Figure 16-15.—Parts of a single-story trestle bent.

PARTS OF A TRESTLE

The principal parts of a trestle and their definitions are as follows:

ABUTMENT.—The ground support at each of the extreme ends of the superstructure. See figures 16-17 and 16-18.

BRACING.—Timbers used to brace a trestle bent, called TRANSVERSE bracing, or timbers used to brace bents to each other, called LONGITUDINAL bracing. Longitudinal bracing is shown in figure 16-16.

CAP.—The uppermost transverse horizontal structural member of a bent, laid across the tops of the posts.

DECKING.—The structure which is laid on the girders to form the roadway across the trestle. The decking in an all-timber trestle consists of a lower layer of timbers called the FLOORING and an upper layer of timbers called the TREADWAY.

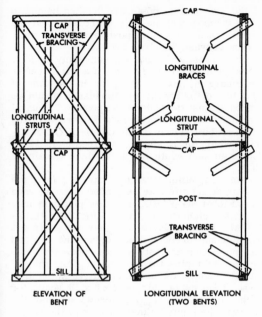

ELEVATION OF
BENT

LONGITUDINAL ELEVATION
(TWO BENTS)

133.200

Figure 16-16.—Two-story trestle bent.

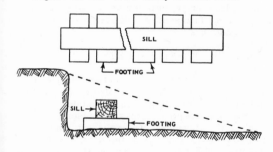

45.524

Figure 16-17.—Abutment sill and footing
and abutment excavation.

FLOORING.—See DECKING.

FOOTINGS.—Supports placed under the sills. In an all-timber trestle the footings consist of a series of short lengths of plank. Whenever possible, however, the footings are made of concrete.

GIRDER.—One of a series of longitudinal supports for the deck, laid on the caps. Also called a STRINGER.

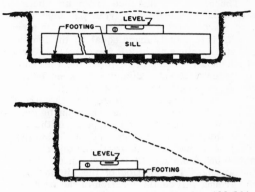

133.201

Figure 16-18.—Placing and leveling abutment footings and abutment sill.

POST.—One of the vertical structural members.

SILL.—Bottom transverse horizontal structural member of a trestle bent, on which the posts are anchored, or transverse horizontal member which supports the ends of the girders at an abutment.

STRINGER.—Same as girder.

SUBSTRUCTURE.—The supporting structure of braced trestle bents, as distinguished from the superstructure.

SUPERSTRUCTURE.—The spanning structure of girders and decking, as distinguished from the substructure.

TREADWAY.—See DECKING.

PARTS OF A PILE BENT

The posts of a pile bent consist of BEARING PILES, or vertical structural members which are driven in the ground. A pile bent does not have footings and a sill; but it does have a cap and transverse bracing similar to those on a trestle bent.

CONSTRUCTING A TRESTLE

After location of the centerline of a trestle has been decided upon, the next step is to locate the abutment on each bank at the desired or prescribed elevation. The abutments are then excavated, to a depth equal to the combined depths of the decking and the stringers, less an allowance for settlement. The abutment footings and the abutments sills are then cut, placed, and leveled as shown in figure 16-18.

441

The horizontal distance from an abutment sill to the first bent, and from one bent to the next, is controlled by the length of the girder stock. It is usually made equal to the length of the stock, minus about 2 ft for overlap. Girder stock usually comes in 14-ft lengths; the center-to-center horizontal distance between bents is therefore usually 14 minus 2, or 12 ft.

The locations of the seats for the trestle bents and the heights of the bents can be determined as follows. Stretch a tape from the abutment along the center line, and use a builder's level or a line level to level the tape. Drop a plumb bob from the 12-ft mark on the tape to the ground. The position of the plumb bob on the ground will be the location of the first bent. The vertical distance from the location of the bob to the horizontal tape, less the thickness of a footing, will be the height of the first bent. Next, stretch the tape from the location of the first bent, level it as before, and again drop a plumb bob from the 12-ft mark. The position of the plumb bob will be the location of the section bent. The vertical distance from the location of the bob to the horizontal tape, PLUS THE HEIGHT OF THE FIRST BENT, less the thickness of a footing, will be the height of the second bent. Next, stretch the tape from the location of the second bent and proceed as before. The vertical distance from the location of the bob to the horizontal tape, plus the height of the second bent, less the thickness of a footing, will be the height of the third bent; and so on. (See fig. 16-19.)

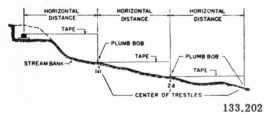

133.202

Figure 16-19.—Locating seats for trestle bents.

CONSTRUCTING TRESTLE BENTS

A trestle bent is laid out and constructed as follows. The length of the posts is equal to the height of the bent, less the combined depths of the cap and sill. In a 4-post bent, the centers

of the two outside posts are located from 1 to 2 1/2 ft inboard of the ends of the sill, and the centers of the two inner posts are spaced equidistant between the other two.

Sills, caps, and posts are commonly made of stock from 12 x 12 to 14 x 16; if a sill or cap is not square in cross-section (as in the case of 14 x 16 stock), the larger dimension should be placed against the ends of the posts. The usual length for a sill or cap is 2 ft more than the width of the roadway on the trestle. The minimum width for a single-lane trestle is 14 ft. The minimum width for a two-lane trestle is 18 ft.

For assembling trestle bents, a part of the terrain at the site may be graded flat and used as a FRAMING YARD, or a low platform may be constructed for use as a FRAMING PLATFORM. To assemble a bent, lay the posts out parallel and properly spaced, set the cap and sill in position against the ends, bore the holes for the drift pins through the cap and the sill into the ends of the posts, and drive in the drift pins. Then cut a pair of 2 x 8 x 18 scabs for each joint and spike, lag-screw, or bolt the scabs to the joints. Finally measure the diagonals to determine the lengths of the transverse diagonal braces, cut the braces to length, and spike, lag-screw, or bolt them to the sills, caps, and posts. Transverse diagonal bracing is usually made of 2 x 8 stock.

ERECTING TRESTLE BENTS

The usual method of erecting trestle bents is as follows. A traveling crane (or, in the absence of a traveling crane, the best available means of transport) brings the assembled first bent to the abutment, swings it out, and sets it in place on the footings at the seat. The bent is carefully plumbed, and temporarily braced with timbers running from the top of the bent to stakes driven at the abutment. The superstructure (girders and decking) is laid from the abutment out to the top of the first bent. The crane then brings the second bent out to the end of the superstructure and sets it in place. The second bent is plumbed, the diagonals are measured to determine the lengths of the longitudinal diagonal braces between the first bent and the second, and the braces are cut and spiked, lag-screwed, or bolted in place. The superstructure is then carried out to the second bent, after which the crane brings the third bent out to the end of the superstructure. This procedure is repeated, usually by parties working out from both abutments, until the entire span is completed. In the absence of a crane, a gin pole or a set of shears is erected and moved out with the superstructure.

ERECTING THE SUPERSTRUCTURE

Timber girders are usually 10 x 16's, 14 ft long, spaced 3 ft 3 1/2 in. O.C. Various methods of fastening timber girders to timber caps are shown in the first view of figure 16-20. Various methods of fastening steel girders to timber caps are shown in the second view of figure 16-20. This view also shows three ways of fastening a timber nailing anchorage for flooring to the top of a steel girder.

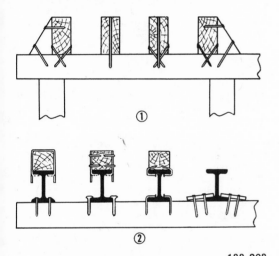

133.203

Figure 16-20.—Methods of fastening timber and steel girders to timber caps.

Timber decking consists of 2 layers of 3-in. planks. The lower layer, called the FLOORING, is laid at right angles to the girders and nailed down with two 60-penny nails to each girder crossing. The upper layer, called the TREADWAY, is laid at 45 degrees to the girders and securely nailed down to the lower layer.

As indicated in figure 16-21, most of the flooring planks and all the treadway planks are cut to lengths which will bring the ends of the planks flush with the outer faces of the outside stringers. At every 5 ft along the superstructure, however, a flooring plank is left long

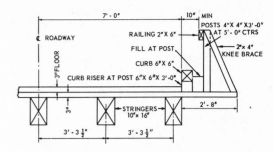

133.204

Figure 16-21.—Details of superstructure of a timber trestle.

enough to extend 2 ft 8 in. beyond the outer faces of the outside stringers. This extension serves as a support for the CURB RISERS, the CURB, and the HANDRAIL POSTS, as shown in the figure. The curb risers consist of 3-ft lengths of 6 x 6, one of which is set in front of each handrail post as shown. A continuous 6 x 6 curb is nailed down to the risers. A continuous 2 x 6 handrail is nailed to 4 x 4 handrail posts. Each handrail post is supported by a 2 x 4 KNEE BRACE, as shown.

As indicated in figure 16-22, an END DAM is set at each end of the superstructure, to prevent the approach road to the trestle from sloughing away into the spaces between the abutment ends of the girders.

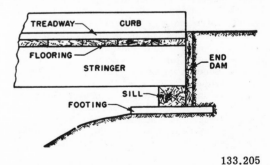

133.205

Figure 16-22.—End dam.

PILES

The principal structural members in many types of waterfront structures are PILES, a pile being a wood, steel, or concrete structural member which is driven into the ground. A vertical pile which sustains a vertical downward pressure is called a BEARING pile. A pile which is set at an angle to sustain a diagonal pressure is called a BATTER pile. Piles which are equipped for edge-joining and which are driven edge-to-edge to form a wall which sustains a lateral (horizontal) pressure, are called SHEET piles.

All piling materials are important, but timber piles are most important. Steel piling ranks next in importance, especially where deliberate construction is planned to accommodate heavy loads or where the foundation is expected to be used over a long period of time. Steel is best suited for use as bearing piles when piles must be driven under the following conditions:

When piles longer than 80 feet are required;

Where column strength is required which exceeds the compressive strength of timber;

To reach bedrock for maximum bearing surface through overlying layers of partially decomposed rock;

To penetrate layers of coarse gravel or soft rock, such as coral; or

To attain greater depth of penetration for stability. An example of this is driving in rock-bedded and swiftly flowing streams where timber piles cannot be driven deep enough for stability.

Concrete and composite piles are used less frequently and require material and equipment not normally available through military supply channels. These are used most frequently where local materials are readily available whereas standard military piling would have to be received in large quantities from CONUS. Interlocking steel sheet piling is most often used in military construction, but field manufactured concrete sheet piling or various types of expendent sheet piling is used when local materials are available.

As you will soon realize: many factors influence the choice of pile type to be used on a given project. In DELIBERATE construction, full weight should be given to the factors listed below (and others, if applicable) in making the selection.

Anticipated pile loads.

Anticipated length of piles and ease of adjusting length, if necessary.

Soil conditions existing at the site.

Ground water conditions existing at the site.

Availability of materials.

Availability of equipment for handling and driving piles.

Time available for construction.

Degree of permanence required and exposure conditions for completed structure.

Physical properties of available pile types.

Accessibility of site and transportation facilities.

Comparative costs.

In HASTY construction, full use is made of any and all readily available materials that can be used to construct a pile foundation capable of supporting the superstructure and maximum load during the short-term period for which use of the structure is intended. The tactical situation and accompanying emphasis placed upon the economy of time and the minimizing of the construction effort will dictate whether construction is of hasty or deliberate nature.

TIMBER BEARING PILES

Timber bearing piles are usually straight tree trunks cut off above ground swell, with branches closely trimmed and bark removed. Occasionally, sawed timbers may be used as bearing piles.

A good timber pile has the following characteristics:

Free of sharp bends, large or loose knots, shakes, splits, and decay.

A straight line between centers of butt and tip lies within the body of the pile.

A uniform taper from butt to tip.

Limiting cross section dimensions of timber used as piles are:

Piles shorter than 40 feet—tip (small end) diameters, 8 to 11 inches, and butt (large end) diameters 12 to 18 inches.

Piles longer than 40 feet—tip diameters, 6 to 8 inches, and butt diameters, 13 to 20 inches. The butt diameter must not be greater than the distance between the pile leads.

Timber piles usually are driven with the tip down.

A typical timber bearing pile is shown in figure 16-23.

Reinforcing of Wood Piles

Piles that have been weakened by marine borers can be strengthened and protected by encasing them in concrete jackets.

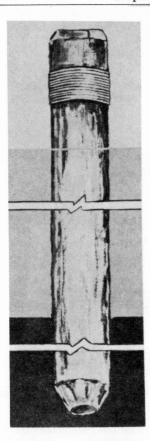

133.392
Figure 16-23.—Typical
timber bearing pile.

Steel reinforcing can be used in the concrete jacket either in the form of bars or wire mesh. Concrete encasement may be used to cover a short section of the pile, where damage is limited; as shown in figure 16-24, or may be extended well below the waterline or to the mud line.

The damaged surface of the pile should be scraped to sound wood. Either metal or wood forms may be used. If wood forms are used, a 2-inch creosoted tongue and groove material should be used and left in place. Fender piles that are broken between the top and bottom wales can be repaired by cutting off the pile just below the break, then installing a new section of pile and fitting. Place and bolt a pile section or timber section directly behind the fender pile from top to bottom wales. A metal wearing strip should be spiked to the wearing edge of the pile.

Preservation of Wood Piles

All timber used for piling and any other structures that are subject to marine borer activity should be pressure-treated with a creosote-coal tar solution containing approximately 30 percent coal tar. The treatment must be thorough and the penetration as deep as possible. The retention should be equivalent to at least 20 pounds of creosote per cubic foot of timber in the case of Douglas fir and 25 pounds per cubic foot in the case of Southern Yellow Pine. The use of untreated wood can seldom be justified, even for temporary structures. Extreme caution should be exercised in the use of untreated wood because it can be destroyed in a very short period of time by marine borers where conditions are unfavorable.

When pressure-treated materials have been cut or bored so as to expose untreated wood, the untreated surface should be field-treated with a hot creosote preservative solution or with generous application of a grease preservative. Holes for bolting should be neat and not oversize and treated with a preservative by the use of a bolt hole treator; or, if this cannot be done, hot creosote should be poured in the holes. Grease-type preservatives can be applied with a grease gun. All cut surfaces should have a minimum of three coats of hot creosote brushed on, or a heavy coating of grease preservative applied immediately after exposure of the surface. If it should be necessary to make emergency repairs of a superstructure above waterline and time will not permit the procurement of pressure-treated wood, the wood used can be treated on the job. After replacement members are cut and bored, soak them in hot creosote, pentachlorophenol, or copper napthenate solution for a minimum of two hours before use. This treatment is NOT a substitute for pressure treatment and should be used only when pressure-treated wood is not available.

STEEL BEARING PILES

The two most common types of steel bearing piles are the H-PILE and the PIPE PILE. The H-pile is a steel beam with a cross-section

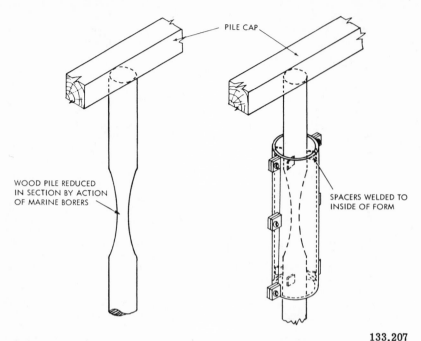

PILE CAP

WOOD PILE REDUCED
IN SECTION BY ACTION
OF MARINE BORERS

SPACERS WELDED TO
INSIDE OF FORM

133.207

Figure 16-24.—Concrete encasement of short section of wood pile.

shaped like an H; it is driven with a special pile-driving cap as shown in figure 16-25. The pipe pile is a steel pipe. An OPEN-END pipe-pile is open at the bottom; a CLOSED-END pipe pile is closed at the bottom.

Reinforcing of Steel Piles

Steel members that have corroded in only limited areas may be repaired by welding fish plates onto the flanges and web. The corroded area should be first thoroughly cleaned and feather edges burned off back to a point where the metal is of sufficient thickness to hold a weld. Fish plates should be of sufficient cross sectional area to develop the full strength of the original section and should extend beyond the top and bottom of the corroded zone as directed by the engineering department. Another method is to encase the corroded section in reinforced concrete. After cleaning the corroded area and cutting back the corroded edges, weld the reinforcing rods to the flanges and web. A form is

then placed around the corroded section and filled with concrete. Figure 16-26 illustrates this procedure for steel "H" pile. The same system can be used for other structural members.

Preservation of Steel Piles

Providing protection against corrosion is the principal and most important consideration in the maintenance of steel structures. In areas above the waterline, this is generally accomplished by the application of protective coatings, or by encasement in concrete. The effectiveness of any coating or covering is its ability to prevent moisture and air from gaining access to the steel. The most commonly used preparation method is sandblasting. If wet sandblasting process is used, a rust inhibitor, such as sodium nitrate, should be used. Power tools are widely used for cleaning, and their use is generally economical; they consist of rotary wire brushes, abrasive disks and wheels, chipping hammers, and rotary impact tools. These may be either

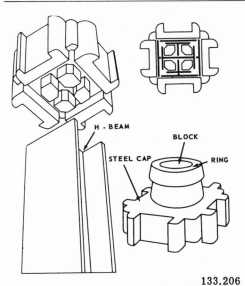

H - BEAM

BLOCK

STEEL CAP   RING

133.206

Figure 16-25.—Steel H-pile and
special cap for driving.

electric or pneumatic. Flame cleaning is often
used for the removal of paint. Handtools should
be used for small areas. Cleaning should remove all rust and scale down to the base metal.
Any oil and grease must be removed by a cleaner
or solvent before protection is applied. All
necessary safety precautions must be observed,
including the use of goggles and respirators.

An economical and most satisfactory coating
is hot coal tar enamel applied over a coal tar
primer. Apply the enamel in two coats at right
angles or in overlapping coats to a total thickness of 3/32 inch. Coal tar enamel is somewhat brittle, and where it is apt to be damaged
by contact with boats or heavy floating debris
or where it is extremely difficult to apply a hot
coating, a cold applied coal tar, can be used.
The material may be applied by a brush or a
spray gun in two coats to provide a thickness of
40 mils (a mil is .001 inch). The first coat
should be permitted to dry for at least 24 hours
before the second coat is applied. To protect
this type of coating from weathering, apply a
coating of bituminous emulsion complying with
Military Specification MIL-C-15203C over the
coal tar. Wet the surface before applying the
emulsion and apply to a thickness of not less
than 10 mils.

CONCRETE BEARING PILES

A concrete bearing pile may be CAST-IN-
PLACE or PRECAST. A cast-in-place concrete
pile may be a SHELL type or a SHELL-LESS
type. A shell type case-in-place pile is constructed as shown in figure 16-27. As you can
see, a steel core called a MANDREL is used to
drive a hollow steel shell into the ground. The
mandrel is then withdrawn and the shell is filled
with concrete. If the shell is strong enough, it
may be driven without a mandrel.

A shell-less cast-in-place concrete pile is
made by placing the concrete in direct contact
with the earth. The hole for the pile may be
made by driving a shell or a mandrel and shell,
or it may be simply bored with an EARTH
AUGER. If a mandrel and shell are used, the
mandrel, and usually also the shell, are removed before the concrete is poured. In one
method, however, a cylindrical mandrel and
shell are used, and only the mandrel is removed
before the concrete is poured. The concrete is
poured into the shell, after which the shell is
extracted.

Casting in place is not usually feasible for
concrete piles used in waterfront structures.
Concrete piles for waterfront structures are
usually PRECAST. Precast concrete piles are
usually either square or octagonal in cross-
section; square-section piles run from 6 to 24
in. square. Concrete piles more than 100 ft long
have been caste, but piles longer than 50 or 60 ft
are usually too heavy for handling.

Repairs above the waterline can be made to
free-standing components for such defects as
spalling or cracks in piles and bracing.
Pressure-applied mortar, epoxy formulations,
normal Portland cement concrete, or grout are
applicable materials. Encasement of damaged
portions in reinforced concrete (fig. 16-28) is
the conventional method of repairing piling. It
is always preferable to place concrete in air if
economical and feasible; however, this requires
cofferdams, pumping and working in the dry and
it is not always an economical solution. When
the situation dictates, concrete can be placed
under water. Forms may be used as shown in
figure 16-28. Additional reinforcing in the form
of rods or mesh is placed around the damaged
pile, and sectional forms are used to hold the
concrete in place until it cures. Forms may be
made of pipe, sheet metal, or wood and are split
in half vertically so that they can be placed
around the pile and bolted together above the

447

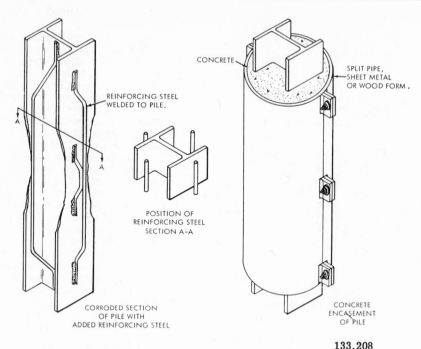

133.208

Figure 16-26.—Concrete encasement of steel piles.

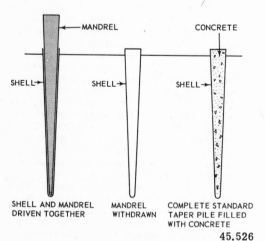

45.526

Figure 16-27.—Shell type cast-in place concrete pile.

water. Each section is then slid into place and new sections added until the desired length is

obtained. The form is then filled with concrete. Forms may be left in place or removed for reuse. Where only a section of the pile is to be encased in concrete and the forms do not extend to the mud line, the lowest section of the forms must be closed to hold the concrete or aggregate and grout in place. Pressure-applied concrete may be used to make sectional forms. These are built upon cylinders of expanded metal lathes shaped to fit around the pile. Wire mesh reinforcement may be used outside of the metal lath where additional strength is required. Pressure-applied concrete is used to make a sectional form one or two inches thick, and the concrete is allowed to set. This form is then dropped into place and filled with concrete.

SHEET PILES

Sheet piles are special shapes of interlocking piles made of steel, wood, or formed concrete, which are used to form a continuous wall to resist horizontal pressures resulting from earth or water loads, and for other purposes. The

448

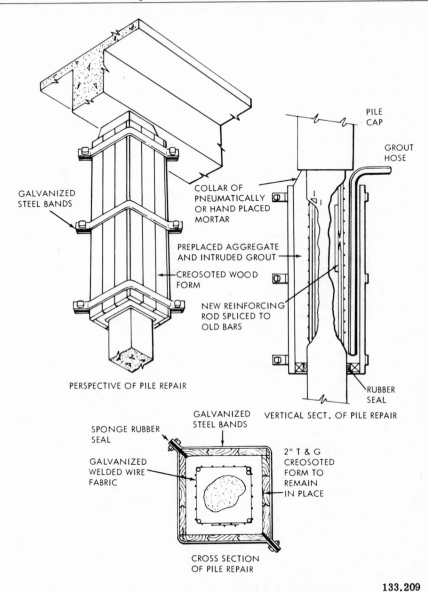

GALVANIZED
STEEL BANDS

COLLAR OF
PNEUMATICALLY
OR HAND PLACED
MORTAR

PREPLACED AGGREGATE
AND INTRUDED GROUT

CREOSOTED WOOD
FORM

NEW REINFORCING
ROD SPLICED TO
OLD BARS

PERSPECTIVE OF PILE REPAIR

PILE
CAP

GROUT
HOSE

RUBBER
SEAL

VERTICAL SECT. OF PILE REPAIR

SPONGE RUBBER
SEAL

GALVANIZED
STEEL BANDS

GALVANIZED
WELDED WIRE
FABRIC

2" T & G
CREOSOTED
FORM TO
REMAIN
IN PLACE

CROSS SECTION
OF PILE REPAIR

133.209

Figure 16-28.—Encasement of damaged piles.

term SHEET PILING is used interchangeably with sheet piles. In selecting the type for a particular installation, consideration should be given to the advantages of each from a standpoint of cost, durability, strength, availability, salvage value, and foundation conditions. A few common uses of sheet piles are as follows:

To resist earth (and water) pressure as a part of a temporary or permanent structure. For example, steel sheet piling is widely used to form the BULKHEADS which are an integral part of many waterfront structures, such as wharves and docks. RETAINING WALLS may be built of sheet piling.

A major use of sheet piles is in the construction of COFFERDAMS, which are built to exclude water and earth from an excavation so that construction can be carried out more easily.

Sheet piles are used in the sheathing of trenches; they are usually braced in such applications.

Sheet piles may be used to form small dams and, more frequently, to form cutoff walls beneath water-retaining structures in order to retard the flow of water through the foundation.

Sheet piles may be used in the construction of piers for bridges and left in place. For example, a pier may be formed by driving steel sheet piling to form a square or rectangular inclosure, excavating the material inside to the desired depth, and then filling the enclosed space with concrete.

Groins and sea walls may be formed from sheet piles.

FABRICATED TIMBER SHEET PILING

When an abundance of timber is available in a theater of operations and the supply of steel sheet piling is limited, timber sheet piling may be fabricated for temporary structures and to resist light lateral pressures. Where marine borers are active or for permanent type structures, timber sheet piling is creosoted. Tongue and groove piling of single thickness (fig. 16-29) is used where on only earth pressures are involved, as in excavating a trench above the water table. For larger pressures and watertightness, planking (fig. 16-30), wakefield (fig. 16-31), or heavy timber (fig. 16-32) piling is used.

STEEL SHEET PILES

The edges of a steel sheet pile are called INTERLOCKS, because they are shaped for

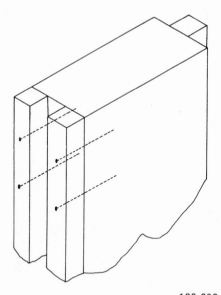

133.393
Figure 16-29.—Fabricated tongue and groove timber sheet piling.

locking the piles edge-to-edge. The part of the pile between the interlocks is called the WEB. Piles are manufactured in 5 standard section shapes: STRAIGHT-WEB (fig. 16-33), ARCH (fig. 16-34), DEEP-ARCH (fig. 16-35), Z-SECTION, and CORNER-SECTION. Sections vary slightly in shape with different manufacturers, each of whom has a particular letter and number symbol for each section he manufactures.

For more examples, figure 16-36 shows the standard sections, other than Z-sections and corner sections, of steel sheet piles manufactured by the Inland Steel Company. The sections designated I-28, I-23, I-21, I-35, and I-31-5 are straight-web sections; the sections designated I-22 and I-31 are arch sections; and the sections designated I-32 and I-27 are deep-arch sections as shown previously. Straight-web sections manufactured by the Bethlehem Steel Company are designated SP-6, SP-7, SP-9, SP-4 and SP-5; arch sections are designated AP-8 and AP-3; and deep-arch sections are designated DP-2 and DP-1. Straight-web sections manufactured by the Jones & Laughlin Steel Company are designated SW-31, SW-35, SW-23, and SW-28; arch sections are designated

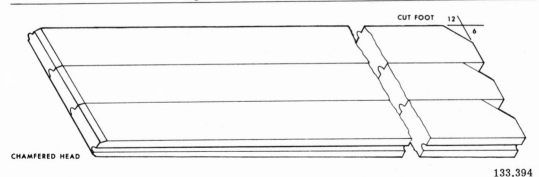

133.394

Figure 16-30.—Timber sheet piling fabricated from planking.

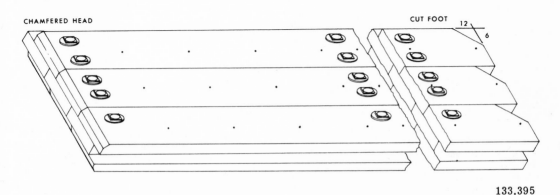

133.395

Figure 16-31.—Fabricated timber sheet piling, wakefield type.

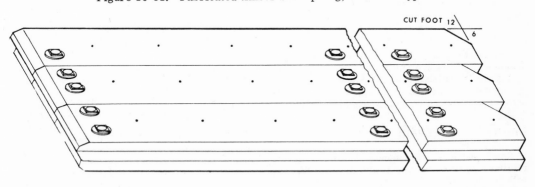

133.396

Figure 16-32.—Timber sheet piling fabricated from heavy timbers.

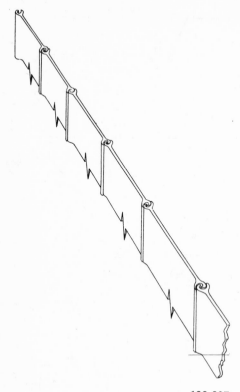

133.397

Figure 16-33.—Standard straight-
web steel sheet pile. (section
type SA-32).

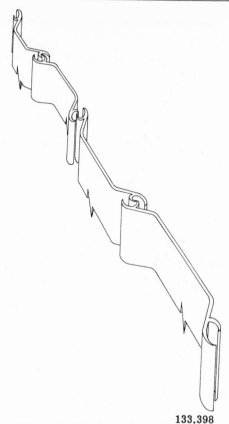

133.398

Figure 16-34.—Standard shallow-
arch steel sheet pile (section
AP-3).

PC-31 and EDC-22; and deep-arch sections are
designated DC-32 and DC-27.

Figure 16-37 shows two types of Z-section
(Bethlehem ZP-38 and ZP-32). Figure 16-38
shows two standard corner sections.

SHEET PILING REPAIR

Sheet piling usually serves as a bulkhead to
retain earth or other fill. Holes in the bulkhead
will result in loss of materials and settlement
behind the bulkhead. Local damage or holes
can be repaired by welding on plates, or sections of steel sheet piling. If the holes are
small, wooden plugs can be used to fill the holes.
Usually it is necessary to install new sheet piling
in the deteriorated areas; however, it may be

feasible to protect the damaged sheet piling with
a concrete facing.

Remove all rust, scale, and marine growth
before placing concrete. Concrete cover, when
applied to the exposed exterior face of the piling,
should be at least 6 inches in thickness and extend well beyond the area of corrosion, damage,
or deterioration. Form work should be of wood,
supported in place by stud bolts that are welded
to the sheet piling. Use heavy zinc coated bolts
and nuts.

CONCRETE SHEET PILES

Concrete sheet piles are reinforced precast
concrete piles of rectangular cross section,

452

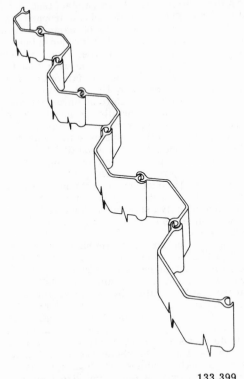

133.399

Figure 16-35.—Standard deep-
arch steel sheet pile (section
type DA-27).

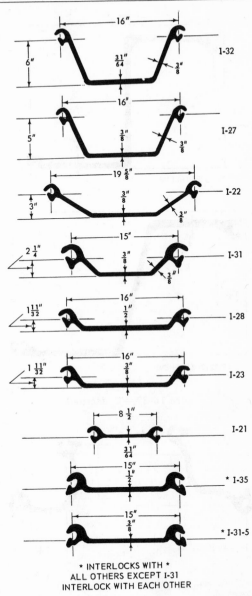

* INTERLOCKS WITH *
ALL OTHERS EXCEPT I-31
INTERLOCK WITH EACH OTHER

133.210

Figure 16-36.—Inland steel sheet piling sections.

with tongue-and-groove interlocks. A working drawing for a concrete sheet pile is shown in figure 16-39.

PILE DRIVING EQUIPMENT

In order to drive piles, the following equipment is needed under normal operating conditions. A piledriver—either a crane-shovel with standard pile-driving attachment or the steel-frame, skid-mounted piledriver—is used to support the leads (hammer guides), raise the pile in the leads, and operate the hammer. A pile-driving hammer delivers the driving blow. Pile-driving leads are used to support and align the pile during driving, and to control the lateral motion of the hammer. Additional support equipment for handling stockpiled piling and for straightening, cutting, capping, and bracing piles must be available. Under special driving conditions, other standard and fabricated equipment may be required.

453

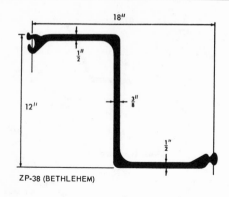

ZP-38 (BETHLEHEM)

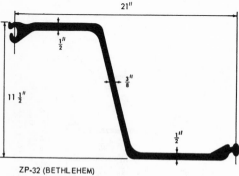

ZP-32 (BETHLEHEM)

133.211

Figure 16-37.—Z-sections.

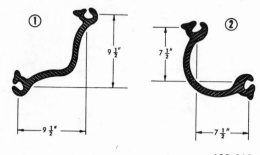

133.212

Figure 16-38.—Two standard
corner sections.

The principal types of pile-driving hammers used by Seabees are the DROP HAMMER, the SINGLE and DOUBLE ACTING AIR or STEAM, and the DIESEL HAMMER.

A drop hammer is a block of steel that is set into a set of leads and raised and dropped onto the lead of a pile. Weights of hammers will vary from 1500 lbs to 12,000 lbs depending on the type of piles being driven. The hammer should weigh 1 1/2 to twice the weight of the pile being driven. The height of fall of the hammer should be from 6 to 15 feet. Blow of the hammer will vary from 15 to 20 blows per minute. A driving cap is installed on most hammers to keep the pile from brooming. The driving cap is a block of steel that slips over the head of a pile with a cushion block of wood fit into the top of the driving cap onto which the hammer falls, as shown in figure 16-40. Under expedient conditions a log hammer or concrete may be used. The advantage of the drop hammer is that it is cheap and quickly assembled. The disadvantage of the hammer is that it is slow and inefficient on large jobs.

Single acting air or steam hammers consist of a stationary cylinder and a moving part called the ram which includes the piston and striking lead. The single acting hammer is designed so that the piston is raised by air or steam pressure and the fall is induced by gravity. The sizes of the single acting hammer will range from 3000 lbs ram to 14,000 lbs ram, and from 50 to 80 blows per minute—stroke 32 inches to 36 inches. The air or steam requirements for the single acting hammer is 80 psi (pounds per square inch), with a minimum size hose of 2 inches. In lubrication of the hammer, an oiler is attached to the hose and oil is regulated into the air hose and onto the piston.

The double acting air or steam hammer piston and ram is raised by air or steam pressure and is also forced down by pressure. The size of the hammer will vary from 5000 lbs to 10,000 lbs ram, and three (3) 3/4 inch to 24 inch stroke, and from 80 to 550 blows per minute depending on the hammer (it is the fastest hammer in use). Steam or pneumatic pile hammers are shown in figure 16-41. Figure 16-42 shows a pile being driven with a pneumatic hammer. The operating pressure for air and steam hammers is usually about 100 psi with a volume of 100 to 600 CFM feed through a 2 inch hose. The driving head will vary from job to job depending on what type of piles you drive. Special driving caps will be used for sheet piling and steel pilings. The double acting hammer generally is used to drive light or average weight piles into soils of average density because the rapidity of blows tend to keep the pile in motion and thereby

454

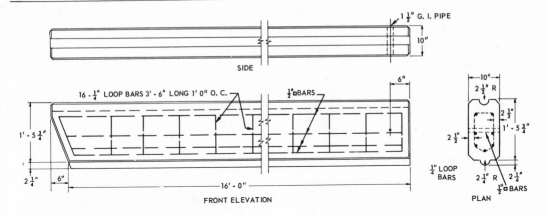

Figure 16-39.—Concrete sheet pile.

133.213

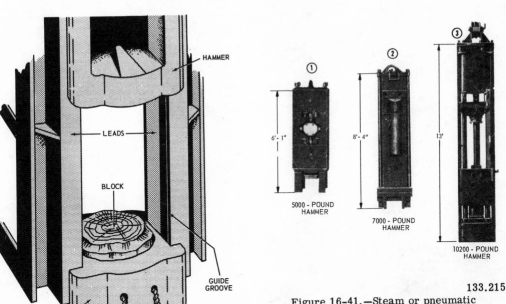

PILE DRIVING CAP

HAMMER SLING

133.214

Figure 16-40.—Cap for driving timber
piles by drop hammer.

5000 - POUND
HAMMER

7000 - POUND
HAMMER

10200 - POUND
HAMMER

133.215

Figure 16-41.—Steam or pneumatic
pile hammers.

reduce the effect of friction. The double acting hammer is faster than the single acting hammer because of its lighter ram and shorter strokes.

The diesel pile hammer is about twice as fast as a conventional pneumatic or steam hammer of comparable size and weight. A conventional

Figure 16-42.—Pile being driven with
a pneumatic hammer.

pneumatic hammer requires a 500-cu ft/min
compressor to operate, while the diesel is a
self-contained unit that is constructed in sizes
capable of delivering up to 22,400 ft lbs of energy per blow.

The McKiernan-Terry pile hammer illustrated in figure 16-43 made up of a cylinder,
ram-piston, fuel pump, built-in fuel tank (which
holds supplies for three days without refueling),
lubricant oil tank (which holds lubricant supplies
for three days), and an inertia oil pump that mechanically lubricates during operation.

133.217
Figure 16-43.—Diesel hammer.

Operation of the McKiernan-Terry diesel pile
hammer is illustrated in figure 16-44. The hammer is worked by a single crane load-line (A).
It is started by lifting the ram-piston (B) with
the load-line until the trip mechanism (C) automatically releases the ram-piston. The

456

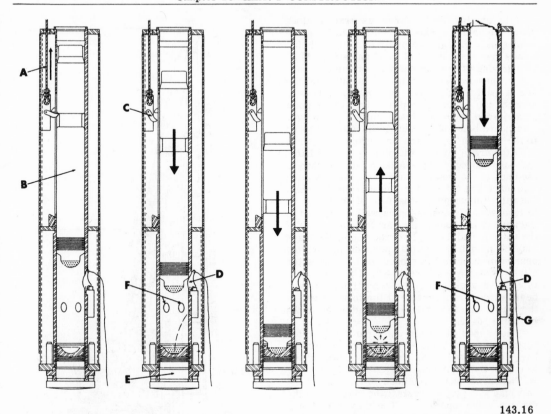

143.16

Figure 16-44.—Operating principles of the McKiernan-Terry diesel pile hammer.

ram-piston falls, actuating the cam of the fuel pump (D), which delivers a measured amount of diesel fuel that falls into a cup formed in the top of the anvil (E). Continuing its downward fall, the ram-piston blocks the exhaust ports (F) and begins compression of air trapped between the ram-piston and the anvil. The compression of the trapped air creates a preloading force upon the anvil, drive cap, and pile. The gravity propelled ram-piston strikes the anvil, delivering its impact energy to the pile.

The rounded end of the ram-piston mates perfectly with the cup in the anvil, displacing the liquid fuel at the precise moment of impact to achieve perfect timing. The fuel is atomized and splattered into the annular (ring-shaped) zone between the ram and the anvil and is ignited by the heat of compression.

The resulting explosive force drives the ram-piston upward and the pile downward, adding a push to the pile to extend the time duration of the total effort to drive the pile.

On the upstroke, the ram-piston opens the exhaust ports (F) to permit scavenging the exhaust gases. The ram-piston continues freely upward until arrested by gravity. The length of the stroke varies with the resistance offered by the pile. The greater the resistance, the longer the stroke.

Having reached the top of its stroke, the ram-piston falls again, repeating the cycle. The hammer is stopped by pulling a rope (G), disengaging the fuel pump cam (D).

The diesel pile hammer which you will use may not be the same make or model as the one described in the preceding paragraphs, but you will find that the operating principles are similar.

457

Pile driving leads serve as tracks along which the hammer runs and as guides for positioning and steadying the pile during the driving. Leads are constructed of wood and steel. Most pile driving is carried out with crawler or mobile cranes for which pile driving attachments are a part of standard equipment. Adapters connect the leads of the pile driver to the point of the crane boom, all leads and adapters have a standard bolt-hole layout. Pulleys are attached to the point of the crane boom and cables run from the crane through the pulleys for the hammer and lifting piling. A ladder is attached to the back of the leads so men can guide the piles into place and unhook the cable from the piles. Catwalk (telescoping)—the foot of the leads is braced with a telescoping catwalk connected to the base of the boom. By varying the length of the catwalk and the angle of the boom, the leads may be held in a vertical position for driving bearing piles or maybe sloped for driving batter piles, as shown in figure 16-45. The moonbeam is used on a skid rig. It is a slightly curved beam placed transversely at the forward end of the skid frame to regulate side batter, as shown in figure 16-46.

Many types of power units can be used for lifting piling and hammer. The unit used must have at least two times the lifting power of the weight of the hammer.

The signalman is the boss of the rig and the only man who gives signals to the operator of the rig and valve operator. The only signal any other man may give that the operator will obey is the EMERGENCY STOP SIGNAL. "Loftman" is the man who works on the lead ladder. He guides the pile under the hammer and into the leads also unlocking the line from the pile. He also helps on the ground around the rig. "Hoisting engineer" is the man who runs the crane or the winches in lifting piles and the hammer. "Valve operator" is the man who operates the air or steam for the hammer. "Hook on man" is the man who hooks the line onto the piling to be driven. He also chamfers and points all the piling to be used and helps set the pile into the leads.

PILE-DRIVING OPERATIONS

When bearing piles are driven on land the position of each pile is usually located by the Engineering Aid and marked with a stake. A common method of locating the positions of a series of pile bents driven in water is a wire

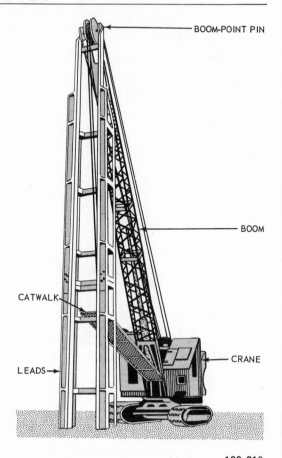

133.218

Figure 16-45.—Crawler crane fitted with pile-driving attachment.

rope long enough to stretch between the abutments and marked with pieces of tape, spaced in accordance with the prescribed or calculated distance between bents.

After the first bent is driven, piles in subsequent bents may be located by the use of a floating TEMPLATE like the one shown in figure 16-47. Pairs of BATTENS, spaced in accordance with the specified spacing between piles in a bent, are nailed across a pair of timbers, spaced in accordance with the specified spacing between bents. The parts of each batten lying beyond the timbers are hinged for raising. The template is lashed to the outer piles in the bent

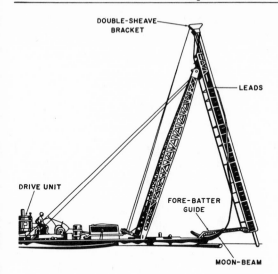

DOUBLE-SHEAVE BRACKET

LEADS

DRIVE UNIT

FORE-BATTER GUIDE

MOON-BEAM

133.219

Figure 16-46.—Steel-frame, skid-mounted pile driver.

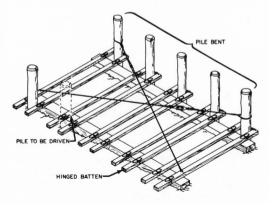

PILE BENT

PILE TO BE DRIVEN

HINGED BATTEN

133.220

Figure 16-47.—Floating template for positioning piles.

already driven by means of a pair of wire ropes, equipped with turnbuckles as shown. After the piles in the new bent are driven, the hinged parts of the battens are raised, the wire ropes are let go, and the template is floated out from between the bents.

Piles can be driven either tip or butt down; they may be driven butt first if a large bearing

area is required or if the pile is to resist an upward force.

DRIVING BEARING PILES

The four major steps in driving a bearing pile with a drop-hammer rig are as follows. (1) The pile driver is brought into position over the pile location, and the hammer and cap are run up to the top of the leads. (2) The pile is brought up to the foot of the leads, the pile whip attached, and the pile is hoisted into the leads. (3) The hammer and cap are lowered onto the top of the pile, and the cap is detached from the hammer. (4) The hammer is raised and dropped to drive the pile.

Driving should be started slowly with a drop hammer; the hammer should be raised only a few inches until the pile is firmly set. The height of the drop should then be gradually increased to a maximum of 10 or 15 ft. Blows should be applied as rapidly as possible, to keep the pile moving and prevent resistance caused by inertia and friction.

With the steam or pneumatic hammer the first blows should be given under reduced pressure, until the pile is firmly set. Pressure should then be gradually increased to the maximum.

DRIVING BATTER PILES

The prescribed angle for a batter pile is indicated on working drawings as shown in figure 16-48. The angle is obtained by setting the leads, which is done on a crane rig by adjusting the length of the catwalk. On a steel-frame, skid-mounted rig it is done by adjusting the length of the fore batter guide, or by adjusting the position of the leads on the moonbeam, or both.

A certain amount of figuring is required, both for setting the leads and for locating the point of penetration of the pile. Let's take the lead-setting problem first. Suppose your leads are 65 ft high and you want to set them for a 1 in 12 (unit of run 1 foot, unit of rise 12 feet) batter. What you need to know is: How far must the foot of the leads be offset from the vertical position to get the required batter?

In this case the working drawings prescribe a unit of run of 1 for every 12 units of rise. The total rise of the leads is the height of the leads, which in this case is 65 ft. The total run of the leads must be offset from the vertical position and must therefore be the value of x in the

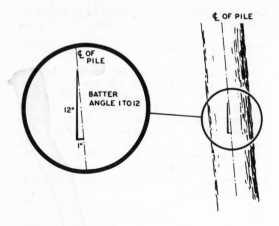

45.525

Figure 16-48.—Batter angle of a pile.

proportional equation 1:12::x:65, or 5 5/12 ft, or 5 ft 5 in.

The problem of locating the point of penetration of a batter pile is illustrated in figure 16-49. From the working drawings you know the location of the head of the pile and the vertical distance of the top of the pile above the ground line after the pile is driven. For a given batter, the point of penetration of the pile will be a given distance away from a point on the ground directly below the location of the head of the pile. Let's say the prescribed batter is again 1 in 12 and the vertical distance of the top of the driven pile above the ground line will be 36 ft. The distance between the point of penetration of the pile and a point on the ground directly below the location of the head of the pile must therefore be the value of x in the proportional equation 1:12::x:36, or 3 ft.

DRIVING SHEET PILES

Sheet piles are frequently driven without leads, as shown in figure 16-50; a hammer used without leads is called a FLYING hammer. The drop hammer is not used to drive sheet piling. The cap of the hammer is equipped with a device which fits over the top of the pile. The crane operator slacks the hammer whip just enough to keep the hammer in contact with the pile as the pile goes down.

When sheet piles are driven with a flying hammer the piles are held upright by one or

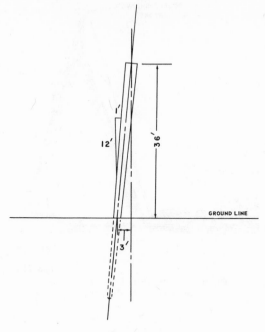

133.221

Figure 16-49.—Locating point of penetration for a batter pile.

more pairs of elevated wales, supported by a braced framework of studs. The wales also guide the alignment of the piles. For piles driven in deep water, a system of floating wales is used.

Steel sheet piles must be locked together as they are driven. After the first pile is driven, or set in place for driving, the next pile must be hoisted high enough to bring its foot level with the head of the pile already in place. A man on the head of the first pile guides the interlock on the second pile into the interlock on the first. This man, who is hoisted to the top of the pile by the pile whip, is supported by a steel STIRRUP which straddles the top of the pile.

When arch or deep-arch steel sheet piles are driven with the arch webs all extending in the same direction, the piles are said to be driven WEBS IN LINE. When the piles are driven with arch webs extending alternately in opposite directions, they are said to be driven WEBS REVERSED. In interlocking, the BALL on the interlock of one pile fits into the SOCKET

133.222

Figure 16-50.—Driving sheet piles
with flying hammer.

on the interlock of the adjoining pile. In driving, the BALL pile is driven first and the socket pile is fitted to it; this is called driving the piles BALL-END LEADING. If the socket pile were driven first, the socket would fill up the soil which would compact under the ball on the ball pile. This could create enough pressure to force open the socket.

SPUDDING

Spudding is driving, raising or dropping of heavy piles to break through a thin layer of hard material or an obstruction. The spud, itself, is a steel, wide-flange or H-beam (12" or 14") use tin place of pile hammer leads. The hammer engages one flange of the beam through spud-clips bolted to one side of the hammer. With a slide connector at the crane boom-point, in place of a fixed connector, a spud can be raised or lowered without changing the operating radius of the crane.

When using the spud be sure to investigate the design of the pile beforehand. Sometime a pilot pile may be used to drive through the thin,

hard layer; the pilot pile is withdrawn and the pile to be used driven in the hole.

LAGGING

Lagging is used to increase the resistance of a friction pile. The extra surface area increases the pile's load-carrying capacity, but tends to make the pile more difficult to drive. Before driving the pile, long, narrow strips of wood or steel are lag screwed to the pile (fig. 16-51). These are attached to the lower part of the pile from approximately 12 inches above the the tip of the limits of the depth the pile is expected to penetrate. Splicing should be done only when piles of sufficient diameter or length are not available.

In the more plastic compressible clays, the bearing value of a steel pile may be small, necessitating the attachment of suitable lagging (fig. 16-52) to the piles to increase their displacement, thus developing more fully the bearing capacity of the soil. A lagged pile is advantageous where extremely long lengths are required, where there is lateral impact (as in the waterfront structures), and where there is a long unsupported length. The lagging is attached throughout the depth of the load-bearing stratum, providing a large section at the point of the pile.

Occasionally, steel pile penetration may be too great in such soils as very saturated sand, sand mixed with a small amount of clay, or loose sand subject to compaction by the vibration of pile-driving operations. The bulk of the piles is increased by the attachment of lagging for 8 to 12 feet near the top of the load-bearing stratum. Attachment of lagging near the bottom will tend to destroy the skin friction above the lagging.

PILE-DRIVING TECHNIQUES
AND TERMINOLOGY

Great care must be taken during driving to avoid damage to the pile, the hammer, or both. The pile driver must be securely ballasted, guyed, anchored, or otherwise fastened in place, to avoid a shift of position. If the pile driver shifts during driving, the blows of the hammer will be out of line with the axis of the pile and both the pile and the hammer will be damaged.

The pile should be carefully watched for any indication of a split or break below ground. If driving suddenly becomes easier, or if the pile suddenly changes direction, a break or split has probably occurred. When this happens, further driving is useless.

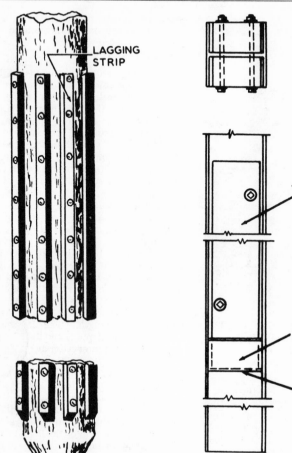

133.400

Figure 16-51.—Lagging
of a timber friction
pile.

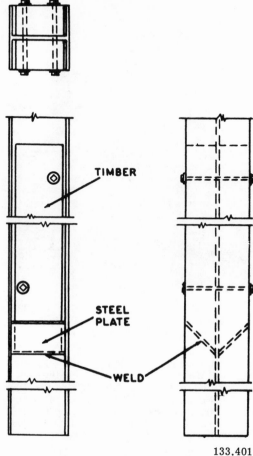

133.401

Figure 16-52.—Lagging a steel pile.

Standard pile-driving safety precautions are as follows:

Each member of a pile-driving crew must be either experienced or carefully instructed in all the details of the work.

Operators and winchmen must not accept signals from any person other than the person authorized to give signals, emergency signals may be given by anyone.

Men handling piles must wear heavy gloves, safety shoes, and protective hats.

Shin and foot guards must be worn by men who are working with adzes or who are heading or pointing piles with axes.

Men working with creosoted piles or timbers must wear goggles and apply protective cream to exposed skin areas.

Men working over the water must wear kapok safety vests or the equivalent, and each rig working over the water must be equipped with life preservers and life lines.

When a pile driver is not in use the hammer must be held in place at the bottom of the

462

leads by a cleat or a timber fastened to the leads.

The main working platform on a pile driver must be kept clear of lumber, ropes, tools, debris, and all other unnecessary obstructions.

Great care must be exercised against bringing booms or leads into contact with any overhead high-tension wires.

A man must never place any part of his body under a suspended hammer unless the hammer is dogged or blocked in the leads.

SPRINGING AND BOUNCING

SPRINGING means an excessive lateral vibration of the pile. It occurs when the pile is crooked, or when the butt is not square, or when the axis of the pile is not in line with the direction of fall of the hammer or ram. If the pile is out of line with the hammer, the head of the pile may be damaged severely, the hammer may be damaged as well, and a great deal of the force of the hammer blow will be lost.

Excessive BOUNCING of the hammer may be caused if the hammer is too light. It is usually caused, however, by a crushed or BROOMED head on a timber pile, or when the tip or foot of the pile has met in underground obstruction, such as a rock or a layer of extra-dense soil. If the butt of a timber plate has been crushed or broomed for more than an inch or so, it should be cut back to solid wood before driving is continued.

With a double-action hammer, excessive bouncing may be caused when the steam or air pressure is too high.

OBSTRUCTION AND REFUSAL

When a pile has reached a level where 6 blows of a drop hammer or 20 blows of a steam or air hammer will not drive it more than an average of 1/8 in. per blow, the pile has either encountered an obstruction or it has been driven to REFUSAL. In either case, further driving is likely to break or split the pile. If the lack of penetration seems to be caused by an obstruction, 10 or 15 blows of less than maximum force may be tried, in the hope that they may cause the pile to displace or penetrate the obstruction. For obstructions which cannot be disposed of in this manner, it is often necessary to PULL (extract) the pile and blast out the obstruction with an explosive lowered to the bottom of the hole.

When a pile has been driven to a depth where further penetration is prevented by friction, the pile has been driven to refusal. A pile which is intended to be supported by skin friction alone is called a FRICTION pile. A pile which is intended to be supported by bedrock or an extra-dense layer of soil at the tip is called an END-BEARING pile. A pile which is intended to be supported partly by skin friction and partly by a substratum of extra-dense soil at the tip is called a COMBINATION END-BEARING AND FRICTION pile.

It is not always necessary to drive a friction pile to refusal; such a pile needs to be driven only to the depth where friction develops the required load-bearing capacity.

PULLING PILES

A pile which has met an obstruction, or which has been driven in the wrong place, or which has split or broken in driving, or which is to be salvaged (steel sheet piles are frequently salvaged for reuse) is usually PULLED (extracted). Pulling should be done as soon as possible after driving; the longer the pile stays in the soil, the more compact the soil becomes, and the greater the resistance to pulling will be. Methods of pulling piles are as follows.

In the DIRECT LIFT method, a crane is used to pull the pile. The crane whip is slung to the pile and a gradually increased pull is applied, up to just a little less than the amount which is expected to start it. Lateral blows from a SKULL CRACKER (heavy steel ball, swung on a crane whip to demolish walls), or a few light blows on the butt or head with a driving hammer, are given to break the skin friction, and the crane pull is then increased to maximum capacity. If the pile still won't start, it may be loosened by jetting, or the lift of the crane may be supplemented by the use of hydraulic jacks.

The 5000-lb double-acting hammer may be used in inverted position to pull piles. The hammer is turned over and a wire rope sling is passed over it and attached to the pile. The hammer whip is heaved taut, and the upward blows of the hammer ram on the sling, plus the pull of the hammer whip, are usually enough to pull the pile.

TIDAL LIFT is often used to pull piles driven in tidewater. Slings on the piles are attached to barges or pontoons at low tide; the rising tide pulls the piles as it lifts the barges or pontoons.

463

A single jet pipe is used as follows. The pile is set in position, with the hammer resting on it for extra weight, and the jet pipe is manipulated to loosen and wash away the soil from under the tip as shown in figure 16-53. As the soil is washed away, the pile sinks under its own weight and that of the hammer. A few hammer blows are struck occasionally to keep the pile moving downward. When it is within a few feet of the desired final position, the jet pipe is withdrawn and the pile is driven the rest of the way with the hammer.

The action of a single jet pipe on one side of a pile tends to send the pile out of plumb. Whenever possible, two pipes are used, lashed to the pile on opposite sides as shown in figure 16-54.

STRAIGHTENING PILES

A pile should be watched closely for misalignment during driving, and any pile which drifts out of alignment should be straightened at once. A strain taken with a block and tackle or with a line or wire to a winch, as shown in figure 16-55, may be sufficient; with a strong strain taken on the pile, the blows of the hammer may jar it back into line. A jet pipe may be used to straighten piles.

WATERFRONT STRUCTURES

Waterfront structures may be broadly divided into 3 main categories, as follows (1) off-shore structures like breakwaters, designed to create a sheltered harbor, (2) alongshore structures like sea walls, designed to establish and maintain a stable shore line, and (3) WHARFAGE structures, designed to make it possible for vessels to lie alongside, in water deeper than their drafts, for loading and discharging.

BREAKWATERS AND JETTIES

A BREAKWATER is an offshore barrier erected to "break" the action of the waves of the open sea and thereby create an area of calm water inside the breakwater. A JETTY is a structure similar to a breakwater, but erected to direct and confine a current and/or tidal flow along the line of a selected channel. Breakwaters and jetties are alike in construction; the chief distinction between them lies in the above-mentioned difference in purpose.

The simplest type of breakwater/jetty is the RUBBLE-MOUND (also called ROCK-MOUND)

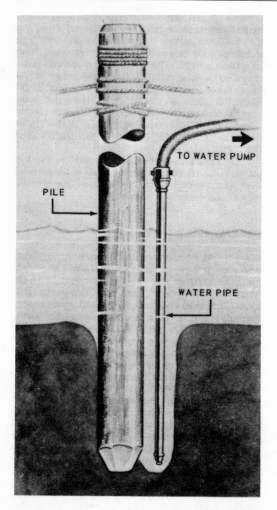

133.223
Figure 16-53.—Jetting with a single jet pile.

PLACING PILES BY JETTING

Pile penetration is often made easier by JETTING, or forcing water under pressure around and under the pile to lubricate and/or displace the surrounding soil as shown in figure 16-53. Jetting equipment consists of a water pump, a length of flexible hose, and a metal JET PIPE; jet pipes run from 2 1/2 in. to 3 1/2 in. in diameter.

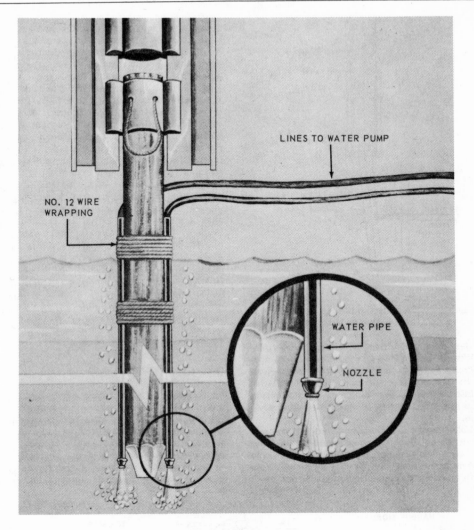

LINES TO WATER PUMP

NO. 12 WIRE WRAPPING

WATER PIPE

NOZZLE

133.224

Figure 16-54.—Jetting with two jet pipes.

type shown in figure 16-56. Rock for a structure of this type is classified according to size as follows:

CAP ROCK: the largest rocks available, approximately rectangular in cross-section, with the smaller cross-section dimension not less than 1/3 of the larger.

CLASS A ROCK: not less than 85 percent consisting of rocks weighing more than 2 tons each.

CLASS B ROCK: not less than 60 percent consisting of rocks weighing more than 100 lbs each.

CLASS C ROCK: rock smaller than class B, technically known as QUARRY WASTE.

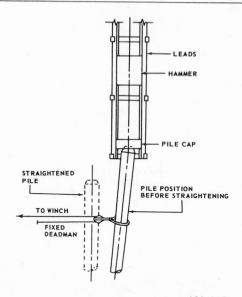

133.225

Figure 16-55.—Straightening a pile by
a strain on a line to a winch.

In designing a rubble mound breakwater/jetty
the width of the CAP is first decided upon; this
width may vary from 15 or 20 ft up to as much
as 70 ft. The width of the base will depend upon
the width of the cap, the height of the structure,
and the specified slopes of the inner and outer
FACES.

Rubble mound breakwaters and jetties are
constructed by dumping underwater rock from
scows, or from rail cars running on temporary
pile-bent structures, and by placing upper rock
and cap rock with floating cranes. As indicated

in figure 16-56, the first rock placed usually
consists of marginal mounds of Class B, extending up to about 20 ft below mean sea level.
A CORE of Class C rock is then dumped between the marginal mounds, also extending up to
about 20 ft below mean sea level. A layer of
Class B rock is then placed as shown; this layer
is usually brought up to the EXPECTED MAXI-
MUM WAVE HEIGHT below MEAN LOW
WATER. The level of mean low water is shown
on the CHART of the area. (Mean low water is
the average sea level at low tide.) The rest of
the breakwater is then built up of Class A rock
and cap rock, as shown.

For a deep-water site, or for one with an
extra-high range between high and low tide, a
rubble mound breakwater-jetty may be topped
with a CAP STRUCTURE to from the COM-
POSITE type of breakwater/jetty shown in figure 16-57. The cap structure in this case consists of a series of precast concrete boxes
called concrete CAISSONS, each of which is
floated over its final location and sunk into place
by filling with Class C rock. A monolithic
(single-piece) concrete cap is then cast in place
on the tops of the caissons. Breakwaters and
jetties are sometimes built entirely of caissons,
as shown in figure 16-58.

GROINS

A GROIN is a structure which is built like a
breakwater or jetty, and which also extends out
from the shore. The chief distinction between
a groin and a breakwater or a jetty lies in the
fact that a groin serves a different purpose from
either of the others. A groin is used where a
shore line is in danger of erosion caused by a
current and/or wave action running obliquely

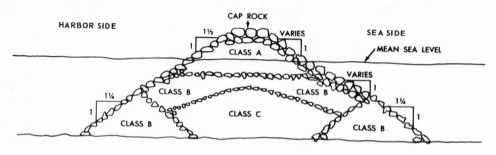

45.527

Figure 16-56.—Rubble mound breakwater/jetty.

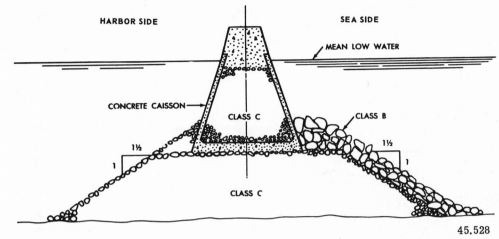

45.528

Figure 16-57.—Composite breakwater/jetty.

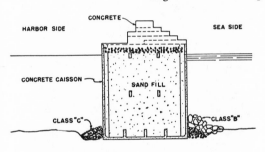

133.228

Figure 16-58.—Caisson breakwater/jetty.

against or parallel to the shore line. The groin is placed so as to check the current or wave action, or to deflect it away from the shore line.

Groins generally consist of tight sheet piling of creosoted timber, steel, or concrete, braced with wales and with round piles of considerable length. The groins are constructed perpendicular to the direction of the littoral drift and follow the general slope of the beach from above maximum high water to low water. Groins are usually built with their tops a few feet above the sloping beach surface that is desired to be maintained or restored.

MOLES

A MOLE is a breakwater which is coincidentally a wharfage structure, alongside which

vessels may lie for loading and discharging. To serve as a mole, the inner or harbor face of the structure must be vertical and the top of the structure must be capable of serving as a deck.

A jetty may also be constructed so as to be capable of serving as a wharfage structure, but a jetty so constructed is still called a jetty.

Seawalls vary widely in details of design and materials, depending on the severity of the exposure, the value of the property to be protected, and other considerations. Basically they consist of some form of barrier designed to break up or reflect the waves and a deep, tight cutoff wall to preclude washing out of the sand or soil behind and under the barrier. The cutoff wall is generally of timber, steel, or concrete sheet piling. Figure 16-59 shows a rubble stone sea wall, built much like a rubble mound breakwater. Stone which is used to protect a shore line against erosion, however, is called RIPRAP, and a rubble stone sea wall is therefore called a RIPRAP sea wall.

Various types of cast-in-place concrete sea walls are the VERTICAL-FACE, the INCLINED-FACE, the CURVED-FACE, the STEPPED-FACE, and the COMBINATION CURVED-FACE and STEPPED-FACE. Note, the sea or harbor bottom along the TOE (bottom of the outside face) of a sea wall is usually protected against erosion (caused by the backpull of receding waves) by riprap piled against the toe.

133.229

Figure 16-59.—Riprap sea wall.

BULKHEADS

A BULKHEAD is used for the same general purpose as a sea wall, namely, to establish and maintain a stable shore line. The chief distinction between the two is that a sea wall is a self-contained, relatively thick wall which is supported by its own weight, while a bulkhead is a relatively thin wall which is supported by a series of TIE WIRES or TIE RODS, running back to a buried ANCHORAGE. A timber bulkhead for a bridge abutment is shown in figure 16-60.

The bulkhead shown in figure 16-60 is made of wood SHEATHING (square edged, single-layer planks), laid horizontally. Most bulkheads,

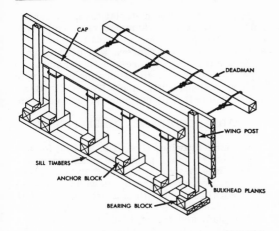

133.230

Figure 16-60.—Timber bulkhead for
bridge abutment.

however, are made of sheet piles, and of the three types of sheet piles (wood, steel, and concrete), steel sheet piles are by far the most frequently used. Figure 16-61 shows a constructed steel sheet pile bulkhead.

The outer ends of the tie rods are anchored to a steel WALE which runs horizontally along the outer face of the bulkhead. This wale is usually made up of pairs of steel CHANNELS bolted together back-to-back. (A channel is a structural steel member with a U-shaped section.) Sometimes the wale is placed on the inner face of the bulkhead and the piles are bolted to it.

In figure 16-61 the anchorage in the figure is covered by backfill. In stable soil above the ground water level the anchorage may consist simply of a buried timber or concrete deadman or a row of driven and buried sheet piles. A more substantial anchorage for each tie rod must be used below the ground water level. Two commonly used types of anchorage are shown in figure 16-62. In figure 16-62 (A) the anchorage for each tie rod consists of a timber CAP, supported by a batter pile which is bolted to a bearing pile. In figure 16-62 (B) the anchorage consists of a reinforced concrete cap, supported by a pair of batter piles. As indicated in the figure, tie rods are supported by supporting piles located midway between the anchorage and the bulkhead.

Bulkheads are constructed from working drawings like those shown in figure 16-63. As

133.231

Figure 16-61.—Constructed steel sheet pile bulkhead.

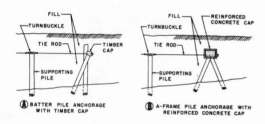

A BATTER PILE ANCHORAGE WITH TIMBER CAP

B A-FRAME PILE ANCHORAGE WITH REINFORCED CONCRETE CAP

133.232

Figure 16-62.—Two types of tie rod anchorages for bulkheads.

indicated in the plan, the anchorage for this bulkhead consists of a row of sheet piles, to which the inner ends of the tie rods are anchored by means of a channel wale.

The order of construction sequences is indicated in the section. The shore and bottom are first excavated to the level of the long, sloping dotted line. The sheet piles for the bulkhead and the anchorage are then driven. The supporting piles for the tie rods are driven next, after which the tie rods between the bulkhead and the anchorage are set in place and the wales are bolted on. The tie rods are prestressed lightly and uniformly, and the backfilling then begins.

The first backfilling operation consists of placing fill over the anchorage, out to the dotted line shown in the plan. The turnbuckles on the tie rods are then set to bring the bulkhead plumb, and the rest of the backfill is worked out to the bulkhead. After the backfilling is completed, the bottom outside the bulkhead is dredged to the desired depth—in this case, 30 ft.

WHARFAGE STRUCTURES

The term WHARF is an overall term applying to any waterfront structure designed to make it possible for vessels to lie alongside for loading and discharging. Figure 16-64 shows the most common types of structures of this kind. The term WHARF is confined in practice to the T-type and U-type MARGINAL WHARVES. The other structures shown are all called PIERS, with the exception of the QUAY.

All the structures shown in figure 16-64 may consist of fill supported by bulkheads, and a QUAY is by definition a structure of this type. A pier or a marginal wharf, however, usually consists of a timber, steel, or concrete super-structure, supported by a series of timber, steel, or concrete pile bents.

Regardless of the material used, the terminology for the structural members of a pile-bent pier or marginal wharf is about the same. As a Builder your chief concern will be with concrete and timber structures, and under advanced base conditions you will be dealing mainly with timber. Consequently, the ADVANCED BASE TIMBER PIER will be your largest concern.

ADVANCED BASE TIMBER PIERS

Working drawings (Dwg. No. 267770) for advanced base timber piers are contained in Advanced Base Drawings, NAVFAC P-140. A pier is designated as to size by its width, the width being equal to the length of a bearing pile cap. Figure 16-65 shows a general plan, figure 16-66 a part plan, and figure 16-67 a section for a 40-ft pier. Included with the drawings is a bill of materials, showing the dimensions and locations of all structural members, drift pins, bolts, hardware, and the like. Figures 16-65, 66, and 67 are parts of NAVFAC Drawing No. 267770.

Each part of a pier lying between adjacent pile bents is called a BAY, and the length of a bay is equal to the spacing of the bents O. C. The general plan shows that the advanced base 40-ft timber pier consists of one 13-ft OUTBOARD bay, one 13-ft INBOARD bay, and as many 12-ft interior bays as desired to suit requirements.

The cross section shows that each bent consists of 6 bearing piles. The bearing piles are braced transversely by diagonal braces. Additional transverse bracing for each bent is provided by a pair of batter piles. The batter is specified as 5 in 12. One pile of each pair is driven on either side of the bent, as shown in the general plan. The butts of the batter piles are joined to 12 in. by 12 in. by 14 ft longitudinal batter pile caps, each of which is bolted to the under sides of two adjacent bearing pile caps with bolts, in the positions shown in the part plan. The batter pile caps are placed 3 ft inboard of the center lines of the outside bearing piles in the bent. They are backed by 6 in. by 14 in. batter pile cap blocks, each of which is bolted to a bearing pile cap with bolts.

Longitudinal bracing between bents consists of 14-ft lengths of 3 x 10 bolted to the bearing piles.

The superstructure consists of a single layer of 4 x 12 planks laid on nineteen 6 in. by 14 in. by 14 ft INSIDE STRINGERS. The inside

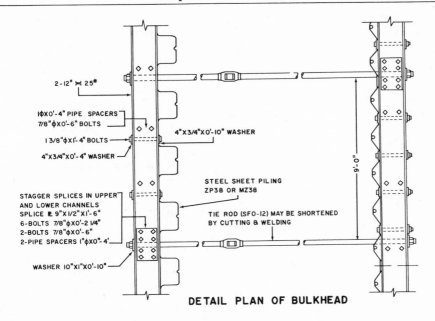

2-12" ⫶ 25#

1⌀X0'-4" PIPE SPACERS
7/8"⌀X0'-6" BOLTS

1 3/8"⌀X1'-4" BOLTS

4"X3/4"X0'-4" WASHER

4"X3/4"X0'-10" WASHER

STEEL SHEET PILING
ZP38 OR MZ38

TIE ROD (SFO-12) MAY BE SHORTENED
BY CUTTING & WELDING

STAGGER SPLICES IN UPPER
AND LOWER CHANNELS
SPLICE ℞ 9"X1/2"X1'-6"
6-BOLTS 7/8"⌀X0'-2 1/4"
2-BOLTS 7/8"⌀X0'-6"
2-PIPE SPACERS 1"⌀X0"- 4'

WASHER 10"X1"X0'-10"

9'-0"

DETAIL PLAN OF BULKHEAD

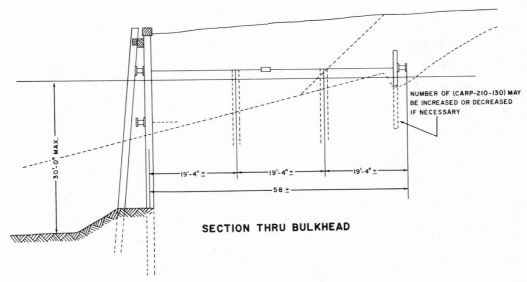

30'-0" MAX.

NUMBER OF (CARP-210-130) MAY
BE INCREASED OR DECREASED
IF NECESSARY

19'-4" ±   19'-4" ±   19'-4" ±

58 ±

SECTION THRU BULKHEAD

45.534

Figure 16-63.—Working drawings for a steel sheet pile bulkhead.

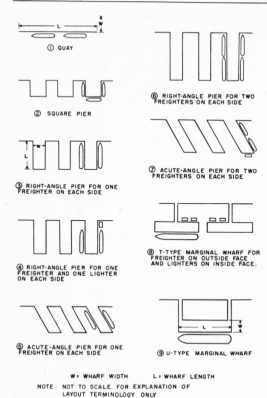

① QUAY

② SQUARE PIER

③ RIGHT-ANGLE PIER FOR ONE
FREIGHTER ON EACH SIDE

④ RIGHT-ANGLE PIER FOR ONE
FREIGHTER AND ONE LIGHTER
ON EACH SIDE

⑤ ACUTE-ANGLE PIER FOR ONE
FREIGHTER ON EACH SIDE

⑥ RIGHT-ANGLE PIER FOR TWO
FREIGHTERS ON EACH SIDE

⑦ ACUTE-ANGLE PIER FOR TWO
FREIGHTERS ON EACH SIDE

⑧ T-TYPE MARGINAL WHARF FOR
FREIGHTER ON OUTSIDE FACE
AND LIGHTERS ON INSIDE FACE.

⑨ U-TYPE MARGINAL WHARF

W = WHARF WIDTH   L = WHARF LENGTH
NOTE: NOT TO SCALE. FOR EXPLANATION OF
LAYOUT TERMINOLOGY ONLY

45.536

Figure 16-64.—Common types of
wharfage structures.

stringers are fastened to the pile caps with drift bolts. The outside stringers are fastened to the pile caps with bolts. The deck planks are fastened to the stringers with 3/8 in. by 8 in. spikes. After the deck is laid, 12-ft lengths of 8 x 10 are laid over the outside stringers to form the CURBING. The lengths of curbing are distributed as shown in the general plan; you can see that the curbing is interrupted wherever there is a CLEAT. The curbing is bolted to the outside stringers with bolts.

The pier is equipped with a FENDER SYSTEM for protection against shock caused by contact with vessels coming or lying alongside. FENDER piles, spaced O.C. as shown in the part plan, are driven along both sides of the pier and bolted to the outside stringers with bolts. The heads of these bolts are countersunk below the surfaces of the piles. An 8 x 10 FENDER WALE is bolted to the backs of the fender piles with bolts. Lengths of 8 x 10 called FENDER PILE CHOCKS are cut to fit between the piles and bolted to the outside stringers and the fender wales. The spacing for these bolts is shown in the part plan.

As indicated in the general plan, the fender system also includes two 14-pile DOLPHINS, located 15 ft beyond the end of the pier. A dolphin is an isolated cluster of piles, constructed as shown in figure 16-68. A similar cluster which is attached to a pier is called a PILE CLUSTER.

MOORING HARDWARE

Various types of metal devices are installed on a wharfage structure for the attachment of ships' mooring lines. These devices are known collectively as MOORING HARDWARE. FENDERS are generally heavy timber piles, frequently of oak, driven at regular intervals along the face of the pier and secured to the pier structure, with timber chocks inserted between the piles to prevent displacement sideways. In some cases hung fenders, consisting of dimension timbers extending from the deck level to near the low-water line, are used and are secured to the pier structure at two or more points. Special spring-mounted and shock-absorbing fenders are occasionally used on heavy piers. Closely spaced planking is employed in front of fenders on piers and wharves used principally for mooring of barges and scows. Fender piles are usually driven to a specified penetration below the final dredged bottom because strength against lateral forces rather than against vertical load is required.

Mooring fittings (BOLLARDS, BITTS, AND CLEATS) are well standardized and will be based on standard plans. As indicated in the plan, cleats, spaced as shown in the plan, are used on the advanced base timber pier. The bill of materials prescribe 42-inch cleats; a 42-inch cleat is shown in figure 16-69. The method of attaching a cleat to the pier is indicated in the part plan. Two 10-inch by 14-inch by 14 ft timbers are bolted on either side of the first inside stringer, and the cleat is bolted down to the timbers. A bollard is shown in figure 16-70 and they are usually located over outside bearing piles. A method of attaching a bollard is shown in figure 16-71.

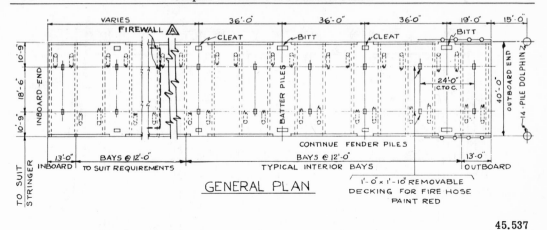

45.537

Figure 16-65.—General plan of advanced base 40 ft timber pier.

PART PLAN

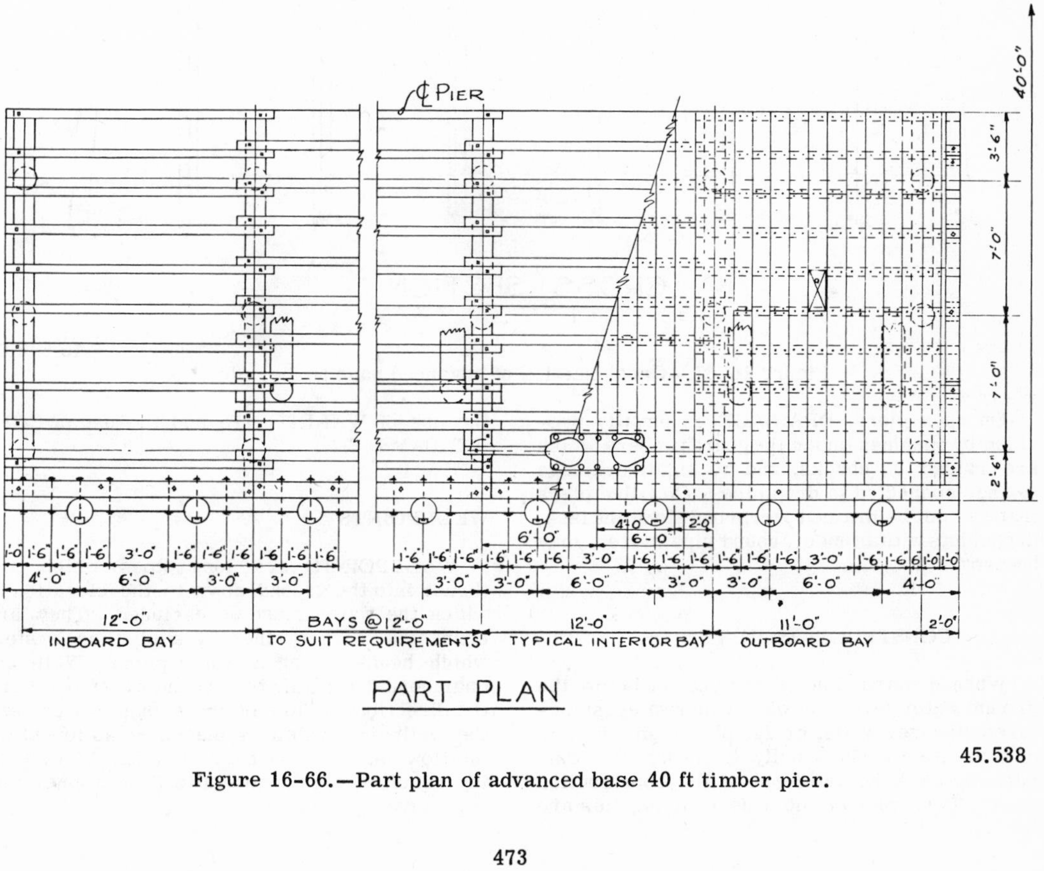

45.538

Figure 16-66.—Part plan of advanced base 40 ft timber pier.

473

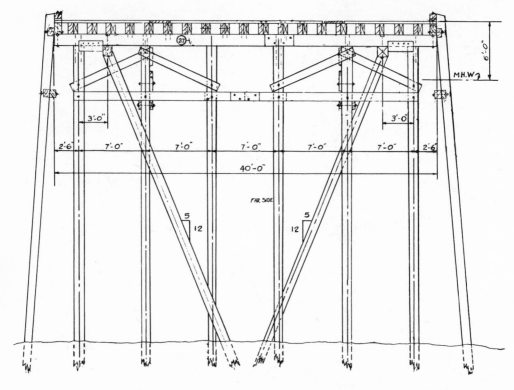

CROSS SECTION

45.538.0

Figure 16-67.—Cross section of advanced base timber pier.

On open piers, DRAINAGE is usually provided by openings under the guard timbers which are raised on chocks, and by small drainage fittings connected to drop pipes. On filled piers that can not be drained overbroad along the face, drop inlets with an underground pipe system may be provided.

CONSTRUCTION IN THE DRY

When construction is carried on below the ground water level, or when underwater structures like sea walls, bridge piers, and the like are erected, it is usually necessary to temporarily keep the water out of the construction area. Two common methods of doing this are

the use of WELLPOINTS and the use of COFFERDAMS.

WELLPOINTS

WELLPOINTS are long pipes which are thrust into the ground down to the elevation to which the water must be excluded. They are connected to each other by a pipeline system which heads up at a water pump. Wellpoint engineers determine the ground water level and the direction of flow of the ground water, and the wellpoint system is placed so as to cut off the flow into the construction area. Wellpointing required highly specialized personnel and expensive equipment.

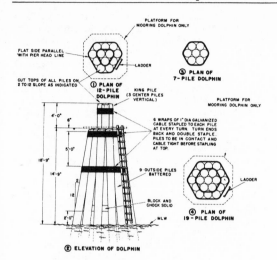

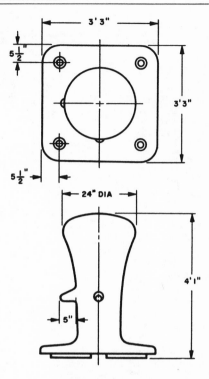

45.539

Figure 16-68.—Dolphins .

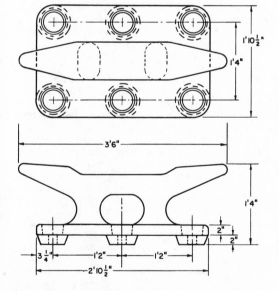

45.541

Figure 16-70.—Bollard.

45.540

Figure 16-69.—Forty-two-in mooring cleat.

COFFERDAMS AND CAISSONS

The COFFERDAM is a temporary structure usually built in place and built tight enough so that the water can be pumped out of the structure and kept out while construction on the foundations is in progress. Common types are the earth cofferdam, the steel-sheeting cofferdam, the cellular type, the wooden sheeting cofferdam, the crib type, and the framed and puddled type. Figure 16-72 shows a cofferdam under construction.

The earth cofferdam is built by dumping into the water an earth fill, shaped so that it will surround the construction area without encroaching upon it. Because swiftly moving currents would carry the material away, the use of earth cofferdams is limited to sluggish waterways where the velocities do not exceed 5 ft per second. The use is also limited to shallow waters, because the quantities of material required in deep waters would be largely due to the flat slopes to which the earth settles when deposited in the water. For this latter reason, the earth

475

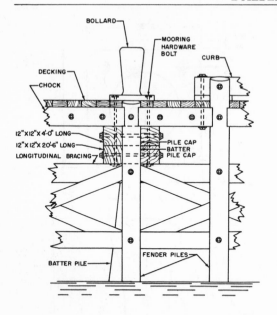

BOLLARD

MOORING HARDWARE BOLT

CURB

DECKING

CHOCK

12"X12"X4'-0" LONG
12"X12"X20'-6" LONG
LONGITUDINAL BRACING

PILE CAP
BATTER PILE CAP

FENDER PILES

BATTER PILE

45.542
Figure 16-71.—Method of attaching a bollard.

type is commonly combined with another type such as sheeting or cribbing to reduce the quantities of earthwork. Steel in the form of piles or pipes is commonly used for cofferdam construction. Steel piling is manufactured in many interlocking designs and in many weights and shapes for varying load conditions. The piling is driven as sheeting in a row to form a relatively tight structure surrounding the construction area. This pile wall is supported in several ways; it may be built in shape of small arches, the abutments of which are supported by cross-members; it may be supported by a framework of stringers and struts; the cofferdam wall might consist of a double row of piles tied together with heavy steel ties and filled with earth, and then this would be built in a square rectangular, circular or oval shape for stability around the construction area. Wooden sheeting in lieu of steel is similarly used in cofferdam constructions. Interlocking timber sheeting is one of the many types used. The timber sheeting is driven as a single wall and supported by stringers and cross struts between walls; or it is driven in double rows as a wall, the sheeting in each row being connected and tied with

braces and the space between being filled with a watertight puddle. Wooden or concrete cribbing may be used in cofferdam construction, by building them to offer stability to the cofferdam wall and then by filling into and against the cribbing with earth and rock to obtain watertightness. Movable cofferdams of timber, steel or concrete have been built, but their uses and designs are very similar to those discussed under boxes and open caissons.

CAISSONS are boxes or chambers used for construction work under water. There are three forms of caissons used in constructing foundations under water; the box caisson, the open caisson, and the pneumatic caisson. If the structure is open at the top and closed at the bottom it is called a box caisson. If it is open both at the top and bottom it is an open caisson. BUT, if it is open at bottom and closed at the top, and compressed air is used, it is a pneumatic caisson. It is sometimes difficult to distinguish between a cofferdam and a caisson. In general, if the structure is self-contained and does not depend upon the surrounding material for support, it is a caisson. However, if the structure requires such support as sheathing or sheet piling, it is a cofferdam. Retaining walls and piers may be built of boxes of wood, steel, or reinforced concrete, floated into place and then filled with various materials. These are known as floating caissons.

Open caissons may be constructed of wood or steel sheet piling. The simplest form of wood-sheet piling consists of wood planks driven side by side as shown in figure 16-73. This structure will hold back earth, but it will not keep out water. The most common form of wood-sheet piling used in waterfront operations is the Wakefield piling, illustrated in figure 16-73. It consists of three planks spiked together to form a tongue and groove. Other forms of wood-sheet piling are shown in figure 16-73. With the exception of the simple planks, all the forms are intended to keep out water as well as to hold back earth. Various forms of steel-sheet piling are shown in figure 16-73, If wood-sheet piling is used, open caissons should preferably be square or rectangular in section. But, if steel piling is used, a circular section will give good results. Wakefield piling will stand the impact of drop hammers. However, steel-sheet piling is usually driven with steam or air hammers. Light wood-sheet piling is sometimes driven with heavy wood mauls.

133.233(133F)

Figure 16-72.—Cofferdam under constructions.

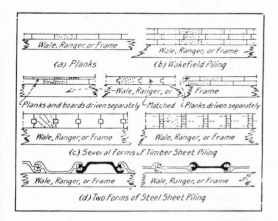

133.402X

Figure 16-73.—Types of sheet piling.

WATER TANKS AND TOWERS

Most water tanks used at advanced bases are 100-bbl, 500-bbl, or 1000-bbl steel tanks (a bbl, liquid measure, equals 31 1/2 U.S. gals), for which the Steelworkers are responsible. However, circumstances occasionally require the use of WOODEN STAVE water tanks, for which the Builders are responsible. In any event, whether a water tank is made of steel or wood it must be supported by a TOWER, and under advanced base conditions a water tank tower is usually made of wood.

Working drawings (Dwg. No. 303776) for wood towers for 100-bbl, 500-bbl, and 1000-bbl tanks are contained in Advanced Base Drawings, NAV-FAC P-140. Figure 16-74 shows drawings for the 100-bbl tank tower. The drawings are self-explanatory.

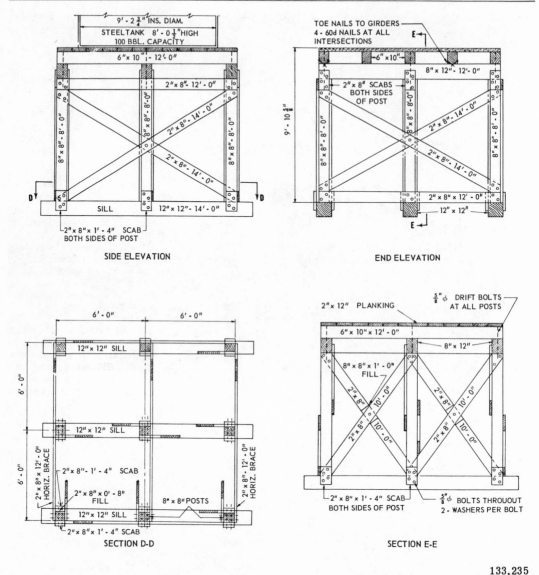

SIDE ELEVATION

END ELEVATION

SECTION D-D

SECTION E-E

133.235

Figure 16-74.—Working drawings for timber tower for 100-bbl water tank.

A wooden stave water tank and the CHINE JOISTS on which it rests are usually prefabricated. The tank consists of the bottom boards (called CANTS), the STAVES, and a number of HOOPS for binding the staves together. Parts for a roof may be included as well.

Manufacturer's instructions for assembling the tank are usually provided and they should be carefully followed. The usual procedure is as follows.

Chine joists are cut so that when they are properly placed their ends form a circle with a diameter about 7 in. less than that of the tank (for tanks with 2-in.-thick staves) or 9 in. less than that of the tank (for tanks with 3-in.-thick staves). Set the chine joists in place on the platform, at right angles to the platform girders, and toenail each joist down with two 60-penny nails at each girder crossing.

Lay the cants in position on the joists, at right angles to the joists. Cants are usually lettered or numbered to show you how they go together. Lay the center cant first and then work outwards, spacing the cants as follows:

1. For tanks up to and including 6 ft in diameter, do not space the cants.

2. For tanks from 13 to 20 ft in diameter, space the cants so that the diameter across the cants exceeds the tank diameter by 3/32 in. for every foot of tank diameter.

3. For tanks over 20 ft in diameter, space the cants so that the diameter across the cants exceeds the tank diameter by 1 in. for every foot of tank diameter.

The spacing of the cants should be worked out evenly, except at the center, where from 2 to 6 cants (depending on the diameter of the tank) should not be spaced at all. After the cants are placed, tack on thin wood strips to hold them in position, as shown in figure 16-75.

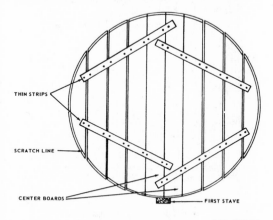

133.236X

Figure 16-75.—Cant spacing for wooden stave water tank.

Each of the staves has a dado called a CROZE cut in it, a few inches up from the bottom, for joining the stave to the cant. Measure the depth of this croze, and gauge a line around the assembled cants, an equal distance away from the ends or edges, as shown in figure 16-75. This line, called the SCRATCH line, serves as a guide when staves are driven onto the cants. A stave which is driven all the way to the line is said to be driven UP TO SCRATCH.

Set the croze on the first stave across the joint between the two center cants, as shown in figure 16-75, and drive the stave half-way up to scratch. For driving, place a softwood block against the stave and strike the block with a mallet or a wooden maul. Do not strike directly against the stave.

Plumb the first stave and brace it with temporary braces running from the inside of the stave, near the top, down to the cants. Then set the other staves in place and drive them all halfway up to scratch. Set the bottoms in contact, but slope the staves outward so that they are slightly separated at the tops, as shown in figure 16-76. Tack on thin wood strips to hold them in place, as shown in the figure, and attach temporary braces to each twelfth stave.

Avoid bringing the joint between any two staves in line with a joint between two cants. Extra staves of various widths are usually provided to make this possible. The last stave placed, called the CLOSURE stave, may require ripping to fit. Measure the width of the closure space at the level of the cants, as shown in figure 16-77, and rip and bevel the stave. You can take the correct bevel angle off another stave with the T-bevel.

When the closure stave has been placed and driven half-way to scratch, set the bottom hoop in place, level with the edges of the cants. The hoop should be placed with the threaded end to the right, and with the turn-buckle located over the joint between two staves as shown in figure 16-78. Set up a slight strain on the hoop with the turnbuckle.

As indicated in figure 16-78 the spacing between hoops is narrower at the bottom of the tank than it is at the top, because of the increased water pressure at the bottom. Correct hoop spacings are given in the manufacturer's instructions. Set the remaining hoops in place, tacking each one in place with enough nails to hold it up. Locate the turnbuckle for the second hoop about 3 ft to the right of the turnbuckle on the first hoop, as shown in the figure. Place the turnbuckles on the others so that they follow a line which spirals upward around the tank, as

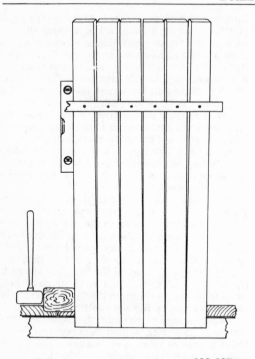

133.237X

Figure 16-76.—Setting staves.

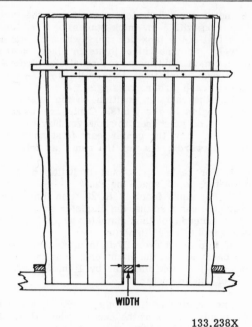

WIDTH

133.238X

Figure 16-77.—Measuring width of closure stave.

also shown. Place each turnbuckle over the joint between two staves.

When all hoops have been placed, tighten them all uniformly and gradually, working several times around the tank and driving staves as required to round out the tank and smooth the joints between staves. When the tank is well rounded and smooth, drive all the staves up to scratch, working several times around, driving a little at a time, and progressively tightening the hoops.

Since heavy construction requires the continuous hoisting and handling of heavy materials, the materials handling safety precautions contained in chapter 5 of this course apply with particular force to men engaged in heavy construction. Since men working on trestles, piers, and the like, are usually working at a considerable height above the ground or water, most of the scaffolding safety precautions in chapter 5 also apply with particular force. Other heavy

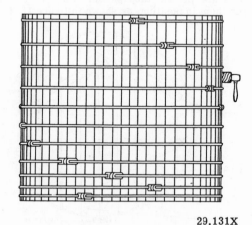

29.131X

Figure 16-78.—Placing hoops.

construction safety precautions are mainly pile-driving precautions. These include precautions which apply to men engaged in any kind of work over the water.

CHAPTER 17
LOGGING OPERATIONS

As a Builder, you must be able to perform the various operations needed to convert a tree into lumber. Therefore, the following sections will explain the duties of the various logging crews. Logging is very dangerous work so special attention is given, throughout this chapter, to safety precautions applicable to various operations involving logging.

LOGGING

Logging is the process of converting standing timber into saw logs or timber products and delivering them to a sawmill for the manufacture of lumber or heavy timber. Logging calls for teamwork. Logging also requires the handling and movement of heavy loads. The operational and organizational maintenance of most of the mobile and heavy equipment needed to handle these loads will be the responsibility of the logging crew. Since the logging crews are engaged in a hazardous operation, rigid safety rules must be established and complied with to prevent serious injuries to personnel and damage to equipment.

The entire logging section is composed of a logging crew. Under the supervision of a logging foreman, each member of the crew may have several duties to perform during a normal logging operation. After the area to be logged has been selected, the foreman is responsible for the planning and construction of woods roads. The foreman is an expediter; it is his responsibility to see that sufficient logs of the correct size and type are cut. In addition to the logging crew, the foreman has supervision over the lumberjacks, the air compressor operator, and the log scaler.

The LUMBERJACKS in the logging crew are normally assigned to fell the trees and saw them into logs (bucking). However, when a new logging operation is started, the lumberjacks will aid in the construction of roads. If necessary, they will construct log-handling and skidding devices. After the new area is prepared, they will resume their normal duties of felling and bucking.

LOGGING EQUIPMENT

The equipment issued to the logging crew is adaptable to nearly every type of logging operation. For the most part, the emphasis is placed on the use of power equipment as a means of facilitating the logging operation.

A pneumatic chain saw sharpener is supplied with the truck-mounted air compressor. It can be used to sharpen both pneumatic and gasoline driven chain saws. The gasoline driven chain saws issued to the logging crew can be used for felling, limbing, trimming, and bucking.

The crawler tractor has a maximum drawbar pull of 24,000 pounds and is equipped with a blade and front and rear-mounted drum winches. The primary use of the tractor is for the transportation of logs by the following methods:

Arch skidding.
Ground skidding.
Log-wagon hauling.
Sled skidding.
Winch; single- or double-drum logging.

In addition to log transportation, the crawler tractor may be used for the following:

Road construction and maintenance.
Construction of fire lanes or guards.
Preparation of camp sites.
Loading of vehicles.
Snow plowing.
Movement of supplies.

WOODS SAFETY

The natural and sometimes unforeseen hazards of woods operations make logging a potentially unsafe operation. The number of persons injured or killed each year is higher in proportion to the number working in other areas. This indicates a need for more attention to safety on the part of everyone working in the woods.

To do this, safety must be considered in the first stages of forest engineering, where the planning of the operation begins. The location of landings and truck and skid roads; the direction of fall of hillside trees; and the schedule of areas to be logged determine, to a great extent, the relative safety of the entire logging operation.

In the road construction which must precede the logging operation, safety must also be considered. The grades, width, and evenness of roads, and the visibility on sharp curves, turnouts, and bridges, must be designed to reduce possible hazards to operators, of crawler tractors, dirt-moving equipment, and trucks.

Supervision of these operations, and those that follow should be carried out with the assistance of a safety organization. This safety organization should consist of one person in charge, and such safety committees as may be practical to check on the details of safe operation.

Personnel should be issued safety (steel-toed) shoes, if obtainable, and safety helmets with liners should be worn by all those actively engaged in the logging operation.

FELLING

Felling is one of the most dangerous and difficult jobs in the logging operation. Trees are felled by chopping a notch in one side of the tree and then cutting from the other side with a chain saw or a crosscut saw. The skills required for felling cannot be attained by reading a few pages of text, but the information presented here may help Builders engaged in felling to avoid some of the more common mistakes.

FELLING CREW DUTIES

A feller equipped with a chain saw is responsible for felling, limbing, and bucking the tree. If the trees are not marked, he selects the tree to be cut. The feller may have an assistant equipped with an ax to increase operating efficiency and to promote greater safety. The assistant removes trash accumulated in cutting, and aids in lifting pieces for their proper cutting.

The crosscut saw crew is a two-man crew, the head feller and the second feller. The head feller carries the saw and one double-bit ax. If the trees have not been previously marked for cutting he selects the tree to be cut. He determines the direction of fall and the size of the undercut. After assuring himself that workers nearby have moved to safe positions, he directs the felling of the tree. Just before the tree falls he gives the warning signal "TIMBER." The

second feller carries one double-bit ax, a sledge hammer, and wedges. He acts as assistant to the head feller. During bucking he is responsible for limbing the tree while the head feller is measuring the tree into log lengths.

LAYOUT OF FELLING JOB

The general layout of the felling job is highly important. Where conditions permit, much time and work can be saved by felling the trees so that the tops and branches can be left where they fall. On some operations where parallel roads are provided, all the trees are felled away from the road so that the tops are windrowed in the middle of the space between the roads (A, fig. 17-1). On other jobs the tops of several trees are felled together in a "jackpot." Tops should never be dropped in a road or skid road if it can possibly be avoided.

It is important, particularly on jobs where the tree trunks are to be skidded out in long lengths, to fell the trees so that they can be removed most easily. This generally means felling them with butts toward the road at about a 45° angle. On some softwood jobs in dense stands of timber exactly the opposite course is followed. (Or the tree can be topped and limbed before it is felled. This will prevent lodging in the dense area.) The trees are felled away from the remaining standing timber, with their tops toward the road (B, fig. 17-1). This reduces lodging (hanging up in an adjacent tree rather than falling free to the ground). Also, a heavier load may be carried when the trees are hauled in top first.

Another method to be considered is to start the felling operation at the far end and top of the logging area and work toward the log landing. This prevents working over and through limbs and tops from previously felled and limbed trees.

DIRECTION OF FALL

Before using the ax or saw on a tree, examine the tree and its location carefully and decide just where the tree should be dropped. The choice is usually limited by the layout of the operation and the location of the tree. Inexperienced fellers may take unnecessary chances of injury by starting the job too hastily. If the tree is leaning not more than 5°, has about the same amount and size of limbs all the way around, and is not being pushed by a strong breeze, the fellers can drop

117.189

A. Felling along parallel roads.   B. Felling with tops toward the road.

Figure 17-1.—Felling patterns.

it in about any direction desired. This is done by the proper location of undercuts and use of wedges to tip it on the stump.

Big trees that lean noticeably or have heavy branches on one side can seldom be thrown in the opposite direction without the use of a block and tackle or other similar equipment, ordinarily not available in the woods. Most of the leaners, however, can be thrown 45° to the right or left of the direction in which they would naturally fall. It is up to the feller to decide just where in this arc his tree should be directed. It can be dangerous to fell a tree into another one. One reason is that the impact may change the direction of fall. Among other things, either tree may have limbs which may snap off and fall on the feller. These limbs are sometimes called "widow makers."

It is also unwise to fell a tree straight up a steep slope. The tree may bounce as it strikes the slope and kick back over the stump to strike the unsuspecting feller who thought he was away from danger. There is no way of telling what the tree will do. The best way is to fell the tree diagonally along the hillside and seek safety on the upper side of the stump away from the direction of the fall. Trees felled straight down a steep slope are likely to be shattered by the fall,

particularly if the ground is rough. It is bad practice to let a tree fall across a large rock, stump, or another log as these tend to break the trunk and cause waste of much of the good timber. Another hazard to be considered in felling a tree is that it may become lodged in the branches of another tree, wasting time and causing trouble. Lodging is possibly the greatest hazard in logging.

CLEARING WORKING SPACE

Once the direction of fall is determined, the next step is to clear away brush, saplings, and low-hanging branches that could interfere with the use of the ax or saw as the feller works at the base of the tree. Small brush is clipped off close to the ground by using the brush hook shown in figure 17-2. Larger brush and saplings can be cut with the single bit belt as shown in the same figure by bending the stem while making slanting downward cuts. Low hanging limbs are removed in the same way.

SAFETY IN BRUSHING OUT

In BRUSHING OUT, ensure that the general safety rules listed below are carefully observed.

483

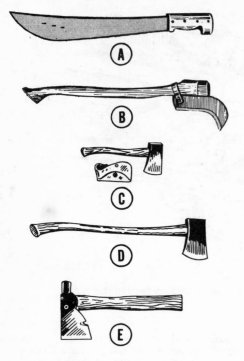

29.83A:.259

A. Machete   C. Single bit belt ax
B. Brush hook   D. Single bit ax
      E. Half hatchet

Figure 17-2.—Field tools.

Check the ax handle for cracks, splits, or splinters. See that the ax head is wedged tight, and that the blade is sharp.

Look over the ground around the tree for rocks, logs, or holes which might cause falls.

Check the tree for hanging branches that might fall on, or be in the way of, men felling the tree.

Wear a hard hat for protection against falling branches.

If carrying a saw, place it on the ground away from the working area before starting to brush. Do not set the saw where it can fall on personnel or where someone is likely to trip over it and get injured.

To prevent concentrations of flammable materials, scatter cut brush and saplings over a wide area.

Never embed a double bladed ax in a stump or tree. Lay it flat on the ground and in the open where it can be easily seen.

MAKING UNDERCUT

Before making an undercut, inspect the tree very carefully for twisted bark. Twisted bark is a strong indication that the tree trunk is twisted and will have a tendency to roll off the stump instead of falling in a direct line.

An undercut is made on the side toward which the tree is to fall. Its functions are to provide a fulcrum and hinge point on which to tip the tree off its stump. The stump should be not more than 12 inches above the ground level on the upper side of the tree. High stumps waste timber and hinder skidding. Exception to the 12-inch rule must be made, of course, when a rock or some other obstruction makes a low stump impossible. If a chain saw is used, the entire undercut is made with the saw. If a crosscut saw is used a horizontal cut is made to a depth of about one-fourth of the diameter of the tree and the notch is chopped out. The usual practice is to chop the notch above the saw cut on a 45° angle, as shown in view A, figure 17-3. A larger notch, like that indicated in view B of the same illustration, requires unnecessary chopping; and a smaller notch, as shown in view C, is too hard to make.

An inexperienced chopper will have trouble in getting the chips to fall out properly. The best method of chopping is to bury only part of the ax edge in the wood at each stroke. If the heel or the nose of the ax is exposed, the chip tends to roll off easily. This can be done by working first the center, then both sides, and repeating the process in that order. In large trees, it is necessary to cut a small notch first and then chip down the full sized notch, as indicated in figure 17-4. In extra large trees it may be best to make two small notches and one large notch, as also indicated in figure 17-4. This prevents binding, thus making the chipping-out easier.

TESTING DIRECTION OF FALL

When the undercut is completed, it is well to check the direction of fall. One simple test

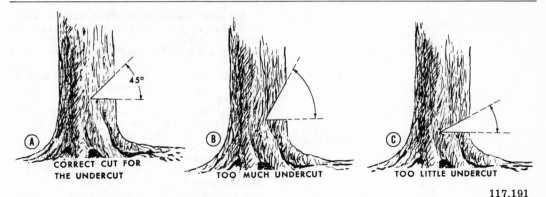

Figure 17-3.—How to make the undercut.

117.191

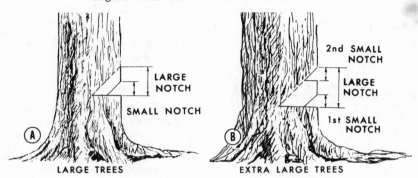

Figure 17-4.—Notching a large tree and an extra large tree.

117.192

is to push the head of a double-bit ax into the crotch made by the undercut, as illustrated in figure 17-5. The handle should then point in the direction in which the tree is to fall. Another method of determining the direction of fall is to use a gun stick, as indicated in figure 17-6. The two points are placed one at each edge of the undercut. The apex then points in the direction of fall.

MAKING BACKCUT

The backcut (A, fig. 17-7) should be approximately 2 inches higher than the bottom of the undercut. The cut normally should be kept parallel with the undercut until only 2 or 3 inches of holding wood is left. If the tree has not fallen by this time, it should be tipped by driving in one or two felling wedges behind

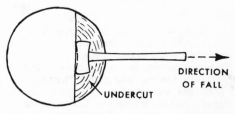

117.193

Figure 17-5.—Use of double-bit ax in testing direction of fall.

the saw. As the sawing is continued, the wedges are driven enough to keep the tree tilted. Do not saw to less than 1 inch of holding wood. This is needed to serve as a hinge (B, fig. 17-7) that will guide the tree as it falls. When a two-man crosscut saw is used to make the backcut,

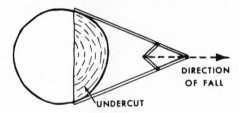

117.194

Figure 17-6.—Use of gun stick in testing
direction of fall.

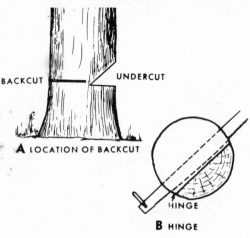

117.195

Figure 17-7.—How to make the backcut
and hinge.

each sawyer should keep his partner informed
of how near the saw is to the undercut so one side
will not be too far ahead of the other.

Before starting to saw a tree, each man
should plan his getaway path. The tree should
be observed closely for any rotten or dead
limbs that would be likely to fall when the tree
is chopped or wedged. Some trees, especially
if they have rot in them, fall quickly. It should
be decided who will remove the saw. The
feller should quickly move back to one side of his
sawing position (preferably behind another tree)
and carefully watch the tree as it falls.

FELLING WITH A CHAIN SAW

The backcut made with a chain saw is similar
to that made with a crosscut saw. The difference

is the speed and flexibility of operation. Extra
care must be taken to prevent cutting through
the hinge. (See fig. 17-8.) While sawing, watch
for widening of the cut and glance at the top of
the tree for indications of motion preceding the
fall. Withdraw the saw from the cut as soon as
the tree is leaning sufficiently to assure a complete fall.

Trees with a larger diameter than the length
of the chain saw guide bar can be felled by
consecutive cuts after the undercut has been
made (see fig. 17-9). It is very important that
the first of the felling cuts be positioned approximately 2 inches above the floor of the undercut,
and that each of the other two cuts follow in the
same plane. The use of wooden wedges is helpful in assuring that the cut will open.

A safe rule to follow is: If the cut cannot be
made with a crosscut saw, it cannot be made
with a chain saw. That is, if the tree or log will
"bind" with a crosscut saw, it will "bind" with
a chain saw.

LEANING TREES

When a tree leans slightly in a direction different from the one in which it should be dropped,
the direction of fall can be changed to a certain
extent by "holding a corner." This is done in
the backcut by simply leaving more wood on the
side opposite the one toward which it leans (A,
fig. 17-10). This acts as a holdback to twist the
tree away from the direction in which it leans.

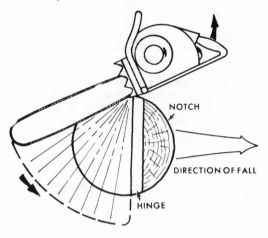

117.196

Figure 17-8.—Normal felling cut.

486

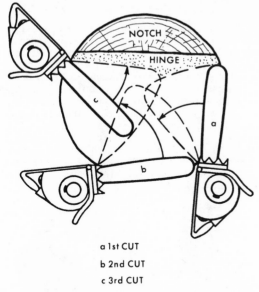

a 1st CUT

b 2nd CUT

c 3rd CUT

117.197

Figure 17-9.—Felling cut, large diameter.

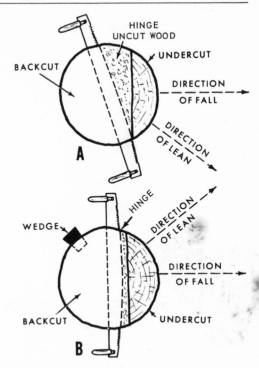

A HOLDING A CORNER IN SAWING A LEANING TREE
B USE OF WEDGE ON A LEANING TREE

117.198

Figure 17-10.—Felling a leaning tree.

Wedging can also be used to alter the direction of a fall. One or more felling wedges are driven into the backcut on the leaning side (B, fig. 17-10) to tip the tree into an upright position from which it can be made to fall in the desired direction.

A gusty wind can sometimes be used to help fell a tree in the direction desired. If the wind is blowing exactly in the desired direction, the fellers merely adjust their rate of sawing so that the last few inches of wood are cut when the breeze is steady enough to take the tree over. If the wind is coming from the opposite direction the problem is much more difficult. The cutters will have to time their work so that their sawing is finished exactly at the time when the wind had died down and the tree is swaying back from the force of the gust. On some days when the wind is changeable, felling may become so dangerous that it should be discontinued altogether. Small trees, of course, can be pushed over in almost any direction by hand.

Trees leaning in the direction of the fall can be dangerous. They usually fall sooner than expected, splintering the butt, and thrashing around in unpredictable directions. One common result is the "barber-chair" stump (fig. 17-11), in which the most valued part of the tree

is spoiled. One method that will usually prevent a leaning tree from splitting in this way is called "sawing off the corners." The backcut is halted before there is any danger that the tree will fall. Then, each corner is sawed off at an angle. The same result can be obtained by chopping out the corners of the undercut (A, fig. 17-12). Another method used to reduce splitting of large bad leaners or hollow-butted trees is to fasten a log chain around the base of the tree just above the backcut (B, fig. 17-12). Wedges driven between the chain and the tree will tighten the chain and prevent serious splitting.

Some valuable leaning trees that can be dropped only in the direction of the lean can be cut three-fourths through from the leaning side by using wedges to prevent pinching the saw. The saw is then removed, and the cut completed from the backcut side. A good general rule to

117.199

Figure 17-11.—A "barber-chair" stump.

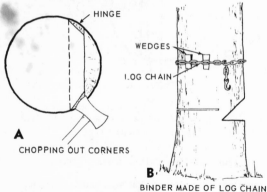

A CHOPPING OUT CORNERS

HINGE

WEDGES

LOG CHAIN

B. BINDER MADE OF LOG CHAIN

117.200

Figure 17-12.—Methods used to prevent splitting of tree.

remember is: THE GREATER THE LEAN, THE DEEPER THE UNDERCUT.

It is possible to fell trees 2 feet in diameter and greater in the opposite direction of lean, if required, providing the lean is not too great. In this operation the backcut is made first on the side of the lean, so that wedges can be applied before the saw is pinched. Sawing and wedging is continued until the tree is in true vertical position after which the undercut is made. After making the undercut, the backcut is completed and wedges are applied until the tree falls.

ROTTEN TREES

Rotten-butted trees present a difficult felling job. Extra precautions will have to be taken to try and anticipate the time and direction of their fall. A large percentage of the most serious accidents occurs in attempting to bring down rotten-butted trees. If possible, the felling cuts are made high enough to avoid most of the rot (A, fig. 17-13). This not only results in safer felling, but also saves the time spent sawing the rotten portion from the butt log. When the rot goes up too high for this, it may be possible to chop or saw around the rot with cornering cuts (B, fig. 17-13) similar to those used for leaning trees.

A STUMP CUT HIGH TO AVOID ROT

B SAWING AROUND ROT

117.201

Figure 17-13.—Felling rotten trees.

When the butt of the tree is badly decayed, it is much safer to chop it down and not use the saw at all. The feller should be more alert than usual when felling a rotten tree. The direction in which it falls is very difficult to control.

HANDLING LODGED TREES

Even the most experienced tree feller sometimes lodges a cut tree in a standing one. An exceptionally sturdy limb on either the tree being felled or the one in its way may fail to bend as expected; or the cut tree may fall or twist out of line. The better and more experienced the felling crew, the fewer trees the crew will lodge. Dislodging may be easy and safe, or it may be very difficult and dangerous, depending on conditions. Cutters must be able to diagnose how firmly a tree is lodged and what method of getting it down is best.

If the tree is lightly lodged, cutting it loose from its stump and prying the butt off to the ground may cause the tree to dislodge and fall. Pushing or twisting it loose is the next step, and is frequently used when only the ends of the limbs are caught. Climbing up the inclined trunk of the lodged tree and attempting to shake it loose by jumping up and down is a dangerous procedure, and is NOT recommended even for the most experienced men.

The safest and most practical way to free a lodged tree is to back the logging tractor to within a safe distance from the tree, attach a winch cable around the butt of the lodged tree, and pull the tree down.

WARNING: Perhaps the most dangerous practice of all is to cut the tree in which the first one is lodged. In doing this, it is difficult to judge the stresses involved, or the way the two trees will fall. If this method becomes necessary, the most experienced and alert man should do the chopping alone, because he will be in a better position for a getaway than a saw crew. Also, working alone, one man can better judge when and in what direction to run.

SAFETY IN FELLING

All personnel performing felling operations should keep safety uppermost in mind. Some of the major safety precautions that should be carefully observed are listed below.

Before making any cuts in the tree, study it carefully for lean, obstructions to the path of fall, wind effect, rolling effect of trunk colliding with adjacent obstacles during its fall, and center of gravity of the tree.

Choose a safe line of retreat from the tree and remove all obstacles which could block the way.

Wear some kind of reinforced head gear—if possible, a safety helmet which will protect your head from falling limbs or other objects.

Two men should not chop together on a tree of less than 20 inches in diameter.

Do not leave a tree which has been started, even at lunch time or at the end of a shift.

Before starting to make the cut, get steady footing to be sure your feet will not slip.

Do not attempt to start a chain saw by holding it in the hand and pulling the starter with the other hand. Place the saw on solid footing and secure it well before attempting to start.

The chain saw's engine and accessories reach high temperatures during operation. Be careful not to touch hot parts. Gloves are a help in case of accidental contact.

Do not check the tension of the chain with the engine running, even though the chain is not moving.

When crews are working several saws together, they should keep a reasonable distance apart so that warning shouts can be heard.

Do not move the saw from one tree to another while it is running.

Watch the fall of the tree to be on guard against limbs of other trees being snapped back.

FIRE PREVENTION RULES
FOR POWER SAWS

In working with power saws, see that the following fire prevention rules are strictly adhered to:

Do not smoke while filling gasoline tanks. Use a gasoline can with a spout or use a funnel. Fill the tank only on an area of bare ground.

Do not start the engine at the place the tank was filled.

Keep the entire saw clean of gasoline, oil, and sawdust. Be sure the muffler is in good condition. Keep the muffler in place at all times while the saw is in operation.

Keep the spark plugs and wire connections tight.

Clear flammable material away from the point of saw cut.

Promptly extinguish any fires. Report fires and possible causes of fires immediately to the proper authority.

LIMBING, BUCKING, AND SCALING

This phase of our discussion deals with operations involving the limbing, bucking, and scaling of logs. Procedures that may be used in carrying out these operations are described in the following sections.

LIMBING

After the tree is on the ground, the next step is the removal of the limbs. This operation is known as LIMBING and is usually done with the ax or chain saw. When using the ax, the limbs should be cut from the lower side, cutting from the base toward the top of the tree. The stub of the limb should be left even with the tree bark. Trees that have been carelessly limbed are hard to skid and load.

Limbing is like other chopping in most ways. The same grip on the handle and the same swing

489

are used. Much of it does, however, have to be performed in restricted areas and from awkward positions. The variation in size of limbs calls for good judgment as to the right amount of force to be put behind the swing of the ax. There is a much greater chance of accident from an ax swung amidst branches than from an ax used in clear chopping, so the axman should clear away any branches that are likely to interfere with chopping. Where possible, the axman should cut limbs on the opposite side of the log (see fig. 17-14) and swing the ax away from himself. The inexperienced chopper should not do any limbing while standing on the tree trunk. As he gains experience and learns control of his ax, he will be able to work safely in positions hazardous for the inexperienced.

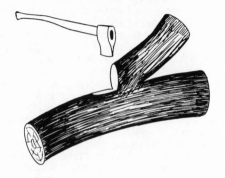

117.203

Figure 17-15.—Cutting off a large limb.

117.202

Figure 17-14.—Cut limbs on the opposite side of the log, where possible.

For large limbs, particularly on hardwoods, it is often necessary to cut a notch similar to that used in cutting down a tree (fig. 17-15). The limb is cut from the lower side and the bottom surface is kept even with the trunk surface. The vertical side of the notch should slope somewhat with the angle of the limb. Often a large notch is easier to cut than a small one. The downward cut is made at a slant with the grain of the wood and not directly across it. Thus chopping should be done slightly at an angle to the grain, and there should be no attempt to twist out the chips. Larger limbs on hardwoods are usually easier to saw off than to chop off.

BUCKING

As logging operations have become more mechanized, the bucking operation (cutting the tree into log lengths) has been shifting from the stump location to the loading dock, or even to the mill where the wood is utilized. There is economy in handling long logs or tree length timber when the quantity to be handled justifies the use of heavy equipment for skidding, loading, and hauling. There is another advantage in bucking at the landing or in the mill yard. Power saws become feasible; logs can be cut to more accurate lengths. A bucking crew that does nothing else will develop maximum skill in cutting the quality logs, especially out of hardwood trees.

Log Grades

Wherever the logs are bucked, the leader of the bucking crew must be familiar with the log grading system used for the species being cut. All grading systems are based on the grade of lumber that can be sawed from the logs. Logs suitable for sawing must meet the minimum standards of length, diameter, quality, and species. For practical purposes in bucking felled trees, the lead bucker should set up a grade of standards similar to that shown in table 17-1. For timber that is to be used for piling or other uses requiring long lengths, a separate table may be necessary.

Table 17-1.—Typical Log Grading System

Log grade	Small end diameter	Requirements	Description
No. 1 (good).......	Over 10".....	All lumber cut from this log must be No. 1 Common or better.	Surface and ends clear of defect, and sapwood bright in color. Two small limb knots are allowed, but two large knots on body knots make it a No. 2 grade. If the knots occur at each end it is a cull log.
No. 2 (common)....	Min 6".......	Two-thirds of the lumber cut from this log must be No. 1 Common or better.	Must not have more than three standard defects (note), or be only slightly wormy.
No. 3 (cull).......	....	One-half of the lumber cut from this log must be No. 2 Common with a little of the better grades.	More than two limb or body knots. Some worm and knot defects.

NOTE. (1) Standard defects are—knots, rot, shakes, season checks, frost cracks, sun, scald, fire scars, seams, wormholes, stain, spiral or crooked grain, cat faces, and crook in the log. Most exterior checking and shallow cat faces are not defects, since they go into the slab only.

(2) No. 1 Common—⅔ of the surface of the board is clear faced.

(3) No. 2 Common—½ of the surface of the board is clear faced.

117.225

The United States maintains the highest grading standards of any nation. In overseas operations it may be necessary to adjust grade standards to the standards which are in use in the area being logged. This will be particularly true if the timber is being purchased from private interests.

Log Lengths

Sawlogs are ordinarily cut in lengths from 8 to 16 feet by 2-foot intervals. Increasingly, as materials become more scarce, the demand is greater for the highest quality logs in the 8- to 16-foot group. However, where special types of construction are being undertaken, specifications frequently call for 20-, 24-, and even 32-foot material. Therefore, good judgment in dividing the tree into logs and a knowledge of the specification requirements cannot be over-emphasized. Accuracy is also important. Ordinarily, a 3-inch trimming allowance for each 16-foot or shorter length is specified in order that any irregularity in the ends can be evened off by the trim saws (A, fig. 17-16), leaving square-end boards of the full specified length. Logs with a greater allowance are penalty scaled for unnecessary wastage (B, fig. 17-16). Logs failing to have this allowance are scaled in the next lower allowable length (C, fig. 17-16).

An accurate log measuring pole (fig. 17-17) showing the specified trimming allowance at the butt should be used. A metal hook on the butt end of the pole is often an aid to its more accurate use.

Bucking Procedures

The first step in bucking sawlogs is to measure the total usable length of the tree (fig. 17-18). This total should be subdivided into the individual log lengths in a way that will obtain both maximum scale and grade. This is done before the crew starts to buck. The following suggestions will aid in obtaining maximum scale and grade.

Saw cuts made below large limbs generally give larger scale in the butt log, since the knots are not included.

Wherever possible, surface defects should be kept in the butt portions of logs, where they will be trimmed off in slabs.

Defects should be grouped in one log if possible. This often means sawing knots, rotten areas, and so on, which is contrary to the natural inclination of the sawyers, but it raises the grade of the product.

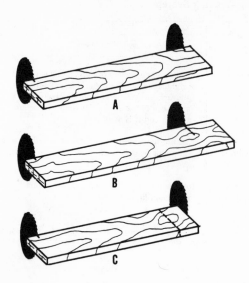

117.204

A. Right length allows just enough for trimming.
B. Extra length causes waste in trimming.
C. Too short for trimming, will be cut to next shorter standard length.

Figure 17-16.—Proper log lengths.

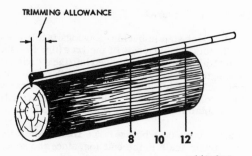

TRIMMING ALLOWANCE

8' 10' 12'

117.205

Figure 17-17.—A log measuring pole.

Sawing too close to the base of a crotch and showing a double heart on the small end of the log should be avoided.

If practicable, cuts should be made at points of the most abrupt crook, leaving the cut logs as straight as possible.

Wedges should be used frequently in bucking to prevent pinching the saw. The crew will ordinarily carry two or three wedges and a maul to drive them.

Before starting to buck, all brush or trash on either side of the log should be cleaned out to get space to work.

Because of the weight of the logs, blocks (fig. 17-19) should be placed alongside the trunk to keep the cutoff section from dropping or rolling on one of the buckers, especially when working on a hillside or sloping ground.

Blocking used under the trunk prevents the log from splitting with a consequent loss of valuable material.

Sometimes, when a heavy trunk is suspended from the two ends, it is necessary to make part of the cut from underneath. This is a more difficult operation because either the power saw or crosscut saw will have to be held into the cut.

Use of Mechanical Equipment

When a tractor and logging arch are being used to haul tree lengths to the log yard, and the bucking is being done at the landing, larger crews can be used to good advantage. The work can be more closely supervised and greater use of mechanical equipment for bucking is feasible. Bucking skids and chutes are sometimes constructed to ease the handling of logs and to avoid the possibility of pinching. Bucking is done on the end of the log which is unsupported. A mechanical bucking chute (fig. 17-20), either hand- or motor-operated, offers several advantages. A series of concave rollers with the front roller fluted or spiked can be used. The front roller is usually hand-crank operated to advance the log for each succeeding cut. The advantage is that the log beyond the saw is unsupported and, therefore, will not pinch the saw. Some mills bring the tree-length logs to the yard for bucking and also construct a motorized bucking plant. These mills are fabricated almost entirely at the site and use circular saws. Some saws are pushed or pulled into the log by a hand lever; others are swung into the log mechanically.

Log Classifying

The most important function of the SEABEE log scaler will be that of classifying uncut logs. By judging the quality of the log, the scaler will determine its eventual use and mark it for

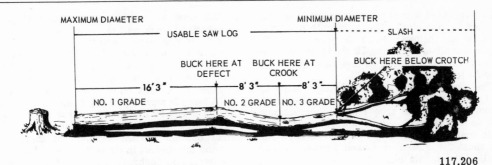

117.206

Figure 17-18.—Log bucking plan.

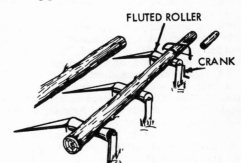

117.208
Figure 17-20.—Mechanical bucking chute.

117.207
Figure 17-19.—Method of propping and bucking a log.

bucking accordingly. If the timber is purchased by the log, his job will include measuring the logs for board- or cubic-foot content. Some of the more common uses and specifications for timber are listed below.

BOLTS are short portions of logs. BILLETS are obtained by halving, quartering, or otherwise splitting bolts or short logs lengthwise. Bolts and billets are used for many purposes such as cooperage, crating, pulp, and so on.

POLE specifications vary greatly. Specifications for poles generally require the material to be of the best quality, of specified dimensions, the butt to be cut square, reasonably straight, well portioned from top to butt, peeled, and with knots trimmed close. Defects looked for in inspection are crookedness, split tops, split butts, sap and butt rot, checks, and shakes.

The classification and grading of PILING depends largely upon its use, whether in fresh water or salt water or on land, and upon its form and size. Very often the kind of wood is not specified, and the requirements refer to straightness, length, and butt diameter measurement 3 feet from the end. Important construction work often calls for specifications similar to the following: All piling shall be cut from sound, live trees of slow growth and firm grain and free from ring heart, wind shakes, decay, large or unsound knots, or any other defects that will impair its strength or durability. The trees shall taper uniformly from butt to tip. Piles shall be so straight that the line joining the centers of the ends will fall entirely within the pile and that, in the opinion of the inspector, they can be subjected to hard driving without injury. No short or reverse bends will be allowed. Bark shall be peeled from the entire length of all piles, and all knots shall be trimmed close. No pile

493

will be accepted with a top measuring less than 6 inches in diameter. The allowable diameter shall be as follows: Butts of piles under 30 feet in length to be from 12 to 16 inches and butts of piles from 30 to 50 feet in length to be from 12 to 18 inches.

The specifications for RAILROAD TIES in most cases are for sound timber of good quality, stripped of bark and free from imperfections, such as shakes and loose or decayed knots, that would impair their strength and durability. The ties must be sawed or hewed smooth on two parallel faces, and ends must be cut square. Pole ties are made of round timber on which are hewed two parallel faces; square ties are hewed or sawed into rectangular shape. Ties are classified according to the species of wood, their wearing and lasting qualities and their need for preservation treatment, and the thickness and width of face, or dimensions.

Any kind of wood measured by the cord and in the form of either round or split sticks is called CORDWOOD. Firewood is measured in standard cords, mostly 4-foot lengths, or short cords of stove wood and other material varying from 12 to 20 inches in length. Wood which is to be used for distillation, extract wood, excelsior, pulp wood, handles, cooperage, and woodenware is frequently sold by the rick or cord. The lengths vary mostly from a minimum of 22 inches for heading and from 5 feet for extract and handle stock. Specifications, if given, refer to the kind of wood, length, average size of the pieces, whether split or round, general soundness, body or limb wood, and degree of dryness.

LOG SCALING

Log lengths can be conveniently measured by the log scaler with a measuring stick 8 feet long. About 3 inches should be added to the nominal length of the log, so that rough ends can be trimmed at the mill. If more than 6 inches of extra length is left, however, carelessness in sawing the trees into logs is indicated. For scaling purposes, the average diameter inside the bark at the small end of the log is measured. Several diameters may be measured where necessary to obtain a fair average. Diameters are rounded off to the nearest inch; that is, 7 1/4 would be considered 7, 7 3/4 would be considered 8, and 7 1/2 should be roughly divided equally between the 7-inch and 8-inch diameters.

As soon as each log is scaled it should be marked, so there will be no danger of scaling it again. If systematic scaling is done, it is desirable to use a special book for this purpose. Each log is recorded in the book with a cross or other mark. When the log is scaled its number is written on the small end of the log.

A sample form for a log scale book is illustrated in figure 17-21. Note that the book has been ruled off into groups of four columns: the first column for the number of the log, the second for its length (in feet), the third for its diameter (in inches), and the fourth for the scale (in board feet). Only one grade of timber should be entered on a page.

A log rule is used by the log scaler to determine the number of board feet in a log. Two types of log rules are illustrated in figure 17-22; they are the International scale log rule and the Scribner decimal C log rule. The scale stick is 48 inches long and calibrated to show the board-foot contents of logs up to 48 inches in diameter.

Scaling Logs in Board Feet by Scribner Decimal C Rule

Scaling is subject to many small differences in practice in different regions with different organizations. The most practical scale is the Scribner decimal C log rule shown in table 17-2.

The maximum and minimum scaling lengths are usually set for each timber cutting operation. Logs longer than the minimum scaling length are scaled in 2-foot increments. Instead of taking the nearest 2 feet, the logs are scaled to the nearest even 2 feet below the actual length. A trimming allowance of 3 inches (for cutting the log off square at the mill and cutting off ends broomed or filled with grit in skidding) is allowed over scaling length. Too large a trimming allowance is corrected by scaling the log as the next longest 2 feet. Ordinarily, all logs over 16 feet are scaled as two or more logs of as nearly the same length as practical. Nominal lengths of either 16 feet or 12 feet are preferable when dividing a long log for scaling.

The length of the log is measured with a tape. The average diameter of the log inside bark at the small end is measured in inches with a scale stick or a ruler (B, fig. 17-22). The scale stick shows diameter in inches on one edge and on the other edge shows the board foot volume, in tens, by the Scribner decimal C rule, for that diameter of different lengths. Except where the small end of the log is perfectly round, the diameter inside

LOG NO.	LENGTH	DIAMETER	SCALE	LOG NO.	LENGTH	DIAMETER	SCALE
	FEET	INCHES	BD. FT.		FEET	INCHES	BD. FT.
1				12			
2				13			
3				14			
4				15			
5				16			
6				17			
7				18			
8				19			
9				20			
10				21			
11				22			

117.209

Figure 17-21.—Sample form for a log scale book.

bark is measured the longest and the shortest way, and the average diameter to the nearest inch is used. Thus, if the diameter inside bark at the small end is 18.5 inches the long way and 16 inches the short way, the average is 17.2 inches and the log would be called a 17-inch log.

For inexperienced scalers, the best rule is to assume even taper on all except butt logs. Thus, a log 40 feet in length, 16 inches in diameter at the small end, and 21 inches in diameter at the large end might be scaled as—a 16-inch log, 12 feet long, a 17-inch log, 12 feet long, and a 19-inch log, 16 feet long. This was figured as follows: total taper in 40 feet equals 21 - 16 = 5 inches; if the log has even taper this amounts to 1/2 inch per 4 feet; the top diameter of the first 12-foot length is the top diameter of the log or 16 inches; the top diameter of the next 12-foot log is the same as the butt diameter of the top 12-foot length of 16 plus 3 x 1/2 = 16 plus 1 1/2, or 17 1/2 inches, rounded off to 17 inches; the top diameter of the 16-foot length is the same as the butt diameter of the preceding 12-foot length or 17 1/2 plus 3 x 1/2 = 19 inches.

For butt logs, inexperienced scalers should use taper tables. In some operations, odd-length lumber can be used. Under these conditions, logs will be scaled to the nearest whole foot in length below the actual length rather than to the nearest even foot.

Deductions for Defect Board Feet,
Using Scribner C Rule

The Scribner C rule is measured from the diameter of the small end of the log inside bark and allows for boards 1 inch thick with a saw kerf (width of cut made by a saw) of 1/4 inch between boards. No allowance is made for taper, and in the tables a certain amount of solid wood around the edges is allowed for slabbing (removing the outer surface of a log in order to obtain a flat surface for sawing lumber). In allowing for defects, therefore, any part of the defect falling in the slabs already deducted by the rule, or in the saw kerf already deducted by the rule, should not be deducted again in scaling. When the defect is in the center of the log, the deduction is

495

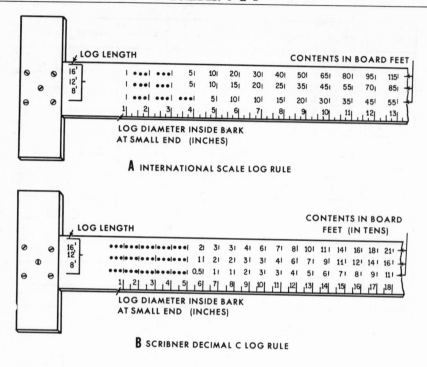

Figure 17-22.—Examples of log rules.

117.210

reduced by the amount of saw kerf only; when the defect comes in from the surface of the log, the deduction is reduced by the amount of taper and slabs, as well as by the amount of saw kerf.

The Scribner rule treats the log as a RIGHT CYLINDER whose diameter is equal to the average diameter inside bark at the small end of the log, and whose length is the scaled length of the log. A right cylinder is a cylinder whose ends are perpendicular to the length. All defects outside the right cylinder of the log are disregarded, since no wood outside the right cylinder has been included in the gross scale of the log as given by the rule. In addition, a certain amount of slabbing has been omitted from the gross scale by the rule. The amount varies with the size of the log, but in allowing for defect it is assumed that it is equivalent to a collar 1 inch thick just inside the edge of the right cylinder. This is illustrated in views I and K, figure 17-23.

The STANDARD RULE for allowing for defects within the right cylinder and within the inside edge of the slab collar is: deduction = $a \times b \times L/15$, in which a is the depth or thickness of the defect, in inches; b is the width of the defect, in inches; and L is the length of the defect, in feet. This deduction is in board feet and must be divided by 10 to obtain tens of board feet corresponding to values given by the Scribner decimal C log rule. It will be noted that the divisor in the rule is 15 instead of 12. This reduces by 20 percent the amount already deducted in the rule for saw kerf. In the case of circular defects in the center of a log, a and b are equal and become D^2 in the formula for deduction. It is customary to add an inch to the actual thickness and width of the defect to allow for sawing around it. The standard rule might be written—for circular defects, taking out a square piece, deduction = $(D + 1)^2 \times L/15$; for defects taking out a rectangular piece, deduction = $(a + 1) (b + 1)L/15$ in which D is the

Table 17-2.—Board Feet Content by the Scribner Decimal C Log Rule

| Diameter (inches) | Length (feet) | | | | | | | | | | | Diameter (inches) |
	6	7	8	9	10	11	12	13	14	15	16	
					Contents (bd ft) in tens							
6	0.5	0.5	0.5	0.5	1	1	1	1	1	1	2	6
7	0.5	1	1	1	1	2	2	2	2	2	3	7
8	1	1	1	1	2	2	2	2	2	2	3	8
9	1	2	2	2	3	3	3	3	3	3	4	9
10	2	2	3	3	3	3	3	4	4	5	6	10
11	2	2	3	3	4	4	4	5	5	6	7	11
12	3	3	4	4	5	5	6	6	7	7	8	12
13	4	4	5	5	6	7	7	8	8	9	10	13
14	4	5	6	6	7	8	9	9	10	11	11	14
15	5	6	7	8	9	10	11	12	12	13	14	15
16	6	7	8	9	10	11	12	13	14	15	16	16
17	7	8	9	10	12	13	14	15	16	17	18	17
18	8	9	11	12	13	15	16	17	19	20	21	18
19	9	10	12	13	15	16	18	19	21	22	24	19
20	11	12	14	16	17	19	21	23	24	26	28	20
21	12	13	15	17	19	21	23	25	27	28	30	21
22	13	15	17	19	21	23	25	27	29	31	33	22
23	14	16	19	21	23	26	28	31	33	35	38	23
24	15	18	21	23	25	28	30	33	35	38	40	24
25	17	20	23	26	29	31	34	37	40	43	46	25
26	19	22	25	28	31	34	37	41	44	47	50	26
27	21	24	27	31	34	38	41	44	48	51	55	27
28	22	25	29	33	36	40	44	47	51	54	58	28
29	23	27	31	35	38	42	46	49	53	57	61	29
30	25	29	33	37	41	45	49	53	57	62	66	30
31	27	31	36	40	44	49	53	58	62	67	71	31
32	28	32	37	41	46	51	55	60	64	69	74	32
33	29	34	39	44	49	54	59	64	69	73	78	33
34	30	35	40	45	50	55	60	65	70	75	80	34
35	33	38	44	49	55	60	66	71	77	82	88	35
36	35	40	46	52	58	63	69	75	81	86	92	36
37	39	45	51	58	64	71	77	84	90	96	103	37
38	40	47	54	60	67	73	80	87	93	100	107	38
39	42	49	56	63	70	77	84	91	98	105	112	39
40	45	53	60	68	75	83	90	98	105	113	120	40
41	48	56	64	72	79	87	95	103	111	119	127	41
42	50	59	67	76	84	92	101	109	117	126	134	42
43	52	61	70	79	87	96	105	113	122	131	140	43
44	56	65	74	83	93	102	111	120	129	139	148	44
45	57	66	76	85	95	104	114	123	133	143	152	45
46	59	69	79	89	99	109	119	129	139	149	159	46
47	62	72	83	93	104	114	124	134	145	155	166	47
48	65	76	86	97	108	119	130	140	151	162	173	48
49	67	79	90	101	112	124	135	146	157	168	180	49
50	70	82	94	105	117	129	140	152	164	175	187	50

117.226

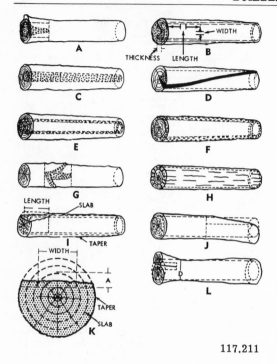

117.211

A. Stump rot
B. Heart check
C. Circular rot
D. Frost check
E. Ring shake
F. Punky sapwood
G. Rotten knots
H. Wind checks
I. Fire scar
J. Crook
K. Fire scar
L. Crotch

Figure 17-23.—Defects in logs.

actual average diameter of the circular defect in inches; a is the actual thickness of the rectangular defect in inches; b is the actual average width of the defect in inches; and L is the length of the defect in feet.

The amount of defect in a log necessary to cause its rejection as a CULL LOG (a log that is economically usable in size but rejected because of defects) varies in different localities and usually is specified for each timber cutting

operation. In general, logs of a valuable species in which less than 33 percent of the gross scale (read from scale stick or log table) is economically usable are considered cull logs, whereas logs of less valuable species in which less than 50 percent of the gross scale is economically usable are considered cull logs. Incidentally, logs of the valuable species are the finer cabinet woods such as walnut and cherry.

Common Defects

There are various types of defects for which deductions must be allowed in scaling logs. Figure 17-23 illustrates some of the common defects of concern to the log scaler. Methods used in making deductions of specific types of defects in logs are discussed below.

STUMP ROT.—Stump rot is found only in butt logs and is illustrated in view A, figure 17-23. Assume that the log illustrated is 12 inches in diameter inside bark at the small end and 16 feet long, and has stump rot with an average diameter of 8 inches at the butt end and estimated to extend 4 feet up the log. By the standard rule the deduction would be— $(8 + 1)^2$ x 4/15 = 22 board feet, or rounded off to the nearest ten, 2.

The gross scale of a 12-inch, 16-foot log is 8 (from table 17-2). The net scale would be 8 - 2 = 6, or 60 board feet. Another method of deducting for stump rot is to reduce the length of the log by the length of the rot. In this instance, the net scale might have been found by looking up the volume of a 12-inch, 12-foot log (16 - 4 = 12). The rule shows 6, or 60 board feet, for such a log. The customary practice is to use whichever method will give the smaller deduction. In this instance it made no difference. Had the average diameter of the rot been 9 inches instead of 8 inches, the deduction by the standard rule would have been 26 board feet, or 3, giving a net scale of only 5, or 50 board feet. In that case, the log would have been scaled as a 12-inch, 12-foot log and the net scale would be 60 board feet as before. On the other hand, if the average diameter of the rot had been 6 inches instead of 8 inches, the deduction by the standard rule would have been 13 board feet, or 1, giving a net scale of 7 or 70 board feet. Under such conditions the standard rule would be used in scaling.

CIRCULAR ROT.—Circular rot may appear at only one or at both ends of the log. If it appears at only one end of the log, the diameter is taken at that end and the length it extends up the log is estimated. The deduction is made exactly the same as that for stump rot, unless it is estimated that the rot extends so far up the log, the remaining sound length is below the minimum length of merchantable board. In this case, the length of the log is used as the length of the rot. Ordinarily, this minimum length of board is 6 feet, but in some sections 6-foot boards are not economically usable.

A log with a circular heart rot showing at both ends is illustrated in view C, figure 17-23. Assume that the log is 12 inches in diameter inside bark at the small end and is 16 feet long. Its gross scale is 8, or 80 board feet. The defect is 4 inches in diameter at the small end and 6 inches in diameter at the large end. For logs 16 feet in length, or shorter, the diameter of the rot is measured at the large end. By the standard rule the deduction is—$(6 + 1)^2$ x 16/15 = 52 board feet, or rounded off to the nearest ten, 5. The net scale would be: 8 - 5 = 3, or 30 board feet. If cull logs are all those whose net scale is less than 50 percent of the gross scale, this log would be cull. If cull logs are those whose net scale is less than 33 percent of the gross scale, this log would be acceptable.

Suppose you are in a region where logs longer than 16 feet are scaled as one log and that the length of the log in view C, figure 17-23 is 18 feet and all other dimensions are the same. In this case the average of the diameters of the defect at the two ends would be used instead of the diameter at the large end. The average diameter of the defect at the two ends would be the average of 6 and 4, or 5 inches. The deduction by the standard rule would be— $(5 + 1)^2$ x 18/15 = 43 board feet, or rounded off to the nearest ten, 4. The gross scale of a 12-inch, 18-foot log is 9, or 90 board feet. The net scale of the log would be: 9 - 4 = 5, or 50 board feet. The log would be more than 50 percent sound and would, therefore, be acceptable.

Now, suppose you are in a locality where logs longer than 16 feet are scaled as two or more logs and that the length of the log in view C, figure 17-23, is 18 feet. In this case, it would be scaled as a 10-foot log and an 8-foot log and taper would be allowed for in the defect as well as in the log. The diameter inside bark at the small end of the log is 12 inches and the diameter inside bark at the large end is 16 inches. The total taper is: 16 - 12 = 4 inches for the

18-foot length; this amounts to 0.22 inches per foot or 1.8 inches in 8 feet. The diameter inside bark at the top of the first 8-foot length would have been the diameter of the log, or 12 inches; the diameter inside bark of the 10-foot length would be 12 + 1.8 = 13.8, or 14 inches. The diameter of the defect at the small end is 4 inches and at the large end, 6 inches; the taper in the defect is 2 inches in 18 feet or 0.11 inches per foot or 0.88 inch in 8 feet. The diameter of the defect at the large end of the first 8-foot length would be 4 + 0.9 = 4.9 or 5 inches; the diameter of the defect at the large end of the 10-foot length is the same as the diameter of the defect at the large end of the log or 6 inches. Applied to the 8-foot length, the standard rule gives a deduction of—$(5 + 1)^2$ x 8/15 = 19 board feet, or rounded off to the nearest ten, 2.

The gross scale of a 12-inch, 8-foot log is 4, or 40 board feet. The net scale of the 8-foot length would be 4 - 2 = 2, or 20 board feet. Applied to the 10-foot length, the standard rule gives a deduction of—$(6 + 1)^2$ x 10/15 = 33 board feet, or rounded off to the nearest ten, 3.

The gross scale of a 14-inch, 10-foot log is 7, or 70 board feet. The net scale of the 10-foot length would be: 7 - 3 = 4, or 40 board feet. The net scale of the whole log would be: 2 + 4 = 6, or 60 board feet. The log would be acceptable.

RING SHAKE.—Ring shake is the separation of the layers of wood along the annual rings. This defect is illustrated in view E, figure 17-23. Ring shake may run only part of the length of the log or it may appear at both ends. It is treated exactly in the same way as a circular rot and deductions are made by the standard rule. Sometimes, however, there is a core of sound wood in the center of the shake which is large enough to be scaled as a merchantable log. In this case, the amount of deduction by the standard rule is reduced by the scale of this core. Assume that the log is 12 inches in diameter inside bark at the small end, 16 inches in diameter inside bark at the large end, and 16 feet long. Let us further assume that the shake is 7 inches in diameter at the small end, 8 inches in diameter at the large end, and extends the full length of the log; also, there is a solid core in the center of the shake 6 inches in diameter at the small end of the log. The deduction by the standard rule is—$(8 + 1)^2$ x 16/15 = 86 board feet, or rounded off to the nearest ten, 9.

The scale of a 6-inch, 16-foot log is 2, or 20 board feet. The net deduction for defect would then be: 9 - 2 = 7. The gross scale of a 12-inch, 16-foot log is 8, or 80 board feet. The net scale of the log is: 8 - 7 = 1, or 10 board feet. In this particular case the volume of the core is the true net volume of the log since the deduction by the standard rule is greater than the gross scale of the core. This log; however, would still be cull.

PITCH RING.—A pitch ring (not illustrated) is a heavy deposit of pitch along an annual ring or group of annual rings. This condition is treated in the same way as shake if the deposit is heavy enough to be a defect.

ROTTEN KNOTS.—Two or more rotten knots on opposite sides of the log and within an area of 2 linear feet are sufficient evidence that there is a limited amount of rot in the log even though the rot does not appear at either end of the log. The best background the scaler can have when allowing for such a defect is a knowledge of how different species of logs in the region showing this evidence of rot saw out in the mill. Where such knowledge is lacking, it is safe to assume that the rot runs down the stem to a point at least 1 foot below the lowest rotten knot and up the log to a point at least 1 foot above the highest rotten knot. This type of defect is illustrated in view G, figure 17-23. Suppose that the log shown is 12 inches in diameter inside bark at the small end and 16 feet long, and with a rotten knot 7 feet from the large end. The deduction is made by reducing the scale by the estimated length of the affected section. Allowing 1 foot below the lowest knot, the rot is estimated to extend within 3 feet of the large end. Allowing 1 foot above the highest knot, the rot is estimated to extend 8 feet from the large end or 8 feet from the small end. Since boards less than 6 feet in length are not economically usable, the sound wood below the rot cannot be included in the net scale. The length of the log must be reduced by 8 feet, therefore, the net scale of the log will be the scale of a 12-inch, 8-foot long log, which is 4, or 40 board feet. The gross scale of a 12-inch, 16-foot log is 8, or 80 board feet; hence, the log is acceptable.

HEART CHECK.—Heart check, illustrated in view B, figure 17-23, is deducted as a rectangle by the standard rule. Of course, if the log has spiral grain and the heart check is thereby twisted in the log, the size of the rectangle must be proportionately larger. This general principle is illustrated in connection with frost check in view D, figure 17-23. When the heart check appears at only one end of the log, the distance it extends into the log must be estimated. In applying the standard rule to heart check, a, the thickness of the rectangle, and b, the width of the rectangle, must be entirely within the right cylinder and the slab. It will be noticed in view B that the part of the heart check extending beyond the right cylinder and slab at the top of the log is disregarded in determining the dimensions of the rectangle, a and b.

Assume that the log shown in view B, figure 17-23 is 12 inches in diameter inside bark at the small end. Assume, too, that the heart check at the large end is 3 inches thick and 9 inches wide within the right cylinder and slab, and is estimated to extend 7 feet up the log. The deduction by the standard rule is—3 x 9 x 7/15 = 13 board feet, or rounded off to the nearest ten, 1.

The gross scale of a 12-inch, 16-foot log is 8, or 80 board feet. The net scale of the log is: 8 - 1 = 7, or 70 board feet. In regions where off-length boards are unmerchantable, the length of the defect would have been taken as 8 feet and the deduction would have been 14 board feet, or rounded off to the nearest ten, 1. The net scale would have been 7, or 70 board feet.

These defects are illustrated in figure 17-23.

FIRE SCAR.—The fire scar type of defect, caused by fire damage to the tree, is illustrated in the log shown in views I and K, figure 17-23. The common method of allowing for this defect is to divide the log in sections and estimate the proportion of loss in the section affected. The diameter inside bark at the small end of the log in view I is 12 inches; the length of the log is 16 feet; the depth of the fire scar at the large end is 6 inches and it extends up the log for a distance of 5 feet. Within the right cylinder and slab, the length of the scar is only 4 feet and the depth of the scar is 3 inches (taper 4 inches in diameter or 2 inches in radius, slab 1 inch in radius; depth of scar 6 - 2 - 1 = 3 inches). The log is divided into 4-foot sections (length of scar inside right cylinder and slab) and the scale volume of each 12-inch, 4-foot section is 2, or 20 board feet. It is estimated that this scar takes up between 1/4 and 1/2 of the total volume of the 4-foot section affected. Assuming 1/3 of the volume of the section is lost in sawing around the defect, the deduction would be 1/3 of 20 or 7 board feet, or rounded off to the nearest ten, 1. The gross scale of a 12-inch, 16-foot log is 8, or 80 board feet. The net scale of the log is 8 - 1 = 7, or 70 board feet.

The deduction for fire scar may also be made by the standard rule. In the log shown in views I and K, suppose that L, the length of the scar within the right cylinder and the slab, is 4 feet; a, the depth of the scar within the right cylinder, is 3 inches (6 inches minus 2 inches for radial taper and 1 inch for slabs); and b, the average width of board lost, is 7 inches. The deduction by the standard rule is—(3 x 7 x 4)/15 = 6 board feet, or rounded off to the nearest ten, 1.

The net scale of the log is: 8 - 1 = 7, or 70 board feet, the same as that obtained by the usual method. It will be noticed from view K that sufficient depth was added in determining a to allow for sawing straight boards inside the fire scar and b was merely the average width of board lost. Wormholes, usually occurring on only one side of the log, may be deducted in the same way as a fire scar.

FROST CHECK.—Frost check is a separation of the wood along the tissue which separates the annual rings, or layers. It follows the grain of the wood. If the grain of the wood is straight, the loss from frost check is comparatively small, but if the log is spiral grained, as in view D, figure 17-23, the loss is considerably greater. The defective part is deducted as a piece whose base is a sector of the cross section of the log. Assume that the log shown in view D is 12-inches at the small end and 16-feet long, and that the affected wood takes up 12 inches of the 50 inches circumference at the large end, or approximately 1/4 of 8 = 2. The net scale of the log would be 8 - 2 = 6, or 60 board feet.

If the frost check enters the log only part way, just the affected part of the sector is deducted. Suppose that the frost check in the log of view D, figure 17-23, had penetrated only 2 inches into the log. The solid core inside the log would have a diameter of 12 - (2 x 2) inches = 12 - 4 = 8 inches inside bark at the small end. The scale of an 8-inch, 16-foot log is 3. The volume of a collar 2 inches thick is, therefore, 8 (scale of 12-in., 16-foot log) minus 3 (scale of 8-in., 16-foot log) equals 5, or 50 board feet. Only 1/4 of this was affected; hence, the deduction is 1/4 of 50, or 12 1/2 board feet, or rounded off to the nearest ten, 1. The net scale of the log would be: 8 - 1 = 7, or 70 board

feet. If the check had spiraled all the way around the tree, the net scale would be the scale of a log inside the check, or 30 board feet.

Where the check extends only part way up the log, the deduction is first made on the basis of a short section including the length of the check. The deduction is then subtracted from the gross volume of the whole log. Lightning scars are treated in the same way as frost checks in scaling.

PUNKY SAPWOOD.—Deduction for punky or broken-down sapwood is made by reducing the diameter inside bark at the small end of the log by twice the radial depth of the defect. A log containing this defect is shown in view F, figure 17-23. Suppose that the log illustrated is 12 inches in diameter inside bark at the small end and 16 feet long, with a gross scale of 8, or 80 board feet. In addition, suppose the sapwood is defective for a depth of 2 inches all around the log. The log is scaled as an 8-inch (12 - 2 x 2 = 8), 16-foot log, having a scale of 3, or 30 board feet. If cull logs are all those whose net scale is less than 50 percent of the gross scale, this log would be cull.

WIND CHECKS.—Deduction for wind checks is made by reducing the small end diameter as for punky sapwood, except that only one-half of the average radial length of check is used as the radial depth of defect. This is due to the fact that the loss from this type of defect is not nearly so great further in the log as it is at the surface. A log with wind checks is illustrated in view H, figure 17-23. Let us assume that the log in view H is 12 inches in diameter inside bark at the small end, is 16 feet long, has a gross scale of 8, or 80 board feet, and has wind checks all around the log entering the log to an average depth of 2 inches. Half the average length of check is 1 inch. The log is scaled as a 10-inch (12 - 2 x 1 = 10), 16-foot log, having a scale of 6, or 60 board feet.

CROOK.—In making deductions for crook or sweep, all the crook or sweep is thrown into the small end of the log and deduction is made from this top half. A right cylinder is drawn with a diameter equal to the small end of the log, but with a length parallel to the lower half of the log. Deductions are made for the part of this right cylinder falling outside the log. A log with a crook is shown in view J, figure 17-23. We will assume that the log in view J has a diameter at the small end of 12 inches and a length of 16 feet. We will also assume that the outside edge of the right cylinder falls 4 inches outside of the outer edge of the log at the small end. It appears that approximately 1/3 of the upper half of the log is affected by the crook. Some 10- and 12-inch boards can be cut in this affected third, but it appears that about 2/3 of this affected portion will be lost. The gross volume of a 12-inch, 16-foot log is 8, or 80 board feet. The upper half includes 1/2 of 80, or 40 board feet. The affected 1/3 of this upper half contains 1/3 of 40, or 13 board feet. The part lost amounts to 2/3 of the affected portion, or 2/3 of 13 = 8 board feet, which, when rounded off to the nearest 10 board feet, gives a deduction of 1. The net scale of the log is: 8 - 1 = 7, or 70 board feet. While this method sounds complicated on paper, an experienced scaler carries on all these calculations in his head while looking at the log and has no difficulty at all in making the deduction rapidly.

CROTCH.—Deduction for crotch in scaling logs is illustrated in view L, figure 17-23. Note that the piece lost due to the crotch is indicated in the illustration. It is taken out as a rectangle by the standard rule. At times the diameter of the log inside bark is measured below the swelling caused by the crotch. Frequently, however, the diameter below the swelling is not actually measured but is computed by subtracting a taper allowance from the diameter inside bark at the large end of the log.

Assume that the log shown in view L has a diameter inside bark below the swelling of 12 inches and a length of 16 feet, with a gross scale of 8, or 80 board feet. Assume, too, that the thickness lost inside the right cylinder and slab, a, is 5 inches; that the average width of the board lost inside the right cylinder and slab, b, is 11 inches; and that the length of the crotch is 3 feet, which will be called 4 feet if off-length boards are not merchantable. By the standard rule the deduction is—(5 x 11 x 4)/15 = 15 board feet, or rounded off to the nearest ten, 1. The net scale is 8 - 1 = 7, or 70 board feet.

Deductions for Defect Board Feet, Using the International 1/4-Inch Rule

In scaling logs by the international 1/4-inch log rule (table 17-3) the procedure is like that for the Scribner decimal C rule, with only such modifications as required by the differences in construction of the two rules. Since there is a deduction of 1/16 inch for shrinkage, in addition to the 1/4-inch saw kerf deduction, the standard rule for defect deductions becomes $(a \times b \times L)/16$, in which a is the thickness or depth of the defect, in inches, b is the width of the defect, in inches, and L is the length of the defect, in feet. This rule is amply generous in its allowance for defect, and it is not desirable to add 1 inch to these dimensions for sawing around the defect. This applies especially to a circular defect for which the standard rule becomes—$(D^2 \times L)/16$, in which D is the average diameter of the defect in inches, and L is the length of the defect in feet. Since the international 1/4-inch rule allows for a taper of 1/2 inch per 4 feet of length, the diameters of any defect appearing at both ends of the log should be averaged in obtaining D, regardless of the length of the log.

Unlike the Scribner decimal C rule, the international 1/4-inch rule does not set up a right cylinder outside of which no deductions should be made. Instead, it sets up a cone frustum (a cone with its top cut off by a plane parallel to the base). The top diameter of the frustum is the top diameter inside bark of the log, and the frustum has a uniform taper of 1/2 inch for every 4 feet of log length. A collar of 1 inch in radial thickness is allowed for slabs within this frustum. Any defect or part of a defect falling outside the cone frustum or its slab collar is disregarded in scaling by the international 1/4-inch log rule. In conformity with the method of constructing the rule, all deductions for defect are rounded off to the nearest 5 board feet.

TRAILER-MOUNTED FIELD SAW

The trailer-mounted field saw is portable and self-contained for field construction use. It has an all-steel chassis on a single axle and is moved about with the aid of a tongue-type drawbar. It is very easy to set-up with its retractable landing jack and standard lunette ring. The trailer-mounted field saw is usually used at remote bases. (A carpenter shop can be installed at a more permanent base.)

One of the machines that you may have an opportunity to operate is shown in figure 17-24. This particular trailer-mounted field saw is 168 inches long and 78 inches wide, thereby making it easy to store or maneuver. If necessary, you can fabricate 4 x 15 x variable length structural and finished lumber on this saw. The

Table 17-3.—Board Feet Content by the International 1/4-Inch Log Rule

Diameter (inches)	Length (feet)												
	8	9	10	11	12	13	14	15	16	17	18	19	20
	Contents (bd ft) in tens												
6............	10	10	10	10	15	15	15	20	20	20	25	25	25
7............	10	15	15	15	20	20	25	25	30	30	35	35	40
8............	15	20	20	25	25	30	35	35	40	40	45	50	50
9............	20	25	30	30	35	40	45	45	50	55	60	65	70
10............	30	35	35	40	45	50	55	60	65	70	75	80	85
11............	35	40	45	50	55	65	70	75	80	85	95	100	105
12............	45	50	55	65	70	75	85	90	95	105	110	120	125
13............	55	60	70	75	85	90	100	105	115	125	135	140	150
14............	65	70	80	90	100	105	115	125	135	145	155	165	175
15............	75	85	95	105	115	125	135	145	160	170	180	190	205
16............	85	95	110	120	130	145	155	170	180	195	205	220	235
17............	95	110	125	135	150	165	180	190	205	220	235	250	265
18............	110	125	140	155	170	185	200	215	230	250	265	280	300
19............	125	140	155	175	190	205	225	245	260	280	300	315	335
20............	135	155	175	195	210	230	250	270	290	310	330	350	370
21............	155	175	195	215	235	255	280	300	320	345	365	390	410
22............	170	190	215	235	260	285	305	330	355	380	405	430	455
23............	185	210	235	260	285	310	335	360	390	415	445	470	495
24............	205	230	255	285	310	340	370	395	425	455	485	515	545
25............	220	250	280	310	340	370	400	430	460	495	525	560	590
26............	240	275	305	335	370	400	435	470	500	535	570	605	640
27............	260	295	330	365	400	435	470	505	540	580	615	655	690
28............	280	320	365	395	430	470	505	545	585	625	665	705	745
29............	305	345	385	425	465	505	545	590	630	670	715	755	800
30............	325	370	410	455	495	540	585	630	675	720	765	810	555
31............	350	395	440	485	530	580	625	675	720	770	820	870	915
32............	375	420	470	520	570	620	670	720	770	820	875	925	980
33............	400	450	500	555	605	660	715	765	820	875	930	985	1,045
34............	425	480	535	590	645	700	760	815	870	930	990	1,050	1,110
35............	450	510	565	625	685	745	805	865	925	990	1,050	1,115	1,175
36............	475	540	600	665	725	790	855	920	980	1,045	1,115	1,180	1,245
37............	505	570	635	700	770	835	905	970	1,040	1,110	1,175	1,245	1,315
38............	535	605	670	740	810	885	955	1,025	1,095	1,170	1,245	1,315	1,390
39............	565	635	710	785	855	930	1,005	1,080	1,155	1,235	1,310	1,390	1,465
40............	595	670	750	825	900	980	1,060	1,140	1,220	1,300	1,380	1,460	1,540

117.227

trailer-mounted field saw shown in figure 17-25 is outfitted with a 16-inch circular saw, a 15 x 48 inch wooden-top saw, and two 15 x 60 inch folding-type roller conveyors with adjustable support legs. This trailer-mounted field saw is designed to aid you in all rough and finish work activities. If any problem arises, check the appropriate manufacturer's manual or consult the petty officer in charge.

Good housekeeping around the saw is very important. Many a man has tripped over the crop end of a board and has fallen into a saw.

Loose clothing should not be worn around the saw. Gloves should NOT be worn while operating the saw. Workmen handling lumber should wear heavy aprons and leather gloves or other suitable hand protection. Goggles should be

133.403
Figure 17-24.—Trailer-mounted field saw.

133.404

Figure 17-25.—Trailer-mounted field saw in operation.

worn while doing work where dust or flying chips are a hazard to the eyes. All workmen handling wood blocks, boards, bundles of shingles, etc., should wear safety shoes or safety-toe clips. Sharp tools should be transported in carrying cases, or with sheathes installed over the cutting edges.

When operating the power saw, the hands should always be kept out of the line of saw travel. Work should not be carried on outdoors during periods of high wind and storms of sufficient violence to endanger workmen, except in case of emergency.

CHAPTER 18
PAINTS AND PRESERVATIVES

Painting is an expensive procedure, involving hours of time preparing the surface and applying the paint. The paint, itself, is expensive—not to mention the brushes, sprayers, respirators, and other associated equipment.

Every petty officer should see that each job of painting is done properly so that the best possible use is made of time, equipment, and material and so that it is not necessary to re-do a job before it would normally be required. Any time thus saved can be well spent training the men to use the advanced and often intricate equipment essential to modern warfare.

PURPOSES OF PAINTING

To employ paint materials and painting man-hours effectively and economically, the fundamental purposes of painting must be borne in mind. The importance of each of these purposes depends, of course, on the particular surface which is to be painted. Following is a brief discussion of each of these fundamental purposes of painting.

PREVENTIVE MAINTENANCE

The primary purpose of painting is protection. This is provided initially with new construction and maintained by a sound and progressive preventive maintenance program.

Resistance to moisture from rain, snow, ice, and condensation constitutes perhaps the greatest single protective characteristic of paint. All things made of metal corrode. Moisture causes wood to swell, warp, and rot. Interior wall finishes of buildings are ruined by neglect of exterior surfaces. Porous masonry is attacked and destroyed by moisture. Paint films must therefore be as impervious to moisture as possible to provide a protective waterproof film over the surface to which applied. Paint also acts as a protective film against attack by acids, alkalies, or marine organisms.

HABITABILITY

Habitability of ships has become of prime interest to the Navy, and scientific tests have proved that, correctly used, painted color on interior surfaces has a soothing effect on the nervous system. The same of course applies to building on shore establishments. A compartment or room painted in pastel tints is more pleasant to live in than a room painted a brilliant red or orange. It can be readily seen that the function paint extends further than merely material protection.

Painting is used as a sanitary measure. A smooth, washable, painted surface which can be cleaned easily, helps produce a clean and healthful atmosphere. Therefore, a painted compartment or room is a healthier place to live in than one that is unpainted.

Another purpose of paint is to reflect light. Used in the interior, light-colored paints reflect and distribute both natural and artificial light, and thus help secure maximum efficiency from the lighting system. Correct illumination helps you to do your job better and easier.

IDENTIFICATION

Another purpose of colored paint is the identification of objects. Red is used to identify firefighting equipment; yellow means caution; green means safety.

PAINTS

The term PAINT is broadly applied to any mixture designed to be spread on a surface in liquid form and to "dry" to a thin, permanent surface coating. By general custom, however, the term PAINT is often restricted to materials containing pigments and designed to obscure the underlying substrata. Oil paint consists of pigments dispersed in a drying oil—usually linseed oil. ENAMELS are paints designed to resist scrubbing and washings. (Enamels are obtainable in flat, semi-gloss and gloss.)

VARNISH is distinguished from paint by the fact that it contains little or no pigment, and is not designed to obscure the surface to which it is applied. OIL varnishes are usually a combination of drying oil with a synthetic resin. When the resin is glyceryl phthalate, the varnish is referred to as an ALKYD VARNISH. SPIRIT VARNISHES are made by dissolving a resin, usually SHELLAC in alcohol.

LACQUERS, which may be clear or pigmented, consist of a cellulose derivative, commonly nitrocellulose, dissolved in a suitable solvent.

Paints which are applied to bare wood or metal surfaces to form undercoats for subsequent coats are called PRIMERS. The most common primers for metal surfaces contain anticorrosive pigments, such as RED LEAD, ZINC DUST, or ZINC CHROMATE. Usually primers for wood are specially formulated to adhere to the wood and to form a good surface for top coats. Paints designed to resist weather and sunlight are called EXTERIOR or OUTSIDE paints; paints not primarily so designed are called INTERIOR or INSIDE paints. Paints which dry to a dull finish are called FLAT paints; paints which dry to a shiny finish are called GLOSS paints; paints with an intermediate surface are called EGGSHELL or SEMI-GLOSS paints.

Paints are composed of various ingredients such as: PIGMENT; NONVOLATILE VEHICLE or BINDER; and SOLVENT or THINNER.

PIGMENTS are insoluble solids, divided finely enough to remain suspended in the vehicle for a considerable time after thorough stirring or shaking. There are several types of pigments.

OPAQUE pigments give the paint its hiding or covering capacity, and contribute other properties. The commonest opaque pigments are WHITE LEAD, ZINC OXIDE, and TITANIUM DIOXIDE.

COLOR pigments give the paint its color. This may be inorganic, such as CHROME GREEN, CHROME YELLOW, or IRON OXIDE; or ORGANIC, such as TOLUIDINE RED or PHTHALOCYANINE BLUE.

TRANSPARENT or EXTENDER pigments contribute bulk, and also control the application properties, durability, and resistance to abrasion of the coating.

MISCELLANEOUS pigments; there are many other pigments that are used for a variety of special purposes. Some of these pigments are;

anticorrosive—metallic zinc dust; safety markings—luminous; and heat resistant—aluminum.

The VEHICLE, or BINDER, of paint is the material that holds the pigment together and also adheres to the surface. In general, the durability of the paint is determined by the resistance of the binder to the exposure conditions.

Formerly, linseed oil was the commonest binder, and it is still used in certain paints. It has however, largely been superseded by various synthetic resins. ALKYD resins are the commonest. These are made by the reaction of glyceryl phthalate and an oil, and may be made with almost any properties desired. Other common synthetic resins, which may be used by themselves or mixed with oil, include PHENOLICS, VINYLS, EPOXIES, URETHANES, POLYESTERS, CHLORINATED RUBBER, etc. Each has its own advantages and disadvantages. It is particularly important in the newer materials that the manufacturer's instructions be followed implicitly.

Certain synthetic materials, called LATEXES, are dispersed in water. Paints made from these are useful because they can be applied to damp surfaces, and tools and spills may be cleaned up easily with water. They have extremely high alkali resistance, and many have excellent durability. They are particularly useful for plaster and masonry surfaces. There are many different chemicals involved in latexes, but the commonest are STYRENE-BUTADIENE (or "synthetic rubber"), POLYVINYL ACETATE ("PVA" or "VINYL"), and ACRYLIC. All are very similar in their performance.

Other common binders are portland cement (in a dry-powder form to be mixed with water) and bituminous material (usually asphalt or coal-tar).

The only purpose of a SOLVENT is to adjust the consistency of the material so that it may be applied readily to the surface. The solvent then evaporates, contributing nothing further to the film. For this reason the cheapest SUITABLE solvent should be used. The solvents most used are MINERAL SPIRITS and NAPTHA. TURPENTINE is sometimes used, but contributes little that other solvents do not, and costs much more. Many synthetic resins require a special solvent, and it is IMPORTANT THAT THE CORRECT ONE BE USED, otherwise the paint may be entirely spoiled. Cement paints usually use water as a solvent.

STORAGE OF MATERIALS

Navy paints, except cement-water paints are usually provided ready-mixed in 1-gal, 5-gal, and 55-gal containers. Large quantities of paint in 1-gal and 5-gal containers should be stored in enclosures with fireproof walls; small quantities should be stored in properly constructed storage cabinets. Metal cabinets should be used if available; if not, cabinets should be constructed of asbestos-cement board not less than 5/32 in. thick. Bottoms and sides should be double thickness, with a 1 1/2-in. air space between the boards. Doors should also be of double thickness, with raised sills 2 in. above the bottoms of the cabinets. Doors should be provided with suitable locks, and a door should be kept closed and locked whenever paint is not being taken from or stored in the cabinet. All doors should be marked DANGER! FLAMMABLE! KEEP FLAME AND EXCESSIVE HEAT AWAY.

All mixed paint must be stored in nearly filled, tightly sealed containers, to prevent skinning over, the loss by evaporation of volatile materials, and the danger of fire.

Paint in storage should be arranged so that the oldest paint of each type is the first available. If old paint must be used with new paint, the entire lot should be blended to ensure uniform gloss and color.

The amount and kinds of EQUIPMENT available will depend on the shop to which you are assigned. This equipment may include either a paint spray outfit of 5-gallon capacity, or a lightweight, portable, 1-quart capacity sprayer, driven either by air or electrically. The equipment may also include a paint mixer of the type used with a portable electric or pneumatic drill, and respirators of the chemical-cartridge or mechanical-filter type. The number and types of brushes available also will vary.

You will have to use your own judgment as to the number of brushes to be kept available for daily use. The equipment should include a stencil-cutting machine with supplies and several sets of metal stenciling letters. (Incidentally, the paper used in stencil-cutting machines is referred to as stencilboard.)

This equipment must be properly maintained to prolong its life and to derive best results from its use. Before new paint brushes are used they should be rinsed with thinner. This tightens the bristles and also removes those which are loose. Brushes should not be soaked in water to tighten the bristles as this will cause the metal ferrule to rust or split due to the swelling of the wooden handle. Brushes that are to be reused the following day should be marked for white, light colors, or dark colors. Excess paint should be removed with thinner and the brushes suspended by the handle with the bristles immersed in thinner or linseed oil to just below the bottom of the ferrule. The weight of the brush must not rest on the bristles as that will cause them to become distorted. Brushes that are not to be reused immediately should be carefully cleaned with thinner, of the type recommended by the manufacturer, washed thoroughly with soap and water, then rinsed. A protective cover and preservative should be applied when appropriate. They should be stored suspended from racks or laid flat.

To clean a frozen brush, soak it in a solvent-type, nonflammable paint and varnish remover, squeeze and scrape the softened paint out of the bristles, and then clean the brush with thinner as previously described.

The spraying equipment used by the Navy is of very high quality and will give excellent service for years if it is given proper care. Most frequent causes of unsatisfactory operation are faulty assembly, improper adjustment, and clogging because of dirt or hardened paint. Spray equipment should be cleaned with an appropriate thinner after each job or at the end of each day.

The paint supply hose should be disconnected from the tank and a container of thinner connected. Pulling the trigger will force the thinner through the paint hose and gun, which cleans out the paint remaining in them. The gun should be taken apart and each part cleaned. Care should be taken not to soak the packing or lubricated parts with thinner, as this will remove the lubricant and cause the packing to become hard. The paint tank should also be cleaned with thinner and wiped dry. All the equipment should be stored in its assigned place. The air and paint hoses should always be coiled before being stored.

The paint-mixing attachment should be removed from the electric or pneumatic drill and cleaned with thinner. The attachment should be removed prior to cleaning, because thinner will cause deterioration of the electric motor. Respirators used in spray-painting should be thoroughly cleaned with thinner after being used, to remove the accumulation of paint. They should then be wiped with a light soap and water solution to remove the thinner, wiped with clear fresh water, and thoroughly dried. If left damp, the metal parts will rust and the rubber will deteriorate.

It is advisable to wipe each respirator with a diluted disinfectant solution, since more than one individual may wear it. The filters or chemical cartridges should be removed and checked after each use and renewed when necessary. Do not use paint remover to clean the respirator, paint hose, mixer, or spray gun, as the corrosive agent contained in the remover will cause deterioration of this equipment.

BRUSHES

Brushes, as any other tools, must be of first quality and maintained in perfect working condition at all times. Brushes are identified, first, by the type of bristle used. Brushes are made with either natural, synthetic or mixed bristles. Chinese hog bristles represent the finest of the natural bristles because of their length, durability and resiliency. Hog bristle has one unique characteristic in that the bristle end forks out like a tree branch. This "flagging" permits more paint to be carried on the brush and leaves finer brush marks on the applied coating which flow together more readily resulting in a smoother finish. Horsehair bristles are used in cheap brushes and are a very unsatisfactory substitute. The ends do not flag, the bristles quickly become limp, they hold far less paint and do not spread it as well. Brush marks left in the applied coating tend to be coarse and do not level out as smoothly. Some brushes contain a mixture of hog bristle and horsehair, and their quality depends upon the percentage of each type used. Animal hair is utilized in very fine brushes for special purposes. Badger hair, for example, produces a particularly good varnish brush. Squirrel and sable are ideal for striping, lining, lettering and free-hand art brushes. Of the synthetics, nylon is by far the most common. By artificially "exploding" the ends and kinking the fibres, manufacturers have increased the paint load nylon can carry, and have reduced the coarseness of brush marks. Nylon is steadily replacing hog bristle because of the difficulties in importing the latter. Nylon is almost always superior to horsehair. The very fact that nylon is a synthetic makes it unsuitable for applying lacquer, shellac, many creosote products and some other coatings that would soften or dissolve

the bristles. Because water does not cause any appreciable swelling of nylon bristles, they are especially recommended for use with latex paints. Brushes are further identified by types, that is, the variety of shapes and sizes as are required for specific painting jobs. Types can be classified as follows: (See figs. 18-1 and 18-2.)

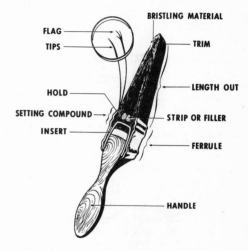

3.210(133F)A
Figure 18-1.—Typical paint brush.

1. WALL BRUSHES: Flat, square-edged brushes ranging in widths from 3" to 6" and used for painting large, continuous surfaces, either interior or exterior.

2. SASH AND TRIM BRUSHES: Available in four shapes, flat square-edged, flat angle-edged, round and oval. These brushes range in width from 1 1/2" to 3" or diameters of 1/2" to 2" and are used for painting window frames, sash, narrow boards, also interior and exterior trim surfaces. For fine-line painting, the edge of the brush is often chisel-shaped to make precise edging easier to accomplish.

3. ENAMELING AND VARNISH BRUSHES: Flat square-edged or chisel-edged brushes available in widths from 2" to 3". The select, fine bristles are comparatively shorter in length to cause relatively high viscosity gloss finishes to lay down in a smooth, even film.

4. STUCCO and MASONRY BRUSHES: These have the general appearance of flat wall brushes and are available in widths ranging from 5" to 6". Bristles can be of hog, other

WALL BRUSH

STUCCO BRUSH

FLATTING
WALL BRUSH

OVAL AND SEMI-OVAL
PAINT AND VARNISH BRUSHES

FLAT VARNISH BRUSH

FLAT SASH
AND TRIM BRUSH

ANGULAR SASH
AND TRIM BRUSH

ENAMELING BRUSH

OVAL SASH BRUSH

DUSTER

3.210(133F)B

Figure 18-2.—Types of brushes.

natural bristle or nylon; the latter is preferred for rough surfaces because of its resistance to abrasion.

Use the right size brush for the job. Avoid a brush that is too small or too large. The latter is particularly important. A large-area job does not necessarily go faster with an over-size brush. If the brush size is out of balance for the type of painting being done, the user tends to apply the coating at an uneven rate, general workmanship declines, and the applicator actually tires faster because of the extra output required per stroke. Synthetic fibre brushes are ready to use when received. The performance of natural bristle brushes is very much improved by a previous 48 hour soak in linseed oil followed by a thorough cleaning in mineral spirits. This process makes the bristles more flexible and serves to swell the bristles in the ferrule of the brush resulting in a better grip so that fewer bristles are apt to work loose when the brush is used.

ROLLERS

A paint roller consists of a cylindrical sleeve or cover which slips on to a rotatable cage to which a handle is attached. (See fig. 18-3.) The cover may be 1 1/2" to 2 1/4" inside diameter, and usually 3", 4", 7" and 9" in length. Special rollers are available in lengths from 1 1/2" to 18". Proper roller application depends on the selection of the specific fabric

and the thickness of fabric (nap length) based on the type of paint used and the smoothness or roughness of the surface to be painted. Special rollers are used for painting pipes, fences and other hard-to-reach areas. (See figs. 18-4 and 18-5.) The fabrics generally used for rollers are lambs wool, mohair, dynel, dacron and rayon.

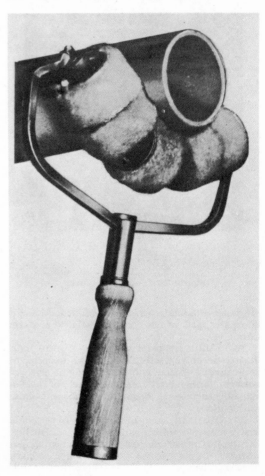

29.140(133F)B
Figure 18-4.—Pipe roller.

LAMBS WOOL (pelt) is the most solvent resistant type of material used and is available in nap lengths up to 1 1/4". It is recommended for synthetic finishes for application on

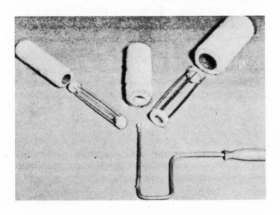

29.140(133F)A
Figure 18-3.—Parts of a roller

29.140(133F)C
Figure 18-5.—Fence roller.

semi-smooth and rough surfaces. It mats badly in water, and is not recommended for water paints.

MOHAIR is made primarily of Angora hair. It also is solvent resistant and is supplied in 3/16 and 1/4 inch nap length. It is recommended for synthetic enamels and for use on smooth surfaces. It can be used with water paints also.

DYNEL is a modified acrylic fibre which has excellent resistance to water. It is best for application of conventional water paints and solvent paints, except those which contain strong solvents, such as ketones. It is available in all nap lengths from 1/4" to 1 1/4".

DACRON is a synthetic fibre which is somewhat softer than DYNEL. It is best suited for exterior oil or latex paints. It is available in nap lengths from 5/16" to 1/2".

RAYON fabric is not recommended because of the poor results generally obtained from its use. Furthermore, rayon mats badly in water. Table 18-1 can be used as a guide for choosing the proper roller cover.

Immediately after use, rollers should be cleaned with the type of thinner recommended for the paint in which the roller was used. After cleaning with thinner, the roller should be thoroughly washed in soap and water, rinsed in clear water, and dried.

SPRAY GUNS

A spray gun is a precision tool that mixes air under pressure with paint, breaks it up into spray, and ejects it out in a controlled pattern.

There are several types, either with a container attached to the gun or with the gun connected to a separate container by means of hoses. There are bleeder or non-bleeder, external- or internal-mix, and pressure-, gravity-, or suction-feed guns.

The BLEEDER type of gun is one in which air is allowed to leak—or bleed—from some part of the gun in order to prevent air pressure from building up in the air hose. In this type of gun the trigger controls the fluid only. It is generally used with small air compressing outfits that have no pressure control on the air line.

The NONBLEEDER gun is equipped with an air valve which shuts off the air when the trigger is released. It is used with compressing outfits having a pressure-controlling device.

An EXTERNAL-MIX gun is one which mixes air and paint outside and in front of the gun's air cap. This type of gun can do a wide variety of work and has the power to throw a very fine spray, even of heavy material. It also permits exact control over the spray pattern. An external-mix air cap is shown in figure 18-6.

An INTERNAL-MIX spray gun mixes the air and fluid inside the air cap as pictured in figure 18-7. It is not as widely used as the external-mix gun.

In a SUCTION-FEED spray gun, the air cap, shown in figure 18-8, is designed to draw the fluid from the container by suction—in somewhat the same way that an insect spray gun operates. The suction-feed spray gun is usually used with 1-quart (or smaller) containers.

A PRESSURE-FEED gun operates by air pressure, which forces the fluid from the container into the gun. This is the type (fig. 18-9) used for large-scale painting.

Table 18-1.—Roller Selection Guide

Type of Paint	*Type of Surface* Smooth (1)	Semi-smooth (2)	Rough (3)
Aluminum	C	A	A
Enamel or Semigloss (Alkyd)	A or B	A	
Enamel undercoat	A or B	A	
Epoxy coatings	B or D	D	D
Exterior House Paint:			
Latex for wood	C	A	
Latex for masonry	A	A	A
Oil or alkyd—wood	C	A	
Oil or alkyd—masonry	A	A	A
Floor enamel—all types	A or B	A	
Interior Wall paint:			
Alkyd or oil	A	A or D	A
Latex	A	A	A
Masonry sealer	B	A or D	A or D
Metal primers	A	A or D	
Varnish—all types	A or B		

*Roller Cover Key**	*Nap Length* (inches)		
A—Dynel (modified acrylic)	¼-⅜	⅜-¾	1-1¼
B—Mohair	3/16-¼		
C—Dacron polyester	¼-⅜	½	
D—Lambswool pelt	¼-⅜	½-¾	1-1¼

(1) Smooth Surface: hardboard, smooth metal, smooth plaster, drywall, etc.

(2) Semi-smooth Surface: sand finished plaster and drywall, light stucco, blasted metal, semi-smooth masonry.

(3) Rough Surface: concrete or cinder block, brick, heavy stucco, wire fence.

* Comprehensive product standards do not exist in the Paint Roller Industry. Roller covers vary significantly in performance between manufacturers and most manufacturers have more than one quality level in the same generic class. This table is based on field experience with first line products of one manufacturer.

133.409

PARTS OF THE SPRAY GUN

The two main assemblies of the spray gun are the gun body assembly and the spray head assembly. Each of these assemblies is a collection of small parts, all of which are designed to do specific jobs.

The principal parts of the gun body assembly are shown in figure 18-10. The air valve controls the supply of air and is operated by the trigger. The spreader adjustment valve regulates the amount of air that is supplied to the spreader horn holes of the air cap, thus varying the paint pattern. It is fitted with a dial which can be set to give the pattern desired. The fluid needle adjustment controls the amount of spray material that passes through the gun. The spray head locking bolt locks the gun body and the removable spray head together.

Most guns are now fitted with a removable spray head assembly. This type has many advantages. It can be cleaned more easily, it permits quick change of the head when you want to use a new color or material, and, if it is damaged, a new head can be put on the old gun body.

The principal parts of the spray head assembly are the air cap, the fluid tip, fluid needles, and spray head barrel, pictured in figure 18-11.

The fluid tip regulates the flow of the spray material into the air stream. The tip encloses the end of the fluid needle. The spray head barrel is the housing which encloses the head mechanism.

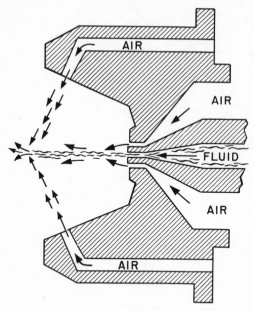

80.233

Figure 18-6.—An external-mix air cap.

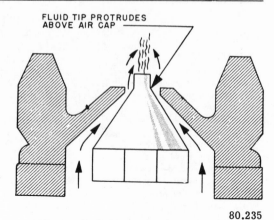

FLUID TIP PROTRUDES ABOVE AIR CAP

80.235

Figure 18-8.—A suction-feed air cap.

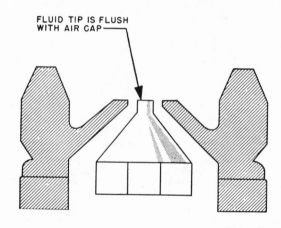

FLUID TIP IS FLUSH WITH AIR CAP

80.236

Figure 18-9.—A pressure-feed air cap.

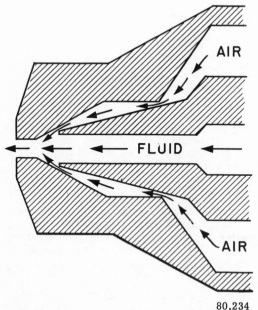

80.234

Figure 18-7.—An internal-mix air cap.

LUBRICATION OF THE SPRAY GUN

Your spray gun also needs lubrication. The fluid needle packing should be removed occasionally and softened with oil. The fluid needle spring should be coated with grease or petrolatum. Figure 18-12 shows where these parts are and also the oil holes in which you occasionally should put a few drops of light oil.

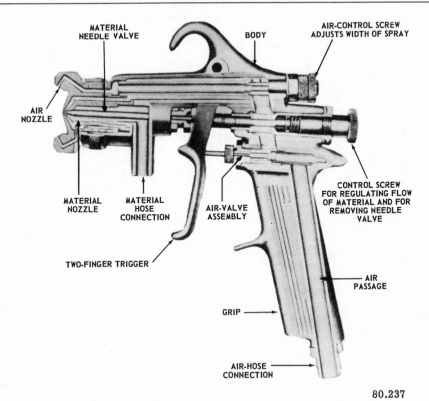

80.237

Figure 18-10.—Cross section of a spray gun.

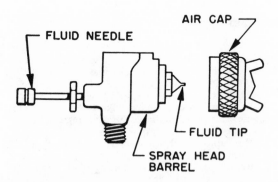

80.238

Figure 18-11.—Principal parts of
the spray head.

SURFACE PREPARATION FOR PAINTING

Proper surface preparation is an essential part of any paint job; paint will not adhere well, provided the required surface protection, or present a good appearance unless the surface has been properly treated. Surface preparation consists of (1) thorough cleaning of the surface, and (2) such mechanical or chemical pretreatment as may be necessary.

FERROUS METALS

CLEANING the ferrous metals (iron and steel) involves the removal of oil, grease, and dirt using one of the cleaners described in Military Specification MIL-C-490, Grade II. This specification describes three types of

515

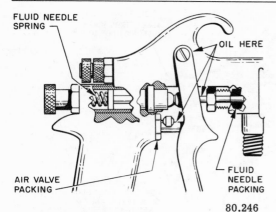

FLUID NEEDLE SPRING

OIL HERE

AIR VALVE PACKING

FLUID NEEDLE PACKING

80.246

Figure 18-12.—Lubrication points of
a spray gun.

ferrous-metal cleaners: Type 2, a HOT ALKA-LINE cleaner; Type 3, a SOLVENT cleaner, and Type 4, an EMULSION cleaner.

PRETREATMENT of the ferrous metals involves the application of a pretreatment coating conforming to Military Specification MIL-C-15328, COATING, PRETREATMENT, METAL FORMULA #117. If a red lead or zinc chromate primer is to be used, however, the pretreatment coating is omitted.

NONFERROUS METALS

The nonferrous metals are brass, bronze, copper, tin, zinc, aluminum, nickel, and other metals which are not derived from iron ore. A galvanized metal is one which has a zinc-coated surface; galvanized metals are therefore treated as non-ferrous metals for painting purposes.

Nonferrous metals are cleaned with a solvent-type cleaner and pretreated by coating with pretreatment coating, metal formula #117.

CONCRETE AND MASONRY

In Navy construction, concrete and masonry are normally not painted unless painting is required for damp-proofing. Cleaning concrete and masonry involves the removal of dirt, mildew and EFFLORESCENCE (a white, powdery, crystalline deposit which often forms on concrete and masonry surfaces).

Dirt and fungus are removed by washing with a solution of TRISODIUM PHOSPHATE; the strength of the solution may vary from 2 oz to 8 oz of trisodium phosphate per gal of water,

depending upon the amount of dirt and/or mildew on the surface. Immediately after washing, rinse off all the trisodium phosphate with clear water. If oil paint is to be used, allow the surface to dry thoroughly before painting.

For efflorescence, first remove as much as possible of the deposit by dry-brushing with a wire brush or a stiff fiber brush. Next, wet the surface thoroughly with clear water, and then scrub with a stiff brush dipped in a 5 percent solution (by weight) of muriatic acid. Allow the acid solution to remain on the surface about 3 minutes before scrubbing, but rinse thoroughly with clear water IMMEDIATELY AFTER scrubbing. Work on small areas, not larger than 4 sq ft in size. Wear rubber gloves, a rubber apron, and goggles when mixing and using the acid solution. In mixing the acid, ALWAYS add acid to water, rather than water to acid.

For a very heavy deposit, the acid solution may be increased to 10 percent and it may be allowed to remain on the surface for 5 minutes before scrubbing.

All defects in a concrete or masonry surface must be repaired before painting. To repair a large crack, cut the crack out to an inverted-V shape and plug it with grout made by mixing 2 or 3 parts of mortar sand, 1 part of portland cement, and enough water to make a putty-like consistency. After the grout sets, damp-cure it by keeping it wet for 48 hours. If oil paint is to be used, allow at least 90 days for weathering before painting over a grout-filled crack.

PLASTER AND WALLBOARD

Whenever possible, new plaster should be aged at least 2 months before painting. Prior to painting, fill all holes and cracks with SPACKLING COMPOUND or PATCHING PLASTER. Cut out the material along the crack or hole in inverted-V shape. To avoid excessive absorption of water from the patching material, wet the edges and bottom of the crack or hole before applying the material. Fill the opening to within 1/4 in. of the surface and allow the material partially to set before you bring the level up flush with the surface. After the material has thoroughly set, smooth it up with fine sandpaper. Allow at least 72 hours for setting before painting. Plaster and wallboard are primed with PRIMER Federal Specification TT-P-56.

WOOD

Prior to painting, a wood surface should be closely inspected for loose boards, defective lumber, protruding nailheads, or any other defects or irregularities. Loose boards should be nailed tight, defective lumber should be replaced, and all nailheads should be countersunk.

A dirty wood surface is cleaned for painting by sweeping, dusting, and washing with solvent or soap and water. When washing wood, take care to avoid excessive wetting, which tends to raise the grain. Wash a small area at a time, and rinse and dry immediately.

Wood which is to be given a NATURAL finish (meaning wood which will not be concealed by an opaque surface coating) may require BLEACHING to a uniform and/or light color. Bleaching is done by applying a solution of 1 lb of OXALIC ACID to 1 gal of hot water. More than one application may be required. After the solution has dried, smooth the surface with fine sandpaper.

Rough wood surfaces must be sanded smooth for painting. Mechanical SANDERS of various types are used for large areas. Hand-sanding of small areas is done by wrapping the sandpaper around a rubber, wood, or metal SANDING BLOCK. For a very rough surface, start with a coarse paper, about No. 2 or 2 1/2; follow up with a No. 1/2, No. 1, or No. 1 1/2; and finish with about a No. 2/0 grit. For fine work, such as furniture work, finish with a still finer grit.

Sap or resin in wood will stain through a coat, or even several coats, of paint. Remove sap or resin by scraping and/or sanding. Knots in resinous wood should be treated with KNOT SEALER, Military Specification MIL-S-12935.

PAINT REMOVERS

Paint and varnish removers generally are used for small areas. Solvent type removers or solvent mixtures are selected according to the type and condition of the old finish as well as the nature of the substrate. Removers are available as flammable or non-flammable types, also liquid or semi-paste in consistency. While most paint removers require scraping or steel wool to physically remove the softened paint, types are available that allow the loosened finish to be flushed off with steam or hot water. Many of the flammable and non-flammable removers contain paraffin wax to retard evaporation. It is absolutely essential that this residue

be removed from the surface prior to painting to prevent loss of adhesion of the applied coating. In such instances, follow the manufacturer's label directions or use mineral spirits to remove any wax residue. As a safety precaution, it should be noted that, while non-flammable removers eliminate fire hazards, they are toxic to a degree (as are all removers). Proper ventilation must be provided whenever they are used.

CONDITIONS, SEALERS, AND FILLERS

Conditioners are often applied on masonry to seal a chalky surface in order to improve adhesion of water-based topcoats. Sealers are used on wood to prevent resin exudation or bleeding. Fillers are used to produce a smooth finish on open grain wood and rough masonry. (See table 18-2.)

Latex (water-thinned) paints do not adhere well to chalky masonry surfaces. To overcome this problem, an oil-based CONDITIONER is applied to the chalky substrate before the latex paint is applied. The entire surface should be vigorously wire brushed by hand or power tools, then dusted to remove all loose particles and chalk residue. The conditioner is then brushed on freely to assure effective penetration and allowed to dry. This surface conditioner is not intended for use as a finish coat.

SEALERS are used on bare wood to prevent resin exudation (bleeding) through applied paint coatings. Freshly exuded resin, while still soft, may be scraped off with a putty knife and the affected area solvent cleaned with alcohol. Hardened resin may be removed by scraping or sanding. Since the sealer is not intended for use as a priming coat, it should be used only when necessary, and applied only over the affected area. When previous paint on pine lumber has become discolored over knots, the sealer should be applied over the old paint before the new paint is applied.

FILLERS are used on porous wood, concrete, and masonry to fill the pores to provide a smoother finish coat.

Wood fillers are used on open-grained hardwoods. In general those hardwoods with pores larger than in birch should be filled. (See table 18-3.) When filling is necessary, it is done after any staining operations. Stain should be allowed to dry for 24 hours before filler is applied. If staining is not warranted, natural

Table 18-2.—Treatment of Various Substrates

| Mechanical | Wood | Metal | | Concrete | Plaster |
		Steel	Other	Masonry	Wallboard
Hand Cleaning	S	S	S	S	S
Power Tool Cleaning	S*	S	......	S	......
Flame Cleaning	......	S	......	......	......
Blast Cleaning:					
Brush-Off	......	S	S	S	......
All Other	......	S	......	......	......
Chemical and Solvent					
Solvent Cleaning	S	S	S	......	......
Alkali Cleaning	......	S	......	S	......
Steam Cleaning	......	S	......	S	......
Acid Cleaning	......	S	......	S	......
Pickling	......	S	......	......	......
Pretreatments					
Hot Phosphate	......	S	......	......	......
Cold Phosphate	......	S	......	......	......
Wash Primers	......	S	S	......	......
Conditioners, Sealers and Fillers					
Conditioners	......	......	......	S	......
Sealers	S	......	......	......	......
Fillers	S	......	......	S	......

S—Satisfactory for use as indicated
*—Sanding only

133.410

(uncolored) filler is applied directly to the bare wood. The filler may be colored with some of the stain in order to accentuate the grain pattern of the wood. To apply, first thin the filler with mineral spirits to a creamy consistency, then liberally brush it across the grain, followed by light brushing along the grain. Allow to stand five to ten minutes until most of the thinner has evaporated, at which time the finish will have lost its glossy appearance. Before it has a chance to set and harden, wipe the filler off ACROSS the grain using burlap or other coarse cloth, rubbing the filler into the pores of the wood while removing the excess. Finish by stroking along the grain with clean rags. It is essential that all excess filler be removed. Knowing when to start wiping is important; wiping too soon will pull the filler out of the pores, while allowing the filler to set too long will make it very difficult to wipe off. A simple test for dryness consists of rubbing a finger across the surface. If a ball is formed, it is time to wipe. If the filler slips under the pressure of the finger, it is still too wet for wiping. Allow the filler to dry for 24 hours before applying finish coats.

Masonry fillers are applied by brush to bare and previously prepared (all loose, powdery, flaking material removed) rough concrete, concrete block, stucco or other masonry surfaces, both new and old. The purpose is to fill the open pores by brushing the filler into the surface to produce a fairly smooth finish. If the voids on the surface are large, it is preferable to apply two coats of filler, rather than one heavy coat, in order to avoid mud-cracking. Allow 1 to 2 hours drying between coats. Allow the final coat to dry for 24 hours before painting.

WEATHER AND TEMPERATURE

Oil-painting and water-painting should not be done in temperatures above 95° or below 45°. Varnishing, shellacking, lacquering, and enameling should not be done in temperatures below 65° or above 95°. No painting except water-painting should be done on a damp surface, or on one which is exposed to hot sunlight.

PAINT MIXING AND CONDITIONING

Most paints used in the Navy are READY-MIXED, meaning that most Navy paints are

Table 18-3.—Characteristics of Wood

Name of Wood	Type .... Soft	Hard		Notes on Finishing
	Grain .... Closed	Open	Closed	
Ash	......	X	......	Requires filler.
Alder	X	......	......	Stains well.
Aspen	......	......	X	Paints well.
Basswood	......	......	X	Paints well.
Beech	......	......	X	Paints poorly; varnishes well.
Birch	......	......	X	Paints and varnishes well.
Cedar	X	......	......	Paints and varnishes well.
Cherry	......	......	X	Varnishes well.
Chestnut	......	X	......	Requires filler; paints poorly.
Cottonwood	......	......	X	Paints well.
Cypress	......	......	X	Paints and varnishes well.
Elm	......	X	......	Requires filler; paints poorly.
Fir	X	......	......	Paints poorly.
Gum	......	......	X	Varnishes well.
Hemlock	X	......	......	Paints fairly well.
Hickory	......	X	......	Requires filler.
Mahogany	......	X	......	Requires filler.
Maple	......	......	X	Varnishes well.
Oak	......	X	......	Requires filler.
Pine	X	......	......	Variable depending on grain.
Teak	......	X	......	Requires filler.
Walnut	......	X	......	Requires filler.
Redwood	X	......	......	Paints well.

Note: Any type finish may be applied unless otherwise specified.

133.411

provided with the ingredients already mixed together in the proper proportions. When oil paints are left in storage for a long while, however, the pigments settle to the bottom, and must be again mixed into the vehicle before the paint is used. This procedure is what is meant by the term "mixing" as used in this section.

MIXING TECHNIQUES

Whenever possible, mix paint in the paint shop. The shop is usually equipped with a mechanical AGITATOR which mixes paint by rapidly shaking the container. In the absence of an agitator, use a strong, smooth, clean wood or metal paddle. If the pigment has settled in a cake, pour the vehicle off into another container and break up the pigment with the paddle. Then pour the vehicle back in, a little at a time, while continuing to work in the pigment. Then BOX the paint by pouring it back and forth from one container to the other. Continue boxing

until the pigment and vehicle form a smooth mixture of uniform consistency and color.

A newly-opened can of ready-mixed paint is usually of the proper consistency for applying. Eventually, however, the paint will thicken as the volatile portion of the thinner evaporates from the open can. When this happens, enough of the appropriate thinner must be added to bring the paint back to working consistency.

The same applies to the drier. When the paint takes longer than it should to dry, the drier has evaporated below the required level, and more drier should be added. Great care must be taken against adding too much drier, however. Paint containing too much drier will dry too rapidly on the surface, which may cause WRINKLING.

Oil paint should be stirred frequently during use, to keep the pigment from settling to the bottom. Varnish and shellac, however, should not be stirred or agitated. Enamel should be mixed with a hand-paddle, not with a shake-type mechanical agitator. A shake-type agitator whips air into enamel, causing it to bubble or froth. Bubbled or frothed enamel must be allowed to stand 6 to 8 hours before it can be used.

CONDITIONING PAINT

When a partially filled can of oil paint is placed in storage, the surface of the paint should be covered with a 1/16-in. layer of the appropriate thinner and the can should be covered as tightly as possible. The layer of thinner will prevent the paint from skinning over, and the tight cover on the can will prevent the thinner from evaporating.

To remove lumps, pieces of skin, or foreign materials from paint, strain the paint through a sieve made of fine wire mesh, silk, or cheesecloth. All paint used in spray guns must be thoroughly strained.

METHODS OF APPLYING PAINT

The most common methods of applying paint are by brush, roller and spray. Dip and flow coat methods are also used but the mechanics of application limit their use to shop work. Of the three designed for field use, brushing is the slowest method, rolling is much faster, and spraying is usually the fastest of all. The choice of method is based on many additional factors such as environment, type of substrate, type of coating to be applied, appearance of finish desired and skill of personnel involved in the operation.

The general surroundings may prohibit the use of spray application because of possible fire hazards or potential damage from overspray. Typical of these are parking lots and open storage areas. Adjacent areas, not to be coated, must be masked when spraying is performed. This results in loss of time and, if extensive, may offset the advantage of the rapidity of spraying operations.

Roller coating is most efficient on large flat surfaces. Corners, edges and odd shapes, however, must be brushed. Spraying also is most suitable for large surfaces, except that it can also be used for round or irregular shapes. Brushing is ideal for small surfaces or for cutting in corners and edges. Dip and flow coat methods are suitable for volume production painting of small items in the shop.

Rapid drying, lacquer type products, e.g., vinyls, should be sprayed. Application of such products by brush or roller may be extremely difficult especially in warm weather or outdoors on breezy days.

Coatings applied by brush may leave brush marks in the dried film; rolling leaves a stippled effect, while spraying yields the smoothest finish, if done properly.

Personnel require the least amount of training to use rollers, and the most training to use spray equipment. The degree of training and experience of personnel will influence the selection of the application method.

BRUSH AND PAINT APPLICATION

Select the type of brush and paint pot needed for the job. The best type of paint pot for brush painting is a 1-gallon paint can from which the lip around the top has been removed. (The lid of the can is fitted to the lip around the top.) you can cut this lip off with a cold chisel. If you leave the lip on the pot, it will fill up with paint as you scrape the brush, and this paint will be continually streaking down the outside of the pot and dripping off.

Dip the brush to only one-third the length of the bristles, and scrape the surplus paint off the lower face of the brush, so there will be no drip as you transfer the brush from the pot to the work.

Here is how to apply paint by brush. For complete coverage, follow the Navy style and first "lay on," then "lay off." Laying on means applying the paint first in long, horizontal strokes. Laying off means crossing your first strokes by working up and down. (See fig. 18-13.)

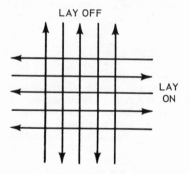

3.212
Figure 18-13.—Laying on and laying off.

By using the laying on and laying off method and crossing your strokes, the paint is distributed evenly over the surface, the surface is completely covered, and a minimum amount of paint is used. A good rule is to "lay on" the paint the shortest distance across the area and "lay off" the longest distance. When painting walls, or any vertical surface, "lay on" in horizontal strokes, "lay off" vertically.

Always paint ceiling first and work from the far corner. By working the ceiling first, you can keep the wall free of drippings by wiping up as you go along.

When painting ceiling surfaces, you will find that paint coats on the ceiling should normally be "lay on" for the shortest ceiling distance and "lay off" for the longest ceiling distance.

To avoid brush marks when finishing up a square, use strokes directed toward the last square finished, gradually lifting the brush near the end of the stroke while the brush is still in motion. Every time the brush touches the painted surface at the start of a stroke, it leaves a mark. For this reason, never finish a square by brushing toward the unpainted area, but always end up by brushing back toward the area already painted.

When painting pipes and stanchions and narrow straps, beams, and angles, lay the paint on diagonally as shown in figure 18-14. Lay off along the long dimension.

Always carry a rag for wiping dripped or smeared paint.

ROLLER METHOD

Pour the pre-mixed paint into the tray to about one-half of the depth of the tray. Immerse the roller completely, then roll it back and forth along the ramp to fill the cover completely and remove any excess paint. As an alternative to using the tray, place a specially designed galvanized wire screen into a five gallon can of the paint. This screen attaches to the can and remains at the correct angle for loading and spreading paint on the roller. (See figs. 18-15 and 18-16.) The first load of paint on a roller should be worked out on newspaper to remove entrapped air from the roller cover. It is then ready for application. As the roller is passed over a surface, thousands of tiny fibres continually compress and expand, metering out the coating and wetting the surface. This is in sharp contrast to other application methods that depends upon the skill and technique

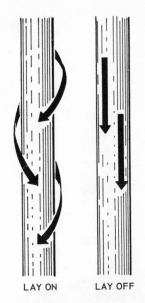

LAY ON   LAY OFF

3.213
Figure 18-14.—Painting pipes and stanchions.

29.140(133F)D
Figure 18-15.—Roller and tray.

of the painter. The uniformity of application by roller is less susceptible to variance in painter ability than other methods. Basic rules must still be followed. Always trim around ceilings, moldings, etc., before rolling the major wall or ceiling surfaces. Then roll as close as possible to maintain the same texture. Trimming is

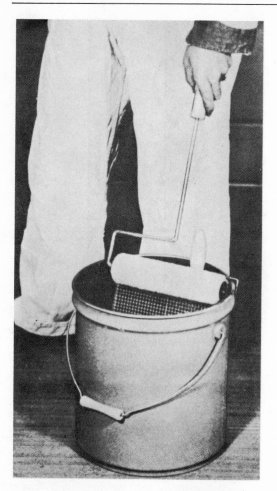

29.140(133F)E
Figure 18-16.—Roller and wire screen
attachment to can.

SPRAY METHOD

Complete instructions for the care, maintenance, and operation of a spray gun are contained in the manufacturer's manual, and these instructions should be carefully followed. Only a few of the major spray-painting techniques can be given here, as follows:

SPRAY GUN ADJUSTMENT

The first essential is the correct adjustment of the AIR CONTROL and MATERIAL CONTROL screws, to produce the type of spray best suited to the nature of the work. The air control screw adjusts the width and the density of the spray. Turning the screw clockwise concentrates the material into a round, more dense spray; turning it counterclockwise widens the spray into a fan-shaped, more diffused spray. As the spray is widened, the flow of material must be increased; if it is not, the spray will break into a fog. Turning the material control screw clockwise increases the flow of material; turning it counterclockwise decreases the flow. The most desirable character of spray (from round and solid to fan-shaped and diffused) depends upon the character of the surface and the type of material being sprayed. Experience and experiment are about the only guides here. Practice spraying should be done on waste material, using different practice adjustments, until a spray is obtained which covers uniformly and adequately.

OPERATIONAL DEFECTS OF
THE SPRAY GUN

Uneven distribution of the spray pattern is caused by clogging of one or more of the air outlets or by incorrect adjustment of the air and/or material controls.

SPITTING is the alternate discharge of paint and air. Common causes of spitting are drying of the packing around the material control needle valve, looseness of the material nozzle, and dirt in the material nozzle seat. To remedy dry packing, back off the material control needle valve and place two drops of machine oil on the packing. To remedy looseness of the material nozzle and dirt on the nozzle seat, remove the nozzle, clean the nozzle and seat with thinner, and screw the nozzle tightly back into place.

usually done with a 3 inch wall brush. Always roll paint onto the surface, working from the dry area into the just-painted area. Never roll completely in the same or one direction. Don't roll too fast and avoid spinning the roller at the end of the stroke. Always feather out final strokes to pick up any excess paint on the surface. This is accomplished by rolling the final stroke out with minimal pressure.

AIR LEAKAGE from the front of the gun is usually caused by improper seating of the air valve in the AIR VALVE ASSEMBLY shown in figure 18-10. Improper seating may be caused by foreign matter on the valve or seat, by wear on or damage to the valve or seat, by a broken valve spring, or by sticking of the valve stem caused by lack of lubrication.

PAINT LEAKAGE from the front of the gun is usually caused by improper seating of the material needle valve. Improper seating may be caused by damage to the valve stem or tip, by foreign matter on the tip or seat, or by a broken valve spring.

SPRAY-GUN STROKE

Figure 18-17 shows the correct method of stroking with a spray gun. Hold the gun 6 to 8 in. from the surface to be painted, keep the axis of the spray perpendicular to the surface, and take strokes back and forth in horizontal lines. Pull the trigger just after you start a stroke, to avoid applying too much paint at the starting and stopping points.

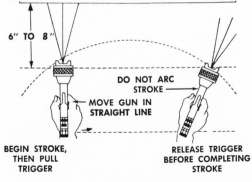

6" TO 8"

DO NOT ARC STROKE →

← MOVE GUN IN STRAIGHT LINE

BEGIN STROKE, THEN PULL TRIGGER

RELEASE TRIGGER BEFORE COMPLETING STROKE

80.243

Figure 18-17.—Correct method of stroking with a spray gun.

Figure 18-18 shows right and wrong methods of spraying an outside corner. If you use the wrong method shown, a good deal of paint will be wasted into the air.

AVERAGE COVERAGE OF PAINT

The area a gallon of paint will cover varies considerably with the nature of the surface, the

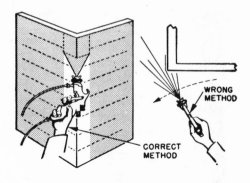

WRONG METHOD

CORRECT METHOD

80.244

Figure 18-18.—Right and wrong methods of spraying an outside corner.

character of the paint, and the method of application. Table 18-4 is intended only to give you a rough estimate of the average coverage per gallon for brush painting.

To plan the work of your crew more competently and, particularly, to make the most effective use of your spray painting teams, you should develop the ability to estimate the number of man-hours and amount of paint required to do the ordinary painting jobs.

It is difficult to list more than a few guidelines for estimating and impossible to lay down any hard and fast rules because of the many variables involved (type of structures, skill of the team, type of paint to be used, and so on).

Keep a set of notes on the jobs that your men do. They will help you with future estimations. Note such things as the number of square feet a gallon of different types of paint will cover when applied by different methods, how much time is required to ready the equipment for spraying, how many square feet of surface a team can paint in an hour, the number of gallons of paint required for each structure and so on.

For example:

Paint coverage per gallon:

1. Enamel—400 ft^2 (square feet) (by brush)
2. Enamel—425 ft^2 (spray)
3. Flat—400 ft^2 (by brush)
4. Flat—430 ft^2 (spray)

Table 18-4.—Average Paint Coverage

Type of Surface	Area in Square Feet per Gallon		
	Primer or First Coat	Second Coat	Third Coat
Exterior			
Wood Siding and Trim			
Flat Oil	300	350	400
Shingle Stain	80	125	
Concrete Masonry Unit			
Cement Base	100	150	200
Latex	150	200	250
Interior			
Plaster Flat Oil	300	350	400
Gloss Oil	300	350	400
Latex	300	350	400
Concrete Masonry Unit			
Cement Base	100	150	200
Latex	150	200	250

133.412

Team #1 (experience_____)
  Readying equipment__ hr. (__helpers)
  Average__ ft^2 per hr.

COLORS

The mixing and use of colored paints to produce a desired color scheme or harmony is technical in nature and difficult to do well. Much could be written about colors, but unless a man works with them and gains experience in this field, he will never fully understand how to use the different colored paints.

MIXING

As you know, there are three primary colors—red, blue, and yellow. These are the only true colors and are the basis for all subsequent shades, tints, and hues that are derived by mixing any combination of these colors in various proportions. Figure 18-19 illustrates a color triangle with one primary color at each of its points. The lettering in the triangle indicates

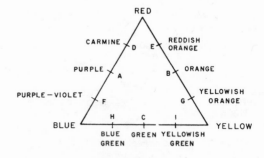

58.150

Figure 18-19.—A color triangle.

the hues that will result when these colors are mixed together as follows:

Equal proportions of red and blue produce a purple.
Equal proportions of red and yellow produce an orange.

Equal parts of blue and yellow produce a green.

Three parts of red to one part of blue will make a carmine.

Three parts of red to one of yellow will result in a reddish-orange.

Three parts of blue to one of red will produce a purple-violet.

Three parts of yellow to one of red will produce a yellowish-orange.

Three parts of blue to one of yellow will result in a blue-green.

Three parts of yellow to one of blue will produce a yellowish-green.

Many other hues may be produced by varying the proportions of the primary colors.

Hues are known as chromatic colors, while black, white, and gray series are known as the achromatic (neutral) colors. The gray series can be produced by mixing black and white in different proportions.

TINTING

Tinting is the process of mixing a colored pigment with a vehicle such as linseed oil, turpentine, or varnish, then blending this combination with a base paint to produce the desired shade or tint.

Some of the most commonly used tinting pigments are lampblack, raw sienna, Venetian red or vermilion, ultra-marine, and the chrome yellow group. Any one of these pigments when mixed with white will result in a lighter tint of the same color. When any one of these pigments (excepting, of course, lampblack) is mixed with a little black and then added to white, it will result in a darker shade of the same color as the pigment.

When tinting oil paints, the pigment is mixed with linseed oil to thin it to the consistency of canned milk. If an enamel paint is to be tinted, the pigment is mixed with varnish or linseed oil to the same consistency as is used for oil paints. After the tint is thoroughly mixed, it should be strained to remove any remaining lumps of pigments. If this isn't done, dark streaks will appear in the tinted paint when it is applied to a surface.

The tint should be added a little at a time to the material being tinted and the mixture spread on a test board so that its color may be compared to the color of the surface being matched. There are differences in the tinting strength of the various brands of tinting colors, and between the colors of one brand. For example: Prussian blue is stronger in tinting strength than other blue tint colors, chrome yellow is stronger than raw sienna or yellow ochre, and vermilion is much stronger than Venetian red. This refers only to their ability to tint or color white paint. However, this does not mean that a satisfactory tinting job cannot be done by using any of the tinting pigments, provided the proper amount of tinting material is blended with the base.

The following are good points to remember when tinting.

1. Colors always appear darker in the mixing can than on a surface.

2. Artificial light causes colors to appear darker than they are in daylight.

3. All colors dry to a lighter shade than they appear before being applied to a surface. Paints should be mixed to a slightly darker shade than the color being matched.

4. The eyes easily become saturated with a color and the colors may seem to fade or change. To assure accuracy when you are mixing colors, it is a good policy to look away from the work for a few minutes and rest your eyes.

DETERIORATION OF PAINT

Paints are not indestructible. Even properly selected protective coatings properly applied on well prepared surfaces will gradually deteriorate and eventually fail. The rate of deterioration under such conditions, however, is slower than when improper painting operations are carried out. Inspectors and personnel responsible for maintenance painting must be familiar with the signs of various stages of deterioration in order to establish an effective and efficient system of inspection and programmed painting. Repainting at the proper time avoids the problems resulting from painting either too soon or too late. Painting scheduled before it is necessary is uneconomical and eventually results in a heavy film buildup leading to abnormal deterioration of the paint system. Painting scheduled too late results in costly surface preparation and may be responsible for damage to the structure, which then may require expensive repairs.

A paint which reaches the end of useful life PREMATURELY is said to have FAILED. The following sections describe the more common types of paint failures, the reasons for such failures, and methods of prevention and/or cure.

CHALKING

Chalking is the result of weathering of the paint at the surface of the coating. The vehicle is broken down by sunlight and other destructive influences, leaving behind loose powdery pigment which can easily be rubbed off with the finger. (See fig. 18-20.) Chalking takes place more rapidly with softer paints such as those based on linseed oil. Chalking is most rapid in areas exposed to large amounts of sunshine. For example, in the northern hemisphere, chalking will be most rapid on the south side of a building. On the other hand, little chalking will take place in areas protected from sunshine and rain such as under eaves or overhangs. Controlled chalking can be an asset, especially in white paints, since it is a self cleaning process and helps to keep the surface clean and white. Furthermore, by gradually wearing away, it reduces the thickness of the coating, thus allowing continuous repainting without making the coating too thick for satisfactory service. Chalked paints are also generally easier to repaint since the underlying paint is in good condition, and, generally, little surface preparation is required. This is not the case when water-thinned paints are to be applied. Their adhesion to chalky surfaces is poor.

ALLIGATORING

Alligatoring describes a pattern in a coating which looks like the hide of an alligator. It is caused by uneven expansion and contraction of a relatively undercoat. (See fig. 18-21.) Alligatoring can be caused by:

1. applying an enamel over an oil primer
2. painting over bituminous paint, asphalt, pitch or shellac
3. painting over grease or wax.

PEELING

PEELING (fig. 18-22) results from inadequate bonding of the top coat with the undercoat or the underlying surface. It is nearly always caused by inadequate surface preparation. A top coat will peel if it is applied to a wet surface, a dirty surface, an oily or waxy surface, or a glossy surface. All glossy surfaces must be sanded before painting.

BLISTERING

BLISTERING (fig. 18-23) is caused by the development of gas or liquid pressure under the paint. The root cause of most blistering, other than that caused by excessive heat, is inadequate ventilation plus some structural defect that allows moisture to accumulate under the paint. Before repainting, the cause of the blistering must be determined and corrected. Blisters should be scraped off, the paint edges around them should be feathered off with sandpaper, and the bare places primed before the blistered area is repainted.

CHECKING AND CRACKING

Checking and cracking describe breaks in the paint film which are formed as the paint becomes hard and brittle. Temperature changes cause the substrate and overlying paint to expand and contract. As the paint becomes hard, it gradually loses its ability to expand without breaking to some extent. Checking is described as tiny breaks which take place only in the

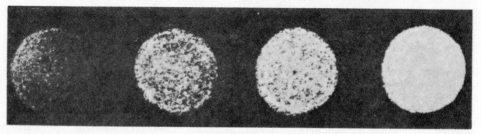

133.405

Figure 18-20.—Degrees of chalk.

133.239(133F)
Figure 18-21.—Alligatoring.

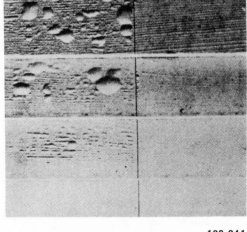

133.241
Figure 18-23.—Blistering.

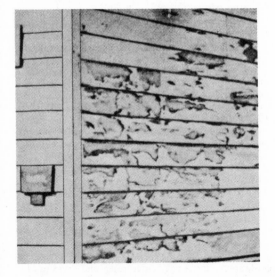

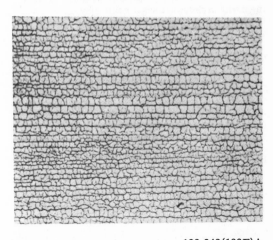

133.242(133F)A
Figure 18-24.—Severe checking.

133.240
Figure 18-22.—Peeling.

upper coat or coats of the paint film without penetrating to the substrate. The pattern is usually similar to a crowsfoot. (See fig. 18-24.) Cracking describes larger and longer breaks which extend through to the substrate. (See fig. 18-25.) Both are a result of stresses in the paint film which exceed the strength of the

coating. Whereas checking arises from stresses within the paint film, cracking is caused by stresses between the film and the substrate. Cracking will generally take place to a greater extent on wood than on other substrates because of its grain. When wood expands, it expands much more across the grain than along the grain. Therefore, the stress in the coating is greatest across the grain causing cracks to

527

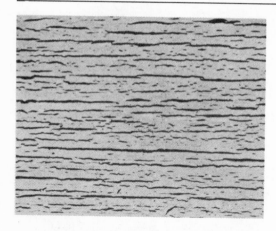

133.242(133F)B
Figure 18-25.—Severe cracking.

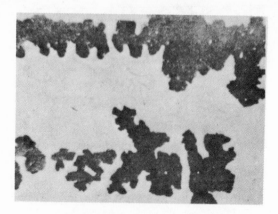

133.406
Figure 18-26.—Crawling.

form parallel to the grain of the wood. Checking and cracking are aggravated by excessively thick coatings because of their reduced elasticity.

CRAWLING

Crawling occurs when the new coating fails to wet and form a continuous film over the preceding coat. Examples are applying latex paints over high gloss enamel or applying paints on concrete or masonry treated with a silicone water repellant. (See fig. 18-26.)

INADEQUATE GLOSS

Sometimes a gloss paint fails to attain the normal amount of gloss. This may be caused by (1) inadequate surface preparation, (2) application over an undercoat which is not thoroughly dry, (3) application in cold or foggy weather.

PROLONGED TACKINESS

A coat of paint is dry when it ceases to be "tacky" to the touch, and prolonged tackiness indicates excessively slow drying. This may be caused by (a) insufficient drier in the paint, (b) a low-quality vehicle in the paint, (c) applying the paint too thickly, (d) painting over an undercoat which is not thoroughly dry, (3) painting over a waxy, oily, or greasy surface, and (f) painting in damp, wet, or foggy weather.

WRINKLING

When paint is applied too thickly, especially in cold weather, the surface of the coat dries to a skin over a layer of undried paint underneath. This usually causes WRINKLING like that shown in figure 18-27. To avoid wrinkling when you are brush-painting or roller-painting, be sure to brush or roll each coat of paint out as thin as possible. To avoid wrinkling when spray painting, be careful to keep the gun in constant motion over the surface whenever you have the trigger down.

PAINTING SAFETY

Every painting assignment exposes Builders to conditions and situations that represent actual or potential danger to themselves and to others in the area. The frequent necessity to use toxic and flammable materials, pressurized equipment, ladders, scaffolding and rigging always presents a potential hazard. Hazards may also be inherent in the very nature of the environment, or caused through ignorance or carelessness of the operator. It is, therefore, extremely important to be aware of all potential hazards, since continuous and automatic precautionary measures will minimize the problem and improve both efficiency and morale of the painting crew.

Painting accident hazards may be broadly divided into three major types as follows:

133.243

Figure 18-27.—Wrinkling.

1. Hazards involved in the use of scaffolds, ladders, and rigging equipment.

2. Fire hazards from flammable materials in paints.

3. Health hazards from toxic (poisonous) materials in paints.

EQUIPMENT HAZARDS

Accidents during painting operations are caused by unsafe working equipment, unsafe working conditions and careless personnel.

Nothing should be taken for granted. Proper use of equipment must be taught to all personnel by qualified Builders. Refresher courses on the use of all equipment must be regularly scheduled.

The following basic procedures in setting up and use of equipment are imperative to assure safety standards and maximum protection of all personnel.

Ladders

1. Store wood ladders in a warm, dry area protected from the weather and ground.

2. Protect wood ladders with clear coatings only, so that cracks, splinters or other defects will be readily visible.

3. Inspect all ladders frequently for loose or bent parts, cracks, breaks or splinters.

4. All straight and extension ladders must have safety shoes. These should be of insulating material for metal ladders. (See fig. 18-28.)

133.407

Figure 18-28.—Ladder safety shoes.

5. Do not use portable ladders greater in length than can be readily carried and placed by two men. Never splice ladders to form a longer ladder.

6. Pre-test all ladders and scaffolding before use by placing horizontally with blocks under ends and "bouncing" in the center or walking along ladder or scaffold.

7. Extension ladders should have a minimum overlap of 15% for each section. (See fig. 18-29.)

8. Do not use stepladders over 12 feet high. Never use one as a straight ladder. Never stand on the top platform.

9. Place ladders so that the horizontal distance from the top support to foot is at least 1/4 of the working length. Be sure that the ladder is securely in place. Rope off all doorways in front of the ladder and place warning signs.

10. Use hand lines to raise or lower tools and materials. Do not overreach when working on ladders. Move the ladder instead.

11. Never use metal ladders in areas where contact with electric power lines is possible.

Scaffolding

1. Inspect all parts before use. Reject metal parts damaged by corrosion and wood parts with defects such as checks, splits, unsound knots and decay.

2. Provide adequate sills or under-pinnings when erecting on filled or soft ground. Be sure that scaffolds are plumb and level. Compensate

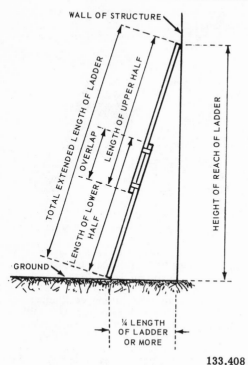

133.408

Figure 18-29.—Ladder stability.

for unevenness of the ground by blocking or using adjusting screws.

3. Anchor scaffolds to the wall about every 28 feet in length and 18 feet in height. Do not force braces to fit. Use horizontal diagonal bracing at bottom and at every 30 feet in height.

4. Lumber should be straight grained. All nails should be driven full length and not subject to direct pull.

5. Provide guard railings regardless of height, on the full length of the scaffold and also on the ends.

6. Erect scaffolding so that ladders are lined up from top to bottom. Always use ladders when climbing scaffolding.

7. Tubular pole scaffolds should be made of two inch O.D. galvanized steel tubing or other corrosion resistant metal of equal strength. They should be erected or dismantled by experienced Builders only.

8. Planking should have at least a two foot overlap. Secure well to wood scaffolding. Platforms should be made of planking of uniform thickness laid close together. They must overlap and be fastened at supports. They must not extend over the edge without being properly supported. An unsupported plank is a deadly trap. Do not use planking for other purposes; paint them only at the ends to identify them. Nominal sizes of planking should be determined from table 18-5. Values are given in pounds for loads at center and allow for weight of planking.

9. Test scaffolds and extensive planking (extended to working length) by raising them one foot off the ground and loading them with weights at least 4 times the anticipated working load.

Table 18-5.—Safe Center Loads for Scaffold Plank.

Span feet	2 x 8*	2 x 10*	2 x 12*	3 x 8*	3 x 10*	3 x 12*
6	200	255	310	525	665	805
8	150	190	230	390	500	605
10	120	155	185	315	400	485
12	100	130	155	265	335	405
14	—	110	135	225	285	346
16	—	—	115	195	250	305

Above values are for planks supported at the ends, wide side of plank face up, and with loads concentrated at the center of the span. For loads uniformly distributed on the wide surface throughout the length, the safe loads may be twice those given in the table. Loads given are net and do not include the weight of the plank. If select structural coast region Douglas fir, merchantable structural longleaf southern pine, or dense structural square edge sound southern pine are used, above loads may be increased 25 percent.

* Dressed sizes of planks, reading left to right, are: 1⅝ x 7½, 1⅝ x 9½, 1⅝ x 11½, 2⅝ x 7½, 2⅝ x 9½, 2⅝ x 11½, respectively.

133.413

Rolling Towers

1. Inspect all tower parts before use. Do not use parts which are damaged by corrosion, deterioration, or misuse.

2. Guy or tie off towers with heights more than three times the minimum base dimension, and fix towers at every 18 feet of elevation. Maintain stability of towers over 25 feet high with out-riggers or handling lines. Use horizontal diagonal bracing at bottom and at every height section.

3. Provide unit lock arms on all towers. Do not use casters less than 6 inches in diameter. Do not extend adjusting screws more than 12 inches.

4. Do not ride towers. Look where you are going when moving them. Do not attempt to move a tower without sufficient help. Apply all caster brakes when tower is stationary.

Swinging Scaffolds, Swing Stages, Bosun Chairs

1. Always read instructions on the proper use and maintenance of the equipment. Follow prescribed load capacities.

2. Stages should be at least 27 inches wide and supplied with guard rails (not rope).

3. Only experienced Builders are to erect or operate stages. Check ropes and blocks before use by suspending stages one foot off the ground and loading at least 4 times the anticipated work load. Before locating on the job site, check for nearby electric power lines.

4. Power stages should have free fall safety devices with hand controls in case of power failure.

Ropes and Cables

1. Store ropes and cables coiled in dry empty drums.

2. Use wire rope at least 3/4 inch diameter for platform slings; use manila rope at least 5/8 inch diameter in bosun chairs and life lines. Use proper clamps with wire rope, and proper knots and hitches when handling materials with manila rope. (See fig. 18-30.)

3. Inspect ropes frequently. Discard if exposed to acid or excessive heat. Check for dry rot, brittleness or excessive wear. Never use frozen rope.

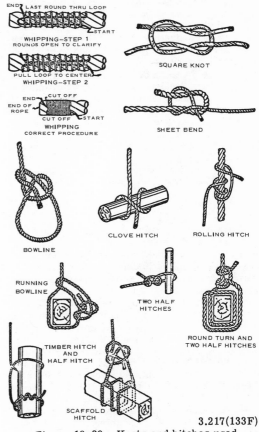

Figure 18-30.—Knots and hitches used in painting operations.

4. Inspect all wire ropes and cables frequently in accordance with current service safety criteria.

5. Do not attempt to salvage rope or cable by splicing.

Pressurized Equipment

These rules apply to all types of equipment used both for spraying and blasting.

1. Use only approved equipment. Use remote control deadman valves on high pressure equipment (60 lbs. or higher). These should be activated by the same air used for blasting or spraying.

2. Conduct a hydrostatic test at least once, preferably twice a year. Test safety relief valves daily.

3. Use conductive hose. Ground nozzles, tanks and pressure equipment when in use, also object being sprayed.

4. Store hose in dry areas. When in use, avoid sharp bends, especially when curved around an object. Secure high pressure hose no more than 10 ft. from operator.

5. Never point gun or nozzle at anyone or any part of the body. When handling or carrying, hold by the grip and remove the fingers from the trigger.

6. Release all pressure before disconnecting any part of the equipment.

FIRE HAZARDS

Certain general rules regarding fire and explosion hazards apply to all situations. All paint materials should have complete label instructions which stipulate the potential fire hazards and precautions to be taken. Painters must be continuously advised and reminded of the fire hazards that exist under the particular conditions of each job, so that they will be aware of the dangers involved and assure that the necessary precautions are taken and maintained. Fire fighting equipment, of the proper type, must always be readily available in the paint shop, spray room and work areas where a potential fire hazard exists. Electric wiring and equipment installed or used in the paint shop, including storage room and spray room, must conform to the applicable requirements of the National Electrical Code for Hazardous Areas. The following precautions against fire must be carefully observed by all paint-handling personnel:

1. Prohibit smoking anywhere that paint is either stored, prepared for use or applied.

2. Provide for adequate ventilation in all of these areas.

3. Perform recurrent spray operations on portable items, e.g., signs, in an approved spray booth equipped with adequate ventilation, a water wash system of fume removal and explosion proof electrical equipment.

4. Wet down spray booth surfaces before cleaning them.

5. Use rubber feet on metal ladders, and be certain that personnel working in hazardous areas use rubber soled shoes.

6. Use non-sparking scrapers and brushes to clean metal surfaces where fire hazards are present.

7. Wet down paint sweepings, rags and waste with water, and store in closed metal containers until disposed of in an approved manner. Do not burn in heaters or furnaces. (See fig. 18-31.)

40.67(133F)

Figure 18-31.—Keep combustible materials in metal waste cans tightly covered.

8. Extinguish all pilot lights on water heaters, furnaces and other open flame equipment on all floors of the structure being painted. Be sure to turn the gas valve off.

9. When painting in confined areas near machinery or electrical equipment, open all switches and tag them to prevent their being turned on inadvertently.

10. Be sure that all mixers, pumps, motors, and lights used in the paint shop, spray room or on the job are explosion proof and electrically grounded.

11. Use pails of sand (never sawdust) near dispensing pumps and spigots to absorb any spillage or overflow.

12. During painting operations keep fire extinguishers nearby. Be sure that they are of the proper type. (See table 18-6.)

13. Check ventilation and temperature regularly when working in confined areas.

14. Consult with the CEs before painting in areas where high voltage lines and equipment are located.

15. Keep all work areas clear of obstructions.

16. Clean up before, during and after painting operations. Dispose of sweepings and waste daily.

HEALTH HAZARDS

A variety of ingredients used in the manufacture of paint materials are injurious to the human body in varying degrees. While the body can withstand nominal quantities of most of these poisons for relatively short periods of time, continuous or over exposure to them may have harmful effects. Furthermore, continued exposure to some may cause the body to become sensitized so that subsequent contact, even in small amounts, may cause an aggravated reaction. To this extent, these materials are a very definite threat to the normally healthy individual and a serious danger to persons with chronic illnesses or disorders. These materials are divided into two major groups, i.e., toxic materials and skin irritating materials.

Nevertheless, health hazards can easily be avoided by a common sense approach of avoiding unnecessary contact with hazardous materials

Table 18-6.—Use the Proper Fire Extinguisher

Three Classes of Fires

Choose from these 5 basic types of extinguishers	CLASS A FIRES Paper, wood, cloth, excelsior, rubbish, etc., where quenching and cooling effect of water is required.	CLASS B FIRES Burning liquids (gasoline oil, paints, cooking fats, etc.) where smothering action is required.	CLASS C FIRES Fires in live electrical equipment (motors, switches, appliances, etc.) where a non-conducting extinguishing agent is required.
CARBON DIOXIDE	Small surface fires only.	**YES** Excellent Carbon dioxide leaves no residue, does not affect equipment or foodstuffs.	**YES** Excellent Carbon doxide is a nonconductor, leaves no residue, will not damage equipment.
DRY CHEMICAL	Small surface fires only.	**YES** Excellent Chemical absorbs heat and releases smothering gas on fire; chemical shields operator from heat.	**YES** Excellent Chemical is a non-conductor; fog of dry chemical shields operator from heat.
WATER	**YES** Excellent Water saturates material and prevents rekindling.	**NO** Water will spread fire, not put it out.	**NO** Water, a conductor, should not be used on live electrical equipment.
FOAM	**YES** Excellent Foam has both smothering and wetting action.	**YES** Excellent Smothering blanket does not dissipate, floats on top of most spilled liquids.	**NO** Foam is a conductor and should never be used on live electrical equipment.
VAPORIZING LIQUID	Small surface fires only.	**YES** Releases heavy smothering gas on fire.	**YES** Liquid is a non-conductor and will not damage equipment.

133.414

and by strict adherence to established safety measures.

The following rules should always be strictly observed:

1. Toxic or dermatitic materials must be properly identified and kept tightly sealed when not in use.

2. Designate a competent person to check the operation of paint spray booths. Check at regular intervals to ensure that the equipment is in a safe and proper operating condition.

3. Be sure that ventilation is adequate in all painting areas. Provide artificial ventilation where natural ventilation is inadequate. Use supplied air respirators, if necessary.

4. Spray all portable items within exhaust ventilated booths especially designed for that purpose.

5. Wear goggles and the proper type of respirator when spraying, blast cleaning or performing any operation where any abnormal amount of vapor, mist or dust is formed.

Table 18-7.—Recommended Preservatives and Retentions for Ties, Lumber, Piles, Poles, and Posts (Fed. Spec. TT-W-571)

Product	Minimum net retention of—(Pounds per cubic foot)				
	Coal-tar creosote (TT-W-556)	Creosote-coal tar solution (TT-W-566)	Creosote-petroleum solution (TT-W-568)	Pentachloro-phenol, 5 percent in petroleum (TT-W-570)	Copper naphthenate (0.75 percent copper metal) in petroleum (AWPA P8)
Ties (crossties, switch ties, and bridge ties)	8	8	9		
Lumber, and structural timbers:					
For use in coastal waters:					
Douglas fir (coast type) lumber and timbers.	14	14			
Southern yellow pine lumber and timbers	20	20			
For use in fresh water, in contact with ground or for important structural members not in contact with ground or water.	10	10	12	10	10
For other use not in contact with ground or water.	6	6	7	6	6
Piles:					
For use in coastal waters:					
Douglas fir (coast type). . . .	17	17			
Southern yellow pine	20	20			
For land or fresh water use . .	12	12	14	12	
Poles (utility and building)	8, 10	. . . .	. . . .	8, 10	8, 10
Posts (round, fence)	6	6	7	6	6

133.415

6. When handling dermatitic materials, use protective creams or preferably gloves, and wear appropriate clothing. Change and clean work clothing regularly.

7. Avoid touching any part of the body, especially the face, when handling dermatitic materials. Wash hands and face thoroughly before eating and at the end of the day.

WOOD PRESERVATIVE

Damage to building and other structures by termites, wood bores, and fungi, is needless waste. Defects in wood have been caused by improper care after preservation treatment. All surfaces of treated wood that are cut or drilled to expose the untreated interior must be treated with the proper application of wood preservative.

The capacity of any wood to resist dry rot, termites, and decay, can be greatly increased by impregnating the wood with a general-purpose wood preservative or fungicide.

Prescribed preservatives are listed in tables 18-7 and 18-8.

Different woods have different capacities for absorbing preservative or other liquids, and in any given wood the sapwood is much more absorbent than the heartwood. Hardwoods are, in general, less absorbent than softwoods. Naturally, the extent to which the preservative affords protection increases directly with the distance to which it penetrates below the surface of the wood. The best penetration is obtained by a pressure process which requires equipment you will not have available. Nonpressure methods of applying preservatives are by dipping and by ordinary surface application with a brush or spray gun.

Figure 18-32 shows how you can improvise long tanks for the dipping process. Absorption is rapid at first, much slower later. A rule of thumb is to the effect that in 3 minutes wood will have absorbed one-half the total amount of preservative it will absorb in 2 hours. However, the extent of the penetration obtained will

Table 18-8.—Minimum Retentions of Water-Borne Preservatives
Recommended in Federal Specification TT-W-571

Preservative	Minimum retentions for uses		Federal Specification covering preservatives
	Not in contact with ground or in water	Involving occasional exposure to rainwater or continually to ground in areas of low rainfall	
	Pounds per cubic foot	Pounds per cubic foot	
Acid copper chromate	0.5	1.00	TT-W-546
Ammoniacal copper arsenite	.3	.5	TT-W-549
Chromated copper arsenate	.35	.75	TT-W-550
Chromated zinc arsenate (including copperized form)	.5	1.00	TT-W-538
Chromated zinc chloride	.75	1.00	TT-W-551
Copperized chromated zinc chloride . . .	.75	1.00	TT-W-562
Fluor-chrome-arsenate-phenol.	.35	.50	TT-W-535

133.416

depend upon the type of wood, its moisture content, and the length of time it remains immersed.

Surface application by brush or spray is, from the standpoint of a desire for maximum penetration, the least satisfactory method of treating wood. However, it is more or less unavoidable in the case of any wood which is already installed, as well as for treated wood which has been cut or drilled to expose the untreated interior.

Pentachruphenol and creosote coal tar are likely to be the only field-mixed preservative used by the Builder. The type of treatment or preservative depends on the severity of exposure and the desired life of the end product. Types and uses of wood preservatives are shown in tables 18-7 and 18-8. However, the Builder should be familiar with NAVFAC-TP-PU 2 PEST CONTROL, and the following safety precautions:

1. Avoid undue skin contact.
2. Avoid touching the face or rubbing the eyes when handling pretreated material.
3. Avoid inhalation of toxic material.

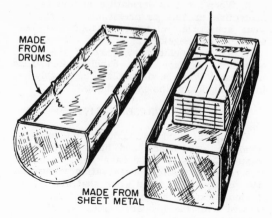

MADE FROM DRUMS

MADE FROM SHEET METAL

133.244

Figure 18-32.—Improvised tanks for dip-treating lumber.

4. The application of preservative is very hazardous; apply only in a properly ventilated space and use approved respirators.
5. Wash with soap and water after contact.

CHAPTER 19

CONSTRUCTION SAFETY AND SUPERVISION

Construction work, whether it is heavy construction, light construction, or shop construction, is highly dangerous work, dangerous to both personnel and material. In accordance with the Navy policy of conserving manpower and material, all naval activities must conduct effective and continuous accident prevention programs. Operating procedures and work methods must be adopted which do not expose personnel unnecessarily to injury or occupational health hazards, or equipment and material to damage. Instruction in appropriate safety precautions must be given by all commands, and disciplinary action must be taken in any cases of willful violations or negligence.

All naval activities are subject to the provisions of one or more authoritative documents relating to safety. Precautions applicable to the operating forces have been set forth in pamphlets, periodicals, and directives, issued by bureaus and offices of the Navy Department. Navy safety precautions indexes are issued as a series of OpNav Notices under the 5100 subject classification number.

The old publication U.S. Navy Safety Precautions, (OpNav 34P1) has been revised and retitled Safety Precautions for Shore Activities, NavSo P-2455.

SAFETY RESPONSIBILITY

The responsibility for the safety of personnel is vested in the commanding officer. Since safety precautions are designed to cover usual situations in naval activities, commanding officers or others in authority may find it necessary to issue special precautions to their commands to cover local conditions and unusual circumstances. In addition to the posting of appropriate precautions, careful instruction and indoctrination of all personnel are necessary to ensure effective compliance.

The commanding officer must require that all personnel under his jurisdiction be instructed and drilled in all applicable safety precautions, that adequate warning signs be posted in dangerous areas, and that all applicable

safety precautions be observed. While he cannot delegate his final responsibility for the safety of personnel under his command, he may delegate his safety authority to the executive officer and to other subordinates.

The basic safety responsibility of supervisory personnel is to ensure that safety precautions are strictly observed and enforced in their own work areas.

Each individual is personally responsible for the strict observance of all safety precautions which are applicable to his work or duty He must make immediate report to his superior of any unsafe condition, equipment, or material he happens to observe. He must warn any other personnel who may be endangered by any existing hazard or by any neglect of safety precautions. He must wear or use any protective clothing or equipment specified or required for the work he is doing. He must report any injury, no matter how slight, to his superior at once.

SAFETY ORGANIZATION

Each command is required to establish a safety organization, to develop, organize, and direct a comprehensive accident prevention program and to provide for the promulgation and enforcement of safety precautions and safe construction techniques.

SAFETY OFFICER

The safety program is usually under the direction of a SAFETY OFFICER designated by the commanding officer. The safety officer has the authority to take immediate steps to stop any operation where there is impending danger of injury to personnel or damage to equipment or material.

The safety officer lays out the safety program, after conducting job analyses and after consultations with the supervisors in charge of the various phases of construction. He maintains an adequate safety library, provides and equips safety bulletin boards, and obtains and distributes safety educational materials like posters, pamphlets, films, books, and visual aids. He initiates and encourages activities designed to stimulate and maintain interest in safety. He cooperates with construction supervisors in the selection and placement of warning signs. He investigates and reports on all accidents, and makes recommendations with regard to the prevention or recurrences.

A chief petty officer may be designated as safety chief in an NMCB to assist the safety officer who usually has other collateral duties.

SUPERVISORY PERSONNEL

The safety duties of supervisory personnel are as follows:

1. They must promulgate and enforce all safety regulations.
2. They must instruct and drill their men in safe practices and provide and enforce the use of applicable personnel protective equipment.
3. They must carry out the safety recommendations of the safety officer or chief and their superiors.
4. They must caution their men repeatedly with regard to occupational hazards.
5. They must conduct regularly scheduled safety inspections in their areas of supervision.
6. They must investigate and analyze the capabilities of their men, to ensure that men are assigned to jobs which are not beyond their technical and physical capabilities.
7. They must report to their superiors at once any accidents which occur within their jurisdictions.
8. They must analyze all accidents which occur within their jurisdictions, ascertain their causes, and recommend appropriate action to prevent recurrences.
9. They must seek and follow the advice of the safety officer and of their superiors with regard to their part in the administration of the accident prevention program.

SAFETY PRECAUTIONS

In order to do their part in the administration of the safety program, supervisory personnel must have a thorough knowledge of the safety precautions which apply to the various types and phases of construction. Safety precautions applying to specific tools, equipment, and types of construction have been inserted in

this manual. The following sections contain construction safety precautions not given elsewhere in this manual.

GENERAL SAFETY

Requirements for personnel safety are designed to cover the dangerous conditions ordinarily experienced by personnel engaged in construction and maintenance work at naval shore establishments and advanced bases. The American Standard Association Safety Code for Building Construction contains additional safety rules for the various fields of activity which constitute the building construction industry. Public works officers and others responsible for the safety of personnel employed on construction and maintenance work should have a current copy of the safety code and be familiar with its provisions.

DRINKING WATER

Fresh and pure drinking water must be supplied on every construction job. Drinking water will be obtained only from sources approved by responsible authority. Any one of the following dispensing methods should be used. Stationary bubbler with guarded orifice installed on an approved water line and fully enclosed water container and individual paper drinking cups. Also, portable sanitary drinking fountains which meet the required specifications. Dipping water out of any container by individual cup, dipper, canteen, or other utensil, is prohibited. Containers must be provided with a covering so designed and fastened as to prevent such use. All containers used to furnish drinking water must be thoroughly sterilized at least once a week, and more frequently if circumstances require, by methods approved by medical authorities.

TEMPORARY TOILET FACILITIES

For every 30 persons or less a latrine or closet space must be provided. It must be constructed so that the occupant thereof will be shielded from view and protected against the weather and falling objects. Latrines must be located so as not to contaminate any domestic water supply used for drinking purposes. They should be so located and banked that surface water cannot flood the pit. Each latrine must be provided with an adequate urinal trough. If sewers are available, connections must be made at once, flush tank closets installed, and running water provided to keep the closet flushed.

At locations where neither a water carriage sewerage system nor chemical toilet is available, the latrine or closet space must contain a fly-tight box constructed over a pit latrine or over pails, or other suitable containers where pits are impracticable. Care must be taken to see that all buildings used as temporary toilets are kept in a clean and sanitary condition. The toilet seats should be scrubbed daily with soap and water, and washed off at least twice a week with an antiseptic solution.

FIRST-AID STATIONS

Where medical facilities are not available at a shore establishment a first-aid station or stations equipped with medicines and supplies common to first-aid treatment, must be established on each project at the beginning of operations and maintained for the duration of the job. On all projects employing fewer than 100 workers, 16-unit first-aid kits must be provided in the ratio of one for each 25 persons employed and these kits must be maintained with all the standard medicines and remedies.

Workmen must report all accidents, no matter how unimportant they seem to be. Minor injuries, when neglected, produce most of the infection cases. All injuries must be given first aid or medical attention immediately. First-aid care must be administered under the direction of qualified personnel.

PERSONAL PROTECTION

Chipper's goggles, welder's goggles, welder's shields, hard hats, safety shoes, rubber boots, safety belts, lifelines, life nets, life preservers or jackets, respirators, and other such protective equipment or clothing, occasioned by the type of work being done must be made available, and their use must be enforced. Personal protective equipment should be properly cleaned before being issued to personnel.

LIGHTING

Stairways, corridors, passageways, excavations, piled materials or obstructions, and working areas must be kept adequately lighted while work is in progress; and where working conditions require the use of artificial lighting

it must be maintained after a shift until workmen have had an opportunity to leave the immediate area.

Outdoor operations must have adequate light for night work.

GAS AND SMOKE

No method of heating must be used which releases smoke or gas within an enclosure where workers are employed. No fire or open flame device should be permitted on a project without the approval of the supervisor or person in charge. Where smoke pipes from stoves or other heating apparatus pass through combustible walls or roof, proper insulating thimbles must be provided. All stoves and other heating apparatus must be mounted on an incombustible base and have proper fire protection at the rear and sides.

HANDLING AND STORING MATERIALS

All material in bags, containers, or bundles, and other material stored in tiers must be stacked, blocked, interlocked, and limited in height so that it will be stable and otherwise safe against sliding or collapsing.

Material stored inside buildings under construction should not be placed within 6 feet of any hoistway or floor opening, nor on any floor above the ground within 10 feet of the outside of the building, unless, the exterior walls extend above the top of the storage pile, in which case the minimum distance must be 6 feet. Material should not be stacked against interior columns or roof supports. Floors must be shored if material stored is heavier than the flooring will support. When any material is stored in public thoroughfares, it must be located so as to prevent the least possible hazard to the public or interference with traffic.

All material must be protected against being hit or knocked over by trucks or other passing vehicles by means of barricades and red flags during the hours of daylight. It should be guarded at night by barricades and an adequate number of red lights located at conspicuous points. When handling materials by hand, workmen should always use the legs in lifting, never the back. Help should be obtained if the load is too heavy or too clumsy to be handled by one man.

PILING LUMBER

Men piling lumber should always wear leather gloves. All lumber must be piled on timber sills to prevent direct contact between stored lumber and the ground. Sills must be level and solidly supported. Lumber must be so piled as to be safe against falling. The height of the pile must not exceed 16 feet. The width of piles must not be less than one-fourth the height. When unpiling, each tier must be completely unpiled before beginning another. Cross strips must be placed in piles which are stacked more than 4 feet high. Used lumber must have all projecting nails withdrawn before it is piled, unless it is burned without further handling.

CEMENT AND LIME

Men handling cement and lime bags should wear goggles and snug-fitting neck and wrist bands. Any susceptibility of their skin to cement and lime burns should be reported. They should always practice personal cleanliness. They must not wear clothing that has become hard and stiff with cement. Such clothing irritates the skin and may cause serious infection. Men who are allergic to cement and lime should be transferred to other jobs.

Bags of cement and lime should not be piled more than 10 bags high on a pallet except when stored in bins or enclosures built for such purposes. The bags around the outside of the pallet should be placed with the mouths of the bags facing the center. To prevent piled bags from falling outward, the first five tiers of bags each way from any corner must be crosspiled and a set-back made commencing with the sixth tier. If necessary to pile above the tenth tier, another set-back must be made. The back tier, when not resting against a wall of sufficient strength to withstand the pressure, should be stepped back one bag every five tiers, the same as the end tiers.

During unpiling, the entire top of the pile should be kept level and the necessary step-backs every five tiers maintained.

Lime must be stored in a dry place to prevent a premature slaking action.

BRICK

Brick should never be piled directly on uneven or soft ground but should always be stacked on planks. Brick must never be stored on scaffolds or runways. This must not prohibit normal supplies on bricklayers' scaffolds during actual bricklaying operations.

Except where stacked in sheds, brick piles should never be more than 7 feet high. When a pile of brick reaches a height of 4 feet it must be tapered back 1 inch in every foot of height above the 4 foot level. The tops of brick piles must be kept level and the taper maintained during unpiling operations.

MASONRY BLOCK AND HOLLOW TILE

Blocks should always be stacked in tiers on solid, level surfaces. Stacked piles should be limited to a height of 6 feet whenever possible. When blocks are stacked higher than 6 feet the pile must be stepped back, braced, and propped, or wood strips placed between tiers to prevent the pile from toppling.

Blocks should not be dropped or thrown from an elevation or delivered through fully enclosed chutes.

REINFORCING AND STRUCTURAL STEEL

Men handling reinforcing steel must wear leather gloves.

Bending of reinforcing steel on the job should be done on substantial benches secured against tipping. Benches should be located on non-slippery level surfaces.

Structural steel must be carefully piled to prevent sliding or tipping over. If there is danger of tipping over, I-beams should be stored with webs horizontal.

SAND, GRAVEL, AND CRUSHED STONE

In withdrawing sand, gravel, and crushed stone from frozen stock piles, no overhang should be permitted at any time. Material should not be dumped against walls or partitions. When this must be done, it should not be stored to a height that will endanger the stability of such walls and partitions.

When men are required to work in hoppers or on high piles of loose material they must be equipped with safety belts and lifelines having no more than 2 feet of slack.

CONCRETE CONSTRUCTION

Good housekeeping must be observed at each new concrete structure. Materials and tools should be kept picked up, and special care must be taken that no boards with protruding nails are allowed to lie around. All workmen placing concrete must wear protective hats wherever the hazard of overhead falling objects exists. Shirt sleeves should be rolled down, gloves should be worn, and every reasonable precaution taken to keep cement and concrete off the skin. Men required to stand in fresh concrete should be provided with watertight boots. Men placing reinforcing steel where there is a falling hazard must be equipped with lifelines and safety belts, firmly secured with a maximum slack of 4 feet. While concreting there should be one Builder, or more if necessary, assigned to tighten wedges and to see that centering supports are not in danger of collapsing. Mud sills should be used on all shoring that rests on the ground, and shoring should be properly placed.

Before decking has been put in place on joists, temporary scaffolding should be erected as necessary to enable men to work safely. Workmen must be particularly careful not to walk out on cantilevered members of the form framing.

Men erecting column forms must always install back braces and side braces so as to prevent any movement out and away from the building. They must also use heavy tie-wire to tie in the tops of wood column forms to the slab reinforcing steel. When the outside beam forms are in place, a continuous length of 3/4-inch manila rope must run from one set of column dowels to the next set of the outside of the building. When outside column forms are being raised from one floor level to another floor level, the area below the place where the column forms are being raised should be roped off. In the setting of shores, all horizontal and cross bracing should tie in all shores with the adjacent ones.

FORM STRIPPING

Only men actually engaged in stripping work should be allowed in areas where stripping is being done. Forms should not be removed prematurely; be sure that the concrete is properly set and that it is not frozen. Before stripping, beam forms should be well supported by shoring. When large panels are removed or handled

by power equipment, rope tag lines should be fastened to the form panels to prevent the wind from swinging them against the men. When tie wires under tension are being cut, care should be taken to prevent a backlash which might hit the body, especially the face, eyes, or throat. Hammer and chisel should not be used to cut tie wires.

Stripped lumber should be removed at once to a separate pile, then cleaned and all nails removed. Workmen cleaning stripped lumber should wear heavy leather gloves and heavy soled safety shoes which are in good condition. Runways that are used for workmen's access should have standard railings on open sides to protect the workmen using them. Runways should be built with such a slope that men will not slip. Cleats should be fastened to sloping runways when the incline exceeds 1-foot rise in a 5-foot run. Runways must be kept free of loose materials, ice, snow, grease, mud, and other causes of insecure footing.

MIXING AND PLACING CONCRETE

Tools such as shovels and hoes should be placed where workmen will not trip over them or bump into them. The mortar box must be placed clear of workmen's access ways.

Workmen must make sure that the transit-mix truck does not back up and pin them between the skip and the truck, or run them down. Transit-mix truck operators must exercise special care in backing up to avoid injuring workmen. The operator should back up only on signal from qualified personnel.

Workmen must be careful not to get too near to moving parts, like revolving drums, cables, etc., thereby running the risk of their clothing being caught and drawing them into the machinery.

When a mixer dumps a load of concrete into a bucket, care must be taken to see that the bucket gate is closed. Extreme care should be taken when planning the working operations so that the bucket will not have to swing over the working men heads. Cables should be checked for defects to prevent the load being dropped.

EQUIPMENT

Operators of construction and weight-handling equipment must be tested and licensed in accordance with the applicable requirements set forth in Testing and Licensing of Construction Equipment Operators, NavDocks P-306.

NOTE: Some NavFac forms are identified by the term "NavDocks" followed by the form number. This is due to a change in name of the activity which is not yet reflected on all the forms. So remember that the two identifying terms refer to the same numbered form.

An apprentice or license applicant should operate equipment only under the direct supervision of a licensed operator. An operator who is not physically able or mentally alert must not be permitted to start work with any piece of equipment.

A frequent and regular inspection should be made of all machines. A well-maintained machine is usually a safe machine. All controls such as steering mechanism, brakes, and operating clutches must be tested by the operator before any work is begun on a new shift. If any of these do not operate properly, they should be adjusted or repaired before any load is moved. Good housekeeping is a prime necessity for safe and efficient operation. An accumulation of grease on a machine can cause falls and invite fires. Refueling of gasoline or diesel-operated equipment should never be done while it is in operation. Frequent inspection of fuel lines and tanks for leaks will prevent fires as well as loss of fuel.

When transporting gasoline from general supply to equipment in 5-gallon quantities, safety cans should be used. If tank truck service is not available, gasoline in quantities in excess of 5 gallons should be transported in steel drums. All bungs must be tight, and the drum itself checked for soundness. When dispensing gasoline from drums an approved pump should be used. An operator should never leave his machine while the engine is running. Upon completion of a work shift, the bucket, skip, etc., must be rested on the ground, and the brakes and clutches set as recommended by the manufacturer.

No one must ever attempt to repair, clean, oil, or grease any part of the equipment while it is in motion.

COLOR CODE

All Navy construction, firefighting, railroad, utility, and weight-handling equipment should be painted in accordance with the instructions contained in NavDocks P-309: The Application of Color to Shore Establishment. Officers should see that all such equipment under their control is painted to meet the accident-prevention standards of that code.

SIGNALS

One person, only, should be designated as signalman, and both he and the equipment operator should be entirely familiar with the standard hand signals. Where possible, the signalman should be given some distinguishing article of dress, such as a brightly colored helmet. He must be in a position to closely observe the load and the workmen or intermediate signalman, and still be in plain sight of the operator at all times. The signals covered in chapter 5 should be understood and used by all hands.

CLEARING

Personal protective equipment or apparel of approved type should be worn by workers for protection against eye, head, leg, or foot injuries, and while working in water or swampy areas and on ice and other hazardous surfaces. Sharp edge tools should be transported in carrying cases or sheaths. Machetes must be kept in sheaths at all times except when in actual use. All hands should stand as far away as possible from moving machines, equipment, or moving logs and taut lines. When operations are conducted at night, adequate artificial illumination should be provided either in the form of headlights or by general lighting of the work area.

All underbrush, vines, small trees, etc., that will interfere with clearing operation, should be cleared before trimming or felling begins. Before felling, all trees must be inspected for rotten hearts, dead or entangled limbs, or similar hazardous conditions. Dead or entangling limbs which endanger personnel should be removed. Trees which present an unusual hazard, such as those with rotten heart, dead, hollow, leaning, lodged or multiple growths, should be felled under the supervision of a skilled foreman. All trees must be properly undercut before felling, with a deep "V" grooved notch on the side where the tree is to fall. Wedges should be used to throw all balanced trees. Persons in the danger areas must be warned prior to the felling of trees. A loud warning call, "TIMBER" must be given at the time of the felling of each tree.

Persons engaged in felling trees should look over the area carefully before starting to fell a tree, and note mentally the existing avenues of escape. Workmen should never climb trees while carrying unguarded sharp-edged tools. Working in or on trees during high winds is prohibited, except in an emergency, and then only under the foreman's direct supervision. After felling a tree, the tree must be lying on the ground and adequately chocked or otherwise secured before leaving it or going to the next tree. Before felled trees are trimmed, they should be properly secured by chocking or other means to prevent them from rolling. Extreme care must be exercised when using chain saws to fell trees. Chain saws must not be used to fell rotten heart or hollow trees.

BURNING

Burning operations must be kept under strict control and not left unattended. They must always be conducted in the clear, where the fire will not ignite leaves, dry wooded areas, or nearby buildings. Workmen should not stand in the smoke. All burning or smoldering material must be completely extinguished before workmen leave the scene. Firing, punching, and placing of material for burning should be done from the windward side. This is especially important when poison oak, poison sumac, or poison ivy is being burned. Workmen should never use flammable liquids on piles of material which are burning or smoldering.

POISONOUS PLANTS

If a workman has been in contact with poison ivy, poison oak, or sumac, his skin should be swabbed with alcohol and scrubbed with laundry soap and water. A brush or a rough cloth should not be used as they might irritate the skin and increase the danger of poisoning. Heavy gloves and clothing should always be worn when handling poisonous plants. The clothing of these workers should be cleaned daily. When burning poisonous vines it is important to keep away from the smoke, which will carry the poison and may be inhaled. If infection develops after contact with poisonous plants, a medical officer should be consulted. Self-medication with poisonous plant immunization or desensitization extracts should never be undertaken. Men who

are extremely sensitive to these poisons should be transferred to other jobs.

EXCAVATION

Where applicable, Federal, State, or local codes, rules, regulations and ordinances governing any and all phases of excavation work should be observed at all times.

Every effort should be made prior to making an excavation to determine whether utility installations (sanitary and storm sewers, water, gas, electric lines, gasoline tanks, etc) are to be encountered. When the excavation approaches the estimated level of such an installation, the installation should be located from blueprints, if available, or by careful probing and digging, and when uncovered, it should be properly supported and protected. Trees, boulders, and other surface encumbrances located so as to create a hazard at any time during operations must be removed before excavation is started.

If the stability of adjoining buildings or walls is endangered by excavations, necessary shoring, bracing, or underpinning must be proved to ensure their safety. Such shoring, bracing, or underpinning should be frequently inspected by a competent person and the protection effectively maintained. If it is necessary to place or operate power shovels, derricks, trucks, material, or other heavy objects on a level above and near an excavation, the side of the excavation must be sheet-piled, shored, and braced as necessary to resist the extra pressure due to such superimposed loads. Wherever any side of an excavation is a masonry wall, such wall should be braced to ensure stability. This should not include reinforced concrete walls known to be of ample strength. Temporary sheet piling which has been installed to permit the construction of a retaining wall must not be removed until such wall has acquired its full strength.

Except in hard rock, excavations below the level of the base or footing of any foundation or retaining wall should not be permitted unless the wall is underpinned and all other precautions taken to ensure the stability of the adjacent walls for the protection of the workmen. Undercutting of earth banks should not be permitted unless they are adequately shored. Excavations should be inspected after every rain storm or other hazard-increasing occurrence, and the protection against slides and cave-ins increased if necessary. All fixed-in-place ladders and stairways giving access to levels 20 or more feet apart should be provided with landing platforms at vertical intervals of not more than 20 feet. Every landing platform should be equipped with standard railings and toeboards.

JACKS

Workmen should always select the proper size jack for the load to be lifted. A jack of too light capacity can strip itself, releasing the load; and a jack with too little height will run itself out before accomplishing the purpose intended. The jack should be inspected before using. If there is any doubt about the jack's condition, it should not be used. The base of the jack should be placed on a level firm footing where it cannot slip or kick away. When the object has been lifted to the desired height, blocking or cribbing must be immediately placed under it.

TRENCHES

Particular attention should be given to shoring of trenches, especially if there are roadways or railroad lines in the vicinity of the excavation or if men are to work in the trench. In the following paragraphs, provisions for shoring and bracing of excavations should apply, except when the full depth of the excavation is in stable solid rock, hard slag, or hard shale or the shoring plan has been designed by the engineering office.

The sides of excavations 4 feet or more in depth, or in which the soil is so unstable that it is not considered safe at lesser depths, should be supported by substantial and adequate sheeting, sheet piling, bracing, shoring, etc., or the sides sloped to the angle of repose. Surface areas adjacent to the sides should be well drained. Trenches in partly saturated, filled, or unstable soils, should be suitably braced.

Excavated or other material must not be stored nearer than 2 feet from the edge of a trench. In the case of extremely deep trenches, material should be stored farther away than 2 feet. The safe storage distance is in proportion to the depth of the trench; the deeper the trench the farther away the material should be stored. Where pedestrian and vehicular traffic is to be maintained over, or adjacent to excavations, proper safeguards should be provided, such as walkways, bridges, guardrails, barricades, warning flags, lights, or illumination.

Where an excavation is close to a cut, particularly when nearer to the cut than its depth, special shoring should be used. Men working in deep trenches should wear hard hats as a protection against falling material. Access to excavations over 5 feet deep should be by ramps, ladders, stairways, or hoists. Workmen should not jump into the trench, nor use the bracing as a stairway.

No tools, materials, or debris should be left on walkways, ramps, struts, or near the edge of an excavation. Such material might be knocked off or cause a worker to lose his footing. Pick-and-shovel men working in trenches must keep sufficient distance apart so they cannot injure each other when working with their shovels.

Extra care should be used in excavating around gas mains, oil tanks, gasoline or oil pipe lines, etc. Smoking or open fires of any kind are prohibited in areas where gaseous conditions are suspected. In such places the air should be tested and, if gas is present, ventilation should be provided by portable blowers or other satisfactory methods. Workmen should put up barricades and lights around the excavation at the end of each work shift for the safety of personnel moving in that area after dark.

EYE HAZARDS

Many operations in an industrial facility involve eye hazards. Certain areas, machines and trades are therefore required to be designated as "eye-hazardous." These include, but are not limited to such operations as arc-welding, the handling of acids, and grinding, chipping and other machining processes which are accompanied by the generation of flying particles.

In order to afford a measure of protection to the casual uniformed visitor, areas and machines which have been designated as "eye-hazardous" should be permanently screened and permanently marked with a black and yellow checkerboard symbol and the phrase, EYE HAZARD, in black on a yellow background. Other areas where personnel are involved in eye-hazardous occupations should be clearly marked with portable screens and signs with the same markings.

Signs similar to the portable sign should be placed on the outside of buildings which are entirely occupied by eye-hazardous processes. These signs should be placed on the door in every case and beside the door if space permits. If space does not permit, the sign beside the door can be replaced by a black and yellow checkerboard which extends from 3 feet above the sill to 7 feet above the sill on both door jambs. Large or multiple doors should have the sign repeated at about 6 foot intervals or repeated on each door, whichever is appropriate. Welding sets in general should be clear blue as for electrical controls. Compressors, generators and other miscellaneous machinery should be painted medium Navy gray.

FLAMMABLE LIQUIDS

Red has been traditionally used on containers for kerosene, gasoline, naphtha, alcohol, solvents and other flammable liquids. This practice is obviously wrong because of conflict with the use of red on fire protection devices. For safety and better visibility, safety cans, small portable tanks and drums used for storage and transportations of gasoline within naval establishments should be painted brilliant yellow throughout and should have the contents conspicuously marked with large black letters. On large fixed tanks, medium Navy gray may be used for the body, with a large area of yellow added with black letters indicating contents.

SAFETY PRECAUTIONS FOR
PORTABLE POWER TOOLS

Portable power tools should be kept cleaned, oiled, and repaired. They should be carefully inspected before use. The switches must operate properly and the cords be clean and free of defects. The plug should be clean and sound.

The casings of all electrically driven tools should be grounded. Double insulated tools from sources qualified under the applicable specification are exempt from this grounding requirement.

Sparking portable electric tools should not be used where flammable vapors, gases, liquids, or exposed explosives are present.

Care should be taken that cords do not come in contact with sharp objects; they should not be allowed to kink, nor left where they might be run over. Cords must not come in contact with oil or grease, hot surfaces, or chemicals. Damaged cords should be replaced. They are not to be patched with tape. Tools should be

stored in a clean, dry place where the cord can be loosely coiled.

POWER TWIST DRILLS

A portable power drill should be grasped firmly during the operation to prevent it from bucking or breaking loose, thereby causing injury or damage. When the work is completed, the drills should be removed, and drill and motor should both be well cleaned.

PNEUMATIC TOOLS

Builders using this type of tool should wear and use necessary protective devices. Only authorized and trained Builders should operate pneumatic tools. Persons with arthritis, neuritis, or circulatory disease should not use vibrating tools such as hammers, chisels, tempers, riveters, or corkers.

When not in use pneumatic tools should be laid down in such a manner that no harm can be done if the switch is accidentally tripped. No idle tool should be left in a standing position. It should be kept in good operating condition, thoroughly inspected at regular intervals with particular attention given to control and exhaust valves, hose connections, guide clips on hammers, and the chucks of reamers and drills.

The valve should be closed and the air exhausted from the line through the pneumatic tool being used before disconnecting the line from the tool. The air hose should be suitable to withstand the pressure required for the tool. Leaking or defective hose should be removed from service. Hose should not be laid over ladders, steps, scaffolds, or walkways in such a manner as to create a tripping hazard. Where hose is run through doorways, the hose should be protected against damage by the door edge.

Compressed air should not be used to clean clothing being worn or to blow dust off the body. An air hose should never be pointed at other persons.

Pneumatic Rock Drills

Under no circumstances should the operator of portable pneumatic drills wear loose or torn clothing. Only trained competent Builders, wearing necessary protective devices, should operate drills.

Bits should be examined for defects; particular attention should be paid to bit flutes which should be ground to uniform size, sharpness, and length. The machine should be held on a straight line with the hole being bored. Tipping of bit is prohibited. The machine should not be fed too fast.

The operator should be on firm footing before commencing operation. All drills should be equipped with a hand-grip switch that will shut off the supply of air when grip is released. This switch should not be modified or bypassed.

Pneumatic Paving Breakers

Suitable goggles should be worn when operating pneumatic paving breakers to protect the eyes from flying particles.

Operators must make sure that the breaker and its accessories are in good working condition. When air is used for power, the valves and connections should be checked carefully. Also, when laying down this pneumatic tool, the operator must be careful to see that the trigger cannot be operated accidentally.

When shock tools are re-dressed the heads should not be tempered, since hard heads will spall and are more dangerous than those which mushroom.

Pneumatic paving breaker operators should never cut off the air supply to the machine by purposely kinking the hose while disconnecting this equipment. Air should be cut off at the source. If the job is near a sidewalk or other thoroughfare, canvas barriers or other suitable screens should be placed on either side to protect others from flying particles.

When using a paving breaker to break up extremely hard materials such as heavy blocks embedded in concrete slabs or with hard and slick surfaces that may cause the tool to slip around instead of biting into the surface, Builders should first use a sledge hammer to roughen the surface. This practice will guard against breaking or cutting the legs or feet.

Power Hammers

No Builder should point any pneumatic hammer at other Builders. Hammers should be operated in a careful and safe manner at all times. All hammers should be equipped with a device for holding the tool in the machine. These safety tool holders should be inspected at frequent intervals.

The operator of a power hammer should not restrict the air exhaust port in any fashion. All pneumatic hammers should be equipped with a hand-grip safety switch. The pneumatic hammer should be used only for those purposes for which intended.

All hammer operators should wear necessary eye, face, and body protection. Operators of pneumatic hammers should wear gloves.

Power Wrenches

Pneumatic wrench operators should use a wrench only for those purposes for which it is intended. All wrenches should be equipped with hand-grip safety switches. All wrenches should be inspected frequently by a competent Builder. Operators of pneumatic wrenches should not wear loose fitting articles of clothing. Wrench operators should use all protective devices provided.

POWDER ACTUATED TOOLS

Powder actuated tools should be operated, repaired, serviced, and handled only by Builders who have been trained and certified by the manufacturer, his authorized representative, or Navy Department certified instructors. In applications to concrete, approval for use of the tool should be given only after it has been ascertained that it will give satisfactory results and create no spalling or "shelling-out."

Each powder-actuated tool to be used at the work site will be presented to the designated representative for inspection and registration. If acceptable, a tool permit will be issued prior to use at the work site. For each powder-actuated tool registered, the following data will be obtained and recorded: trade name; manufacturer; model and size; serial number; ownership. The use of powder-actuated tools in explosive or flammable atmospheres is prohibited.

The tool operator, together with other personnel in the vicinity, should wear safety goggles or other approved safety-type face and eye protective devices and a hard hat. Powder-actuated tools and the powder charges will be secured to prevent unauthorized possession. Upon the detection of any defect in the operation of a powder-actuated tool, the tool will be removed from service until the deficiency is corrected. Powder-actuated, fastener-type tools which, by means of a powder charge propellant, discharge an object for the purpose of affixing it to or penetrating another object, should meet the following requirements:

The muzzle end of the tool, including barrel extensions, should have a protective shield or guard at least 3 inches in diameter, securely attached, perpendicular to the barrel, designed to confine the flying particles and arrest the ricochet of the projectiles; or, in lieu of such shield or guard, a jig providing equivalent protection may be used. The tool should be made incapable of firing if not equipped with either a standard guard or a special guard, fixture, or jig of the manufacturer's design. The tool should not be operated against other than a flat work surface unless it is equipped with a special head or jig to accommodate the curvature of the surface. The tool should be so designed that it will not operate, when equipped with the standard guard indexed to the center position, if the bearing surface of the guard is tilted more than eight degrees from contact with the work surface.

Fasteners should not be driven directly into materials such as brick or concrete closer than 3 inches from the edge or corner, or into steel surfaces closer than one-half inch from the edge or corner, unless a special guard, fixture, or jig is used. Penetration must not endanger personnel, equipment, materials, or surroundings on the opposite side of the object to which the fastener is being affixed.

All powder-actuated tools and their use should comply with such Federal, State and local laws as are applicable.

POWER SAWS

In addition to the general precautions for portable electrical and pneumatic tools contained in this chapter, the precautions common to both electrical and pneumatic portable saws are as follows:

All circular portable power saws should be provided with guards that fully encompass the unused portion of the blades.

Circular saw blades should be installed by a qualified Builder and only when the source of power is disconnected from the tool.

Only a hand grip switch, electric or pneumatic, should be used.

Never use a blade which has a speed rating less than the saw on which it is being used. If the saw begins to "lug down," back it out slowly and firmly in a straight line.

SAFETY PRECAUTIONS FOR ASPHALT AND CONCRETE EQUIPMENT

Where safety precautions are considered to be necessary but have not been provided, or where existing precautions are judged to be inadequate, the Builder in charge will issue new or supplementary precautions that are deemed necessary for the protection of personnel and property. Listed below are some specific rules for asphalt and concrete equipment.

ASPHALT EQUIPMENT

Paint, or otherwise mark, pipes through which heated asphalt is flowing. Bare skin contact with such lines may result in severe burns. Place heating devices, such as the asphalt melter, on a level, firm foundation and protect it against traffic, accidental tipping, or similar hazards. Provide adequate fire extinguishers at the location of heating devices.

Allow hot equipment, such as the aggregate dryer, to cool sufficiently before attempting to clean or otherwise maintain it.

Maintain a minimum 3-inch covering of asphalt over the top of heating tubes when heating asphalt in equipment that utilizes an open flame heating system. Perform all heating in a level, well-ventilated area, with the item of equipment in which the asphalt is being heated at a halt. Make sure fire extinguishers are on hand and properly charged in the event of fire.

When dedrumming or heating asphalt cement, do not smoke or use open flames within 50 feet of the equipment. When heating, dedrumming, or manufacturing asphalt cutbacks, extend this distance to 100 feet.

Do not climb on equipment or stand on aggregate stockpiles in bins while equipment is in operation.

Do not use open flames around asphalt or fuel storage tanks.

Do not stand between the asphalt finisher and haul trucks.

CONCRETE EQUIPMENT

Keep the area beneath batching plants as free of personnel as possible. Be sure that men operating haul equipment have left their vehicles before commencing batching.

Empty batching plants before attempting repairs. Work on fully or partially loaded plants must be carried out only in cases of extreme urgency.

Guard against the possibility of shock when undertaking to maintain such electrically powered apparatus as the central mix plant or the slip-form paver by ensuring that they are shut down and by using only approved insulated tools.

Wear hard hats around the batch and central mix plants.

BUTANE OR BLOWTORCH SAFETY

Every blowtorch should be provided with a complete set of operating instructions (i.e., directions for filling, pumping up the air pressure, lighting, and extinguishing), and no one should use a blowtorch until he has read and is familiar with the operating instructions.

The blowtorch should, preferably, be filled out-of-doors. If it is filled indoors, it should be filled at a point remote from open flame, sparks, or other source of ignition. The torch should not be filled while hot. Safety cans should be used when blowtorches are being filled. Gasoline containing lead compounds or benzol should not be used.

Laundry soap may be used on threads of the filler plug to ensure a tight seal. The filler plug should be tightened gently; force may ruin the gasket or strip the threads of the plug. The filler plug should not be loosened while the burner is hot.

Alterations on torches which would permit pumping up the pressure by any method other than the use of pumping devices provided by the torch manufacturers should not be made. No device other than the pump supplied with the torch should be used to obtain working pressure. Preferably, pressure should not be pumped up while the torch is lighted. Torches should not at any time be pumped up to excessive pressure. Five to fifteen strokes of the pump are enough, depending upon the size of the tank and the amount of gasoline in it.

Before torches are stored the pressure in the tanks should be released and the valves secured.

Before torches are lighted they should be examined carefully for leaks. All torches should be inspected and tested at frequent and regular intervals by a competent Builder to make sure that the torches are in proper operating condition. Any defect found in torches should be reported at once to the supervisor. No torch which is defective in any way should be used until after such defect has been properly repaired.

The priming cup should not be overfilled, as the gasoline may flow over the tank and become ignited, thus furnishing sufficient heat to develop a dangerous pressure within the tank. If gasoline should flow over the tank it should be carefully wiped off before the torch is lighted. When heating tile, care should be taken to prevent igniting of the material being heated.

Torches should not be lighted until the gasoline in the priming cup has nearly all been consumed. Immediately after the torch has been lighted the flame should be shielded from the wind. Windbreaks should be made of noncombustible material, without bottoms and easily removable. Torches should preferably be preheated and lighted out-of-doors.

Stuffing boxes should be kept tight so as to prevent leaks around the valve stem. They should not be tightened while torches are in use.

A torch should not be used in a small unventilated space. It may heat up and thus become a source of danger, and it may exhaust the supply of oxygen, causing the operator to lose consciousness or even his life from suffocation. When such use is unavoidable, it is necessary to provide airfed respiratory protective equipment for the workers. Torches should not be dragged across the floor or abused in any other way.

Torches fired with petroleum gases are preferred to those fired by gasoline because of the fewer hazards. However, liquified petroleum gases, which are composed of propane, propylene, butane, or butylene, present a hazard comparable to that of any flammable natural of manufactured gas and in addition they are heavier than air. Therefore, there must be adequate ventilation of spaces in which the gas is used. Precautions should be taken to assure that control valves are tightly closed after use and that there are no leaky valves or connections.

SAFETY HOUSEKEEPING

Good housekeeping in working areas is as important to safety as it is to efficiency. Beside the idea of "a place for everything and everything in its place," good housekeeping includes the matter of keeping working areas and thoroughfares clear of rubbish, debris, nonessential articles, and the like, which tend to create tripping and/or fire hazards.

OUTDOOR HOUSEKEEPING

To reduce fire hazard, any natural growth on an area which is to be used for the storage of lumber or other combustible material must be burned off or otherwise cleared before material is stored in the area. A margin 50 ft wide should be cleared beyond the outer boundaries of the area.

To reduce fire hazard, crawl spaces must be kept clear of vegetation and debris, and they must not be used for the storage of combustible material. A margin at least 50 ft wide should be cleared, and kept clear, beyond the outer boundaries of any structure.

Waste flammable liquids must not be poured into sewers or drains. They should be collected in steel drums or other fireproof receptacles and disposed of as recommended by the safety officer. Definite areas for the dumping of refuse must be set aside and plainly identified, and refuse must not be dumped or allowed to accumulate anywhere else.

All thoroughfares must be kept clear. Ice or snow must be removed at once if possible. If not, slipperiness must be reduced by spreading gritty material, such as sand, gravel, or ashes. On any structure where a water hazard exists, life rings must be provided at intervals of not more than 200 ft. All men working over the water must be provided with life jackets, and the jackets must be worn.

All outdoor traffic hazards, such as stock piles, excavations, low overhangs, and the like must be marked with suitable warning signs, flags, barricades, lights, for other markers.

INDOOR HOUSEKEEPING

All working spaces, construction areas, and repair areas must be regularly policed, to maintain order and cleanliness and to eliminate tripping and fire hazards.

All indoor traffic hazards, such as stock piles, floor openings, low overhangs, changes in floor level, and the like must be barricaded or marked with suitable warning signs.

All rubbish, scrap material, and the like must be placed in appropriate identified receptacles. All working areas must be kept clear of rubbish and scrap, and all such material must be removed from structures at least once a day. Oily rags, steel wool, waste paper, and other flammable waste materials must be placed in tightly closed fireproof containers, and the contents of these containers must be disposed of, as recommended by the safety officer, at the end of each working day.

Ample and well-defined thoroughfares should be laid out in structures, and traffic should be confined to them as much as possible. Thoroughfares must be kept clear of obstructions and debris. Collision hazards at blind corners should be eliminated by the installation of mirrors. Running, which is often the cause of slipping, tripping, and collision accidents, must be prohibited. Floors and decks must be kept free of protruding nails, splinters, holes, and loose boards.

Stairway openings must be guarded by railings not less than 36 in. nor more than 42 in. above the floor surface. A stairway between 22 and 44 in. wide must have at least one handrail. A stairway over 44 in. but less than 88 in. wide must have a handrail on each side. A stairway 88 in. wide or wider must have a handrail on each side and another down the center. Handrails must not be less than 30 in. nor more than 34 in. high, as measured from the top of a tread at the face of a riser.

Stairways must be kept well lighted, clean, dry, and free of slippery substances, refuse, and obstructions. There must be no storage of materials on stairways.

SUPERVISION

As a Builder, you must know and observe all safety precautions for the equipment you use and the work you do. In addition, it is your responsibility to ensure that all men working under your supervision also observe the proper safety rules. You must make certain, for instance, that every man in the shop knows the location of the portable firefighting equipment and that he knows how to use it.

There are dozens of precautions that must be observed; make frequent checks to see that they are. When you are giving your men instructions, either formally or informally, teach safety as an integral part of the program. Follow all applicable safety precautions.

Accident prevention is both a science and an art. It represents, above all other things, control—scientific control of personnel performance, machine performance, and physical environment. From the standpoint of handling people so that they willingly work safely, accident prevention is an art.

Safety plays a major role in any supervisory job and, to a considerable degree, affects the supervisor's ability to meet the demands required of him.

The attitude of the supervisor influences the attitudes of his men. When a supervisor has the attitude that safety does not pay, he can be sure that his men will ignore safety. When a supervisor is safety-conscious, his men will be safety-conscious. If you are one of the few supervisors who think that safety is unimportant, consider how you would feel if one of your men were injured or killed because of your negligence. Would you want it on your conscience? Could you face the family of the man?

SAFETY EDUCATION

Many supervisors feel that it is only necessary to provide safeguards and safety will then take care of itself. Provision of safeguards is a move in the right direction, but it alone will not get good results. To maintain a good safety record, the supervisor needs to employ a combination of safety devices and safety training. If each man has had sound safety training, he will be able to guard against even those hazards where safety devices are impracticable. The supervisor must, however, train every man in the use of safeguards, explaining why, as well as how, they should be used. How many supervisors have seen a man shut off the power on a machine and then walk away from it before it has stopped turning? Such a man uses a safeguard, but he does not know why he uses it. By providing the necessary training, an alert supervisor will make sure that such careless uses of safeguards do not happen again.

Standup safety meetings should be held in every shop once every week. The meetings should be held at or near the work place. Instead of a routine safety lecture, it is much better to hold a group discussion of specific accidents that are to be guarded against or that may have happened in the unit. The men should be encouraged to express their ideas. A group conclusion as to how specific accidents can be prevented should be reached.

Another type of safety meeting is one in which the supervisor presents a safety problem that has developed because of new work or new equipment. Again, the men should be invited to express their ideas.

A third type of safety meeting is one in which actual demonstrations and practice by the group are carried out. You might demonstrate how to lift, and then have the men practice lifting. Also, to make the reasons for lifting in this manner more realistic, a little lesson on the classes of tools and a little problem in ratio and proportion should prove interesting.

If you are demonstrating how to use a saw, bring in a saw and use it—don't just talk about how to use it. Then, again, let the men practice.

Making these meetings interesting is of the utmost importance. The supervisor should not complain or scold, and the meetings should be limited in time. The subject should be thought out carefully in advance and it should be timely. Considerable ingenuity is required to keep these meetings from degenerating into dull, routine affairs. Some supervisors have the men themselves rotate as leaders of the safety meetings—an excellent device to maintain interest. Hundreds of good motion pictures and other visual aids are available on safety subjects. Use them.

ACCIDENT REPORTING

When an accident occurs in your shop, office, or within your crew, you must fill out a OpNav Form 5100/1, Accidental Injury/Death Report. (See figs. 19-1 through 19-4.) This form provides a method of recording the essential facts concerning an accident, from which data for use in accident prevention can be compiled. Item 27—"Corrective action taken/recommended"—is the most important part of this report. The manner in which this question is answered provides a clue to the attitude of the supervisor. Too many supervisors answer this question with, "The man has been warned to be more careful." This type of answer does not mean a thing. The answer to this question should tie in with the rest of the report. If an unsafe condition is the cause of the accident, you cannot correct it by warning the man to be more careful. Study the report; analyse it; then take the proper corrective action. This report is one of your best accident prevention tools if properly used. In many cases the difference between a minor accident and a major one is a matter of luck. Do not ignore the small cuts and bruises; investigate the reasons for them and correct the causes. If you do this, you will have a safe shop or office and an efficient one.

ACCIDENT INVESTIGATION

To fill out a OpNav Form 5100/1 properly, as shown in figures 19-1 and 19-2, an accident

ACCIDENTAL INJURY/DEATH REPORT			FOR OFFICIAL USE ONLY	

OPNAV FORM 5100/1 (5-69) S/N-0107-776-0010

SPECIAL HANDLING REQUIRED IN ACCORDANCE WITH OPNAVINST 5100.11   REPORT SYMBOL OPNAV 5100-3

TO: COMMANDER, NAVAL SAFETY CENTER, NAVAL AIR STATION, NORFOLK, VA. 23511

1. REPORTING COMMAND	2A. COMMAND AUTHORITY EXERCISED BY:	3. REPORT NUMBER
Training Publications Division Washington Navy Yard, Wash. D.C.	Naval Station 2B. GCM AUTHORITY EXERCISED BY:	5

4. NAME OF PERSON INJURED/KILLED (FIRST, MIDDLE, LAST)	5A. SERVICE/BADGE NO. B472465	6. RANK & DESIGNATOR/RATE AND NEC/CIVILIAN OCCUPATION
Jimmie Lee Don	5B. SOCIAL SECURITY NO. 247-83-2448	BU3

7. SEX	8. AGE	9A. TIME IN SERVICE (MIL ONLY)	10A. MIL: [x] USN [ ] USNR [ ] OTHER
M	19	1 Year / 9B. YEARS EXPERIENCE (CIV ONLY)	10B. CIV: [ ] EMPLOYEE [ ] DEPENDENT [ ] OTHER

11A. DUTY STATUS	11B. DUTY STATUS
MIL [ ] EXT ACT DU [x] ACDUTRA [ ] DRILL [ ] TRAVEL [ ] LV/LIB [ ] UA [ ] OTHER	CIV: [ ] REG. [ ] UNAUTH WORK [ ] TEMP. [ ] OTHER [ ] TRAVEL

12. DATE AND TIME OF INJURY				13. PLACE OF OCCURRENCE	14. DAYS LOST/CHARGED
HOUR	DATE	MONTH YEAR	DAY OF WEEK	[ ] ABOARD SHIP [x] ASHORE	5
1600	12	April 1970	Friday	DESCRIBE LOCATION Carpenter shop	

15. WEATHER/NATURAL DISASTER	16. LIGHT CONDITIONS AT SITE
NA	Good

17. DESCRIPTION OF EVENTS: (DESCRIBE THE CONTRIBUTING EVENTS LEADING UP TO THE INJURY/DEATH SO THAT THE REVIEWING OFFICIAL WILL HAVE A CLEAR PICTURE OF WHAT CAUSED THE INJURY/DEATH, SELECT THE APPROPRIATE ENTRY FROM EACH MAJOR FACTOR CATEGORY LISTED ON BACK OF INSTRUCTION SHEET AND ENTER IT WITH AMPLIFYING DETAIL IN BOXES 18 THROUGH 25 BELOW.)

> While brushing shavings from a surfacer, Don's right hand slipped and struck the cutterhead of the surfacer. Even though the current had been turned off, the knives had not stopped. Therefore, Don lost the first joint of his index finger on his right hand.

WITNESSES: NAME, RANK/RATE, ADDRESS

18. KIND OF INJURY:	19. BODY PART INJURED:
Amputation.	Index finger on right hand.

20. SOURCE OF INJURY (OBJECT, SUBSTANCE, ETC.) WHICH CONTACTED THE BODY AND INJURED PERSON):	21. KIND OF ACCIDENT (FALL, CRUSHED, STRUCK BY, ETC.):
Machine-electric motor powered.	Cut by machine.

22. HAZARDOUS CONDITION (WHAT CONDITION CAUSED, PERMITTED, CONTRIBUTED TO ACCIDENT WHICH RESULTED IN INJURY): [x] NOT APPLICABLE	23. AGENCY (AND AGENCY PART) OF ACCIDENT (OBJECT, SUBSTANCE, ETC. TO WHICH THE HAZARDOUS CONDITION APPLIED): [x] NOT APPLICABLE

24. UNSAFE ACT (WHAT PERSONAL ACTION CAUSED OR ALLOWED ACCIDENT TO OCCUR): [x] BY INJURED MAN [ ] BY ANOTHER [ ] NOT APPLICABLE	25. UNSAFE PERSONAL FACTOR (MENTAL OR PHYSICAL CONDITION WHICH RESULTED IN OR CONTRIBUTED TO THE UNSAFE ACT): Inattention to surroundings.

26. REASON FOR BEING ON GOVERNMENT PROPERTY (REGULAR DUTY ASSIGNMENT, CIV EMP, PATIENT, VISITOR, BUSINESS, ETC.):

Regular duty assignment.

29.52.1(2D)

Figure 19-1.—Accidental Injury/Death Report OpNav Form 5100/1 (front).

OPNAV FORM 5100/I (5-69) (BACK)

27. CORRECTIVE ACTION TAKEN/RECOMMENDED (WHAT ACTION WILL HELP PREVENT ANOTHER ACCIDENT OF THIS TYPE?):

Don should have waited a few seconds longer to clean the machine. A safety lecture on shop hazards, emphasizing "Haste Makes Waste", was assigned to Don.

28. SIGNATURE OF PERSON PREPARING REPORT	29. TITLE AND GRADE	30. DATE
[signature]	CUCM, USN	12 April 1970

31. REVIEW AND COMMENTS OF SAFETY OFFICER OR COMMANDING OFFICER

32. SIGNATURE	33. TITLE AND GRADE	34. DATE

ADDITIONAL INFORMATION WHEN REQUIRED BY JAG

35. CONDITION OF INDIVIDUAL AT TIME OF THIS OCCURRENCE:

UNDER THE INFLUENCE OF: ☐ ALCOHOL ☐ NARCOTICS ☐ BARBI-TURATES ☐ OTHER (SPECIFY) _____ ☐ NOT APPLICABLE

☐ UNABLE TO DETERMINE DUE TO PHYSICAL CONDITION

EXAMINER _____

36. BASIS FOR ABOVE OPINION:
A. CLINICAL FINDINGS: _____

B. BIOLOGICAL SPECIMEN TAKEN: ☐ NO ☐ YES TIME _____ LABORATORY TO WHICH SPECIMEN SENT _____

TYPE OF TEST _____ RESULT _____ OTHER TESTS/RESULTS _____

37. MEDICAL OFFICER'S FINDINGS RELATIVE TO NATURE AND EXTENT OF INJURY: _____

38. WAS SUBJECT HOSPITALIZED AS A RESULT OF THIS OCCURRENCE? ☐ YES ☐ NO

39. IF THE SUBJECT WERE ALREADY ON THE SICK LIST FOR OTHER REASONS AT TIME OF INJURY WOULD THIS INJURY IN ITSELF HAVE REQUIRED HOSPITALIZATION? ☐ YES ☐ NO ☐ NOT APPLICABLE

40. IT IS POSSIBLE THAT THE FOLLOWING DISABILITY MAY RESULT: ☐ PERMANENT PARTIAL ☐ PERMANENT TOTAL

41. DATE OF EXPIRATION OF ENLISTMENT/TERM OF OBLIGATED SERVICE:

42. IF DECEASED, WAS AUTOPSY CONDUCTED? ☐ YES ☐ NO IF YES, ATTACH COPY OF AUTOPSY PROTOCOL

43. ADDITIONAL INFORMATION FOR RESERVISTS: IF RESERVIST WAS ENGAGED IN ACTIVE-DUTY TRAINING OR INACTIVE DUTY (DRILL) SUPPLY THE FOLLOWING INFORMATION:

MEMBER REPORTED FOR DUTY OR DRILL		DISMISSED FROM DUTY OR DRILL		INJURY	
DATE	TIME	DATE	TIME	DATE	TIME

44. MEDICAL OFFICER'S SIGNATURE	45. GRADE	46. DATE

47. IT IS THE OPINION OF THE UNDERSIGNED THAT THE INJURY/DEATH IN QUESTION WAS INCURRED IN THE LINE OF DUTY AND NOT AS THE RESULT OF THE SUBJECT MAN'S OWN MISCONDUCT. ☐ YES ☐ NO

COMMANDING OFFICER (OR ONE AUTHORIZED TO SIGN BY HIS DIRECTION - IF LATTER SO INDICATE)

48. SIGNATURE	49. TYPED NAME AND GRADE	50. DATE

51. ACTION OF OFFICER EXERCISING GENERAL COURT-MARTIAL JURISDICTION:

DATE: _____

FROM:

TO: JUDGE ADVOCATE GENERAL OF THE NAVY

SIGNATURE AND TYPED NAME OF OFFICER EXERCISING GCM AUTHORITY (OR ONE AUTHORIZED TO SIGN BY DIRECTION)

29.52.2(2D)

Figure 19-2.—Accidental Injury/Death Report OpNav Form 5100/1 (back).

ACCIDENTAL INJURY/DEATH REPORT
OPNAV FORM 5100/1 (5-69)

Print with pen or type; items not applicable or contributory to the injury/death will be marked N.A.

INSTRUCTIONS FOR ACCIDENTAL INJURY/DEATH REPORT

Block 1. Reporting Command - Self-explanatory.

Block 2A. Command Authority Exercised By. In the case of ships and air units this is the Type Commander. For shore activities this is the command that provides command and support (ie COMSERVLANT in the case of NAVSTA NORVA, COMNAVSHIPSYSCOM in the case of a ship yard, etc.)

Block 2B. GCM Authority Exercised By. Self-explanatory. Use only when report is required by JAG.

Block 3. Report Number. Reports will be serialized consecutively by each reporting command/activity during the fiscal year. (ie 2-69 is the second report of fiscal year 1969)

Block 4. Name of Person Injured/Killed. Self-explanatory.

Block 5A. Service/Badge Number. Self-explanatory.

Block 5B. Social Security Number. Self-explanatory.

Block 6. Rank & Designator/Rate & NEC/Civilian Occupation. Self-explanatory.

Block 7. Sex. Self-explanatory.

Block 8. Age. Self-explanatory

Block 9A. Time in Service (Mil Only). Indicate in years only.

Block 9B. Years Experience (Civ. Only). Indicate number of years experience in present occupation, including years of experience gained in that occupation in other government or private industry employment. In cases of injury or death to civilians other than employees of the Department of the Navy, mark "N.A.".

Block 10. Employment Status. In the event the line "Other" is selected for either military or civilian, specify as contract employee, visitor, Army, Air Force, etc.

Block 11. Duty Status. For either military or civilian check all applicable boxes.

Block 12. Date and Time of Injury. Give the hour on the basis of the 24 hour clock using four digits. Use two digits each for the date, month and year.

Block 13. Place of Occurrence. In describing the location enter paint locker, weather deck, flight deck, machine shop, galley, etc. as appropriate.

Block 14. Days Lost/Charged. For fatal injury or missing persons, enter 6000 days. For all other injuries enter the number of calendar days of disability, or time charges using the schedule of charges, Table 1, Appendix I. Whenever the schedule of charges is used the actual number of calendar days of disability is not entered.

Block 15. Weather/Natural Disaster. If a factor, describe weather conditions or natural disaster which contributed to the injury.

Block 16. Light Conditions at Site. Describe outside or internal lighting conditions, as applicable, existing at the immediate site and time of accident.

Block 17. Description of Events. Enter narrative description of circumstances and events which directly or indirectly led to the injury, physical impairment or death. Include sufficient information to clarify or expand upon the character and scope of data to be entered in blocks 18 through 25 of the report. Accidental injury/death reports in all cases resulting from a ship accident will reference the applicable ship accident report serial in this block. Include in this block, as appropriate, comments on the following:

    a. Time injured person first seen by medical officer/representative.
    b. Disposition of injured person; i.e. treated and retained aboard or transferred to another ship (military personnel) or transferred to a hospital for treatment (military and civilian personnel).
    c. In cases of exposure to toxic fumes/chemical poisons, describe type of substance, concentration and type of exposure.
    d. Describe additional causative/contributing factors not described in blocks 20 through 25 and indicate (D) for a definite cause, (S) for a suspected cause and (P) for condition present but not a factor. Enter name, rank/rate or grade and address of witnesses to the accident. If none, so indicate.

Block 18. Kind of Injury. Enter words from Block 18 (on reverse side of this sheet) which best describes nature of injury.

Block 19. Body Part Injured. Enter word(s) from block 19 (on reverse side of this sheet) which best describes body part affected by nature of injury

Block 20. Source of Injury. Enter object or environment from block 20 (on reverse side of this sheet) which best describes source of injury. (NOTE: A direct logical relationship between "Source of Injury" and "Kind of Injury" must be established.)

Block 21. Kind of Accident. Enter action, motion or type of contact from block 21 (on reverse side of this sheet) which best describes means by which injured person came in contact with previously selected "Source of Injury". (NOTE: A direct logical relationship between the "Source of Injury" and "Kind of Accident" must be established.)

Block 22. Hazardous Condition. Enter the condition from block 22 (on reverse side of this sheet) which best describes the hazardous condition which permitted or occasioned occurrence of previously selected "kind of Accident". (NOTE: A direct logical relationship between "Kind of Accident", "Hazardous Condition", and "Agency of Accident", which is to follow, must be established).

Block 23. Agency (and Agency Part) of Accident. Enter the object or environment from Block 20 (on reverse side of this sheet) which best describes the agency to which the hazardous condition applies. In addition, describe the part of the agency which is unsafe. For instance, if the agency is a table saw from which the blade guard has been removed, enter the words "cross cut saw - blade." In some agencies such as a length of pipe, rope, lumber, etc., no agency part is required to be named. The rule for agency part is - if corrective or preventive action for the part involved is different from the action on any other part of the agency, name the agency part involved. (NOTE: A direct logical relationship between "Hazardous Condition" and "Agency of Accident" must be established). If there is no hazardous condition there can be no agency or agency part of accident, and all three items shall be described as "Not Applicable"

Block 24. Unsafe Act. Enter the act or omission from Block 24 (on reverse side of this sheet) which best describes unsafe act which permitted or caused occurrence of previously named kind of accident. (NOTE: A direct logical relationship between "Unsafe Act" and "Kind of Accident" must be established).

Block 25. Unsafe Personal Factor. Enter the reason from Block 25 (on reverse side of this sheet) which best describes the unsafe personal factor which led to the "Unsafe Act" or contributed to the injury. (NOTE: If there was an unsafe act committed, an unsafe personal factor should always be selected. If no unsafe act was committed there may still, however, be an unsafe personal factor which contributed to the accident).

Block 26. Reason for Being on Government Property. Self-explanatory.

Block 27. Corrective Action Taken/Recommended. List specific remedial actions which have been or should be taken to prevent recurrence of similar injury. If an entry of "unknown" or "none" seems appropriate, an explanation shall be given as to why corrective action can not be recommended. Specify whether actions have been taken or are only recommended. If the latter, what action is expected?

Blocks 28 through 30. First Signature Line. Report is to be signed and dated by the individual who prepared the report to this point.

Block 31. Review and Comments of Safety Officer or Commanding Officer. Additional recommendations may be made if appropriate.

Blocks 32 through 34. Second Signature Line. Self-explanatory.

The remainder of the report form will only be filled out in those instances where the injury/death to the military member is reportable to JAG.

    a. Blocks 1-34. Prepared in accordance with above instructions.
    b. Blocks 35-50. Self-explanatory.
    c. Blocks 35 through 40, 42, and 44 through 46 shall be completed and signed by the medical officer on the basis of his observation or examination of the injured or deceased member and information then available to him.
    d. Blocks 41, 43 and 47 through 50 shall be completed and signed by the commanding officer on the basis of his investigation (or by an officer authorized and directed by the commanding officer to investigate the incident and sign the report by direction).

29.52.3(127E)

Figure 19-3.—Instructions for Accidental Injury/Death Report (front).

BLOCK 18. KIND OF INJURY

AMPUTATION OR ENUCLEATION
ASPHYXIA, STRANGULATION
BURN OR SCALD (THERMAL)
BURN (CHEMICAL)
CAISSON DISEASE, BENDS
CONCUSSION, BRAIN
CONTUSION, CRUSHING, BRUISE
CUT, LACERATION, PUNCTURE, OPEN WOUND
DISLOCATION
DROWNING
ELECTRIC SHOCK, ELECTROCUTION
FOREIGN BODY LOOSE (DUST, RUST, SOOT)
FOREIGN BODY, RETAINED OR EMBEDDED
FRACTURE
FREEZING, FROSTBITE
HEARING LOSS, OR IMPAIRMENT
HEAT STROKE, SUNSTROKE, HEAT EXHAUSTION
HERNIA
• INJURIES, INTERNAL
• POISONING, SYSTEMIC
RADIATION, IONIZING
RADIATION, NONIONIZING
RADIATION, ACTINIC
SCRATCHES, ABRASIONS
SPRAINS, STRAINS
SUBMERSION, NONFATAL
• MULTIPLE INJURIES
UNDETERMINED
• OCCUPATIONAL DISEASE, NEC
• OTHER INJURY, NEC

BLOCK 19. BODY PART INJURED

• HEAD (INCLUDING FACE)
• NECK
• UPPER EXTREMITIES
• TRUNK
• LOWER EXTREMITIES
• MULTIPLE PARTS
• BODY SYSTEM
• BODY PARTS, NEC

BLOCKS 20 & 23. SOURCE OF INJURY AND
AGENCY OF ACCIDENT

• AIR PRESSURE
• ANIMALS
• BODILY MOTION
• BOILERS, PRESSURE VESSELS - PARTS
• BOXES, BARRELS, CONTAINERS, PACKAGES
  (EMPTY OR FULL, EXCEPT GLASS)
• BUILDINGS & STRUCTURES - PARTS
• CHEMICALS & CHEMICAL COMPOUNDS
• CLOTHING, APPAREL, SHOES
• COAL AND PETROLEUM PRODUCTS
• CONSTRUCTION MATERIALS (NOT PART OF A
  STRUCTURE)
• CONVEYORS, GRAVITY OR POWERED
  (EXCEPT PLANT & INDUSTRIAL VEHICLES)
• DRUGS AND MEDICINES

• ELECTRIC & ELECTRONIC APPARATUS, NEC
• FLAME, FIRE, SMOKE
• FOREIGN BODIES OR UNIDENTIFIED ARTICLES
• FURNITURE, FIXTURES, FURNISHINGS
• GLASS & CERAMIC ITEMS, NEC
• HAND TOOLS (NOT POWERED; WHEN IN USE,
  CARRIED BY A PERSON)
• HAND TOOLS (MECH. & ELEC. MOTOR POWERED;
  IN USE, CARRIED AND HELD BY A PERSON)
• HEATING EQUIPMENT, NEC (NOT ELEC.) WHEN IN
  USE (FOR ELEC. FURNACES SEE ELECTRONIC
  APPARATUS)
• HOISTING APPARATUS
• ELEVATORS
• HUMAN BEING
• INSTRUMENTALITIES OF WAR
• MACHINES (PORTABLE & FIXED, EXCEPT
  WHEELED VEHICLES)
• METAL ITEMS, NEC
• MINERAL ITEMS, NEC
• NATURAL POISONS AND TOXIC AGENTS, NEC
  NOISE
• PERSONNEL SUPPORTING SURFACES (DECK,
  LADDER, STAGE, BROW, PLATFORM)
• PLASTIC ITEMS, NEC
• PUMPS, ENGINES, TURBINES (NOT ELEC.)
• RADIATING SUBSTANCES AND EQUIPMENT (USE
  ONLY FOR RADIATION INJURIES)
• SCRAP, DEBRIS, WASTE MATERIAL, ETC., NEC
  (EXCEPT RADIOACTIVE)
• SHIP STRUCTURE - PARTS
• SPORTS
• TEMPERATURE (ATMOSPHERIC, ENVIRONMENTAL)
• TEXTILE ITEMS, NEC
• VEHICLES, (AIR, LAND, SEA) INCLUDING
  MILITARY AND INDUSTRIAL
  WATER AND STEAM
• WOOD ITEMS, NEC
• MISCELLANEOUS, NEC
  UNDETERMINED
• OTHER, NEC

BLOCK 21. KIND OF ACCIDENT

• STRUCK AGAINST
• STRUCK BY
• FALL OR JUMP FROM ELEVATION
• FALL OR JUMP ON SAME LEVEL
• CAUGHT IN, UNDER, OR BETWEEN
  BITE OR STING, VENOMOUS AND NON-VENOMOUS
• RUBBED, ABRADED, PUNCTURED OR CUT
  BODILY REACTION OR MOTION
• OVEREXERTION
• CONTACT WITH
  UNDETERMINED
• OTHER, NEC

BLOCK 22. HAZARDOUS CONDITION

• DEFECT OF THE AGENCY OF ACCIDENT
• DRESS OR APPAREL HAZARD
• IMPROPER ILLUMINATION
• IMPROPER VENTILATION

• ENVIRONMENTAL HAZARD, NEC
• HAZARD OF OUTSIDE WORK
  ENVIRONMENT - OTHER
• INADEQUATELY GUARDED
• PLACEMENT HAZARD
• PUBLIC HAZARD
  UNDETERMINED
  NO HAZARDOUS CONDITION
• HAZARDOUS CONDITION, NEC

BLOCK 24. UNSAFE ACT

• WORKING ON MOVING OR DANGEROUS
  EQUIPMENT
• DRIVING ERRORS BY VEHICLE
  OPERATOR
• FAILURE TO USE PERSONAL
  PROTECTIVE EQUIPMENT
  FAILURE TO WEAR SAFE PERSONAL
  ATTIRE
• FAILURE TO SECURE OR WARN
  HORSEPLAY AND SKYLARKING
  QUARRELING OR FIGHTING
• IMPROPER USE OF EQUIPMENT
• IMPROPER USE OF HANDS OR BODY
  PARTS
  INATTENTION TO FOOTING OR
  SURROUNDINGS
• FAILURE TO USE SAFETY DEVICES
• OPERATING OR WORKING AT UNSAFE
  SPEED
• TAKING UNSAFE POSITION OR
  POSTURE
• UNSAFE PLACING, MIXING,
  COMBINING, ETC.
• USING UNSAFE EQUIPMENT
• OTHER UNSAFE ACTS, NEC
  UNDETERMINED
  NO UNSAFE ACT
  NEC - NOT ELSEWHERE CLASSIFIED

BLOCK 25. UNSAFE PERSONAL
FACTOR

UNDER INFLUENCE DRUG/ALCOHOL
FATIGUE
ILLNESS
• IMPROPER ATTITUDE
• LACK OF KNOWLEDGE OR SKILL
• BODILY DEFECTS
  UNDETERMINED
  NO UNSAFE PERSONAL FACTOR
• OTHER UNSAFE PERSONAL FACTOR,
  NEC

• SPECIFY/DETAIL

29.52.4(127E)

Figure 19-4.—Instructions for Accidental Injury/Death Report (back).

investigation must be conducted. Here are six important factors you should consider:

1. Unsafe conditions. Was the equipment improperly guarded, unguarded, inadequately guarded? Was the equipment or material rough, slippery, sharp-edged, decayed, worn, cracked? Was there a hazardous arrangement, such as congested work space, lack of proper lifting equipment, unsafe planning? Was there proper illumination, ventilation? Was the man dressed properly for the job? Was he provided with the proper respirator goggles/gloves?

2. Type of Accident. Was he struck by some object? Did he fall at the same level or to a different level? Was he caught in or between objects? Did he slip (not fall) or overexert himself?

3. Unsafe Act. Was he operating a machine without authority? Was he working at an unsafe speed, too fast or too slow? Was any safety device made inoperative (for example, blocked out or removed)? Was any load made unsafe, or were tools or equipment put in an unsafe place where they would fall? Did someone fail to wipe up oil, water, grease, paint, etc., on working surfaces? Did the injured man take an unsafe position of posture? Did he lift with a bent back or while in an awkward position? Did he lift jerkily? Was he riding in an unsafe position on a vehicle? Was he using improper means of ascending or descending? Was the injury caused by failure to wear the provided safe attire or personal protective devices such as goggles, gloves, masks, aprons, safety shoes?

4. Unsafe Personal Factor. Was he absent-minded or inattentive? Did he fail to understand instructions, regulations, safety rules? Did he willfully disregard instructions or safety rules? Was he unaware of safe practices, unpracticed, unskilled? Was he unable to recognize or appreciate the hazard? Did he have a bodily defect, such as poor eyesight, defective hearing, hernia?

5. Type of Injury. Did he sustain a cut, bruise, sprain, strain, hernia, fracture? Generally you should get this information from a doctor, because it is often difficult for a layman to diagnose injuries.

6. Part of Body Affected. Did the injury involve arm, leg, ribs, feet, fingers, head, etc.? This information should also be obtained from the doctor.

The factors cited above will give you an idea of some of the things which a supervisor must investigate and report when accidents occur. It is not all-inclusive. Each accident is different, and each should be investigated and judged on its merits. Do not jump to conclusions. Start each investigation with an open mind. The most important factor in any accident investigation is to determine how to prevent a similar accident.

PLANNING

The planning of day to day assignments for team/work crews can be a frustrating job unless the crew leaders are familiar with the capabilities of his men and equipment needed to complete the work projects assigned. This is particularly true in a combat zone where the priorities of construction may change every day. You may have your best team/work crew on a prefabricating project when suddenly an emergency comes up that requires your team/work crews plus a good portion of equipment to be dispatched to another jobsite. Since the project has to be completed, you must be able to re-organize and assign team/work crews to continue work on the original project. By knowing your men and their capabilities you should be able to control the various projects and:

1. Plan work to avoid wasted or poorly utilized manpower.
2. Be sure that each element in a project is really necessary. Eliminate or combine operations.
3. Arrange priorities of projects and have second or third projects ready so that a crew can shift work if delayed on a primary project.
4. Make sure tools, supplies, and materials are on hand.
5. Distinguish types of manpower required for different projects.
6. Establish rate of work. How many hours should a particular project take under normal conditions, and under adverse conditions.

The above points are necessary for getting the project finished; as well as aiding you in controlling the project operations. Never forget these three words—ORGANIZE, SUPERVISE and ANALYZE.

REQUISITIONING

As a crew leader or supervisor, you will realize that battalions operations require a complex variety of material. Equipment and equipment parts are usually the most critical shortages. Long-lead times and long-distance shipment require careful advance planning and action for procurement as soon as needs are established. In time of emergency mobilization, all items become comparatively scarce; therefore waste, hoarding or oversupply in one area can act to the detriment of others. Shipping space, port capacity and materials handling capacity are determining factors in military supply operations and only essential cargo can be carried. Under such conditions, many items become critical and their improper requisition or use can have severe adverse effects. Delivery of serviceable material to the location where it is needed requires cooperation among planning staffs, supply sources, and using activities. Because of the long-lead time, needs must be anticipated and acted upon as quickly as possible under the operational circumstances. The initiative for this logistic support lies with staff planners who have at their disposal information which cannot easily be made available to field activities. However, failures may happen between the source and the user through human oversight, unforeseen wear, improper maintenance, accidents, careless use of materials, storms or enemy action. To the extent that this situation permits, each Mobile Construction Battalion (MCB) and Amphibious

Construction Battalion (ACB) supervisor must know what arrangements have been made to support his operation, and take action to provide for any development which was not anticipated. He must have sufficient familiarity with the working of the supply system to obtain the material he needs, to maintain and use it, to repair or replace it if necessary, and to get along without it in an emergency.

To assist the Supply Officer to obtain material needed by crew leaders they must submit their request on DD Form 1348, DOD Single Line Item Requisition System Document (Manual), indicating the date the material is needed and completely identifying the items required. See figure 19-5. Since many tools, etc., are called by various names, the originator of the request must describe the item as it is listed in the Federal Stock Catalog. For example, to describe a tool as a "jackhammer" would cause delay in proper identification and processing by the supply system because, although "jackhammer" is a commonly used construction term, this tool is listed as a "pavement breaker" in the catalog. Identification must also include the specific stock number. For example, suppose the Supply Officer received a requisition for 2,000 board feet of 2 x 4s. He would find in the catalog, numerous stock numbers for 2 x 4s depending upon the type and grade of the wood and the number of finished sides. Since he

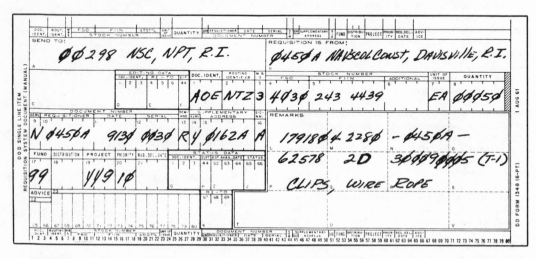

43.24

Figure 19-5.—DOD Single Line Item Requisition System Document (Manual), DD Form 1348.

would not know how the lumber is to be used, he must go back and ask the originator for more information.

When the Supply Officer must go to another Navy Supply Activity for the material, he prepares the requisition on the DD Form 1348, citing the accounting data and placing a priority number on the requisition. The number is a combination of a Force/Activity Designator (FAD) assigned by higher authority which reflects the battalion's employment (combat, positioned, ready or reserve and support) and the Urgency of Need Designator which runs from emergency requirements for material without which the activity is "unable to perform assigned operational missions" to material required "in preparation for a scheduled deployment."

Requests for material available at local government salvage yards or for surplus supplies of other activities on a "no funds involved" basis, will also be prepared on DD Form 1348, and submitted to the Supply Officer. Procurement of any surplus or salvage material or equipment of any nature whatsoever from any source must follow standard procedures. The requirements for custody and records on equipment procured from salvage yards are the same as for items procured new through regular channels.

TIMEKEEPING

In order to record and measure the number of man-hours the battalion spends on various functions, a labor accounting system is necessary. This system must permit the day-by-day accumulation of labor utilization data in sufficient detail and in a manner that allows ready compilation of information required by the unit in the management of its labor forces and in the preparation of the required reports to higher authority. Each battalion must account for:

    a. Forty (40) man-hours per week (normal work week) for all enlisted men assigned to the battalion for the full work week; plus,

    b. All man-hours actually expended above the normal work week; plus,

    c. All indigenous civilian man-hours actually charged to the battalion.

While the system may vary slightly between battalions, they are so similar that the one

described in this chapter can be considered typical.

During the planning and scheduling phases each work element of each project is given an identifying number. For example, "clear and grub site" may be the first task of project R-15 and therefore would be identified as work element R-15a. All man or machine hours used in clearing and grubbing that project site would simply be listed under R-15a. In like manner indirect labor would have a series of codes as would training and overhead. An example of some indirect codes are listed below:

X01   Construction Equipment Maintenance Report and Records.

X02   Operations and Engineering. Includes planning and estimating, material take-off, drafting, surveying, testing, photography, safety chief, inspectors and all other phases of project support.

X03   Project Supervision. Labor spent by field and shop personnel in supervising project work. When over 50% of a man's time is spent in supervision, all his time shall be charged to supervision.

X04   Project Material Expediting (Shop Planner). Labor spent in arranging for equipment and tools, scheduling for utility outages, coordinating with other crews, etc.

X05   Location Moving. Moving equipment, tools, field offices, etc., to and from project sites as well as time spent on mobilizing resources at the job site.

X06   Project Material Support. Includes material liaison functions, receipt, storage, issue and on-site delivery of project materials.

X07   Tool and Spare Parts Issue. Includes issue and tool room repairs and maintenance.

X08   Other. Used for reportable items not covered above and should be explained fully when used.

These codes are used by the supervisors or crew leaders when reporting the hours spent by each member of their crew. Reports are usually made as simple as possible and take the form of a card such as the one shown in figure 19-6. Supervisors or crew leaders submit

TYPICAL TIMEKEEPING CARD

CREW LEADER HUTSON BU1 | CREW | CREW SIZE 6 | TRANSFERS THIS DATE NONE

PROJECT POL SYSTEM | DATE 15 NOV 19—

NAME	PRODUCTIVE: DIRECT LABOR CODE R 9C	PRODUCTIVE: DIRECT LABOR CODE R 9D	PRODUCTIVE: INDIRECT LABOR CODE X04	MILITARY LABOR CODE	OVERHEAD: ADMINISTRATIVE LABOR CODE	OVERHEAD: MISCELLANEOUS LABOR CODE Y01	OVERHEAD: MISCELLANEOUS LABOR CODE Z04	
HUTSON	4	4						8
AARON		6	2					8
FRITZ		8						8
GONDA		7				1		8
SANTZ	8							8
MANUEL	7						1	8
TOTAL	19	25	2			1	1	48

DAILY LABOR DISTRIBUTION

2.295(133F)

Figure 19-6.—Typical Timekeeping Card.

these cards to the Operations Department daily. The man-hours expended by all crews in the battalion are summarized by the operations clerk. All man-hours expended on each work element are correlated by the S-3 with measurements of work-in-place to determine progress with respect to the schedule. These figures can also be used to determine the daily percentages of direct, indirect and overhead labor. At the end of each month the mandays in every category are summarized and used to fill out the Labor Distribution Report which is usually an enclosure to the monthly report. An example is included as figure 19-7. If more information is needed on how the timekeeping records are to be kept just ask the Chief in charge.

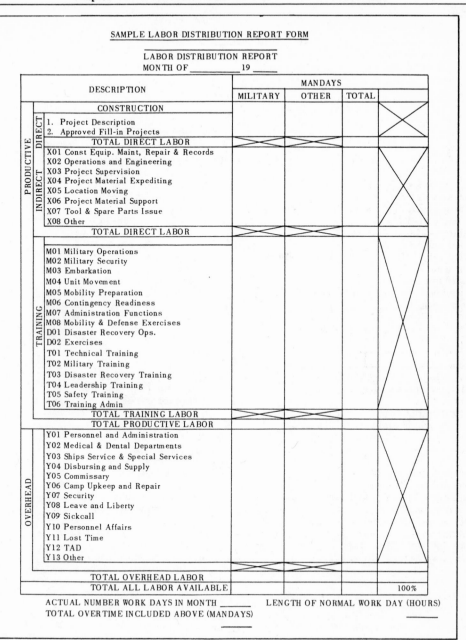

SAMPLE LABOR DISTRIBUTION REPORT FORM

LABOR DISTRIBUTION REPORT
MONTH OF _____ 19 ____

DESCRIPTION	MANDAYS			
	MILITARY	OTHER	TOTAL	
CONSTRUCTION				
1. Project Description				
2. Approved Fill-in Projects				
TOTAL DIRECT LABOR				
X01 Const Equip. Maint, Repair & Records				
X02 Operations and Engineering				
X03 Project Supervision				
X04 Project Material Expediting				
X05 Location Moving				
X06 Project Material Support				
X07 Tool & Spare Parts Issue				
X08 Other				
TOTAL DIRECT LABOR				
M01 Military Operations				
M02 Military Security				
M03 Embarkation				
M04 Unit Movement				
M05 Mobility Preparation				
M06 Contingency Readiness				
M07 Administration Functions				
M08 Mobility & Defense Exercises				
D01 Disaster Recovery Ops.				
D02 Exercises				
T01 Technical Training				
T02 Military Training				
T03 Disaster Recovery Training				
T04 Leadership Training				
T05 Safety Training				
T06 Training Admin				
TOTAL TRAINING LABOR				
TOTAL PRODUCTIVE LABOR				
Y01 Personnel and Administration				
Y02 Medical & Dental Departments				
Y03 Ships Service & Special Services				
Y04 Disbursing and Supply				
Y05 Commissary				
Y06 Camp Upkeep and Repair				
Y07 Security				
Y08 Leave and Liberty				
Y09 Sickcall				
Y10 Personnel Affairs				
Y11 Lost Time				
Y12 TAD				
Y13 Other				
TOTAL OVERHEAD LABOR				
TOTAL ALL LABOR AVAILABLE				100%

(Left vertical labels: PRODUCTIVE — DIRECT, INDIRECT, TRAINING; OVERHEAD)

ACTUAL NUMBER WORK DAYS IN MONTH _____   LENGTH OF NORMAL WORK DAY (HOURS) _____
TOTAL OVERTIME INCLUDED ABOVE (MANDAYS) _____

133.417

Figure 19-7.—Sample Labor Distribution Report Form.

INDEX

A

Abrasive tools and equipment, 227-230
  abrasive grinders, 228
  care and maintenance of abrasive equipment, 228-230
  oilstone, 228
  rasps and files, 227
Accident Injury/Death Report OpNav Form 5100/1, 551-552
Adhesive application, 400
Advanced base timber piers, 470-472
Advancement, 4-10
  how to prepare for advancement, 5-10
  how to qualify for advancement, 5
Aggregate, 98-101, 388
Application of plaster, 397-399
Applying plaster, 394-399
  application of plaster, 397-399
  plastering crews, 396
  plastering tools, 395
Arithmetical operations, 26-30
Asbestos-cement siding, 356-359
  application of siding to wall, 358
  cant strip, 359
  care of material, 357
  corner finishing, 358
  first and odd-numbered courses, 359
  flashing at openings and corners, 357
  preparation, 357
  second and succeeding even numbered courses, 359
Asphalt and vinyl tiles, 379
Average coverage of paint, 523

B

Baseboards, 384
Basic erection procedures, 403
Basic structural erection, 410-416
Batching, 106-108
  batching plant, 108
  measuring aggregate, 107

Batching—continued
  measuring aggregate, 107
  measuring cement, 107
  measuring water, 107
Batter boards, 53
Block and tackle, 65-74
  allowance for friction, 68
  block nomenclature, 66
  construction of blocks, 66
  erecting, 74
  lifting a given weight, 72
  mechanical advantage, 67
  ratio of size of block to size of line or wire used, 67
  reeving blocks, 70
  rigging, 74
  safe working load of a tackle, 71
  shear legs, 73
  size of line to use in a tackle, 72
  tackle safety precautions, 73
  tackle terms, 65
  types of cargo blocks, 67
  types of tackle, 68
Block nomenclature, 66
Bracket scaffolding, 83
Brick masonry, 168-202
  brick classification, 169
  brick construction, 181-198
  bricklaying methods, 172-180
  brick terminology, 169
  fire resistance, 171
  general characteristics of brick masonry, 172
  mortar for brick masonry, 170
  reinforced brick masonry, 198-202
  resistance to weathering, 171
  types of bricks, 170
Bridging, 298-300
Brushes, 509
Bucking, 490-494
Builder rating, 1-4
  navy enlisted classification codes, 1
  practical leadership aspects, 4
  types of billets, 2-4